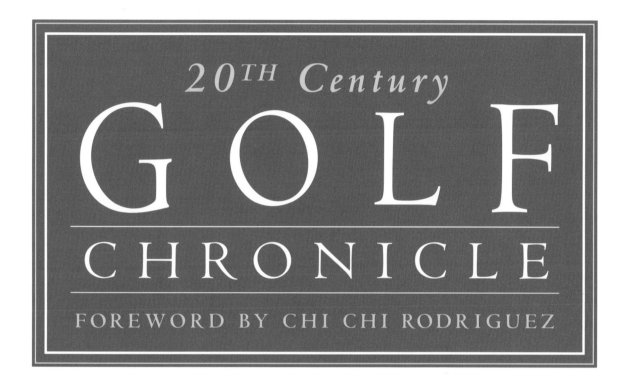

20TH Century GOLF CHRONICLE

FOREWORD BY CHI CHI RODRIGUEZ

Contributing Writers

Al Barkow
David Barrett
David Earl
Rhonda Glenn
Pat Seelig

Consultants

David Barrett
Cal Brown
Patrick Leahy

PUBLICATIONS INTERNATIONAL, LTD.

Al Barkow is the former editor-in-chief of *Golf Illustrated* and *Golf*. He is editor and publisher of *Al Barkow's Golf Report* and has been a freelance writer for sports magazines, including *Golf Digest*, *Sport*, and *Golf Journal*.

David Barrett is a senior editor at *Golf*. He was a contributing writer to *Golf in America: The First One Hundred Years* and *The PGA Championship: 1916–1984*. He compiled the records and statistics section for *Grand Slam Golf*.

Cal Brown is a former editor and writer for *Golf Digest* and editor of Golf Digest Books. He is the author of several books, including *The Golf Courses of the Monterey Peninsula, Great Shots* (with Bob Sommers), and *Golf Course Designs* (with Tom Fazio).

David Earl has served as editor for several national golf magazines, including *Golf* and *Golf Illustrated*. He has contributed articles on golf and many other subjects to magazines ranging from *Sports Illustrated* to *SPY*. He is a member of the Golf Writers Association of America.

Rhonda Glenn is the author of five golf books, including the award-winning *The Illustrated History of Women's Golf*. She is a frequent contributor to golf magazines, is a member of the USGA Women's Mid-Amateur Committee, and is a golf commentator for ABC.

Patrick Leahy is a noted golf historian and chronologist. He is a former editor of *Golf World*.

Pat Seelig is a contributing writer to golf magazines, including *Golf Journal, PGA Magazine*, and *Golf*. He is the author of *America's Most Historic Golf Courses* and is a co-founder and past president of the Texas Golf Writers Association.

Special thanks to the following for their help with photo research: Marge Dewey and Saundra Sheffer of the Ralph W. Miller Golf Library/Museum; David Earl and Andrew Mutch; Tom Gilbert of Wide World Photos; and Deborah Goodsite of Bettmann.

Allsport USA: Cover, 501, 514, 516, 530, 533, 554; Howard Boylan: 566; Simon Bruty: 543, 555, 557-558; David Cannon: Cover, 447, 485-486, 491, 497-499, 500-503, 505-507, 509-511, 513-519, 521-523, 525-527, 529-530, 532, 538, 541, 543, 545-547, 549-550, 554, 556, 558, 561, 565; Tim DeFrisco: 537; Stephen Dunn: 546, 549-551, 555-556, 559, 562; Scott Halleran: 543; Rusty Jarrett: 551; Diane Johnson: 531; Ken Levine: 546, 556, 562-563; Steve Munday: 553; Gary Newkirk: 523, 559, 562-567; Mike Powell: 515, 530-531, 539, 548; J. Rettaliata: 9, 532, 535; Keith Simonian: 534; Rick Stewart: 538-541, 567; Damina Strohmeyer: 567; Budd Symes: 499, 522, 524; **AP/Wide World Photos:** Cover, 8-9, 67, 75, 81, 93, 116, 155, 178, 182, 189-190, 193, 195-197, 199-203, 205-209, 211-215, 217-221, 223-227, 229-233, 235-239, 241-245, 247-251, 254-257, 259-263, 265-269, 272-275, 278-281, 283-287, 290-295, 297-303, 305-311, 313-319, 321-327, 329-331, 333-334, 337-343, 346-351, 354-359, 363-367, 369, 371-373, 377-378, 380-383, 386-388, 391, 394-395, 398-399, 402-403, 405, 407, 410-411, 413, 419-422, 427-428, 435-437, 439, 441, 443, 445, 450, 453-454, 458, 460, 466, 469, 471, 474-477, 484-485, 490-491, 493-494, 500, 506, 508-509, 511, 517, 519, 523-524, 526-527, 531, 534-535, 538, 540, 542, 547-549, 551, 554-555, 557-558, 566; **The Bettmann Archive:** Cover, 12, 16, 25, 27, 36, 40, 47, 49, 51, 55, 72-73, 76, 80-81, 88, 99, 118, 127, 135, 137, 140, 143, 145-148, 165-166, 170, 172, 177, 179, 191, 194, 202, 207, 208, 214-215, 220, 248, 251, 253-255, 261-262, 273, 277, 279, 284, 287, 289-291, 293, 316, 319, 324, 330-332, 335, 338-339, 341-342, 347, 354-355, 357, 359, 362, 364-365, 367, 370, 373-375, 379-380, 383, 385, 395, 401, 404, 411, 413, 417, 422, 426, 429, 434, 442, 446, 451-452, 454, 459, 461-462, 465, 467-468, 470, 477, 479, 482, 484, 490-493; Peter E. Georgiady: 16, 20, 28, 33, 64; Leonard Kamsler: Cover, 386-391, 394, 398-399, 402, 404-407, 409-412, 414-415, 418-423, 425, 427-428, 430-431, 433, 435-438, 442-447, 450, 452-455, 458, 460-461, 473; **Ralph W. Miller Golf Library:** Cover, 13, 20-21, 24-25, 32-33, 35, 40-41, 44, 52, 69, 72, 84-85, 92, 96-97, 100, 103-105, 108-109, 111-113, 116-117, 119, 121-125, 128-131, 133-137, 140-142, 147-149, 152-154, 159-161, 163-164, 166, 169, 171, 175-177, 179, 182, 185, 187-191, 194, 209, 214, 230, 236, 239, 242, 256, 280, 302, 316, 335, 347, 353, 361-362, 370, 375, 390, 393, 406, 414, 419, 421, 426-427, 429, 431, 434, 437-439, 449-450, 457, 461, 463, 466-468, 474, 476-477, 484, 487; **Old Chicago Golf Shop/Leo M. Kelly Jr.:** 32, 45; **John M. Olman & Morton W. Olman/Golf Antiques/Market Street Press:** 17, 19, 23, 28, 33, 36, 40, 43-44; **Royal Canadian Golf Association:** 28-29, 49, 56, 84; **The Tufts Archives of Given Memorial Library, Pinehurst, N.C.:** 15, 17, 29, 31, 36, 39, 41, 44-45, 60, 65; **United States Golf Association, Far Hills, N.J.:** Cover, 11-13, 16-17, 20-21, 24-25, 29, 48-49, 52-53, 56-57, 59-61, 63-65, 68-69, 71, 73, 76-77, 79-81, 83-85, 87-89, 91-93, 95-97, 100-101, 104-105, 107-109, 112-113, 115, 117, 119, 122-124, 131, 134-135, 137, 139, 141-143, 146, 148-149, 151-152, 155, 157-160, 164-167, 170-171, 173, 176-179, 181, 183-185, 188-189, 191, 244, 271, 345; Ruffin Beckwith: 462, 471; Dost & Evans: 510; Joann Dost: 483, 486, 495, 516; Ed Karakul: 463; John Kelly: 478, 490, 494-495, 507, 518; Kelly/Russell: 460, 467, 475-476, 481; Bob LaRouche: 479; McKenzie-Dickerson: 469; Warren Morgan: 478, 485; Larry Petrillo: 489, 541; Barry Rabinowitz: 469; Greg Russell: 533; David Walberg: 455, 482, 487, 494; Randy Wood: 483.

CONTENTS

CONTENTS

CONTENTS

By Chi Chi Rodriguez

For those of us on the Senior Tour, *20th Century Golf Chronicle* is a treasure chest of memories. Most of us have played golf since the 1950s, 1940s, and—for some—even the 1930s, and the book gives us a chance to remember our old heroes, our old rivals, and many of our old friends. When given the opportunity to reflect on the game of golf for this foreword, I began to sift through my many wonderful memories—memories that go back more than 50 years.

My early recollections of golf began when I was a young boy growing up in Puerto Rico. I made my own clubs out of guava limbs, and my golf balls were made out of tin cans. My friends and I would dig holes at the baseball park, and we would play our own version of golf. I could hit them about 100 yards. I would also sneak onto the golf course at night and practice.

At age seven, I got a job at Berwind Country Club as a forecaddie, and then at age nine I started to caddie. This is when visions of fame and riches began to enter my head about golf. My friends and I used to sit in the big banyan tree by the entrance at the clubhouse and watch the fancy convertibles drive through the gate, and there I was without shoes, telling my friends that someday I'd own a car like that. They all laughed, of course, but I knew it would be true. I also told my friends that someday I would beat Ben Hogan and Sam Snead, and once again they laughed and said, "There has never been a touring pro from Puerto Rico." They told me I was a hound dreaming about pork chops.

During my two years in the Army, I tried out for a baseball team and watched a former major leaguer take his cuts. I realized then I could never play baseball. So the answer was golf. After returning from the Army to Puerto Rico, I talked Ed Dudley into hiring me as a caddie master at the new Dorado Beach resort. Soon after, I went under the tutelage of PGA professional Pete Cooper, who prepared me for the mental and emotional strains of Tour life.

I played little tournament golf in Puerto Rico, preferring instead to measure myself against Pete. When I began to feel more confident, I told Pete, "I'm going on Tour with you." Pete said that I would have to prove I could beat him before I could go. We played 16 matches, and I beat him every time. Pete then told me to go pack my bags. I traveled with Pete in a used Pontiac, and once at the Motor City Open in Detroit, the security guard thought I was Pete's caddie and wouldn't let me enter.

The early days on Tour were tough on everyone. In those days, there were times we could not find a hotel room and had to sleep in our cars. Furthermore, you didn't play to make money; you played to become the home pro at a good club, and you played for prestige.

Upon looking back at my years on the PGA Tour, I'm very proud of my accomplishments and earnings, but one of my most humiliating experiences occurred during that time. When I arrived on the Tour, my humorous antics were not welcomed by many of the players, and as a result I was fined and warned by the PGA for conduct "unbecoming of a professional." But the most devastating moment was when my idol, Arnold Palmer, criticized me at the 1964 Masters for my antics. I went to my locker room and cried.

As I approached age 50, I was not sure about joining the Senior Tour. But when Jack Nicklaus asked me to endorse a line of clubs for MacGregor Golf Company and told me I could still play, his confidence in me meant a lot. Therefore, I thought to myself that maybe I could be a star on the senior circuit. I also remembered Pete Cooper telling me that he played better golf after age 50.

One of my most emotional moments was when I won the 1987 PGA Seniors Championship, and I kissed a man for the first time. I kissed Pete Cooper, who traveled with me all those years and helped me improve my game, making it the way it is today. Winning usually does not make me an emotional guy, but Pete mentioned in passing that day that he could use a new pickup truck, and knowing that he needed a truck and that I could buy it for him made me very emotional.

I enjoy golf. It has not only given me a living but it has also allowed me to accomplish things I never dreamed of. One of those accomplishments, which is the most satisfying, is helping kids. In 1979, I co-founded the Chi Chi Rodriguez Foundation in Clearwater, Florida, which is a counseling and education service for troubled, abused, and disadvantaged children.

When I retire from competitive golf, I hope to devote more time working with the kids. Until then, I will continue to play the game I love, and cherish the wonderful memories that I have gathered throughout my long career. The *20th Century Golf Chronicle* is sure to inspire some of my favorite memories of golf, and I hope the book does the same for each and every reader.

Chi Chi Rodriguez

Chi Chi Rodriguez

Unlike baseball, America's other century-long passion, the history of American golf has been difficult to trace. Major League Baseball can boast of two distinct leagues since 1900 with detailed records kept for each season. But the sport of golf hasn't been so lucky.

In the early years of this century, pro golf consisted of a few tournaments scattered across the

country, plus exhibition matches that popped up here and there. In the first third of this century, reporters who tried to cover tournaments were not always welcomed, and thus had to scrounge around for information. The PGA Tour has no set beginning; it just slowly evolved, becoming official—more or less—in the mid-1930s. And despite many classic books and outstanding magazines on golf, there hasn't been one publication fans could turn to to find a chronology of golf history.

In short, American golf's Big Picture has been a little fuzzy, and somewhat incomplete. The *20th Century Golf Chronicle* was created to put a clearer focus on the Big Picture, to package golf history into a well-organized, comprehensive volume.

The *Chronicle* neatly lays out more than 1,000 short articles and an equal number of photos. By strolling through the 576 pages, fans can see golf progress, step by step, from 1900 through 1992. The book captures every significant moment of the century. The focus is on American golf, but important developments in Great Britain, Canada, and other countries are noted as well.

Chronicling golf's history has never been an easy task. Although the PGA Tour has stabilized in recent decades, tournament results are still difficult to trace. PGA and LPGA Tour events have come and gone over the years (there once were such short-lived tourneys as the Rubber City Open, Hardscrabble Open, and Girl Talk Classic), and neither fans nor the media have had easy access to their results.

Moreover, the simple nature of golf doesn't lend itself to neat packaging, since the expanse of the sport is enormous. On each summer weekend, numerous amateur tournaments are staged on some of the thousands of American golf courses. On the same weekends, prestigious events are held in countries throughout the world.

INTRODUCTION

Indeed, sifting through and organizing 20th Century golf was a tough task. It took a team of seven top golf historians with a combined 150 years of golf-writing experience—not to mention a group of experienced photo researchers—to help pull it off.

The *20th Century Golf Chronicle* is divided into individual years, 1900–92. Each year begins with a feature on the season's biggest story. The year 1930, for example, opens with a feature story on Bobby Jones's Grand Slam, while 1990's main story probes the ugly Shoal Creek episode.

The following pages of each year recap other big events that made headlines. While Shoal Creek was the No. 1 story of 1990, Hale Irwin's third U.S. Open triumph was also significant. If you flip to the 1990 section, you'll find a short story on Irwin's victory as well as an accompanying photograph. Fifteen other important stories are presented in 1990, each with an adjoining photo.

Perhaps the most unique aspect of *20th Century Golf Chronicle* is its century-long timeline, which runs along the bottom of each page of the book. The timeline notes the results of each year's significant tournaments, including all the majors. The timeline also lists items of historical significance, such as major breakthroughs in equipment, changes in the Rules of Golf, grand openings of esteemed golf courses, and birthdates of Hall of Famers.

The timeline is also peppered with little-known yet fascinating facts. The 1911 timeline notes that when the National Golf Links of America opened, one of its charter members was Robert Todd Lincoln, son of President Abraham Lincoln. The 1982 timeline points out that Wayne Levi won a PGA Tour event, the Hawaiian Open, with an orange ball, thus becoming the first golfer to do so.

And so every significant golf event of this century is explored in the *Chronicle,* be it something as grand as Gene Sarazen's double eagle in the Masters, or something as trivial as Jerry Pate's

swan-dive into a lake. The *20th Century Golf Chronicle* packages thousands of such moments together, brings them to life with over 1,000 photographs, and puts a clearer focus on American golf's Big Picture.

Opposite page, top: Harry Vardon, Francis Ouimet, Ted Ray; bottom: Bobby Jones. This page, top: Jack Nicklaus; right: Nancy Lopez; bottom: Raymond Floyd.

VARDON COMES TO AMERICA, WINS OPEN

At the turn of the century, golf was on a popularity roll in America. From five member clubs at its establishment in 1894, the U.S. Golf Association now boasted 168 clubs. Entries in the Open grew more than fivefold. As a result, the demand for golf equipment ballooned, and companies like A.G. Spalding produced more and more clubs and balls. Spalding didn't have the market locked up, however, as other equipment makers began to make strides.

What Spalding needed to increase its market share was a figurehead. And who better, the Spalding big-wigs reasoned, than Harry Vardon? Vardon had won three British Opens in the past four years. He enjoyed the reputation, and probably deservedly so, of being the best golfer in the world. A couple of years before, Spalding had produced a line of clubs bearing his name, and a new golf ball—the Vardon Flyer—was scheduled for release.

The Spalding execs approached Harry with an offer he couldn't refuse: Vardon would tour America and play a series of exhibition matches—with

Spalding's clubs and balls, of course. He would also compete in the U.S. Open and obviously enjoy the role of pre-tournament favorite. With this much attention on Vardon, Spalding figured, sales would rocket.

Things couldn't have worked out better for the Massachusetts club- and ball-makers. Vardon arrived early in the year, with a 20,000-mile itinerary set out for him. He visited courses and played matches from Canada to Florida. "The tour was a roaring personal success for Vardon and an absolute revelation to American golfers," wrote Robert Sommers.

The results of his matches speak for themselves. He won 50, halved two, and lost 13. What impressed the American golfers as much as his successes was his stylishness.

Eminent British golfer/author Horace Hutchinson summed it up thusly: "The quietness and control of the swing are reflected in the modest confidence of his manner. He is universally, we believe, liked as a man; universally, we are sure, feared as a golfer."

And with good reason. In October, Harry defeated long-time rival J.H. Taylor by two strokes to win the U.S. Open at Chicago Golf Club, becoming the first foreign professional to win the title. The nearest American-based pro, David Ball, was 10 strokes back of Vardon. Incidentally, Harry did take one break, returning to Britain for the British Open. There, the order of finish was reversed, with Taylor capturing the championship by eight strokes over Vardon at St. Andrews.

The impact of Vardon's American sojourn cannot be exaggerated. It "showed decisively that British golfers were still the best," wrote Sommers. It also propelled Spalding into a dominant market position in the burgeoning golf equipment business, and it fed the fire of American enthusiasm for the game.

1900

- June 7: The Great Triumvirate of J.H. Taylor, Harry Vardon, and James Braid finishes 1-2-3 in the British Open at St. Andrews, Scotland, where dogs are banned on the Old Course during the championship.

- July 7: Australian-born Walter J. Travis earns medalist honors, then

posts a 2-up U.S. Amateur victory over Findlay S. Douglas in a storm-wrecked final at Garden City G.C. in New York.

- September 1: Philadelphian Frances C. Griscom beats Margaret Curtis, 6 & 5, for the U.S. Women's Amateur title at Shinnecock Hills G.C.

- October 4: American Charles Sands wins the Olympic golf competition over the Compiegne course near Paris, France.

- October 5: Margaret Abbott wins the women's Olympic golf competition and is credited as the first American woman to win an Olympic gold medal.

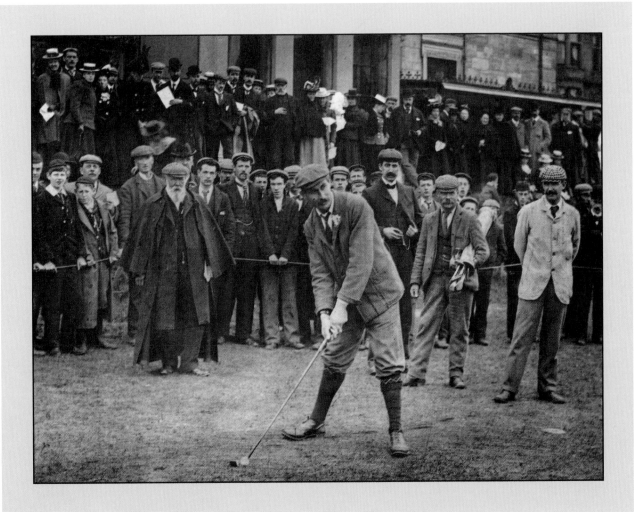

Globetrotting Harry Vardon was at the peak of his game at the turn of the century.
On a trip to America sponsored by ball- and clubmaker A.G. Spalding, he captured
the U.S. Open at Chicago G.C. by two strokes over J.H. Taylor. His 313 total
included a whiff on the final green when he stabbed at a one-inch putt.

• October 5: Harry Vardon edges fellow Britisher J.H. Taylor by two shots for the U.S. Open title at Chicago G.C., despite whiffing a short putt on the final green.

• Harold Hilton cracks the British Amateur's winner's circle at Royal St. George's in Sandwich, England, defeating James Robb, 8 & 7.

• Popular Rhona Adair captures the British and Irish ladies championships and also wins a long-driving contest at Royal Lytham and St. Annes with a 173-yard poke.

• After a bang-up start in 1899, the Western Open is inexplicably canceled. It will resume in 1901.

• W.M. Mollison invents and patents the perforated leather grip for golf clubs. To this day, it's still used.

• Although persimmon has been used previously in clubheads, it doesn't become the material of choice until now, supplanting beech and other hardwoods.

Rhoda Fuller, Charles Sands

Sands Captures the Medal at Paris Olympics

Golf has rarely been played in the Olympics, but the Games did host the sport in 1900, on the Compiegne course near Paris, France. There were two divisions, scratch and handicap, and Charles Sands *(right)* took the scratch medal. Ironically, Sands's strong suit was thought to be lawn tennis.

Britain's Great Tait Dies in the Boer War

One of the tragic stories of early golf was that of Freddie Tait, a universally loved and respected golfer who died in February 1900 in South Africa, serving Great Britain in the Boer War. Tait was a daring player whose power and charismatic personality became legend—sort of an early version of Arnold Palmer.

Freddie Tait

Harold H. Hilton

Hilton's Vicious Swing Leads to Big-Time Success

Harold H. Hilton was golf's version of the Tasmanian Devil. Wrote Bernard Darwin of Hilton: "One had a wild and whirling vision of a little man jumping on his toes and throwing himself and his club after the ball with almost frantic abandon." Hilton, who won two British Opens in the 1890s, won his first of four British Amateurs in 1900.

• John Gammeter develops a thread-winding machine that allows Haskell Golf Ball Company to mass-produce rubber-cored golf balls.

• John Laing Low's book *F.G. Tait: A Record* chronicles the two-time British Amateur champion's life until his death on February 7, 1900, while in the Boer War.

• Two-time British Amateur champion Horace G. Hutchinson brings two books to the market, *Aspects of Golf* and *Golf: A Complete History of the Game.*

• Three-time U.S. Women's Amateur champion Beatrix Hoyt retires from national competition at age 20.

• Chicagoan William Walter wins the Western Amateur at the Onwentsia Club in Lake Forest, Illinois.

• Robert Foulis, a St. Andrews native, is hard at work on Normandie G.C. in St. Louis, considered the first public course west of the Mississippi.

Walter J. Travis

Los Angeles C.C. Was Once a Dump

Members of Los Angeles C.C. pose for a photo taken in 1900. Few clubs' beginnings are as humble as those of L.A. C.C. In 1897, members rented a 16-acre plot that was once a garbage dump. On it, they created a nine-hole course using tomato cans for holes. Ed Tufts *(middle row, left)* served as the club's president from 1912–46.

Los Angeles Country Club Members

Travis Learns Golf Fast, Wins Amateur

Walter J. Travis, a native Australian who moved to the United States as a boy, didn't take up golf until he was a 35-year-old man in 1897. Incredibly, he reached the semifinals of the U.S. Amateur the following year. In 1900, Travis took the whole ball of wax, defeating Findlay Douglas in the U.S. Amateur's final round.

Royal Montreal Golf Club

Royal Montreal Dates to 1873

Pictured is Royal Montreal G.C., the oldest continuous golf club in North America. Royal Montreal dates back to 1873, 15 years earlier than the United States' oldest club, St. Andrews in New York. Royal Montreal, which hosted the 1900 Canadian Amateur, relocated in 1959. Its new Blue Course featured huge greens and became one of the very best in Canada.

- Frances C. Griscom wins a tourney at Baltusrol G.C. in Springfield, New Jersey. It's the largest women's golf event to date—113 entries.

- Walter J. Travis becomes a match-play juggernaut, annexing the Metropolitan, Atlantic City, Oakland, Shinnecock, Tuxedo, and Lakewood amateur tourneys.

- Robert H. Robertson of Shinnecock Hills G.C. is named USGA president.

- George Cumming, the Dean of Canadian Golf Professionals, begins his 50-year tenure at Toronto G.C.

- All-around athlete George S. Lyon wins his second Canadian Amateur.

- James W. Tufts hires Donald J. Ross from Dornoch, Scotland, to serve as golf pro at his new Pinehurst, North Carolina, course.

- A.G. Spalding sends British great Harry Vardon on a U.S. exhibition tour to promote its new "Vardon Flyer" golf ball.

BRITAIN'S GREAT TRIUMVIRATE RULES SUPREME

In ancient Rome, the job of leadership was, for a time, shared by three men—a "triumvirate," from the Latin. Leadership of the world of golf in 1901 was also the property of a triumvirate: Harry Vardon, John Henry Taylor, and James Braid. Among them, these three Britons stood as surely as Roman rulers at the pinnacle of championship play. Like Hogan, Nelson, and Snead after them, oddly enough, they were all born within one year.

How dominant was the Great Triumvirate? One merely has to examine the record. In the 21-year span from 1894–1914, the three compiled 16 first-place finishes and a dozen seconds in the British Open. In golf-mad Britain, Vardon, Braid, and Taylor were heroes. A painting by Clement Flower almost echoes the idealistic style of Roman statuary: Vardon, with his perfect balance, drives the ball as a seated Taylor and Braid, with his driver tucked under his arm, watch impassively. The Three Wise Men couldn't have been portrayed more heroically.

It can be argued that these three brought respectability to the position of golf professional. Each held that job at some of Britain's

most respected clubs. Taylor worked at Burnham in Somerset, as well as Winchester, Wimbledon, and Royal Mid-Surrey. Braid took the job at Walton Heath, where he remained all his life. And Vardon served at Ganton and South Herts. In fact, J.H. Taylor is given credit for playing the leading role in the formation of the British Professional Golfers Association.

Stories of their prowess abound. In a 1905 match over four different courses and 72 holes, Vardon and Taylor beat Braid and Sandy Herd, 11 holes and 10 to play. The fray was mostly decided at Troon, in Scotland, where Harry and J.H. won 14 of the 18

holes, even though Vardon had suffered a hemorrhage the previous evening.

Wherever they played, the Triumvirate was followed by adoring, tumultuous galleries. The newspapers of the time were full of praise for their prowess, photographs, and endless descriptions of matches, strokes, and victories. But none phrased it better than Horace Hutchinson, the great English amateur and author, when he wrote: "The three great men...had this in common, that they all took the game earnestly and kept themselves very fit and well, in order to do their best in it; therein marking a point of departure from the usual mode of the Scottish professional of the old days, who was a happy-go-lucky fellow, not taking all the care of himself that he should if he was to excel in such a strenuous game as golf. The example of these men was infectious."

Indeed it was. One wonders if it hadn't been for the Triumvirate, would golf have ever attained the station in society it now occupies? Or would we all be playing croquet, lawn bowling, and/or cricket?

1901

• June 6: James Braid outduels Triumvirate foes Harry Vardon and J.H. Taylor to win his first of five British Opens. Scottish supporters at Muirfield cheer their first homebred Open champion since 1893.

• June 17: Willie Anderson and Alex Smith post the highest 72-hole score (331) ever to lead the U.S. Open,

then Anderson takes the first Open playoff, 85-86, at Myopia Hunt Club near Boston.

• August 20: Transplanted Scot Laurie Auchterlonie wins the second Western Open, at Midlothian C.C. in Illinois, by two strokes over host pro David Bell under very windy conditions.

• August 29: The USGA delineates 13 ways golfers can forfeit their amateur status, including caddying from age 15 up and competing professionally in any other sport.

• September 21: Walter J. Travis repeats as U.S. Amateur champ, beating Walter Egan, 5 & 4, at C.C. of Atlantic City.

1901

James Braid quit school in his early teens, became a clubmaker, and—in his free time—played amateur golf. Though not quite the legend of Harry Vardon, Braid was nearly Vardon's equal. James won five British Opens, the first coming in 1901. In that tournament, he edged out Vardon and J.H. Taylor, the other two members of the Great Triumvirate.

• October 12: Genevieve Hecker routs Lucy Herron, 5 & 3, for the U.S. Women's Amateur title in the first national championship staged at Baltusrol G.C.

• November 17: Joyce Wethered, who will win five consecutive Women's English Championships, is born in England.

• A.T. Saunders obtains British patent No. 8069 for his invention of a golf ball with a compressed-air center. The air is injected with a hypodermic needle.

• Genevieve Hecker completes her first two-year hold on the Women's Metropolitan (New York) championship.

• At Atlantic City, Harvard's H. Lindsley wins the individual National Collegiate championship, and his school takes the team title.

• Harold Hilton becomes the first repeat British Amateur champion since 1887, outlasting John L. Low by one hole on the Old Course at St. Andrews.

1901

Forgan Crown Cleekmark

The Crown Cleekmark Honors King Edward

Clubmakers in the early days identified their work with cleekmarks, stamped into the backs of iron clubs and the tops of wooden clubs. The Forgan family was one of Scotland's clubmaking dynasties, employing almost 50 workers around the turn of the century. Their cleekmark, a crown, reflected the ascendancy of Prince Edward to the throne of England in 1901.

Laurence Auchterlonie

Auchterlonie Prevails in Western Open

Laurence Auchterlonie was one of many Scottish professionals who crossed the Atlantic to staff American golf clubs—and, incidentally, to play in the ever-increasing number of competitions. Auchterlonie captured the 1901 Western Open and won the U.S. Open the following year.

Walter Travis

Travis Wins Another Amateur, Writes a Book

Walter Travis, who often posed with his trademark cigar, successfully defended his U.S. Amateur championship in 1901, as he defeated Walter Egan of Chicago in the final, 5 & 4, at Atlantic City C.C. Travis was also an esteemed writer, and in 1901 he completed one of America's earliest instruction books, called *Practical Golf.*

- America's hottest golfer, Walter J. Travis, publishes his classic instruction book, *Practical Golf.*

- George C. Dutton wins the inaugural North and South Amateur, debuting at the sand-green Pinehurst C.C. layout in North Carolina.

- Molly Graham unseats Rhona Adair as Ladies' British Open Amateur champion, at Aberdovey G.C. in Wales.

- Phelps B. Hoyt wins the Western Amateur championship, at Midlothian C.C. in Blue Island, Illinois.

- R.H. Lyttleton publishes one of the rarest of golf books, *Out-Door Games: Cricket and Golf.*

- Findlay S. Douglas wins the prestigious Metropolitan Amateur at Apawamis Club in Rye, New York.

- John Stuart captures the inaugural Trans-Mississippi Golf Association

Horace Hutchinson

Hutchinson Proves His Diversity as a Writer

Horace Hutchinson, British Amateur champion in 1886–87, achieved greater success as a writer. Hutchinson's instruction book *Golf: The Badminton Library* went into its seventh printing in 1901. He also wrote history and fiction golf books. This lithograph of Hutchinson, which appeared in *Vanity Fair* in 1890, was created by Sir Leslie Ward.

Hecker Wins Women's Amateur at Baltusrol

From 1895–1945, the USGA staged only one event for women, the U.S. Women's Amateur championship—which was simply called the Women's Championship during the early years. Though Beatrix Hoyt grabbed three titles in the 1890s, Genevieve Hecker won it in 1901. It was the first USGA event held at Baltusrol G.C. in Springfield, New Jersey.

Willie Anderson

Anderson Wins First of His Four U.S. Opens

The 1901 U.S. Open brought a new hero to American golf. Willie Anderson, a native Scot, won his first of four U.S. Opens at Myopia Hunt Club in Massachusetts. After 72 holes, the leaders were Anderson and Alex Smith, who had tied at 331, the highest winning score ever in the Open. Anderson won an 18-hole playoff, 85-86.

Genevieve Hecker

Amateur championship, held at Kansas City C.C.

• A British sculptor named Cassidy creates one of the earliest golf bronzes—a 12-inch classic statue of British star Harold Hilton.

• Clubmaker Robert Forgan & Son, Ltd., of St. Andrews, becomes authorized to use the "King's Crown" cleekmark when the Prince of Wales becomes King Edward VII.

• The British Professional Golfers Association organizes to promote its members' trade interests. J.H. Taylor is its first chairman and James Braid its first captain.

• Bessie Anthony wins the inaugural Women's Western Amateur at Onwentsia Club in Lake Forest, Illinois. Her three consecutive titles (1901–03) will never be equalled.

• Horace G. Hutchinson's *Golf: The Badminton Library* volume begins its seventh printing since 1890.

HASKELL'S NEW BALL IS A SMASHING SUCCESS

As much as any factor, the golf ball has served to define the parameters of the game of golf. Clubs are designed to accommodate the ball's characteristics; courses are defined by the ball's properties of distance and roll; and even the golf swing itself has changed again and again because of the peculiar behavior of the tiny sphere.

In the earliest years, the ball was of wood. Somewhere, centuries ago, someone invented the featherie, a leather sack filled with compressed goose feathers. It reigned until the mid-19th Century, when the "guttie," or gutta-percha ball—made from the rubber-like sap of an Asian tree—supplanted it for reasons of cost, distance, and durability.

With the imminent coming of the 20th Century, a change was in the wind. Coburn Haskell, a Cleveland resident, with some collaboration from Bertram Work of Akron, came up with the idea that a golf ball consisting of rubber thread wound around a core—with a gutta-percha cover—might be just the ticket. This insight occurred in 1898, but the process involved laborious hand-winding. That is, until John Gammeter perfected a machine that would wind the threads mechanically. He was granted a patent in 1900 for the device.

According to Henderson and Stirk in their *Golf in the Making*, "the early Haskells were not a great success.... They exhibited the same tendency to duck and dart as smooth guttas had done.... The problem was solved when the new ball was given a bramble pattern cover." The cover design, of course, gave the ball improved aerodynamic properties, and the ball's reputation for unpredictability—it was at one point nicknamed the "Bounding Billy"—was eradicated.

Soon, the reputation of Coburn Haskell's new ball spread, and it wasn't long before the top players gave it a try. The results were, predictably, compelling. In 1901, the first title went to a Haskell user, when Walter J. Travis took the U.S. Amateur with it. The 1902 championships were dominated by those who had adopted the design: Sandy Herd in the British Open, Laurence Auchterlonie in the U.S. Open, and Charles Hutchings in the British Amateur.

The gutta-percha was doomed, obviously. Because of the ease of producing large quantities of Haskells, the ball soon was found everywhere. Its advantages were apparent to all who played it. Primarily, it was measurably longer. Interestingly, a legal problem arose over the Haskell ball. It turned out that in Britain the idea of the rubber-thread winding had occurred as early as 1871! After laborious wrangling in the courts in 1905, Haskell's patent was disallowed in the British Isles.

How good an idea was the rubber winding? Most balls played by the pros, and low-handicap golfers, use the design today—more than 90 years after the first Haskell ball hit the shelves.

1902

• February 27: Eugenio Sarazeni, better known as Gene Sarazen, who will go on to win 57 career tournaments, is born in Harrison, New York.

• March 17: Robert Tyre "Bobby" Jones Jr., who will become the greatest amateur golfer of all time, is born in Atlanta.

• June 5: Alexander "Sandy" Herd's decision to use the new Haskell ball in the British Open leads to victory at Hoylake, England.

• July 19: Louis N. James, age 19 and the 64th and last qualifier, beats Eben M. Byers, 4 & 2, in the U.S. Amateur final at his home Glen View Club in Golf, Illinois.

• September 17: Willie Anderson wins the Western Open at the Euclid Club in Cleveland with a historic 299. No golfer has previously broken 300 for 72 holes in America.

• October 4: Defending U.S. Women's Amateur champion Genevieve Hecker retains the Robert Cox Cup by defeating Louisa Wells,

1902

Pictured is an assortment of gutta-percha balls from the mid- to late 19th Century. These balls were made entirely from gutta percha, a rubber-like sap imported from Asia. The new Haskell ball looked like the Spalding ball on the far right. However, the Haskell used gutta percha only as a cover; its inside contained rubber thread wound around a rubber core.

4 & 3, on her home turf at The Country Club in Brookline, Massachusetts.

• October 11: Laurie Auchterlonie becomes the first golfer to break 80 all four rounds in a U.S. Open (78-78-74-77—307), as the new Haskell rubber-cored ball contributes to lower scoring at Garden City G.C.

• November 18: The USGA appoints a committee composed of leading golf authorities Charles B. Macdonald, Walter J. Travis, and G. Herbert Windeler to recommend possible changes in the Rules of Golf.

• J.H. Taylor's book *Taylor on Golf: Impressions, Comments and*

Hints enjoys wide distribution in Great Britain and the United States.

• Charles Hutchings, age 53, trims Sidney Fry, 1 up, to win the British Amateur at Hoylake, England.

• May Hezlet of Ireland wins her second of three Ladies' British Open Amateur championships.

Rib-faced Iron

New Rib-Faced Irons Impart Needed Backspin

In 1902, E. Burr of England broke new ground when he received a patent for "rib-faced" irons. Burr claimed that the exaggerated pattern helped impart much-needed backspin to the golf ball. This was especially important in Britain, where the greens were firm and fast. Engineers would tinker with the design of grooved irons throughout the century.

Taylor on Golf

Taylor Offers a Few Hints

When you're a champion, you're often in demand as an author—especially when the subject is golf instruction. Such was the case for Devon's John Henry Taylor, who published his magnum opus in 1902. The book was called *Taylor On Golf: Impressions, Comments and Hints* and became an immediate best-seller.

Harry Vardon

Vardon Challenges Again in the British Open

In his prime, Harry Vardon expected to win every British Open he entered—and he darn nearly did. Vardon didn't win the championship in 1902, but he did finish second for the third consecutive year. In fact, from the years 1896–1903, Vardon won the British title four times and finished second three times.

• The Bridgeport (Connecticut) Gun and Implement Company debuts its first golf ball, called the Champion Flyer.

• Charles B. Corey wins the second-annual North and South Amateur championship at Pinehurst C.C. in North Carolina.

• Career lawyer Fritz Martin outlasts Bertie Cassels in a 36-hole Canadian Amateur final at Royal Montreal G.C.

• E. Burr of England obtains the first patent for rib-faced irons, leading ultimately to a spate of deep grooves and regulations as to their extent.

• A.F. Schwartz of New Orleans claims the prestigious Southern Amateur, played for the first time, in Nashville, Tennessee.

• Yale wins the Intercollegiate Golf Association's spring championship at Garden City G.C. in New York. Charles Hitchcock Jr. of the Elis garners individual honors.

Del Monte Resort

Vacationers Flock to Monterey Peninsula

The stunning scenery of the Monterey Peninsula in California drew tourists even as early as 1902. These well-to-do folks hang out near the Del Monte hotel, which featured a nine-hole course nearby. Eventually, of course, the peninsula would become a golf mecca, with courses like Pebble Beach, Cypress Point, and Spyglass Hill gaining fame.

After Slow Start, James Nabs Amateur

Louis N. James was only 19 years old, but he was good enough to win the 1902 U.S. Amateur. James barely qualified for match play at the Glen View Club near Chicago, as his 94 was the worst of the 64 players who survived. Nevertheless, James roared to victory, defeating Eben M. Byers in the final, 4 & 2.

Louis N. James

Curtis Makes Her Mark in Amateur

Margaret Curtis didn't win the 1902 U.S. Women's Amateur, but she tied for the qualifying medal for the second year in a row, shooting a record 89. Curtis, who first entered the championship in 1897 at age 13, would win the title three times. She would also claim a national doubles championship in tennis in 1908.

Margaret Curtis

• H. Chandler Egan and his Harvard Crimson mates sweep individual and team honors in the Intercollegiate Golf Association's autumn championship at Morris County G.C. in New Jersey.

• Walter J. Travis wins his second of four Metropolitan titles at Tuxedo G.C. in New York.

• H. Chandler Egan wins his first of four Western Amateur titles at Chicago G.C.

• Canadian Mabel Thomson, regarded as her nation's first great female golfer, collects her first of five Canadian national championships at Toronto G.C.

• Alex Ross, younger brother of famed architect Donald, wins his first of six North and South Open titles at Pinehurst C.C.

• The Chicago-based *Golfers Magazine* commences publication.

• Andrew Herd Scott becomes the clubmaker to the Prince of Wales.

IN THE EARLY DAYS, FAMILIES FORGE THE CLUBS

In the 1902 U.S. Open, the champion scored four rounds in the 70s for the first time. The fashioner of this feat was Laurence Auchterlonie, a Scot from St. Andrews. The name of Auchterlonie doesn't ring through the annals of golf when one thinks of players. Rather, it has become almost synonymous with makers of golf clubs.

In golf's early years, clubmakers were some of the sport's most important and respected figures. Through almost the first four centuries of golf, clubmaking was a family business, pure and simple. Names from Philps and Forgan to Patrick and Parks bore the burden of providing golf implements to the golfers of their time.

The first, and earliest, of the families were the Philps and Forgans. To this day, long-nose clubs made by Hugh Philp, the patriarch, are hailed as the standard when it comes to craftsmanship. Hugh was born in Cameron but moved to St. Andrews and plied his trade. He became successful enough to be appointed clubmaker to the Society of St. Andrews, later to become the Royal and Ancient. In

1852, nearing the end of his life, he brought in his nephew, Robert Forgan. The Forgans carried on Philp's tradition of quality workmanship, and their business thrived. As late as 1937, more than 70 people were employed by the family business.

The name of McEwan echoed through the early days of Scottish golf. In 1770, the founder, James McEwan, set up residence hard by Bruntsfield Links, near Edinburgh. A decade later, he went into a partnership of sorts with ball-maker Douglas Gourlay, effectively becoming a full-service golf business. The McEwan shop supplied other centers of Scottish

golf as well. In the 1840s, however, the golf societies moved to the Musselburgh links, in the Edinburgh suburbs, and McEwan followed. Through the following decades, the business continued to thrive. An especially profitable era was the 1880s, when golf enjoyed a boom in the British Isles.

Also carrying a great influence were the Patricks, of Leven, and the Parks, of Musselburgh. The Patrick patriarch, John, had four sons, all fine clubmakers, and the business lasted for a century. The Parks enjoyed dual careers as clubmakers and champion players, claiming seven British Open championships among Willie Sr., Mungo, and Willie Jr. Young Willie also became respected, as Sir Guy Campbell put it, as the layer of "the foundation stone of golf course architecture."

And we come to the Auchterlonies. William began his club-making career as a Forgan apprentice, but he soon set up business with his brother David. The Auchterlonie business thrives to this day and, if you are lucky enough to visit St. Andrews, their shop stands on Links Road, just across from the 18th fairway of the Shrine of Golf.

1903

- June 11: An exhausted Harry Vardon struggles to his fourth British Open title at Prestwick, Scotland, before his illness is diagnosed as tuberculosis.

- June 20: Glenna Collett, who will win a record six Women's Amateurs and appear on four Curtis Cup teams, is born in Connecticut.

- June 29: Willie Anderson becomes the first golfer to win the U.S. Open twice in playoffs, as he outduels David Brown, 82–84, at Baltusrol G.C. after both deadlocked at 307.

- July 17: Alex Smith wins the Western Open at Milwaukee C.C. with the highest winning total (318) in the event's history.

- September 5: Walter J. Travis, known as the Old Man in his 41st year, wins the last of his U.S. Amateurs, at Nassau C.C. in Glen Cove, New York.

- October 3: Bessie Anthony wins the first U.S. Women's Amateur held in the West, clobbering J.A. Carpenter, 7 & 6, at Chicago G.C.

1903

Willie Auchterlonie stands in front of his shop in St. Andrews, Scotland. Auchterlonie, who opened this business with brother David in 1897, became the honorary professional to the Royal and Ancient Golf Club. His son Laurie assumed the title. The Auchterlonie shop is still in business and continues to hand-craft clubs.

• Harvard continues its domination of the Intercollegiate Golf Association's championship, but a new individual champion emerges—F.O. Reinhart of Princeton.

• Myra D. Paterson wins the inaugural Women's North and South Amateur at Pinehurst C.C. for her first of three titles.

• John Laing Low's *Concerning Golf* codifies the principles of golf course architecture.

• James Ross Brown patents a golf club with open slots "resembling a comb or rake" in the head.

• Bessie Anthony, the National Women's Amateur champion, adds her third consecutive Women's Western Amateur title at Exmoor C.C. in Illinois.

• Two-time British Amateur champion Horace Hutchinson continues his foray into golf fiction by publishing *Bert Edward, the Golf Caddie.*

1903

Nassau Country Club

Smith, Travers Call Nassau C.C. Home

Nassau C.C. on Long Island, which hosted the 1903 U.S. Amateur, was one of the premier venues of the early 20th Century. Nassau is where future Hall of Famer Jerry Travers learned to play the game. Around 1902, Travers was just a young duffer when Nassau's club pro, Alex Smith, gave him instruction. In coming years, both men would win the U.S. Open.

Oakmont Course Opens For Play

William and Henry Fownes completed their famous Oakmont C.C. course in 1903. Set atop a hill north of Pittsburgh, the course quickly became known for its difficulty. Greens were super slick and heavily contoured. Oakmont's most famous feature remains the "church pew" bunker, which lays between the 3rd and 4th fairways.

Oakmont Country Club

• Arthur Franklin Knight of Schenectady, New York, patents the controversial "Schenectady" center-shafted, mallet-style putter.

• Robert Maxwell will win both of his British Amateur titles at Muirfield six years apart, the first being a 7 & 5 drubbing of Horace Hutchinson in 1903.

• Walter Egan wins the fifth-annual Western Amateur championship, at the Euclid Club in Cleveland, reversing last year's result against his brother, Chandler.

• A.W. Gaines wins the second Southern Amateur, at Asheville, North Carolina.

• Charles Dana Gibson's "Gibson Girls" are the subject of Royal Doulton golf-themed ceramics.

• James Braid wins the inaugural *News of the World* pro match-play championship in England.

• Rhona Adair, billed as "the foremost woman golfer in the

1903

Bessie Anthony

Anthony Prevails in Women's Amateur

Bessie Anthony reached the semifinals of the U.S. Women's Amateur only once, in 1903, and she ended up going all the way. The championship was held at Chicago G.C., a few miles from her home club in Golf, Illinois. Anthony defeated J.A. Carpenter in the final round by the then-record margin of 7 & 6.

Walter Travis

Travis Beats Seven Foes to Win U.S. Amateur

Walter Travis, winner of the 1900 and '01 U.S. Amateurs, must have cringed when he arrived at the 1903 championship at Nassau C.C. on Long Island. The USGA had expanded the match-play bracket to include 128 golfers, meaning Travis would have to win seven head-to-head matches. But the Old Man did just that, beating Eben M. Byers in the final.

Alex Smith

Smith Weathers the Rain to Win the Western

Golfers sloshed through the 1903 Western Open, as heavy rain fell on the Milwaukee C.C. course. Alex Smith won the tournament, but he needed an all-time tournament-high 318 whacks to do it. The Smith brothers captured the Western Open a total of six times. Willie won once, Alex twice, and Macdonald three times.

world," plants the seed of competition between American and British women players while on a tour of U.S. courses.

• William and Henry Fownes guide the design and construction of the Oakmont C.C. outside Pittsburgh, which features lightning-fast greens and church-pew bunkers.

• Rhona Adair recaptures the Ladies' British Open Amateur at Portrush G.C. in Northern Ireland.

• Donald Ross, whose name and reputation will become synonymous with the Pinehurst C.C., wins his first of three North and South Opens there.

• T. Sterling Beckwith wins the Men's North and South Amateur at Pinehurst C.C.

• George S. Lyon wins his third Canadian Amateur at Toronto G.C.

• The Oxford and Cambridge Golfing Society embarks on its first overseas tour to the United States.

OLD MAN TRAVIS SAILS TO ENGLAND, WINS BRITISH AMATEUR

As long as the championships of Great Britain and America had been played, they had been the province of players from England and Scotland, with rare exception. That is, until The Old Man came on the scene.

Walter J. Travis didn't take up golf until after his 30th year, but his natural athletic ability, combined with a dogged determination and a highly competitive personality, made him one of the top golfers of his time. The Old Man was born in Australia of well-to-do parents and emigrated to America, settling in the suburbs of New York. He was rarely seen without a black cigar clutched firmly in his mouth.

Travis's first U.S. Amateur title came in 1900, when he was 38, at his home club, Garden City Golf Club on Long Island. He led the qualifying and went on to beat Findlay Douglas, 2 up, in the final match. The next year, 1901, he was even better, as he used the wound-rubber Haskell ball to set a record qualifying score of 157 at Atlantic City Country Club. The *USGA Record Book* relates that "he used (it) with such success that the gutta-percha ball was soon discarded." Though the final match was delayed a week because of President McKinley's death, Travis easily defeated Walter Egan, 5 & 4.

His run continued unabated, as he tied for second in the 1902 U.S. Open. The next year, he took the U.S. Amateur again, giving him three Amateur titles in four years. In 1904, Travis journeyed across the sea in search of further honors, entering the British Amateur at Sandwich. The story has it that he became frustrated at his inability to putt well in practice rounds and on the practice green. A friend noticed his difficulties and offered him the center-shafted Schenectady putter.

Travis began holing everything he looked at, and he adopted the new implement.

Walter's performance in the British Amateur was based on his putting, and a solid base it was. He was never a long driver, as he used wooden clubs on many of his approach shots, but his accuracy and his impeccable putting stroke gave him match-play victories over some of the greatest British amateurs of the time, among them James Robb, Harold Hilton, and Horace Hutchinson. In the final match of 1904, he never looked back, and he took the measure of Edward Blackwell on the 15th.

The Old Man was never to win a national championship again, but his talents in other areas were to manifest themselves until his death in 1927. He wrote books and articles, including one that would have great influence in shaping the course rating and handicap systems in use today. He also proved to be a skilled golf course architect, and he became editor of *The American Golfer*, arguably the best-ever golf magazine. And finally, his nickname changed. In the last years of his life, they called Walter Travis the Grand Old Man.

1904

- May 2: Bing Crosby, the entertainer who will lend his name to the world's most famous celebrity pro-am, is born in Tacoma, Washington.

- June 10: Jack White, a golf pro and clubmaker, wins the British Open at Royal St. George's in Sandwich, England, with a record score of 296.

- June 10: Runner-up J.H. Taylor's closing 68 is a British Open standard for the next 30 years.

- July 1: Willie Anderson becomes the first two-time Western Open champion with a winning 304 total, as he dethrones defender Alex Smith at Michigan's Kent C.C., which features a windmill green.

- July 9: At Glen View Club in Golf, Illinois, Willie Anderson becomes the first three-time U.S. Open champion and the first to successfully defend. His 303 total sets an Open record.

- August 6: Harry Cooper, who will go on to win 31 PGA tournaments, is born in Leatherhead, England.

Walter Travis packed a lot of excitement into 1904. Travis, the favorite in the U.S. Amateur, lost in the quarterfinals when George Ormiston holed a cleek shot for an eagle. Travis also co-authored a book, won the North and South Amateur, and became the first American to win the British Amateur, using the controversial Schenectady center-shafted putter.

• September 10: Recent Harvard graduate H. Chandler Egan begins a two-year reign as U.S. Amateur champion with a 8 & 6 victory over Fred Herreshoff at Baltusrol G.C.

• September 17–24: Glen Echo C.C. in St. Louis hosts golf's last hurrah as an Olympic sport.

• September 17: The Western G.A., led by U.S. and Western Amateur champion H. Chandler Egan, defeats Trans-Mississippi G.A. for the Olympic team title.

• September 24: Canada's George S. Lyon, age 46, wins the individual gold medal by beating H. Chandler Egan, 3 & 2, then—at the awards dinner—walks the length of the dining room on his hands.

• October 15: Merion Cricket Club, outside Philadelphia, makes its national championship debut, hosting Georgianna Bishop's 5 & 3 U.S. Women's Amateur victory over Mrs. E.F. Sanford.

Olympic Golf Medal

Golf Held at Olympics for the Last Time

Pictured is a golf medal from the 1904 Olympic Games, held in St. Louis. This turned out to be the last golf competition ever held in the Olympics. Before the Games were held in London in 1908, the Royal and Ancient Golf Club of St. Andrews said that golf wasn't suitable for the Olympics, so the sport was discontinued.

Harry Vardon Bronze

Vardon Immortalized in Statue

Elkington & Co., Ltd. produced this bronze of Harry Vardon in 1904. The statue, sculpted by Hal Ludlow, is the finest of its kind. So precise was Ludlow that he even captured Vardon's best follow-through. Even Harry himself was impressed. "When I finish like that," he said, "I've hit one of the best."

Hecker and Hezlet Author New Books for Women

Few women had a chance to write about golf in 1904, but Genevieve Hecker and May Hezlet were something special. Hecker, a two-time U.S. Women's Amateur champion, penned *Golf for Women* in '04. The same year, Ireland's Hezlet—a three-time winner of the Ladies' British Open Amateur—offered *Ladies' Golf*.

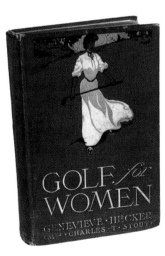

Golf for Women

Bizarre New Putter Features Four Faces

Some of the clubmakers in the early 1900s had wild imaginations, receiving patents for bizarre, sometimes nonsensical, creations. William Davis of New Jersey was granted a patent for this wacky putter, which has four striking faces! It's apparently for ambidextrous golfers who also like to hit forward and backward.

Four-sided Putter

• Royal Ottawa professional John H. Oke wins the inaugural Canadian Open by two strokes, with a two-round total of 156 at Royal Montreal G.C.

• Harvard wins its fourth straight National Collegiate team title, led by individual champion A.L. White, at Myopia Hunt Club near Boston.

• Myra D. Paterson repeats as Women's North and South Amateur champion at Pinehurst C.C.

• In the U.S. Amateur, defending title-holder Walter J. Travis is eliminated, 3 & 1, in the second round when George Ormiston of Oakmont C.C. holes a cleek shot for an eagle 2.

• The era's great women golfers take pen in hand. May Hezlet publishes *Ladies' Golf*, and Genevieve Hecker releases *Golf for Women*.

• Two champions co-author a book on "the game within a game," as Walter Travis and Jack White conspire to write *The Art of Putting*.

1904

J.H. Oke

Oke Claims the First Canadian Open Title

J.H. Oke, club pro at Royal Ottawa G.C., won the inaugural Canadian Open, held in 1904 and sponsored by the Royal Canadian Golf Association. Oke shot 156 in the 36-hole tournament, which was played at the venerable Royal Montreal G.C. Among modern-day PGA Tour events, only the U.S. and Western Opens date farther back than the Canadian.

H. Chandler Egan

Harvard Grad Egan Wins U.S. Amateur Title

H. Chandler Egan did his family proud in 1904, as he graduated from Harvard, won a national golf championship, and nearly took an Olympic gold medal. At the U.S. Amateur, Egan crushed Fred Herreshoff in the final, 8 & 6, at Baltusrol G.C. Egan, who also won the Western Amateur, lost his gold-medal match with George S. Lyon in the Olympic Games.

Willie Anderson

Anderson Repeats as U.S. Open Champion

Willie Anderson claimed his second straight U.S. Open title—and third in four years—by winning the 1904 version at the Glen View Club in Illinois. Anderson set the U.S. Open scoring record with a 303, and his closing round of 72 set an 18-hole tournament record. A week earlier, Anderson captured his second Western Open championship.

• Five-time Wimbledon tennis champion Lottie Dod edges out May Hezlet for the Ladies' British Open Amateur championship.

• Walter J. Travis wins the first of three North and South Amateurs.

• Alex Ross regains his North and South Open crown.

• Michael Scott, an English amateur affiliated with Royal Melbourne G.C., captures the inaugural Australian Open at Kensington.

• H. Chandler Egan recaptures the Western Amateur title with a convincing 6 & 5 victory over D.E. Sawyer at Exmoor C.C.

• At Royal St. George's, Walter J. Travis employs the controversial Schenectady center-shafted putter to become the first overseas British Amateur champion.

• James Braid is appointed golf professional for the new Walton Heath G.C. in Surrey, England.

ANDERSON NABS HIS THIRD STRAIGHT U.S. OPEN

Since the U.S. Open debuted in 1895, only one man has ever won three Opens in a row: Willie Anderson. Born the son of a greenkeeper in North Berwick, Scotland, Anderson emigrated to the United States at the age of 17 and took a club pro job in Rhode Island. The first inklings of his consummate skill came in the 1897 U.S. Open, when he finished in second place, only one stroke back of Joe Lloyd.

The dour, unflappable Scot continued to hone his competitive skills despite often changing club jobs—he was to hold 10 positions as professional in the 14 years he lived in America. In the 1901 U.S. Open, despite posting a bloated four-round total of 331, he tied Alex Smith and prevailed in a playoff, 85-86.

Anderson also excelled in the Western Open, winning it four times, but the U.S. Open is what he's remembered for. The 1903 Open, at Baltusrol Golf Club in New Jersey (one of Anderson's places of employ), saw him tie David Brown in regulation with a total of 307, including a record score of 73 in the first round. Anderson then beat Brown in the playoff by two strokes, 82-84. The

next year, the Open moved west, to Chicago's Glen View Club. There, Willie didn't need a playoff, as he prevailed by five strokes with a 303 total, including a 72 in the final round. Both scores were records.

Myopia Hunt Club was the venue in 1905. At first, it looked as if Anderson was out of the running for a third straight title. Scores of 81 and 80 left him five strokes behind his longtime rival, Alex Smith, and Stewart Gardner. But after the 4th hole of the third round, Willie stood 2-under for the day, and it's reported that he turned to the gallery and said, "That's the championship." He

was as good as his word. From there in, he ate away at the lead, then moved in front, steadily and inexorably. By the 70th hole, he had a four-stroke lead, and he held it together to prevail by two over Smith.

How significant is Willie Anderson's feat? Only three other players have won four Opens; their names are Jones, Hogan, and Nicklaus. No one else has ever won four Opens in five years. At the time, he was 27 years old, and most followers of the game would have wagered that he would continue his reign as long as age would permit.

Alas, it was not to be. Although he would continue to play well, he would only threaten in the Open once more, in 1906. Gradually, his health declined, and so did his game. By 1907, he was under a doctor's care as he played, and by 1910, the signs were clear. After the Open, in which he finished 11th, he set out on a series of exhibition matches. Two days after a 36-hole round, when he and Gil Nicholls lost on the last hole to amateurs Eben Byers and William Fownes, Anderson died at his Philadelphia home. Will we ever see his equal?

1905

- April 4: Fred Corcoran, tournament director of the LPGA during its formative years, is born in Cambridge, Massachusetts.

- June 9: James Braid wins his second British Open despite problems with railway fencing at the 15th and 16th holes in the final round at St. Andrews.

- July 31: Arthur Smith uses a pneumatic golf ball to win the Western Open at Cincinnati G.C., where he posts a record 278 total.

- August 12: H. Chandler Egan repeats as U.S. Amateur champion, easily handling fellow Chicagoan D.E. Sawyer, 6 & 5, in the final at Chicago G.C.

- September 22: Willie Anderson wins his third straight U.S. Open and a record fourth overall, at Myopia Hunt Club near Boston.

- October 14: Pauline Mackay wins the closest match-play final since the U.S. Women's Amateur began, defeating Margaret Curtis, 1 up, at Morris County G.C. in New Jersey.

In 1905, dour Scotsman Willie Anderson became the only man ever to win three consecutive U.S. Open championships. Anderson prevailed by two strokes over Alex Smith at Myopia Hunt Club in Hamilton, Massachusetts. This was also Anderson's fourth career Open title. Only three others have won four U.S. Opens: Bobby Jones, Ben Hogan, and Jack Nicklaus.

• Leighton Calkins's *A System for Club Handicapping* helps the USGA establish eligibility criteria for U.S. Amateur entrants.

• George S. Lyon wins his fourth Canadian Amateur title at Toronto G.C., defeating R.S. Strath by the same record margin, 12 & 11, that he established in 1898.

• Brothers Chandler and Walter Egan meet in the Western Amateur final for the third time. Chandler prevails, 3 & 2, at the Glen View Club in Illinois.

• An informal team match in England between top women golfers from the U.S. and Great Britain sows the seeds for what eventually will become the Curtis Cup Match. The Brits win, 6-1.

• George Cumming wins the Canadian Open with a 148 total.

• James D. Foot wins the U.S. Senior Golf Association's inaugural championship at Apawamis Club in Rye, New York.

1905

Taylor Gets It Right with Dimpled Ball

Early on, ball-makers had experimented with all sorts of wild geometries. But in Great Britain in 1905, William Taylor discovered the pattern that is still used to this day, patenting a cover with a concave dimple pattern *(right)*. The dimpled ball was more aerodynamic than other versions, such as the one on the left.

Dimpled Golf Ball

Spalding Golf Guides

Golf Mags Flourish in Early 1900s

In 1905, Spalding put out its 10th-annual *Golf Guide,* which not only promoted golf but undoubtedly boosted sales of Spalding golf balls and clubs. Actually, quite a few golf publications hit the stands in the early 1900s, including *The American Golfer, Golfers Magazine, Golfing, Golf and Lawn Tennis,* and *Golf,* which was not related to the *Golf* magazine we know today.

Morris Winds Down a Legendary Career

In 1905, Old Tom Morris served his final stint as starter at the British Open. Morris was born in St. Andrews, Scotland, where he learned clubmaking and greenkeeping under Allan Robertson. Morris was the greenkeeper at Prestwick for 30 years, then returned to St. Andrews from 1865 through the turn of the century. As a player, Morris won four British Opens.

Old Tom Morris

- England's nonpareil Harry Vardon publishes one of the best-selling golf books of the era, *The Complete Golfer.*

- Briton William Taylor patents a dimple-cover golf ball design, considered more aerodynamically sound than the popular bramble cover.

- A.G. Spalding introduces the Spalding Dimple, the first dimpled golf ball.

- Former U.S. Open champion James Foulis patents the first concave-face clubhead design.

- The Yale golf team breaks Harvard's string in the National Collegiate championships. Robert Abbott of Yale takes the individual title, at Garden City G.C.

- Dr. L. Lee Harban wins the North and South Amateur championship at Pinehurst C.C.

- Mary H. Dutton wins the Women's North and South Amateur.

1905

Crombie Pokes Fun at Golf's Rules

In 1905, Charles Crombie's *Rules of Golf* were published in book form by Perrier of France. The book included 24 illustrations, all similar to Rule I. Rule XVII, which states that "any loose impediments may be removed from the putting green," features a golfer carting two winos off the green in a wheelbarrow.

H. Chandler Egan

Rules of Golf

Egan Breezes to Victory in Windy City

Chicago was golf's kind of town in 1905. Chicagoans H. Chandler Egan *(pictured)* and D.E. Sawyer met in the final of the U.S. Amateur at Chicago G.C., with Egan prevailing, 6 & 5. And in the Western Amateur, Chandler defeated his brother Walter in the final. The site for that event? The Glen View Club in suburban Chicago.

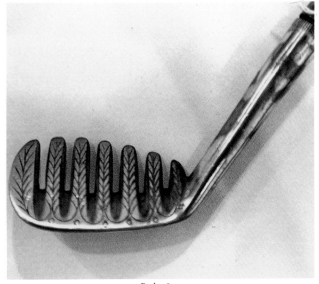

Rake Iron

New Rake Iron Helps Golfers Hit from Rough

In 1905, James Ross Brown received a U.S. patent for a "rake iron." It was designed to "rake" the club through heavy grass when trying to extricate the ball from deep rough. Many other specialty clubs were created in the century's early years. An example was the rut iron, which helped golfers play balls from the wagon ruts in roads and paths.

• The Ross family's domination of the North and South Open continues as Donald edges brother Alex for his second title at Pinehurst C.C.

• Goodyear Tire and Rubber Company's pneumatic golf ball has one chief drawback: its compressed-air center tends to explode in hot weather.

• The U.S.-based Haskell Golf Ball Company sues Hutchison, Main and Company of Glasgow, Scotland, for a patent infringement on its rubber-cored golf ball. A court declares the Haskell patent void in Great Britain.

• Old Tom Morris serves as British Open starter for the last time.

• James Braid wins the *News of the World* professional match-play championship for the second time in three years, at Walton Heath.

• St. Andrews University student A. Gordon Barry defeats Hon. Osmund Scott, 3 & 2, in a rain-swept British Amateur final at Prestwick, Scotland.

BRIDESMAID SMITH FINALLY WINS THE U.S. OPEN

The saying "always a bridesmaid, never a bride" must have been in Scottish professional Alex Smith's mind after Willie Anderson's incredible third consecutive U.S. Open championship in 1905. Alex seemed doomed to second place in the Open. Three times—in 1898, 1901, and 1905—he finished second banana. A single victory in the 1903 Western Open must have been small consolation.

Alex Smith was a proud man, proud of his talent as a golfer. Later in his career, he would garner a fine reputation as a teacher of the game, and he's credited with being the major influence in the careers of both Jerry Travers and Glenna Collett, who became two of the best players of their era.

Smith was born in the Scottish golfing town of Carnoustie in 1872. He came from a family that lived and breathed the game. His brother Willie, in fact, won the 1899 U.S. Open, setting a still-unbroken record with his 11-stroke margin of victory. Another Smith brother, Macdonald, would also make his mark in the annals of American competitive golf. Alex was a fine figure of a man.

Unlike other professionals, he spent most of his career at one club, at Nassau Country Club on Long Island, and was known as one of the most congenial members of his calling.

Alex's first appearance at the Open, in 1898, was also his first runner-up finish. He started the first day of competition with a rousing 78, but he couldn't break 85 thereafter and fell away. Alex kept trying. The next year, he finished eighth, 15 strokes off the pace. In 1900, he was even farther back, 27 blows worse than the winner.

In 1901, the Open was held at Myopia Hunt Club, and although Smith's total of 331 was a stroke higher than in 1899, it was good enough to tie him for the lead with Anderson. In the playoff, however, Anderson was one better than Alex; 85 beat 86, and the silver medal, symbolic of the runner-up, was again in Alex's possession.

The same scenario, in essence, took place in 1905, again at Myopia. Anderson's two-stroke victory, his third consecutive Open championship, again relegated Alex to the role of runner-up. At the beginning of the fourth round, Alex actually held a one-stroke lead, but Anderson's 77 did its job, as the best Smith could muster was 80.

Finally, Smith prevailed in the Open in 1906, and in no uncertain terms. At the Onwentsia Club in Illinois, he led after each round, and his 295 was seven better than the runner-up, brother Willie. It was the first time that the 300 barrier had been broken in either a U.S. or a British Open. Alex Smith would go on to win a second U.S. Open, in 1910. Ironically, that victory came over his *other* brother, Macdonald. Thus, the tale of Alex Smith was bittersweet. He finally won the U.S. Open, but he did so at the expense of his flesh and blood.

1906

• June 15: James Braid becomes the first golfer to win the British Open twice at Muirfield. The Great Triumvirate finishes 1-2-3 for the third and final time, as Braid's 300 bests J.H. Taylor by four and Harry Vardon by five.

• June 20: Golf course architect Robert Trent Jones is born in Ince, Lancashire, England. He will design more than 600 courses world-wide.

• June 22: Alex Smith wins his second Western Open by three shots over Jack Hobens at Homewood C.C. in Illinois.

• June 29: Alex Smith becomes the first golfer in U.S. Open history to break 300 for 72 holes when he posts a 295 for a seven-stroke victory over his brother, Willie, at Onwentsia Club in Illinois.

• July 14: Eben M. Byers beats George S. Lyon, 2 up, in the U.S. Amateur final at Englewood G.C. in New Jersey. Byers had finished second on two previous occasions.

Brothers Alex Smith *(left)* and Willie Smith *(center)* pose with fellow golfer David Bell. Willie had won the U.S. Open in 1899, and in 1906 he duked it out with Alex at the Onwentsia Club near Chicago. This time, Alex prevailed, shooting 295 to Willie's second-place total of 302. In 1910, Alex beat his other brother, Macdonald, in a playoff for the U.S. Open title.

• October 13: Harriot Curtis, of the golfing Curtis sisters, wins her only U.S. Women's Amateur, at Brae Burn C.C. in Massachusetts. She defeats Mary Adams, 2 & 1, in the title match.

• C.T. Jaffrey wins the Trans-Mississippi Golf Association's title at the Omaha Field Club in Nebraska.

• George S. Lyon is in peak form in winning his fifth Canadian Amateur, 5 & 4, over New York-born Douglas Laird at Royal Ottawa G.C.

• Top British golfer James Braid takes pen in hand and releases his first book, *Golf Guide and How to Play Golf,* on both sides of the Atlantic.

• Fanny Osgood, who will become a powerful golf administrator in years to come, is crowned the inaugural Women's Eastern Amateur champion.

• England's Horace Hutchinson continues his prolific writing, this time exploring agronomy in *Golf Greens and Greenkeeping.*

1906

Lenox Golf Ceramics

Golf Ceramics a Hot Item in Early 1900s

Golf collectors of today seek out more than just clubs and balls. In fact, many collectors pay big money for golf-decorated ceramics—like this beautiful sampling of Lenox mugs. Royal Doulton produced the largest amount of golf ceramics in England, while Lenox led the way in the U.S. The trend became popular in the 1890s and fizzled out in the 1930s.

Inventor's Gadget Cuts Holes into Greens

Early-day inventors didn't limit themselves to clubmaking. In fact, one smart fellow developed this contraption, used to cut holes into greens. Golf course maintenance was a difficult and respected trade. Horace Hutchinson wrote an entire book on the subject in 1906: *Golf Greens and Greenkeeping.*

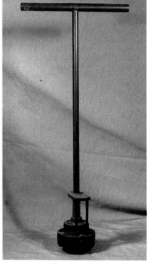

Golf Hole Puncher

Lyon Roars to Victory in Canadian, U.S. Amateurs

In 1906, George S. Lyon reigned as the best amateur golfer in Canada. Lyon captured his fifth Canadian Amateur championship and also made quite a showing in the U.S. Amateur, falling to Eben M. Byers in the final at Englewood G.C. in New Jersey. Two years earlier, Lyon won the Olympic gold medal.

George S. Lyon

- A.M. Maude obtains a British patent for a hinged mirror attached to a putter shaft, which is to be used as an aiming device.

- Royal Montreal professional Charles Murray wins his first of two Canadian Opens, despite rounds of 84-86 at Royal Ottawa G.C.

- The practice of publishing golf club histories gains momentum, notably the *History of the Edinburgh Burgess Golfing Society.*

- Myra D. Paterson wins her third Women's North and South title.

- Warren K. Wood wins the Men's North and South Amateur.

- Mrs. C.L. Dering wins a second consecutive Women's Western Amateur title, at Exmoor G.C. in Illinois.

- In Great Britain, the Hartley brothers obtain a patent for a golf ball with a core of gelatin-wound elastic bands and a gutta-percha cover.

James Braid

Braid Wins Third of Five British Open Titles

In 1906, James Braid won his second consecutive British Open, and third of his career, by shooting 300 at Muirfield in Scotland. All of Braid's five British Open titles would come on golf's grandest courses—two at St. Andrews, two at Muirfield, and one at Prestwick. Also in 1906, Braid released his first book, *Golf Guide and How to Play Golf*.

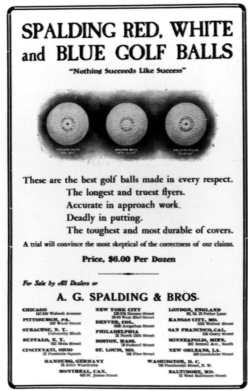

Spalding "Dot" Golf Balls

Spalding Introduces Its Pricey "Dot" Golf Balls

In 1906, A.G. Spalding debuted its famous dot-labeled golf balls. Pictured here are the Spalding White ("red dot"), Spalding White ("with click"), and Spalding Wizard ("blue dot"). Spalding's "click" balls were so named because they made a neat "click" sound when hit. Note the price of these new pellets—$6 a dozen!

Harriot Curtis

Harriot One-Ups Her Sister, Wins Amateur

Harriot Curtis *(pictured)* wasn't quite as good a golfer as her younger sister Margaret, but Harriot was the first of the two to win the U.S. Women's Amateur, claiming the 1906 title at Brae Burn C.C. near Boston. Each sister reached the quarterfinals in 1905. In 1907, they met in the final match.

• Yale wins the National Collegiate championship, at Garden City G.C. Yale's W.E. Clow Jr. captures the individual competition.

• Leigh Carroll wins the Southern Amateur at New Orleans C.C.

• Arnaud Massy wins the inaugural French Open at his home club, La Boulie. It's his first of four wins in this event.

• A.G. Spalding introduces its "Dot" label on golf balls.

• Donald Ross becomes the first three-time North and South Open champion.

• Alexander "Sandy" Herd wins the *News of the World* professional match-play championship at Hollinwell.

• George Low Sr. wins the Metropolitan Open at Hollywood G.C. in New Jersey, beating U.S. Open champ Alex Smith.

ROSS'S BRILLIANT CAREER BEGINS IN PINEHURST

He was the son of a Dornoch stonemason, and he began his career as a lowly journeyman carpenter. However, the destiny of Donald James Ross would not be crafting stone or wood. Instead, he would craft the finest playing fields of golf. Ross would design courses that would host America's greatest championships.

Ross received his initial training from one of the greats of golf, Old Tom Morris, the keeper of the green at St. Andrews. In addition, Ross studied the craft of clubmaking at the firm of David Forgan. Lessons learned, Ross returned to Dornoch, serving the fine course there as both professional and greenkeeper. At the age of 25, in 1898, he emigrated to the U.S.

This move was influenced by a professor at Harvard University, one Robert Wilson. Wilson took Ross under his arm, and upon the Scot's arrival in Boston, the professor got him the job of professional at Oakley Country Club in Massachusetts. There, Ross met the well-to-do Tufts family, who were in the process of constructing the Pinehurst resort. They convinced Ross to take a position as winter professional in the North Carolina sandhills.

Ross was also an exceptional golfer, but his primary calling, to North Carolina and the Tufts empire, would be his ticket to immortality. He soon became a permanent fixture at the Pinehurst resort. There, he was given the responsibility of planning, designing, and maintaining the complex's golf courses, and his talent and skill in doing so brought him national attention. Golf-mad America soon clamored for Donald Ross golf courses. As Cornish and Whitten wrote in *The Golf Course*, "From 1912 until his death in 1948, Ross was considered by many to be America's best-known and most active course designer."

Ross was indeed prolific. More than 500 courses benefitted from his skill, either from construction or renovation, and many of these layouts are considered among the finest in the United States. Besides his masterpiece, Pinehurst No. 2, which he honed and refined for decades, his credits include Seminole in Florida, Oakland Hills in Michigan, Scioto and Inverness in Ohio, and Oak Hill in New York.

To a golfer with an eye for architecture, a Ross course is almost instantly recognizable. His primary skill was the fashioning of greens and green surrounds. Like his native Dornoch, they feature a natural look, with putting surfaces that fall off to their edges, and bunkers, hillocks, and contours just off the green that, in Cornish and Whitten's words, "put a premium on short recovery shots."

One of the founders of the American Society of Golf Course Architects, Donald Ross is considered by many to be the organization's patron saint. He left a lasting legacy to golf, a legacy that will be appreciated as long as club strikes ball.

1907

- January 26: Henry Cotton, who will win three British Opens and play on three Ryder Cup teams, is born in London, England.

- June 21: Arnaud Massy, described as a "Frenchman with the soul of a Scot," becomes the first overseas British Open champion, by two strokes over J.H. Taylor at Hoylake.

- June 21: Alex Ross stages a mild rally to win the U.S. Open on the old St. Martin's Course at Philadelphia Cricket Club. In searing heat, he shoots 302.

- June 21: Third-round U.S. Open leader Jack Hobens finishes with an 85 to lose by seven. He had made the first U.S. Open hole-in-one.

- June 28: After an opening 84, Robert Simpson caps a remarkable comeback to win the Western Open at Hinsdale G.C. in Illinois.

- July 13: Inspired by Scottish bagpipe music in the wee hours of the morning of the championship match, Jerome D. Travers takes his first of four U.S. Amateur titles,

Donald Ross emigrated from Scotland to the United States in 1898, and in the early 1900s developed the great Pinehurst resort courses in North Carolina. In his career, Ross designed more than 500 golf courses, including Pinehurst No. 2, Oakland Hills, Oak Hill, Seminole, and Inverness. More than 50 national championships have been played on Ross courses.

6 & 5, over Archibald Graham at Euclid Club in Cleveland.

• October 12: Two sisters meet in the U.S. Women's Amateur championship match for the only time in history. Margaret Curtis defeats her defending champion sister, Harriot Curtis, 7 & 6, at Midlothian C.C. in Illinois.

• November 17: Joe Dey, executive director of the USGA for more than 30 years, is born in Norfolk, Virginia.

• As his great career continues unabated, two-time British Open champion Harold Hilton publishes his biography, *My Golfing Reminiscences.*

• One of the classic golf books, Henry Leach's *Great Golfers in the Making,* is published simultaneously in Great Britain and the U.S.

• Margaret and Harriot Curtis travel to England in their quest to establish an international competition, but Margaret grabs more headlines for her feathered hats.

James Braid

Ward's Lithograph Pokes Fun at James Braid

Caricaturist Sir Leslie Ward created this lithograph of the laconic James Braid, one of the members of the Great Triumvirate. Ward, who went under the pseudonym "Spy," created this piece of work for *Vanity Fair* magazine. Ward also spoofed other golfers in his lithographs, including John H. Taylor, Harold Hilton, and Horace Hutchinson.

Nelson Whitney

Whitney Captures the Budding Southern Amateur

Another regional amateur tournament, the Southern Amateur, was beginning to command respect in the early 1900s. The 1907 title went to Nelson Whitney, who would win this tournament five times in all. The '07 tourney took place at East Lake in Atlanta, the course where Bobby Jones would soon learn his golf.

Golf Ball Paint

Golf Ball Paint Used to Whiten Old Pellets

In the early portion of the century, golf balls were white and bright—but only when they were brand new. After a few whacks, the paint would begin to chip off, and golfers needed to smear them with golf ball paint in order to get them white again. This two-inch-high can says its paint "does not turn yellow or chip off the ball."

• Ellis Knowles of Yale wins the individual National Collegiate championship and leads the Elis to their third straight team title.

• Molly B. Adams, winner of the year's Women's North and South championship, also takes the Women's Eastern Amateur in Atlantic City, New Jersey.

• A. and J. Dey patent an apparatus similar to a pop-up toaster, to eject the ball from the hole.

• Alex Smith skips his U.S. Open title defense to compete in the British Open, but he finishes 21 shots back.

• For the fourth time in six years, Chandler Egan wins the Western

Amateur, this time by 5 & 4 over Herbert Jones, at Chicago G.C.

• Nelson Whitney captures his first of five Southern Amateur titles, at East Lake C.C. in Atlanta.

• Arnaud Massy repeats as French Open champion, again on his home turf at La Boulie.

1907

Alex and Donald Ross

Alex Ross Wins Open as Donald Finishes 10th

Alex Ross *(left)*, posing with older brother Donald, won the 1907 U.S. Open at the Philadelphia Cricket Club. Ross shot 302 to defeat runner-up Gil Nicholls by two strokes. Donald, by the way, finished 10th in the tournament—his fourth career top-10 showing. Also in 1906, Alex won his third of six North and South Opens.

Crawford House Golf Club

Folks Vacation at Numerous Golf Resorts

These fine people smiled for the camera in 1907 at Crawford House G.C. in New Hampshire. Some may be surprised to learn that golf resorts date back to the turn of the century. The Pinehurst resort in North Carolina was one of numerous golf getaways. Others were built in Atlantic City, on Cape Cod, and in the Adirondack Mountains.

Mary B. Adams

Adams Prevails in Big-Name Tourneys

Mary B. Adams, also known as Molly Adams, captured two of the most prestigious ladies' events in 1907—the Women's North and South championship and the Women's Eastern Amateur. Adams had made her presence felt in the 1906 U.S. Women's Amateur, losing in the final to Harriot Curtis. In the 1907 Amateur, she fell in the third round, as Margaret Curtis beat sister Harriot in the final match.

• May Hezlet defeats her sister, Florence, 2 & 1, in the Ladies' British Open Amateur final at Newcastle County Down.

• James Braid wins his third of four *News of the World* professional match-play titles, at Sunningdale, England.

• John Ball wins his sixth of eight British Amateurs, but it's his first on the Old Course at St. Andrews, where he routs C.A. Palmer, 6 & 4.

• Alex Ross wins his third of six North and South Opens.

• Allan Lard begins a two-year reign as North and South Amateur champ.

• George S. Lyon wins his third straight Canadian Amateur (sixth overall) but his first at his home Lambton G.C. in Toronto.

• Percy Barrett, a Harry Vardon protégé, wins the first Canadian Open held over 72 holes at Lambton G.C., where he serves as golf professional.

LONG-NOSES EVOLVE INTO BULGERS, BRASSIES

Let us now speak of the wooden club, the implement that propels the golf ball over such prodigious distances, and let us examine how, like the very game itself, it has continuously evolved in terms of shape, make-up, and efficiency.

For the first four hundred years, wooden golf clubs carried the general appellation of "long-nose clubs." Crafted entirely by hand, for machine production didn't begin until the end of the 19th Century, long-noses had a whippy, flexible shaft fashioned from a variety of woods—from ash to hazel and hickory. The clubheads were of fruit woods— apple, thorn, and pear—and beech.

The shaft and clubhead were joined together by a splice or "scare" joint, secured by glue and a wrapping or whipping of pitched twine. The joint was then varnished and fitted with grips of leather wrapped over wool. Aesthetically, the best long-noses were considered to be those made by Hugh Philp of Scotland, who worked in the late 18th and early 19th Centuries.

Lo and behold, along came the gutta-percha ball, replacing the featherie around 1850. The much harder "guttie" wreaked havoc on the long-nose's softwood clubface. Clubmakers tried to remedy the situation by using harder woods for the head—eventually most clubmakers found persimmon the best—or they added an insert, a harder material set into the face to resist the shock of impact.

In addition, a stronger, thicker joint was also needed, as was a thicker, stiffer wooden shaft. Through their experimentation, the makers also discovered that a more compact head provided better playing characteristics. So, as the 19th Century came to a close, the head shortened and deepened, first into a semi-long-nose, then into the bulger.

The bulger incorporated another scientific concept, called by some "gear effect." The face had a concave cross-section, and balls struck on the toe or heel had a spin imparted to them that had the effect of minimizing any inaccuracy.

Also at this time, other methods of fitting the head to the shaft were tried, including the socket joint, where the shaft was inserted into the head, then glued and whipped—today's method. Lastly, to protect the sole of the club, a brass plate was added—therefore, the "brassie."

There was no end to innovation as the golf boom of the early 1900s took hold. Aluminum and synthetic clubheads were marketed, and head shapes assumed aerodynamic characteristics. Then, along came the Haskell ball. Its rubber winding and, eventually, rubber cover softened the shock of impact. Clubhead speeds increased, and heads grew slightly larger again to provide a larger "sweet spot." Of course, changes in woods have continued throughout the century, as manufacturers look for an edge in the marketplace and players look for an edge on the course.

1908

- May 22: Horton Smith, who will win both the 1934 and 1936 Masters, is born in Springfield, Missouri.

- May 24: Old Tom Morris, a four-time British Open champion in the 1860s, dies at age 86 from a concussion caused by a fall down a flight of stairs.

- June 18: Willie Anderson becomes the first three-time Western Open champ. His 299 at Normandie Park G.C. in St. Louis edges Fred McLeod by one shot.

- June 19: James Braid wins his fourth British Open, at Prestwick, Scotland, lowering the 72-hole standard to 291.

- July 12: Paul Runyan, who will win the 1934 and 1938 PGA Championships, is born in Hot Springs, Arkansas.

- August 29: Fred McLeod, who weighs just 108 pounds, tops Willie Smith in a U.S. Open playoff, 77-83, after they had tied at Myopia Hunt Club near Boston.

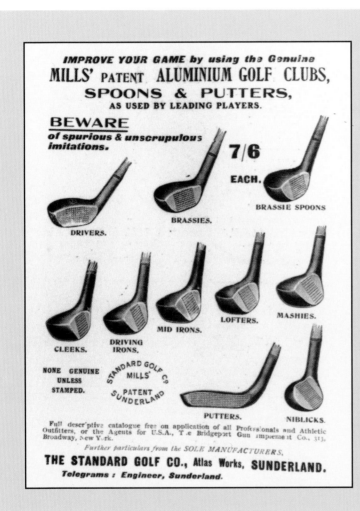

With the advent of the hard gutta-percha balls in the mid-1800s, soft-wooded long-nose clubs *(right)* became passe. The long-nose clubheads evolved into the shorter and more compact bulgers, and then into the brass-plated brassies. Around the turn of the century, even aluminum clubs hit the market. The ad on the left offers a sampling.

• September 18: Walter Travis, winner of the U.S. Amateur's qualifying medalist honors for the sixth time, loses the semifinal match to Jerome D. Travers, 2 up.

• September 19: Jerry Travers tops Max Behr, 8 & 7, to successfully defend his U.S. Amateur crown at Garden City G.C. in New York.

• October 24: Katherine Harley coasts to a 6 & 5 U.S. Women's Amateur victory over Mrs. T.H. Polhemus at Chevy Chase Club in Maryland.

• Harry C. Lee begins his club-importing business in New York City, achieving great success that will last for two decades. His clubs are marked with a cleekmark shaped like an acorn.

• W.W. Tulloch releases a 440-copy limited first edition of *The Life of Tom Morris.*

• Mabel Thomson wins her fifth Canadian Ladies title (fourth in a row) at Lambton G.C.

Golf Magazines

American Golfer *Hits the Stands*

In 1908, Walter Travis founded *The American Golfer*, considered by many to be the finest golf magazine of all time. So prestigious was the publication that the legendary Grantland Rice succeeded Travis as the magazine's editor. *Golfers Magazine*, another prestigious publication, commenced in 1902 and was edited by Charles Evans Jr.

Tulloch's New Book Honors Tom Morris

Upon the death of Old Tom Morris, who passed away in 1908, W.W. Tulloch completed the biography *The Life of Tom Morris*. The first edition was a limited run of 440 copies, making it one of golf's more collectible books. However, a trade edition followed closely on its heels and proved to be one of the most popular golf books of its era, going into several printings.

The Life of Tom Morris

James Braid

Braid Wins British with Rousing 291

James Braid, sketched here with his famous bushy mustache, won the 1908 British Open championship at Prestwick in Scotland. Braid shot an eyebrow-raising 291, setting a British Open standard that wouldn't be equaled until 1926, when Bobby Jones would shoot the same score. Also in 1908, Braid released *Advanced Golf*, a highly acclaimed instruction book.

• Albert Murray becomes the youngest Canadian Open champion ever at age 20 and 10 months, posting an even 300 at Royal Montreal G.C.

• James Braid's *Advanced Golf*, possibly the best instruction book of its era, is published in both Great Britain and the United States.

• Maude Titterton prevails over Dorothy Campbell on the 19th hole to win the Ladies' British Open Amateur, held on the Old Course at St. Andrews.

• J.H. Taylor becomes the first non-Frenchman to win the French Open, at La Boulie.

• Mason Phelps captures his first of two Western Amateur championships at Arsenal G.C. in Rock Island, Illinois.

• Last year's U.S. Women's Amateur champion, Margaret Curtis, crosses over to tennis and wins the National Doubles title with Evelyn Sears.

Fred McLeod

Tiny McLeod Plays Big in U.S. Open Playoff

Fred McLeod, a wisp of a man at 108 pounds, won the 1908 U.S. Open at Myopia Hunt Club in Massachusetts. McLeod tied Willie Smith with a rather bloated score of 322, then downed Smith in an 18-hole playoff, 77-83. McLeod would never again win the Open, but he'd finish a shot out of a playoff in both 1910 and 1911.

Old Tom Morris

Legendary Morris Passes Away at the Age of 86

Old Tom Morris, the pioneer of modern golf, died in 1908 at age 86 after falling down a flight of stairs. Morris outlived his son by 33 years. Young Tom Morris, who had won four consecutive British Opens, died at age 24 in 1875. Young Tom, traumatized by the sudden death of his wife, died a few months after her death from a ruptured blood vessel.

Walter Travis

Travis Takes the Medal in U.S. Amateur

Though he turned 46 years old in 1908, Walter Travis had hardly lost a step. In the U.S. Amateur, he earned medalist honors with a score of 153—nine strokes better than anyone else. This was the sixth time that Travis had won the medal, a feat that only Bobby Jones would ever match. Travis lost in the Amateur's semifinals to Jerry Travers.

- Walter J. Travis is the founder and first editor of *The American Golfer.*

- Ford Desborough, president of the British Olympic Committee, invites Royal St. George's G.C. to host the golf competition, but the idea is scrapped when St. Andrews protests that golf is not suitable for the Olympics.

- E.A. Lassen is the surprise British Amateur champion, trouncing H.E. Taylor in the final-round match at Royal St. George's in Sandwich, England.

- Allan Lard becomes the first repeat North and South Amateur champion at Pinehurst, North Carolina.

- Alex Ross wins his fourth of six North and South Open titles at Pinehurst C.C.

- Yale wins its fourth consecutive National Collegiate title, and Harvard's H.H. Wilder takes individual honors, at Brae Burn C.C. in Massachusettes.

TEENAGE GARDNER SWINGS, SINGS WAY TO TOP

Talk about your all-around athletes! Here's a guy who not only was—and still is—the youngest player ever to win the U.S. Amateur, but he also set an American record in the pole vault. An All-American boy, Robert Abbe Gardner had a beautiful singing voice, was as handsome as a movie star, and served his country with distinction as an Army officer in World War I. Do you need more?

Bob Gardner was born in 1890 in Illinois and took to golf like the proverbial duck to water. Just after completing his freshman year at Yale University, he entered the 1909 U.S. Amateur, which was at Chicago Golf Club, only a few miles from his home. Who would have thought that, at only 19 years and five months of age, he would qualify as co-medalist with Charles "Chick" Evans at 151? Who could have predicted that he would move steadily through match play and prevail each time, including a solid defeat of Chandler Egan in the final? Indeed, Gardner was almost a neophyte. He hadn't made any sort of mark for himself in any championship of consequence up to that exalted point. But, as they

say, talent will win out.

From 1910–13, Gardner's play wasn't up to his usual standard. Although he qualified for match play in the 1911 and 1913 U.S. Amateurs, he lost his first-round match in each. In 1914, he regained that "ease and lack of effort that was the envy of all his contemporaries," as the *Encyclopedia of Golf* put it, and he made it to the round of eight before losing to eventual champion Francis Ouimet.

In 1915, however, no one could beat Gardner. Again, he swept through the U.S. Amateur, at the Country Club of Detroit, defeating John Anderson in the final. In 1916, he almost took the title again, falling to Chick Evans in

the final after beating a young Bobby Jones in the earlier matches.

World War I put a stop to Gardner's golf, but following the Armistice, he was back on the competitive trail again. In the 1920 British Amateur, he narrowly lost to Cyril Tolley in an explosive final match. Gardner birdied the last hole of regulation to tie the match, but Tolley birdied the first extra hole to claim the crown. The next year, he fell to Jesse Guilford in the U.S. Amateur final, his fourth such appearance in a dozen years.

And Gardner wasn't done yet. He played on the first U.S. Walker Cup team in 1922, and he was the team's playing captain in 1923 and 1924, going undefeated both years. Gardner is perhaps best remembered, at least in the context of the Walker Cup, for singing. Following the 1923 Match, he led the St. Andrews crowd in song. Standing on the steps of the Royal and Ancient clubhouse, the multitudes intoned the old Scots anthem, "A Wee Doch and Doris." More than likely, it was the first time they had seen a golf champion who sung as well as he swung.

1909

• June 11: J.H. Taylor wins his fourth British Open with a 295 total at Deal G.C. in England, which joins the championship rota.

• June 24: David Hunter posts the first sub-70 round in U.S. Open history with a 68 in the morning, but he balloons to an 84 in the brutal afternoon heat.

• June 25: English-born George Sargent wins the U.S. Open at Englewood G.C. in New Jersey, lowering the 72-hole record to 290.

• September 11: Robert Gardner becomes the youngest U.S. Amateur champion ever at 19 years and five months, defeating H. Chandler Egan, 4 & 3, at the Chicago G.C.

• September 15: Willie Anderson wins a fourth Western Open and second in a row at Skokie C.C. in Illinois.

• October 9: Dorothy Iona Campbell completes the double by winning the U.S. Women's Amateur over Nonna Barlow at Merion Cricket Club, just a few months

Robert Gardner came out of nowhere to win the 1909 U.S. Amateur at Chicago G.C. Gardner defeated H. Chandler Egan in the final to become the youngest champion ever at 19 years and five months. The well-rounded Gardner also set an American record in the pole vault, served his country as an Army officer in World War I, and displayed a fine singing voice.

after capturing the Ladies' British Open Amateur.

• Karl Keffer becomes the first Canadian-born golfer to win the Canadian Open, as he wins at his home club, Toronto G.C.

• British instructor Maud Robertson taps the growing women's market

with her first book, *Hints to the Lady Golfers.*

• Douglas Grant, who years later will work with Jack Neville on the design of Pebble Beach G.L., wins the Pacific Northwest Amateur.

• J.H. Taylor successfully defends his French Open crown at La Boulie.

• The USGA offers to donate a cup for an international women's team match, but the British Ladies Golf Union declines, saying it would be too difficult to field a team.

• Edward Legge defeats Glen Moss, 1 up, for the Canadian Amateur title at the Toronto G.C., but he'll never again enter another national title.

John H. Taylor

Taylor Tallies His Fourth Win in British Open

John H. Taylor, the least famous of the Great Triumvirate, captured his fourth British Open championship in 1909 at Deal G.C. in England. Taylor, who learned golf as a caddie at Westward Ho! in Devonshire, was a stocky golfer who played flat-footed. He had a short, quick swing and was known for his accuracy.

George Sargent

Sargent Wins U.S. Open with Record Total Score

George Sargent broke new ground in 1909, as he lowered the U.S. Open scoring record to 290—the same score that Jack Nicklaus would win with in 1972. Sargent shot 75-72-72-71 to prevail by four strokes at Englewood G.C. in New Jersey. In 1912, Sargent became the first to break 300 in the Canadian Open.

Campbell is the First to Do the Double

Despite the rigors of trans-Atlantic travel, Britain's Dorothy Campbell completed an unprecedented double in 1909. In early summer, she defeated May Hezlet in the final of the Ladies' British Open Amateur. In October, Campbell won the U.S. Women's Amateur at Merion Cricket Club, beating Nonna Barlow in the final, 3 & 2.

Dorothy Campbell

- James D. Foot wins his second consecutive U.S. Senior Golf Association championship, at Apawamis Club in Rye, New York.

- Yale takes its fifth straight National Collegiate title, and Princeton's Albert Seckel earns individual honors, at Apawamis Club in New York.

- The Royal and Ancient Golf Club intends to outlaw the controversial Schenectady center-shafted putter, which would force British clubmakers to scrap thousands of models.

- Charles "Chick" Evans and Vida Llewellyn win their respective Western Amateur titles at Homewood C.C. in Illinois.

- Robert Maxwell beats Cecil Hutchison for his second British Amateur title, at Muirfield in Scotland.

- James D. Standish Jr. and Mary Fownes win their respective North and South Amateur titles at Pinehurst C.C.

William Howard Taft

Pupil Beats Teacher in Canadian Open

Karl Keffer *(pictured)*, who had learned his golf from George Cumming, the longtime pro at Toronto G.C., upset his teacher at Cumming's home course to win the 1909 Canadian Open. Cumming, who won the tournament in 1905, finished second three of the next four years, this time by three strokes.

Taft's Love of Golf Spreads to the Masses

William Howard Taft *(pictured)* succeeded President Theodore Roosevelt in 1909, giving the game of golf a big boost. While Roosevelt disliked golf, Taft was obsessed with it. Big Bill sung its praises and encouraged Americans to take up the game, which added to the popularity of the growing sport.

Karl Keffer

Golf Competitors

Hunter Is the First to Break 70 in U.S. Open

Dave Hunter *(back row, third from right)* achieved a notable feat in the 1909 U.S. Open. In the first round, Hunter shot a 68 to become the first to ever break 70 in the championship. Unfortunately, Hunter skied to an 84 in the second round and finished 23 shots off the pace of winner George Sargent.

• Fred McLeod becomes the first golfer other than the Ross brothers to win the North and South Open at Pinehurst.

• The Western Golf Association considers a name change to "American Golf Association" as a challenge to the USGA's authority.

• Outgoing President Theodore Roosevelt advises his successor, William Howard Taft, against playing golf. He considers it too undemocratic and too much of a sissy game for a public man.

• The USGA tightens its definition of the amateur golfer, targeting for exclusion pro athletes in other sports as well as caddies, caddie masters, and greenkeepers after age 16.

• Royal Doulton's famed "Toby" ceramics, portraying a character taken from the novel *Tristam Shandy* who engages in games including golf, are placed on the market.

'BIG BILL' TAFT PRESIDES OVER THE GAME

Who really brought the round ball to the Oval Office? Although Presidents before him dabbled and palavered about golf, the largest influence—pun intended—on making golf acceptable in the highest reaches of U.S. government had to be William Howard "Big Bill" Taft.

Taft, who served as U.S. President between 1909 and 1912—and as Chief Justice of the Supreme Court thereafter—was gaga about the game. As he told a California crowd during an electioneering swing in 1908: "I don't know of any game that after a while makes you so ashamed of your profanity. It is a game full of moments of self-abasement, with only a few moments of self-exaltation. And we Americans, who are not celebrated for our modesty, may find such a game excellent training."

Prophetic words? Would Americans hit the links with even greater zeal than ever before? It sure looked like it, considering what was going on in the world of professional golf. In the 1909 U.S. Open, American-born Tom MacNamara parlayed a second-round 69 into a second-place finish, the highest by a native to

that point. The *USGA Record Book* commented, "...the era of the homebreds was dawning." Then, in the middle of Taft's term, another Yank, Johnny McDermott, took two U.S. Open titles in a row, in 1911 and 1912. Francis Ouimet made it three home wins in 1913, and Walter Hagen took it to four in a row in 1914.

During his term, wrote historian Jim Apfelbaum, Taft's game became the object of media attention. It "was well covered during his Presidency," Apfelbaum wrote. "While he enjoyed the mashie, his putting was problematic.... He had animated conversations with the ball.... Once he lightly referred to his game as 'bumble puppy golf.'"

How gung-ho was Big Bill? Very. He was informed once that a foreign head of state had arrived in the Capitol. "I'll be damned if I will give up my game to see this fellow," he told the messenger, and blissfully played on.

History records that, following Taft, many other Presidents found solace and challenge on the course. The roster of Presidential hackers grew as the years passed, from Woodrow Wilson and Warren G. Harding (who donated a trophy to the USGA as a prize in the Amateur Public Links championship) through Dwight D. Eisenhower, John F. Kennedy, Richard Nixon, and Gerald Ford. President George Herbert Walker Bush was a tough competitor on the course. (His maternal grandfather, George Herbert Walker, was the president of the USGA who inaugurated the Walker Cup.) Even workaholic Bill Clinton finds time now and then for a round of golf.

However, Taft set the standard for those Presidents who followed. So obsessed was Taft that he once opined: "The beauty of golf is that you cannot play if you permit yourself to think of anything else."

1910

• May 25: Jimmy Demaret, who will win three Masters and appear for the U.S. on three Ryder Cup teams, is born in Houston.

• June 20: Alex Smith wins his second U.S. Open in the first three-way playoff. Smith (71) beats his brother, Macdonald (77), and Johnny McDermott (75) at the

Philadelphia Cricket Club. They were tied at 298.

• June 24: James Braid wins his fifth British Open and his second at St. Andrews, as the Open celebrates its Golden Jubilee (1860–1910).

• September 2: Charles Evans Jr., age 20, becomes the first amateur to

win the Western Open, at Beverly C.C. in Chicago. This Open is conducted at match play.

• September 17: William C. Fownes Jr., a future president of the USGA, wins his only U.S. Amateur, defeating Warren K. Wood, 4 & 3, in the final at The Country Club in Massachusetts.

1910

President William Howard Taft became hooked on golf in 1896 and couldn't give it up. For Taft, it seemed, a round on the links took precedence over his duties in the Oval Office. Witnesses said that he was serious business on the course—rarely joking around. The weakness of his game was his putting, as one might imagine for a man his size. He weighed nearly 300 pounds.

• October 15: Dorothy Campbell—who had earlier won the Canadian Amateur—captures her second consecutive U.S. Women's Amateur title, at Homewood C.C. in Flossmoor, Illinois.

• October 25: Four-time U.S. Open champion Willie Anderson, who has played three 36-hole matches in the last six days, dies at age 31 at his Chestnut Hill, Philadelphia, home, reportedly from arteriosclerosis.

• British author Bernard Darwin publishes his classic book, *Golf Courses of the British Isles.* Even the watercolor illustrations by Harry Rountree are held in high esteem.

• At Royal North Devon G.C., Miss Grant Suttie tops Miss L. Moore in their final-round match to win the Ladies' British Open Amateur championship, 6 & 4.

• Arthur F. Knight of Schenectady, New York, obtains a patent for a seamed, tubular steel golf shaft.

Caddies of Del Monte and San Francisco Golf Clubs

Caddies Tote the Bags at an Early Age

Caddies at Del Monte G.C. and San Francisco G.C. posed for this photo in September 1910. They look to be a mixed and somewhat surly lot, and some seem smaller than the bags they toted. Young loopers were not unusual. In fact, when Francis Ouimet won the 1913 U.S. Open, his caddie, Eddie Lowery, was only 10 years old.

Evans Beats the Pros in Western Open

Until 1910, the Western Open had been the province of the professionals. But 20-year-old amateur Charles Evans Jr. changed all that, winning the 1910 version—conducted at match play—at Beverly C.C. in his hometown of Chicago. Throughout his career, Evans often struggled with his putting. His iron play, though, was outstanding.

Charles Evans Jr.

Tillinghast a Good Golfer Himself

Albert W. Tillinghast played in the 1910 U.S. Open and finished 25th. But Tillie soon realized that his talents lay more in creating courses, not playing them. He completed his first layout at age 32. His company achieved success after success, and his creation of courses like Winged Foot and Baltusrol eventually made him a millionaire.

Albert W. Tillinghast

• Florence Vanderbeck and Walter J. Travis win their respective North and South Amateur titles at Pinehurst C.C.

• Mason Phelps wins his second Western Amateur, unseating the defending champion, Charles Evans Jr., 2 & 1, at the Minikahda Club in Minneapolis.

• F.G. Byrd wins the Southern Amateur championship.

• For the first time, advertising appears on a golf tee, as A.W. Hill patents a cardboard collar that fastens into a ball support.

• Daniel Kenny claims the Canadian Open at Lambton G.C.

• For the sixth straight year, the Yale team takes the National Collegiate title. Yale is led by Robert Hunter, who wins the individual championship.

• Alex Ross wins his fifth of six North and South Open titles at Pinehurst C.C.

James Braid

Braid Claims Win No. 5 in British Open

James Braid, the most taciturn member of the Great Triumvirate, won the 1910 British Open. Braid toured the Old Course at St. Andrews in 299 strokes for four rounds, beating Alexander Herd by four shots. The old-school Scottish professional had thus won his fifth Open championship. He would never again challenge for the title.

William Fownes

Future President Fownes Wins U.S. Amateur

He would go on to become president of the USGA, but in 1910 William Fownes was on the front lines of golf, both as a designer of courses and as an amateur player. Fownes won the 1910 U.S. Amateur, rallying to beat Charles Evans Jr. in the semifinals and then knocking off Warren Wood in the final, at The Country Club in Massachusetts.

Bernard Darwin

Darwin, Rountree Create a Classic Book

Though a fine golfer in his own right, Bernard Darwin's greatest gift was writing and reporting about the game. Perhaps his finest work was *Golf Courses of the British Isles*, a classic that hit the shelves in 1910. Darwin's precise and intuitive prose served as the perfect foil for Harry Rountree's moody watercolor illustrations.

• Fritz Martin wins the Canadian Amateur by defeating George S. Lyon in a 37-hole championship match on Lyon's home Lambton G.C. turf in Toronto.

• A.F. Dimmock receives a patent for a golf ball composed of a nucleus of small rubber balls wound inside a regular ball.

• John Ball wins his seventh British Amateur at his home Royal Liverpool G.C. in Hoylake, where he won earlier in 1890 and 1894.

• *Golf Monthly* magazine commences publication in Scotland.

• Fanny Osgood wins her third Women's Eastern Amateur.

• Great Britain's James Braid braves the chops of the English Channel to win the French Open title at La Boulie.

• Michael Scott becomes the first three-time Australian Amateur champion, all coming at Royal Melbourne G.C.

HILTON BRAVES THE SEA TO DO THE DOUBLE

In the days before World War I, trans-Atlantic travel was certainly no picnic. The so-called luxury liners took the grueling and stormy North Atlantic route to save fuel, belching coal byproducts from their multiple stacks. Generally speaking, voyagers could count on a week of cooped-up, claustrophobic conditions. However, this prospect didn't deter premier British amateur Harold H. Hilton. In 1911, he packed his hickories and his plus-fours and booked passage to America, intending to take his chances against the best amateurs America had to offer in the national championship.

It certainly wasn't the fiery enthusiasm of youth that propelled Hilton across the sea. At the age of 42, he had compiled a stellar record in his native land. In fact, the Liverpudlian had proved victorious in the 1892 and 1897 British Opens and the 1900 and 1901 British Amateurs, finishing as runner-up in that event three times as well. Early in 1911, he made it three British Am titles, prevailing over E.A. Lassen and 144 other entrants at Prestwick, claiming the trophy with a 4 & 3 victory in the final match.

Yes, Hilton had plenty of experience—and it showed in the 1911 U.S. Amateur. He dominated the 36 holes of stroke-play qualifying, posting a 150 total at the Apawamis Club in Rye, New York. HHH must have liked mid-September at Apawamis, just north of the hustle and bustle of New York City. He started at the top of the bracket in match play, defeating S.J. Graham of Greenwich, Connecticut, 3 & 2. He then coasted by R.C. Watson, requiring only 26 of the 36 holes to post an 11 & 10 win.

Jerome "Jerry" Travers was Hilton's next hurdle, and he was no pushover. Travers would go on to become Amateur champion in 1912 and 1913, and finish second in 1914. However, Hilton was able to topple Travers, winning by three holes with two to play. In the semifinals, he came up against C.W. Inslee, playing out of Wykagyl, just down the road from Apawamis. Inslee's 37-hole victory in the quarterfinals, over P.W. Whittemore of The Country Club in Brookline, Massachusetts, must have taken a lot out of him, though, as Hilton had another easy win, this time by the count of 8 & 6.

So the final match was set, Hilton versus Fred Herreshoff. It was a terrific match. Herreshoff was six down with 13 to play, then won the 6th, 8th, 9th, 11th, 12th, and 16th to tie it, and missed putts of five and seven feet on the 17th and 18th. On the first extra hole, Hilton's shot got a favorable bounce off a slope to the right, ending up on the green, 20 feet from the hole. He won there when Herreshoff bogeyed.

Like the sportsman he was, Hilton returned the next year to defend his title, although he lost in his first-round match. However, his 1911 win would stand in the annals, as he was the first golfer ever to take the double, the British and U.S. Amateurs, in the same year.

1911

- June 26: Johnny McDermott becomes the first American-born man and the youngest golfer (19 years, 10 months) to win the U.S. Open. He prevails in a playoff (80-82-85) at Chicago G.C.

- June 30: Robert Simpson wins his second Western Open, 2 & 1, over Tom McNamara in the final at Kent

C.C. in Grand Rapids, Michigan. Many pros boycotted in a protest over the match-play format.

- June 30: Harry Vardon lunches on a chicken wing and a cup of tea midway through a British Open playoff win over Arnaud Massy at Royal St. George's. It's his record-tying fifth Open victory.

- July 7: Some 20 professional golfers organize the Canadian Professional Golfers Association during the Canadian Open.

- October 14: Margaret Curtis wins her second U.S. Women's Amateur title, topping Lillian B. Hyde, 5 & 3, in the final at Baltusrol G.C. in New Jersey.

Harold H. Hilton used an extremely short-shafted putter, and he had a habit of swinging with a lit cigarette in his mouth. Nevertheless, HHH was an outstanding amateur player. In 1911, he took the Amateur titles of both Britain and the U.S., defeating E.A. Lassen and Fred Herreshoff in the finals of the respective tournaments.

• November 22: Ralph Guldahl, winner of the 1937 and 1938 U.S. Opens and the 1939 Masters, is born in Dallas.

• Charles Murray posts the highest winning score (314) in Canadian Open history, defeating runner-up Davie Black by two strokes at Royal Ottawa G.C.

• George Hutton wins the Canadian Amateur, defeating Bert Austin in a record 39-hole championship match, at Royal Ottawa G.C.

• For the fifth time in seven years, James D. Foot prevails in the U.S. Senior Golf Association championship.

• Mrs. Roger Smith of Nashville, Tennessee, wins the inaugural Women's Southern Amateur championship.

• George Stanley of Yale takes the individual title at the National Collegiate championships, leading his team to its seventh title in a row.

Canadian Open Champions

Canadian Open Titles Won by the Canadians

Prior to World War I, the Canadian Open was dominated by Canadians, including four in this photo. Charles Murray *(far left)* won in 1906 and 1911, while Albert Murray *(third from right)* prevailed in 1908 and 1913. Other champs included Karl Keffer *(center)*, who won in 1909 and 1914, and George Cumming *(far right)*, the winner in 1905.

Vardon Nabs His Fifth Open Title

After James Braid captured his record fifth British Open in 1910, Harry Vardon claimed a fifth title of his own in 1911. Vardon and Arnaud Massy tied at 303 after 72 holes at Royal St. George's in England, then met in a 36-hole playoff the next day. On the 35th hole trailing by seven strokes, Massy conceded the match.

Harry Vardon

Barlow Wins First Eastern Amateur

Nonna Barlow was one of the finest women players of the early part of the century. Twice she made it to the final match of the U.S. Women's Amateur; twice more she reached the semifinals. But her true province was the Women's Eastern Amateur, which she won six times. Her first victory came in 1911.

Nonna Barlow

• Charles Evans Jr. and Louise Elkins win their respective North and South Amateur titles at Pinehurst C.C.

• The first reminder grip, with a ridge on the side of the grip opposite to the clubhead, is patented in Great Britain by H. Cawsey.

• Cecil Leitch, a 20-year-old British golfer, publishes her first book, *Golf for Girls.*

• Charles Blair Macdonald's National Golf Links of America is opened for play on Long Island, New York. Charter members include Robert Todd Lincoln, son of President Abraham Lincoln.

• The USGA establishes par as "perfect play without flukes and under ordinary weather conditions, always allowing two strokes on each putting green."

• Arnaud Massy becomes the first three-time French Open champ, at La Boulie.

Macdonald Unveils National Golf Links

Charles Blair Macdonald helped pioneer golf in the U.S. He was one of the prime movers of the fledgling USGA, and he won the first U.S. Amateur title in 1895. However, his fame has lasted longer as an architect. His crowning achievement, the National Golf Links of America, opened in Southampton, New York, in 1911.

Johnny McDermott

Charles Blair Macdonald

American-Born McDermott Prevails in U.S. Open

Johnny McDermott became the first homebred American to win the U.S. Open, as he claimed the 1911 title in a playoff at Chicago G.C. McDermott, Mike Brady, and George Simpson all ended regulation tied at 307. But McDermott, who had lost a U.S. Open playoff in 1910, posted an 80 to defeat Brady by two strokes and Simpson by five.

• Charles Evans Jr. defeats John G. Anderson in a 38-hole French Amateur final at La Boulie.

• James Braid wins his fourth and final *News of the World* professional match-play title at Walton Heath.

• Dorothy Campbell wins her second Ladies' British Open

Amateur title, defeating Violet Hezlet, 3 & 2, at Portrush G.C. in Northern Ireland.

• Portrush G.C. hosts an informal match called "American and Colonial versus Great Britain." The British women's team triumphs by the score of 7-2.

• Gil Nicholls wins his first of two North and South Open titles, matching Alex Ross's 36-hole winning total of 141 set last year.

• Carnegie Clark becomes the first three-time Australian Open champion, winning at his home Royal Sydney G.C.

ENGLAND'S BALL POCKETS WIN NO. 8 IN BRITISH AMATEUR

Is it poetic justice, or merely happy coincidence, that the greatest British amateur ever to play the game was named Ball? For indeed, there can be no argument: Just as Bobby Jones now—and probably forever—will bear the designation of America's greatest amateur golfer, so will Johnny Ball stand in British golf history. In 1912, Ball won his eighth British Amateur championship, a feat that no one has ever approached. Michael Bonallack, with five wins, has come closest.

The argument could be made that John Ball was born to golf. It was only natural that he should take to the game since his father was owner and proprietor of the Royal Hotel of Hoylake, which was the Royal Liverpool Golf Club's first headquarters. Johnny began golf at an early age, and by the time he was 17, in 1878, he fashioned a fourth-place finish in the British Open.

After this auspicious beginning, Ball was slow to develop. "He would not do himself any kind of justice at the beginning of his career," wrote Horace Hutchinson, "and this failure was a source of bitter disappointment to his friends at home." Learning

and persevering, Ball began to improve, and he finally took the British Amateur title in 1888 after losing on the final hole to Hutchinson the year before. "Johnny Ball, at his best, was a terror," Hutchinson allowed.

What a terror! The victory in 1888 ignited the fire in Ball's game, and it was to burn for decades thereafter. In 1890, he was the first Englishman and the first amateur to win the British Open. Ball's dominance of the game seemed to last forever; he won the British Amateur in 1890, 1892, and 1894, finished second in 1895, and won again in 1899. After spending three years in South Africa in the Boer War, Ball won the British Amateur in 1907,

1910, and finally 1912. What's more, he almost won the British Open championship a second time in 1892, finishing second by three strokes to Harold Hilton. As Hutchinson said, "Johnny Ball is the best amateur that has ever been seen."

Pundits throughout Great Britain heaped praise on the mighty Ball. No less than Bernard Darwin wrote, "I have derived greater aesthetic and emotional pleasure from watching John Ball than from any other spectacle in the game."

The 1912 British Amateur took place at the Royal North Devon Golf Club in Westward Ho!, England, long held to be a classic links. Ball reached the finals against Abe Mitchell, described by many as "the best golfer who never won a British Open." The match-up was certainly a stirring spectacle, to use Darwin's word. On the 36th hole, Mitchell had a four-foot putt for the title—but missed. The pair played two extra holes before Ball won his last title. Is it any wonder Mitchell turned pro the next year? He probably couldn't stand the thought of another loss to the incomparable Johnny Ball.

1912

- February 4: Byron Nelson, winner of 52 PGA Tour events including 11 in a row in 1945, is born in Waxahachie, Texas.

- May 27: Sam Snead, winner of three Masters, three PGAs, and a record 81 PGA Tour events, is born in Hot Springs, Virginia.

- June 25: Edward "Ted" Ray wins his only British Open title, at Muirfield in Scotland. He equals the record score of 295.

- August 2: Johnny McDermott defends his U.S. Open crown and becomes the first golfer to break par for 72 holes when he shoots 294 on the par-74 C.C. of Buffalo course.

- August 13: Ben Hogan, winner of four U.S. Opens and golf's best player in the middle of the century, is born in Dublin, Texas.

- September 7: Jerry Travers takes his third U.S. Amateur in six years, defeating Charles Evans Jr., 7 & 6, in the final at Chicago G.C.

1912

In 1912, Johnny Ball won his eighth British Amateur title, setting an all-time record for victories in a major championship—amateur or professional, men's or women's. Even more amazing is that Ball didn't play any competitive golf for a period of three years. Instead, he served in the British Army during the Boer War in South Africa.

• October 5: Margaret Curtis repeats as U.S. Women's Amateur champion, defeating Nonna Barlow, 3 & 2, at her home Essex C.C. in Massachusetts.

• Macdonald Smith earns a comeback Western Open victory over Alex Robertson at the Idlewild G.C. in Chicago.

• George Sargent becomes the first golfer in Canadian Open history to break 300 (299), at Rosedale G.C. in Toronto. Walter Hagen, age 19, makes his first appearance in the event.

• Charlie Murray wins the inaugural Canadian PGA championship at the Mississauga Golf and C.C.

• To determine eligibility to enter the U.S. Amateur, the USGA issues a national handicap list, showing 471 eligible players with handicaps from zero to six, but only 86 enter.

• Englishman Harold Hilton collaborates with golf writer Garden C. Smith to publish the classic *Royal and Ancient Game of Golf.*

Jerry Travers

Travers Strolls to an Easy Victory in U.S. Amateur

It appeared that the 1912 U.S. Amateur would be a battle between two-time champ Jerry Travers *(pictured)* and Harold Hilton, the defending champion. Both tied for the medal at 152. But while Hilton lost in the first round, Travers rolled to four easy victories. He beat Chick Evans in the final, 7 & 6, at Chicago G.C. for his third of four Amateur titles.

Edward "Ted" Ray

Merion's East Course Opens

The East Course at Merion Cricket Club opened in 1912. Its designer, Hugh Wilson, created a short but complex course that remains one of the world's best. Bobby Jones, with a victory in the U.S. Amateur, clinched his Grand Slam at Merion in 1930. Ben Hogan, in his classic comeback from an auto accident, won the U.S. Open there in 1950.

Merion Cricket Club

Ray Beats the Triumvirate in British Open

Edward "Ted" Ray often played second fiddle to the Great Triumvirate, but Ray outshined them all in 1912 as he won his only British Open. The long-driving, wild-swinging Jersey native fired a record-tying 295 for the four rounds at Muirfield in Scotland. He defeated old rival Harry Vardon by four shots.

• It's eight British Amateur championships for John Ball, as he nips Abe Mitchell on the second extra hole at Royal North Devon G.C. at Westward Ho!.

• Dorothy Campbell three-peats as Canadian Women's Amateur champ, at Rosedale G.C. in Toronto.

• Yale's string of National Collegiate championships continues, as the Elis take their eighth title in a row. F.C. Davison of Harvard garners individual honors at Ekwanok G.C. in Vermont.

• George S. Lyon rebounds from last year's withdrawal due to hay fever to win his seventh Canadian Amateur, winning the final match, 6 & 5, over A.E. Hutcheson at Royal Montreal G.C.

• The Western Amateur moves farther west, to Denver C.C., where Chick Evans wins his first title.

• Minnesota golf legend Harry G. Legg wins his fourth straight Trans-

Walter J. Travis

Old Man Travis Wins Third North and South

Walter J. Travis took up golf in his 30s. He used the baseball grip, as well as a very long-shafted driver to gain more length. But despite his late start and unorthodox ways, Travis enjoyed a long reign as an amateur star. In 1912, he won his third North and South Amateur—at the tender age of 50.

Harold Hilton

Golfing Great Hilton Pens His First Book

After nearly two decades of success on the links, British golfer Harold Hilton took pen in hand. Hilton, with the help of golf writer Garden C. Smith, got down to work on his first book, the *Royal and Ancient Game of Golf*. The book was released in 1912, and today it's considered eminently collectible.

Macdonald Smith

Smith's Western Wins Come Many Years Apart

It's hard to find a peak in the career of Macdonald Smith. For example, he finished second in both the 1910 and 1930 U.S. Opens and never reached such a height in between those years. His performance in the Western Open was similar. He won his first of three Western titles in 1912. The others came in 1925 and 1933.

Mississippi G.A. championship, at the Minikahda Club in Minnesota.

• Walter J. Travis captures the North and South Amateur, his third and final victory in the event.

• Hugh Wilson's creation of the East Course for the Merion Cricket Club opens in Ardmore, Pennsylvania.

• Arthur Ryerson, a USGA founding father and a Chicago delegate at its 1894 organizational meeting, perishes when the *Titanic* sinks in the North Atlantic.

• Tom McNamara begins a two-year reign as North and South Open champion at Pinehurst C.C.

• Ivo Whitton, youngest Australian Open champion ever at age 19, win his first of five titles, at Royal Melbourne G.C.

• J.H. Taylor joins forces with Frederick G. Hawtree to form the British Golf Greenkeepers Association.

OUIMET SLAYS THE GIANTS IN CLASSIC U.S. OPEN

David and two Goliaths? Yes, yes. With slingshot-bearer Eddie Lowery by his side, frail Francis Ouimet vanquished the giants of Britain—sweet-swinging Harry Vardon and burly, pipe-clenching Ted Ray. In the process, golf in America came of age.

If they'd had a Caesar's Palace sports book back in 1913, the odds of local boy Francis Ouimet winning the U.S. Open would have been toward the bottom, in the three-figure category. He had to face two legends of golf, who sailed imperiously across the sea with the sole purpose of carting home the U.S. Open trophy. The only question seemed to be: Which one of the two would prevail?

Harry Vardon had already built a resumé that was envied world-wide. Thirteen years ago, he came to the States and crushed the opposition in the Open; his only challenger was a fellow member of the Triumvirate, John Henry Taylor, who finished second to Vardon by two strokes. There wasn't an American contender who even came close. In his native land, Vardon had won the British Open five times (he would win a sixth in 1914) and had finished second four times. Ray was no slouch either, winning in 1912 and finishing second in 1913.

The only advantage Ouimet could have had in the 1913 U.S. Open was local knowledge. The 20-year-old knew The Country Club, in Brookline, Massachusetts, like the back of his hand. He had learned golf there as a caddie and had honed his game over the course as an amateur. However, before 1913 he had never even qualified for match play in his own country's amateur championship and was the darkest of all darkhorses entering the Open.

Who can explain what happened? After the first round, Mac Smith led with a sterling 71. Vardon stood four back with a 75, Ouimet was two farther with a 77, and Ray was struggling at 79. In the second round, the British masters found their form, when Ray fired a 70 and Vardon shot a 72. Francis? He could do no better than 74. However, Ouimet's third-round 74 was just fine, as Vardon ballooned to 78 and Ray shot 76. Entering the final round, these three shared the lead.

The final day of the Open may as well not have been played. All three golfers posted 79s, although Ouimet needed to play the last six holes in 2-under to achieve that number. The stage was set, and the playoff began. You can almost imagine the scene at the first tee, with 10-year-old caddie Eddie Lowery hovering like a shadow next to Ouimet, and the two grand Brits chatting in another corner. Then the drives hit the first fairway, and the legend took shape.

When the playoff ended, the results were shocking. Ouimet's steady round of 72 prevailed over Vardon's 77 and Ray's 78. A photograph shows Francis, with the flush of glory, hoisted on the shoulders of the adoring gallery. A small step for man; a giant step for golf in America.

1913

• June 24: J.H. Taylor joins Harry Vardon and James Braid as five-time British Open champions, winning by eight at Hoylake.

• September 6: Jerry Travers becomes the first four-time U.S. Amateur champion by defeating John G. Anderson, 5 & 4, in the final at Garden City G.C.

• September 20: Former caddie Francis Ouimet defeats England's Harry Vardon and Ted Ray in a playoff for the U.S. Open championship, at The Country Club in Brookline, Massachusetts. Ouimet is the first amateur to win the Open.

• October 11: A visiting British women's team defeats an American contingent, led by Margaret and Harriot Curtis, 4-3, in an informal skirmish preceding the U.S. Women's Amateur, at Wilmington C.C in Delaware.

• October 17: Johnny McDermott leads wire-to-wire for a seven-stroke Western Open victory over Mike Brady at the Memphis C.C.

1913

Pictured is one of the most famous golf photos of the early 1900s. Francis Ouimet *(center)* poses with Harry Vardon *(left)* and Ted Ray. Ouimet, a 20-year-old American amateur, defeated the two British legends in a playoff for the 1913 U.S. Open, at The Country Club in Massachusetts. It was hailed as the greatest achievement in the history of American golf.

• October 18: Gladys Ravenscroft wins her only U.S. Women's Amateur, prevailing by 2 up in the final over Marion Hollins, at Wilmington C.C.

• Harold H. Hilton's *Modern Golf,* an extensive instructional treatise, is published in Great Britain.

• Jerry Travers's first golf book is primarily a volume of instruction tips, titled *Travers' Golf Book*.

• Albert Murray wins his second Canadian Open, defeating Nicol Thompson and Jack Burke Sr. by six strokes with a record 72-hole total of 295, at Royal Montreal G.C.

• Geoff Turpin takes his only Canadian Amateur championship, defeating Gerald Lees, 1 up, at Toronto G.C.

• Nathaniel Wheeler's win in the individual National Collegiate championship leads Yale to its ninth straight title, at Huntington Valley C.C. in Pennsylvania.

U.S. Open Playoff

Fans Weather the Rain to Watch Ouimet

Pictured is the last hole of the 1913 U.S. Open playoff at The Country Club in Brookline, Massachusetts. Francis Ouimet, who learned the game here as a caddie, won the playoff with a 72 to Harry Vardon's 77 and Ted Ray's 78. Though rain fell throughout the round, an estimated 10,000 fans showed up to watch the local boy make history. He didn't disappoint.

Gladys Ravenscroft

Ravenscroft Shines in Women's Amateur

Some golfers have but one moment of glory, and such a player was Gladys Ravenscroft. Although she had played well in Britain, she was barely known in the States until she competed in the 1913 U.S. Women's Amateur at Wilmington C.C. in Delaware. Her large, powerful frame served her well, as she beat Marion Hollins in the final, 2 up.

New Irons Make the Game Easier

Pictured is the stepped-face iron patented by Willie Park Jr. in 1913. Many players of the era embraced the grooved irons, which gave their shots more backspin and thus gave the golfers more control. Traditionalists, however, howled that the new clubs made the game too easy. Debate over grooved clubs would continue through the 1990s.

Stepped-face Iron

- Walter Fairbanks of Denver wins his only U.S. Senior Golf Association championship.

- For the first time, a golf patent mentions the use of a motion-picture camera, as W. and T. Avery and J.M. McGrath invent a device to measure weight transfer during the stroke.

- Nelson Whitney and Mrs. E.W. Daley win their respective Southern Amateur titles.

- Henry Topping and Lillian Hyde win their respective North and South Amateur titles at Pinehurst C.C.

- Tom McNamara repeats as North and South Open champion.

- Robert Simpson of Carnoustie, Scotland, takes out a patent on a rounded-sole iron club, designed to ease passage through the turf.

- Nonna Barlow wins her third consecutive Women's Eastern Amateur championship, at Brae Burn C.C. in Massachusetts.

1913

Willie Park Jr.

Innovative Park Designs Stepped-Face Iron

One of the most innovative of the early clubmakers was Willie Park Jr. of Scotland. Park was the first to develop both the wry-neck putter and the track-sole wood (which he named the Pik-up). In 1913, Park designed an iron club with a stepped face. Players loved the club since it was able to impart maximum backspin.

Flower's "Triumvirate" to Become a Classic

In 1913, Clement Flower painted "The Triumvirate," perhaps the most famous golf painting of all time. Flower portrayed the members of Britain's "Great Triumvirate": J.H. Taylor, James Braid, and Harry Vardon *(left to right)*. The painting is almost life-size, and the players' names and records are etched directly onto the canvas.

"The Triumvirate"

• Scottish clubmaker Willie Park patents an iron club with a stepped face, the intention being to impart backspin.

• Clement Flower's "The Triumvirate," featuring Harry Vardon, J.H. Taylor, and James Braid, will become one of the most recognized of all golf paintings.

• Davie Black wins his first of four Canadian PGA championships.

• Harold H. Hilton wins his fourth British Amateur, defeating Robert Harris, 6 & 5, at St. Andrews.

• Muriel Dodd, winner of the Canadian Amateur, also captures the British Amateur title.

• George Duncan, winner of the French Open at Chantilly, also nabs the *News of the World* professional match-play championship at Walton Heath.

• Warren Wood and Myra Helmer win their respective Western Amateur titles.

VARDON, 44 YEARS OLD, CAPTURES ONE MORE BRITISH OPEN

Two shots shaped the year of 1914, that of the assassin of the Archduke Ferdinand at Sarajevo—which plunged the world into "the war to end all wars"—and the certainly less significant stroke of Harry Vardon that would give him his record sixth victory in the British Open.

For Britain, of course, the assassin's bullet would prove to be a horrific prelude to nearly five years of sadness and tragedy. Vardon's victory, though considered relatively insignificant at the time, will probably place him at the top of British golfers as long as the inhabitants of that sceptered isle pursue the royal and ancient game.

The 1914 British Open was paying its penultimate visit to the Prestwick links, which had hosted the first 12 Opens. Overall, this would be the 23rd time in 50 years that the Cup was vied for over the Scottish sandhills, just south of Troon on the seacoast. In what possibly could have been a harbinger of the coming hostilities, the number of golfers qualifying for the 1914 Open dropped, from 269 the previous year to 194.

The 1914 Open was once again a contest between two old rivals, two members of the famed Triumvirate. Vardon opened the 72 holes of medal play with a strong 73, a stroke ahead of John Henry Taylor and James Braid. Two off the pace was T. Williamson of Notts Golf Club, as well as J. Ockenden. Vardon shot 77 in the second round, keeping him a stroke ahead of Ockenden and two ahead of Taylor.

But John Henry wasn't done, not by a long shot, as he fired a solid 74. The Mid-Surrey professional, who had also claimed five British Open championships up to this point, set his sights on the historic sixth triumph. As the third round concluded, Taylor led Vardon by two strokes and everyone else by at least six shots. The final round would be a two-man race.

The next day, things didn't look promising for the 44-year-old Vardon, who awoke beset with an unexplained illness. Nonetheless, he was able to maintain his shot-making, hole putts when he needed to, and post a 78. Taylor saw strokes slip away through the round, and when play was done, he staggered in with a disappointing 83. No other player threatened to win, although H.B. Simpson fired a 75 and finished in sole possession of third.

The day, and the title, was Vardon's. He was to regard this grueling victory as the "best of his accomplishments," reported the *Encyclopedia of Golf*, "for he was so unwell that he nearly fainted several times during the round." Vardon nor any member of the Triumvirate would get a realistic chance to win another British Open, as the event would be canceled from 1915–19 due to the First World War.

1914

- May 15: Cecil Leitch defeats Gladys Ravenscroft, 2 & 1, to win her first of four Ladies' British Open Amateur championships, at Huntstanton G.C. in England.

- May 23: Glasgow native J.L.C. Jenkins defeats Charles O. Hezlet, 3 & 2, for the British Amateur title, at Royal St. Georges in England.

- May 28: Francis Ouimet wins the French Amateur at La Boulie.

- June 2: Mrs. H. Arnold Jackson wins the Women's Eastern Amateur.

- June 19: Harry Vardon, age 44, wins an unprecedented sixth British Open, the last of the Great Triumvirate.

- June 26: Mildred "Babe" Didrickson, who will capture three U.S. Women's Opens, is born in Port Arthur, Texas.

- June 27: Jack Neville of San Francisco, who will be co-designer of Pebble Beach G.L. with Douglas Grant, wins the Pacific Northwest Men's Amateur.

Through 1913, each member of the Great Triumvirate had won the British Open five times. In 1914, Harry Vardon battled wind and rain on the Prestwick links in Scotland to claim the title. Because the Great War would suspend play from 1915–19, the other members of the Triumvirate—James Braid and John H. Taylor—would never get a realistic chance to match his six victories.

• July 4: George S. Lyon wins his record eighth and final Canadian Amateur, 8 & 7, over Brice Evans at the Royal Ottawa G.C.

• July 23: Charles Grimes wins the inaugural Western Junior championship, defeating Lawson Watts, 6 & 5, at Chicago G.C.

• August 1: Charles Evans Jr. wins his third Western Amateur title, crunching James D. Standish Jr., 11 & 9, at the Kent C.C. in Grand Rapids, Michigan.

• August 10: George Cumming wins the Canadian PGA title at Lakeview G.C. in Toronto.

• August 15: Just 11 days after Canada enters World War I, Karl Keffer wins his second Canadian Open, at Toronto G.C.

• August 21: Walter Hagen recovers from food poisoning (lobster dinner) to become the first golfer to lead a U.S. Open after every round, at Midlothian C.C. near Chicago.

Walter Hagen

Young Hagen Follows in Ouimet's Footsteps

A year after Francis Ouimet's stirring victory, another young, American-born star emerged in the U.S. Open. Walter Hagen, a 21-year-old pro from Rochester, New York, won the 1914 U.S. Open by a stroke at Midlothian C.C. in Illinois. Charles Evans Jr. finished a shot back, as his pitch on the final hole popped out of the cup.

Pebble Beach Designer Wins Amateur Tourney

Architecture buffs know that the design of Pebble Beach G.L. is credited to Douglas Grant and Jack Neville. But how many could tell you that both were fine amateur players too? In 1914, Neville *(pictured)* won the Pacific Northwest Amateur. Coincidentally, his design partner had won the event five years previously.

Jack Neville

Jim Barnes

Barnes Storms to Victory in Western Open

Long Jim Barnes was a golfer with character and purpose, one who had fierce competitive drive and concentration. Through his career, he was feared and respected by fellow golfers, and he was able to take his play to the highest level. Barnes proved himself in the 1914 Western Open, shooting 1-over-par to win his first of three Western titles.

• August 26: English-born James Martin "Long Jim" Barnes wins his first of three Western Open titles, edging Willie Kidd by one at Interlachen C.C. It's the first pro competition held in Minnesota.

• September 5: Francis Ouimet becomes the first golfer with career U.S. Open and U.S. Amateur

victories, beating defending champion Jerry Travers in the Amateur, 6 & 5, at the Ekwanok C.C. in Vermont.

• September 19: Mrs. H. Arnold Jackson wins her second U.S. Women's Amateur at Nassau C.C. on Long Island.

• The first English-language version of Frenchman Arnaud Massy's book, titled *Golf,* is published.

• With its first National Collegiate team championship, Princeton finally breaks Yale's nine-year stranglehold. Harvard's Edward Allis wins the individual title, at Garden City G.C.

Kate Harley

Leitch Wins the Top Two British Titles

The writers of her time, in referring to Cecil Leitch, lauded her skills in both wood and iron play. In 1914, Leitch was only 23 years old when she won the two premier British women's events—the English Ladies' Amateur and the Ladies' British Open Amateur. In the latter, she edged Gladys Ravenscroft in the final.

Cecil Leitch

Harley, Or Mrs. Jackson, Wins Women's Amateur

Miss Kate Harley won the 1908 U.S. Women's Amateur, but when she entered the 1914 championship, she played under her husband's name and was referred to as Mrs. H. Arnold Jackson. Such was the custom of the time. Nevertheless, Mrs. Jackson—or Kate, if you will—won the 1914 Women's Amateur title, edging Elaine Rosenthal, 1 up, at Nassau C.C. on Long Island.

San Francisco Golf Club

San Francisco G.C. Opens for Play

San Francisco G.C. opened at its present-day site in 1914, and though few tournaments have been played there—the members have preferred a low-key atmosphere—the A.W. Tillinghast course remains one of the country's best. It has changed very little over the years; however, some of the club's caddies have said the breaks in the greens are different since the earthquake of 1989.

- Reginald Worthington and Florence Harvey win their respective North and South Amateur titles at Pinehurst C.C.

- Nelson Whitney and Mrs. Frank Jones each win their respective Southern Amateur titles for the second time.

- The first published instruction manual on the art of bag-toting, *How to Caddie*, is written by Ernest A. Baughman.

- Opponents of deep-groove irons complain they produce excessive backspin that makes the game of golf easier.

- Gil Nicholls wins his second North and South Open at Pinehurst C.C.

- The New York-based *Golf Illustrated* makes its publishing debut with its April issue.

- Springfield, New Jersey's Frank Wright wins his only U.S. Senior Golf Association title.

AFTER FOUR AMATEUR VICTORIES, TRAVERS NABS U.S. OPEN

If there was talk of a dominant player in the decade preceding the First World War, the name of Jerome Dunstan Travers was probably heard as often as any other. The scion of a well-to-do New York family, he parlayed his strong all-around game into an impressive competitive record.

Travers had the early advantage of a fine teacher, Alex Smith, who was impressed by Jerry's even temperament. In fact, Smith once commented that it was impossible to tell whether Travers was winning or losing. However, an examination of the Travers resumé shows that he won far more than his share.

His earliest significant victory came in the prestigious Nassau Invitational, where he prevailed in 1904 at the tender age of 16. Travers had qualified for the U.S. Amateur in 1903 but lost in the second round of the grueling all-match-play format. In 1904 and '05, he fell in match play in the first round. In 1906, he lost in the third round.

Starting in 1907, however, Travers rolled into the top echelons and stayed there, aided, possibly, by his adoption of the Schenectady putter design. (In fact, he was to market such a putter under his own manufacture—with his address on it!) In '07, at Cleveland's Euclid Club, Travers forged his way to the U.S. Amateur championship, winning his semifinal and final matches by the equal—and dominant— margin of 6 & 5. He captured the Havemeyer Trophy again in 1908, prevailing by a couple of narrow margins en route to the final. In the championship match, he destroyed future *Golf Illustrated* editor Max Behr, 8 & 7.

Inexplicably, after two consecutive championships, Travers's name doesn't appear in the match-play player rolls for the next two years. Why? the *Encyclopedia of Golf* offers the theory that "...his habit of playing only when he felt inclined to was carried to the point that he omitted to enter...the Amateur championship for which he was the title-holder."

Be that as it may, Travers was back at the Amateur in 1912, defeating Chick Evans in the final, 7 & 6. Travers won again in 1913, knocking off Francis Ouimet, Fred Herreshoff, and John Anderson (in that order) in the last three matches. He finished second in 1914, losing to Ouimet in the final match.

In 1915, the U.S. Open's venue, Baltusrol Golf Club in New Jersey, was conveniently close to Travers's home turf. After two rounds, he stood two strokes behind "Long Jim" Barnes and Louis Tellier, and he closed the margin to one with a 73 in the second morning's round. In spite of a shaky start in the afternoon, Travers played the final six holes in 1-under-par and won by a stroke over Tom McNamara, totaling 297. Later that year, Travers lost early in the Amateur—then never played competitively again. Like Bobby Jones 15 years later, Travers retired his bag at age 28.

1915

- March 27: Alex Ross wins the last of his record six North and South Open titles at Pinehurst C.C.

- May 29: Alexa Stirling of Atlanta wins her first of three Women's Southern Amateur titles.

- June 2: Florence Vanderbeck captures her only Women's Eastern Amateur championship, at the Merion Cricket Club in Ardmore, Pennsylvania.

- June 12: Alden B. Swift captures the Trans-Mississippi Golf Association championship.

- June 18: Jerry Travers becomes the second amateur in three years to win the U.S. Open, nipping three-time runner-up Tom McNamara by a single stroke at Baltusrol G.C.

- July 24: Charles Evans Jr. again dominates James D. Standish Jr. in the Western Amateur, 7 & 6, for his fourth title in seven years, at the Mayfield C.C. in Cleveland.

At the end of 1915, Jerry Travers retired from competition at the age of 28. But before the year was out, he won the U.S. Open at Baltusrol G.C. in New Jersey. Travers didn't win the year's U.S. Amateur (it would have been his fifth), but he made his mark in the first round, routing George A. Crump by the count of 14 & 13.

• August 19: Tom McNamara wins the Western Open at Glen Oak C.C. in Illinois, despite posting the last 300-plus winning total in the event's history.

• September 1: Jerry Travers sets a U.S. Amateur championship record by drubbing George A. Crump, 14 & 13, in a first-round match.

• September 4: Robert A. Gardner wins his second U.S. Amateur by defeating John G. Anderson, 5 & 4, in the final at the C.C. of Detroit.

• September 11: Florence Vanderbeck tops Margaret Gavin, 3 & 2, to win the U.S. Women's Amateur at Onwentsia Club near Chicago. Vanderbeck survived a 22-hole semifinal match against Alexa Stirling.

• September 24: James A. Tyng wins his second U.S. Senior Golf Association championship.

• Because of the onset of World War I, all British championships are canceled. They will resume in 1920.

W.C. Fields

Fields Loves Golf But Is No Fan of Geese

In the 1910s, W.C. Fields kept fans in stitches with his comic golf routine. Fields loved golf and once bought a house adjacent to a golf course—although the geese that flocked around a water hazard often got on his nerves. One morning, Fields stormed out of his house in a bathrobe, waving a niblick. "Either poop green or get off my lawn!" he screamed.

Rosenthal Grabs First of Three Western Amateurs

Elaine V. Rosenthal captured the 1915 Women's Western Amateur, her first of three victories in the prestigious event. Rosenthal, who would tour with the famed Dixie Kids during World War I, was put through the ringer in the 1914 U.S. Women's Amateur. She won on the 19th hole in the quarterfinals, won 1 up in the semis, and lost 1 up in the final match.

Elaine V. Rosenthal

• The Canadian Open, Amateur, and PGA championships are put on hold owing to World War I. They will not resume until 1919.

• Golf course architect Albert W. Tillinghast takes pen in hand and writes a short book, *Cobble Valley Golf Yarns and Other Sketches*.

• Clubmaker Alex Shepherd of Inverness, Scotland, continues the tradition of custom cleekmarks when he begins marking his clubs with an arm grasping a shepherd's crook.

• *Spalding's Official Golf Guide*, the longest-published yearly reference book on golf, prints its 20th edition.

• Jerry Travers and sports writer Grantland Rice collaborate on a book, *Winning Shot*, published in Great Britain.

• Former U.S. Amateur champion H. Chandler Egan, nowadays a golf course designer, wins his first of five Pacific Northwest Amateur titles.

1915

McNamara Falls Short in U.S. Open

Tom McNamara of Boston won the 1915 Western Open and nearly took the U.S. Open. He lost by a stroke to Jerry Travers, who played 1-under golf over the last six holes. McNamara frequently challenged in the U.S. Open but never quite reached the top. He finished runner-up three times and placed in the top 20 on seven other occasions.

Florence Vanderbeck

Tom McNamara

Vanderbeck Prevails in Women's Amateur

Florence Vanderbeck challenged in the 1913 and '14 U.S. Women's Amateurs, and in 1915 she went all the way. Vanderbeck led the qualifying with an 85 at the Onwentsia Club near Chicago, then went tooth and nail with Alexa Stirling in the semis—finally winning on the 22nd hole. Vanderbeck beat Mrs. William Gavin in the final match by the count of 3 & 2.

Baltusrol Golf Club

Storied Baltusrol Plays Host to U.S. Open

Pictured is the clubhouse of Baltusrol G.C. in Springfield, New Jersey, which hosted the 1915 U.S. Open. Baltusrol opened as a nine-hole course in 1895 and was named after Baltus Roll, a farmer who was killed on the land years earlier. It expanded to 18 holes in 1901 and would go on to host seven U.S. Opens.

- E.C. Robinson wins the inaugural Southwestern Amateur.

- Yale regains the National Collegiate team championship. Yale's Francis Blossom takes the individual title.

- Canada's first golf magazine, *Canadian Golfer*, makes its debut.

- Fillmore Robeson and Nonna Barlow win their respective North and South Amateur titles.

- W.C. Fields commits his famous comic golf routine to film in *His Lordship's Dilemma*.

- Elaine V. Rosenthal wins her first Women's Western Amateur title.

- The USGA elects its first president from west of the Mississippi River—the controversial Frank L. Woodward of Denver.

- Samuel F.B. Morse forms Del Monte Properties, which will undertake the development of the Pebble Beach G.L.

20TH Century Golf Chronicle

1916

PROS BAN TOGETHER TO FORM PGA OF AMERICA

During the early years of golf, the professional didn't get much respect. Pros were essentially looked upon as artisans, clubmakers, gamblers, and—in many cases, sadly—frequent drinkers. They were of a different social class than the members of the clubs they served.

However, this stereotype began to disappear when the likes of Walter Hagen entered the professional ranks. It was time for a change, time for a new image. As Al Barkow wrote in *The History of the PGA Tour,* "As more and more American-born men became golf professionals, there was less and less a feeling of subservience to the membership. The historical American egalitarian spirit began to prevail."

It was only natural, therefore, that the golf professionals adopt the practice of organizing. On January 17, 1916, a meeting was held for that purpose at the Taplow Club in New York City. The luncheon was attended by prominent professional and influential amateur golfers, among the amateurs being Rodman Wanamaker, the heir to the Wanamaker's department-store fortune. Wanamaker helped

spearhead the formation of the Professional Golfers Association of America, as he offered to donate the trophy and the prize money for the first PGA Championship.

In June, the PGA of America held its first annual meeting at the Hotel Radisson in Minneapolis. At the meeting, Robert White of Wykagyl Country Club in New Rochelle, New York, was elected PGA president, and other significant actions were taken. Members established a definition of "golf professional" to exclude pretenders and frauds, and they set up a benevolent fund for PGA members.

The main effect of organizing, wrote Barkow, was to give

credibility to the collection of tournaments that eventually would evolve into the PGA Tour: "Many of the players who were most instrumental in forming a tournament circuit were members, (and) the association was the logical organization to nurture the circuit and give it credence."

In October, the first PGA Championship, for pros only, was held at Siwanoy Country Club in Bronxville, New York. Just 31 players teed it up in the match-play format and, in the final, Jim Barnes prevailed over Jock Hutchison, 1 up. The championship would be suspended for the next two years, as would most of the country's golf events, because of the entry of the U.S. into World War I.

The only drawback to the pros-only PGA Championship was an obvious one. "Any tournament that excluded Bobby Jones," wrote Mike Bryan in *Golf in America: The First One Hundred Years,* "was a championship of somewhat tainted value." Nonetheless, the popularity of Walter Hagen, and his domination of professional golf in the 1920s, gave the fledgling PGA the publicity and credibility it needed.

1916

- January 14: The USGA determines that golfers who capitalize on their fame and skill to promote the sale of golf goods will lose their amateur status.

- January 15: Francis Ouimet intends to open a Boston sporting goods business despite the USGA ruling.

- January 17: The Professional Golfers Association is founded when Rodman Wanamaker gathers influential pro and amateur golfers for a luncheon meeting at the Taplow Club in New York City.

- March 29: Nonna Barlow repeats as Women's North and South Amateur champ at Pinehurst C.C.

- April 1: Jim Barnes wins his first North and South Open at Pinehurst.

- April 7: Philip V.G. Carter captures his only North and South Amateur, at Pinehurst.

- May 16: USGA President Frank L. Woodward reveals that Francis Ouimet has acknowledged by letter

1916

In 1916, Rodman Wanamaker keyed the formation of the Professional Golfers Association. Wanamaker felt that pro golfers needed to be organized, so he gathered the country's influential golfers at a luncheon meeting in New York City. Wanamaker, a wealthy businessman, later donated the trophy and the prize money for the first PGA Championship.

that he fully understands the amateur-status edict that will bar him from further tournament activity.

• May 27: R.G. Bush Jr. wins his only Southern Amateur, in Dallas.

• May 28: The Western Golf Association threatens to form a breakaway organization with plenary powers over all U.S. golfers in protest of the USGA's controversial decision in the Francis Ouimet amateur-status case.

• June 7: Margaret Gavin wins the Women's Eastern Amateur championship, one of the few women's tournaments that will suspend activity for two full years due to World War I.

• June 26: The PGA of America conducts its first annual meeting at the Hotel Radisson in Minneapolis.

• June 26: Robert White, a native of St. Andrews, Scotland, is named the first PGA president.

1916

USGA Executive Committee

Woodward Puts Squeeze on Ouimet

The Executive Committee of the USGA posed for this photo in 1916. Frank L. Woodward *(seated, center)* was named president of the USGA a year earlier. In 1916, he stripped amateur status from Francis Ouimet because Ouimet intended to open a sporting goods store. Ouimet wouldn't be reinstated until 1918.

Charles Evans Jr.

Father of American Golf, Reid, Passes Away

John Reid, the first president of the USGA and the founder of New York's St. Andrews G.C. (the oldest golf club in America) died in 1916 at the age of 76. Reid was universally liked. He gave his life to the game and was a powerful influence in its growth and development. Reid, in fact, is sometimes referred to as the Father of American Golf.

John Reid

Evans Claims U.S. Open, U.S. Amateur

Of the top 38 finishers in the 1916 U.S. Open, only one was an amateur. But that man, Charles Evans Jr., beat out all the pros at the Minikahda Club in Minneapolis. In fact, Evans's score of 286 would not be bettered in the Open until 1936. Later in the year, Evans won his first U.S. Amateur, beating Robert Gardner in the final at Merion Cricket Club.

• June 30: Amateur Charles Evans Jr. wins the U.S. Open with a record 286 total that will stand for 20 years, at the Minikahda Club in Minneapolis.

• July 22: Heinrich Schmidt wins the Western Amateur at Del Monte Golf & C.C. on California's Monterey Peninsula.

• August 18: After summer wins in the Metropolitan Open and the Shawnee Open, Walter Hagen wins the Western Open, at Blue Mound C.C. in Wisconsin.

• September 7: Bobby Jones, age 14, makes his first appearance in a U.S. Amateur, losing in the quarterfinals to Bob Gardner, 5 & 3.

• September 9: Chick Evans completes his USGA double, capturing the U.S. Amateur. He defeats Bob Gardner, 4 & 3, at Merion Cricket Club.

• September 16: Princeton emerges as the new college powerhouse, winning the National Collegiate title at Oakmont C.C.

1916

Barnes Prevails in First PGA Championship

Who was the first PGA Champion? None other than Long Jim Barnes, a transplanted Cornishman. Barnes, who got his nickname for his prodigious length off the tee, won the inaugural event in 1916 at Siwanoy C.C. in Bronxville, New York. Barnes nipped Jock Hutchison in the final, 1 up, to take the Wanamaker Trophy.

Mildred Caverly, Alexa Stirling

Stirling Downs Caverly in Women's Amateur

The 1916 Women's Amateur came down to a duel between Mildred Caverly *(left)* and the young Alexa Stirling *(right)*, who grew up in Atlanta with Bobby Jones. Stirling stayed close with her outstanding short game and uncanny putting and defeated Caverly, 2 & 1, at Belmont Springs C.C. in Massachusetts. Stirling would win again after the war.

Jim Barnes

- October 7: Alexa Stirling wins her first of three successive U.S. Women's Amateur titles, defeating Mildred Caverly, 2 & 1, at Belmont Springs C.C. in Massachusetts.

- October 14: Jim Barnes wins the inaugural PGA Championship, for the Rodman Wanamaker Trophy, by defeating Jock Hutchison Sr., 1 up, at the Siwanoy C.C. in Bronxville, New York.

- P.C. Pulver publishes the first edition of *American Annual Golf Guide and Year Book.*

- Cartoonist Clare Briggs publishes his first book, *Golf: The Book of a Thousand Chuckles.*

- Pinehurst, North Carolina, claims the world's first miniature golf course when James Barber creates an 18-hole "Lilliputian" layout on his private estate near the Carolina Hotel.

- Harry Vardon's primer on equipment, called *Golf Club Selection,* hits the store bookshelves.

TOP PROS, DIXIE KIDS HELP AID WAR EFFORT

We won't go into detail as to why the United States entered the First World War. Various torpedoings, ship sinkings, and the U.S.'s need to support its European allies against the threat of the Kaiser's war machine will serve sufficiently to provide a reminder of history. At least of geopolitical history. As one might expect, the war also affected the world of golf.

In 1917, as Pershing's battalions and the American Expeditionary Force joined the conflict, the USGA suspended its national championships. On the home front, many golfers weren't qualified to join the bayonet-wielding, trench-defending troops. Nevertheless, these golfers were still able to contribute to the war effort.

How did they help? Through charity exhibitions. The U.S. Open was supplanted by a competition among those golfers who didn't head for France and the war. Jock Hutchison came up with the idea for the competition, and the event was named the Open Patriotic Tournament. The tourney was held at Whitemarsh Valley C.C., just outside Philadelphia, and Hutchison took the top prize with

a total of 292, defeating Tom McNamara by seven.

A number of other fund-raising exhibitions popped up during the war. The newly designated professional golfers, among them Walter Hagen, Jesse Guilford, and Mike Brady, put mile after mile on their odometers—although in most cases, public transportation was the chosen mode for travel, rather than private cars, since gasoline and other material essential to defense were needed elsewhere. Hagen and the rest made tours for charities, including Red Cross promotions, solicitations for bond donations, and the like. Amateurs like Francis Ouimet and Charles Evans Jr. also barnstormed around the country,

putting their talents on display for the worthiest of causes.

One of the premier attractions, one that drew considerable galleries as they made their way around the nation, was an aggregation known popularly as the Dixie Kids. Keyed by the 16-year-old Bobby Jones, the quartet also featured Alexa Stirling, Perry Adair, and Elaine Rosenthal. The Kids toured for months, performing exhibition matches and pleasing wartime galleries hungry for high-quality golf, from border to border and coast to coast. The Atlanta teens raised more than $150,000 for the coffers of the Red Cross.

One more significant event took place during World War I. Francis Ouimet, a hero of American golf since his 1913 U.S. Open victory over Ted Ray and Harry Vardon, found himself embroiled in a controversy. His amateur status was revoked since he worked for a sporting goods company. After some highly publicized brouhaha, however, he was reinstated in 1917. Finally, the Armistice was signed, on November 11, 1918, and the world was able to lay down arms and take up golf clubs again.

1917

- January 12: The USGA tightens its definition of the golf professional to read: "Engaging in any business connected with the game of golf wherein one's usefulness or profits arise because of skill or prominence in the game of golf."

- March 29: Elaine Rosenthal wins the Women's North and South.

- March 31: Michael J. Brady wins the North and South Open.

- April 7: Norman H. Maxwell wins the North and South Amateur.

- April 9: The PGA of America adopts a permanent constitution patterned after the British PGA bylaws.

- April 23: This year's U.S. Open is canceled due to World War I.

- June 9: Bobby Jones, age 15, wins his first of three Southern Amateur titles at the C.C. of Birmingham.

- June 22: Jock Hutchison Sr. wins the Open Patriotic Tournament—a replacement for the U.S. Open—at

1917-18

Even the youngsters lent a hand to the war effort. Teenage friends Bobby Jones *(left)* and Alexa Stirling *(right)* headed a traveling group known as the Dixie Kids, who put on exhibitions to raise money for the Red Cross. Fellow Atlantan Perry Adair and Chicagoan Elaine Rosenthal were also part of the group.

Pennsylvania's Whitemarsh Valley C.C. It benefits the Red Cross.

• July 4: On behalf of the American Red Cross, some 485 U.S. golf clubs conduct Liberty Tournaments.

• July 14: Francis Ouimet captures his only Western Amateur at Chicago's Midlothian C.C.

• September 15: Jim Barnes breaks the Western Open 72-hole record with a 283, at Westmoreland C.C. in Chicago.

• November 20: Bobby Locke, who will go on to win four British Opens in the 1940s and '50s, is born in Transvaal, South Africa.

• The PGA Championship suspends play for 1917 and 1918.

• Future golf great Tommy Armour incurs severe wounds and impaired vision while serving in the British Tank Corps during the war.

• Fannie Osgood is named the first USGA women's golf chairman.

Robert Gardner, Charles Evans Jr., Perry Adair, Bobby Jones

Amateur Stars Tee It Up for War-Time Charities

In an intriguing match-up, these amateur greats met in a Red Cross benefit match in Chicago in June 1917. Pictured are *(left to right)* Robert Gardner, Charles Evans Jr., Perry Adair, and Bobby Jones. Evans was the king of exhibitions, traveling 26,000 miles to 41 cities on behalf of war-time charities.

Mrs. F.C. Letts

Hutchison Wins Open Patriotic Tourney

Though the USGA suspended its championships during 1917 and '18, the staff didn't go unemployed. In 1917, the USGA held a U.S. Open substitute called the Open Patriotic Tournament, with proceeds going to the Red Cross. Jock Hutchison won the event at Whitemarsh Valley C.C. in Pennsylvania.

Jock Hutchison

Letts Again Captures Western Amateur

One of the few tournaments that made it through World War I without interruption was the Women's Western Amateur. Not even the Western Open or Amateur made it through unscathed. Mrs. F.C. Letts, the winner in 1916, again captured the title in 1917. Though not one of the great women players of the era, Mrs. Letts certainly excelled in this event, as she won it again in 1920.

1918

- January 24: Pine Valley founder George Crump dies, leaving the 12th through 15th holes unfinished at his dream golf course in the New Jersey sandhills.

- January 25: The USGA reinstates Francis Ouimet as an amateur golfer in good standing during its annual meeting in Philadelphia.

- February 13: Patty Berg, who will go on to win 15 major titles, is born in Minneapolis.

- March 27: Dorothy Campbell Hurd wins the Women's North and South Amateur.

- March 30: Walter Hagen wins his first of three North and South Open titles with a 293 total, as the event expands to 72 holes.

- April 6: Irving S. Robeson claims the North and South Amateur title.

- November 10: After winning a war-effort exhibition, Walter J. Travis auctions off his famous Schenectady putter for $1,700.

1917-18

Francis Ouimet

Western G.A. Opens Its Arms to Ouimet

The USGA stripped Francis Ouimet of his amateur status in 1916, but the Western Golf Association—a frequent rival of the USGA—was more than happy to let the popular Ouimet play in its tournaments. In fact, Ouimet won the 1917 Western Amateur. While the Western Amateur and Open were played in 1917, USGA events were not.

World War I Rally

Courses Used as Gardens, Grazing Fields During War

During the war, the priority of golf course maintenance fell to a low ebb. It was considered that prime land was far more valuable for food production than for recreation, so many courses were converted into vegetable gardens, cornfields, or grazing areas for cattle. Imagine the work the greenkeepers faced after the Armistice was signed!

Bobby Jones

Jones, 15, Prevails in Southern Amateur

In 1917, Bobby Jones was a tanned teenager with skinny arms, but oh, what a golf swing.... The 15-year-old was good enough to capture that year's Southern Amateur in Birmingham, Alabama. Jones had first played golf on a dirt road-way at the age of six. At age nine, he won a junior tour-nament sponsored by the Atlanta Athletic Club.

• The hostilities affect everyday golf. Rubber for golf balls is unavailable, and courses are appropriated for everything from airfields to gardens.

• In a wartime fund-raising effort, Charles Evans Jr. travels 26,000 miles to 41 cities to play exhibition matches.

• "Dixie Kids" Bobby Jones, Perry Adair, and Alexa Stirling of Atlanta—and Elaine Rosenthal of Chicago—barnstorm the United States in a series of exhibition matches on behalf of the American Red Cross.

• The RADIO golf ball is advertised as the Ball of Mystery that never

loses life or shape due to its inherent radioactive properties.

• Despite the impression that golf activity is waning due to World War I, statistics indicate that golfers on the United States' 2,002 courses have spent $10.5 million on golf balls in the last 12 months.

FLAMBOYANT HAGEN CAPTURES SECOND U.S. OPEN

Because he had married in 1917, Walter Hagen was exempted from military service during the Great War. These extra years of practice apparently did him good. The Haig, showing a new-found touch from 100 yards in and on the greens, dominated competitive golf in the years after the war.

Hagen began to make a name for himself a few years earlier. In 1913, the year of Francis Ouimet's triumph, he finished fourth in the U.S. Open, but he was so little known that a newspaper called him William Hagan. The scribes spelled his name right the next year, though, when he took the championship with scores that included a record single-round figure of 68—although the win was only by a stroke over Chick Evans.

After the 1914 Open, Hagen claimed that anyone could win the U.S. title once, but only a great player could do it twice. In 1919, Hagen proved his greatness with his second win in the U.S. Open, defeating Mike Brady in a playoff. Hagen burned up the course over the last six holes of regulation, going 1-under to total a 75 at Brae Burn Country Club near Boston.

Hagen then squeaked by in a playoff sullied by a Rules controversy, shooting 77 to Brady's 78. A month later, Hagen went to New York and defended his Metropolitan Open title, defeating Emmet French by three strokes.

Besides his great play, Hagen also became famous for his personality. Flamboyant as they come, The Haig starred in a series of anecdotes and incidents that, deservedly or not, made him the subject of conversation whenever golfers of his era, and those to the present day, talked about the game and its legends. The stories are innumerable: pretending to get drunk while surreptitiously pouring brandies into planters; showing up on first tees with rumpled tuxedos that were purposely rumpled to give the appearance of nights of debauchery; and sending caddies 150 yards ahead to pull the flagstick.

What was the effect of Hagen's panache? For one, he brought respect to his profession. No doubt existed in the minds of his fans (and his detractors) that he was, plain and simple, a gentleman. Hagen's charm and attitude brought him into the eye and the heart of the public. Ironically, his gentlemanly behavior also gave him an edge on his opponents. No less than Bernard Darwin wrote, "His demeanor toward his opponents, though entirely correct, had a certain suppressed truculence; he exhibited so supreme a confidence that they could not get it out of their minds and could not live against it."

Walter Hagen would go on to dominate the ranks of the professionals. Four victories in the Western Open, six appearances on the Ryder Cup team, five PGA Championships, and four British Open titles assured his position among the all-time greats. Hagen always put on a show, and in more ways than one.

1919

- March 26: Nonna Barlow wins her third Women's North and South Amateur.

- March 29: Jim Barnes wins his second North and South Open.

- May 31: Alexa Stirling wins her third Women's Southern Amateur.

- June 3: Nonna Barlow begins her second three-year reign as Women's Eastern Amateur champion.

- June 9: The U.S. Open is scheduled over three days for the first time. Eighteen holes will be played each of the first two days, and the third day will feature a 36-hole double round.

- June 9: In West Newton, Massachusetts, Willie Chisholm sets a U.S. Open record for highest score on a par-3 hole, taking an 18 on Brae Burn C.C.'s 185-yard 8th in the first round.

- June 12: After playing the final six holes in 1-under to tie Mike Brady in regulation, Walter Hagen wins his

1919

After winning the U.S. Open in 1914, Walter Hagen dropped to 10th in the event in 1915 and seventh in '16. However, Hagen worked on his game during the war years and, when the national championships resumed in 1919, he stood as the game's best player. In 1919, Hagen defeated Mike Brady in a U.S. Open playoff, 77-78, at Brae Burn C.C. in Massachusetts.

second U.S. Open in a playoff, 77-78. The event is plagued by several Rules controversies.

• June 21: Harry G. Legg wins the Western Amateur championship.

• June 25: The National Collegiate championships are resumed, with Princeton winning the team title.

• June 28: A.L. Walker Jr. of Columbia captures individual honors at the National Collegiate championships.

• June 28: Nelson Whitney wins his fifth Southern Amateur.

• July 30: British-born professional J. Douglas Edgar wins his first

Canadian Open title by 16 strokes, posting a 278 that lowers the standard by 17 shots, at Hamilton G.C. in Ontario.

• July 5: William McLuckie wins the Canadian Amateur, billed as the "Peace Year Championship," at Lambton G.C. in Toronto.

Gleneagles Hotel

Gleneagles Opens for Business

After the Armistice was signed, hoteliers and course builders were anxious to accommodate the golfers' return. In Perthshire, Scotland, the magnificent Gleneagles Hotel and its adjacent King's and Queen's Courses opened. The King's Course has a dramatic, gothic feel.

J. Douglas Edgar

Chisholm Lives Through a Nightmare at Brae Burn

Brae Burn C.C. in West Newton, Massachusetts, hosted the 1919 U.S. Open, and it proved to be a bear of a course. Not only didn't anyone break 300 on the sinuous track, but no one shot a subpar round during the entire tournament. Willie Chisholm fared the worst of the 142 entrants. In the first round on the par-3, 185-yard 8th hole, Chisholm took 18 strokes.

Brae Burn Country Club

Edgar Claims Canadian Open—By 16 Strokes

In 1919, Bobby Jones broke the Canadian Open scoring record at Hamilton G.C. in Ontario, yet he didn't even come close to winning. Amazingly, J. Douglas Edgar *(pictured)* won by a whopping 16 strokes over runner-up Jones, as his 278 total broke the tourney record by 17. Edgar would win the Open again in 1920—although that would come in a playoff.

• July 25: Jim Barnes wins his second straight Western Open at Mayfield C.C. in Cleveland.

• August 23: S. Davidson "Davey" Herron wins the U.S. Amateur at his home Oakmont C.C. near Pittsburgh. He defeats Bobby Jones, 5 & 4, in the final match.

• September 20: Jim Barnes repeats in the PGA Championship with a 6 & 5 victory over Fred McLeod at Engineers C.C. in New York.

• October 4: Alexa Stirling retains the U.S. Women's Amateur crown with a 6 & 5 win over Mrs. W.A. Gavin, at Shawnee C.C. in Pennsylvania.

• December 8: At a meeting of 26 British clubs, the Royal and Ancient Golf Club assumes management authority over the British Open and Amateur.

• In St. Andrews, Scotland, Tom Auchterlonie opens his golf equipment shop, which will still be in business in the 1990s.

Alexa Stirling

Herron Tops Jones in U.S. Amateur

Bobby Jones reached the final of the 1919 U.S. Amateur, but he couldn't conquer 20-year-old S. Davidson Herron, who beat Jones, 5 & 4, at Oakmont C.C. Oakmont was known for its slick greens, described by one writer as "like a marble tabletop." However, this was Herron's home course, which gave him a clear advantage.

S. Davidson Herron

Stirling Wins Amateur, Inspires a Young Collett

Alexa Stirling, who won the U.S. Women's Amateur in 1916, took it again when the championship resumed in 1919. Stirling rolled past Mrs. W.A. Gavin in the final, 6 & 5, at Shawnee C.C. in Pennsylvania. Legend has it that Glenna Collett first became interested in golf after admiring Stirling's play on a summer afternoon.

Abe Mitchell

Mitchell Wins *the* News of the World Tourney

Abe Mitchell was one of the finer British professionals of his era, and in 1919 he won the prestigious *News of the World* championship in England, which resumed after a six-year hiatus. In 1920, Mitchell led the British Open after 36 holes, only to see George Duncan—13 strokes behind—overtake him for the title.

- Jim Barnes publishes *Picture Analysis of Golf Strokes,* which is the first such book to depend primarily on photography as an instruction tool.

- The Gleneagles Hotel and its golf complex, including the King's and Queen's Courses, open in Scotland.

- Horace Hutchinson publishes his universally acclaimed memoirs, *Fifty Years of Golf.*

- The Kroydon Company, which will develop into one of the largest manufacturers of golf equipment, opens for business in Maplewood, New Jersey.

- Architect John Russell Pope builds a Georgian mansion for the Thomas H. Frothingham family in Far Hills, New Jersey. It will become the present-day USGA Golf Museum and Library.

- Plans to resume the Ladies' British Open Amateur are abandoned due to a railway strike.

RAY, AGE 43, WON'T GO DOWN WITHOUT A FIGHT

Is there a photograph of Edward "Ted" Ray that doesn't show him with a pipe clenched between his teeth? Doubtful. This large, lumbering man wore the briar and his trilby hat like a badge of authority. In his career, Ray won one British Open and one U.S. Open, the latter coming in 1920 at the age of 43.

Few people know that Ray was born on Jersey—that jewel of Britain's Channel Islands—seven years after Harry Vardon. Vardon took the spotlight as the isle's best, and so it remained for the big man with the big heart. When the famed Triumvirate is mentioned in golf history, Ray is always doomed to an afterthought, the fourth of the three. The first entry in the *Encyclopedia of Golf* lists him as "runner-up" in the British Professional Match Play, then admits his supporting role. "In some ways," it reads, "he was overshadowed by (Vardon, Braid, and Taylor)...."

Big Ted had his moments, though. It must have been gratifying to, at long last, clutch the Cup at the 1912 British Open and stare out at his long-time conquerors. Ray's game was characterized by power. An oft-

told anecdote relates that, when asked by an amateur how to get more distance on his drive, Ted replied, "Hit it a bloody sight harder, mate!"

No less a source than Bobby Jones tells of an incident that summarizes the power of Ray's game—and his almost callous disregard of intimidation. Jones was among the attendees at an exhibition match and, on one hole, Ray was in what appeared to be an impossible situation: 150 yards from the green and totally blocked by a stand of towering trees. Eschewing prudence, which would have dictated a safe play out to the fairway, Ray chose his

niblick (a club with about the loft of an 8½ iron) and, taking a tremendous swing at the ball, cleared the trees and landed in birdie range on the green. For Bob Jones to have written in such laudatory terms about the shot speaks volumes.

So, with a history of being almost always an also-ran, 43-year-old Ted Ray came to America to take his chances in the U.S. Open. Thanks to the newly established USGA Green Section, the course at Inverness in Toledo, Ohio, was in top shape—and so was Ted's game. With only seven holes remaining, 50-year-old Harry Vardon had fashioned a five-stroke lead, but strong winds blew up out of the north, and Vardon faltered.

Ray finally had his chance. Ted held on to score a final-round 75 and, by a stroke, took the title. Second place was crowded; beside Vardon, Jock Hutchison, Jack Burke, and Leo Diegel (of the awkward and amazing putting stroke, arms akimbo) shared the runner-up role. With the win, Ted Ray had his last fling at glory. He remained the oldest Open champion until Raymond Floyd in 1986, 66 years later.

1920

- March 3: Julius Boros, who will win two U.S. Opens, win a PGA Championship, and play on four Ryder Cup teams, is born in Connecticut.

- March 27: Dorothy Campbell Hurd wins her second Women's North and South Amateur title in three years.

- March 30: Fred McLeod wins his second North and South Open, and first in 11 years.

- April 6: Francis Ouimet wins his only North and South Amateur title, 5 & 4, over Samuel Graham.

- June 8: Nonna Barlow wins her fifth Women's Eastern Amateur.

- June 13: Plans to send a U.S. Olympic golf team to Belgium are abandoned when only Bobby Jones and Max Marston confirm their willingness to compete.

- June 18: USGA President George Herbert Walker, grandfather of U.S. President George Bush, meets with the R&A concerning standardization

Finally, it was Ted Ray's turn. In 1920, the genial, pipe-smoking giant accompanied Harry Vardon across the Atlantic to take one final stab at a U.S. Open title. With seven holes to go at the Inverness Club in Toledo, Ohio, Vardon led by five strokes. But then the winds howled and Vardon lost strokes left and right. Ray rallied to win the championship by a shot.

of the golf ball and the abolition of the stymie, neither of which is resolved.

• July 1: George Duncan, 13 strokes behind leader Abe Mitchell after 36 holes, stages the greatest comeback in British Open history to win by two strokes over Sandy Herd at Deal G.C. in England, where the championship resumes following WWI.

• July 7: Walter Hagen becomes the first American-born golfer to win the French Open, at La Boulie.

• July 10: Bobby Jones wins his second of three Southern Amateur titles, in Chattanooga, Tennessee.

• July 17: Charles Evans Jr., already a four-time Western Amateur champion, begins a four-year stranglehold on the title.

• July 31: Walter Hagen captures his third consecutive Metropolitan Open in a playoff with Jim Barnes, at the Greenwich C.C. in Connecticut.

George Duncan (left)

Duncan Wins First Post-War British Open Championship

With the Great Triumvirate now deep into middle age, a new breed of players had a chance to win the 1920 British Open championship—held for the first time since 1914. George Duncan *(left)* opened with a pair of 80s, but then caught fire and gained strokes as the others fell away. He ended up with a two-stroke victory over Alexander Herd, at Deal in England.

Cyril Tolley

Tolley Takes Title at British Amateur

In 1920, the British Amateur resumed for the first time in six years, at Muirfield G.C. in Scotland, and it certainly didn't lack in drama—especially the final match. Cyril Tolley *(pictured)* was tied at the end of 36 holes with American Robert Gardner, but Tolley birdied the first extra hole to take the title. Tolley would win the British Amateur crown again, but not until 1929.

Evans Nabs U.S. Amateur

George Herbert Walker *(right)* presents the U.S. Amateur trophy to 1920 champion Charles Evans Jr. Evans defeated Francis Ouimet, 7 & 6, in the final at Engineers C.C. in Roslyn, New York. Evans prevailed thanks to great iron play and a hot putter. He also won his fifth of eight Western Amateurs in 1920.

Charles Evans Jr., George Herbert Walker

• August 5: Jim Barnes captures the Western Open at Olympia Fields C.C. in Illinois.

• August 13: Edward "Ted" Ray, at age 43, becomes the second overseas golfer to win the U.S. Open, overcoming a five-stroke Harry Vardon lead at the Inverness Club in Toledo, Ohio.

• August 21: Jock Hutchison enters the PGA Championship as an alternate, then fights his way to a 1-up victory over J. Douglas Edgar in the final at the Flossmoor C.C. in Chicago.

• August 28: J. Douglas Edgar becomes the first back-to-back Canadian Open champion, winning in a playoff over Charlie Murray and Tommy Armour at Rivermead G.C. in Ottawa.

• September 11: Charles Evans Jr. wins his second U.S. Amateur title, defeating former champion Francis Ouimet, 7 & 6, in the final at the Engineers C.C. in Roslyn, New York.

Max Marston

Marston, Jones Say Yes to Olympics

With peace restored, talk arose about bringing golf back to the Olympics. Although some countries expressed interest, the only two noteworthy Americans who agreed to make the trip to Belgium were Bobby Jones and three-time Walker Cup player Max Marston *(pictured)*. Because of the lack of interest, the U.S. decided not to field a team.

Alister Mackenzie (right)

Mackenzie Unveils His Secrets in New Book

In 1920, golf course architect Alister Mackenzie *(right)* published *Golf Architecture,* a must read for anyone remotely interested in the subject. In his career, Mackenzie designed some of the world's great courses, including Cypress Point, Royal Melbourne, Pasatiempo, and Augusta National (with Bobby Jones).

Marion Hollins

Hollins Makes Presence Felt at Amateur

Marion Hollins was a natural athlete who combined power with finesse. In the 1920 U.S. Women's Amateur, Hollins took the qualifying medal with an 82, breaking the record by three strokes. Alexa Stirling won her third straight Women's Amateur in 1920, but Hollins would prevail the following year.

• October 2: J. Douglas Edgar, the British-born professional affiliated with the Druid Hills G.C. in Atlanta, wins the Southern Open.

• October 9: Atlanta's Alexa Stirling captures her third consecutive U.S. Women's Amateur, defeating Dorothy Campbell Hurd, 5 & 4, at Mayfield C.C. in Cleveland.

• November 30: The USGA Green Section is created to distribute authoritative scientific knowledge about golf course upkeep.

• British golf course architect Dr. Alister Mackenzie publishes *Golf Architecture,* considered a classic of its genre.

• One of the classic golf instruction books, *The Art of Putting,* is published by two-time British Open champion Willie Park Jr.

• Conde Nast is the new publisher of *The American Golfer,* and Grantland Rice succeeds Walter J. Travis as its editor.

HUTCHISON'S IN A GROOVE, NABS THE BRITISH OPEN

Scottish-born Jock Hutchison had little to prove by the time the 1921 British Open rolled around. The St. Andrews native had, like so many of his professional contemporaries, emigrated to the United States to ply his trade in the early 1900s. At championships, he had compiled an enviable record, with two runner-up finishes in the U.S. Open and victories in the 1920 PGA Championship and '20 Western Open, as well as a slew of lesser wins.

In 1921, Jock had the opportunity to visit Scotland with a dual purpose. The British Open was being held at the Old Course in his hometown; thus, he could play in the championship as well as rekindle his family relationships. As the *Encyclopedia of Golf* put it, "He sailed to Britain early in the year and while staying with relatives played the Old Course dozens of times in preparation."

Like many other players, Hutchison had been quick to recognize the advantages of deep-grooved iron clubs. The additional backspin that such clubs imparted to the ball enabled shots to check up quickly, even on the hardest greens. At the seaside courses on the British Open rota, ever-present winds and sand-based soils conspired to dry and harden putting surfaces into almost table-top consistency, so clubs with deep grooves would certainly be of help.

Before 1910, most iron clubs had smooth faces, but players observed that routine mainte-nance—the wiping of the face with emery cloth—roughened the surface and gave shots more spin. Soon, face markings were the norm, and around 1914, club-makers began to make the grooves deeper and deeper. (Incidentally, these clubs are big among collectors today.)

Hutchison wasn't concerned with potential collectibility, however, but with function. His deep-grooved irons were what the doctor ordered. In the first round of the '21 British Open, he shot 72, coming close to the unprece-dented feat of two consecutive holes-in-one. After acing the 8th hole, he drove the 9th, but the ball missed the hole by a whisker. "Spectators were astounded by Hutchison's pitching and by the amount of backspin he could impart to the ball," observed the *Encyclopedia of Golf.*

His game deteriorated through the second and third rounds. He fired a 75 and then a 79, which dropped him four strokes off the lead. In the fourth round, Hutchison regained his uncanny touch, though, shooting a 70 to tie English amateur Roger Wethered at the end of regulation with a score of 296. He then crushed Wethered in a 36-hole playoff by nine strokes.

The Royal and Ancient took notice of Hutchison and his clubs. Once before, after Walter Travis had won the 1904 British Amateur with his center-shafted Schenectady putter, the Royal and Ancient banned the design. And here again they acted, putting deep grooves on the list of forbidden clubs.

1921

- January 6: Cary Middlecoff, who will win two U.S. Opens and a Masters, is born in Tennessee.

- January 7: George Herbert Walker donates the International Challenge Trophy to be competed for by any country that can field an amateur team. Journalists dub it the Walker Cup, much to his chagrin.

- January 15: The Western G.A. defers for one year its intention to split with the USGA.

- March 30: Dorothy Campbell Hurd repeats as Women's North and South champion.

- April 2: Jock Hutchison wins the North and South Open.

- April 9: B.P. Merriman inflicts a 9 & 8 defeat on Gardiner W. White in the North and South Amateur final.

- May 27: Willie Hunter wins the British Amateur, 12 & 11, over Allan Graham at Hoylake, England.

- June 6: Nonna Barlow three-peats as Women's Eastern Amateur

1921

Jock Hutchison gained a huge advantage on his opponents in the 1921 British Open at St. Andrews, as his bag included the new deep-grooved irons. Able to impart tremendous backspin, Hutchison scored a hole-in-one and nearly another on the next hole. Jock tied Roger Wethered at 296, then defeated him in a playoff, 150-159.

champion, winning her sixth overall, at The Country Club in Brookline, Massachusetts.

• June 25: Perry Adair succeeds childhood pal Bobby Jones as Southern Amateur champion.

• June 25: Jock Hutchison wins the British Open using "ribbed" clubs

that will become illegal. He prevails by nine strokes in a 36-hole playoff over amateur Roger Wethered at the Old Course at St. Andrews.

• July 2: Dartmouth wins its first National Collegiate team title, at Greenwich C.C. in Connecticut. Princeton's Simpson Dean wins the individual crown.

• July 22: Jim Barnes wins the U.S. Open by nine strokes over Walter Hagen and Fred McLeod at the Columbia C.C. in Chevy Chase, Maryland.

• July 22: U.S. President Warren Harding presents the U.S. Open championship trophy to Jim Barnes.

Los Angeles Country Club

Los Angeles C.C. Opens For Play

Another fine West Coast course opened for play in 1921, the George Thomas-designed North Course at Los Angeles C.C. To this day, the North Course is ranked among the top 25 layouts in America. The layout features no water; but hills, trees, and long, tight fairways make it a difficult track. The course hosted the first L.A. Open in 1926.

Jesse Guilford

Broadmoor Course Opens in Colorado

As the western United States grew in population, quality golf courses also arose. One of the best was built at the Broadmoor G.C. in Colorado Springs, Colorado. A great course required a championship, so the Broadmoor Invitational—to this day considered a premier amateur event—was inaugurated. The first championship, in 1921, went to local player J.H. Potter.

Broadmoor Golf Club

U.S. Amateur Moves West; Guilford Prevails

Jesse Guilford won the 1921 U.S. Amateur, played west of the Mississippi River for the first time. On a rainy day, Guilford outclassed Robert Gardner in the final, 7 & 6, at St. Louis C.C. In the semis, Guilford had nipped Charles Evans Jr. Like a number of top amateurs at the time, Guilford decided against turning pro because he could make a better living in the business world.

• July 25: Charles Evans Jr. wins his sixth Western Amateur title.

• August 2: Mike Brady's triple bogey at the Toronto G.C.'s "Graveyard" hole enables Michigan's W.H. Trovinger to become the first American-born Canadian Open champion.

• August 26: Walter Hagen charges to a five-stroke Western Open victory over Jock Hutchison, closing with three consecutive birdies at the Oakwood Club in Cleveland.

• September 5: U.S. Open champion Jim Barnes defeats British Open champ Jock Hutchison, 5 & 4, for the unofficial supremacy of world

golf, at the Sound View G.C. in Great Neck, New York.

• September 23: Cecil Leitch, winner of this year's British Open Amateur and French Ladies' titles, wins the Canadian Ladies' Amateur, crushing little lefty Molly McBride, 17 & 15, at Rivermead G.C. in Ottawa.

Marion Hollins

Harding Honors Barnes at U.S. Open

U.S. President Warren G. Harding presents the 1921 U.S. Open trophy to Long Jim Barnes. Barnes shot a classy 69 in the first round, then coasted to a nine-stroke victory at Columbia C.C. in Chevy Chase, Maryland. Harding, a quality golfer himself, preferred a good time to the daily duties of the White House.

Hollins Ousts Stirling in Women's Amateur

Marion Hollins triumphed in the 1921 U.S. Women's Amateur, thus ending Alexa Stirling's three-year stranglehold on the title. Hollins defeated Stirling head-to-head in the final match, 5 & 4, at Hollywood G.C. in Deal, New Jersey. In 1922, Hollins would help start the Women's National Golf and Tennis Club in Glen Head, New York.

Warren G. Harding, Jim Barnes

Walter Hagen

Hagen Triumphs in Western Open, PGA

Walter Hagen moved into his prime in the years following World War I. He won the 1921 Western Open by five strokes, then became the first American-born golfer to win the PGA Championship. With a strong all-around game and spectacular putting, Hagen defeated Jim Barnes in the PGA final, 3 & 2, at Inwood C.C. in Far Rockaway, New York.

• September 24: Jesse P. Guilford tops Robert A. Gardner, 7 & 6, at the St. Louis C.C., as the U.S. Amateur travels west of the Mississippi for the first time.

• October 1: Walter Hagen becomes the first American-born PGA Championship winner, edging Jim Barnes, 3 & 2, at the Inwood C.C.

in Far Rockaway, New York. It's his first of five titles.

• October 8: Marion Hollins ends Alexa Stirling's bid for a fourth straight U.S. Women's Amateur title, winning 5 & 4 in the first 36-hole final, at the Hollywood G.C. in Deal, New Jersey.

• The USGA rules that the standard golf ball for championship play will not be less then 1.62 inches in diameter and not greater than 1.62 ounces.

• J.H. Potter wins the inaugural Broadmoor Invitation Tournament, at Broadmoor G.C. in Colorado Springs.

As a young man, muffin-faced Eugenio Saraceni didn't look like an athlete at all. Short and stubby, he didn't project the lithe quickness that characterizes the natural. And he was saddled with another disadvantage, that of a poor, working-class background. A sixth-grade dropout who caddied for nickels, dimes, and quarters, he seemed doomed to the obscurity that would be the fate of so many of his New York-area brethren.

As we now know, however, this young man was the exception. He changed his name to Gene Sarazen, which symbolized the change in his life that ensued when he found he could play golf. Oh, could Sarazen play! His career would eventually last more than a half-century, and he would go on to win all four majors, one of only four players in the history of the game to do so.

Gene's first appearance in the U.S. Open came in 1920. It wasn't all that distinguished, as he finished back in the field, 16 strokes off the winning pace. But his determination and skills were developing at a rapid pace, and by 1922 he was ready to compete with—and beat—the best of the

RAGS-TO-RICHES SARAZEN COPS U.S. OPEN AND PGA

era. Only 20 years old, he found July in Illinois to his liking. Although he stood four strokes back after the third round, he put it all together over the final 18 holes and shot 68, including an 18th-hole birdie, to win by a stroke over Bob Jones and John Black. The 68 tied a last-round record that would stand until Sarazen himself would break it with a 66, 10 years down the road.

The breakthrough was just what the doctor ordered for Sarazen. At the PGA Championship, he continued to beat all he faced. He moved through match play with alacrity and, in the final,

bested Emmet French, 4 & 3, to claim the Wanamaker Trophy.

Still, though, there were those who weren't convinced that Sarazen could handle all the competition. They pointed out that Walter Hagen had declined to defend the PGA title in '22, and without The Haig, Gene's victory was somehow sullied. To prove who was better, both players agreed to meet head-to-head, in a 72-hole match called the Golf Championship of the World.

The prize fund for the match was huge—$2,000 for the winner, $1,000 to the loser. After the first two rounds at Oakmont, Sarazen stood two down. Moreover, he was ill on the train that evening, en route to Westchester-Biltmore Country Club in New York. Sarazen later wrote, "I really shouldn't have played that day, but I knew if I backed out of the match, everyone would say I was afraid of losing."

In spite of his pain and the weather—it poured throughout the match—Gene reached down and wound up the winner, 3 & 2. The next day, he had an emergency appendectomy. From that point on, no one ever again doubted Sarazen's skill and mettle.

1922

- January 18: Marion Hollins spearheads the formation of the Women's National Golf and Tennis Club at Glen Head, New York.

- February 4: Bob MacDonald wins the inaugural Texas Open, at Brackenridge Park in San Antonio, with a score of 281.

- March 4: Gene Sarazen wins his first notable professional title, the Southern Open, just five days past his 20th birthday.

- March 29: Glenna Collett begins her three-year reign (first of six titles overall) as Women's North and South Amateur champion.

- April 1: Pat O'Hara wins the only North and South Open held over 54 holes.

- April 5: The USGA continues to prohibit the use of steel-shafted clubs in championship play.

- May 19: Joyce Wethered wins her first of a record four Ladies' British

1922

Gene Sarazen, only 20 years old, won the 1922 U.S. Open at Skokie C.C. near Chicago. Trailing by four strokes after 54 holes, Sarazen shot a record final round of 68, capped by a last-hole birdie. He finished one stroke ahead of Bobby Jones and John Black. Sarazen also won the 1922 PGA Championship, beating Emmet French in the final by the count of 4 & 3.

Open Amateurs, blitzing defending champion Cecil Leitch, 9 & 7, at Princes G.C. in Sandwich, England.

• June 7: Glenna Collett wins her first of six Women's Eastern Amateur titles.

• June 23: Walter Hagen becomes the first American-born British Open champion, winning his first of four titles at Royal St. George's G.C.

• June 24: In his final Southern Amateur appearance, Bobby Jones wins for the third time at his home East Lake course in Atlanta.

• July 1: Charles Evans Jr. wins the Western Amateur for the seventh time, topping George Von Elm, 5 & 4, at the Hillcrest C.C. in Kansas City, Missouri.

• July 15: Gene Sarazen, age 20, wins the U.S. Open by one shot over Bobby Jones and 43-year-old grandfather John Black, at Skokie C.C. in Illinois. For the first time, a spectator admission fee is charged.

Jesse Sweetser

Sweetser Beats the Best in U.S. Amateur

Jesse Sweetser grabbed his first and only U.S. Amateur championship in 1922, at The Country Club in Brookline, Massachusetts. Sweetser cut quite a swath through match play, defeating such standout golfers as Willie Hunter, Jesse Guilford, Bobby Jones, and Charles Evans Jr. He defeated Evans in the final, 3 & 2.

Joyce Wethered

Wethered Defeats Leitch, Impresses Jones

Joyce Wethered won the 1922 Ladies' British Open Amateur, routing Cecil Leitch, 9 & 7, in the final. Wethered also won her third of five straight English Ladies' titles. After playing a round with Wethered, Bobby Jones once said, "I have not played golf with anyone, man or woman, amateur or professional, who made me feel so utterly outclassed."

• July 29: Al Watrous wins the Canadian Open at Mount Bruno G.C. in Montreal, where an innovative scoreboard system is the main topic of conversation.

• August 18: Gene Sarazen wins the PGA Championship, topping Emmet French, 4 & 3, at Oakmont C.C. near Pittsburgh. He becomes the first golfer to win the U.S. Open and PGA title in the same year.

• August 25: At Oakland Hills C.C. in Michigan, host professional Mike Brady wins the Western Open by 10 strokes, as defending champion Walter Hagen mixes his dates and doesn't show.

• August 29: The U.S. defeats Great Britain, 8-4, in the first Walker Cup Match, at the National Golf Links of America on Long Island.

• August 29: When a British player becomes ill and can't compete in the Walker Cup, British golf writer Bernard Darwin fills in and beats William Fownes, 3 & 1.

Walker Cup Match Competitors

U.S. Tops the British in First Walker Cup

The first-ever Walker Cup Match, pitting amateurs from the United States against those of Great Britain/Ireland, took place in 1922 at the National Golf Links of America on Long Island. It was certainly a friendly competition as shown by this photo, in which members of both teams commiserate together. The U.S. won the event, 8-4.

Mike Brady

Fans Dip into Their Wallets at U.S. Open

In 1922, the USGA charged admission for the first time at the U.S. Open, held at Skokie C.C. near Chicago. The fans certainly got their money's worth, as 20-year-old phenom Gene Sarazen defeated Bobby Jones and 43-year-old grandfather John Black by a stroke. In 1923, fans at the Canadian Open were charged an admission fee ($1) for the first time.

Golf Gallery

Brady Wins Western Open on Home Course

Mike Brady had been a perennial runner-up in the Western Open, but his eyes lighted up when he learned that the 1922 version would be held at Oakland Hills C.C. in Birmingham, Michigan. Brady, club pro at Oakland Hills, obviously knew the layout well, and he proved it with a score of 291 and a commanding 10-stroke victory.

• August 31: The USGA inaugurates the Amateur Public Links championship. The first event, at Ottawa Park in Toledo, Ohio, is won by Edmund R. Held.

• September 9: Jess W. Sweetser wins his only U.S. Amateur, crunching Bobby Jones, 8 & 7, in the semis and Charles Evans Jr.,

3 & 2, in the final, at The Country Club in Massachusetts.

• October 7: Gene Sarazen beats Walter Hagen, 3 & 2, in a 72-hole marathon match for the unofficial world title, concluding at the Westchester-Biltmore C.C. in Rye, New York.

• October 8: Gene Sarazen suffers an attack of appendicitis and will be operated on tomorrow.

• Two-time U.S. Open champion Walter Hagen founds the Walter Hagen Golf Products Corporation, in Longwood, Florida. Its main product is Hagen-signature golf clubs.

It's indisputable that golf enjoys the most beautiful playing fields of any game or sport. An almost infinite variety of landscape provides challenge, reward, and aesthetics to all those who take club in hand and set out to get the ball in the hole in as few strokes as possible.

Albert Warren Tillinghast, a Philadelphian, will forever stand among the greats of the elusive art of golf course architecture. He was also among the game's most colorful personalities. In *The Golf Course,* the young Tillinghast is described as one of a group of teenage thugs named "the Kelly Street Gang, who seemed bent on engaging in the most scandalous behavior that could be attempted in the late 1890s."

With adulthood, though, Tillie turned his life completely around, becoming a fine husband, sportsman, and antique buff, and adopting the trappings of near-aristocracy. A visit to St. Andrews, the Shrine of Golf, worked on him as it did so many others. Tillinghast was also a fine player, reaching the match-play bracket of the U.S. Amateur championship in 1909 and 1912, losing to Charles Evans Jr. in 1912.

TILLINGHAST OUTDOES HIMSELF WITH DESIGN OF WINGED FOOT

It was as a course builder, however, that Tillie gained renown. In 1906, without a whit of experience, he was engaged to lay out Shawnee Country Club in Pennsylvania. Not only did he do a fine job, but he fell in love with the craft. Setting up a golf course construction company, he traveled around America, giving birth to outstanding tracks like San Francisco Golf Club in 1914 and, in New Jersey, Somerset Hills Country Club in 1918. He also completed both Baltusrol courses in 1922. It was in Mamaroneck, New York, though, that he constructed perhaps his best-known efforts, the legendary Winged Foot Country Club courses, which opened in 1923.

"A controlled shot to a closely guarded green," Tillie once wrote, "is the surest test of any man's game." Nowhere is that philosophy better executed than at Winged Foot's West Course. The club approached him in 1921, cognizant of his fine work and his devotion to detail. He didn't disappoint his employers by any stretch of the imagination, as time has proven. Winged Foot has hosted four U.S. Opens, and the West Course has been perennially ranked among the top 10 courses in the world.

How good was Tillinghast? Frank Hannigan, former USGA executive director, wrote that "35 national championships of the USGA or PGA of America...have been played on 19 different Tillinghast courses." The times were right for his ascendancy. In addition to Tillinghast, a roster of architects—Donald Ross, Alister Mackenzie, and a host of others—found the 1910s and 1920s a time for manifesting their creative gifts. It's no wonder that these two decades have been designated "The Golden Age of Golf Course Architecture."

1923

- January 28: Walter Hagen wins his only Texas Open title, with a 279 total at Brackenridge Park in San Antonio.

- March 17: Walter Hagen rolls to his third straight Florida West Coast championship, winning by 10 strokes. His 276 total includes a 62, billed as a "world record."

- March 28: Glenna Collett takes her second consecutive title in the Women's North and South.

- March 30: Walter Hagen wins his second North and South Open.

- April 14: Roberto De Vicenzo, who will win national championships in more than a dozen countries, is born in Buenos Aires, Argentina.

- May 5: William C. Campbell, who will be both president of the USGA and captain of the Royal and Ancient Golf Club—and a seven-time Walker Cupper—is born in Huntington, West Virginia.

Pictured is the clubhouse of Winged Foot G.C., which opened in 1923 in Mamaroneck, New York. Winged Foot's West Course, the greatest of all A.W. Tillinghast designs, perennially ranks among the top 10 or 15 courses in America. Impressively, Winged Foot's East Course, which also opened in '23, ranks among the country's top 50 courses.

• May 11: Doris Chambers interrupts Joyce Wethered's stranglehold on the Ladies' British Open Amateur title.

• May 12: Roger Wethered clubs Robert Harris, 7 & 6, to win the British Amateur, at Deal G.C. in England.

• May 19: The U.S. Walker Cup team, minus Bobby Jones who is concentrating on his Harvard studies, ekes out a 6-5 victory over Great Britain at St. Andrews, Scotland.

• June 15: Arthur C. Havers's British Open victory, by one stroke over Walter Hagen at Troon G.C. in

Scotland, will be the last by a British subject for 11 years. Havers posts a score of 295.

• June 23: Perry Adair once again succeeds Bobby Jones as Southern Amateur champion, this time prevailing at the C.C. of Birmingham in Alabama.

Jesse Sweetser, Max Marston, Robert Gardner

Marston Nips Sweetser in U.S. Amateur

Max Marston *(center)* locks arms with Jesse Sweetser *(left)* and Robert Gardner. Marston, playing out of the new Pine Valley G.C. in Clementon, New Jersey, beat Sweetser in the final of the 1923 U.S. Amateur at Flossmoor C.C. in Illinois. After topping Bobby Jones and Francis Ouimet in earlier rounds, Marston bested Sweetser on the 38th hole.

Havers Holds Off Hagen in British Open

Tall Englishman Arthur Havers won the 1923 British Open championship, topping a field that included such legends as Bobby Jones, Walter Hagen, and Gene Sarazen. Holding a two-stroke lead over Hagen going into the final round at Troon in Scotland, he hung on to win by one stroke. Havers would play on three Ryder Cup teams for Great Britain.

Arthur Havers

Adair Nabs Southern Amateur

Perry Adair, a close friend of Bobby Jones, duked it out with Jones in the Southern Amateur. While Jones won the championship in both 1920 and 1922, Adair took the title in 1921 and 1923. Jones and Adair were two of the Dixie Kids who put on fund-raising exhibitions during World War I. Adair, however, never made it past the second round in the U.S. Amateur.

Perry Adair

• June 27: The U.S. Amateur Public Links championship now includes a four-man team event for the Warren G. Harding Trophy. Chicago wins the inaugural competition.

• June 29: Secretary of State Charles Evans Hughes presents the James D. Standish Cup to the new U.S. Amateur Public Links champion,

Richard J. Walsh, at East Potomac Park in Washington, D.C.

• July 14: H. Chandler Egan wins his third Pacific Northwest Amateur.

• July 15: Bobby Jones finally wins a USGA national title, defeating Bobby Cruickshank, 76-78, in a U.S. Open playoff at Inwood C.C. in

New York, after Jones lost a three-shot lead on the 72nd hole.

• July 28: Charles Evans Jr.'s fourth consecutive Western Amateur title, at Mayfield C.C. in Cleveland, is also a record eighth overall.

• August 4: The Royal Canadian G.A. makes spectators pay a $1

Collett Cops Another North and South Title

Though Glenna Collett didn't win the 1923 U.S. Women's Amateur—she fell to Florence Vanderbeck in the semifinals—she did capture her second straight Women's North and South Amateur. Collett, who turned 20 in 1923, loved all sports as a kid. In fact, she was a regular on her brother Ned's baseball team.

Bobby Jones

The Jones Era Begins; Bobby Wins U.S. Open

In 1923, Bobby Jones's seven lean years ended and his seven fat years began. After a series of frustrations and near-misses, Jones won the U.S. Open at Inwood C.C. in New York. Bobby almost lost this one too, as he double bogied the 72nd hole to fall into a playoff with Bobby Cruickshank. However, Jones prevailed in the extra 18 holes, 76-78.

Glenna Collett

admission charge for the first time. They watch Clarence Hackney win the Canadian Open at Lakeview G.C. in Toronto.

• September 7: Louise Suggs, who will win the amateur championships of both the U.S. and Great Britain as well as two Women's Opens, is born in Atlanta.

• September 22: Max Marston beats Bobby Jones, Francis Ouimet, and Jess Sweetser en route to his only U.S. Amateur triumph, at the Flossmoor C.C. in Illinois.

• September 29: Gene Sarazen repeats as PGA Champion, beating Walter Hagen on the 38th hole at Pelham C.C. in New York.

• October 6: Edith Cummings, sister of Collegiate champion Dexter, defeats Alexa Stirling, 3 & 2, in the U.S. Women's Amateur championship match at Westchester-Biltmore C.C. in Rye, New York.

• October 12: Jock Hutchison wins his second Western Open at Colonial C.C. in Tennessee.

FINALLY, JONES PREVAILS IN U.S. AMATEUR CHAMPIONSHIP

With his self-described "seven lean years" behind him, Robert Tyre "Bobby" Jones Jr. was making his move in 1924. The year before, he finally got off the schneide, taking his first U.S. Open title in a July playoff over another Bobby, last name of Cruickshank, with a wonderful shot from the rough on the final hole.

But the man who would go on to become the greatest amateur ever to play the game still hadn't captured the U.S. Amateur championship. Despite a half-dozen attempts, including a final-match appearance in 1919 and a semifinal showing in both 1920 and 1922, he had fallen short, seemingly unable to make the breakthrough.

The 1924 Amateur was held at Merion Cricket Club in Ardmore, Pennsylvania, where Jones had made his debut in USGA championships at the tender age of 14. Now he was 22 and had played well during the previous months, coming in second while defending his U.S. Open title and representing America in the Walker Cup, winning his singles match. In addition, he had experienced the test of British championships;

visiting the Isles for the first time in 1921, he'd acquitted himself fairly well.

In the '24 Amateur, Bobby was determined not to come up short again. A 144 in the 36-hole stroke-play qualifying augured well for his prospects in match play—and he would not disappoint his many adherents. His first-round match against Canada's W.J. Thompson set the tone, as Jones easily prevailed by the count of 6 & 5. The toughest test was his next opponent, medalist D. Clarke Corkran, who had made it to the semifinal match in 1916 before falling to eventual champion Charles Evans Jr. Jones struggled with Corkran but

wound up beating him, 3 & 2.

Then it was Easy Street for the Atlantan. He took the measure of Rudolf Knepper of Iowa, 6 & 4; embarrassed Francis Ouimet in the semifinal, taking only 26 holes before claiming victory, 11 & 10; and in an almost anticlimactic final, hammered George Von Elm on the 28th hole of the match, 9 & 8. That margin of victory, oddly enough, would prove to be Jones's average winning margin in semifinal and final matches for the five U.S. Amateur championships he would win in his career.

Ever hear a golfer say, "I've got it now"? Never was the old saying more true than for Bobby Jones after the '24 Amateur. Following this victory, he went on to compile a record that is the stuff of legend, a resumé that would place him forever at the pinnacle of amateur golf: four more U.S. Amateur championships, three more U.S. Opens, three British Opens, and his only British Amateur—that in the incredible year of 1930, when he took them all in the Grand Slam. With Bobby's commanding Amateur victory in 1924, it was certain that the tow-headed kid from East Lake would never be forgotten.

1924

- January 18: On Jekyll Island, Georgia, the USGA begins tests to determine the standard golf ball of the future.

- February 27: Pro golfer and trick-shot artist Joe Kirkwood wins the Houston Open, after capturing the Texas Open and Corpus Christi Open in the two previous weeks.

- March 28: Glenna Collett captures her third consecutive title in the Women's North and South Amateur.

- April 1: Walter Hagen successfully defends his North and South Open title, shooting a record 283.

- April 5: Arthur Havers defeats Bobby Jones, 2 & 1, at Jones's home

East Lake C.C. in Atlanta, where the two National Open champions battle for the unofficial world title.

- May: The USGA introduces regional qualifying for U.S. Open berths, with elimination rounds in Massachusetts and Illinois. Each sends the top 40 players and ties to the championship proper.

1924

Bobby Jones *(left of trophies)* must have wondered whether he'd ever win a U.S. Amateur. In six previous tries, he had lost once in the final, twice in the semis, and twice in the round of eight. In 1924, however, he routed Francis Ouimet in the semis, 11 & 10, and George Von Elm *(right of trophies)* in the final, 9 & 8.

• June 3: Glenna Collett wins her third straight Women's Eastern Amateur.

• June 6: Cyril Walker (weighing 118 pounds) beats Bobby Jones by three strokes to win the U.S. Open at Oakland Hills C.C. near Detroit, as the steel-shafted putter is permitted for the first time.

• June 25: Yale wins its 14th National Collegiate team championship, though its first since 1915, at Greenwich C.C. in Connecticut.

• June 27: Ten consecutive years of U.S. domination of the British Open begins with Walter Hagen's second title, a one-stroke victory at Royal Liverpool G.C. in Hoylake, England.

• June 28: Yale's Dexter Cummings becomes the first to capture back-to-back National Collegiate titles.

• June 28: Philadelphia waiter Joseph Coble tops Henry Decker, 2 & 1, to win the U.S. Amateur Public Links title at Community C.C. in Dayton, Ohio.

1924

Gene Sarazen

Sarazen Tees It Up After the Sun Goes Down

Gene Sarazen was never afraid to try something different, and in 1924 he put on a night-golf demonstration for the Illuminating Engineers Society in New York. After winning the 1923 PGA Championship, Sarazen fell into a three-year slump—blaming the drought on a poor grip. Gene did finish second in the '24 Western Open.

Leo Diegel

Despite Odd Ways, Diegel Triumphs in Canada

Leo Diegel had his ups and downs, especially on the putting green, where he developed one of the most unusual styles ever seen. His elbows stuck out horizontally, and the method earned him the name "Diegeling." In the 1924 Canadian Open, however, whatever style Leo may have used seemed to work. He won the event with a 285.

Merion Hosts U.S. Amateur

Bobby Jones *(on green, right)* aligns a putt during the 1924 U.S. Amateur at Merion Cricket Club in Ardmore, Pennsylvania. Merion is known for its small, undulating greens, its strategic design, and its famous white-faced bunkers. Then as now, woven baskets adorned the "flagsticks." Jones's caddie holds one of them in the far right of this photo.

Merion Cricket Club

• July 6: American John G. Anderson wins the French Amateur over Cyril Tolley at La Boulie, where Tolley won the French Open four days earlier.

• August 2: Leo Diegel wins his first of four Canadian Opens by two strokes over Gene Sarazen, at Mount Bruno G.C. in Montreal.

• August 25: Reigning U.S. Women's Amateur champion Edith Cummings becomes the first golfer to grace the cover of *Time* magazine.

• September 6: Dorothy Campbell Hurd, age 41, wins her third U.S. Women's Amateur title, defeating former national tennis champ Mary K. Browne, at Rhode Island C.C.

• September 6: "Wild Bill" Mehlhorn scores an eight-stroke Western Open victory over Al Watrous at Chicago's Calumet C.C.

• September 13: The U.S. dominates the Walker Cup Match, 9-3, at Garden City G.C. in New York. The match will be held biennially hereafter due to the financial strain.

1924

Cyril Walker

Pencil-Thin Walker Prevails in U.S. Open

Cyril Walker, a skinny Englishman who weighed less than 120 pounds, won the 1924 U.S. Open at Oakland Hills C.C. in Birmingham, Michigan. Walker and Bobby Jones were tied at 222 after three rounds, but Cyril outplayed Jones in the final round, 75-78. It was Walker's only victory in a major championship.

Walter Hagen

Hagen Edges Barnes in PGA Championship

Walter Hagen, a lover of the sweeter things in life, won his first of four straight PGA Championships in 1924 at French Lick C.C. in Indiana. Hagen's mere presence often gave him a stroke or two advantage on his opponent. He needed it in the final of the PGA, as he defeated Jim Barnes, 2 up.

Bill Mehlhorn

Mehlhorn Wins the Western by Eight Shots

The long-hitting Bill Mehlhorn splashed onto the scene in 1924–25, challenging in three different major championships. Mehlhorn romped to an eight-stroke victory in the 1924 Western Open and finished third in the '24 U.S. Open, losing by four. The following year, he fell to Walter Hagen in the final of the PGA Championship.

• September 20: Walter Hagen's second PGA Championship also begins his four-year lock on the title, as he beats Jim Barnes, 2 up, at French Lick C.C. in Indiana.

• September 27: Bobby Jones wins the U.S. Amateur, defeating George Von Elm, 9 & 8, at Merion Cricket Club in Pennsylvania.

• The USGA okays the use of steel-shafted golf clubs in championship play after April 11.

• Congressional C.C., which will go on to host many championships of note including the 1964 U.S. Open, is opened for play in Bethesda, Maryland.

• Executive Secretary Thomas J. McMahon will now manage the USGA's burgeoning activities from its new Manhattan offices.

• The USGA declines an invitation to supervise an international match among women golfers from the United States, Great Britain, and Canada, similar to the Walker Cup.

"She was our Bobby Jones." That was USGA Secretary Judy Bell's succinct summation of Glenna Collett Vare's influence on women's golf, spoken at Glenna's funeral ceremony in 1989. Bell couldn't have said it better. As a player, the native of New Haven, Connecticut, compiled a record that, in all likelihood, will never be surpassed: She won six U.S. Women's Amateurs, the second of which came in 1925. Collett also provided an example of class and sportsmanship the equal of Jones.

As in the lives of many champions, Collett's family had a heavy influence. Her father was quite the athlete, capturing the American bicycle-racing championship in 1899. He must have been a source of inspiration to young Glenna, but—like many doting parents— he was a source of pressure as well. Rhonda Glenn, in her *Illustrated History of Women's Golf,* quotes Glenna on the topic: "(He was) my most enthusiastic supporter, who expected such extravagant things of me."

Glenna did live up to expectations. At age 18, she astounded onlookers with a measured drive of 307 yards, helped by a tip from Alexa Stirling and the steady

COLLETT PILES UP THE AMATEUR CROWNS

tutelage of her long-time mentor and teacher, Alex Smith. As her game improved, Collett began to bring home the titles. In 1921, she was the medalist in the Women's Amateur, shooting 85. Soon thereafter, she defeated Cecil Leitch to take the Berthellyn Cup, a top-drawer Philadelphia competition. In 1922, Collett captured both the Women's North and South and the Eastern Amateur, then traveled to White Sulphur Springs in Virginia and fired an 81 to again lead the qualifying for the Women's Amateur. She went on to win, and at age 19 had her first national championship.

That was but a prelude to a great career. A loss in the 1923

Women's Amateur, when she fell in the third round, actually served as a blessing in disguise. The loss of her title, she was to recall, gave her a sense "of relaxation and freedom."

In 1925, she found herself again in position to take a national championship. The Women's Amateur was hosted by St. Louis Country Club, the first site west of the Mississippi to hold the women's championship. Making her way through match play with some difficulty—twice winning only by the narrow margin of 1 up—Collett found herself paired in the final with her old friend, confidante, and nemesis Alexa Stirling, now Mrs. Fraser and a Canadian resident. Friendship be damned, Collett must have thought, and she went on to beat Alexa, 9 & 8.

Remarkably, she would go on to take four more Women's Amateurs (1928–30 and 1935). Only JoAnne Gunderson Carner, with five wins in the event, would ever come close. In 1953, in honor of Glenna Collett Vare, the LPGA unveiled the Vare Trophy, presented to the Tour player with the lowest scoring average on the year.

1925

- February 4: Walter Hagen defeats Cyril Walker, 17 & 15, for the unofficial world championship, at St. Petersburg, Florida.

- February 14: Joe Turnesa, one of seven golfing brothers, claims his only Texas Open title at the Brackenridge Park course in San Antonio.

- April 2: Mac Smith unseats reigning North and South Open champion Walter Hagen, firing a record 281.

- May 21: Although the R&A still does not sanction steel-shafted clubs, the Royal Canadian G.A. joins the USGA in approving them for championship play.

- May 29: Robert Harris, age 43, finally wins the elusive British Amateur championship, at Royal North Devon G.C. in England. He clubs Kenneth Fradgley, 13 & 12.

- June 3: Willie Macfarlane, the first champion to wear eyeglasses during a U.S. Open, fires an Open-record 67 (4-under-par) in the second

Glenna Collett captured her second U.S. Women's Amateur in 1925, routing Alexa Stirling, 9 & 8, in the final at St. Louis C.C. Collett also played in the Ladies' British Open Amateur championship and, in the third round, went head-to-head with Joyce Wethered, Britain's great woman player. Wethered won the classic match-up, 4 & 3.

round, at Worcester C.C. in Massachusetts.

• June 5: Willie Macfarlane wins the U.S. Open, defeating Bobby Jones by one stroke over 36 playoff holes after both shot 291 in regulation.

• June 9: Maureen Orcutt wins her first of seven Women's Eastern

Amateurs, at Greenwich C.C. in Connecticut.

• June 26: Jim Barnes wins the 24th and final British Open held at Prestwick in Scotland, where bad crowd control is blamed for Macdonald Smith's final-round collapse (82).

• June 27: Yale wins its second consecutive National Collegiate team championship (15th overall), at Montclair G.C. in New Jersey.

• July 2: Donald D. Carrick, age 18, becomes the youngest Canadian Amateur winner ever, defeating C. Ross "Sandy" Somerville, 5 & 4, at Royal Ottawa G.C. in Ontario.

Pebble Beach Golf Links

Fans Live on the Edge at Pebble Beach

The 8th hole at Pebble Beach G.L. has always been treacherous—especially in the early days, when spectators were just a slippery spot away from plunging to their death. Rocky coastline lines the entire right side of the par-4 8th hole. The approach shot must carry ocean and rocks to the green, which is just 12 feet away from the steep cliff.

Orcutt Wins Her First Eastern Amateur

In the early years, it seemed that each of the great women players found one tournament to dominate year after year. Maureen Orcutt was no exception. In 1925, Orcutt won the first of seven Eastern Amateurs. She would also win three straight North and South Women's Amateurs, from 1931–33.

Maureen Orcutt

Diegel Wins Second of Four in Canada

Leo Diegel seemed to like it north of the border. Though he often fell short in major U.S. championships, Diegel won his second straight Canadian Open in 1925. He also won the title in 1928 and '29. Diegel seemed to heat up in the cold; he once shot a 65 in a Ryder Cup match in frigid weather.

Leo Diegel

• August 1: Leo Diegel wins his second consecutive Canadian Open, at Lambton G.C. in Toronto.

• August 8: Raymond J. McAuliffe wins the Amateur Public Links title, defeating William F. Serrick, 6 & 5, in the final at Salisbury C.C. in Garden City, New York.

• August 22: Macdonald Smith wins his second Western Open, at Youngstown C.C. in Ohio.

• August 29: Elaine Rosenthal Reinhardt captures her third Western Amateur championship.

• September 5: Bobby Jones captures his second consecutive U.S. Amateur

title, defeating his friend Watts Gunn, 8 & 7, in the final match at Oakmont C.C. in Pennsylvania.

• September 17: Jim Barnes pastes Willie Macfarlane, 12 & 11, for the unofficial world championship, which concludes at Columbia C.C. near Washington D.C.

Macfarlane Beats the Legends in U.S. Open

After 72 holes, six men were within two strokes of the lead in the 1925 U.S. Open—including legends Bobby Jones, Francis Ouimet, Gene Sarazen, and Walter Hagen. But who prevailed? This fellow, Willie Macfarlane. Willie tied Jones at 291 at Worcester C.C. in Massachusetts, then outlasted him in two playoffs, 75-72 to 75-73.

Mary and Bobby Jones

No Contest: Jones Cruises in U.S. Amateur

Bobby Jones, shown here with his wife Mary, battled for 108 holes before falling in the 1925 U.S. Open. However, Jones hardly broke a sweat in winning the '25 U.S. Amateur, at Oakmont C.C. near Pittsburgh. In the four rounds of match play, Jones won 11 & 10, 6 & 5, 7 & 6, and 8 & 7. The victim in the final was his friend, Watts Gunn.

Willie Macfarlane

• September 26: Walter Hagen eagles the first hole en route to his 6 & 5 victory over Bill Mehlhorn in the PGA Championship, at Olympia Fields C.C. in Illinois. It's his second straight PGA title.

• October 4: Glenna Collett wins her second U.S. Women's Amateur, drubbing Alexa Stirling Fraser, 9 & 8, at St. Louis C.C., as the event crosses the Mississippi for the first time.

• October 9: Arnaud Massy wins a record fourth French Open, at Chantilly.

• November 22: The Havemeyer Trophy, emblematic of U.S. Amateur supremacy, is destroyed in a fire at Atlanta's East Lake C.C., home of current national champion Bobby Jones.

• Golf writer Oscar Baun Keeler, who will become known as Bobby Jones's Boswell, publishes his first book, *Autobiography of an Average Golfer*.

FAN-FAVORITE JONES PREVAILS IN U.S OPEN, BRITISH OPEN

It was somewhat ironic that the two major championships Bobby Jones won in 1926 were those in which the professionals played—the British and U.S. Opens—while the two he did not win were the ones he of all people, the greatest amateur golfer in the game's history, would seem most likely to capture—the U.S. and British Amateurs.

This lends credence to the argument that match play is the more difficult of the two basic competitive formats by which to win a tournament. It is always possible for a lesser player to get hot for a few hours and topple a top seed who happens to be a little off his game at the moment. By contrast, a 72-hole stroke-play competition takes long-lasting mechanical and psychological consistency, and therefore is a truer way to define a golf champion.

In any case, no matter how he fared, Jones was now the focus of golfdom's eye. His victories were hailed while his losses were taken with deep regret by the multitudes in the United States and Great Britain. He transcended feelings of national pride. He was golf's Everyman.

Jones's popularity may have been due to his patrician manner as much as his brilliant play. Golf was increasingly being dominated by the professionals, most of whom came from the caddie ranks. They brought with them a more proletarian character marked by a certain gamesmanship and showmanship that would take some getting used to. It was as if Jones was the last vestige of a gentler time, the last of the gentleman amateur era in sports. This point was made, however subtly, by Anthony Spalding of *The New York Times* in his concluding remarks after Jones's 1926 British Open victory: "He goes about the game without doing anything to the disadvantage of his opponents. He is silent, and his cap is homespun and fits his head."

All of which gave Bobby's two Open victories in 1926 even more resonance. At Royal Lytham in England, Jones finished two shots ahead of Michigan pro Al Watrous. In the U.S. Open at Scioto Country Club in Ohio, Jones came from behind to beat the leader of the First Family of American Professionals, Joe Turnesa, by a stroke. At the latter championship, Jones did something that would be recalled time and again as the most poignant articulation of the quintessential sportsman.

During the second round, Jones called a penalty on himself when his ball turned over as he addressed it to hit a putt. He was lauded for his action. To be sure, professionals as a whole then and always were just as honorable. But it was Jones's response to the acclaim he received that gave such behavior a perspective that has rung down through the ages: "To praise me for that," he said, "is to congratulate someone for not robbing a bank."

1926

• January 10: Harry Cooper earns his "Lighthorse" tag from writer Damon Runyon en route to his victory in the inaugural $10,000 Los Angeles Open at Los Angeles C.C.

• January 15: Macdonald Smith wins the Texas Open, at the Brackenridge Park course in San Antonio.

• February 22: Alex Findlay, a native Scot who pioneered American golf west of the Mississippi, reveals that he failed to convince the Pope to build a six-hole course on Vatican grounds.

• March 7: In a 72-hole challenge match billed as the "World Championship," Walter Hagen soundly defeats the golfing world's other great star, Bobby Jones, 12 & 11, over the Whitfield Estates and Pasadena golf courses in Sarasota, Florida.

• March 26: The city of Chicago opens free public golf schools modeled after its regular school system. Charles Evans Jr., a former

In 1926, Bobby Jones won his second U.S. Open, beating Joe Turnesa by a stroke at Scioto C.C. in Columbus, Ohio. Jones's swing, though elegantly graceful, also produced surprising power. Such was the makeup of Jones himself: noble and graceful on the outside, but fiercely driven within.

U.S. Open and U.S. Amateur champion, is named principal.

• April 4: Bobby Cruickshank wins his first of three North and South Open titles at Pinehurst C.C.

• April 7: The first national golf exhibition and merchandise show opens in Chicago.

• May 29: Although suffering from the flu, Jesse Sweetser becomes the first American-born golfer to win the British Amateur, at the Muirfield G.C. in Scotland.

• June 3: The U.S. Walker Cup team defeats the Great Britain/Ireland team, 6½-5½, on the Old Course at St. Andrews.

• June 5: British professionals thump their U.S. counterparts, 13½-1½, in an unofficial skirmish at Wentworth, England. It's a preliminary to next year's Ryder Cup series.

• June 24: Cecil Leitch wins her record fourth Ladies' British Open Amateur.

1926

Los Angeles Open

Los Angeles Open Debuts at L.A. C.C.

In 1926, the Los Angeles C.C. hosted the first Los Angeles Open, a breakthrough event in the development of the PGA Tour. With its $10,000 total purse, it associated the pro game with the glamour of show business, and it reflected the upbeat "go west young man" spirit of America's Roaring '20s. Harry Cooper won the inaugural event with a score of 279.

Rice Helps *Write* Duffer's Handbook

The Duffer's Handbook of Golf, one of the most humorous of all golf books, was published in 1926. Grantland Rice, co-author of the book, once said: "Golf is 20 percent mechanics and technique. The other 80 percent is philosophy, humor, tragedy, romance, melodrama, companionship, camaraderie, cussedness, and conversation."

The Duffer's Handbook of Golf

Fownes Is Named USGA President

William Fownes became president of the USGA in 1926. Years before, he and his father co-designed the Oakmont C.C. course near Pittsburgh. They created a fearsome layout with unique deep-furrowed bunkers and exceptionally fast greens. Their stern philosophy was, "A shot poorly played should be a shot irrevocably lost."

William Fownes

• June 25: Bobby Jones wins his first of three British Opens, at Royal Lytham & St. Annes in England.

• June 30: Yale wins its third consecutive (16th overall) National Intercollegiate championship at the Merion Cricket Club in Ardmore, Pennsylvania.

• July 3: Tulane's Fred Lamprecht successfully defends his individual title.

• July 10: Bobby Jones wins his second U.S. Open, by one stroke over Joe Turnesa, at Scioto C.C. in Columbus, Ohio. He becomes the first golfer to win the U.S. Open and British Open titles in the same year.

• July 24: Macdonald Smith wins his second of three Metropolitan Open titles at the Salisbury C.C. in New York. Smith and Gene Sarazen tie at 286, then need three 18-hole playoffs to settle the issue: Smith (70-72-66) and Sarazen (70-72-70).

• July 25: A *New York Times* article notes that two million Americans are

1926

George Von Elm

Von Elm Tops Jones in U.S. Amateur

George Von Elm won the 1926 U.S. Amateur, upsetting defending champion Bobby Jones in the final, 2 & 1, at Baltusrol G.C. in Springfield, New Jersey. Von Elm, a dashing Californian, gained sufficient revenge on Jones. In the 1924 U.S. Amateur, Jones humiliated him in the final, 9 & 8; in 1925, Jones beat him in the semifinals, 7 & 6.

Bing Crosby

Young Bing Triumphs in Musicians Championship

Bing Crosby has appeared in innumerable golf photographs, but very few before the 1930s. Here he's shown at the 1926 U.S. Musicians championship in Rancho Santa Fe, California—which he won. Crosby, who turned 22 in May 1926, took an interest in the game at age 12, when he became a caddie in Tacoma, Washington.

Mr. and Mrs. George Thomas

Thomas Designs California's Top Courses

George C. Thomas designed such classic California golf courses as Los Angeles C.C. (North), Bel Air C.C., and Riviera C.C., the latter of which opened in 1926. Thomas's book, *Golf Architecture in America: Its Strategy and Construction*, was published in 1927 and is a seminal work on the subject.

---

playing golf, and $468 million is spent annually on the game.

• August 7: Macdonald Smith wins the Canadian Open with a score of 283 at the Royal Montreal G.C.

• August 28: Walter Hagen wins his third Western Open title, by nine strokes over Harry Cooper and

Gene Sarazen at the Highland Golf & C.C. in Indiana.

• September 18: George Von Elm wins the U.S. Amateur, upsetting Bobby Jones, 2 & 1, in the final at Baltusrol G.C. in New Jersey.

• October 2: Helen Stetson defeats Elizabeth Goss, 3 & 1, in the final

match to capture the U.S. Women's Amateur championship at the Merion Cricket Club in Ardmore, Pennsylvania.

• The Oak Hill C.C.'s East Course, designed by Donald Ross and site of three memorable U.S. Opens and a PGA Championship, opens for play.

HAGEN EKES OUT HIS FOURTH STRAIGHT PGA TITLE

Although Walter Hagen won the great majority of his 40 career victories at stroke play, his flamboyant style made him all the more daunting at match play. With his loose swing, Hagen could spray a driver with the worst of them. But his never-quit spirit and remarkable flair for recovery from horrendous places, backed up by nerveless chipping and putting, allowed him to steal many a victory from the jaws of defeat.

From the 1916 inaugural PGA Championship through 1927 (it was at match play until 1958), Hagen won 35 matches and lost three. So it came as no surprise every time he won the event—and he won it five times. The first title came in 1921, which he chose not to defend. Then, from 1924–27, Hagen won four in a row.

The 1927 PGA was played in November, at the Cedar Crest Country Club in Dallas. Hagen, of course, was the favorite, but a cakewalk was not expected. He had played his annual heavy and tiring world-wide exhibition schedule, and a batch of young and hungry pros had arisen who were anxious to make their mark. Hagen was ready for them. At the

time, even the defending champion had to qualify for one of the 32 match-play berths, and Hagen won the medal by three strokes with rounds of 72-69.

His first match, against Jack Farrell, a relative unknown who had beaten out Leo Diegel for the last qualifying spot, was tough. Hagen was four down after the first 18 (all the matches were scheduled for 36 holes), but the grandmaster whittled away and won, 3 & 2. Hagen then met Tony Manero, winner of the U.S. Open nine years later but not yet ready for The Haig, who romped, 11 & 10. Next was Tommy Armour, winner of the U.S. Open

in June and who, in six previous head-to-head confrontations with Hagen (in other than the PGA), had never lost. Never mind. Hagen beat him soundly, 4 & 3.

Now came Al Espinosa, the Spaniard out of Chicago who was beginning to tilt a few golfing windmills—he would go to the PGA final in 1928. Indeed, Espinosa had Hagen one down with one to play before falling to "majors fever." He three-putted the 18th from 25 feet, while Hagen got down in two with a great chip from a tough lie. When Espinosa three-putted again on the first extra hole, it was over. Hagen admitted he was lucky to win, then added, "What are you going to do? You give these boys a chance and they don't take it."

In the final against Joe Turnesa, runner-up to Jones in the 1926 U.S. Open and conqueror of Gene Sarazen earlier in the week, Hagen was two down after 18 holes. But when Turnesa gave Hagen a chance with poor play at the 21st and 22nd holes, the champion took it and went on to win, 1 up. Hagen had now won five of the first 10 U.S. PGA Championships, and he played in only eight of them.

1927

- January 4: Gene Sarazen continues his sweep through the Miami portion of the winter tour, winning the Miami Beach Open. He finishes at 7-under-par 277.

- January 7: The Federal Court of Claims rules on initiation fees to private country clubs, saying that golf club securities are non-taxable.

- January 9: Bobby Cruickshank wins the Los Angeles Open for his first of three tour victories in five weeks.

- January 23: Tommy Armour begins his rise to prominence as a tournament player by winning his second event on the winter circuit. After capturing the Long Beach

Open on January 2, he wins the El Paso Open.

- February: The Royal and Ancient Golf Club of St. Andrews comes out in favor of the lighter and bigger golf ball. No final decision is reached.

- February 1: The Boyce Thompson Institute reports that American bent

1927

Walter Hagen, at the pinnacle of his career in 1927, won that year's PGA
Championship—his fourth in a row. Also in '27, The Haig captured his fourth
Western Open title and, to top it off, captained the United States team in the first-ever
Ryder Cup Matches. Hagen's team won, 9½-2½.

grass is the best type of grass for golf courses.

• February 5: The U.S. Department of Agriculture announces it has developed "the perfect putting green grass," creeping bent, which it claims will never have weeds, brown spots, ant hills, or worm hills.

• February 6: Harry Cooper drubs Walter Hagen, 10 & 9, in a 72-hole exhibition match in Dallas.

• February 22: Billy Burke, who until the previous year was a caddie who didn't think he was good enough to play against the pros, wins the Florida Open.

• February 23: Bobby Jones scores his first ace, holing out a 4-iron on the 170-yard 11th hole of the East Lake C.C., his home course, during a practice round.

• February 24: Mr. Doe Graham, in his quest to drive a golf ball from Mobile, Alabama, to Los Angeles, gets as far as New Orleans.

Gene Sarazen

City-Bred Sarazen Does His Best Work in Miami

Gene Sarazen, a native of Harrison, New York, enjoyed uncanny success in Miami. On New Years Eve, 1926, he won his first Miami Open. Days later, he captured the Miami Beach Open. A year later, he again won these two back-to-back plus won the Miami International 4-Ball. Sarazen wound up winning the Miami Open five straight times.

Graffis Brothers Launch Golfdom

In 1927, Herb Graffis and his brother Joe started *Golfdom* magazine, which stressed the business side of golf. Herb Graffis was an experienced journalist who had a lifelong infatuation with golf. Besides *Golfdom*, he founded *Chicago Golfer* and *Golfing*. He also assisted Tommy Armour in writing golf instructional books and helped found the Golf Writers Association of America.

Golfdom *Magazine*

Joe Turnesa

Turnesa Just Misses in PGA Championship

Joe Turnesa was nipped by Walter Hagen, 1 up, in the final of the 1927 PGA Championship, at Cedar Crest C.C. in Dallas. Turnesa had a chance to tie on the last hole, but his putt hung on the lip of the cup. Joe, one of seven brothers who made an indelible mark on American golf, also played in the inaugural Ryder Cup Match in '27.

• February 27: Walter Hagen defeats Gene Sarazen in a 72-hole exhibition match. Total gate receipts reach $6,000, considered a good "take."

• March 10: Tommy Armour and Bobby Cruickshank, the hottest golfers on the winter tour, win the prestigious Miami International 4-Ball tournament.

• March 26: Bobby Jones wins the Southern Open. The strangest moment occurs when Joe Turnesa's driver head flies off at the top of his backswing. The local committee assesses a penalty, even though he did not begin his downswing.

• March 30: Glenna Collett, beginning to make her mark as one of the greatest women golfers in history, wins her fourth Women's North and South Amateur championship.

• April: Bobby Jones publishes *Down the Fairway,* destined to become one of the best-selling golf books ever. Co-author is O.B. Keeler.

Quartet of Stars Boast Nine Amateur Championships

Bobby Jones

Four U.S. Amateur champions pose together. From left to right stand George Von Elm, Max Marston, Bobby Jones, and Bob Gardner. Von Elm won the Amateur in 1926; Marston took it in 1923; Jones prevailed in 1924–25, 1927–28, and 1930; and Gardner grabbed the crown in 1909 and 1915.

U.S. Amateur Champions

Jones Wins Two Majors, Publishes a New Book

In 1927, Bobby Jones won the British Open, captured the U.S. Amateur, scored his first hole-in-one, and published a book—*Down the Fairway.* Here he uses one of the new motion-picture cameras that were coming into vogue. In 1931, Jones went to Hollywood to film the first-ever instructional movies, called *How I Play Golf.*

Bobby Cruickshank

Pint-Sized Cruickshank Burns It Up Early

"Wee" Bobby Cruickshank was red-hot in early 1927, winning three tour events in a five-week period, including the Los Angeles Open. Cruickshank, one of the most successful of the native-born Scottish golfers to emigrate to the United States, was no bigger than a jockey but had a lion-sized heart.

- April 1: Bobby Cruickshank successfully defends his North and South Open title, outlasting Walter Hagen at Pinehurst C.C.

- May 27: Johnny Farrell edges Bobby Cruickshank by a stroke to win his only Metropolitan Open, at the Wykagyl C.C. in New Rochelle, New York.

- May 28: Dr. William Tweddell beats Eustace Landale, 7 & 6, for the British Amateur title at Hoylake.

- June 4: The Ryder Cup series begins with a 9½-2½ U.S. victory over Great Britain at the Worcester C.C. in Massachusetts. Walter Hagen captains the winning side; Ted Ray heads the losing effort.

- June 17: Tommy Armour and Harry Cooper complete 72 holes of the U.S. Open at Oakmont C.C. with 301 totals, the last time a 300-plus score will lead the Open. Armour wins the playoff, 76-79.

- June 30: Johnny Farrell begins a summer winning binge with a victory in the Massachusetts Open.

Babe Ruth

Ruth Blasts Mammoth Homers, Behemoth Drives

When he wasn't cracking home runs for the New York Yankees (he hit 60 in 1927), Babe Ruth spent considerable time on the golf course. In 1929, he reportedly drove a golf ball 325 yards using his 45-inch-long "bludgeon," and in 1932 he was named president of the American Lefthanders Golf Association.

Little-Known Horn Wins Women's Amateur

Miriam Burns Horn won the 1927 U.S. Women's Amateur, at Cherry Valley Club in Garden City, New York. Horn, from Kansas City, Missouri, thus became the first woman from west of the Mississippi to win the event. Glenna Collett, Helen Hicks, and Virginia Van Wie—much bigger names— would win the next eight Amateurs.

Miriam Burns Horn

• July: Princeton wins the National Intercollegiate championship for the seventh time, at the Garden City G.C. in New York.

• July: Watts Gunn of Georgia Tech captures the individual title at the National Intercollegiate championship.

• July 14: Bobby Jones successfully defends his British Open crown, setting a new Open record (285) at the Old Course at St. Andrews.

• July 31: Walter Travis, the first overseas golfer to win the British Amateur and the founder of *The American Golfer* magazine, dies at the age of 65.

• August 27: Bobby Jones, fresh from his British Open triumph, outclasses Charles Evans Jr., 8 & 7, in the U.S. Amateur final at the Minikahda Club in Minneapolis.

• September 10: Walter Hagen coasts to his fourth Western Open title by four strokes, at the Olympia Fields C.C. in Illinois.

Bernice Wall, Glenna Collett

Collett's the Women's Equal of Bobby Jones

Glenna Collett *(right)* captured her fourth North and South Amateur in 1927. Collett was called the Bobby Jones of women's golf, and the comparison was fitting. While Jones won five U.S. Amateurs from 1924–30, Collett captured five U.S. Women's Amateurs from 1922–30—plus another in 1935.

Johnny Farrell

Armour Hits the Big Time, Wins Open

Tommy Armour rose to prominence in 1927 by winning the U.S. Open, beating Harry Cooper in a playoff, 76-79, at Oakmont C.C. Armour was a college-educated Scot who lost an eye during World War I. After emigrating to the United States, he became the club secretary at the fashionable Congressional C.C. in Washington, D.C.

Tommy Armour

Farrell Wins Seven Tour Events on the Year

Former caddie Johnny Farrell, at the age of 26, established himself as one of the premier American professionals in 1927, as he won seven tournaments on a circuit he was instrumental in shaping. Farrell, from White Plains, New York, won half of his 22 career victories on the East Coast.

- September 24: Miriam Burns Horn defeats Maureen Orcutt, 5 & 4, in the U.S. Women's Amateur at the Cherry Valley Club in New York.

- November 5: Walter Hagen wins his fifth PGA Championship and fourth in a row, nipping Joe Turnesa, 1 up, in the final at Cedar Crest C.C. in Dallas.

- December 23: Youngsters Byron Nelson and Ben Hogan, each 15 years old, meet in a playoff for the Glen Garden C.C. caddie championship in Fort Worth. Nelson prevails by a stroke.

- Miss Harriott Curtis and her sister Margaret offer a cup in their name to be played for by teams of American and British women amateurs. The USGA withholds acceptance.

- Riviera C.C. in Pacific Palisades, California, opens for play.

- Brothers Herb and Joe Graffis launch *Golfdom*, the first periodical devoted to the business side of golf.

DIEGEL FIGHTS OFF NERVES, WINS HIS FIRST MAJOR TITLE

When Leo Diegel won the 1928 PGA Championship, there was a sigh of relief among the golfing public and his tournament-playing peers—not unlike when Tom Kite won the 1992 U.S. Open. In both cases, a very fine player finally broke through to win a big one. Diegel had been close numerous times before. In at least eight U.S. or British Open championships, he had clear chances to win but always found a way to lose. Over the last six holes of the '25 U.S. Open, for example, he went 9-over-par. An 8 on the last hole capped this dismal fall, and he finished five shots off the pace.

Diegel was a magnificent iron player capable of fantastically low rounds—he once shot a 65 in a Ryder Cup match on a bitterly cold day. Yet he was his own worst enemy. High-strung by nature, he forever fought nervousness. He became famous for a peculiar putting style designed to steady his stroke. He held his elbows akimbo and looked like a bat over the ball. A bright and self-aware man, Diegel stole a march by some 60 years on the current rage for sports psychology. He saw a psychoanalyst in an effort to find the calm so important to great golf.

Of course, Diegel had his bright moments as well. He won 29 times on the Tour, including four prestigious Canadian Opens and two PGA Championships. Not surprising for a man of his mental makeup, Diegel was superstitious and believed he could not win in certain places, could win in others. One of the latter was the state of Maryland, and sure enough that's where his major breakthrough occurred. He won the 1928 PGA Championship at Five Farms Country Club in Baltimore. It was in no way a fluke, as he beat the best golfers of his day.

In the first round at Five Farms, Diegel smashed a helpless Tony Manero, 10 & 8, with a withering run of sub-par golf. He played nine straight holes in 31 strokes. But the most satisfying victory was in the quarterfinals, when he defeated his good friend and nemesis, Walter Hagen, the master gamesman who had easy pickings with Diegel's psyche. Diegel had lost twice to Hagen in the past. In the 1925 PGA Championship, he blew a 3-up lead with four holes to play, then lost on the fourth extra hole. In the final of the 1926 PGA, Diegel was five holes up on Hagen at one point but went on to lose, 5 & 3.

But at Five Farms in 1928, Leo got his druthers. On the 35th hole against Hagen, he canned a four-foot birdie putt to clinch a 2 & 1 victory. Once past that enormously gratifying hurdle, there was no stopping him. Diegel next defeated Gene Sarazen by an impressive 9 & 8 score. In the final, which was in a sense anticlimactic, Diegel beat Al Espinosa, 6 & 5. The past seven PGA Championships had been won by either Hagen or Sarazen, the Nicklaus-Palmer of their era. Diegel broke the mold.

1928

• January 1: The Penn Athletic Club opens an 18-hole miniature golf course on the roof of its building in Philadelphia.

• January 8: Macdonald Smith wins his first of four Los Angeles Opens.

• January 8: Less than a week after winning the Miami Beach Open, Gene Sarazen captures the Miami Open title.

• January 12: The Pacific Coast Long Driving Contest is won by Leonard Schmutte with drives of 289, 272, and 275 yards.

• February 3: After studying the golf course from an airplane, Glenna Collett wins the Women's Mid-South tournament.

• February 5: Golf ball manufacturers agree not to pay professionals secret salaries for using certain brands of balls in competition.

• February 7: It is reported that a blackbird is sentenced to death by

1928

Only pretty women could separate Walter Hagen *(left)* and Leo Diegel *(right)*, who
were fast friends off the golf course. On the course, in serious competition, Hagen had
a way of playing on the nerves of his pal. But in 1928, Diegel prevailed to win the
PGA Championship and stop Hagen's four-straight win streak in the event.

French golfers for stealing 30 golf balls off the Saint-Germain course near Paris.

• March 13: Johnny Farrell and Gene Sarazen team up to win the Miami International 4-Ball.

• March 31: Billy Burke unseats Bobby Cruickshank as the North

and South Open champion at Pinehurst C.C.

• April 5: Opal S. Hill, later a pioneer of women's professional golf, wins the Women's North and South Amateur at Pinehurst C.C.

• April 28: Archie Compston hands Walter Hagen an embarrassing

18 & 17 defeat in their special challenge match at Moor Park in London, England.

• May 4: Betsy Rawls, winner of 55 tournaments on the LPGA Tour, including four U.S. Women's Opens, is born in Spartanburg, South Carolina.

1928

Smith Proves Versatility in Los Angeles Open

Macdonald Smith won a bunch of prestigious tournaments, including one Canadian Open, two Western Opens, and four Los Angeles Opens, his first L.A. title coming in 1928. Impressively, the four L.A. wins came on four different courses. He proved he could win on a short track (Wilshire C.C.; 6,442 yards) or a long one (Riviera C.C.; 7,029).

Cypress Point Club

Breathtaking Cypress Point Opens for Play

The spectacular Cypress Point Club course, designed by Alister Mackenzie, opened in 1928. Pictured is the world-famous 16th hole, a par-3 that measures 233 frightening yards. Seven people have aced this hole. Bing Crosby, a member of the club, aced it in 1948. Jerry Pate remains the only professional to do so.

Macdonald Smith

• May 11: Walter Hagen wins his third British Open, by two strokes over chief rival Gene Sarazen, at Royal St. George's in Sandwich, England.

• May 26: Phil Perkins beats Roger Wethered, 6 & 4, in the British Amateur final at Prestwick, Scotland.

• June 24: Johnny Farrell defeats Bobby Jones, 143-144, in a 36-hole playoff for the U.S. Open at Olympia Fields C.C. in Illinois.

• June 29: Princeton wins the National Collegiate title at the Apawamis Club in Rye, New York. Maurice McCarthy of Georgetown wins the individual title.

• July 13: British Professional star Archie Compston wins his only American tour event, the Eastern Open, before returning home.

• July 20: After winning the Pennsylvania Open on July 3, Tommy Armour captures the Metropolitan Open by two strokes over Johnny Farrell.

Compston Humiliates Hagen in Exhibition

Great Britain's Archie Compston, a giant of a man at well over six feet, played a 72-hole exhibition match against Walter Hagen a week before the 1928 British Open and handed The Haig the worst defeat of his career— 18 & 17. But once Hagen got his bearings after the long voyage across, he defeated Compston and all others to win his third British Open.

Johnny Farrell

Farrell Nips Jones in U.S. Open Playoff

Johnny Farrell's only major championship came in the 1928 U.S. Open, a tension-filled affair. Farrell edged Bobby Jones, 143-144, in a 36-hole playoff for the title, at Olympia Fields C.C. in Illinois. Farrell never again reached such heights. He finished out his career with a long tenure as head pro at the famed Baltusrol G.C.

Walter Hagen

Hagen Wins One in Britain, None in the U.S.

Walter Hagen *(left)* captured the 1928 British Open, by two strokes over Gene Sarazen, at Royal St. George's in Sandwich, England. Ironically, Hagen didn't win any American tournaments in 1928, ending a 10-year streak. This, of course, did not deter him from celebrating any occasion that might crop up.

Archie Compston

• July 25: Congressman Fiorello LaGuardia participates in an aerial golf match at the Dunwoodie G.C. in Yonkers, New York.

• July 28: Leo Diegel wins his third Canadian Open title by two strokes over Walter Hagen, Macdonald Smith, and Archie Compston at Rosedale G.C. in Toronto.

• July 28: Abe Espinosa wins the Western Open at the North Shore C.C. in Illinois. He becomes the first Hispanic-American to win a big-time American pro tourney.

• August 7: The R&A presents its plan for a uniform golf ball. It is the same as the USGA model—1.68 inches in diameter and 1.55 ounces.

• August 25: Frank Dolp wins his second Western Amateur title in three years, 4 & 3, over Gus Novotny at the Bob O'Link G.C. near Chicago.

• August 31: First-time captain Bobby Jones leads the United States team to its fifth consecutive Walker Cup victory at Chicago G.C.

1928

Glenna Collett

Collett Christens New-Look Pebble Beach

When the famed Pebble Beach G.L. was revised by H. Chandler Egan in 1928, reigning U.S. Women's Amateur champion Glenna Collett played an exhibition to break it in. This is Glenna playing her third shot to the green of the par-5 6th hole, with its grand vista overlooking Monterey Bay.

Espinosas Among the Best Mexican-Americans

Al Espinosa *(pictured)* and his brother Abe were the two best Mexican-American golfers before Lee Trevino hit the scene in the 1960s. Al Espinosa played on two U.S. Ryder Cup teams and, in 1928, captured two of his nine career victories on the PGA Tour. The following year, he lost a playoff for the U.S. Open to Bobby Jones.

Al Espinosa

Jones Routs Perkins at the U.S. Amateur

In 1928, Bobby Jones won his fourth U.S. Amateur, at Brae Burn C.C. in West Newton, Massachusetts. Jones romped to a 10 & 9 final-match victory over Phil Perkins, the same guy whom he humiliated in his 1928 Walker Cup match. This was the largest margin of victory in an Amateur final since the inaugural year of 1895.

Bobby Jones

- September 1: William Wrigley, the chewing gum magnate, announces he will stage a pro tournament (December 20–23) on his Catalina Island, off the coast of Southern California.

- September 5: In a special American Ryder Cup benefit match to raise money for the team's expenses, Walter Hagen and Gene Sarazen defeat the team of Bobby Jones and Johnny Farrell.

- September 9: Walter Hagen's plan to fly in a private plane from Philadelphia to Massachusetts to play a tournament is halted. Fear of flying at night terminates the flight in Rhode Island.

- September 15: Bobby Jones wins his fourth U.S. Amateur in five years, downing Phil Perkins, 10 & 9, at the Brae Burn C.C. in West Newton, Massachusetts.

- September 16: Walter Hagen defeats Johnny Farrell for the mythical World Championship of Golf.

1928

Bobby Jones

In Walker Cup Match, Jones Again Crushes Perkins

In 1928, Bobby Jones captained the U.S. Walker Cup team for the first time, and he led his club to an 11-1 blowout over Great Britain/Ireland, at Chicago G.C. Jones's singles victory was over Phil Perkins, whom he crushed, 13 & 12. This set a Walker Cup record for the largest rout in a 36-hole singles match.

Santa Catalina Island Clubhouse

Wrigley's Catalina Island Hosts Tourney

In 1928, chewing gum magnate William Wrigley opened for play an 18-hole golf course on the mountainous Catalina Island, just off the coast of Southern California. Wrigley actually owned the island. A number of PGA Tour events would be held on the course, and the inaugural event, held in December 1928, was won by Horton Smith.

- September 29: Glenna Collett wins her third U.S. Women's Amateur title by crushing up-and-comer Virginia Van Wie, 13 & 12, at the Virginia Hot Springs Golf and Tennis Club.

- October 6: Leo Diegel breaks the seven-year Sarazen/Hagen stranglehold on the PGA Championship. He wins it at the Five Farms C.C. in Baltimore with a 6 & 5 victory in the final over Al Espinosa.

- December 5: The Hawaiian Open is inaugurated in the biggest geographic expansion of the winter tour. Bill Mehlhorn wins it in a playoff with Fred Morrison.

- Cypress Point Club, on California's Monterey Peninsula, is opened for play. The Alister Mackenzie layout is almost immediately designated one of golf's most beautiful courses.

- Glenna Collett publishes *Ladies in the Rough,* which contains a foreword by Bobby Jones.

OLD HICKORIES HELP BRITS CAPTURE RYDER CUP

The seed from which the Ryder Cup Match grew was sown by a golf magazine out to build circulation. In 1921, Jim Harnett of *Golf Illustrated* in Chicago raised the money to send 10 top American pros to play their counterparts in Great Britain. It was a way of promoting golf and, of course, his magazine. The magazine eventually foundered, but the concept it engendered flowered into one of golf's most prestigious fixtures.

The 1921 confrontation, in Great Britain, went to the home team. Another unofficial match occurred in 1926, again in Great Britain, and the United States was thoroughly trounced, 13½-1½. Still, all concerned liked the concept, and in 1927 Samuel Ryder—an English golf enthusiast and seed merchant who supplied golf course superintendents in both Great Britain and the United States—donated a cup and the Match took his name and became official. It would be played every other year on a home-and-home basis. In 1927, the United States won, 9½-2½, at Worcester Country Club in Massachusetts.

Entering the 1929 Matches, it seemed Great Britain would have an advantage. First of all, the competition would be on home turf, Moortown Golf Club in Leeds, England. Secondly, the Americans would be forced to revert to hickory-shafted clubs because steel had not yet been approved by the R&A. Nevertheless, the United States entered the Matches as the favorite. America had begun to dominate world golf, which at the time constituted competition in these two countries. Only one Briton had won his National Open between 1921 and 1928. Before the '29 Matches, British Ryder Cup captain George Duncan put his squad through a "training camp" that emphasized the American playing style; i.e., "taking the game very seriously." It worked.

On the first day of the two-day event, held in blustery cold spring weather, the alternate-shot foursomes were contested and the Americans took a 2½-1½ lead. It might have been more had captain Walter Hagen not opted to sit Horton Smith down even though he was coming off a brilliant winter tour in which he had won eight tournaments. Instead, Ed Dudley partnered Gene Sarazen and they registered the only U.S. loss that day.

Smith played the singles the following day, and he won handily. But it was not enough to stem Britain's rising tide, which saw the home squad win five matches, lose two, tie one, and capture the Cup by the score of 7-5. If the reversion to hickory shafts had an effect on the Americans' play, no one mentioned it—probably because they had all learned the game with wood shafts and had only been using steel for a couple of years. The British approved steel the following November, but they would win only two Ryder Cups in the next 23 renewals.

1929

- January 12: A week after winning the Miami Open for the fourth time, Gene Sarazen captures the Miami Beach Open for the third time, at LaGorce C.C.

- January 14: Macdonald Smith wins his second consecutive Los Angeles Open, which finishes in total darkness at the Riviera C.C.

- February: The True Temper Co. patents a seamless, steel golf shaft with a stepdown taper, which will become the industry standard.

- February 4: Bill Mehlhorn wins the South Central Open after winning the El Paso and Texas Opens the previous two weeks.

- February 17: Mr. George Orth reportedly watches two golfers play 13 holes, then tries it himself. With his first shot, he scores an ace.

- March: The Seminole G.C. in North Palm Beach, Florida, opens for play. A Donald Ross masterwork, it'll become the course that Ben Hogan calls home.

1929

The 1929 U.S. Ryder Cup team poses in front of the map of the Old Course at St. Andrews, Scotland. Pictured left to right are: Bob Harlow (team manager), Johnny Golden, Joe Turnesa, Al Watrous, Ed Dudley, Horton Smith, Johnny Farrell, and Leo Diegel. The three American team members not pictured are Walter Hagen, Gene Sarazen, and Al Espinosa.

• March 6: Horton Smith, the 20-year-old Missouri flash, wins the Fort Myers Open to start a four-week winning streak. He'll follow with victories in the Florida, LaGorce, and North and South Opens.

• March 12: U.S. equipment manufacturers introduce an anti-shock iron with a rubber joint between the shaft and heel, claiming that it eliminates shock to the hands at impact.

• April 5: Glenna Collett wins her fifth Women's North and South Amateur championship in eight years, at Pinehurst C.C.

• April 13: George Voigt wins his third consecutive North and South Amateur, 9 & 8, over William C. Fownes Jr. at Pinehurst C.C.

• April 27: British captain George Duncan lambastes Walter Hagen, 10 & 8, en route to a 7-5 victory over the U.S. team in the Ryder Cup Matches in Leeds, England.

1929

Walter Hagen, A.J. Coleman, Leo Diegel, Charlie Seaver

Pro-Ams Becoming Popular

The pro-am team tournament was coming into vogue in 1929. It was an effort to maintain the amateur connection to the game, which was being lost as the pros became significantly better players. Here, Walter Hagen and partner A.J. Coleman *(left)* are pictured with Leo Diegel and Charlie Seaver. Seaver *(far right)* fathered baseball great Tom Seaver.

Horton Smith

Hagen Claims His Fourth British Open

A thick crowd lines the course at Muirfield, Scotland, during the final round of the 1929 British Open. All eyes are on the 12th green, where the great Walter Hagen prepares to putt. Hagen won the championship by six strokes over another American, Johnny Farrell. It was Hagen's second British Open title in a row and his fourth British victory in the last eight years.

British Open

Smith Rises to Top with Eight Tour Victories

In 1929, Horton Smith, known as the "Joplin Ghost," had a phenomenal year that put him on the highest rung of American golf. The smooth-swinging Missourian with the brilliant putting touch won eight tournaments on the burgeoning PGA Tour. Wins included the prestigious Florida and North and South Opens.

• **April 30:** The R&A votes down movement for change to a bigger and lighter golf ball, saying it makes the game too difficult. The USGA says that's the idea, in light of so many better players now in the game.

• **May 10:** Walter Hagen repeats as British Open champion (his fourth title overall) by six strokes over fellow American Johnny Farrell at the Muirfield G.C. in Scotland.

• **May 17:** Joyce Wethered joins Cecil Leitch as the only four-time Ladies' British Open Amateur champs, defeating Glenna Collett, 3 & 1, in their historic showdown at the Old Course at St. Andrews.

• **May 17:** Italian dictator Benito Mussolini is an interested spectator at a Gene Sarazen/Johnny Farrell exhibition, arranged through the American Embassy, at Rome C.C.

• **June 15:** Cyril Tolley closes the 1920s as he began, winning the British Amateur, this time at Royal St. George's G.C. in England.

1929

Pebble Beach Golf Links

U.S. Amateur Travels to the West Coast

The 1929 U.S. Amateur was played for the first time west of the Rocky Mountains when it was held at Pebble Beach G.L. (then known as Del Monte Golf and C.C.). Here, a sizable gallery encircles the 10th green. Pebble Beach would host the Amateur twice more—in 1947 and in 1961, when Jack Nicklaus won before turning professional.

Riviera Hosts Its First Los Angeles Open

Pictured is the slick-looking program of the 1929 Los Angeles Open. In the background is the distinctive clubhouse of Riviera C.C., which hosted the tourney for the first time in '29. Riviera again played host in 1930, 1941, 1945–53, and 1973 through the present. In 1929, Macdonald Smith won his second consecutive Los Angeles Open.

L.A. Open Program

Ouimet and Winton Play Under the Lights

Six years before major-league baseball played its first night game, Francis Ouimet played the first noted golf match at night. In July 1929, Ouimet played William Winton at Winchester C.C. in Massachusetts, as portable lights lit the course. Winton won the match, which ended at midnight.

Francis Ouimet

• June 28: Princeton wins its ninth National Collegiate title (and third in a row) at the Hollywood G.C. in New Jersey. Tom Aycock of Yale wins the individual title.

• July 15: Francis Ouimet plays a night match against William Winton at Winchester C.C. in Massachusetts. Portable lights show the way.

• July 27: Leo Diegel wins his fourth and final Canadian Open title, with a record score of 274, at the Kanawaki G.C. in Montreal.

• August 9: Babe Ruth whacks a 325-yard drive at the St. Albans G.C. in New York. He uses his 45-inch-long, 16-ounce "bludgeon" (driver).

• August 10: Carl Kauffmann wins his third straight U.S. Public Links title, at Forest Park G.C. in St. Louis.

• August 17: The Los Angeles Open tournament committee uses a Goodyear blimp to inspect courses from the air and sticks with Riviera C.C. as its host club.

1929

Johnny Goodman, Bobby Jones

Mackenzie Designs a Gem in Pasatiempo

Pasatiempo Golf Course, a highly acclaimed public layout, opened in 1929 in Santa Cruz, California. Pasatiempo, founded by amateur star Marion Hollins, was designed by Alister Mackenzie, the creator of Cypress Point. Mackenzie was so pleased with this course that he built his home off the 6th hole.

Pasatiempo Golf Course

Goodman Shocks Jones in a First-Round Match

Bobby Jones congratulates Johnny Goodman after Goodman beat him, 1 up, in the first round of the 1929 U.S. Amateur. Goodman rode a cattle car from Nebraska to Pebble Beach to compete in the championship. The loss was a shocking blow to Jones, who had won four of the five previous Amateurs and was co-medalist in '29.

Glenna Collett, Leona Pressler

Collett Wins Her Fourth Women's Amateur

In 1929, Glenna Collett *(left)* became the first four-time winner of the U.S. Women's Amateur. Collett defeated Leona Pressler *(right)* in the final, 4 & 3, at Oakland Hills C.C. near Detroit. Earlier in the year, Collett was runner-up in the Ladies' British Open Amateur championship.

• August 23: Peter Thomson, a five-time British Open champion, is born in Melbourne, Australia.

• August 24: Tommy Armour wins the Western Open with a 273 total that shatters Arthur Smith's 24-year-old scoring record by five strokes, at Ozaukee C.C. in Milwaukee.

• August 24: St. Louis native Eddie Held becomes the first American-born golfer to carry off the Canadian Amateur title, downing Gardiner White, 3 & 2, at the Jasper Park G.C. in Alberta.

• August 30: Bobby Jones scores a course-record 67 at Pebble Beach in California during a U.S. Amateur

Open practice round. He rips seven birdies from the 6th through the 14th holes.

• September 7: In the first U.S. Amateur played west of the Rockies, at the Del Monte G.C. in Pebble Beach, California, Minnesota's Harrison Johnston defeats Dr. Oscar F. Willing, 4 & 3.

1929

Johnston Prevails in Wide-Open U.S. Amateur

After Bobby Jones was eliminated in the first round of the 1929 U.S. Amateur by Johnny Goodman, Goodman was stopped in the next round by Lawson Little. The title was won by Minnesota's Harrison R. Johnston *(pictured)*, who beat Francis Ouimet in the semifinals and Dr. O.F. Willing in the final, 4 & 3.

Leo Diegel

Harrison R. Johnston

Diegel in Good Spirits After Winning the PGA

Leo Diegel enjoyed his celebrity after winning his second straight PGA Championship by accepting a lucrative head pro post at a fine club in California. He spent little time in the pro shop, though, as he continued to play in many tournaments and do numerous exhibitions, in which he tried to pull off sensational trick shots.

• September 10: Arnold Palmer, perhaps the most popular golfer of all time, is born in Latrobe, Pennsylvania.

• September 17: Billy Burke chips in for birdie on the ninth playoff hole to win the inaugural Glens Falls Open in upstate New York over Bill Mehlhorn.

• October 5: Glenna Collett wins her fourth U.S. Women's Amateur, defeating Leona Pressler, 4 & 3, at Oakland Hills C.C. in Birmingham, Michigan.

• November 28: The R&A makes a landmark decision when it finally sanctions the use of steel-shafted clubs within its jurisdiction.

• December 7: Leo Diegel repeats as PGA Champion, defeating Johnny Farrell, 6 & 4, in the final at Hillcrest C.C. in Los Angeles.

• Bob Harlow signs on as the first official PGA Tournament Bureau manager. It's a major step toward the development of a full-time tournament circuit.

JONES MAKES HISTORY, WINS ALL FOUR MAJORS

It wasn't entirely unthinkable that Bobby Jones could win in one year the four major championships of his era—the U.S. and British Amateurs and Opens. Early in the year, Bobby Cruickshank predicted it, bet on it, and won a large sum of money. Surely Jones entered every national championship intending to win. But all four in one season? It had crossed his mind, but he was never so presumptuous to make public such a notion. Still, he seemed to have something afoot.

Early in 1930, he began an exercise routine to combat a tendency to gain weight in the off-season. Jones also entered a couple of winter tour events, which he seldom did, and played with an ardor he normally reserved only for championships. In the Savannah Open in February, he shot a 67 and a 65 among his four rounds. He finished second by a shot to Horton Smith. A month later, Jones won the Southeastern Open by 13 strokes.

It is certain Jones was after the British Amateur crown, for it was the only one of the four majors he had never won. He played it only when the Walker Cup Matches were held in Great Britain—every other even-numbered year—and he was by now intimating a readiness to retire from competition to raise his young family and earn his living practicing law. This might be his last chance for that elusive title, and so the great journey began.

Jones's most anxious moment in the British Amateur, at St. Andrews, was in the fourth round, when Cyril Tolley had a 12-foot birdie putt on the last hole to win 1 up. He missed, and Jones won on the first extra hole after laying a stymie on his foe. At Hoylake two weeks later, Jones led the British Open through the first three rounds and broke the 72-hole course record by 10 strokes.

On to Minnesota and the U.S. Open, the third leg. At the Interlachen Country Club, Jones took a five-shot lead with a third-round 68—the lowest he ever shot in this his 11th and last U.S. Open. Nevertheless, he had to birdie three of the last six holes in the final round to win by two over Macdonald Smith. A 40-foot birdie putt on the last green was the clincher.

Given his own momentum, and the undoubted awe everyone had for Jones by the time the U.S. Amateur came around, his victory in that championship was practically assured. Jones won the 36-hole qualifying medal at Merion Cricket Club in Pennsylvania with 69-73. In the matches, he was never down to any opponent. Jones then retired for all time from championship golf. He was just 28 years old.

George Trevor, in *The New York Sun,* called Jones's feat "the impregnable quadrilateral." No one before or since has won all four championships in one year, and with the Opens now dominated by pros, it's unthinkable that anyone ever will.

1930

- January 5: Gene Sarazen wins his fifth consecutive Miami Open title, at the Miami C.C.

- January 14: Denny Shute, an emerging professional star, wins the Los Angeles Open at the Riviera C.C. with the highest winning score (296) in the event's history.

- January 23: The $25,000 Agua Caliente Open, the richest tournament ever, is held in Tijuana, Mexico. Gene Sarazen wins the $10,000 first prize.

- February 1: Walter Hagen and Joe Kirkwood begin an extended exhibition tour of the Orient and Australia.

- February 2: Denny Shute continues his superb play, taking the Texas Open by three strokes at the Brackenridge Park course in San Antonio.

- February 9: Al Espinosa wins the first Houston Open with a 281 total at the Rio Rico C.C.

It was not all a cakewalk for Bobby Jones on his way to his Grand Slam in 1930. At the Old Course at St. Andrews during the British Amateur, Jones had to play from Swilcan Burn, the ditch cutting across the front edge of the 1st green. Despite a tough fourth-round match against Cyril Tolley, Jones easily won the final, 7 & 6, over Britain's Roger Wethered.

• February 22: Horton Smith deals Bobby Jones the final tournament loss of his active competitive career, winning the Savannah Open by one. Jones's prize as low amateur is a double-barreled shotgun.

• March 15: Walter Hagen says he will not defend his British Open crown, causing controversy.

• March 28: Paul Runyan wins his first North and South Open title, at Pinehurst C.C.

• April: Horton Smith is the leading money winner on the winter pro tournament swing, with five victories and total earnings of $15,500.

• April 1: Bobby Jones wins the Southeastern Open by 13 strokes over Horton Smith at the Forrest Hills-Ricker golf course in Augusta, Georgia.

• April 5: Glenna Collett wins her sixth and last Women's North and South title, at Pinehurst C.C.

Bill Mehlhorn

Mehlhorn Claims His Last Pro Victory

"Wild Bill" Mehlhorn, who won the last of his 21 career victories in 1930—the LaGorce Open—got his nickname not from having a golf temper, but for the ability to go wild and shoot terrifically low scores. Mehlhorn never won a major title, but he was a superb shot-maker. Ben Hogan said he was the best he'd ever seen.

Gene Sarazen

Sarazen Wheels Out of Mexico with $10,000

In January 1930, the Agua Caliente Open in Tijuana, Mexico, offered a purse of $25,000—the largest purse ever seen at that time. Gene Sarazen needed a wheelbarrow to cart off his $10,000 first prize. Ironically, Sarazen had lost a bundle in the famous stock market crash, which occurred just months earlier.

Joe Kirkwood

Kirkwood, Hagen Take Their Show Abroad

Joe Kirkwood, the great trick-shot artist, was the first Australian-born golfer to make his fortune in the United States. At least he was based in the U.S., for he traveled often on worldwide exhibition tours. In 1930, he and Walter Hagen toured the Far East and played golf before the Emperor of Japan.

• May 1: Molly Gourlay leads her British team to an 8½-6½ victory over Glenna Collett's American contingent at Sunningdale, England. The success of the event makes inevitable the inauguration of the Curtis Cup series.

• May 16: Captain Bobby Jones wins two matches, leading the U.S.

Walker Cup team to victory over Great Britain/Ireland, 10-2, at the Royal St. George's G.C. in Sandwich, England.

• May 31: Bobby Jones goes one extra hole to defeat Cyril Tolley in the fourth round of the British Amateur at St. Andrews. He goes on to win the championship.

• June 18–20: Bobby Jones's run for the Grand Slam spurs the first radio reports of the British Open to the U.S. from Great Britain. O.B. Keeler does the summaries for NBC.

• June 20: Bobby Jones wins the British Open with a score of 291, breaking the course record at Hoylake by 10 strokes.

Merion Cricket Club

Merion Site of Dramatic U.S. Amateur

The Merion Cricket Club *(pictured)* installed a state-of-the-art watering system prior to the 1930 U.S. Amateur. Fans witnessed great drama throughout the championship. Not only did Bobby Jones clinch his Grand Slam here, but in the second round Maurice McCarthy and George Von Elm battled 10 extra holes before McCarthy prevailed.

Horton Smith

Golf's Not Pretty at Tijuana Tournament

A quality field of golfers and a pretty good crowd showed up at the 1930 Agua Caliente Open in Tijuana, Mexico. Undoubtedly, the golfers were more impressed with the $25,000 purse than with aesthetics: This desert course wasn't the prettiest layout in the world. Sand traps and wasteland served as the hazards.

Agua Caliente Open

Smith Takes a Liking to New Sand Wedge

Horton Smith holds a 25-ounce sand wedge with a rounded soul, which was designed by a Texan named MacLain. Smith invested heavily in the club, but it was eventually deemed illegal because it had a concave face. Bobby Jones used the club once, when it was still legal, while winning the 1930 British Open.

• June 28: Princeton wins its 10th national collegiate title (fourth in a row) at the Oakmont C.C. Princeton's George T. Dunlap Jr. wins the individual title.

• July: Americans who bet on Bobby Jones at 10-to-1 to win the British Amateur wait in vain for the payoff from a Welsh bookmaker.

• July 10: Ted Husing is the play-by-play announcer for the first radio broadcast of a U.S. Open.

• July 12: Bobby Jones wins the third leg of the Grand Slam, the U.S. Open, at the Interlachen C.C. in Minnesota. Jones birdies three of the last six holes to win by two over Macdonald Smith.

• July 21: Gene Littler, winner of the 1953 U.S. Amateur, 1961 U.S. Open, and 29 PGA Tour events, is born in San Diego.

• July 25: The Merion Cricket Club announces its new, state-of-the-art watering system installed for the upcoming U.S. Amateur championship.

1930

Jones Honored with Ticker-Tape Parade in New York

So beloved was Bobby Jones that New Yorkers gave him a ticker-tape parade after he won the 1930 British Amateur and British Open. Ironically, Jones was only halfway done, as his U.S. Open wouldn't come until 10 days later, and his U.S. Amateur victory wouldn't take place until late September.

Bobby Jones

Popluar Jones Poses for Pix at British Amateur

Although on a mission to win the British Amateur for the first time in 1930, Bobby Jones could still be compliant enough to pose for press pictures before teeing off. His victory here, at the Old Course at St. Andrews, was the first win of his Grand Slam. He defeated Roger Wethered in the final.

Parade for Bobby Jones

- July 30: "Tom Thumb," or miniature golf, becomes all the rage. A new "course" is installed in Ile de France.

- July 30: Tommy Armour unseats defending champion Leo Diegel in a 36-hole Canadian Open playoff at the Hamilton G.C. in Ontario.

- August 9: Robert E. Wingate becomes the first golfer to win the U.S. Amateur Public Links in his hometown, as he defeats Joseph E. Greene, 1 up, at the Jacksonville Municipal G.C. in Florida.

- August 11: The U.S. Department of Commerce estimates that $125 million has been invested in Tom Thumb golf courses.

- August 17: Minnesota joins the tour with a bang, putting on the $10,000 St. Paul Open. Harry Cooper wins the $2,500 first prize.

- August 23: Gene Sarazen pulls away to a seven-stroke victory over

1930

Tommy Armour

United States Captures Another Walker Cup

In 1930, the U.S. Walker Cup team *(pictured)* won for the sixth straight time, at Royal St. George's G.C. in Sandwich, England. Standing are *(left to right)* George Von Elm, Don Moe, Roland MacKenzie, and Bobby Jones. Sitting are *(left to right)* Harrison Johnston, Francis Ouimet, Dr. O.F. Willing, and George Voigt.

U.S. Walker Cup Team

Armour Nips Sarazen in Tense PGA Championship

Tommy Armour *(pictured)* defeated Gene Sarazen, 1 up, in the final of the 1930 PGA Championship, at Fresh Meadows C.C. in Flushing, New York. The final, called "the greatest golf match I ever saw" by Leo Diegel, was a nail-biter throughout. Armour won by canning a 14-foot putt on the 36th hole. Tommy also won the 1930 Canadian Open.

"Tom Thumb" Golf Course

Tom Thumb Courses Pop Up All Over

Miniature golf courses, also known as "Tom Thumbs," were a big fad in the 1920s and 1930s. In fact, by the summer of 1930, it was estimated that $125 million had been invested in Tom Thumbs in the United States. This little layout was constructed in New York City. Note the lights strung on the lines above, indicating night play.

Al Espinosa in the Western Open at the Indianwood Golf & C.C. near Detroit.

• September 13: Tommy Armour wins the PGA Championship by nipping Gene Sarazen, 1 up, in a hard-fought final at the Fresh Meadow C.C. in Flushing, New York.

• September 21: Civic rivalry prompts St. Louis to follow St. Paul onto the tour. It stages the $10,000 St. Louis Open, which is won by Tommy Armour.

• September 27: Bobby Jones achieves the Grand Slam by winning the U.S. Amateur at the Merion Cricket Club in Pennsylvania. Jones trounces Eugene V. Homans, 8 & 7, in the final.

• October 18: Glenna Collett collects her third straight U.S. Women's Amateur title, defeating Virginia Van Wie, 6 & 5, at the Los Angeles C.C. in Beverly Hills, California.

IN SEARCH OF A HERO, GOLF TURNS TO ARMOUR

It was no surprise that Tommy Armour was a go-for-broke golfer who never feared the chancy, heroic shot. Armour would never be nervous on the golf course after what he experienced in World War I, when he was a soldier in the Black Watch Regiment of Highlanders. In the Great War, Armour's left arm was severely and permanently damaged by shrapnel. Also, as the result of a mustard gas attack, he ended up with sight in only his right eye. These were the physical and emotional scars (or attributes) he brought to each and every golf tournament he entered.

A fair amateur golfer at home, Armour emigrated to the United States from his native Scotland after the war was over. He was 25 years old when he made the move. Once in the U.S., Armour took a job as club secretary at the Congressional Country Club in Bethesda, Maryland, then later became its head professional. All the while, he honed his game to become one of the great long-iron and fairway-wood players in golf history.

Armour won the U.S. and Canadian Opens in 1927, the PGA Championship in 1930, and

the Canadian Open again in 1930 and 1934. And when he captured the British Open in 1931, Armour became the first professional golfer to ever hold four major national titles. The British Open victory was perhaps the most satisfying, for it came not far from his Braid Hills birthplace (near Edinburgh). It was also played for the first time at Carnoustie Golf Club, one of golf's most difficult courses. What's more, at 36 years of age, he captured the crown with a wonderful final round of 71 that tied the course record. He needed just that to come from sixth place and overtake the brilliant Argentine, Jose Jurado, and win by one stroke with a score of 296.

It was a stroke of luck for golf that Armour won this most honored championship when he did, for golf was in a kind of interregnum. The great Walter Hagen was nearing the end of his fabled career, Bobby Jones had called it quits after his 1930 Grand Slam, and Gene Sarazen was seemingly at the end of his reign. No one with their magnetism and ability to win big had yet come forward. Armour was tall and slender with wavy silver hair; he was intelligent and glib with a stage actor's delivery. He may not have had the stuff of broad public appeal, but he was picturesque.

William Richardson of *The New York Times* called Armour the "Lawrence (as in Arabia) of the Links." And to be sure, he could hit marvelous shots when he needed them. On the 72nd hole of the 1927 U.S. Open, he rifled a 3-iron approach to within 10 feet of the cup, then holed the putt for a birdie. That put him into a playoff, which he won. Two of his Canadian Open victories were achieved with brassies on par-5s that brought him eagles. Golf needed a hero in the early 1930s, and Armour was just the man to fit the bill.

1931

- January 1: The new larger (1.68-inch), lighter (1.55-ounce) "balloon" golf ball, USGA-approved from this date, will prove very unpopular.

- January 4: Joe Turnesa wins the Miami Open, earning a meager $400 from a purse made up of players' entry fees, gate receipts, and a $500 local contribution.

- January 12: Ed Dudley wins the Los Angeles Open, which rotates to the Wilshire C.C. once again.

- February 1: Abe Espinosa wins the Texas Open, overcoming a six-stroke Denny Shute lead at the Brackenridge Park course in San Antonio.

- February 16: Henry Cotton is officially barred from the British Ryder Cup team after he insists on the right to travel separately from the team to and from the matches at Columbus, Ohio.

- February 24: Bobby Jones leaves for the Warner Bros. studios in Hollywood to film the first-ever

Tommy Armour holds the prized claret jug symbolic of victory in the British Open. Armour won the 1931 title at the Carnoustie G.C., not far from the small town near Edinburgh, Scotland, where he was born and raised. Armour played with only one functioning eye and a permanently damaged left arm, the result of combat service in the first World War.

instructional movies, *How I Play Golf.* Slow-motion sequences will stun teaching pros, who see swing movements they didn't think happened.

• March 3: The USGA bans the concave-faced sand wedge, introduced the previous year, deeming it an "illegal instrument."

• March 21: Gene Sarazen wins the LaGorce Open for his 14th career victory on the Florida circuit.

• March 23: The PGA of America approves a plan that insists that each prospective member serve a three-year apprenticeship learning the art of clubmaking.

• March 28: Wiffy Cox sheds his reputation as a poor finisher by winning the North and South Open at Pinehurst C.C.

• April 4: Maureen Orcutt begins her three-year reign as Women's North and South Amateur champ at Pinehurst C.C.

1931

Jones Breaks New Ground in Hollywood

In 1931, Bobby Jones went to Hollywood to help make the first-ever instructional movies, *How I Play Golf*. By playing the film in slow-motion, golf teachers could better analyze the mechanics of the swing. Pictured here are *(left to right)* film star Ben Lyon, director George Marshall, Jones, and actress Bebe Daniels.

Ben Lyon, George Marshall, Bobby Jones, Bebe Daniels

Turnesa's Miami Open Victory Worth Just $400

Joe Turnesa won the Miami Open in January 1931. His first-place check was only $400, as the Depression was beginning to pinch the tour's purses. Turnesa had to work hard for his money too, as he won by just one stroke over three others. Later in the year, Joe's brother Mike won the Mid-South Open Title.

Joe Turnesa

- April 11: George T. Dunlap Jr. wins his first of a record seven North and South Amateur titles, 6 & 5, over future U.S. Open champion Sam Parks at Pinehurst C.C.

- May 7: The USGA decides to assume financial responsibility for the U.S. Curtis Cup team. It will undertake administration of the matches against the British women's team beginning next year.

- June 5: Tommy Armour wins the British Open by one stroke over little Argentinean Jose Jurado, at Carnoustie in Scotland.

- June 12: Enid Wilson beats Wanda Morgan, 7 & 6, for her first of three consecutive Ladies' British Open Amateur titles.

- June 20: Ed Dudley wins the Western Open by four strokes over Walter Hagen at the Miami Valley G.C. in Ohio.

- June 23: Yale, ending a four-year drought, wins its 17th National

Wiffy Cox

Foul-Mouthed Cox Wins North and South Open

Wiffy Cox was a crusty professional from Brooklyn who often used strong language when things weren't going well on the course. Cox was good enough to win a few pro tournaments, including the 1931 North and South. He was also one of the first to use steel shafts. Cox finished his career as head pro at Congressional C.C.

Billy Burke

Burke Wins U.S. Open Title with Steel Shafts

Billy Burke, an American of Lithuanian heritage, won the 1931 U.S. Open, at the Inverness Club in Toledo, Ohio. The one-time iron worker in the mills of Cleveland was the first winner of the national championship to use steel-shafted clubs—and the last to use the experimental "balloon" golf ball, which weighed only 1.55 ounces.

George Von Elm

Von Elm Loses 72-Hole U.S. Open Playoff

George Von Elm, a sleek swinger with all the shots, suffered a heartbreaker in the 1931 U.S. Open. He and Billy Burke tied at 292 after regulation, then tied at 149 after a 36-hole playoff. Burke beat him in a second playoff, 148-149. Von Elm stayed alive by birdieing both the last hole of regulation and the last hole of the first playoff.

Intercollegiate championship at the Olympia Fields C.C. outside Chicago, its farthest west site to date.

• June 24: Billy Casper, winner of 51 tournaments as a professional and a member of eight U.S. Ryder Cup teams, is born in San Diego.

• June 27: Princeton's George T. Dunlap Jr. repeats as the individual champion in National Intercollegiate play at Olympia Fields C.C.

• June 27: The United States hands Great Britain a crushing 9-3 Ryder Cup defeat in sweltering heat at Scioto C.C. in Columbus, Ohio.

• July 4: Four Tom Thumb miniature golf courses are now open in Peiping, China.

• July 6: Billy Burke wins the U.S. Open at the Inverness Club in Toledo, Ohio, by one stroke over George Von Elm in the longest playoff in major championship history (72 holes).

Ed Dudley

Ferrera Beats 15-Year-Old in U.S. Publinx

Charles Ferrera, who worked as a riverter in San Francisco, won the 1931 U.S. Amateur Public Links championship at the Keller Golf Course in St. Paul, Minnesota, the same course on which the St. Paul Open was played. Ferrera defeated a 15-year-old, Joe Nichols, in the final, 5 & 4.

Dudley Wins Los Angeles and Western Open Titles

Ed Dudley, a slow-moving Southerner with a languid swing, won two highly regarded events in 1931—the Los Angeles Open and the Western Open, the latter considered a major at the time. Dudley, who once shot a 68 on the famously difficult Pine Valley G.C, also played on the 1929 and 1933 U.S. Ryder Cup teams.

Charles Ferrera

Walter Hagen, Walter Hagen Jr.

Walter Jr. Follows in His Father's Footsteps

Walter Hagen gives a few pointers to his one and only son, Walter Hagen Jr., in a photo taken in March 1931. Not only did Junior look and dress like his dad, but he was a pretty good golfer too. In 1938, Hagen Jr. played for Notre Dame in the NCAA championships. Hagen Sr. won the Canadian Open in 1931.

• July 14: Walter Hagen's superior approach shots are the difference in his 36-hole playoff victory in the Canadian Open over Percy Alliss at the Mississauga Golf & C.C. in Toronto.

• August 8: Charles Ferrera, a San Francisco riveter, defeats 15-year-old schoolboy Joe Nichols in the final of the U.S. Public Links, 5 & 4, at the Keller G.C. in St. Paul, Minnesota.

• August 10: Ed Dudley, destined to become Augusta National G.C.'s first professional, is struck by lightning while playing in the Philadelphia Open. He'll still manage to finish second to Clarence Hackney the following day.

• September 5: Seventeen years after his first U.S. Amateur victory, Francis Ouimet wins a second time, defeating Jack Westland, 6 & 5, in the final at Beverly C.C. in Chicago.

• September 26: Helen Hicks dethrones Glenna Collett Vare, 2 & 1, in the U.S. Women's Amateur final, at the C.C. of Buffalo.

Helen Hicks

Hicks Dethrones Vare to Win U.S. Amateur Title

Helen Hicks, a long-hitting 20-year-old, won the 1931 U.S. Women's Amateur at the Country Club of Buffalo. Hicks defeated reigning British women's champion Enid Wilson in the semifinals, then beat defending U.S. champion Glenna Collett Vare in the final, 2 & 1. Hicks later became the first U.S. Women's Amateur champion to turn pro.

R. Asaami, Dewey Longworth, T. Miyamoto

Japanese Professionals Arrive to Play U.S. Tour

In December 1931, Messrs. Asaami *(left)* and Miyamoto *(right)* became the first Japanese golfers to come to the United States to play on the pro tour. The pair played in the National Match-Play championship in Lake Merced, California. Pictured with them is Dewey Longworth, a Northern California pro champ.

• September 30: The USGA adopts a rule that will permit golfers to remove loose impediments on putting surfaces during competitions.

• November 18: At its national convention in Boston, the PGA of America considers turning the Ryder Cup Matches into a worldwide competition, rather than one exclusively between the U.S. and Great Britain.

• November 20: The USGA reverses its decision on the new golf ball and adopts a ball that is the same size (1.68 inches) but heavier (1.62 ounces), effective January 1, 1932.

• November 23: In England, Mr. G. Ashdown wins a match and a bet by driving his golf ball on every hole from a tee strapped to a girl's head.

• In building the Bayside Links on Long Island, Alister Mackenzie makes notable use of modern course construction equipment—trenchers, tractors, and power shovels.

1932

In 1922, 20-year-old Gene Sarazen came from four strokes off the pace to win the U.S. Open. He won by a stroke with a birdie on the final hole that capped a round of 68. Later that year, he won the PGA Championship. Barely known on the national golf scene a week before his Open victory, he became an indelible star in the game's annals. A short, tightly built man with a feisty, no-nonsense manner and a golf swing to match, Sarazen put together a career that was marked by periodic bursts of utter, perfectly timed brilliance.

Although he won the PGA Championship again in 1923, it was one of only three victories Sarazen gained between then and 1926. He counted the decline to a poor grip. He fixed it, and was off again. From 1927 through 1930, he won 17 official tournaments and played regularly on the U.S. Ryder Cup team. But it was in 1932 when he confirmed his high place in the game, and at the same time made another contribution that effectively changed for all time the way all people played golf.

Like golfers at every level of the game in his time, Sarazen had

SARAZEN WINS BRITISH OPEN WITH NEWFANGLED WEDGE

trouble playing out of greenside bunkers. He felt it was not technique so much as equipment. The shots had to be played with thin-bladed niblicks that too readily dug too deeply into the sand. Inspired by watching ducks landing on a pond, skimming in with their rounded bellies just barely submerging, he soldered lead onto the back of his niblick to create an angled, belly-like flange. Now he could hit behind the ball and the club would make only a shallow plunge beneath and explode the ball up and forward by the weightier force of impact.

After practicing with the new wedge for numerous hours, Sarazen was ready to test it in the

British Open. Unfortunately, he almost didn't travel to the event, held at the Prince's Golf Club in England, because he didn't think he could afford the trip—he had lost a great deal of money in the stock market crash of 1929. However, Gene's wife, Mary, bought him his tickets, urging him to go. As it would turn out, his newfangled club would more than pay for the traveling expenses.

In the practice rounds of the British Open, Sarazen made frequent use of his wedge and was wonderfully effective from the bunkers. All who watched him marveled at these shots and exclaimed about Sarazen's new "weapon," but he never let anyone, especially tournament officials, inspect it. He was sure they would ban it. Every night, he took it to his room under his overcoat.

In the championship, he was a demon from the sand, and he won his first and only British Open with a new 72-hole record of 283. Later that month, Sarazen won the U.S. Open, shooting 286 to set that event's record as well. In upcoming years, the wedge became standard equipment in every golfer's armory of weapons.

1932

• January: The Miami-Biltmore Open sponsors get around a federal tax problem by donating profits to polio research. This gives birth to the March of Dimes program and previews the concept of pro tournaments played for charity.

• January: Fred Morrison wins the Agua Caliente Open. His brother

Alex will have a greater impact on golf as a legendary golf teacher.

• January 11: Macdonald Smith wins the Los Angeles Open, the $5,000 purse guaranteed by movie star Richard Arlen.

• February 14: Gene Sarazen wins the New Orleans Open. His first

career victory came in this event in 1922, when he was 19 years old.

• April: Henry Picard wins the Mid-South Open, the first of 25 career PGA Tour victories.

• April: Women members of the Century C.C. in New York protest against having "laborers" and old

In 1932, the doughty Gene Sarazen returned to championship form by winning his second U.S. Open and his first British Open. In the latter, Sarazen unveiled his new invention, the sand wedge, and wowed fans with his deft touch from the bunkers. Sarazen shot 283 to break the British Open scoring record.

men caddying for them. The club says it will train idle men for the work.

• April: The winner of a tournament played in Kansas receives a 35,000-pound carload of crushed rock salt.

• April: Byron Nelson, who turned pro six months earlier, counts winnings totaling $12.50 on his first winter tour swing.

• April 15: Bob Harlow is forced to retire as manager of the PGA Tour.

• May: At Hot Springs, Virginia, John Fischer of the University of Michigan becomes the first Midwesterner to win the NCAA individual title. Yale wins the NCAA team championship.

• May: The Handicap Golfers Association of America announces a plan to eliminate par as the arbitrary measurement of golf performance in favor of a system based on course rating.

1932

Picard Wins Mid-South for First Pro Title

Henry Picard, who was born and raised in Massachusetts but made his career out of South Carolina, won his first tournament in 1932, the Mid-South Open. Picard would considerably influence the careers of Sam Snead and Ben Hogan, getting them equipment contracts, offering financial help, and helping them with their golf games.

Henry Picard

A Guy Named R. L. Wins U.S. Public Links Title

The 1932 U. S. Public Links championship, held at the Shawnee G.C. in Louisville, was won by R.L. Miller, who said his initials didn't stand for anything. The 21-year-old from Jacksonville, Florida, defeated Pete Miller in the final, 4 & 2. R.L. had recently been reinstated to amateur status after working for a year in a pro shop.

R.L. Miller

Johnny Fischer

Fischer, of Michigan, Wins NCAA Championship

In 1932, John Fischer of the University of Michigan won the NCAA championship, making him the first golfer from a Midwest university to claim the coveted crown. The 34 previous titles were claimed by golfers of Ivy League schools (30), Southern schools (three), and Georgetown (one).

• May 21: Played in one day, the first Curtis Cup Match between U.S. and British women amateurs is held. The U.S. wins, 5½-3½.

• June: A letter concerning the game of golf is found in Savannah, Georgia. It supports those who believe the game was first played in the U.S. in that city.

• June: A photoelectric device is introduced that can time the swing of a golf club.

• June 4: At Chicago's Soldier Field, Craig Wood wins the World's Fair Long-Drive contest with an average of 247 yards. His best is 253½ yards. He wins $1,000.

• June 7: Harry Vardon plays his last round of championship golf while trying to qualify for the British Open, which he had won six times. Only two spectators are on hand to watch as he shoots in the high 80s.

• June 10: With help from his new invention, the sand wedge, Gene Sarazen wins the British Open with a

1932

Jim Reynolds

New Machine Measures Speed of the Golf Swing

This contraption, using an "electric eye," was created in 1932 to time the swing of a golf club. Here, former national driving champion Jim Reynolds tees it up in a General Electric laboratory in Schenectady, New York. The machine measured Reynolds's swing at 125 miles per hour.

Gene Sarazen

Smith Wins His Third L.A. Open

Tournament officials Harvey Humphrey *(left)* and Don Forker *(right)* congratulate Macdonald Smith for winning his third Los Angeles Open. Later in 1932, Smith finished runner-up to Gene Sarazen in the British Open. If British officials had banned Sarazen's wedge, Smith might have captured his first and only major championship.

Los Angeles Open

Sarazen Captures the U.S. Open Title Too

One of golf's great moments was Gene Sarazen's victory in the 1932 British Open, but often overlooked was his win in the U.S. Open just two weeks later. At Fresh Meadows C.C. in Flushing, New York, Sarazen trailed by seven strokes with 28 holes to play. However, he played his last 28 holes in 100 strokes to win by three.

---

tournament-record 283 at Prince's G.C. in England.

• June 25: At the Fresh Meadow C.C. in Flushing, New York, Gene Sarazen wins the U.S. Open with a tournament-record score of 286. It comes 10 years after his first Open victory.

• July 2: Walter Hagen wins his fifth and last Western Open, at Canterbury G.C. in Cleveland.

• July 9: Harry Cooper wins the Canadian Open.

• July 13: The American Lefthanders Golf Association is founded. Babe Ruth is elected president.

• July 23: The U.S. Amateur Public Links championship is won by R.L. Miller at the Shawnee C.C. in Louisville.

• August: Gene Sarazen, winner of this year's U.S. and British Opens, fails to qualify for the PGA Championship.

C. Ross "Sandy" Somerville

Van Wie, Hollins Make Strides in Women's Golf

Posing left to right are Marion Hollins, Virginia Van Wie, and Leona Cheney. Van Wie won her first of three straight U.S. Women's Amateurs in 1932. Hollins founded the first women's golf club, Women's National in New York, as well as Pasatiempo G.C. in Santa Cruz, California.

Marion Hollins, Virginia Van Wie, Leona Cheney

Canadian Somerville Wins U.S. Amateur

The first Canadian to win the U.S. Amateur championship was C. Ross "Sandy" Somerville, from London, Ontario, who took the title in 1932 at the Five Farms East Course of the Baltimore C.C. Somerville, who had already won the Canadian Amateur four times and would win it twice more, defeated Johnny Goodman in the final, 2 & 1.

Caddie Instruction

Big Wigs Caddie During Depression

John B. Cenerich *(wearing derby)*, public safety commissioner of White Plains, New York, teaches a group of men the art of caddying in April 1932. During the Depression, thousands of unemployed men worked as caddies in and around New York City. Among them were former bankers, executives, and surgeons.

• August 9: The PGA of America declares war on racketeers with pari-mutual machines, as well as lotteries based on golf tournaments.

• August 25: Olin Dutra wins the PGA Championship at Keller Municipal Golf Course in St. Paul, Minnesota. He defeats Frank Walsh in the final, 4 & 3. It is the first time the championship is played on a public course.

• August 27: Mr. C.H. Calhoun and his son score holes-in-one on the same hole during the same round of golf.

• September: John Campbell brings back to the U.S. from Scotland rare antique golf clubs and balls that will form the nucleus of one of American golf's first museums, which will be at the James River C.C. in Virginia.

• September 2: The U.S. team wins the Walker Cup Match for the seventh time in a row, 9½-2½, at The Country Club in Brookline, Massachusetts.

1932

Dutra Defeats Lesser-Knowns for PGA Title

Olin Dutra, of Spanish descent and born and raised in Monterey, California, began his rise to the golfing heights by winning the 1932 PGA Championship, at the Keller Golf Course in St. Paul, Minnesota. Dutra defeated Ed Dudley in the semis and Frank Walsh in the final. Most of the favorites were knocked off in the early rounds.

Francis Ouimet, Johnny Goodman

Ouimet Falls to Goodman in U.S. Amateur Final

Francis Ouimet *(left)* attempted to defend his U.S. Amateur title in 1932. Ouimet won his first-round match after shooting a 30 for nine holes. He won each of his next two rounds by the score of 1 up, then lost in the semifinals to Johnny Goodman *(right)*, 4 & 2. Goodman lost in the final to C. Ross Somerville.

Olin Dutra

• September 17: The U.S. Amateur is won by C.R. Somerville at the Five Farms C.C. in Baltimore. The event takes in some $17,000 in receipts.

• October 1: Virginia Van Wie routs five-time champion Glenna Collett Vare in the final, 10 & 8, to win her first U.S. Women's Amateur championship, at Los Angeles C.C.

• November: A court finds that a golfer is immune from damages for injury to his own caddie, but he's liable if he hits another player's caddie.

• December: Gene Sarazen is voted the Associated Press Athlete of the Year.

• December: The PGA of America forms an unemployment relief committee to provide aid for needy professionals and their families.

• December: It is reported that the PGA Tour's total purse money for the year reached an all-time high of $130,000.

JONES, MACKENZIE UNVEIL AUGUSTA NATIONAL

The Augusta National Golf Club was destined to become one of golf's shrines from the moment of its conception. For it was the idea of Bobby Jones, the most idolized golfer of his time and a man who carried off his celebrity and monumental talent as a player with quiet intelligence and unpretentious elegance. Everyone was sure his golf course would be a reflection of him, and it was.

Jones built the course on rolling Georgia terrain already in a state of horticultural grace. It had been the property of Baron Berckmans, a Belgian with a love of and keen eye for landscaping and gardening. To work with him on the layout of the 18 holes, and oversee their construction, Jones hired Dr. Alister Mackenzie, an Englishman who forsook his training as a physician to build golf courses and had gained a worldwide reputation in this field. His Cypress Point Club on the cliffs of the Monterey Peninsula had become one of the great wonders of the golf world.

Jones clearly articulated his criteria for the new course. It would give the average golfer a fair chance, while requiring the utmost from top players. To that end, there would be over 300 yards difference between the championship and members tees. But most significantly, the fairways would be wide, there would be no rough, and the course would include only 29 bunkers. The correct placement of shots would be paramount to negotiating the undulating ground. For Jones, golf was mainly a game of control, and his course would reflect that.

Construction began in early 1932, with Jones hitting many shots from the projected tees and fairways to ascertain the proper angles, sight lines, distances, and playability of each hole. Many features of the Old Course at St. Andrews, Jones's favorite, were incorporated into the design. The grand opening was on January 13, 1933, a Friday; so much for that superstition. People came from around the world for the unveiling. The weather didn't cooperate but golf was played, and Jones, on January 14, shot a round of 69. Augusta National had been properly christened.

The creation was meant from the start to be an exclusive private club with members coming from around the nation—hence, the name Augusta National. It might well have faded from public attention as Jones, who three years earlier retired from competition, inevitably slipped farther and farther from the limelight. However, Jones also decided to hold a tournament every spring on his course for the game's best pros and amateurs. It would be a kind of gathering of the clan to conclude the winter tour. Originally called the Augusta National Invitational, Horton Smith won the inaugural, in 1934. Soon after, it would be known as the Masters. The rest is woven inextricably into the fabric of golf.

1933

- January: It is announced that the total purse for the late-winter/spring tour will be about $23,000.

- January: George Jacobus begins a seven-year reign as an autocratic president of the PGA of America.

- January: Francis Powers is named new manager of the PGA Tour.

- January 2: Johnny Revolta, coming to the front as a top touring pro, wins his first tour event, the Miami Open. He will win 18 in all, including a PGA Championship.

- January 10: Gene Sarazen urges an eight-inch-diameter cup, saying the game "needs greater thrills." Later in the month, the eight-inch cup will be tested in the Gasparilla Open in Tampa, Florida.

- January 13: Bobby Jones's Augusta National G.C. in Augusta, Georgia, is officially opened. Jones shoots a 69 in the dedication round.

- January 14: Paul Runyan wins the Agua Caliente Open.

1933

Augusta National G.C., Bobby Jones's dream come true, opened to fanfare in January 1933. Friends of Jones came from all over the world to be at the inaugural, and there was a parade through the streets of downtown Augusta, Georgia, to celebrate the occasion. The area shown here would become the practice putting green.

• February: Walter Hagen wins the first open tournament ever played in Charleston, South Carolina, where golf was said to be first played in North America.

• March: The USGA announces it will keep the U.S. Open's total purse at $5,000, despite the hard economic times gripping the nation.

• March: Walter Hagen sponsors an open tournament that's named for him and played in Jacksonville, Florida. Hagen wins the event and declines the purse.

• April: Tommy Armour denounces the PGA of America for not selecting Billy Burke to the 1933 U.S. Ryder Cup team.

• June: Canadians boast of having the "most exclusive golf club in the world." On the north shore of Hudson Bay, its four members include two missionaries. The membership fee is 10 polar bear teeth.

• June: Billy Burke is selected to the U.S. Ryder Cup team.

Johnny Revolta

Revolta Wins with Brilliant Short Game

Johnny Revolta was born in St. Louis but played out of Milwaukee and Chicago for most of his career. In 1933, he began his rise to prominence with a victory in the Miami Open. A short hitter off the tee, he would set a new standard for short-game excellence. He subsequently became an outstanding teacher.

Joyce Wethered

Wethered Stands Tall Among Women Golfers

Joyce Wethered, sister of British amateur star Roger, was a tall woman with a classic golf swing. In 1933, a British golf writer called her "the greatest woman golfer in the world." Although she never played in any American championships, Wethered in her prime was thought to be the equal of all but a half-dozen men golfers in the British Isles.

Johnny Goodman

Goodman Becomes Last Amateur to Win Open

Johnny Goodman scored a shocking upset when he defeated Bobby Jones in the first round of the 1929 U.S. Amateur. But Goodman's greatest achievement was his victory in the 1933 U.S. Open, which he won by a stroke over Ralph Guldahl at North Shore C.C. in Glenview, Illinois. Goodman became the fifth and last amateur to win this title.

• June: Yale wins its third straight NCAA championship. Walter Emery of the University of Oklahoma wins the individual title.

• June 9: Wilfred Wherle, an 18-year-old amateur, scores a birdie, eagle, par, and "buzzard" (double bogey) on the first four holes of his second round of the U.S. Open. He shoots 77 and makes the cut by one stroke.

• June 10: Johnny Goodman wins the U.S. Open. He defeats Ralph Guldahl by one stroke at the North Shore C.C. in Glenview, Illinois. He is the fifth amateur to ever win the title and, to date, the last.

• June 13: Billy Burke is declared eligible to compete in the British Open, despite his late entry. His selection to the Ryder Cup team paved the way.

• June 27: The Ryder Cup Match is won by the British team, 6½-5½, at the Southport and Ainsdale courses in England.

Ralph Guldahl

Hagen Lets the Good Times Roll

Walter Hagen *(seated, left)* often made a remark that epitomized his lifestyle. "Be sure to smell the flowers along the way," he said. Hagen, who journeyed all over the world giving exhibitions, traveled in a wide range of vehicles: fast trains, airplanes, Rolls-Royce automobiles, and even the occasional rickshaw, as shown here.

Walter Hagen

Guldahl Bogeys Last Hole to Lose U.S. Open

A young Ralph Guldahl lost by a stroke to amateur Johnny Goodman in the 1933 U.S. Open. Guldahl could have tied Goodman on the last hole, but he hit into a greenside bunker and made bogey. Ralph developed his game faster than Sam Snead, Ben Hogan, and Byron Nelson. All four Hall of Famers were born in 1912.

Turnesa Brothers

Willie, Jim Best of the Turnesas

The renowned Turnesa brothers get together at Elmsford, New York, in May 1933. They include the lone amateur of the bunch, Willie *(left)*, and four of his professional brothers, Phil, Frank, Mike, and Joe *(left to right)*. Willie won the 1938 U.S. Amateur. Jim, not pictured, was the most successful of the pros, winning the 1952 PGA Championship.

- July 8: Densmore "Denny" Shute wins the British Open in a 36-hole playoff with Craig Wood. Shute becomes the ninth homebred American to win the championship in the past 12 renewals.

- July 29: Walter Hagen defeats up-and-coming British star Henry Cotton, 3 & 2, in a challenge match played in England. Hagen wins the £100 "side bet."

- August: Insurance brokers with Lloyds of London reserve a decision on the approximate odds against a hole-in-one. Mr. D. Cox, an independent London insurance broker, sets the odds at 100-1 against scoring an ace.

- August: An increase in the purchase of first-grade golf balls rather than second-grade golf balls is said to indicate a return to economic prosperity in England.

- August 2: In a club championship match, Mr. D. Ahern hits a ball 20 feet high into a tree, plays the ball from the tree, and halves the hole.

Maurene Orcutt, Virginia Van Wie, Helen Hicks

Orcutt Falls Short in U.S. Women's Amateur

Maureen Orcutt, Virginia Van Wie, and Helen Hicks *(left to right)* were all semifinalists in the 1933 U.S. Women's Amateur. Orcutt lost to Hicks, who in turn lost to Van Wie in the final. Often a contender, Orcutt could never quite win the championship. She eventually became a golf writer and covered the women's game for *The New York Times.*

Kirkwood's Big Win Comes in Canadian Open

In 1933, Joe Kirkwood proved he was more than a trick-shot artist when he captured the prestigious Canadian Open, played at Toronto's Royal York G.C. for the first and only time. Kirkwood's score was a very respectable 282. However, the Canadian was the only big-name event he would ever win on the pro tour.

Joe Kirkwood

- August 13: Gene Sarazen wins his third PGA Championship and first in 10 years, beating Willie Goggin in the final at Blue Mound C.C. in Milwaukee. Goggin led after 18 holes, 1 up, but Sarazen stormed to a 5 & 4 victory.

- August 19: Joe Kirkwood Sr. wins the Canadian Open, proving he is more than the best trick-shot artist in golf.

- September 2: Virginia Van Wie wins her second consecutive U.S. Women's Amateur championship, defeating Helen Hicks in the final at Exmoor C.C. in Highland Park, Illinois.

- September 11: Johnny Fischer posts the lowest qualifying score in the history of the U.S. Amateur championship, a 141, which includes a 69. The event is staged at Kenwood C.C. in Cincinnati.

- September 12: Johnny Fischer loses his second-round match in the U.S. Amateur.

Johnny Fischer

Fischer Sets Qualifying Record at Amateur

In 1933, while a law student at the University of Michigan, Johnny Fischer set a new qualifying record at the U.S. Amateur. He shot 69-72—141 at the Kenwood C.C. in Cincinnati. Fischer lost his second-round match, to Sid Noyes, but he would win the title in 1936 and play on three U.S. Walker Cup teams.

Denny Shute

Shute Becomes the Latest American to Win British

In 1933, Densmore "Denny" Shute, from Cleveland, became the 10th consecutive American to win the British Open. He defeated another American, Craig Wood, in a playoff at St. Andrews for his first major championship victory. An American wouldn't win the British Open again until 1946, largely because of the Depression and World War II.

George T. Dunlap Jr.

Dunlap Succeeds Jones as Top Amateur

George T. Dunlap Jr. was perhaps the premier American amateur in the wake of Bobby Jones's retirement. Twice winner of the NCAA individual title while attending Princeton, Dunlap in 1933 won both the North and South Amateur and the U.S. Amateur. He also reached the quarterfinals of the British Amateur.

• September 16: George T. Dunlap Jr. establishes himself as the premier American amateur now that Bobby Jones is retired. After winning the North and South Amateur in April, he wins the U.S. Amateur, beating Max Marston, 6 & 5, in the final.

• October: The first Handicap Golfers Association of America national championship is won by J.B. Bass.

• November: Bob Harlow returns as manager of the PGA Tour.

• December: Bobby Jones announces he will compete in the inaugural Augusta National Invitational to be held next spring.

• December 1: Ralph Guldahl, on the rise as a tournament pro, sets a course record with a 65 in a practice round preceding the Miami-Biltmore Open.

• December 30: Bobby Jones plays a municipal course in Atlanta that is named for him and dedicates it with a round of 67.

20TH Century Golf Chronicle

1934

DESPITE THE DEPRESSION, PGA TOUR TAKES ROOT

It says something for the appeal of golf that in the heart of the worst economic crisis in American history—the Great Depression of the 1930s—the professional tournament circuit not only survived but began its expansion to a year-round, nationwide tour. All the pieces were already in place, thanks in large measure to Bob Harlow, who was Walter Hagen's personal manager and, in 1930, was hired as the first manager of the PGA Tournament Bureau.

A newspaper man by profession, Harlow understood well how to promote a tournament circuit. He also had organizing skills to pull it off. An urbane man with a prep school background, he was also an effective negotiator with tournament sponsors. Harlow instituted practices that remain the foundation blocks on which today's Tour stands: a logical geographic order to the circuit; a Tournament Record Book with player biographies and complete statistics to convenience press coverage; and pairings and tee times announced the day before so that golf fans could anticipate, and plan, their attendance.

Harlow also made sure banners were strung across Main Street trumpeting the tournament that was in town, and that players were doing interviews on the local radio stations. He got sponsors to provide courtesy transportation to the players, and he enlisted volunteers to help run the tournaments. He also put together fund-raising dinners with a Walter Hagen or a Gene Sarazen as the feature speaker. It all sounds simplistic and obvious to modern ears, but in his time Harlow was innovative. The immediate result was that the total purse money for the entire Tour rose in one year from $70,000 to a full-blown $130,000.

The increase was due in good part to two new tournaments on the 1930 schedule, each with a $10,000 purse—the St. Paul Open and the St. Louis Open. The money aside, the entry of these cities sounded the bell for the development of a summer circuit. Chambers of commerce all over the country, looking for ways to keep their heads above water in trying times, were sold on the notion that a professional golf tournament featuring the biggest names in the game was a good way to enhance the image of their city as a fine place to visit, to do business, to live. Here was the keystone to the growth of the PGA Tour.

The Tour's legitimacy was codified in 1934, when it crowned its first official leading money winner. It was Paul Runyan, with $6,767. Also in '34, the first official records were kept and the first media guide compiled. The Tour could have fizzled during these troubled times, but with the help of Harlow, it only grew stronger. In years to come, the total Tour purse would reach $1 million in 1958, $10 million in 1978, and a fruitful $50 million in 1992.

1934

- January: Sam Snead turns pro, beginning as an assistant at The Homestead in West Virginia.

- January 8: Macdonald Smith wins his fourth Los Angeles Open, at Los Angeles C.C.

- February: The PGA of America issues a statement encouraging golf professionals to give free lessons to children to help popularize the game.

- February 9–11: In the revived Texas Open, Byron Nelson leads through the first three rounds and finishes second. Ben Hogan, who made a hole-in-one, finishes in the money. Wiffy Cox wins.

- March 2: Bobby Jones sets the unofficial course record at his Augusta National G.C. with a 65.

- March 22–25: The first Augusta National Invitational, hereafter called the Masters, begins. Horton Smith is the winner by one stroke over Craig Wood. Bobby Jones finishes in a tie for 13th.

In 1934, Paul Runyan became the first official leading money winner on the PGA Tour with a total of $6,767. He had to win seven tournaments (he won nine the previous year) to reach that financial height. One of his '34 victories was the PGA Championship, which he captured in a playoff with Craig Wood.

• May: Californian Lawson Little wins the British Amateur and is honored with personal congratulations from President Franklin Roosevelt, himself a fine golfer before being struck with polio.

• May 12: Using the new standard golf ball approved by the USGA, the U.S. Walker Cup team retains the Cup, 9½-2½, at the Old Course at St. Andrews.

• May 19: Ky Laffoon makes claim to a new world record for a standard 18-hole golf course with a 72-hole score of 266. He shoots it while winning the Park Hill Open in Denver.

• June: The University of Michigan becomes the first non-Ivy League school to win the NCAA championship. Charles Yates of Georgia Tech is the individual champion.

• June 9: Olin Dutra, just out of the hospital after suffering a severe stomach ailment, wins the U.S. Open at the Merion Cricket Club.

Henry Cotton

Ailing Dutra Musters the Victory in U.S. Open

Olin Dutra came out of a sick bed to win the 1934 U.S. Open, at the Merion Cricket Club in Pennsylvania. Eight strokes off the lead after 36 holes, and having suffered a serious stomach ailment the night before the final day of play, Dutra shot 71-72 to emerge the winner by one stroke over Gene Sarazen.

Native Son Cotton Prevails in British Open

Henry Cotton came to the rescue of British golf when he became the first resident Briton since 1923 to win his country's Open. His fine score of 283, at Royal St. George's G.C., augured well for Cotton's future. He would win the cherished title three times in all and become the doyen of the game in Europe for the next two decades.

Olin Dutra

• **June 20:** Helen Hicks becomes one of the first women professionals in American golf when she signs a contract with the Wilson-Western Sporting Goods Co.

• **June 23:** Jim Ford claims a golf marathon mark when he plays 335 holes in a row in Portland, Oregon. He averages 4.9 shots per hole.

• **June 29:** Henry Cotton becomes the first Briton to win the British Open in 11 years, taking the title at the Royal St. George's G.C. in England.

• **July 10:** Ky Laffoon continues his rise to stardom with a victory in the Glens Falls Open. It is his third victory of the year.

• **July 30:** Paul Runyan becomes the smallest winner of the PGA Championship when he defeats long-hitting Craig Wood, 1 up, over 38 holes at the Park C.C. in Williamsville, New York.

• **August:** The U.S. Amateur championship format is changed to a six-day event with no 36-hole

1934

Craig Wood

Wood Just Misses Again in Masters and PGA

In 1934, Craig Wood, one of the few college-educated professionals of his era, continued a pattern of finishing a close second or losing playoffs for major titles. He lost the '34 Masters by one stroke to Horton Smith, then lost the '34 PGA title to Paul Runyan on the second extra hole.

Tommy Armour

Armour Captures His Third Canadian Open

Tommy Armour, the Silver Scot, prevailed in the 1934 Canadian Open, which he also won in 1927 and 1930. Armour was known as one of the games great iron players. His exceptionally large hands—described as "two stalks of bananas" by sports writer Grantland Rice—helped him control his shots.

Horton Smith

Smith Wins by One in First Masters

Horton Smith won the first Masters Tournament (known then as Augusta National Invitational) with rounds of 70-72-70-72—284. Smith canned a 20-foot birdie putt on the 17th to take a one-stroke lead over Craig Wood, who had finished. Horton maintained his lead with a par on the final hole. Smith would capture the Masters title again in 1936.

---

stroke-play qualifying at the tournament site. The semis and finals will be 36-hole matches.

• August: The Metropolis and Elmsford clubs in New York ban women and men from wearing shorts on the course. Five women had worn shorts in a tournament in late July.

• August 4: Tommy Armour wins the Canadian Open at the Lakeview G.C. in Toronto. He becomes the second golfer to win the event more than twice.

• August 5: The Met Women's Golf Association in New York bans shorts.

• August 6: The Northern California Women's Golf Association criticizes the MWGA's decision to ban shorts.

• August 10: Leo Diegel, one of Walter Hagen's favorite playing partners, wins the inaugural Rochester-Walter Hagen Testimonial Open at Oak Hill C.C. in Rochester, New York.

1934

Water Golf

Golfers Stretch Their Imaginations

In 1934, "silly" golf was at its peak. Marathons were a big fad, with real golfers playing as many holes as they could in the shortest possible time. Also, miniature or "Pee Wee" golf was all the rage in big cities and small towns. Even water golf—seen here being played in Pasadena, California—had its customers.

Prescott S. Bush

Bobby Jones Chats with Another Bobby Jones

Amateur great Bobby Jones *(left)* talks with another Bobby Jones, this one from suburban Detroit. The latter looked like the former in the first round of the 1934 U.S. Amateur, as the youngster beat legendary Francis Ouimet in the first round, 1 up. In later years, an annual tournament would be held in Detroit exclusively for people named Bobby Jones.

Bobby Jones, Bobby Jones

George's Father Named President of the USGA

In 1934, Prescott S. Bush was named president of the USGA. One of his sons, George, would become the President of the United States. The latter's maternal grandfather, George Herbert Walker, had been the USGA president in 1920 when a competition between British and American amateurs was proposed. It was named after him—the Walker Cup.

• August 24: Bobby Cruickshank completes a run of 20 consecutive rounds under par on par-72 courses.

• September 15: Lawson Little wins the U.S. Amateur, defeating David Goldman in the final at The Country Club in Massachusetts. Coupled with his British Amateur victory, he accomplishes the "Little Slam."

• September 20: Leo Diegel wins the last of his 29 career victories when he captures the New England PGA.

• September 28: The U.S. Curtis Cup team beats the British, 6½-2½, at the Chevy Chase Club in Maryland.

• October: The first official PGA Tour ends. Paul Runyan is the leading money winner, earning $6,767 out of the $70,000 in total purse money offered. He finishes with six victories.

• October: Ky Laffoon wins the Radix Cup, precursor of the Vardon Trophy, with the lowest stroke average on the Tour for the year.

Little Wins Both the U.S. and British Amateurs

In 1934, burly, long-hitting Lawson Little Jr., the son of a California-based Army officer, fulfilled the great promise he had been showing by winning both the British Amateur and U.S. Amateur championships. The achievement came to be called the "Little Slam." Little would repeat the performance the following year.

Bobby Cruickshank

Cruickshank Bangs His Head at U.S. Open

In 1934, Bobby Cruickshank literally knocked himself out of a chance to win the U.S. Open. On the 64th hole at Merion Cricket Club, his poor approach hit a rock and bounced onto the green. Elated, he threw his club into the air. It landed on his head and knocked him out. He recovered but finished with a 76, two shots behind the winner.

Lawson Little Jr.

- October 6: Virginia Van Wie wins her third consecutive U.S. Women's Amateur championship, at Whitemarsh Valley C.C. in Chestnut Hill, Pennsylvania.

- November 8: Prescott S. Bush, father of future U.S. President George Bush, becomes president of the USGA.

- November 20: U.S. Olympic star Mildred "Babe" Didrikson, only a few years a golfer, leads the qualifying for the Ft. Worth Women's Golf Association championship.

- December: Australian golf authorities consider a Ryder Cup-style match with American pros.

Gene Sarazen puts up $250 to bring two top Aussie players to compete in the U.S. and Great Britain during the upcoming summer.

- December 10: Joseph P. Dey Jr. becomes executive secretary of the USGA, a post he will hold for over three decades.

SARAZEN PLAYS PAR-5 HOLE IN TWO, WINS MASTERS

Perhaps the Masters tournament didn't need it. Perhaps on the strength of its founder's personality and reputation—as well as the quality of the course and the competitive field—it would have become the great championship it is today. But it didn't hurt at all that, in the second year of its existence, Gene Sarazen hit one golf shot that will forever be associated with the Masters tournament, not to mention Sarazen's own legend.

In the late afternoon on the last day of play in the '35 Masters, Sarazen came to the 15th hole of the Augusta National Golf Club as the only player on the course with any chance at all of catching Craig Wood, who was putting the finishing touches on a round of 282. But even Sarazen's chance was remote, as he needed to go 3-under for the last four holes to tie Wood. The 15th, at the time a 485-yard par-5 (it's now at 500 yards), was an easy birdie chance and even an eagle opportunity, because with a good drive it could be reached in two.

At the 15th tee, Sarazen drove the ball well, some 250 yards into the right side of the fairway. However, his lie was not ideal, as

the ball was a touch low in soggy grass. Of course, that would not stop him from going for the green. However, the lie dictated he go at it with a 4-wood rather than the 3-wood that the distance really called for, and the 4-wood is what he chose.

As was his wont—it was Sarazen who made popular the phrase "miss 'em quick"—Sarazen wasted no time over the ball. But he didn't miss. The ball was sent like a bullet on a low trajectory toward the right corner of the green. A bunker is now at that corner, but not then. The ball landed on the corner, kicked toward the hole, and—following

the contour of the green—glided into the cup. A double eagle! With one swing of the club, Sarazen had made up his entire deficit. He now needed only to par the remaining three holes to gain a tie with Wood.

Clearly buoyed by his fantastic stroke of luck at the 15th, Sarazen cruised home with three consecutive pars to tie Wood at 6-under-par 282. The hapless Wood would have to meet Sarazen the next day in a 36-hole playoff. Wood, according to one reporter, "looked like a man who had won a sweepstakes and then had lost the ticket on the way to the payoff window." In the playoff, Sarazen shot a ho-hum even par, but he won by five strokes, as Wood shot a discouraging 149.

Thousands of people would say, in the years to come, that they saw The Shot. In reality, only a relative handful of people were there. Sarazen's playing partner, Walter Hagen, was one of them, as was Bobby Jones. Ironically, nobody speaks of attending the playoff. It was porridge compared to the *creme de la creme* of golf shots, Sarazen's 4-wood, certainly one of the most astonishing single golf strokes ever played.

1935

- January: The PGA Tour gets under way, with a projected total purse for the year of $134,700.

- January 22: Robert "Chief" Coy claims the world's golf marathon record by playing 459 holes non-stop in Los Angeles. Afterward, he goes directly to a hospital with badly swollen ankles.

- January 29: After taking the Sacramento Open a week earlier, rising star Harold "Jug" McSpaden captures the San Francisco Match-Play title.

- February: Ky Laffoon wins the first Phoenix Open, which will become one of the longest-lasting Tour events in American golf.

- February: Gene Sarazen complains that the purses are being spread too far down the line of finishers.

- February: Walter Hagen wins the last individual tournament of his career—the Gasparilla Open.

- February 4: Mickey Wright, winner of 82 LPGA events including

In the 1935 Masters, Gene Sarazen, the only player left on the course with a chance to catch Craig Wood, holed a 4-wood second shot on the par-5 15th for a double eagle. Sarazen parred in from there to tie Wood, then beat him in a playoff the following day. The double eagle is probably the most famous single golf shot ever struck.

four U.S. Women's Opens, is born in San Diego.

• February 7: Gene Sarazen assails pari-mutual betting on golf tournaments.

• February 13: Contestants in the Agua Caliente Open favor betting on the outcome of the event.

• March 17: The first Amateur-Pro National Match-Play championship is played, in St. Augustine, Florida. T. Suffern Tailer and Jimmy Hines are the winning team.

• April 7: In the final round of the Masters, Gene Sarazen and Craig Wood finish tied at 282. Sarazen scores a double eagle on the par-5,

485-yard 15th, as he holes a 4-wood from a soggy lie.

• April 8: Gene Sarazen defeats Craig Wood, 144-149, in a 36-hole playoff to win the Masters.

• April 21: A *New York Times* editorial discusses how golf is competing with church attendance.

Agua Caliente Open

Cox, Photog Have Fun in Mexico

A trio of characters enjoy the festivities at the 1935 Agua Caliente Open in Mexico. Wiffy Cox, who won the tournament, stands far left, while golf writer Darsie L. Darsie stands beside him. The fellow in the sombrero and kilt is D. Scott Chisholm, a big-name golf photographer of the era who occasionally appeared in his own shots.

Harold "Jug" McSpaden

Crosby Knocks Handicap Down to 2

Bing Crosby *(center)* poses with Macdonald Smith *(left)* and Walter Hagen. Crosby, a caddie as a child, revived his interest in the game around 1930. In the early '30s, he pared his handicap down to 2. In 1937, he hosted the first Bing Crosby Pro-Am, which he presided over for the remaining 40 years of his life.

Macdonald Smith, Bing Crosby, Walter Hagen

McSpaden Wins His First Pro Tournaments

Harold "Jug" McSpaden, a big hitter from Kansas, won two tournaments on the pro Tour in 1935—the Sacramento Open and the San Francisco Match-Play—establishing himself as a young comer in American golf. He would garner 17 victories during his 12-year Tour career, including the Los Angeles and Canadian Opens.

• May: Lawson Little repeats as the British Amateur champion. He is the first repeat victor since Harold Hilton in 1900–01.

• May 9: The Bethpage State Park's Blue Course in Farmingdale, New York, destined to become one of the best public courses in the game, is opened for play.

• May 20: Gene Sarazen, playing a tournament in Pittsburgh, says he'll need a special flight to New York to catch the fast boat to England for the British Open. He won't make it.

• June: The University of Michigan wins its second straight NCAA championship, at the Congressional C.C. in Bethesda, Maryland. Ed

White of the University of Texas is the individual champion.

• June 1: Babe Didrikson is ruled ineligible for amateur competitions because of her professional activities in other sports.

• June 8: Sam Parks Jr. becomes one of the darkest darkhorse winners of

Sam Parks

Parks Comes Out of Nowhere to Win U.S. Open

In 1935, Sam Parks Jr. became one of the darkest of darkhorse winners of the U.S. Open when he took the title at Oakmont C.C. Parks had been playing the PGA Tour, but his only victory before the Open was in the Western Pennsylvania Junior. Sam was a member of Oakmont and his local knowledge held him in good stead.

Perry Ties Tourney Record in British Open

Like Sam Parks in the U.S. Open, Alfred Perry *(pictured)* pulled a big upset by winning the 1935 British Open, at Muirfield in Scotland. Moreover, Perry shot 283, tying the tournament record. In the third round, he set a Muirfield record with a score of 67. Another Alfred, Padgham, finished in second place.

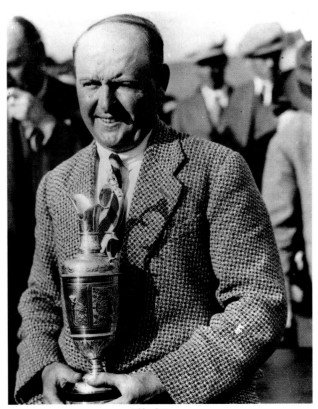

Alfred Perry

the U.S. Open, taking the title at his home course, Oakmont C.C.

• June 28: In the battle of Alfreds, Alfred Perry beats Alfred Padgham in the British Open at Muirfield.

• July 16: Babe Didrikson plays the first of a series of exhibition matches with Gene Sarazen.

• August: Byron Nelson makes his first mark as a tournament player when he wins the New Jersey Open, defeating such stars as Paul Runyan, Craig Wood, and Vic Ghezzi.

• August 14: Mr. E.D. Searle wins the annual New York World Telegram hole-in-one contest for the second time.

• August 31: Glenna Collett Vare wins her sixth U.S. Women's Amateur championship, defeating Patty Berg, 3 & 2, in the final at Interlachen C.C. in Minneapolis.

• September: A confident British Ryder Cup team, holder of the trophy, insures it for its return journey.

Didrikson Turns Her Attention to Golf

Mildred "Babe" Didrikson, who won two gold medals in track and field in the 1932 Olympics, began playing golf seriously in 1935. Because she had played professional baseball, her amateur status in golf was not approved. Instead, she made an exhibition swing with Gene Sarazen.

Babe Didrikson

Nelson Nabs His First Pro Victory

John Byron Nelson, a rangy young Texan with promise, won his first-ever pro tournament in 1935, the New Jersey State Open. The event sounds regional in nature, but the field consisted of such outstanding golfers as Craig Wood, Paul Runyan, and Tommy Armour, who were resident club pros in the New York-New Jersey area during the summer.

Byron Nelson

U.S. Ryder Cup Team

Americans Grab the Ryder Cup

The 1935 American Ryder Cup team smiles proudly after beating Great Britain/Ireland, 9-3, at Ridgewood C.C. in New Jersey. Left to right are: Paul Runyan, Horton Smith, Ky Laffoon, Henry Picard, Johnny Revolta, Walter Hagen, George Jacobus, Gene Sarazen, Sam Parks, Craig Wood, and Olin Dutra. Jacobus, president of the PGA, did not play.

• September 14: Lawson Little completes his second successive Little Slam when he defends his U.S. Amateur crown with a 4 & 2 victory over Walter Emery, at The Country Club in Chagrin Falls, Ohio.

• September 29: The U.S. wins the Ryder Cup Match, 9-3, at Ridgewood C.C. in New Jersey.

• October 4: Dr. John Monteith Jr. announces the creation of a mechanical niblick to test the reaction of a spinning ball to different kinds of grass.

• October 23: Johnny Revolta defeats Tommy Armour in the final to win the PGA Championship at Twin Hills C.C. in Oklahoma City.

• October 23: Juan "Chi Chi" Rodriguez, one of the sport's greatest characters, is born in Puerto Rico.

• November 1: Gary Player, one of only four golfers to win all four major championships, is born in Johannesburg, South Africa.

Johnny Revolta

Revolta Knocks Off Armour in PGA Final

Johnny Revolta defeated Tommy Armour in the final of the 1935 PGA Championship, 5 & 4, at Twin Hills C.C. in Oklahoma City. Although Revolta was considered a fine golfer, no one expected him to take Armour in a head-to-head duel. Revolta prevailed thanks to adept skill with the wedge, chipper, and putter.

Glenna Collett Vare

Vare Beats Berg for Sixth Women's Amateur

Glenna Collett Vare won an unprecedented sixth U.S. Women's Amateur championship in 1935. In the final, she beat 17-year-old Patty Berg at the Interlachen C.C. in Minneapolis, Berg's home course. It was the last of Vare's eight appearances in the Amateur final, as she retired from competition afterward.

Lawson Little

Little Again Wins British, U.S. Amateurs

In 1935, Lawson Little cinched his place in golf history when he successfully defended his British and U.S. Amateur crowns. In the former event, Little was playing with a painful heel injury. The sturdy walls of amateurism were continually being threatened at this time, yet Little denied rumors he would turn pro. He did, though, in 1936.

• November 10: In Moscow, Robert Miller III of Duxbury, Massachusetts, hits the first golf ball ever on Soviet turf. At the same time, Chicago golf architect Leo Macomber negotiates to build three courses in Moscow.

• December: Johnny Revolta becomes the years's leading money winner on the Tour with a total of $9,543.

• December: Johnny Revolta and Henry Picard lead the Tour in season victories with five each.

• December: Gene Sarazen announces he will not play in the Agua Caliente Open because of the pari-mutual betting that takes place on the tournament.

• A new steel shaft is introduced with a thinner tip and increased flexibility that "will increase clubhead speed by 21 percent and give a double-wrist action." It will wholesale for $4.80.

DARKHORSE MANERO NIPS LIGHTHORSE COOPER IN U.S. OPEN

In the long history of the U.S. Open, there have been few winners without established credentials going into the event. Ironically, two of the few "darkhorses" came in succession. In 1935, Sam Parks Jr., who played undistinguished college and amateur golf only a few years earlier, won at Oakmont Country Club outside Pittsburgh. His 11-over-par total of 299 attested to the exceptional difficulty of the course, with its notorious furrowed bunkers and glass-fast greens. Parks would admit he was a beneficiary of having learned his golf as a member of the club.

Tony Manero didn't have that advantage in 1936, yet he broke the Open record with a 72-hole total of 282. The venue, the Upper Course of the Baltusrol Golf Club in New Jersey, played much easier than Oakmont, but Manero's effort was nonetheless superb. A slightly built man of 31 who learned the game as a caddie in nearby Westchester County, New York, Manero had been playing the tournament circuit for the past few years. In that time, he managed to win six events.

But in the midst of a U.S. Open championship featuring Gene Sarazen, Walter Hagen, Harry Cooper, Tommy Armour, Macdonald and Horton Smith, Ralph Guldahl, and other stars, Manero was hardly noticed. Tony's opening 73 did little to bring him forward. A second-round 69 augured well, but still not much attention was paid him. A third-round 73 kept him more or less within range, but given his past record, he was not expected to be a factor in the fourth round.

But then Manero got hot. He scorched the final round's front nine in 33 to pull within two shots of Lighthorse Harry Cooper. While Cooper made a couple of mistakes on the homeward nine, he finished at 284 to break the Open scoring record by two strokes. But Manero hung in there, aided by the steadying influence of his playing partner, Sarazen, a fellow Italian-American who had come up in golf in the same way and place.

Cooper's 72-hole scoring record lasted only an hour. With a two-shot lead going to the final hole, Manero had to wait a full 10 minutes on the tee before he could play. When he finally got his chance, he drove the ball well, drilled a long-iron approach onto the putting surface, and calmly two-putted for a 67. It was the lowest round of the week, and it helped Tony post a four-round total of 282. Manero did little as a competitor from then on, but he showed the stuff of a champion in his one grab at immortality.

For Cooper, the loss was another heartbreaker. It was Harry's second runner-up finish in a U.S. Open (he lost a playoff in 1927), and he was second twice in the Masters (1936 and '38). It had been said of Macdonald Smith, but it was even more apropos of Cooper—winner of 31 tournaments—that he was the best golfer to never win a major championship.

1936

- January 13: Jimmy Hines, on his way to his best season on the Tour, wins the season opener, the Los Angeles Open. The following week, he'll win the Riverside Open in California.

- February 19: The will of Samuel Ryder, donator of the Ryder Cup and otherwise a great supporter of golf, is read. In it there is no mention whatsoever of golf.

- March 29: Henry Picard, developing into one of the all-time best American Tour players, wins the prestigious North and South Open for the second time, at Pinehurst C.C. in North Carolina.

- March 31: Patty Berg, on her rise to high accomplishment, wins the Florida Women's Amateur championship at the Miami-Biltmore course. She'll be named to the U.S. Curtis Cup team.

- March 31: George Dunlap Jr. captures his fourth straight North and South Amateur title, the longest

1936

Tony Manero became the second consecutive darkhorse winner of the U.S. Open when he won the title in 1936, at Baltusrol G.C. in New Jersey. Although Manero had won six times on the PGA Tour, he was never a contender in major competitions. But when he got his chance, he made good, coming from four off the pace with a final-round 67 to defeat Harry Cooper.

such streak in this event's history. In all, Dunlap will win it seven times.

• April: Bobby Jones offers his services as an adviser to the Works Progress Administration, which is planning 600 golf course.

• April 1: After two straight Little Slams, Lawson Little turns pro.

• April 5: Harry Cooper, a great tournament player who will never win a major, leads the Masters by three strokes going into the final round. After a round of 76, he loses by a shot. Horton Smith wins for the second time.

• April 9: The Western Golf Association drops the stymie rule

from its events, which include the important Western Open.

• May 6: In the Curtis Cup Match, at the King's Course in Gleneagles, Scotland, the American and British teams play to a draw, 4½-4½. The British team declines sharing possession of the Cup, declaring it had not won any claim to it.

Picard Captures North and South Open

Rangy Henry Picard made it clear to one and all that he was going to be a major player on the Tour when, in 1936, he won the North and South Open for the second time in three years. Played on the great Pinehurst No. 2 Course in North Carolina, the North and South was, in the estimation of American golfers, a major title.

Henry Picard

Cooper Comes Up Short Again

When Harry Cooper *(pictured)* was edged out by Horton Smith in the 1936 Masters, he said to Bobby Jones: "It seems that it was not intended for me to ever win a major tournament." His prophecy was fulfilled later that year when he set a new scoring record for the U.S. Open only to have it broken a half-hour later by Tony Manero, the tournament's winner.

Harry Cooper

Masters Tournament

Smith Wins His Second Masters

Horton Smith putts on the 18th green during the final round of the 1936 Masters, on a gray, chilly day at Augusta National G.C. Smith won by one stroke, just like he did in the 1934 Masters. On each occasion, Smith took the lead on the next-to-last hole. His victims were Craig Wood in '34 and Harry Cooper in '36.

• May 24: Byron Nelson wins his first important tournament, the Metropolitan Open in New York. The field includes Paul Runyan, Craig Wood, and Tommy Armour.

• May 29: Olin Dutra wins the True Temper Open, the first Tour event sponsored by a golf equipment manufacturer.

• June: Yale wins its 20th NCAA championship, at the North Shore C.C. in Glenview, Illinois. Charles Kocsis of the University of Michigan wins the individual title.

• June 6: Tony Manero becomes the second straight darkhorse winner of the U.S. Open, as he defeats runner-up Harry Cooper at Baltusrol G.C.

• June 27: The British Open is won by Briton Alf Padgham, at Hoylake in England. Thirteen Americans enter, in defiance of the hard economic times.

• July: The R&A, concerned that the golf ball is becoming too lively, invites golf ball manufacturers to produce a "slower" ball.

Jimmy Hines

Hines Makes His Mark with Three Tour Wins

Jimmy Hines, a native of Mineola, New York, who had an unusual pigeon-toed stance at address, began to make some noise on the tournament circuit in 1936. He won three events that year—the Los Angeles, Riverside, and Glens Falls Opens. Furthermore, Hines finished in the top 10 11 times during the year.

Denny Shute

Steady Shute Prevails in PGA Championship

Denny Shute captured his second major championship when he won the 1936 PGA Championship. In the final match, he toppled the game's best long-ball hitter, Jimmy Thomson, 3 & 2, on the No. 2 Course at Pinehurst, North Carolina. Shute played a solid game from tee to green that was the envy of his peers.

Ralph Guldahl

Guldahl's Three Wins Tie for PGA Tour Lead

Ralph Guldahl, the laconic, round-shouldered Texan, began his rise to prominence in 1936 when he won the Western, Augusta, and Miami-Biltmore Opens. Equally impressive, he finished in the top 10 18 times. Guldahl's three victories tied him for the Tour lead. Henry Picard and Jimmy Hines also won thrice.

• July: As an experiment, the Massachusetts Golf Association drops the stymie rule for one year.

• July: Ralph Guldahl begins his rise to prominence on the Tour with a victory in the Western Open.

• July 25: In the U.S. Amateur Public Links championship, B. Patrick

Abbott defeats Claude Rippy, 4 & 3, in the final at Bethpage State Park G.C. in Farmingdale, New York.

• August 4: In the first Tour event played in the Pacific Northwest, Macdonald Smith wins the Seattle Open in a playoff with Ralph Guldahl.

• September: The USGA says it will retain the stymie rule but asks for opinions on its viability. Few like it, and it is predicted the USGA will drop it from the Rules.

• September 2: Babe Didrikson wins the Eastern Women's Open. It is only the third tournament she has entered since learning to play golf.

U.S. Shuts Out Brits in Walker Cup

Britain's Harry G. Bentley plays from a 5th-hole bunker during the 1936 Walker Cup Match, at Pine Valley G.C. in Clementon, New Jersey. Bentley halved this singles match with American George T. Dunlap. Britain also halved two other matches, but the U.S. posted a 9-0 shutout—the only whitewash in Walker Cup history.

Harry G. Bentley

Dunlap Nabs Another North and South

In 1936, George T. Dunlap Jr. won his fourth consecutive North and South Amateur, at Pinehurst, North Carolina. Dunlap became famous for winning this event—he'd claim seven such titles overall—but he also excelled in USGA events. Dunlap won the 1933 U.S. Amateur and played on the 1932, 1934, and 1936 Walker Cup teams.

George T. Dunlap Jr.

Curtis Cup Matches

U.S. and Britain Tie in Curtis Cup Match

Patty Berg, age 18, diligently lines up a putt during the 1936 Curtis Cup Matches, at the King's Course in Gleneagles, Scotland. In a foursomes match, Berg teamed with the great Glenna Collett Vare, yet they only halved their match with Britain's Wanda Morgan and Marjorie Ross Garon. The two teams tied overall, 4½-4½.

• September 3: In the Walker Cup Match, played at Pine Valley G.C. in Clementon, New Jersey, the U.S. defeats the British, 9-0, for the only shutout in the history of the competition.

• September 19: John Fischer defeats Jack McLean of Scotland, 1 up on the 37th hole, to win the U.S.

Amateur at the Garden City G.C. in New York.

• October 3: In the U.S. Women's Amateur, Pamela Barton defeats Maureen Orcutt, 4 & 3, in the final at Canoe Brook C.C. in New Jersey.

• November 11: The PGA of America says it favors the elimina-

tion of unnecessary sand traps on golf courses.

• November 23: Denny Shute wins the PGA Championship, topping Jimmy Thomson in the final at Pinehurst C.C.

• December: Ralph Guldahl, Henry Picard, and Jimmy Hines share

Patty Berg

Berg Has Her Own Way of Doing Things

Freckle-faced Patty Berg ushered in a new era in women's golf with an aggressive style of play, and by rejecting formal golfing attire for more comfortable garb. In 1936, Berg captured the Florida Women's Amateur championship, a prestigious title, and was named to the U.S. Curtis Cup team.

Tommy Armour, Gene Sarazen

Sarazen Prefers the Head-On Competitions

Gene Sarazen *(right)* never missed a chance to promote golf, and himself, often creating "news events" to back up various assertions. In 1936, he said all golf tournaments should be at match play because the head-to-head confrontations were, like football, more exciting than stroke-play tournaments. Here, Sarazen kids around with Tommy Armour.

Alf Padgham

Another Brit, Padgham, Wins British Open Title

Alf Padgham claimed the 1936 British Open at Hoylake, making him the third British professional in three years to win his country's national championship (Henry Cotton won in 1934 and Alfred Perry won in '35). Americans would argue that the poor world economy kept them from entering the event in the 1930s, although 13 Yanks fell to Padgham in '36.

---

honors for most wins on the PGA Tour with three each. Horton Smith is the leading money winner, with a total of $7,682.

• December: Bob Harlow is dismissed again as PGA Tour manager, this time for good. Fred Corcoran is appointed to the position.

• December 2: Gene Sarazen, ever stirring up controversy in the interest of promoting golf, suggests that all Tour events be played at match play, because "stroke play week after week is too boring." The comment will fall on deaf ears.

• December 17: Dr. John Monteith Jr. announces the development of a

green dye for use on grass that turns brown in the fall.

• December 17: The Works Progress Administration announces that $10,500,000 of Relief Funds will be spent to build new public golf courses and improve existing public courses.

GOLF WORLD OPENS ITS ARMS TO SLAMMIN' SAMMY

Walter Hagen, Gene Sarazen, and Bobby Jones formed the first triumvirate of great American-born golfers who, as a group, stimulated interest in the game by making almost every event on the tournament calendar a little more special. By 1937, the next trio was shaping up. Byron Nelson won the Masters that year while Ben Hogan would arrive in 1940. In the middle was Samuel Jackson Snead, who at age 24 came out of the mountains of Virginia to make his debut on the national golf scene at the start of the 1937 winter tour. It had all the flavor of an opening-night hit show on Broadway.

In only his third official Tour event, Snead won the Oakland Open in California with rounds of 69-65-67-69—270, a splendid run of golf elevated to stratospheric heights by a swing as graceful and powerful as a panther on the hunt. He quickly became known as Slammin' Sammy. What made Snead even more attractive was a disarming country-boy naivete. After winning in Oakland, he was shown a copy of *The New York Times* with his picture in it. He asked how that could be, being that he had never been in New York. Even if he was being coy, and years later he would suggest that he was, it was harmless fun that everyone enjoyed.

Snead had a way of spinning a yarn, of telling a joke that was a refreshing change from the dour manner of many of his fellow Tour pros. The press followed his every step and took down his every word. If they missed anything, Fred Corcoran, who had taken over from Bob Harlow as manager of the Tour and had his predecessor's nose for a good story, filled their notebooks with Sneadisms.

All the characterizations of Snead as a personality would have been a sidebar, though, if he were only a flash in the competitive pan. That was decidedly not the case. Shortly after his Oakland victory, Snead traveled down to the Rancho Santa Fe Country Club, near San Diego, to play in the first Bing Crosby National Pro-Am. Snead won with a 68. (Scheduled for 36 holes, rain shortened it to one round.) The Bing Crosby win was perfect timing for Snead. With his wonderfully fluid swing and his own flair for the stage, he made good in the midst of Hollywood celebrities who commanded a much wider audience than did Fred Corcoran.

Snead continued his hot play into the spring and summer. He was continually in contention for the remainder of 1937 and won three more tournaments for a total of five on the year. In 1938, he would win eight times and top the money list with a then-phenomenal $19,534. The Tour had a new star, and one that would shine for an uncommonly long time. Throughout the 1940s, 1950s, and, yes, even the 1960s, golf fans would cheer on the friendly country boy with the big swing, Sam Snead.

1937

- January: The USGA announces it is returning to a previous format for the U.S. Amateur: 36-hole, stroke-play qualifying at the tournament site among those who have qualified in their section.

- January: Ray Mangrum, older brother of the more-famous Lloyd Mangrum, wins the Miami Open.

- January 1: The USGA announces there will be a limit of 14 clubs in a set during a round, the new rule to go into effect in 1938.

- January 2: Charles "Chick" Evans, the former U.S. Amateur and Open champion, comes out in favor of a 10-club limit.

- January 5: The R&A rejects the club limit that's to be invoked by the USGA.

- January 11: Harry Cooper wins his second Los Angeles Open, now worth only $5,000 in total purse money. His share is $2,500—$1,000 less than for his 1926 victory.

1937

Playing in his first U.S. Open, Sam Snead *(left)* immediately felt the sting of near-victory in this the only major championship he would never win. Leading by a stroke after three rounds, he shot a very respectable 71 but finished second to a charging Ralph Guldahl *(right)*, who shot a 69 and set a new Open record of 281.

• January 16: A brewing controversy over the stymie rule surfaces. The USGA says it is considering the issue.

• January 17: Sam Snead wins the Oakland Open.

• January 24: Sam Byrd, who replaced Babe Ruth in right field for the New York Yankees and who will become a fine PGA Tour player, wins the Baseball Players Tournament.

• February: In London, Sir J. Simon announces his invention of a golf ball that makes a sound that leads to it being found.

• February 7: Sam Snead wins the first Bing Crosby Pro-Am at Rancho Santa Fe C.C. in San Diego.

• March: Byron Nelson breaks through once and for all time, winning the Masters with a score of 283. It is only his third official PGA Tour victory.

Mangrum's Gambling Affects His Golf Game

Tall, razor-thin Ray Mangrum won the 1937 Miami Open and looked to be an upcoming star on the PGA Tour. He would win a few more tournaments, but his penchant for gambling at cards, horses, and golf deflected his attention from tournament golf. The Mangrum name would become celebrated through the play of Ray's brother, Lloyd.

Ray Mangrum

Byron Nelson

Nelson Wins Masters, Humbled in U.S. Open

Byron Nelson prevailed in the 1937 Masters, making up six strokes on Ralph Guldahl during the stretch run. It was Byron's third pro victory and first in a major. Nelson, though, got a dose of humility in the '37 U.S. Open at Michigan's Oakland Hills C.C., as he shot 295, tied for 20th with nine others, and took home winnings of $50.

- March: Patty Berg wins the first Titleholders Championship, at Augusta C.C. in Georgia.

- April 23: The New York State Golf Association announces it will try the new stymie rule in its events.

- April 28: The Westchester County Golf Association in New York announces it is abandoning the stymie rule for one year, as a trial.

- May: The Internal Revenue Service announces that Tour golf pros are exempt from social security tax if they are not employed by a club.

- May 10: It is announced that the Vardon Trophy will be awarded.

A point system based on where a player finishes in tournaments is used.

- May 30: Denny Shute wins his second consecutive PGA Championship. He has to go 37 holes to defeat Harold McSpaden in the final at Pittsburgh Field Club.

1937

Harry Cooper

Thomson Puts on a Show with Big Drives

Jimmy Thomson's capacity to hit long drives made the long-drive contest an integral part of the PGA Tour's "pre-game show." Thomson, shown here loosening up like a slugger in the on-deck circle, won a 1937 contest by averaging 340 yards. The tee was 164 yards above the fairway.

Jimmy Thomson

Cooper Sweeps the Postseason Honors

Harry Cooper enjoyed his best season in 1937, leading the Tour in victories with eight and in earnings with a record $14,138.69. Highlights included triumphs in the Canadian and Los Angeles Opens. Also in '37, Cooper won the first Vardon Trophy, which was based on a point system that depended on where a player finished in tournaments.

Ryder Cup Presentation

U.S. Wins Last Ryder Cup Before the War

Lord Wadlington presents the Ryder Cup trophy to Walter Hagen, captain of the 1937 team that defeated Great Britain/Ireland, 8-4, at Southport and Ainsdale G.C. in England. Hagen, a non-playing captain, guided his team to its first victory on British soil. It would be the last Ryder Cup until 1947, owing to World War II.

• June 12: In the U.S. Open, Ralph Guldahl sets a new scoring record by winning with a 7-under-par 281 over the Oakland Hills C.C. course in Birmingham, Michigan. Sam Snead, in his first U.S. Open, is second.

• June 30: In the Ryder Cup Match at the Southport and Ainsdale courses in Southport, England, the U.S. team defeats Great Britain/Ireland, 8-4. It's Walter Hagen's swan song as team captain, a position he held for the first six Matches.

• July 1: The Federal Trade Commission charges the PGA of America and golf ball manufacturers in the United States with running monopolies.

• July 4: In the NCAA championships, Freddie Haas Jr. of Louisiana State is the individual champion.

• July 4: Princeton takes the NCAA team title.

Johnny Goodman

Goodman Achieves a Personal Little Slam

In 1937, Nebraskan Johnny Goodman, who turned golfdom's head when he won the 1933 U.S. Open as an amateur, completed his personal career "Little Slam" by winning the U.S. Amateur championship. He defeated Ray Billows in the final, 2 up, at Alderwood C.C. in Portland, Oregon. It was the first Amateur held in the Pacific Northwest.

Hutchison Claims the First PGA Seniors

In 1937, Jock Hutchison won the first PGA Seniors Championship, for golfers age 50 and older. At the urging of Bobby Jones, the championship was held at his Augusta National G.C. Alfred S. Bourne, a "friend of the pros," contributed a $1,500 trophy. Hutchison shot 7-over-par 223 but still won by eight strokes.

Jock Hutchison

• July 7: Jimmy Thomson wins a driving contest in Canada with an average of 340 yards for 10 hits. The tee is 164 yards above the fairway.

• July 9: Henry Cotton wins his second British Open, finishing two strokes ahead of Reg Whitcombe at Carnoustie, Scotland.

• July 13: Henry Cotton secures his place at the top of European golf by defeating Denny Shute, 6 & 5, in a specially arranged match.

• August 14: In the U.S. Amateur Public Links championship, Bruce McCormick defeats medalist Don Erickson in the final, 1 up, at Harding Park G.C. in San Francisco.

• August 28: Johnny Goodman wins the U.S. Amateur by defeating Ray Billows in the final, 2 up, at the Alderwood C.C. in Portland, Oregon. It's the first Amateur held in the Pacific Northwest.

• September 2: Opal Hill fires a round of 66 to set a world record for women golfers.

Bill Frawley, Walter Hagen, John Montague

Montague Does Wonders with His Hoes and Rakes

Walter Hagen throws his arm around actor Bill Frawley, of *I Love Lucy* fame, and talks with John "Mysterious" Montague, a man of uncertain origin. Montague could hit golf balls well with hoes, rakes, and shovels, and he apparently made his living betting he could hit shots with them. Frawley competed in the inaugural Bing Crosby Pro-Am in 1937.

Page Rolls Past Berg in Women's Amateur

Estelle Lawson Page of North Carolina won the 1937 U.S. Women's Amateur, trouncing 19-year-old Patty Berg, 7 & 6, in the final at Memphis C.C. Though she would never enjoy the celebrity of Berg, Lawson was a legitimate champion: She captured the U.S. Women's Amateur qualifying medal in 1936, '37, and '38.

Estelle Lawson Page

Bruce McCormick

McCormick Wins the U.S. Public Links Title

In the 1937 U.S. Public Links final, 28-year-old Bruce McCormick of Los Angeles defeated a fellow Californian, Don Erickson, who had tied the qualifying record by shooting 67-72—139. The tournament was played on the Harding Park G.C. in San Francisco, where future pro star Ken Venturi learned his golf.

• September 5: Henry Picard continues to hone his skills by winning the Hershey Open.

• September 19: Ralph Guldahl wins his second straight Western Open, at Canterbury C.C. in Cleveland.

• October 9: Estelle Lawson, the medalist, wins the U.S. Women's

Amateur by defeating Patty Berg, 7 & 6, in the championship match at Memphis C.C.

• November 18: John Montague, a noted trick-shot golfer, plays a match against Babe Ruth that draws some 10,000 people. The money raised is given to the Poor Children's Fund.

• December: Harry Cooper wins the first Vardon Trophy with a total of 500 points. He also leads in money winnings with $14,139, and victories with seven. Rookie Sam Snead has five.

• December 2: Jock Hutchison wins the first PGA Seniors Championship, at Augusta National G.C.

GULDAHL'S ODD WAYS LEAD TO MAJOR SUCCESS

Ralph Guldahl was considered one of the greatest natural golfers to ever play the game. A tall, round-shouldered Texan with a shock of raven-black hair, Guldahl had never bothered much with the mechanics of the golf swing—at least not classic mechanics. Learning his golf on a public course in Dallas, he found his own somewhat unorthodox way, which he combined with extraordinary instincts for the game that seemed to serve him best in major championships.

Counting the Western Open as a major, which was considered so in his day—and which Guldahl won in 1936, 1937, and 1938—six of his 16 career victories were majors. What made his record especially interesting, and in a way peculiar, was that all those major victories came within a four-year period—from 1936 through 1939—including exceedingly rare back-to-back U.S. Opens in 1937 and 1938. Before him, in the era that began after World War I, only Bobby Jones had managed to defend that title.

Guldahl's victory in the 1937 U.S. Open at Oakland Hills Country Club in Michigan produced the first Open champion to play all four rounds in even par or less (three rounds were under par). Knowing midway through his last round that he could ill afford to slack off, for Sam Snead, playing ahead of him, had made a rush to the finish with a fine 71—283, Guldahl rang up a 69 to win by two.

In 1938, Guldahl made sure that sort of pressure would be unnecessary. At the Cherry Hills Country Club in Colorado, he opened with a 3-over-par 74, then put it all together and kept it that way with rounds of 70-71-69 to defeat Dick Metz by six shots. Omitting U.S. Opens decided in playoffs, this was the largest margin of victory in the championship since the steel shaft had been made legal in the United States.

For an instinctive golfer, Guldahl had machine-like consistency once he got on a roll. This was reflected by his plodding on-course manner. He stood over a putt for what seemed an hour before making the stroke. His unique style helped him win the Masters in 1939 and capture five more Tour events through 1940 (two with partners in four-ball competitions). Then at age 29, he virtually disappeared from the competitive scene. Yes, Guldahl served in the military during World War II, but so did such contemporaries as Ben Hogan, Jimmy Demaret, and Snead, who afterward picked up where they left off to play superlative competitive golf.

Guldahl said years later that injuries ended his career. He also said that he worked on a golf instruction book without the usual ghost writer. Holing up in a hotel room for over a week with a full-length mirror, he tried to articulate how he did it for the first time in his life. Paralysis by analysis?

1938

- January: PGA Tour players will vie for $158,000 in 38 events.

- January: Babe Didrikson competes in the Los Angeles Open. It's the only time a woman has ever played on the men's tour.

- January: The caddies at the four courses on the Monterey Peninsula are put on notice that they better improve their English and manners—"or else."

- January 8: The USGA modifies the stymie rule, allowing a ball within six inches of another and within six inches of the hole to be lifted until the other golfer has played.

- February 3: The American Golf Institute, a clearing house of golf information and promotion, is formed and headed by Bobby Jones.

- February 13: Jimmy Demaret, who will become one of golf's best players and most colorful personalities, wins for the first time on Tour, at the San Francisco Open.

In 1938, Ralph Guldahl became the fourth player to win back-to-back U.S. Opens (only two others have done it since Guldahl). This time he made it easy, winning by six strokes at Cherry Hills Country Club in Denver. In the second round, Ray Ainsley set a tournament record by taking 19 strokes on a hole.

• March 1: The Federal Trade Commission orders eight manufacturers and the PGA of America to quit golf ball price-fixing.

• March 28: Sam Snead wins the first Greater Greensboro Open in North Carolina. It's the first of his eight career victories in this event over a 27-year period.

• April 4: Henry Picard wins the Masters when he fires a 70 in the final round to defeat Harry Cooper and Ralph Guldahl by two strokes.

• May 7: The New York Museum of Science and Industry announces a program to help golfers: slow-motion motion pictures of their swings to be analyzed by pros.

• May 25: Walter Hagen and Joe Kirkwood complete another world exhibition tour and become the most traveled golfers in history.

• June: Walter Hagen Jr., his famous father's only child, competes for Notre Dame in the NCAA championships.

Picard Prevails in Another Tight Masters

Henry Picard, shown playing out of trouble in the Western Open, won the 1938 Masters. He closed with a 70 to beat runners-up Ralph Guldahl and Harry Cooper by two strokes—the longest winning margin to date. Picard won 26 Tour events from 1925–50.

George and Babe Zaharias

Babe Misses the Cut But Gains a Husband

In 1938, Babe Didrikson became the first (and to date the only) woman to qualify for a PGA Tour event, the Los Angeles Open. She played poorly and did not make the 36-hole cut, but at the tournament she met one-time professional wrestler George Zaharias, who enjoyed a good laugh just as Babe always did. They were married later in the year.

Henry Picard

• June 4: In the Walker Cup Match at St. Andrews, Scotland, the British/Irish team wins for the first time in 10 tries, by a margin of 7-4.

• June 11: Ralph Guldahl wins his second consecutive U.S. Open, defeating Dick Metz by six strokes at Cherry Hills C.C. in Denver.

• June 19: Ralph Guldahl wins the Western Open for an unprecedented third straight time, at the Westwood C.C. in St. Louis.

• June 26: Sam Snead wins the Cincinnati Goodall Invitational, one of the earliest Tour events with a corporate sponsor. Goodall is a clothing manufacturer.

• July 2: Stanford becomes the first Western school to win the NCAA team championship. John Burke of Georgetown wins the individual crown.

• July 2: In the unofficial American Champions Match, PGA Champion Denny Shute defeats U.S. Open winner Ralph Guldahl, 2 & 1.

Jimmy Demaret

Demaret Makes a Fashion Statement

Jimmy Demaret, who would sometimes moonlight as a nightclub singer, won his first Tour event in 1938, the San Francisco Match-Play. Demaret would have a fine competitive career—and would also change the dress styles of American golfers. Jimmy had a flair for colored shoes, silky sport shirts in bright colors, and an unusual collection of hats.

Paul Runyan

Runyan Slays a Goliath in PGA Championship

In a storied final, tiny Paul Runyan (pictured) defeated Sam Snead, 8 & 7, in the 1938 PGA Championship at Shawnee C.C. in Pennsylvania. Runyan was outdriven by Snead by an average of 40 yards per hole. However, he could hit his approaches with a 4-wood closer to the hole than Snead could with short irons. It was Runyan's second PGA title.

Walter Burkemo

Burkemo Gets It Going at U.S. Publinx

Walter Burkemo, a 20-year-old from Detroit, made his first mark on the national scene in 1938 when he won the qualifying medal for the U.S. Amateur Public Links championship, at the Highland Park Municipal G.C. in Cleveland. Burkemo lost his second-round match, but 15 years later he'd win the PGA Championship.

• July 8: England's Reg Whitcombe wins the British Open with a final-round 78 in howling winds, which demolish the exhibition tent at Royal St. George's G.C. in Sandwich, England.

• July 14: The PGA Tour sets a purse minimum of $5,000 for a 72-hole event, $3,000 for a 54-holer.

• July 16: Paul Runyan, outdriven by some 40 yards on almost every hole, defeats Sam Snead in the final of the PGA Championship, at Shawnee-on-the-Delaware C.C. in Pennsylvania.

• July 24: Sam Snead continues his torrid pace by winning the $5,000 Chicago Open.

• August 2: The USGA Greens Committee announces availability of an insecticide that is dyed green for use on golf courses.

• August 5: J.S. Ferebee bets $2,500 and half of his plantation that he can play 144 holes of golf and average less than 95 per round. He wins.

Al Leach

Leach Hangs on to Win U.S. Public Links Title

The 1938 U.S. Amateur Public Links champion was Al Leach, a 26-year-old Works Projects Administration worker from Cleveland. In an exciting final against Louis Cyr, Leach saw his 6-up lead after 23 holes dwindle to a tie at the 34th. But with a resurgent effort, he pulled the match out on the last hole.

Hogan's First Victory Comes in Four-Ball

In 1938, at age 26 and still struggling with a hook, Ben Hogan finally broke into the win column. It was only a partial victory, however, for the event was the Hershey Four-Ball tournament. Vic Ghezzi was Hogan's partner. Afterward, Hogan signed to represent Hershey C.C., site of the Four-Ball, on the Tour.

Ben Hogan

Harold "Jug" McSpaden

McSpaden Wins Miami and Houston Open Titles

Harold "Jug" McSpaden was coming into his own in 1938, winning both the Miami Open and the Houston Open. In the '38 U.S. Open, the Massachusetts-born McSpaden had the lowest single round, a 67, but finished in a tie for 16th place. Jug would turn in another spectacular round in the 1939 Texas Open.

• August 22: Sam Snead defeats defending champion Harry Cooper in a playoff for the Canadian Open title.

• August 29: Al Leach wins the U.S. Amateur Public Links championship—but loses his $73.50-a-month WPA job for being absent too many days in a row.

• September 4: Vic Ghezzi and Ben Hogan win the Hershey Four-Ball Open. It is Hogan's first victory of any kind on the Tour.

• September 9: The U.S. wins the Curtis Cup Match in Manchester, Massachusetts, 5½-3½, when the American team takes five of six singles matches during the last day.

• September 17: Willie Turnesa, the only member of his illustrious golfing family to remain an amateur, wins the U.S. Amateur, defeating Pat Abbott, 8 & 7, in the final at Oakmont C.C. near Pittsburgh.

• September 24: Patty Berg wins the U.S. Women's Amateur at Westmoreland C.C. in Illinois.

Sam Snead

Berg Turns the Tables in Women's Amateur

In 1938, Patty Berg finally broke through to win the U.S. Women's Amateur championship, at Westmoreland C.C. in Wilmette, Illinois. Berg defeated Estelle Lawson in the final, 6 & 5. A year earlier, Berg lost to Lawson in the final. In her first-round match in '38, scheduled for 18 holes, Berg won by a score of 10 & 8.

Snead Wins Eight Tourneys and 19 Grand

In 1938, Sam Snead won eight PGA Tour events and led in earnings with over $19,000. Short-sighted pros of the time said no one would ever again win that much money in a single year on the Tour. At the same time, Snead had one of his poorest U.S. Opens, a tournament that would be his career nemesis. He tied for 38th and never broke 76.

Patty Berg

Joe Kirkwood

Kirkwood Reaches into His Bag of Tricks

In 1938, Joe Kirkwood completed yet another of his world tours giving trick-shot exhibitions. By now, he had accumulated an incredible array of clubs with which he performed feats that amazed his audiences. Kirkwood was the first golfer to make his living doing trick shots, and a good living it was. Eventually, he retired to Vermont.

• October 18: Woman amateur star Opal Hill turns pro. She will play an important role in the development of a women's pro tour.

• November 16: Tommy Armour wins his last Tour event, the Mid-South Open. He won 24 tournaments in all, including three of the modern-day major championships.

• December: Sam Snead is the leading money winner on Tour with $19,534. He won eight tournaments. He also captures the Vardon Trophy.

• December 18: Professor A.M. Low announces he has invented a putter that lights up when swung correctly.

• December 18: Harold "Jug" McSpaden—the nickname derived from his prominent jaw—wins the Miami Open.

• The five Turnesa brothers, playing a course in New York, defeat the five Fry brothers, playing in California, in a telegraphic match.

NELSON'S 1-IRON WINS FRENETIC U.S. OPEN

Although he was indeed heroic in achieving the victory, the fact of Byron Nelson winning the 1939 U.S. Open was overshadowed at the time, and historically, by the loss of the championship by two other golfers. In the end, though, everyone could not help but realize Nelson's enormous talent and recall a single shot of his that best exemplified it.

Going into the final round, on the Spring Mill Course of the Philadelphia Country Club—which at close to 6,800 yards was playing to a par of 69—Johnny Bulla led with a score of 211. Sam Snead, Craig Wood, Denny Shute, and Clayton Heafner were just one stroke behind Bulla, and Nelson was in 12th place, five shots off the pace. But in the final round, Nelson posted a 68. Only three others in the field made that score during the entire event. It appeared, though, that his 284 total wouldn't do.

Sam Snead came to the 71st hole needing just two pars for 282. The popular young belter seemed a shoo-in, even after he missed a six-foot putt for a par on the 17th. A par-5 on the fairly easy last hole would do it. But after driving into thick rough,

disaster struck. Not certain a par was enough, as Wood and Shute were playing behind him, Snead felt he needed a birdie and used a 2-wood in an effort to either reach or come close to the green. He pushed his ball badly into a bunker some 100 yards from the green, took two shots in the sand, and eventually three-putted for an incredible 8. He lost by two strokes and would be haunted ever after in the U.S. Open, the only championship he would never win.

With rounds of 72, Wood and Shute made it a three-way playoff with Nelson. Wood, who birdied the 72nd hole by hitting the green in two, was the favorite of the gallery. A handsome big hitter, he

thrice before came oh-so-close to a major title only to be thwarted (he lost playoffs in the 1933 British Open, '34 PGA Championship, and '35 Masters). In this playoff, he fired a 68. But Nelson rolled in a sizeable putt on the last green that he needed to force a second 18-hole playoff. It would be Nelson vs. Wood, as Shute had faded out with a 76.

Nelson would win the second playoff on the strength of a spectacular approach shot. Entering the tournament, golf fans were talking about Nelson's accuracy from tee to green with a swing he had purposefully devised for the steel shaft. It was not uncommon for him to hit the pin from goodly distances. And at the par-4 4th hole in the afternoon, he went one better by holing a 1-iron shot for an eagle 2.

Although it was still early in the round, the shot surely shook Wood, who had had that sort of thing happen to him at the Masters four years earlier, when Gene Sarazen canned his 4-wood for a double eagle. Nelson won this second playoff by a score of 70-73. It would be his only U.S. Open victory, but it was surely one to remember.

1939

- January: PGA Tour players will play for $121,000 in 28 events.

- January: In the Phoenix Open, Byron Nelson shoots 66-65-65 in the first three rounds to set a 54-hole record. He goes on to win.

- January: In a practice round for the Texas Open, Jug McSpaden

shoots a round of 59. In the tournament proper, he shoots a 63. E.J. "Dutch" Harrison wins the tournament.

- January 7: The USGA, fearing the manufacturers will make ever-longer-flying golf balls, announces an effort to "stabilize" the golf ball at its current maximum distance.

- January 9: Jimmy Demaret makes his first important mark as a future great with a victory in the Los Angeles Open.

- January 22: After winning the Oakland Open a week earlier, handsome, smooth-swinging Dick Metz captures the San Francisco Match-Play Open.

Not only did Byron Nelson win the U.S. Open in 1939, but he also captured the North and South Open and the Western Open—both prestigious events. In the same year, Nelson won the Vardon Trophy, which from 1937–41 was based on where a player finished in tournaments.

• February: It is announced that the Ryder Cup Match, scheduled to be played in the U.S., is canceled because of the war in Europe.

• April 2: Ralph Guldahl completes a phenomenal run of major championship golf by winning the Masters, his sixth major in three years (including three Western Opens).

• April 4: JoAnne Gunderson, destined to become one of the best women amateur and professional golfers in history, is born in Kirkland, Washington.

• April 12: PGA Tour manager Fred Corcoran comments that the par of a hole should be revised to account for its comparative difficulty to another hole of the same par. He says a longer, tougher par-4 should be a par-4⁴/₁₀.

• June 4: Harry Cooper wins the Goodall Round-Robin tournament. It is his last official PGA Tour victory, capping a superb 30-victory career.

Sam Snead, Harold "Jug" McSpaden

McSpaden Shoots 59 in Practice

Sam Snead *(left)* and Harold "Jug" McSpaden examine a scorecard together. McSpaden opened some eyes in January 1939 when he fired a 59 in a Texas Open practice round, at Brackenridge Park in San Antonio. Of course, no Tour player had ever broken 60 in an official round of golf—and wouldn't until 1977. Later in '39, Jug won the Canadian Open championship.

Ralph Guldahl

Demaret Prevails in L.A. Open

Jimmy Demaret, indicated by the jumbo-sized arrow, holes out to win the 1939 Los Angeles Open. This was the third and final year that this tournament was held at Griffith Park, where the winning scores (274, 273, and 274) were exceptionally low by L.A. Open standards. Demaret, 28 years old, was just coming into his own on Tour.

Los Angeles Open

Guldahl Achieves Unparalleled Success

Ralph Guldahl won the 1939 Masters, the last important championship in his phenomenal four-year run of victories in majors. In this photo, Guldahl takes the club well past parallel, which was not uncommon in his time. Bobby Jones and a young Ben Hogan, among others, took the club to the same length with the driver.

• June 10: Byron Nelson, Craig Wood, and Denny Shute tie at 284 at the end of the U.S. Open at Philadelphia C.C.

• June 11: After an 18-hole playoff for the U.S. Open, Byron Nelson and Craig Wood tie at 68. Nelson defeats Wood in another 18-hole playoff, 70-73.

• June 11: Denny Shute's entry to the PGA Championship is not accepted because he paid his annual dues two days late. At the tournament, the star players will refuse to play unless Shute is allowed in. He will be.

• July 1: In the NCAA championships, Stanford repeats as team champion. Vincent D'Antoni of Tulane wins the individual honors.

• July 7: Briton Richard Burton wins the British Open at St. Andrews in Scotland. Johnny Bulla finishes second, two strokes off the pace.

• July 15: At the Pomonok C.C. in Flushing, New York, Henry Picard

Henry Picard

Snead Nipped by Guldahl at Masters

Sam Snead gets a ground-level view of this putt at the 1939 Masters. Snead finished at 280 but lost to Ralph Guldahl by one stroke. Guldahl prevailed by playing the last nine holes in 3-under, which included an eagle on No. 13. Snead also lost the 1939 U.S. Open when he fell apart on the last two holes.

Sam Snead

Picard Nips Nelson in the PGA Championship

Henry Picard won the 1939 PGA Championship by edging Byron Nelson in the final, 1 up in 37 holes, at Pomonok C.C. in Flushing, New York. Henry birdied the last two holes for the victory. Picard won seven other tournaments in '39 to lead the Tour in victories, and was the year's leading money winner with $10,303.

Dick Metz

Metz's Big Year Includes Four Tourney Victories

Dick Metz, the smooth-swinging Kansan, claimed four tournaments in 1939, his best single year on the PGA Tour. Metz captured the St. Paul, Oakland, and Asheville Opens, plus the San Francisco Match-Play tournament. He also won a place on the 1939 Ryder Cup team, although the Matches were canceled due to the war in Europe.

defeats Byron Nelson in the PGA Championship with a 1-up victory on the first extra hole.

• July 23: Byron Nelson wins the Western Open, at the Medinah C.C. in Chicago, with a score of 281.

• July 29: The U.S. Amateur Public Links championship is won by burly Andy Szwedko at the Mt. Pleasant Park G.C. in Baltimore. The team championship is claimed by Los Angeles.

• August 14: In Pittsburgh, Ralph Guldahl wins the Dapper Dan Open, one of the earliest Tour events used to raise money for charity.

• August 25: Cliff Strickland wins the National Negro Open for the second time in a row. Dr. Remus Robinson wins the amateur title.

• August 26: Betty Jameson wins the U.S. Women's Amateur by beating Dorothy Kirby in the final, 3 & 2, at Wee Burn Club in Darien, Connecticut.

Evans's Brilliant Career Comes to an End

In 1939, Charles "Chick" Evans formally retired from national championship competition, concluding a long and illustrious career. His most enduring legacy, though, would be the caddie scholarship foundation that he started. The foundation has given thousands of needy young people a higher education.

Chick Evans

Betty Jameson

Jameson Beats Kirby in U.S. Women's Amateur

Betty Jameson watches her tee shot fly at the 1939 U.S. Women's Amateur championship at Wee Burn C.C. in Darien, Connecticut. Jameson defeated Dorothy Kirby in the final, 3 & 2, for her first of two consecutive Women's Amateur titles. Jameson, just 20 years old in '39, was one of golf's first glamour girls.

• September: The Curtis Cup Match, scheduled to be played in Great Britain in 1940, is canceled due to the war.

• September 16: Byron Nelson is given the $300 he would have won if a spectator had not mistakenly picked up his ball at the Hershey Open, which cost him a penalty.

• September 16: Marvin "Bud" Ward wins the U.S. Amateur championship at the North Shore C.C. in Glenview, Illinois. He wins by one-putting 29 greens in his last two matches.

• September 27: Kathy Whitworth, seven-time LPGA Player of the Year and winner of 88 tournaments on the LPGA circuit, is born in Monahans, Texas.

• October 21: Head pro Wiffy Cox shoots 33 skunks that had dug up his Congressional C.C. course.

• November 16: Fred Corcoran is reappointed the manager of the PGA Tour.

Marvin "Bud" Ward

Steel Worker Szwedko Wins U.S. Public Links Title

The U.S. Public Links championship was created to give the everyday working man a chance to win a national title. In 1939, Andy Szwedko —a brawny, 32-year-old Pittsburgh steel-mill worker—realized his dream. Szwedko *(left)* beat Californian Phil Gordon *(right)*, 1 up, in the final at Mt. Pleasant Park G.C. in Baltimore.

Andy Swedko, Charles Rainwater, Phil Gordon

Ward All Smiles After Winning U.S. Amateur

Marvin "Bud" Ward wore a grim expression when on the golf course, but he could crack a wonderful smile when it was over—especially after winning the 1939 U.S. Amateur. He played 170 holes in 11-under-par on the superb North Shore C.C. course in Glenview, Illinois. In the final, he defeated Ray Billows, 7 & 5.

William Shankland, A.T. Kyle, Richard Burton, Henry Cotton

British Players Contribute to War Effort

Soon after Great Britain entered World War II in September 1939, the nation's best golfers began staging exhibitions to raise funds for the Red Cross. These four men played an exhibition at Moortown, Leeds, in December 1939, raising £725. The four are *(left to right)* Bill Shankland, A.T. Kyle, Richard Burton, and Henry Cotton.

• December: Henry Picard is the leading money winner on the Tour with a total of $10,303. Picard leads the Tour with six victories. Byron Nelson, Dick Metz, and Ralph Guldahl each have four.

• December: Byron Nelson wins the Vardon Trophy.

• December: For the Tour year, Jimmy Thomson averaged 290 yards with his driver, hitting one drive an estimated 410 yards.

• December 1: Lee Trevino, two-time winner of the U.S. Open, British Open, and PGA Championship, is born in Dallas.

• December 7: Chuck Kocsis is at the forefront of a developing trend—outstanding amateur golfers turning professional.

• Caddies at Carnoustie G.C. in Scotland carry theirs and their golfers' gas masks in the event of a German attack.

HOGAN BREAKS THROUGH— WITH A VENGEANCE

Sam Snead, Byron Nelson, and Ben Hogan were all born in 1912. But while Snead and Nelson began their part of the triumvirate's dominance of the PGA Tour in 1937, Hogan took three more years—difficult, discouraging years. He had more than enough power for a smallish man (5'9", 140 pounds) but was plagued by a hook. Could Hogan find a method for controlling the flight of his ball? His determination to succeed was without question, and it led to the solution.

With the help of Henry Picard, Hogan adjusted his grip and shortened his swing. He then hit hundreds upon thousands of practice balls to build up "muscle memory," a phrase he may not have coined but surely made popular. Indeed, Hogan made practice itself fashionable—and his success made it *de rigueur*.

By 1940, Hogan was putting his game together, and early in the year he came very close to his first victory. Jimmy Demaret and Ed Oliver nipped him at the wire in Oakland and Phoenix, and Byron Nelson beat him in a playoff for the Texas Open. Hogan was about due; and when he struck, it was with a vengeance.

Hogan's first victory came in mid-March in the prestigious North and South Open, considered a major title at the time. Playing on one of the best courses in the world, Pinehurst No. 2 in North Carolina, Hogan shot 66-67 in the first two rounds to set a new 36-hole Tour scoring record. He led by seven strokes. Hogan weakened a bit in the third round with a 74, but then the 27-year-old Texan closed with a 70 to hold off a fast-finishing Sam Snead by four shots. Byron Nelson was third. The triumvirate was in place.

After his first taste of victory, Hogan became voracious. It had been so long coming that he had some catching up to do. Two days after the North and South, the Greensboro Open got under way. Hogan and Clayton Heafner shot 69s to take the first-round lead, then snow and bitter cold canceled play for three days. When they resumed, no one got close to Hogan. He fired rounds of 68, 66, and 67 to win by nine strokes. The very next day, the Land of the Sky Open began in Asheville, North Carolina. Hogan shot 67-68-69-69 to beat Ralph Guldahl by three strokes.

In the space of 10 days of tournament golf, Hogan played 12 rounds—216 holes—in 34-under-par. Ten of the rounds were in the 60s. He had retained his length off the tee but now had a degree of accuracy—and consistent accuracy the likes of which had not been seen before. He hit fairway after fairway and green after green in regulation. His golf was as close to perfection as it could get. Hogan would keep up his style for so long, and with such success, that he would eventually transcend all the champions that came before him and set the standard for all those who would follow.

1940

• January: PGA Tour players will play in 27 tournaments for $117,000.

• January 6: Jack Burke Jr., eldest son of one of American golf's most renowned teachers, turns pro. He will win 17 Tour events, including four in a row in 1952.

• January 21: Jack Nicklaus is born in Columbus, Ohio.

• February 6: The Greens Superintendents of America say they will make an extra effort to combat the dreaded Japanese beetle.

• February 12: Byron Nelson wins the Texas Open. It will be the first of

only five tourneys he will win in his native state out of a career victory total of 52.

• February 21: Jimmy Demaret wins the Western Open at River Oaks C.C. in Houston.

• February 23: Walter Burkemo takes his first step into big-time Tour

1940

Before he adopted the white cap that would become his trademark, Ben Hogan broke through in 1940 to win his first individual pro title, the North and South Open. He also won three Tour events, which brought him the first of his three consecutive money-winning titles.

golf with a victory in the Southern Florida Open.

• March: Lloyd Mangrum wins his first Tour event, the Thomasville Open. He will win 36 in all.

• March 10: Patty Berg continues her rise in women's golf. After a victory in the Mid-Florida Women's

Open on February 24, she takes the East Coast Women's championship in the same state.

• April 6: George Dunlap Jr. wins his fifth North and South Amateur, at Pinehurst C.C.

• April 7: Jimmy Demaret wins his first of three Masters titles by four

strokes over Lloyd Mangrum, who broke the tournament record with a 64 in the first round. Demaret finishes at 280.

• April 9: The USGA announces cancellation of the Walter Cup Match scheduled for later in the year due to the war over in Europe.

1940

George T. Dunlap Jr., Judge M. Fred O'Connell, Jack Ryerson

Dunlap Does It Again in North and South Amateur

Judge M. Fred O'Connell presents George T. Dunlap Jr. with the prize for winning the 1940 North and South Amateur, in Pinehurst, North Carolina. Dunlap defeated Jack Ryerson, 7 & 6, in the 36-hole final. This was getting to be old hat for Dunlap, who had won five previous North and South titles— and would win another.

Who's Who of Golf Shows Up at Goodall

A field of elite golfers appeared in the 1940 Goodall Round-Robin, at the Freshmeadow C.C. in New York. Pictured are *(front row, left to right)* Ben Hogan, Byron Nelson, Jimmy Demaret, Dick Metz, Craig Wood, Paul Runyan, and Clayton Heafner. Also *(back row, left to right)* Henry Picard, Martin Pose, Jimmy Hines, Horton Smith, Gene Sarazen, Lawson Little, Jimmy Thompson, and Sam Snead.

Goodall Round-Robin

- April 9: The R&A cancels the British Open and Amateur for the duration of the war.

- May 27: Ben Hogan, the year's leading player, fails to qualify for the U.S. Open.

- June: The first NCAA championship tie occurs when Louisiana State and Princeton finish with 601 strokes each. Dixon Brooke of Virginia wins the individual honors.

- June 6: A heavy favorite in the U.S. Open, Jimmy Demaret opens with an 81 and does not turn in his card.

- June 7: The golf balls of many players in the U.S. Open are examined by the USGA, after rumors that a ball was being used that could be driven "unheard-of distances and might have a magnetic core."

- June 8: At the U.S. Open, Ed "Porky" Oliver's 287 total that ties for the title does not count, as he is disqualified for starting his last

Snakebit Wood Shoots 264 in Metropolitan

By 1940, Craig Wood had lost playoffs for three major titles—the British and U.S. Opens and the Masters—yet he was an amenable man who would pose for a photo symbolic of those disappointments. In the 1940 Metropolitan Open, Wood made even the greatest players take notice when he shot a 264, the best total to that point on a regulation course.

Jimmy Demaret

Colorful Demaret Wins Masters, Western

Texan Jimmy Demaret, who had done some crooning in a Galveston nightclub before hitting the golf circuit, made his infectious smile and snappy clothes a permanent feature on the pro Tour. In 1940, he led the circuit with six tournament victories, including the Masters and the Western Open.

Patty Berg

Amateur Star Berg Joins Professional Ranks

In 1940, the loquacious redhead from Minnesota, Patty Berg, turned professional after winning 29 amateur events in a seven-year period. Unfortunately, in 1940 there were very few pro women's tournaments for Berg to compete in. She mostly gave clinics and exhibitions for Wilson Sporting Goods Company.

Craig Wood

round before he was officially scheduled. He and five others teed off early to try and beat a storm.

• June 9: Lawson Little wins the U.S. Open, at the Canterbury G.C. in Cleveland, in a playoff with the venerable Gene Sarazen, who won his first Open 18 years earlier.

• June 28: Betty Jameson wins her second straight U.S. Women's Amateur, at the Del Monte Golf & C.C. in Pebble Beach, California.

• July: In winning the Metropolitan Open, Craig Wood sets a new 72-hole scoring record on a regulation course with rounds of 64-66-68-66—264.

• July 27: Ed Furgol, the 1954 U.S. Open champion, is medalist in the U.S. Amateur Public Links, but he loses in the semifinal to the eventual winner, Robert C. Clark.

• August 19: Sam Snead defeats Harry Cooper in a playoff for the Canadian Open, at the Scarborough Golf & C.C. in Toronto.

W.B. "Duff" McCullough, Dick Chapman

Chapman's Right at Home in U.S. Amateur

Dick Chapman *(right)* played in the 1940 U.S. Amateur on his home course, Winged Foot G.C. in New York, and he took advantage of it. Chapman earned medalist honors and, in the final, obliterated W.B. "Duff" McCullough *(left)*, 11 & 9. During the course of his victory, Chapman played 157 holes in 8-under-par.

Mighty Little Triumphs in U.S. Open

Lawson Little, the son of an Army officer, won the 1940 U.S. Open in a playoff with Gene Sarazen, 70-73, at Canterbury G.C. in Cleveland. Little was a powerful ball-striker who was not always accurate. However, he often used his power to help him out of the trouble he got himself into. Little whacked this shot to within four feet of the hole.

Lawson Little

• August 26: The USGA rules Australian amateur star Jim Ferrier ineligible for the U.S. Amateur for purportedly writing a golf instructional book for which he received royalties.

• August 26: Henry Cotton notes that most courses in Great Britain have been torn up and covered with posts and poles to stop German war planes from landing, but that play continues.

• September 2: Two emergent giants of the pro Tour, Byron Nelson and Sam Snead, play in the final for the PGA Championship at the Hershey C.C. in Pennsylvania. Nelson wins, 1 up.

• September 14: Dick Chapman, the medalist and playing on his home course, wins the U.S. Amateur at Winged Foot G.C. in Mamaroneck, New York.

• September 20: The Italian sports paper *Littoriale,* noting that virile, young Italian fascists are playing golf, says the game was first played

1940

Sam Snead

Snead Wins Canadian Open

Sam Snead, who had shown great promise as a baseball and football player in high school, gave his wonderfully graceful athleticism to golf. Each of his swings ended with a picture finish that was the envy of the golf world. In 1940, he displayed his skills in the Canadian Open, where he defeated Harry Cooper in a playoff.

Betty Jameson

Nelson Nips Snead to Claim PGA Championship

Byron Nelson *(left)* won the 1940 PGA Championship in a thriller, 1 up over Sam Snead *(right)*, at Hershey C.C. in Pennsylvania. Tom Walsh, president of the PGA of America, presented the trophy. Nelson's victory made up for the previous year, when he lost to Henry Picard in the PGA final.

Byron Nelson, Tom Walsh, Sam Snead

Jameson Repeats in U.S. Women's Amateur

Oklahoma's Betty Jameson won her second straight U.S. Women's Amateur championship in 1940. She would claim a total of 14 amateur championships before turning professional in 1945 and later became one of the founders of the LPGA. One of Jameson's most notable feats was her victory in the 1932 Texas Public Links. She was 13 years old.

---

in Umbria, Italy, and centuries later spread to Holland and Scotland.

• December: Porky Oliver is named the unofficial Rookie of the Year on the strength of his three PGA Tour victories.

• December: Ben Hogan wins the Vardon Trophy with a 423 total and

also tops the Tour in earnings with $10,655.

• December 3: A committee of leading golf writers is formed to help select inductees to a proposed PGA Hall of Fame.

• December 16: The USGA adopts new specifications for iron clubs, in

which the grooves must be no wider than ¹/₃₂ of an inch and the distance between grooves not less than three times the width of the groove.

• Golf clubs in the London area post wartime rules that include: "Competitors during gunfire or while bombs are falling may take cover without penalty."

IN TROUBLED WAR YEARS, THE GAME OF GOLF MARCHES ON

When Craig Wood finally broke through in major championship golf, he won two of them in one year—the 1941 Masters and U.S. Open. But in a way, his bad luck did not change. His victories became but a murmur beside the terrible thunder that arose a few months later with the bombing of Pearl Harbor and the onset of World War II. In early 1942, the USGA canceled all of its championships; the British championships had been canceled in 1940.

Although they would be canceled in 1943, the Masters and the PGA Championship were played in 1942. In the '42 Masters, Byron Nelson beat Ben Hogan by one stroke in a playoff when he picked up five shots over an 11-hole stretch, which Hogan himself played in 1-under-par. Later that year, Sam Snead cajoled his recruiting officer to give him a few extra days before entering the Navy so he could go to New Jersey and play in the PGA. Snead won, for his first major title, with a 2 & 1 victory over Jim Turnesa.

In early 1942, PGA of America President Ed Dudley took a lead from President Roosevelt's statement that America's profes-

sional sports organizations should keep going as best they could. The reason? To provide the nation with some diversion from the agony of war and the effort to fight it. So, like major league baseball, the PGA Tour continued throughout most of the war, although it had to significantly curtail its schedule because—for transportation—golfers were dependent on gas that was now rationed. But there was a '42 Tour schedule, along with many Red Cross fund-raising tournaments and exhibitions.

The most notable fund-raising tournament in 1942 was staged in Chicago by the USGA, the Chicago District Golf Association,

and the PGA of America. It was called the Hale America National Open, and it raised over $25,000 for Navy Relief and the USO. The "Hale America" in the title was a subsidiary promotion of exercise to keep home-front war-workers healthy and strong. It was conceived by John Kelly, a champion sculler and father of future actress and princess Grace Kelly.

Hogan won the Hale America with a 271, four shots better than Jimmy Demaret and Mike Turnesa. In subsequent years, Hogan would occasionally allude that this victory represented his fifth U.S. Open title. While there was U.S. Open-style regional qualifying for the event—and it did have National Open in the title—no one has ever taken Hogan's intimation seriously, if only because the venue was hardly up to U.S. Open standards. The Ridgemoor Country Club layout on which it was played was a well-designed course, but only 6,519 yards long and not as rigorously prepared as Open courses generally are. Hogan's winning total was a full 10 strokes better than any U.S. Open winning score up to that time.

1941

• January: PGA Tour players will play for a total of $169,200 in 30 events.

• February 28: The United States War Department orders a survey of 200 golf courses in the New York City area that can be used as emergency landing fields.

• April: In a reversion to golf's earliest days, it is announced that 150 sheep will be allowed to graze the golf courses of St. Andrews, Scotland, as part of the war effort.

• April 6: Craig Wood, who finished second in the first two Masters, finally wins it and sheds his bridesmaid reputation.

• June 2: The USGA announces it will put a limit on the distance qualities of golf balls.

• June 7: Craig Wood wins the last U.S. Open until 1946, at the Colonial Club in Fort Worth, Texas. Wood plays the tournament in a back brace.

Johnny Bulla, winner of the 1941 Los Angeles Open and twice a runner-up in the British Open (1939 and '46), became a pilot with Eastern Air Lines during the war. In 1945, Bulla bought a small transport plane and soon after flew himself and many pros to stops on the tournament circuit.

• June 28: In the NCAA championships, Stanford wins for the third time in the last four years. Earl Stewart of Louisiana State wins the individual title.

• July 13: At Cherry Hills C.C. in Denver, Vic Ghezzi upsets Byron Nelson in the PGA Championship—1 up on the 38th hole.

• August 9: The USGA rules that players may discontinue play on their own volition during thunderstorms.

• August 24: The World Blind Golfers championship is won by Clint Russell, when he holes a 10-foot putt on the last hole.

• August 30: Marvin "Bud" Ward wins his second U.S. Amateur, defeating B. Patrick Abbott in the final at the Omaha Field Club.

• September 13: Betty Hicks Newell wins in the U.S. Women's Amateur at The Country Club in Brookline, Massachusetts. Immediately afterward, she turns professional.

1941-42

Vic Ghezzi, Tom Walsh, Byron Nelson

Ghezzi's Precision Earns Him PGA Trophy

Big Vic Ghezzi *(left)* accepts the PGA Championship trophy from Tom Walsh after defeating Byron Nelson, 1 up, in the final at the Cherry Hills C.C. in Denver. Although a short hitter, Ghezzi was a most accurate ball-striker. This would be his one day in the sun, as he would never again win a major title.

Masters Victory Ends Wood's Major Drought

After years of frustration, Craig Wood finally crashed the barrier that had denied him major championships, and he did so in spades. In 1941, he won both the Masters and the U.S. Open. Wood was runner-up in each of the first two Masters, including 1935 when Gene Sarazen holed his world-famous double eagle.

Craig Wood

- November 10: The PGA of America names its 1941 Ryder Cup team, with Craig Wood as the captain. There will be no Ryder Cup this year.

- December: Sam Snead leads the PGA Tour with six victories. Ben Hogan wins five events and is second 11 times.

- December: Ben Hogan leads the PGA Tour money list with $18,358. He wins the Vardon Trophy.

- December 13: PGA of America President Ed Dudley informs President Franklin Roosevelt that his organization is ready to do anything to help the war effort, especially fund-raising exhibitions.

- December 17: The Office of Price Administration issues an order reducing the production of new golf balls by 80 percent.

- December 18: In response to the OPA's golf ball restrictions, golfers in major cities are reportedly rushing to buy balls before the order goes into effect.

Denny Shute, Craig Wood

Wood Wins U.S. Open; Shute Is Second Again

An elated Craig Wood *(right)* poses with Densmore "Denny" Shute after Wood defeated Shute by three strokes for the 1941 U.S. Open crown. It was Shute's second runner-up finish in three years in the national championship. In 1939, he and Wood lost to Byron Nelson in a playoff for the title.

Marvin "Bud" Ward

Hicks Slips Past Sigel in Women's Amateur

Betty Hicks Newell *(right)* defeated Helen Sigel *(left)* in the final of the 1941 U.S. Women's Amateur, at The Country Club in Brookline, Massachusetts. Hicks would become a pioneer in the development of the women's pro circuit. Sigel would again finish runner-up in this event, in 1948.

Helen Sigel, Betty Hicks Newell

Nothing Stops Ward from Second U.S. Amateur

Marvin "Bud" Ward, a grimly determined competitor who had won the U.S. Amateur in 1939, was undeterred by tree trouble in his semifinal match in the 1941 Amateur. Ward won this hole and the match, at Omaha Field Club in Nebraska, then defeated Patrick Abbott, 4 & 3, in the final.

1942

• January: In an abbreviated Tour of 21 events, PGA players will play for $116,650.

• January 11: The USGA says all of its championships will be canceled for the duration of the war.

• February 8: Herman Barron wins the last Western Open until 1946, and he becomes the first Jewish golfer to win an important American golf event.

• March 26: The USGA urges that driving ranges and putting greens be installed at Army camps.

• March 28: The U.S. Rubber Co. announces the development of a method for re-covering and reprocessing golf balls without using war-critical rubber.

• April 9: The United States' War Production Board orders that the manufacturing of golf equipment be stopped completely as of May 31, 1942.

Herman Barron

Barron Ends Drought at Western Open

At the age of 32, and after 13 years of Tour golf without a victory, Herman Barron won the 1942 Western Open with a brilliant 8-under-par 276 over the Phoenix G.C. course. With the victory, Barron became the first Jewish golfer to win a major title.

U.S. Ryder Cup Team

U.S. Names Its Ryder Cuppers—Just in Case

In 1942, the U.S. named its Ryder Cup team in case World War II ended before the next scheduled meeting (1943). The U.S. team, pictured here, was headed by honorary captain Walter Hagen *(front row, second from left)*. If the war had ended, this mighty squad—with Hogan, Nelson, Snead, McSpaden, etc.—likely would have routed the British.

Sam Snead

Snead Claims PGA Title, Then Enters Navy

Slammin' Sam Snead plays from beside a bunker on his way to his first major crown, the 1942 PGA Championship. Snead would win this title three times in all. He was able to play in this one because, at Snead's request, his draft board gave him an extra 10 days before making him report for induction into the Navy.

• April 13: Byron Nelson wins his second Masters, defeating Ben Hogan in an 18-hole playoff by one stroke, 69-70.

• May 12: The WPB amends its order of April 9 and permits manufacturers to make new clubs with material on hand.

• May 12: The Falk bill is passed in New York, barring race discrimination on the state's public courses.

• May 31: After getting an extension of his military induction date so he could play in the PGA Championship, Sam Snead wins the title at the Seaview C.C. in Atlantic City, New Jersey.

• June 13: The PGA of America announces it will present an annual Walter Hagen Award to the person contributing the most to the game of golf.

• June 21: Ben Hogan wins the Hale America National Open, a substitute for the U.S. Open and sponsored by the USGA.

1941–42

Ben Hogan

Hogan Leads in Earnings, Wins Hale America Tourney

Ben Hogan chips from the sand in a practice round for the 1941 U.S. Open. He finished in a tie for third, five strokes behind Craig Wood's winning 284, but he was the year's leading money winner. In 1942, Hogan would win the Hale America National Open, a fund-raising event that filled the void of the canceled U.S. Open.

Quartet of Stars Meets in the PGA's Semifinals

From left to right sit Sam Snead, Jimmy Demaret, Byron Nelson, and Jim Turnesa, semifinalists in the 1942 PGA Championship. Snead defeated Turnesa in the final, 2 & 1, at the Seaview C.C. in New Jersey. Turnesa had already joined the military service, while Demaret would join the Navy shortly after. Nelson was exempt from service because of hemophilia.

Sam Snead, Jimmy Demaret, Byron Nelson, Jim Turnesa

• June 27: In the NCAA championships, Louisiana State and Stanford tie for the team title. Stanford's Frank Tatum wins the individual championship.

• August: Ben Hogan leads an abbreviated PGA Tour with six victories. He also leads in earnings with $13,143.

• August 8: In the Canadian Open in Toronto, caddies wear numbers for the first time to help the gallery identify the players. Craig Wood wins the tournament.

• September 4: Raymond Floyd, winner of two PGA Championships, a Masters, and a U.S. Open, is born at Ft. Bragg, North Carolina.

• October 3: It is announced that the Masters will be canceled for the duration of the war.

• November 1: A patent is issued on a golf club that automatically applauds players starting their backswing correctly by giving them a mechanized "razzberry."

GOLF WIPED OUT AS WAR EFFORT HEIGHTENED

In 1943, when the war was going badly for the United States, golf at every level was deep in the doldrums. Gas rationing restricted travel to courses. The manufacturing of new golf balls was virtually banned. Sam Snead remembered, many years later, of starting a tournament with a quality pre-war ball he luckily acquired. It was so precious that he ended up using it for the entire 72 holes. Even the re-covering of used balls was severely limited because of the rationing of rubber. This led to experimentation within the chemical industry on synthetic materials for golf ball covers, which eventually came to dominate the game.

There were only three Tour events in 1943, and no official prize money was listed for the year. The main event was staged in Chicago by an individual promoter named George S. May. May began his involvement in tournament golf in 1941, when he staged an open at his Tam O'Shanter Country Club course with a purse of $10,000. This was the genesis of what became an annual two-week tournament extravaganza that May would put on through the mid-1950s; it featured men's and women's pro and amateur tournaments. His chief attraction would be called the "World Championship," which eventually would be worth a phenomenal $100,000 to the winner.

In 1944, as the fortunes of war began to turn in favor of the United States and its allies, golf too began to stir. Twenty-two tournaments were played on the Tour in '44, for a total of $150,500. All the money was paid out in U.S. War Bonds (which were worth about 75 percent of their face value). The golf equipment manufacturers put up a portion of that money, a contribution meant to keep the game alive during the difficult times. But

George S. May was the Tour's biggest benefactor, offering a $42,000 purse for his 1944 open. Byron Nelson earned $13,462 for winning it. It was the largest first prize in the PGA Tour's history and was part of the nearly $40,000 he won to lead the year's money-winning list.

By 1944, the PGA felt it could resume its championship, and the first major in two years was played the week before the Tam O'Shanter tournament, at the Manito Golf and Country Club in Spokane, Washington. Nelson was the 1-10 favorite to take the title, but in the final he was the victim of "the most spectacular upset in the tournament's history." Bob Hamilton, out of Evansville, Indiana, and playing in his first PGA, had not done much Tour playing up until then but did have a reputation as a good money player. He defeated Nelson, 1 up, in a stirring final that went to the 36th hole, on which both men scored birdies. Proceeds of the event went to two local Army hospitals.

The Allies were not quite out of the war woods yet, and neither was golf, but both could see a gap through the branches.

1943

• January: The PGA Tour will consist of just three Tour events worth a total of $17,000.

• January 7: It is announced that 50 head of cattle will graze the Augusta National G.C., which is closed for the duration of World War II, to aid the war effort.

• January 22: The Chicago District Golf Association announces plans to stage another National Open-type championship to aid the war effort.

• January 31: It is reported that leftover golf ball centers are being used in the manufacturing of baseballs.

• February: Byron Nelson, ineligible for military service because of a blood disorder, plays his 35th war-relief benefit match.

• March: It is reported that, in Great Britain, golf remains popular despite restrictions that include fences around greens to keep off grazing sheep.

1943-44

Sam Byrd, the man who replaced Babe Ruth as the New York Yankees' right fielder and who later turned to professional golf, was one of many Tour players drafted into military service during World War II. Here, Byrd reads his notice to report at Fort McClellan, Alabama, to take his physical.

• March 25: Bobby Cruickshank, 48 years old, wins the North and South Open with a 292, 21 strokes higher than Ben Hogan's winning score of a year ago.

• April 3: The USGA announces it has given 1,000 golf balls for distribution to the armed forces.

• June 4: The Chicago District Golf Association initiates a Dime-a-Round program, whereby golfers deposit a dime in a milk bottle at the first tee of all courses, with the money going to war relief.

• July 1: The NCAA team championship is won by Yale. It is the school's 21st victory since the inception of the competition in 1897. Wallace Ulrich of Carleton College captures the individual championship.

• July 4: A New York City golf pro is arrested for operating a gambling game in which golfers tried to win a new ball after giving up an old one.

Louise and Byron Nelson

Things Looking Up for Allies, as Well as Nelson

Byron Nelson's wife, Louise, was his constant companion on the tournament circuit. In 1944, as World War II was beginning to tilt toward an Allied victory, the Tour began to regain its momentum. There was close to a full schedule of events, and Nelson won eight of them to lead the circuit.

Porky Gets Special Treatment at St. Paul Open

The Red Cross was on hand at most PGA Tour events, and it was a good thing for Ed "Porky" Oliver. Well-qualified medical aid was available at the 1944 St. Paul Open when he strained his wrist while shooting a round of 66.

Bobby Cruickshank

Grandpa Cruickshank Wins North and South

The 1943 North and South Open more or less pre-empted today's Senior Tour when, in a concession to World War II, it limited its field to golfers 38 years old or older. The winner was Bobby Cruickshank, a World War I veteran and a 48-year-old grandfather. He won with a total of 291.

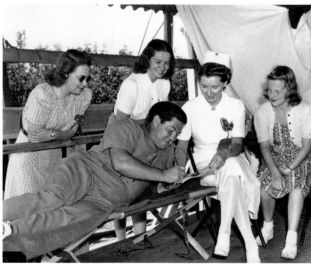

Ed "Porky" Oliver

• July 11: Ensign Willie Turnesa wins the Florida Open Links tournament in Orlando, with a 5-under-par 279. Professional Pete Cooper is second.

• July 11: Byron Nelson wins the Kentucky Open by three shots over Melvin "Chick" Harbert. Nelson earns a $1,000 war bond.

• July 27: The Tam O'Shanter All-American Open, with a $10,000 purse, is won by Jug McSpaden. The event promotes the sale of an estimated $900,000 in war bonds.

• July 30: A patent is issued to Emery Lunkenbill on a golf club with a variable face angle and a variable length shaft.

• October 10: The unofficial U.S. Professional Championship is won by Jug McSpaden at Chicago's Tam O'Shanter C.C.

• November 4: Baltusrol G.C. announces it has made an unexpected profit raising livestock on its two courses, which was intended to alleviate the nation's meat shortage.

Joe Louis, Byron Nelson

McSpaden Wins an All-American Thriller

A ring of spectators watches Harold "Jug" McSpaden sink a 25-foot putt to win the 1943 All-American Open, at Tam O'Shanter C.C. near Chicago. The putt came on the 18th hole of a playoff to beat Buck White by one stroke. The event promoted the sale of about $900,000 in war bonds.

Harold "Jug" McSpaden

Boxer Louis Takes a Shot at Tam O'Shanter

Heavyweight champion Joe Louis, an avid golfer, was invited to play in the 1943 Tam O'Shanter All-American Amateur tournament in Chicago. Louis, on furlough from the Army, didn't qualify but stayed on to play exhibitions to raise money for the War Fund. Here, Louis shakes hands with Byron Nelson.

Steve Warga

Warga Wins the War-Depleted Miami Open

In 1943, the PGA Tour was an unofficial circuit with only three tournaments on its schedule. With almost all of the circuit's top players in the service, unknown Steve Warga, a pro working as an airline radio operator, won the Miami Open, etching his name in the Tour record book for all time.

1944

• December 8: Gene Sarazen urges golfers to get their old balls reprocessed or "next year you'll be swinging at potatoes."

• December 19: Steve Warga, a young pro working as an airline radio operator, wins the Miami Open by three shots over Sam Byrd.

• January: The PGA Tour will consist of 22 events with a total purse of $150,500 (in war bonds).

• January 10: After a one-year cancellation due to the war, the Los Angeles Open is again played. Jug McSpaden wins it at the Wilshire C.C. with a total of 278.

• January 15: Babe Didrikson Zaharias is reinstated as an amateur. So is Johnny Dawson.

• January 20: Betty Hicks offers a proposal for the founding of a Women's Professional Golf Association that would have a tour similar to that of the PGA Tour.

Sam Byrd

Former Yankee Byrd Prevails in New Orleans

Sam Byrd became the best cross-over athlete in Tour history. The one-time New York Yankees outfielder, seen here playing in a best-ball tournament prior to the 1943 National Victory Open, won two Tour events. One of the victories came in February 1943, when he captured the New Orleans Open.

Sullivan Captures Tourney in South Pacific

Ivan S. Sandberg, commander of a naval construction unit on an island in the South Pacific, hands a trophy to First Class Metalsmith Tim Sullivan. Servicemen had carved out a golf course on the island and played a tournament using homemade clubs. Sullivan won the tourney and received the trophy, hammered out of a 105-millimeter shell.

Ivan S. Sandberg, Tim Sullivan

• February 6: The Phoenix Open, canceled from 1941–43, is renewed, and Jug McSpaden wins it in a playoff.

• February 14: Johnny Revolta wins the last of his 18 career Tour events, the Texas Open, at Willow Springs G.C. in San Antonio.

• February 28: Sam Byrd completes his transition from major-league baseball player to major-league golfer by winning the New Orleans Open.

• March 16: Bob Hamilton, making his first full winter tour, wins the North and South Open by seven strokes over Bobby Cruickshank.

• June 26: Notre Dame wins its first (and only) NCAA team championship, at the Inverness Club in Toledo, Ohio. Louis Lick of the University of Minnesota wins the individual title.

• August 20: Bob Hamilton wins the PGA Championship, upsetting 1-10 favorite Byron Nelson, 1 up, in the

Bob Hamilton

Journeyman Hamilton Stuns Nelson in PGA

Bob Hamilton, a pro from Indiana with a thin resumé, surprised the golf world by reaching the finals of the 1944 PGA Championship, then defeating Byron Nelson for the title. Hamilton was a 1-10 underdog going into the match, but he seemed unfazed as he made one fine swing after another and won, 1 up.

Revolta's Last Win Comes in Texas

Johnny Revolta proved that a short hitter off the tee could win big with a good short game. Acknowledged as one of the best chippers and putters in golf history, Revolta won the 18th and final event of his career at the 1944 Texas Open. Ironically, it was held at the relatively long Willow Springs G.C. in San Antonio.

Johnny Revolta

Eisenhower Sneaks in a Round

General Dwight D. Eisenhower obviously had more important things to do during the war, but he had to get a few swings in now and then. Ike took golf seriously but never became a great player. Bothered by an old football injury to his left knee, he was unable to fully shift his weight to his left side during his downswing.

General Dwight D. Eisenhower

final match. This is the only major championship held this year, and it's staged at Manito Golf & C.C. in Spokane, Washington.

• August 28: Byron Nelson wins $13,462, twice the year's next biggest first prize, at the Tam O'Shanter Open.

• September 10: Byron Nelson wins his third straight event, the Texas Victory Open.

• December: Byron Nelson leads the PGA Tour with eight victories. Harold McSpaden wins five events.

• December: Byron Nelson leads the PGA Tour money list with $37,968

in war bonds (worth 75 percent face value). Nelson takes home one-quarter of the season's total purse.

• December: Amid rumors that the U.S. Open will be renewed before the end of World War II, Craig Wood says it should not be renewed until the war is officially over.

At the end of the 1944 season, in which he won twice as much money as any player ever had in one year of Tour golf, Byron Nelson sat down with his notebook and figured out where his game was weakest. He decided it was his chipping, which he took to practicing at length. Nelson then went on to set a standard of excellence that goes beyond mere dominance of a sport. How does one describe a golfer who, in one year, wins 18 official tournaments—and 11 of them in a row?

The Streak was the feature story. It began in March when Nelson and his partner, Jug McSpaden, won the Miami International 4-Ball. After that, Nelson was on his own, although the second straight win was a close one. In the Charlotte Open, Nelson needed a blistering 33 on the final nine just to tie Sam Snead. They also tied in the playoff, the lead changing hands four times. In the second playoff, Nelson won by four with a 69.

From then on, Nelson made every effort to avoid close calls, often by making inspired rushes of brilliant golf in the closing rounds—streaks within The Streak. At Greensboro, he played

WHEW! NELSON RIPS OFF 11 WINS IN A ROW

the last 36 holes in 68-66 to win by eight shots. At Durham, Nelson closed with a 65 to win by five. In Atlanta, he finished with 65-65 to win by nine. A final-round 63, featuring birdies on the last four holes, clinched the Philadelphia Inquirer Open. Nelson's second-round match in the PGA Championship was his toughest. He was two down with four to go against Mike Turnesa, but he went 4-under-par with two birdies and an eagle to win, 1 up.

Nelson would one day admit that the competition was not as tough as it might have been. Snead played in all but three, but in a few he was recovering from a broken wrist. Ben Hogan and Jimmy Demaret competed in only

two each of the events that made up The Streak. Other young stars also in the military at the time—Vic Ghezzi, Ed Oliver, Lloyd Mangrum, Clayton Heafner, Dutch Harrison—played perhaps two each. Yet, one must not downplay the brilliance of Byron's play. In 38 rounds at straight stroke play, Nelson was 113-under-par, averaging 67.92 per round.

Ironically, his streak ended when an amateur, Freddie Haas Jr., won the Memphis Open. Nelson was third. Haas, though, was one of the country's best amateurs, played against the pros regularly, and soon after began a successful career on the Tour. Nelson played only one more year of full-time tournament golf, retiring after a six-victory campaign in 1946, even though he was only 34. His sustained excellence may well have worn him out. He would suggest as much. As a result, while Nelson would play the occasional tournament in the next few years, he retired too soon for younger golf fans to see for themselves how good he really was. With a glance at his record, though, everyone gets the idea.

1945

- January: PGA Tour players will compete in 36 events for a total purse of $435,300 (in war bonds).

- January 13: It is announced that PGA golf pros will offer free golf lessons to returning American GIs.

- January 13: Despite indications that the war is ending, the USGA

decides that it will not play any of its championships in 1945.

- March 7: PGA Tour manager Fred Corcoran says golf balls are so scarce that the top pros are paying up to $4 for a "pre-war pellet."

- March 8: Cary Middlecoff becomes one of the few amateurs to

ever beat the pros in an open event when he wins the North and South.

- March 11: Byron Nelson and Jug McSpaden, called the Gold Dust Twins because they are winning so much during the war years, team up to win the Miami International 4-Ball, defeating Lt. Ben Hogan and Ed Dudley in the final.

1945

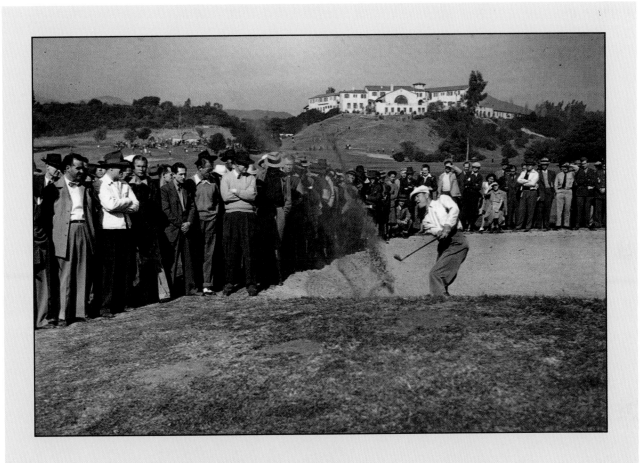

Prior to 1945, the one thing Byron Nelson needed to work on was his chipping. After refining that phase of his game, Nelson took off on the hottest streak in the history of golf. He is shown here chipping in the Los Angeles Open. Nelson finished back in the pack in this tournament. He would go on to win 18 events during the year.

• April 8: Byron Nelson sets a new PGA Tour 72-hole scoring record of 263 in winning the Iron Lung Open in Atlanta. It is his fifth consecutive victory.

• May 1: The War Production Board announces permission for manufacturers to make golf balls with synthetic rubber interiors.

• May 7: George Fazio, destined to become an outstanding golf architect, wins the California State Open.

• May 31: The WPB lifts its ban altogether on the manufacturing of golf balls.

• June: Ohio State becomes the first winner of the NCAA championship on a school-owned course—its own Scarlet Course.

• June 3: Hale Irwin, three-time winner of the U.S. Open, is born in Joplin, Missouri.

• June 6: Betty Jameson, two-time winner of the U.S. Women's Amateur, turns professional.

Cary Middlecoff

Amateur Middlecoff Nabs North and South

Lt. Cary Middlecoff, a dentist from Memphis, became one of golf's best-ever players. Winner of 40 events, including two U.S. Opens and a Masters, he began his rise to prominence by winning the 1945 North and South Open as an amateur. He was one of the first simon-pures to ever win a PGA Tour event.

Betty Jameson

Fazio Drives to Victory in California

Sweet-swinging George Fazio sold cars to pay his way on the pro Tour before becoming a high-quality player. Fazio won the California State Open in 1945 and the Canadian Open in 1946. Of course, he would go on to become one of golf's leading course architects, with Jupiter Hills Club in Florida among his many accomplishments.

George Fazio

Jameson No Match for the Babe

Texan Betty Jameson, the 1939 and 1940 U.S. Women's Amateur champion, turned professional in June 1945. Here, she plays from a bunker during a 72-hole challenge match against Babe Zaharias at the Los Angeles C.C. Jameson was four down after 36 holes and finally lost the marathon contest before a gallery that reached 3,000 spectators.

• **June 10:** The PGA Tour returns after a two-month break, and Byron Nelson makes the Montreal Open his sixth consecutive victory.

• **June 17:** Byron Nelson birdies five of the last six holes to beat Harold McSpaden by one shot at the Philadelphia Inquirer Invitational. It is Nelson's seventh straight win.

• **June 23:** Babe Zaharias becomes the first woman to win the Women's Western Amateur three times.

• **July 15:** Byron Nelson wins the PGA Championship at Moraine C.C. in Dayton, Ohio, defeating Sam Byrd in the final. It is Nelson's ninth straight win.

• **July 21:** Byron Nelson doesn't play in the St. Paul Open because of a sore back. Dutch Harrison wins.

• **July 29:** Byron Nelson is back for the Tam O'Shanter Open and scores his 10th consecutive victory.

• **August 2:** Ray McDonnell, a veteran left with the use of only one

1945

Nelson Claims PGA for Ninth Win in a Row

In the 1945 PGA Championship at the Moraine C.C. in Dayton, Ohio, Byron Nelson played Sam Byrd in the final. At the 26th hole of their match, scheduled for 36 holes, Nelson hit this short pitch that helped him to a 4 & 3 victory. It was his ninth consecutive victory—and he wasn't done yet.

Byron Nelson

Byron Nelson

Nelson Wins O'Shanter for 10th Straight

In the Tam O'Shanter All-American Open, Byron Nelson tries for a birdie on the 12th hole of the third round. He missed this one but not many more, as he eventually finished six shots ahead of the field. His win at Tam O'Shanter was his 10th in a row. He captured the event with his usual combination of accurate driving and pinpoint iron play.

---

arm, wins a closest-to-the-hole contest with a shot that comes within five feet of the cup.

• August 4: Byron Nelson extends his winning streak to 11 by capturing the Canadian Open.

• August 19: Amateur Fred Haas breaks Byron Nelson's winning

streak by taking the Memphis Invitational. Nelson is fourth.

• August 22: The U.S. Rubber Co. says its synthetic rubber golf balls will soon be in production.

• September: USGA officials announce that they will renew their championships in 1946.

• September 26: The British PGA rejects an offer to resume the Ryder Cup Match immediately, saying British players and courses need time to recover from the war.

• September 30: Ben Hogan breaks the PGA Tour's 72-hole scoring record with a 261 at the Portland Invitational.

Harold "Jug" McSpaden, Buck White

Gold Dust Twins Team Up for 4-Ball Victory

Harold "Jug" McSpaden *(left)* wraps his arm around Buck White. McSpaden, the lantern-jawed long-knocker from Kansas, bowed often to fellow Gold Dust Twin Byron Nelson in 1945, but Jug did team up to win the Miami International 4-Ball. His partner? Nelson, of course. They defeated Ed Dudley and Lt. Ben Hogan in the final.

Bobby Locke

Babe Wins Her Third Western Open

Babe Zaharias picked up golf in the mid-1930s and quickly became a sensation in a series of exhibitions with Gene Sarazen and others. She remained a professional through 1944, when she applied for and received reinstatement as an amateur. In 1945, she won her third Women's Western Open.

Babe Zaharias

Locke Foils Snead in Exhibitions

Bobby Locke of South Africa was a wizard with the putter. In 1945, he soundly defeated Sam Snead in a long series of exhibitions on his home courses. Byron Nelson was offered $10,000 to face Locke in a series of matches in South Africa, but Nelson turned it down because of traveling considerations.

• October 14: Byron Nelson is offered $10,000 to play a series of matches in South Africa against Bobby Locke, the local golf hero. Nelson declines, owing to the poor travel situation in the world.

• October 14: In the Seattle Open, Byron Nelson breaks Ben Hogan's record with a 72-hole total of 259.

• October 21: Babe Zaharias wins the Texas Women's Open, further proof of her fast-developing skills.

• October 29: The R&A announces it will resume all of its championships starting in 1946.

• November 4: All-time tennis great Ellsworth Vines wins his first golf tournament as a pro, the Southern California Open.

• November 15: The PGA announces it will limit its open events to 100 players, plus exemptions. The 100 will be decided through an 18-hole qualifying round.

Harold "Jug" McSpaden, Libby Walker, Henry Picard

Picard Wins in Miami; McSpaden Second Again

Orange Bowl queen Libby Walker presents a first-place check to Henry Picard, winner of the 1945 Miami Open. To the left is runner-up Harold "Jug" McSpaden, who finished five strokes back. For Jug, this scene became all too familiar in 1945 and 1946; he finished in second place an amazing 13 times, mostly to Byron Nelson.

Tennis Champ Vines Also Excels on the Links

Ellsworth Vines, a great tennis champion of the 1930s, eventually crossed over into professional golf and, in 1945, won the Southern California Open. Though never a winner on the PGA Tour, Vines possessed a very sound golf swing that got him into the money on many occasions. He later became an excellent teacher of the game.

Ellsworth Vines

- December: Byron Nelson finishes the year with a record 18 victories. Sam Snead won six events and Ben Hogan five.

- December: Byron Nelson leads the PGA Tour money list with $63,336, much of it in war bonds. He wins 15 percent of the total purse.

- December: Byron Nelson's 68.3 scoring average is the best ever.

- December 11: Tour pro Johnny Bulla, a licensed pilot, buys a passenger airplane and begins flying pros around the tournament circuit.

- December 17: The Veterans Administration, citing the recupera- tive benefits of golf, reports that there are 19 V.A. hospital golf courses—and six more are under construction.

- December 21: The USGA an- nounces it will increase the purse to $8,000 for the 1946 U.S. Open—the first to be played after the war.

HOGAN'S GREAT YEAR MARRED BY FINAL-HOLE THREE-PUTTS

The year 1946 was one of those rare seasons in which three of history's best players—Byron Nelson, Ben Hogan, and Sam Snead—inspired each other to great play. But the year would belong to Hogan, and it marked the emergence of a pure champion. Ending a 2½-year stint in the Army Air Corps, Hogan had played in 19 tournaments in 1945 and won five of them. In 1946, he hit the Tour full stride. He played an iron-man schedule of 32 tournaments, won 13, and finished in second place seven times.

In 1946, Hogan couldn't match Nelson's 1945 record of 11 wins in a row, but Ben had several streaks of his own. He won three straight at one point, and four straight at another. Ironically, though, Hogan suffered heart-breaks in two major championships in '46, the result of three-putting two greens.

The first setback came at the Masters. Herman Keiser started the final round five strokes ahead of Hogan but closed with a 74. Hogan, playing smoothly, was 3-under-par for the day as he stood on the tee of the par-4 18th hole. When he hit the green with his second shot, he needed but two

putts to tie and go into a playoff. But Hogan missed a 12-foot putt, then a 2½-footer, and Keiser won the Masters.

Hogan and Nelson were both in the thick of the fight at the '46 U.S. Open at Canterbury Country Club in Cleveland. With a record 12,000 fans tromping over the course the final day, Hogan and Vic Ghezzi had a two-stroke lead over Nelson. The unruly crowd may well have cost Byron the championship. Fans crowded around every shot and were so close to Nelson's ball on the 13th hole that his caddie stumbled under a rope and accidentally kicked the ball, costing Nelson a penalty stroke. But Nelson shot a 69 and held the 54-hole lead with

211, two ahead of Hogan.

Through 71 holes, Hogan had a chance to win. On the last hole, he could win with a birdie or tie with a par. His approach shot settled 18 feet above the hole, leaving him a slick downhill putt. He stroked his putt boldly for the win and his ball finished two feet past the cup. He missed coming back and wound up one stroke out of a tie for the U.S. Open lead. Nelson, Mangrum, and Ghezzi tied for the championship at 284 and Mangrum won the playoff the following day.

At the PGA Championship, played at match play at Portland G.C. in Oregon, Hogan got his revenge. In the semifinals, he romped over pal Jimmy Demaret, 10 & 9. When asked what the dour Hogan said to him during their match, Demaret answered, "The only thing I ever heard him say was, 'You're away.'" Hogan next met Porky Oliver in the final, and after the morning 18, Oliver was three up. Hogan roared back after lunch and played the front nine in 30 strokes, beating Oliver, 6 & 4, to win his first PGA Championship. By season's end, Hogan had won $42,556 and was the new king of golf.

1946

- January: Players on the PGA Tour will vie for $411,533 in prize money in 37 official events. The Athletic Institute, a group of golf equipment manufacturers, contributes $25,000 to keep the Tour going.

- January: Tommy Bolt turns professional.

- January 7: Byron Nelson, who won 11 tournaments in a row in 1945, wins the first tournament of the year, the Los Angeles Open at Riviera C.C., by five strokes.

- January 8: Eddie Williams wins the PGA Seniors Championship for the third year in a row.

- January 13: Byron Nelson wins the Tour's second event, the San Francisco Open at Olympic C.C., by nine strokes. Having now won three in a row, Nelson decides to take time off.

- February 10: With a 72-hole score of 264, Ben Hogan wins the Texas Open.

In his first full season after a stint in the Army Air Corps, Ben Hogan picked up 13 first-prize checks in 1946. Hogan *(right)* received this $3,000 payoff from Amon Carter, tournament chairman, when he won the Colonial NIT in Fort Worth, Texas, on May 19. He shot a course-record 65 in the final round for the victory.

• February 17: Byron Nelson wins the New Orleans Open.

• March 24: Sam Snead wins the Greater Greensboro Open for the second time. His first victory was in 1938.

• April: Amateur Louise Suggs wins the prestigious Titleholders Championship. She'll also capture the Women's Western Open later in the year.

• April: Frank Stranahan of Toledo, Ohio, heir to a sparkplug fortune, wins the North and South Amateur.

• April 7: Ben Hogan three-putts the 72nd green to lose the Masters by a single stroke. Hogan finishes the tournament with a 72-hole score of 283 and is beaten by Herman Keiser, who shoots 282.

• May 12: Byron Nelson wins the first Houston Open, shooting 274 for 72 holes at River Oaks C.C. in Houston.

1946

Ben Hogan, Herman Keiser, Bobby Jones

Keiser Prevails in Masters—By That Much

Herman Keiser *(center)* won his only major championship when he captured the 1946 Masters, after Ben Hogan missed a 30-inch putt on the final hole. Hogan shows Keiser and tournament host Bobby Jones the size of his missed putt, which gave him a total of 283. Keiser's 282 was enough to win.

Williams Best Again in PGA Seniors

Eddie Williams of Chicago was an early pioneer of PGA Seniors competition. In 1946, Williams won his second straight PGA Seniors Championship, which was held at PGA National G.C. in Dunedin, Florida, its longtime home. In '46, Williams defeated former and future champ Jock Hutchison in a playoff.

Eddie Williams

Frank Stranahan

Stranahan Takes Two Amateurs

Frank Stranahan—the Toledo, Ohio, strongman—picked up two important amateur titles in 1946 when he won the North and South and the Western Amateur. The long-hitting Stranahan, heir to the Champion Spark-plug fortune, could afford to play the Tour as an amateur before turning pro.

- May 19: Ben Hogan wins the National Invitation Tournament at Colonial C.C. in Fort Worth, Texas.

- May 26: In the first Western Open since 1943, Ben Hogan wins with a 271 at Sunset C.C. in St. Louis.

- June: George Hamer of the University of Georgia wins the NCAA individual championship, and Stanford takes the team title.

- June 2: Ben Hogan wins the Goodall Round-Robin, his third consecutive victory.

- June 13: The U.S. Open is resumed for the first time since World War II, at Canterbury G.C. in Cleveland.

- June 15: In the U.S. Open's third round, Byron Nelson is leading by a stroke when his caddie inadvertently steps on his ball, costing Nelson a penalty stroke.

- June 15: In the second of Saturday's double round at the U.S. Open, Byron Nelson pulls into a three-way tie with Vic Ghezzi and

1946

Louise Suggs

Amateur Suggs Proves Better Than the Pros

Amateur Louise Suggs, nicknamed "Sweet Swinger" and "Miss Sluggs," burst onto the national scene in 1946. Suggs, shown on her way to defeating Patty Berg for the 1946 Western Open, also won the Titleholders. Both were pro events, although Louise wouldn't turn pro until 1947.

Sam Snead

Nelson Says Goodbye to PGA Tour

Coming off his sensational 1945 season, Byron Nelson won the 1946 San Francisco Open. Nelson got down in two from this bunker at the Olympic Club. After winning the L.A. Open, Nelson took time off. He lost a playoff for the 1946 U.S. Open and officially retired from the Tour later in the year.

Byron Nelson

Snead Wins the British But Loses Money

Sam Snead's powerfully smooth swing led him to a victory in the 1946 British Open, held for the first time since 1939. Snead was one of the few Americans to compete in the British, making the trip at the urging of his equipment company. Although he won the $600 first prize, Snead claimed the trip cost him $1,000.

Lloyd Mangrum. Ben Hogan finishes a stroke back.

• June 16: Lloyd Mangrum, Byron Nelson, and Vic Ghezzi shoot identical scores of 72 in the 18-hole playoff for the U.S. Open and are forced into another 18-hole round. Mangrum shoots 72, to Nelson's and Ghezzi's 73s, and wins the title.

• July 5: Sam Snead wins the British Open at the Old Course at St. Andrews, Scotland, by four strokes over runners-up Bobby Locke and Johnny Bulla.

• August 20: At the PGA Championship, reporters Charles Bartlett and Herb Graffis and PGA Tournament Director Fred Corcoran

plan an organization of golf writers. The group becomes the Golf Writers Association of America.

• August 24: Ben Hogan routs future Hall of Famer Jimmy Demaret, 10 & 9, in the semifinals of the PGA Championship at Portland G.C. in Oregon.

1946

Ted Bishop, Smiley Quick

Bishop Nips Quick in U.S. Amateur Championship

Ted Bishop *(left)* shakes hands with Smiley Quick, the man he would defeat the following day to win the first post-war U.S. Amateur championship, at New Jersey's Baltusrol G.C. Bishop, of Dedham, Massachusetts, was forced to go 37 holes in the final match before defeating Quick, 1 up.

Louise Suggs, Patty Berg

Berg Prevails in the First Women's Open

Patty Berg *(right)* chats with amateur Louise Suggs. Berg was a savvy player with an efficient swing who, in 1946, won the first U.S. Women's Open. Her career included a record 15 major wins. Berg and Suggs battled for supremacy in the early 1950s and both wound up in the LPGA Hall of Fame.

Britain Still Prefers the Smaller Golf Ball

British golfers still played with the small golf ball in 1946. British Open champion Richard Burton *(left)* compares the smaller British ball with the American size being held by Fred Corcoran, PGA tournament manager. Burton arrived in New York via ocean liner to compete in American tournaments.

Richard Burton, Fred Corcoran

- **August 25:** Ben Hogan wins his first major championship, the PGA, with a 6 & 4 victory over Ed "Porky" Oliver in the 36-hole final. Hogan fires a 30 on the front nine in the afternoon.

- **August:** Patty Berg wins the qualifying medal at the first U.S. Women's Open.

- **September 1:** At Spokane C.C. in Washington, Patty Berg wins the U.S. Women's Open, and $5,600 in bonds. She defeats Betty Jameson, 5 & 4, in the final.

- **September 2:** Ben Hogan wins the Golden State Open. It's the second time this year he's won three straight events.

- **September 8:** Sam Snead wins George S. May's first World Championship, at Tam O'Shanter C.C. near Chicago.

- **September 14:** At Baltusrol G.C. in Springfield, New Jersey, Stanley Bishop wins the U.S. Amateur, 1 up, over Smiley Quick in a 37-hole final.

Mangrum Nabs Open in Three-Way Playoff

Lloyd Mangrum, who played with the nerve of a riverboat gambler, made his move in 1946. The colorful Mangrum, shown here in the Chicago Victory National Open, won the U.S. Open in a 36-hole playoff with Vic Ghezzi and Byron Nelson. The three tied after 18 holes (at 72), and Mangrum edged Ghezzi and Nelson in the second 18 (72-73-73).

Lloyd Mangrum

Ben Hogan

Hogan Rolls to an Easy Win in PGA

Ben Hogan choked away both the Masters and the U.S. Open in 1946, but he wouldn't be denied in the PGA Championship. At Portland G.C. in Oregon, Hogan walloped future Hall of Famer Jimmy Demaret in the semis, 10 & 9, then buried Ed "Porky" Oliver in the final, 6 & 4.

• September 28: Babe Zaharias wins the U.S. Women's Amateur at Southern Hills C.C. in Tulsa, Oklahoma, defeating Clara Sherman in the final, 11 & 9.

• September 29: Ben Hogan shoots 284 and wins the Dallas Open. Hogan had predicted that a 284 would be the winning score.

• December: Patty Berg leads the Women's Professional Golf Association Tour with four victories on the year.

• December: Ben Hogan leads the PGA Tour with 13 victories, second only to Byron Nelson's 18 wins in 1945.

• December: Ben Hogan is the PGA Tour's leading money winner with $42,556.16. His total is nearly double that of Herman Barron, who is second with $23,003.

• December: Byron Nelson, who won six tournaments during the season, announces his retirement. He is 34 years old.

SOUTH AFRICAN LOCKE CLEANS UP ON PGA TOUR

Bobby Locke of South Africa made a name for himself in the winter of 1946–47, when he defeated Sam Snead in 12 of 16 matches during a tour of South Africa. Thoroughly impressed, Snead told Locke to come to America and give the PGA Tour a try. Locke took the advice, and in 1947 he stood the PGA Tour on its ear.

Arthur D'Arcy Locke arrived in the United States in April of '47. His ample features and unchanging expression prompted the American pros to dub him Muffin Face, an altogether uncomplimentary nickname perhaps spurred by Locke's raids on their prize money. Locke gave the pros reason to remember him: In 1947, he won six Tour events and finished second twice.

Locke's success in the United States won him few friends. Players moaned about his pace, which was slow and deliberate. Locke, dressed in his trademark plus fours, white shoes, and stockings, sailed slowly down the fairway, stately as a great clipper ship. His style of play, while somewhat eccentric, was world-class. Locke was history's premier putter. Using a method he picked up from Walter Hagen, he took the putter back on the inside. But the blade, hooded for more overspin, was always square. Combined with a superior ability to read greens, Locke's putting was deadly.

Locke's goal was to always keep the ball in play. To this end, he drove mostly with a brassie. Locke's swing was unorthodox, at best. Allowing for the right-to-left shot he preferred, he aligned his stance far to the right, then hit shots that climbed out over the right rough and curved back to the fairway in a huge hook. "His critics, and in their envy there were many," wrote Pat Ward-Thomas, "used to deride his method of hitting the ball."

But how he could play! In 1947, Locke won the Houston Open and the Canadian Open. By the end of the year, he had added the Philadelphia Inquirer Open, the All-American Open, the Columbus Open, and the Goodall Round-Robin to his list of victories. He also won an unofficial event, the Carolinas Open, which gave him four wins in a five-week period. In 1947's official earnings, he was barely edged by Jimmy Demaret.

Locke returned to the PGA Tour in 1948 and won the Chicago Victory National Championship by 16 strokes, a new record margin on the Tour. In 1949, he won the Goodall Round-Robin a week after Tour officials announced he wouldn't be invited to play in the PGA Championship because he was neither a PGA member nor a "guest player." Locke was understandably more comfortable in Europe, and his favorite championship was the British Open. He would go on to win the event in 1949, 1950, 1952, and—at age 40—1957. Three years later, Locke was seriously injured in an auto accident and never again returned to his old form.

1947

- January: PGA Tour players will compete in 31 events with a total season purse of $352,500.

- January 6: Ben Hogan shoots 280 to win the Los Angeles Open.

- January 10: The Bing Crosby Pro-Am moves to California's Monterey Peninsula, and is held at Cypress Point C.C., Monterey Peninsula C.C., and Pebble Beach G.L.

- January 12: Ed Furgol and George Fazio tie for first and are declared co-winners of the Bing Crosby Pro-Am, the first since the war.

- January 26: Ben Hogan sets a tournament record when he shoots 270 to win the Phoenix Open for the second straight time.

- February 2: Jimmy Demaret wins his second straight Tucson Open with a 264, a tournament record.

- March: Babe Zaharias, still an amateur, wins the Titleholders Championship.

1947

South African Bobby Locke invaded the U.S. PGA Tour in 1947 and nearly broke the bank. Locke *(left)*, shaking hands with runner-up Porky Oliver, won the Canadian Open and picked up five other titles on the American circuit that year. While Oliver looks gracious enough, many American pros resented Locke's success in the U.S.

• March 1: The USGA revises and simplifies the Rules of Golf, cutting the number of rules from 61 to 21. The R&A fails to join the effort.

• April 6: Jimmy Demaret, on top after all four rounds, becomes the third two-time winner of the Masters. Byron Nelson and amateur Frank Stranahan tie for second.

• May 11: Bobby Locke bursts into the winner's circle at the Houston Open. It's his first of six official victories on the 1947 PGA Tour.

• May 15: The Walker Cup Match, originally scheduled in the U.S., begins tomorrow at St. Andrews, Scotland, because travel is too difficult for a post-war British team.

• May 17: For the first time in 11 years, the United States wins the Walker Cup, 8-4. Joe Carr marks the first of a record 10 appearances on the British side.

• May 18: Ben Hogan wins the Colonial NIT by shooting 279, the same score with which he won in 1946.

Ed Furgol, George Fazio, Peter Hay

Furgol, Fazio Split the Dough at Crosby Pro-Am

Ed Furgol *(left)* and George Fazio *(center)* receive identical prize checks from Peter Hay, after they tied for first in the Bing Crosby Pro-Am and were declared co-winners. Despite a withered left arm, Furgol would go on to win the 1954 U.S. Open. Fazio would become one of the world's finest golf course architects.

Jimmy Demaret, Byron Nelson

Palmer Sets the Western Open Scoring Record

Johnny Palmer

Little-known Johnny Palmer startled the world of golf when he won the prestigious Western Open in 1947 at the Salt Lake City C.C. Not only that, but Palmer's 270 for 72 holes set a new tournament record. The native of Bodine, North Carolina, had been a gunner on a B-29 in World War II.

Demaret Beats Out Nelson for Second Masters Win

Tied for the first-round lead at the 1947 Masters, Jimmy Demaret *(left)* and Byron Nelson check their scorecards. Demaret led or was tied for the lead after every round and went on to become the third two-time winner of the event. Nelson and amateur Frank Stranahan tied for second.

• June: Babe Zaharias becomes the first American to win the British Ladies' Open Amateur when she defeats Jacqueline Gordon, 4 & 2, in the final at Gullane, Scotland.

• June 14: The U.S. Open at St. Louis C.C. becomes the first U.S. Open to be televised locally.

• June 14: Amateur James McHale Jr. sets a U.S. Open scoring record of 65 in the third round at St. Louis C.C., though he'll tie for 23rd at the end of the championship.

• June 14: Sam Snead makes an 18-foot birdie putt on the final hole to tie Lew Worsham for the U.S. Open championship.

• June 15: In the 18-hole playoff for the U.S. Open, Lew Worsham halts play to ask for a measurement as Sam Snead addresses a short putt on the final hole. Snead misses. Lew makes his putt and wins, 69-70.

• June 24: Australian-born Jim Ferrier beats Chick Harbert, 2 & 1,

1947

St. Louis Country Club

St. Louis C.C. Plays Host to U.S. Open Championship

The 17th was one of the most picturesque holes at the St. Louis C.C., site of the 1947 U.S. Open. The course was designed by Charles Blair Macdonald, a reknowned architect from 1893 through 1926. Macdonald never accepted a fee for his design work. The '47 U.S. Open was the first Open to be televised locally.

Lew Worsham, Sam Snead

Daly Wins British; Few Americans Compete

Despite a third round of 78, 35-year-old Irishman Fred Daly won the 1947 British Open at Hoylake. Although Sam Snead had won the British the previous year, few American pros competed in '47. Amateur Frank Stranahan of Toledo, Ohio, who was also runner-up in the 1947 Masters, finished second to Daly.

Fred Daly

Snead Doesn't Quite Measure Up in U.S. Open

Lew Worsham *(left)* checks the putter that Sam Snead used to tie him in the U.S. Open. Snead made an 18-footer on the 72nd hole. But on the last hole of the 18-hole playoff, Snead was addressing a short putt when Worsham halted play to ask for a measurement. A rattled Snead missed the putt and shot 70. Worsham won with a 69.

to win the PGA Championship at Plum Hollow C.C. near Detroit.

• June 29: In the first U.S. Women's Open conducted at stroke play, Betty Jameson's winning 295 marks the first time a woman has broken 300 for 72 holes. The event is held at Starmount Forest C.C. in Greensboro, North Carolina.

• July 4: Fred Daly wins the British Open at Hoylake, England, despite a third round of 78. American amateur Frank Stranahan finishes tied for second.

• July 19: South African Bobby Locke wins the Canadian Open at Scarborough Golf and C.C. in Toronto.

• August: Babe Zaharias, whose amateur status was revoked in 1935 by the USGA, turns pro again.

• August: Amateur Louise Suggs wins the Women's Western Open.

• September 1: Johnny Palmer wins the Western Open at Salt Lake City C.C. in Utah.

Jameson Breaks 300 in the U.S. Women's Open

Betty Jameson takes a practice swing prior to the third round of her record-breaking performance in the 1947 U.S. Women's Open. At Starmount Forest C.C. in Greensboro, North Carolina, Jameson shot 295 to win and became the first woman to break 300 for a 72-hole event. The Women's Open was played at stroke play for the first time.

Jim Ferrier

Betty Jameson

Ferrier Edges Harbert in PGA Championship

Australian Jim Ferrier urges a putt toward the cup on the 22nd hole of his final-round match in the 1947 PGA Championship, at the Plum Hollow C.C. near Detroit. Ferrier won the match by defeating Chick Harbert, 2 & 1, in 36 holes. This was the first and only major championship ever held at the rather unheralded Plum Hollow.

• September 13: The U.S. Amateur returns to an all-match-play format. Robert "Skee" Riegel defeats John Dawson, 2 & 1, in the final at the Del Monte Golf and C.C.

• September 27: Two Georgians, Louise Suggs and Dorothy Kirby, meet in the final of the U.S.

Women's Amateur at Franklin Hills C.C. in Michigan. Suggs wins, 2 up.

• September 28: Promoter George S. May adds the World Championship to his All-American Open for men and women professionals and amateurs at Tam O'Shanter C.C. in Chicago. Ben Hogan wins the new event.

• November 2: The British Ryder Cup team avoids a whitewash when Sam King wins the final singles match. The U.S. wins, 11-1, and Lew Worsham and Porky Oliver team for the largest foursomes win, 10 & 9, in Ryder Cup history.

• December: For the third straight year, Babe Zaharias is named

Skee Riegel

Overdue Riegel Crowned U.S. Amateur Champion

At the 14th hole at Pebble Beach, Skee Riegel emerges from the crowd to play his second shot in the final of the U.S. Amateur. Riegel, of Pennsylvania, defeated Johnny Dawson, 2 & 1, to win the championship. Riegel was due; in 1946, he had set a new U.S. Amateur qualifying record of 69-67—136.

Curtis Enters One More Women's Amateur

Margaret Curtis, 63, teed off in the 1947 U.S. Women's Amateur. Curtis first played in the Women's Amateur exactly 50 years earlier, at the age of 13. She won it in 1907, 1911, and 1912. With her sister Harriot, Margaret donated the Curtis Cup for competition between women amateurs from the U.S. and Great Britain/Ireland.

Margaret Curtis

Louise Suggs

Suggs Proves the Victor in U.S. Amateur

Slender Louise Suggs kisses the putter she used to win the 1947 U.S. Women's Amateur. Suggs beat Dorothy Kirby, another Atlanta amateur, 2 up, at Franklin Hills C.C. in suburban Detroit. Suggs would win the British Women's Amateur the following spring and then go on to a 35-year professional career.

Woman Athlete of the Year by the Associated Press.

• December 14: Ben Hogan leads all players on the PGA Tour with seven official victories for the year.

• December 14: Jimmy Demaret is the PGA Tour's leading money winner with $27,936.83.

• December 14: For the first time, the Vardon Trophy is awarded based on average strokes per round. Jimmy Demaret leads the Tour with an average of 69.90 strokes.

• In the first all-American final, William Turnesa defeats Dick Chapman to win the British Amateur at Carnoustie, Scotland.

• Robert E. Harlow publishes the first *Golf World*, a weekly magazine devoted to golf news, in Pinehurst, North Carolina.

• The Dunes Golf and Beach Club, designed by Robert Trent Jones, opens in Myrtle Beach, South Carolina. It's the first resort course to open after World War II.

BERG, ZAHARIAS KICK-START LPGA

The LPGA officially dates its birth to 1950, the year in which it was chartered. But the concept for the LPGA was actually worked out two years earlier at a private meeting in Miami, headed by the world's two best women golfers, Patty Berg and Babe Zaharias.

The women's pro tour, such as it was, was on shaky ground. In 1944, Hope Seignious, Betty Hicks, and Ellen Griffin had founded the women's pro circuit under the name of the Women's Professional Golf Association. The WPGA tour in those days included the Western Open, the Tampa Open, George S. May's World and All-American Championships, the Titleholders, and several smaller events. But the WPGA was floundering. Seignious had used her own money to finance the tour, with help from her father, a cotton broker, and now she was nearly broke.

By January 1948, the WPGA was only a figurehead organization. Berg and Zaharias decided something had to be done if a women's pro golf tour was to survive. They met at Miami's Venetian Hotel, inviting Babe's husband, George Zaharias, and an

astute sports promoter, Fred Corcoran, who was Babe's manager. The meeting was a sort of mutiny. Berg was the WPGA's president and Babe was its biggest star. "You have to give a lot of credit to Hope Seignious, and her dad," Berg recalled. "She had tremendous vision, but I thought that we just had to get going."

Berg and Zaharias decided to start a new women's pro golf association, and try to draft WPGA players to join them. Throughout 1948, they lobbied for a new association. By 1949, they appeared to have enough support. In May, Berg, Zaharias, Betty Jameson, Helen Dettweiler, Betty Hicks, and Betty Mims Danoff met at the Eastern Open and named Fred Corcoran

tournament manager of their new group. At another meeting at the U.S. Women's Open, Alice and Marlene Bauer, Opal Hill, Sally Sessions, Shirley Spork, Louise Suggs, and Marilynn Smith hopped on board. Berg was elected president.

Corcoran was a key to their success. He worked for the new association through the courtesy of Wilson Sporting Goods Company. Berg and Zaharias were affiliated with Wilson, which also had Corcoran on its payroll. Corcoran named the group the Ladies Professional Golf Association, and he issued a press release.

Corcoran began rounding up tournaments and enlisted several loyal sponsors to see the LPGA through its early struggling years. The association was formally chartered in 1950. Under the guidance of Corcoran and Berg, and with the outspoken input of Zaharias, the LPGA was on the road to success. By 1952, the Tour boasted a schedule of 21 events, nearly triple the tournaments offered only two years before. The LPGA would eventually become the most successful women's professional sports organization in the world.

1948

- January: PGA Tour players will compete in 34 events with a total season purse of $427,000.

- January: For the first time, the PGA Tour agrees to conduct tournaments by USGA Rules.

- January: Patty Berg, president of the Women's Professional Golf

Association, meets with Babe and George Zaharias at Miami's Venetian Hotel to plan a new women's pro tour.

- January 5: Ben Hogan wins the Los Angeles Open with a 275.

- January 18: Black professionals Ted Rhodes, Bill Spiller, and

Madison Gunter sue the PGA Tour when they're barred from entering the Richmond Open in California.

- February 1: Johnny Palmer sets a 36-hole PGA Tour scoring record with 62-64 in the Tucson Open. He'll finish second to Skip Alexander, who shoots 67-63-72-62—264.

1948

In 1948, Patty Berg *(left)* and Babe Zaharias kicked off the founding of the Ladies Professional Golf Association. Berg and Zaharias worked with sports promoter Fred Corcoran and the Wilson Sporting Goods Company to form the association, which replaced the struggling Women's Professional Golf Association.

• February 8: Sam Snead wins the Texas Open, shooting 66-65-65-68—264 and tying Skip Alexander for the year's best 72-hole score.

• March: Patty Berg wins her fourth Titleholders Championship.

• April: The famed Pinehurst resort celebrates its 50th anniversary.

• April 11: In the final round at the Masters, Claude Harmon knocks his ball out of the water fronting Augusta National's 13th green, pars, and wins with four sub-par rounds.

• May: Louise Suggs becomes the second American to win the British Ladies' Open Amateur. She then turns pro.

• May: Sam Snead wins the long-driving contest at the PGA Championship in St. Louis with a 320-yard wallop.

• May 22: The United States defeats Great Britain/Ireland, 6½-2½, in the first post-war Curtis Cup Match, in Birkdale, England.

Ben Hogan

Hogan Claims First of Four U.S. Opens

In the second round of the 1948 U.S. Open, Ben Hogan rammed home this 30-foot birdie putt on the 2nd hole at Riviera C.C. in Los Angeles. He went on to win for his first U.S. Open title. Moreover, Hogan's 72-hole total of 276 set an Open record that would stand until 1967. Hogan would win four U.S. Open titles in six years.

Bing Crosby, Walter Winchell

Locke's Hot Putter Leads to 16-Stroke Victory

Bobby Locke, perhaps golf's greatest putter, shows youngsters the instrument he used to one-putt nine greens at Chicago's Midlothian C.C. for a blistering 65 in the 1948 Chicago Victory Open. The South African won the tournament by 16 strokes—still a PGA Tour record.

Bobby Locke

Crosby Aces the Famed 16th Hole at Cypress

Bing Crosby *(left)*, shown here with Walter Winchell, made golf history in February 1948. Crosby made a hole-in-one on the 16th at Cypress Point Club—a 233-yard hole with a green surrounded by rocks and crashing ocean waves. Through 1992, Crosby remained one of just seven golfers to ever ace the famous hole.

- May 25: Ben Hogan beats Mike Turnesa, 7 & 6, in the PGA Championship at Norwood Hills C.C.

- June: San Jose State sweeps the team title, individual title, and qualifying medal at the NCAAs.

- June: Babe Zaharias wins her first U.S. Women's Open, sponsored by the Women's Professional Golf Association, at Atlantic City C.C.

- June: South African Bobby Locke wins the Chicago Victory National Championship by 16 strokes—a record margin on the PGA Tour.

- June 12: Ben Hogan returns to Riviera C.C. in Los Angeles and wins his first U.S. Open. He shoots 276, a championship record.

- June 12: Father and son Joe Kirkwood Sr. and Jr. finish 28th and 21st, respectively, in the U.S. Open.

- July: Ted Rhodes shoots a 62 and wins a first prize of $800 in the Ray Robinson Open in the Caribbean.

Henry Cotton

After 14 Years, Cotton Wins Second British Open

The elegant Henry Cotton putts on the 13th hole on his way to winning his second British Open. It was a sentimental occasion for British golf fans, as Cotton's first victory came in 1934. Cotton was one of Britain's greatest players, and in 1938 he led the Order of Merit, the ranking standard for European professionals.

Harmon Wins Masters in Record Fashion

Claude Harmon

Claude Harmon hugs his wife after shooting 209 to take the third-round lead at the 1948 Masters. The following day, Harmon hit into the creek on the 13th hole, but he played the ball out of the water to the green and got his par. Harmon won the Masters with a 279, tying the tournament record.

Zaharias Wins U.S. Open by Eight Shots

Babe Zaharias, Betty Jameson, Peggy Kirk

Babe Zaharias *(left)*, pictured with fellow leaders Betty Jameson and Peggy Kirk, went on to win her first U.S. Women's Open in 1948. She won by a record eight strokes at the Atlantic City C.C. The 1948 championship was sponsored by the Women's Professional Golf Association for the third and final time.

• July: The polio epidemic forces cancellation of the Carolinas Junior Girls' championship.

• July 2: Henry Cotton, at the age of 41, wins his third British Open, at Muirfield in Scotland.

• August: Cross-handed golfer Howard Wheeler wins his third consecutive open championship of the United Golf Association, the organization for black golfers.

• August 1: At the Western Open, Ben Hogan beats Porky Oliver by seven in an 18-hole playoff.

• August 6: Lloyd Mangrum wins the All-American Open.

• August 8: Lloyd Mangrum wins the 36-hole World Championship to collect $10,000 and sweep George S. May's two tournaments at Tam O'Shanter C.C.

• August 14: Dean Lind, age 17, defeats Ken Venturi in the final of the first U.S. Junior Amateur, which attracts 495 entries.

Gene Dahlbender, Willie Turnesa

Turnesa's the Champ as Amateur Moves South

Willie Turnesa, last year's British Amateur champ, strokes a putt on the 13th hole of his semifinal match against Gene Dahlbender in the 1948 U.S. Amateur. Turnesa won the '48 championship at Memphis C.C. This was the first time a U.S. Amateur was held at a Southern venue.

Frank Stranahan, Fred Corcoran

Corcoran Bestows High Honor on Stranahan

Although he didn't win the U.S. title in 1948, Frank Stranahan (left) dominated world amateur golf. Stranahan won the amateur titles of Britain, Canada, and Mexico. He was picked by Fred Corcoran (right), the golf promoter and editor of a golf guide, as the Amateur of the Year.

• September: In the final of the Women's Texas Open, Babe Zaharias loses to amateur Polly Riley, 10 & 9. It's Babe's largest losing margin.

• September: Black pros Ted Rhodes, Bill Spiller, and Madison Gunter drop their lawsuit against the PGA Tour after the PGA promises that no players will be barred from open events because of color.

• September 4: Willie Turnesa wins the U.S. Amateur, his second, at Memphis C.C., the championship's first Southern venue.

• September 18: Grace Lenczyk, Canadian Women's Amateur champion, wins the U.S. Women's Amateur at Del Monte Golf and C.C. in Pebble Beach, California.

• September 19: Porky Oliver wins a five-way playoff for the Tacoma Open title.

• December: Frank Stranahan, who won the amateur championships of

1948

Ken Venturi, Dean Lind

Lind Tops Venturi in First Junior Amateur

In 1948, 17-year-old Dean Lind *(right)*, of Rockford, Illinois, defeated Ken Venturi *(left)* to win the first edition of the U.S. Junior Amateur championship. Lind beat Venturi, a San Francisco junior, 4 & 2, in the final. Venturi was somewhat hampered by a sore back. The first Junior Amateur attracted 495 contestants.

Helen Sigel, Grace Lenczyk

Hogan Wins His Second PGA Title

A beaming Ben Hogan *(right)* receives the Wanamaker Trophy from PGA President Ed Dudley *(left)* after defeating Mike Turnesa, 7 & 6, to win his second PGA Championship. Later that year, Hogan would win the U.S. Open. The man with his eyes closed is Jerry Tegeler, president of the host Norwood Hills C.C. in St. Louis.

Ed Dudley, Jerry Tegeler, Ben Hogan

Lenczyk Downs Sigel in Women's Amateur

Helen Sigel *(left)* and Grace Lenczyk smile away after surviving their semifinal matches in the 1948 U.S. Women's Amateur at Pebble Beach. The two met in the 36-hole final the following day and Lenczyk outlasted Sigel, 4 & 3. The next year, Lenczyk would shoot a 66 in Western Open qualifying.

Britain, Canada, and Mexico, is named Amateur of the Year by *Golf World*.

• December: By year's end, Ben Hogan's book *Power Golf* has sold 54,000 copies.

• December 16: Ben Hogan wins the Vardon Trophy, averaging 69.30.

• December 16: Ben Hogan—whose 10 victories include the U.S. Open, the PGA Championship, and the Western Open—is leading money winner with $32,112. He is named the PGA Tour's Player of the Year.

• December 16: Lloyd Mangrum finishes with seven PGA Tour wins on the year.

• The USGA announces that women golfers are barred from playing in the men's U.S. Open after Babe Zaharias said she planned to enter the championship.

• The USGA begins publication of *Golf Journal*, which would still be in operation in the 1990s.

Golf greats Sam Snead, Byron Nelson, and Ben Hogan were all born in the same year, 1912, but in the immediate post-war years, Nelson and then Hogan were the marquee attractions—not Snead. Sammy fell to the middle of the pack in 1948, as putting problems dropped him to 18th on the money list. With Nelson now retired, Hogan was the main man entering 1949. As the year began, Ben graced the cover of *Time* magazine—the first golfer ever to do so—then proceeded to win the first two tournaments of the year. In the third, the Phoenix Open, he lost to Jimmy Demaret in a playoff.

But fate intervened. On February 2, near Van Horn, Texas, a bus collided with Hogan's car and nearly killed him. He was hospitalized with multiple injuries, and it appeared that his career was over. With Hogan facing a long recuperation, the tournament fields were wide-open. Who would step forward? Many thought it would be Demaret, Lloyd Mangrum, or South African Bobby Locke. But as it turned out, it was Sam Snead.

In March, Snead beat Mangrum in a playoff in the Greensboro

SNEAD RISES AGAIN—ALL THE WAY TO No. 1

Open and then, at Augusta, captured his first Masters in resounding fashion. One stroke behind leader Johnny Palmer as the final round began, Snead fired a magnificent 67 to win by three strokes over Mangrum and Johnny Bulla. "Eight times during the final round the countryside reverberated with the cheers of the multitudes," wrote one golf scribe, "as one of the South's favorite golfing sons rapped that ball into the hole to hit the jackpot." After the tournament, Ben Hogan telephoned Snead with congratulations. As dusk settled, Snead sat in the clubhouse telling reporters he believed he was cured of a mysterious putting ailment he called "the yips."

In May, Snead won his second major of the year, the PGA Championship at the Hermitage Golf Club in Richmond, Virginia. Again the crowd's favorite, Snead beat Johnny Palmer in the final. June brought a disappointment in the U.S. Open. Snead fired a final-round 70 at Medinah Country Club in Illinois to finish one stroke behind Cary Middlecoff. It was one of four runner-up finishes in the Open for Sam. Years later, he would speculate of his failure to win a U.S. Open: "I once figured out that if I'd shot 69 in the final round of all U.S. Opens, I would have won seven of them."

In July, Sam won the Washington Star tournament, firing a 64 in the second round. In August, he shattered the 72-hole scoring record at the Western Open, shooting 268 at Keller Golf Course in St. Paul, Minnesota, to win by four strokes. In November, he sailed through the North and South Open, winning by six.

Snead ended the year with six tournament wins, including two majors, and was the Tour's leading money winner with $31,593. He also captured the Vardon Trophy and was easily the PGA Tour's Player of the Year.

1949

- January: PGA Tour players will compete in 25 events with a total season purse of $338,200.

- January 3: Alice Bauer, the first woman to enter the L.A. Open, misses qualifying by eight shots.

- January 10: Ben Hogan graces the cover of *Time* magazine.

- January 23: Patty Berg shoots a 68, a Women's Professional Golf Association record, on her way to a one-stroke victory over Babe Zaharias in the Tampa Women's Open.

- January 24: Ben Hogan defeats Jimmy Demaret in a playoff for the Long Beach Open title.

- January 30: Jimmy Demaret defeats Ben Hogan in a playoff for the Phoenix Open title.

- February 2: Ben Hogan suffers a fractured collar bone, a fractured rib, two cracked bones in his left ankle, and two pelvis fractures when a bus collides with his automobile near Van Horn, Texas.

It's little wonder Sam Snead *(left)* grinned after the 1949 Masters Tournament. Snead made eight birdies on Sunday and shot a 67 for a three-stroke victory. The Slammer's two 67s in the final two rounds remained the best two finishing rounds in the Masters until Jack Nicklaus scored 64-69 in 1965.

• February 9: The Women's Professional Golf Association hires sports promoter Fred Corcoran as tournament manager, replacing WPGA founder Hope Seignious.

• March 3: Ben Hogan is flown to El Paso, Texas, for emergency surgery after blood clots are discovered in his abdomen and crushed left leg, but he's reported in good condition following the surgery.

• April 1: Ben Hogan returns to his home in Fort Worth, Texas, after nearly two months in the hospital and says he will try to play golf again.

• April 10: Sam Snead closes with 67-67, including eight birdies in the final round, to win the Masters by three strokes over Lloyd Mangrum.

• May 11: The PGA Tour announces that South African Bobby Locke won't be invited to the PGA Championship since Locke is neither a PGA member nor a "guest player."

Ben Hogan's Car

Hogan's Car Totaled in Near-Fatal Accident

On February 2, 1949, the driver's side of Ben Hogan's car was demolished after a collision with a bus on a fog-shrouded highway near Van Horn, Texas. The car's steering column was shoved through the driver's seat. Ben's life was probably saved when he threw himself to the right to shield his wife Valerie from the crash.

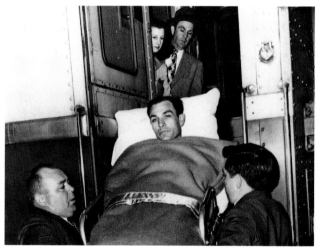

Ben Hogan

Hope Tops Crosby in Celebrity Tourney

In his day, Bob Hope had a handicap as low as five or six. One of his brightest moments came in the 1949 National Celebrities tournament in Washington, D.C., where Hope shot 74-73 to beat Bing Crosby by two strokes and win his division. Hope and Crosby are the only two entertainers in the PGA World Golf Hall of Fame.

Bob Hope

Hogan Begins the Long Road to Recovery

On April 1, 1949, Ben Hogan went home to Fort Worth, Texas, after nearly losing his life in an auto accident. Hogan's extensive injuries resulted in life-threatening surgery and a long, painful recuperation. Here, his wife Valerie and brother Royal look on as Ben's stretcher is lowered from the railroad car that brought him home.

• May 22: Joe Kirkwood Jr., "Joe Palooka" in the television series, wins the PGA Tour's Philadelphia Inquirer Invitational, firing a competitive course-record 66 in the third round.

• May 29: Tournament manager Fred Corcoran changes the name of the Women's Professional Golf Association to the Ladies Professional Golf Association.

• May 29: Patty Berg is elected LPGA president. Betty Jameson, Babe Zaharias, and several others join the new association.

• May 31: Babe Zaharias wins the Eastern Women's Open by 13 shots.

• May 31: Sam Snead wins his second major of the year by edging Johnny Palmer in the final of the PGA Championship, at Hermitage C.C. in Richmond, Virginia.

• June: Semi-retired Byron Nelson shoots 60 in an exhibition at Santa Rosa C.C. in California.

Snead Goes Home to Virginia, Wins PGA

Sam Snead escapes from an ugly lie in the 1949 PGA Championship, held at Hermitage C.C. in Virginia, Snead's home state. Snead defeated Johnny Palmer in the 36-hole final, 3 & 2. It was Snead's second win in the PGA and, after his April victory at the Masters, his second major championship of the year.

Cary Middlecoff

Sam Snead

Phew! 11 Extra Holes and Still No Winner

Cary Middlecoff dueled Lloyd Mangrum in a sudden-death playoff for the 1949 Motor City Open title. Mangrum and Middlecoff tied after regulation and went 11 extra holes before they were declared co-winners. Here, Middlecoff bends over backwards hoping for the ball to drop on the playoff's third hole, but it doesn't.

Gabriel Wilson, Joe Kirkwood Jr.

TV's Joe Palooka Prevails in Philly

Golf professional and actor Joe Kirkwood Jr. *(right)*, who played the lead in television's *Joe Palooka*, flashes a winning smile after capturing the Philadelphia Inquirer Invitational. Kirkwood won by four strokes. Whitemarsh C.C. President Gabriel Wilson hands Kirkwood a $2,600 check.

• June 5: In the National Celebrities tournament in Washington, D.C., Bob Hope shoots 74-73 to edge Bing Crosby by two strokes and win his division.

• June 11: Cary Middlecoff captures the U.S. Open at Medinah C.C. near Chicago, edging Sam Snead and Clayton Heafner by one stroke.

• June 19: Cary Middlecoff and Lloyd Mangrum, unable to break a tie after 11 holes of sudden-death, declare they are co-winners of Detroit's Motor City Open.

• June 25: Rookie pro Louise Suggs wins her third Women's Western Open.

• July 2: Nineteen-year-old Arnold Palmer of Wake Forest is medalist at the NCAA championship in Ames, Iowa.

• July 8: Bobby Locke wins the British Open at Royal St. George's in England in a playoff with Harry Bradshaw.

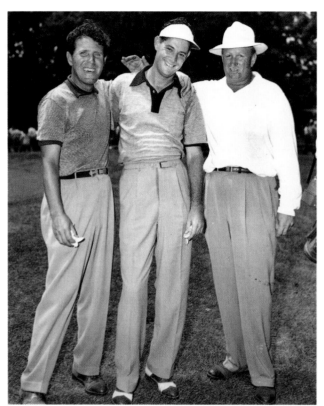

Buck White, Cary Middlecoff, Clayton Heafner

Middlecoff Wins U.S. Open Down the Stretch

At the 1949 U.S. Open at Chicago's Medinah C.C., Cary Middlecoff *(center)* and Clayton Heafner *(right)* were tied going into the final nine. Buck White *(left)* was only two strokes behind the leaders at the 63rd hole, but Middlecoff prevailed and won by one stroke over Heafner and Sam Snead. White tied for sixth.

Bauer, 15, Wins the First Girls' Junior

Marlene Bauer, a mere 15 years old in 1949, captured the trophy for the first U.S. Girls' Junior championship. Along with her sister Alice, the Los Angeles youngster turned pro later in the year and became a big attraction on the LPGA Tour.

Marlene Bauer

Rufus King, Charles Coe, Fielding Wallace

Coe Clobbers King for U.S. Amateur Title

Charles Coe *(center)* accepts the trophy from USGA President Fielding Wallace at the 1949 U.S. Amateur at Oak Hill C.C. in Rochester, New York. The lanky Coe beat top amateurs Bob Sweeney, Harvie Ward, and Bill Campbell on his way to the final. In that 36-hole match, Coe trounced Rufus King *(left)*, 11 & 10.

• **August:** Johnny Palmer wins George S. May's World Championship and Lloyd Mangrum wins the All-American. Babe Zaharias and Louise Suggs win the respective women's events.

• **August 19:** Marlene Bauer, 15, wins the inaugural U.S. Girls' Junior championship, at Philadelphia C.C.

• **August 20:** The U.S. Walker Cup team defeats Great Britain/Ireland, 10-2, at Winged Foot G.C. in New York.

• **September 3:** Charles Coe, a 25-year-old insurance broker, defeats Rufus King, 11 & 10, to win the U.S. Amateur at Oak Hill C.C. in Rochester, New York.

• **September 4:** Tom Watson, winner of five British Opens, is born in Kansas City, Missouri.

• **September 17:** The Ryder Cup Match is played without U.S. Open winner Cary Middlecoff or British Open champ Bobby Locke, who were ineligible. The U.S. wins, 7-5, at Ganton G.C. in England.

1949

D. Roddick, Bobby Locke

Locke Claims First of Four British Titles

Bobby Locke (right) began his reign as British Open champion by receiving the cup and a check from D. Roddick, captain of Royal St. George's G.C. To win, the South African beat Irishman Harry Bradshaw by 12 strokes in a 36-hole playoff. Locke would win three more British Open championships over the next eight years.

Top LPGA Stars

Babe, Berg, and Suggs Monkey Around

Babe Zaharias (top) clowns around with Patty Berg (far left), Louise Suggs (far right), and Betty Mims Danoff. All but Danoff were multiple winners in 1949, with Suggs winning both the U.S. Women's Open and the Western Open. With the LPGA about to begin in 1950, these were indeed joyous days for the women stars.

Teenage Palmer Makes His Mark at NCAAs

Arnold Palmer, age 19, blasts from the bunker during a U.S. Amateur practice round at Oak Hill C.C. in Rochester, New York. Young Palmer was beginning to make his presence felt. The Wake Forest student had been medalist at the NCAA championship in the summer.

Arnold Palmer

• September 25: Louise Suggs wins the LPGA-sponsored U.S. Women's Open by a record 14-stroke margin over runner-up Babe Zaharias at Prince George's Golf and C.C. in Landover, Maryland.

• October 5: Sports writer Robert Ruark interviews the ailing Bobby Jones and reports that Jones's rare spinal ailment will keep him from playing golf again.

• October 22: Patty Berg wins the Hardscrabble Open. She defeats Marlene Bauer, 15, who beat Babe Zaharias in the semifinals.

• December 12: Ben Hogan says he is playing Colonial C.C. in Fort Worth, Texas, using a motorized golf cart.

• December 18: Sam Snead leads the Tour in earnings with $31,593.83 and wins the Vardon Trophy with a scoring average of 69.37. Snead ties Cary Middlecoff with six wins and is named the PGA Tour's Player of the Year.

HOGAN WINS U.S. OPEN IN MIRACULOUS COMEBACK

Less than a year after a near-fatal head-on car crash, Ben Hogan was back in the thick of the battle. Just 10 months before, doctors had hesitated to predict whether he would survive the injuries he suffered when a bus collided with his car. His left leg was crushed, and his collar bone, pelvis, and a rib were fractured. In March, he underwent emergency surgery to remove life-threatening blood clots. Two months later, he began a long, painful recuperation.

By December, Hogan was attempting to play Fort Worth's Colonial Country Club using a motorized golf cart. Despite reports that Hogan had shot rounds of 70 and 71, he refused to verify the scores. Still, fans were amazed when he entered the L.A. Open at Riviera Country Club in January. More than 9,000 fans showed up the first day, most of whom doubted Hogan could even walk 72 holes. But an unsteady 73 was followed by three sizzling rounds of 69 and, incredibly, Hogan led the tournament.

When Sam Snead birdied the final two holes, the two men were tied. The outcome of the 18-hole playoff was predictable. Although

Hogan used a shooting stick to rest his legs, his weary body couldn't rally for another great round. Snead won, 72-76. Hogan also challenged in the Masters before a final-round 76. Amazingly, he proved the victor in the Greenbrier Pro-Am, and he was primed to do the same at the U.S. Open at Merion.

After studying the Merion course meticulously, Hogan opened with rounds of 72-69, good for a tie for fifth. Each night, Ben unwrapped the bandages that stretched from his ankles to his thighs and soaked in a tub of hot water. Saturday, he would have to play 36 holes.

Hogan shot a 72 in the morning, putting him two strokes

behind leader Lloyd Mangrum. One round to play. Playing ahead, Mangrum shot 76 to tie George Fazio at 287. Hogan was three strokes ahead, but his legs throbbed in pain and his caddie had to pick his ball out of the hole. Hitting his tee shot at the 12th, he nearly fell. He staggered toward Harry Radix, a friend standing nearby. "Let me hang on to you, Harry," he gasped. "My God, I don't think I can finish."

With 13,000 fans swarming around him, progress was slow. Hogan three-putted the 12th and 15th and bogied the 17th. He had fallen back into a tie. On the second shot of the final hole, he pulled out a 1-iron and hit one of the most famous shots in golf. With his familiar, precise swing, Hogan hit a low, boring shot that climbed to the top of a perfect arc and settled safely on the green, 40 feet from the hole. In agony, he two-putted for a tie.

He had already accomplished a miracle, but the following day Hogan provided a fairy-tale ending, shooting 69 to Mangrum's 73 and Fazio's 75. After nearly losing his life, Ben Hogan had beaten the odds to win his second U.S. Open.

1950

- January: PGA Tour players will compete in 33 events with a total season purse of $459,950.

- January: In the LPGA Tour's first season, players will compete in nine events with a total purse of $50,000.

- January 8: On wobbly legs, Ben Hogan ties Sam Snead for the L.A.

Open title. It's his first tournament since a near-fatal accident 11 months ago.

- January 16: Sam Snead beats Ben Hogan in an 18-hole playoff, 72-76, for the Los Angeles Open title. The playoff was postponed a week because of rain.

- January 22: Amateur Polly Riley stuns women professionals by winning the Tampa Open, the first-ever LPGA Tour event.

- February: A poll of Associated Press sports editors names Bobby Jones as the greatest golfer of the first half of the 20th Century.

Incredibly, Ben Hogan was back. Just a year after an automobile accident nearly took his life, Hogan was in a playoff with Sam Snead for the 1950 Los Angeles Open title. Hogan found tree trouble here on the 5th hole and bogied, but his presence in the playoff was considered nothing short of a miracle.

• February 12: Sam Snead cards successive 63s, smashing the PGA Tour record for the final 36 holes, and wins the Texas Open by a single stroke over Jimmy Demaret.

• March 19: After lessons from Tommy Armour, Babe Zaharias wins the Titleholders by eight strokes.

• April 1: The Associated Press says Jimmy Demaret, Ben Hogan, Cary Middlecoff, and Sam Snead are among 11 pros organizing as the Professional Golf Players Division of the PGA, which seeks to operate the Tour.

• April 8: Jimmy Demaret, Sam Snead, Ben Hogan, and eight other pros drop efforts to organize as a separate Tour players division and settle for four seats on the PGA's tournament committee.

• April 9: Jimmy Demaret becomes the first three-time winner of the Masters. Though four strokes behind Jim Ferrier entering the final round, he wins with a closing 69.

Sam Snead, Ben Hogan

Hogan Forced to Rest His Weary Legs

A fatigued Ben Hogan *(right)* was forced to rest on a shooting stick in his Los Angeles Open playoff battle with Sam Snead. Hogan's legs, severely injured in a highway crash the previous year, couldn't stand the strain of his fifth straight competitive round. Snead won the playoff, 72-76.

Ed Furgol

Bauer and Bauer Big Hits on LPGA Tour

The Bauer sisters were the first glamour girls of the budding LPGA Tour. Alice *(left)*, 18, and Marlene, 15, were the LPGA's youngest players when they turned pro in 1950. Earlier in the year, Marlene beat Alice in the final of the Palm Beach Championship on the women's winter amateur year.

Alice and Marlene Bauer

Furgol Challenges on Tour, Despite Bad Arm

Ed Furgol took the first-round lead in the 1950 Houston Open with a score of 66, and he eventually finished tied for eighth. Furgol, whose left elbow was shattered and left arm permanently crooked in a playground accident when he was 12, perfected his own swing to conquer the handicap. He would win the U.S. Open in 1954.

• May 7: Ben Hogan ties Byron Nelson's 72-hole scoring record on a par-70 course when he wins the Greenbrier Spring Festival at White Sulphur Springs, West Virginia. He shoots 64-64-65-66—259.

• May 18: Bobby Jones undergoes a life-threatening spinal operation in Boston.

• May 22: American Frank Stranahan wins his second British Amateur championship by defeating a match-play field that included singer Bing Crosby, who lost in the first round.

• May 28: Sam Snead wins the Colonial NIT a week after taking the Western Open.

• June 8: Lee Mackey, an unknown ex-Army private from Birmingham, Alabama, shoots a tournament-record 64 on Merion's East Course for the first-round lead in the U.S. Open, but he'll balloon to 81 in the second round.

• June 10: A weary Ben Hogan fires 72-74 over the final 36 holes and

Jack Harden

Harden Shoots a Record 62 in Los Angeles Open

Little-known Jack Harden had his moment of glory at the 1950 Los Angeles Open, at Riviera C.C. Harden fired an opening 62 to set a new single-round scoring record on the PGA Tour. However, reality set in and Harden ballooned to 77 in the next round. He finished 70-68 to tie for 14th.

Amateur Riley Wins the First-Ever LPGA Event

Polly Riley of Fort Worth, Texas, stunned women touring pros by winning the 1950 Tampa Women's Open. The Tampa Open, the first official event of the new Ladies Professional Golf Association, was designed to showcase the women pros. Riley was an amateur. She added insult to injury by shooting 295, tying the tournament record.

Polly Riley

---

ties Lloyd Mangrum and George Fazio for first place in the U.S. Open.

• June 11: Ben Hogan fires a 69 in a playoff with Lloyd Mangrum (73) and George Fazio (75) to win his second U.S. Open, just 16 months after his near-fatal automobile accident.

• June 12: Ben Hogan says he won't play the upcoming PGA Championship because its match-play format calls for seven straight days of play.

• June 27: Chandler Harper of Portsmouth, Virginia, wins the PGA Championship with a final-match victory over Henry Williams Jr., at Scioto C.C. in Columbus, Ohio.

• July 7: Bobby Locke wins his second consecutive British Open championship, at Troon, Scotland. Locke sets the tournament record with a 279 total.

• August: Babe Zaharias wins the women's All-American and World Championships at George S. May's annual golf festival near Chicago.

Bobby Locke

Locke Repeats as British Open Champion

South African Bobby Locke, refreshed after his raids on U.S. PGA Tour prize money, won his second consecutive British Open in 1950. Locke, shown here driving, shot a 279 at Troon G.C. in Scotland to defeat Roberto De Vicenzo by two strokes. Locke broke the British Open record by four shots.

Jimmy Demaret

Friends Mob Urzetta, the Amateur Champ

Sam Urzetta, the pride of East Rochester, New York, was mobbed by friends when he arrived home after winning the 1950 U.S. Amateur. The final was a classic David and Goliath match-up. Urzetta, a former caddie, defeated Frank Stranahan, a wealthy two-time Walker Cup player, 1 up in 39 holes, at Minneapolis G.C.

Sam Urzetta

Demaret Becomes First to Win Three Masters

In 1950, Jaunty Jimmy Demaret became the first three-time champion in Masters history when he closed with a 69. Demaret's hot finish enabled him to vault from four strokes behind Jim Ferrier to take the title. Also in 1950, Demaret appeared in the Ben Hogan movie *Follow the Sun,* which would be released in March 1951.

• August: Henry Ransom wins George S. May's men's World title and Bobby Locke wins the men's All-American.

• August 26: Sam Urzetta of East Rochester, New York, defeats Frank Stranahan, 1 up, 39 holes, in the final of the U.S. Amateur at the Minneapolis G.C.

• September 5: The United States defeats Great Britain/Ireland, 7½-1½, to win the Curtis Cup at the C.C. of Buffalo in Williamsville, New York.

• September 24: Skip Alexander, fourth in today's Kansas City Open, is the lone survivor of a plane crash near Evansville, Indiana. He's in

critical condition with third-degree burns and a broken leg.

• October 1: Babe Zaharias ties the U.S. Women's Open scoring record of 291 to win her second Women's Open, at Rolling Hills C.C. in Wichita, Kansas. She wins by nine strokes over runner-up Betsy Rawls, an amateur.

Chandler Harper

Harper Hacks Out of Trouble to Win PGA Title

In the final of the 1950 PGA Championship, Chandler Harper managed to extricate his ball from this shrubbery on the 13th hole at Scioto C.C. in Columbus, Ohio. Harper scrambled for a 5, halving the hole with Henry Williams Jr., his opponent. Harper became PGA Champion when he won the match, 4 & 3.

Alexander Badly Injured in Plane Crash

Skip Alexander, a member of the 1949 U.S. Ryder Cup team, had just picked up a fourth-place finish in the 1950 Kansas City Open when he boarded a private plane. The plane crashed near Evansville, Indiana, and Alexander was critically injured with third-degree burns and a broken leg.

Skip Alexander

Babe Zaharias

Babe Receives A.P.'s Top Honor— Once Again

Babe Zaharias was named 1950's Woman Athlete of the Year by the Associated Press after winning all three majors: the Titleholders, Western Open, and U.S. Women's Open. Zaharias was also the LPGA's leading money winner with $14,800. It was the fifth of six times A.P. bestowed the honor upon her.

• October 1: Babe Zaharias is the LPGA's leading money winner with $14,800 for the year.

• October 22: Marvin "Bud" Worsham, 20, brother of professional Lew Worsham and Wake Forest golf teammate of Arnold Palmer, dies in an auto accident in North Carolina.

• November 1: A poll of sports writers makes U.S. Open champion Ben Hogan the overwhelming choice as the PGA Tour's Player of the Year.

• November 3: Four professionals— Mike Turnesa, Steve Doctor, Harry Dee, and Art Doering—make holes-in-one during the North and South

Open, a PGA Tour event in Pinehurst, North Carolina. Sam Snead wins.

• December 17: Sam Snead wins the Vardon Trophy with an average of 69.23, and he's leading money winner with $35,758.83. His 11 victories also lead the circuit.

HOGAN BRINGS THE MONSTER TO ITS KNEES

When the script was completed for *Follow the Sun*, the movie about Ben Hogan's comeback, the story was far from over. The film, starring Glenn Ford and Anne Baxter—and featuring Sam Snead, Jimmy Demaret, and Cary Middlecoff—premiered in Hogan's hometown of Fort Worth, Texas, on March 23, 1951. Recounting Hogan's struggle to become a great player, his near death in a horrifying automobile accident, and his courageous comeback, *Follow the Sun* is one of the most famous golf movies ever made.

Some of Hogan's greatest victories, however, were just ahead, including two in 1951. Hogan, still playing on damaged legs, was forced to limit his play to events he particularly liked as well as major championships. One event he would never play again, though, was the PGA Championship, since his legs could not stand the strain of repeated 36-hole days.

Hogan's first major championship of 1951 was the Masters, where he had a strong record. Since 1939, he had never finished out of the top 10 and twice finished second. This year, Hogan

fired rounds of 70-72-70, putting him one stroke behind Skee Riegel. He then fired a masterful 68 to Riegel's 71, and by two strokes captured the first of two Masters victories. The win, coupled with his 1950 U.S. Open title, signaled that Hogan had clearly returned to his championship form of old.

The 1951 U.S. Open was to be played at Oakland Hills Country Club near Detroit, which recently had been renovated by architect Robert Trent Jones, who turned the track into a terror. The course, now a par-70, demanded defensive golf and Hogan, for one, didn't like the changes. Believing that Jones's more narrow fairways made driving for position nearly impossible, Hogan looked for safe shots. Playing conservatively, he

opened with a 76, followed by a 73, and was five strokes off Bobby Locke's lead after 36 holes.

Soaking his legs that night, Hogan decided to change to an attack strategy. The next morning, he fired a 71 for 220, two strokes behind Locke and Jimmy Demaret. On the 1st tee for the afternoon round, he grimly told Ike Grainger, the referee, "I'm going to burn it up." His front nine was, instead, lukewarm: even-par 35. But birdies at the 10th, 13th, and 15th (and a bogey at 14) put him 2-under-par through 17 holes. Again, Hogan had attracted a huge crowd, and nearly 18,000 people stampeded the course.

As the other players fell back, Hogan believed a par-4 on the final hole would win by a stroke. With the gallery surrounding the 18th, Hogan lashed a perfect drive over fairway bunkers, then floated a 6-iron to within 15 feet of the hole. His putt trickled downhill and into the hole for a birdie. Playing in near anger, Hogan had closed with a 67, the low round of the tournament, and won his third U.S. Open. "I'm glad," he said, "that I brought this course, this monster, to its knees."

1951

- January: PGA Tour players will compete in 30 events with a total season purse of $460,200.

- January: LPGA Tour players will compete in 14 events with a total purse of $70,000.

- January 8: Marlene Bauer, a 16-year-old professional, is runner-up

to Babe Zaharias in the first LPGA event of the year, the Ponte Vedra Beach Women's Open.

- January 14: Semi-retired Byron Nelson wins the Bing Crosby Pro-Am at Pebble Beach.

- February 10: Al Brosch breaks the 18-hole PGA Tour record by one

stroke. He fires a 60 on the Brackenridge Park course in San Antonio in the third round of the Texas Open.

- February 15: PGA Tour stars jump ship. They skip the Tour's Rio Grande Valley Open in Harlingen, Texas, to play in the Mexican Open for hefty guarantees.

1951

Ben Hogan *(left)* poses with Anne Baxter and Glenn Ford, stars of *Follow the Sun,* the film version of Hogan's life. Ford played the part of Hogan. It was a heck of a year for Ben in 1951. First, the movie premiered in Hogan's hometown of Fort Worth, Texas, and then he won both the Masters and the U.S. Open.

• March: The No. 4 Course at Pinehurst, North Carolina, opens with a dedication ceremony.

• March 17: At Augusta C.C., the first Women's Golf Hall of Fame inducts Beatrix Hoyt, Margaret Curtis, Alexa Stirling Fraser, Dorothy Campbell Hurd, Glenna Collett Vare, and Virginia Van Wie.

• March 18: Amateur Pat O'Sullivan wins the Titleholders Championship.

• March 19: Jim Ferrier wins the Jacksonville Open by 11 strokes at Hyde Park C.C. It's his third victory in a row.

• March 23: *Follow the Sun,* a movie of Ben Hogan's life starring Glenn Ford and Anne Baxter, premieres in Fort Worth, Texas, Hogan's hometown.

• March 30: Amateur Jerome D. Travers, 64, who was 1915 U.S. Open champion and a four-time winner of the U.S. Amateur, dies a pauper. In 1938, he raffled off a mashie to feed his wife and children.

Pat O'Sullivan

Unknown O'Sullivan Wins Titleholders Championship

Pat O'Sullivan, a relatively obscure amateur from Race Brook, Connecticut, beat a field of pros and top amateurs to win the prestigious Titleholders Championship in 1951. O'Sullivan, who had never been in the national spotlight, made the Curtis Cup team the following year.

Brosch Becomes the First on Tour to Shoot 60

Few knew his name, but Al Brosch fired one of the lowest rounds in PGA Tour history in 1951. Brosch broke the Tour's 18-hole record by one stroke when he shot a 60 in the third round of the Texas Open, on the Brackenridge Park course in San Antonio. He finished fourth in the event.

Al Brosch

• April 6: Patty Berg, Babe Zaharias, Louise Suggs, and Betty Jameson are inducted into the Women's Golf Hall of Fame, which will become the LPGA Hall of Fame.

• April 8: Third-round co-leader Sam Snead balloons to an 80 in the final round and Ben Hogan fires a 68 to win his first Masters title.

Tournament officials say the gallery is the largest in Augusta National G.C. history.

• April 15: After opening with an 83, Babe Zaharias fires a women's course record of 66 at Lakewood C.C. to win a Weathervane tournament in Dallas.

• May 12: In the Walker Cup Match at Royal Birkdale, England, three foursomes matches are decided on the final hole, but the United States eases past Great Britain, 6-3.

• May 26: Dick Chapman, 1940 U.S. Amateur champion, wins the British Amateur on his 15th try, at Royal Porthcawl in Wales.

1951

Masters Tournament

Patty Berg, Betty Jameson

Four Stars Enter New Hall of Fame

Patty Berg *(left)* and Betty Jameson *(right)*, along with Babe Zaharias and Louise Suggs, were inducted into the new Women's Golf Hall of Fame at Augusta C.C. The hall included pros and amateurs named by a selection committee. The pros eventually became members of the LPGA Hall of Fame.

Record Number of Fans Flock to See Masters

The largest gallery in Masters history, inspired by the heroics of Ben Hogan's comeback and the film version of his life, trailed Hogan throughout the 1951 tournament at Augusta National G.C. Hogan *(right center)* rewarded the gallery by lofting this 35-yard chip to within eight inches of the cup on the 72nd hole.

Ferrier Racks Up Three Wins in the Month of March

Jim Ferrier's 1951 season got off to a bang when he won three straight PGA Tour tournaments. Ferrier won the St. Petersburg Open on March 4, the Miami Open on March 11, and the Jacksonville Open by 11 strokes on March 19. Ferrier, an Australian who had moved to San Francisco, was the 1947 PGA Champion.

Jim Ferrier

• June 16: Ben Hogan tames Detroit's Oakland Hills C.C., the course he dubs "The Monster." In Saturday's double round, he shoots 71-67 to vault over 15 players and win his third U.S. Open.

• June 17: Patty Berg nips Babe Zaharias by one stroke, 146-147, to win a 36-hole playoff for the LPGA's Weathervane title, in White Plains, New York.

• July 6: With no top American pros in the field, the British Open at Royal Portrush, Ireland, is won by England's Max Faulkner.

• July 28: Lloyd Mangrum shoots a third-round 62 to take a four-stroke lead in the St. Paul Open. He receives a midnight telephone call advising that, if he wins, he won't leave town alive.

• July 29: Lloyd Mangrum, under police protection after receiving death threats, shoots a final-round 70 and wins the St. Paul Open by one stroke.

Detroit Turns 250; Hogan Wins the U.S. Open

Ben Hogan, after winning the 1951 U.S. Open at Oakland Hills C.C. near Detroit, cuts into a cake commemorating Detroit's 250th birthday. Hogan's dramatic finish of 71-67 on the brutal course allowed him to vault over 15 players to win. USGA President James Standish and club official Spike Briggs watch Hogan cut the cake.

Ben Hogan, James Standish, Spike Briggs

Ben Hogan

Hogan Closes with a 68 to Win Masters

Surrounded by admirers—and at least two photographers—Ben Hogan chips to the 7th green during the third round of the 1951 Masters. While he bogied the hole, it was one of Hogan's few miscues. On Sunday, while Sam Snead ballooned to an 80, Ben fired a 68 for a winning score of 280.

- August 3: Jim Frisina, an amateur from Taylorville, Illinois, beats out Ben Hogan and Byron Nelson to win the 36-hole Decatur Invitation.

- August 12: Ben Hogan wins golf's top prize of $12,500 when he shoots a final-round 66 to win George S. May's World Championship.

- August 12: Babe Zaharias, who won George S. May's All-American title by 10 strokes, wins May's World Championship by six strokes for $3,100 in prize money.

- August 19: Skip Alexander, badly burned in a plane crash last September, returns to action in the Sioux City Open. He ties for 27th.

- August 20: Dorothy Kirby wins the U.S. Women's Amateur championship at the Town and Country Club in St. Paul.

- September 15: Billy Maxwell wins the U.S. Amateur at Saucon Valley C.C. in Bethlehem, Pennsylvania. Tommy Jacobs, 16, makes it to the semifinals.

U.S. Women's Open Competitors

Betsy Rawls

Rawls Hangs Onto Lead at U.S. Open

Rookie professional Betsy Rawls got off to a hot start in the 1951 U.S. Women's Open, as she proudly points out. She fired 73-71—144 at Atlanta's Druid Hills G.C. and led by four strokes after 36 holes. Rawls finished at 293 for a five-stroke victory, giving her the first of her four U.S. Women's Open titles.

Top Women Pros Hope to Knock Off Zaharias

The nation's best women golfers gathered at Druid Hills G.C. in Atlanta to vie for the 1951 U.S. Women's Open title. Strolling down the fairway are *(left to right)* Pat Lesser, Helen Dettweiler, Pat Garner, Betsy Rawls, Beverly Hanson, and Pat Grant. All hoped to dethrone Babe Zaharias.

Maxwell the Best of 1,416 in U.S. Amateur

Billy Maxwell *(right)* was a student at North Texas State College when he cut through a record field of 1,416 competitors to win the 1951 U.S. Amateur. Maxwell, comparing scores with third-round victim Bo Wininger, beat lawyer Joseph Gagliardi, 4 & 3, in the final at Saucon Valley C.C. in Bethlehem, Pennsylvania.

Bo Wininger, Billy Maxwell

- September 16: Rookie Betsy Rawls wins her first U.S. Women's Open, at Druid Hills G.C. in Atlanta.

- September 16: Babe Zaharias is the LPGA Tour's leading money winner with $15,087.50.

- November 4: The U.S. Ryder Cup team breezes past Great Britain/ Ireland, 9½-2½, on the No. 2 Course at Pinehurst, North Carolina. Skip Alexander, injured in a plane crash last year, wins his singles match.

- December 14: The USGA and the R&A announce that the stymie rule goes out of effect January 1, 1952.

- December 16: Lloyd Mangrum tops the PGA Tour with $26,088.83. He also wins the Vardon Trophy with a 70.05 scoring average.

- December 16: Cary Middlecoff leads the PGA Tour with six wins. Ben Hogan is Player of the Year.

- *Golf Digest* begins publication.

EISENHOWER TAKES OFFICE, THEN TEES IT UP

In 1952, American golf gained a champion when a new man was elected to the White House—U.S. President Dwight D. Eisenhower. Eisenhower, elected in November 1952, did as much as Ben Hogan to popularize the game. The president relished golf and played at every opportunity. In Washington, he'd dash out to Burning Tree for a quick round. In summer, Ike's vacations were largely spent on the courses around Denver. Even the so-called "Little White House" was a cottage near the practice green of Augusta National Golf Club.

After his election, Ike vacationed at Augusta National, where he was a member. The club offered privacy and serenity, and its famous founder, Bob Jones, was one of Ike's close friends. In fact, Jones—a former lieutenant colonel in the Ninth Air Force who saw action under Eisenhower—had strongly influenced Eisenhower to accept the Republican presidential nomination. During Ike's campaign, Jones was a member of Georgia Democrats for Eisenhower and appeared on his behalf at a number of campaign rallies.

Ike was only an average golfer. Hampered by an old West Point football injury to his left knee, he was unable to fully shift his weight to his left side during his downswing. But he never stopped trying. Over the years, he took lessons from several favored instructors, including Arnold Palmer (who would become a good friend) and Ed Dudley, Augusta National's pro.

"Ike goes about his game determinedly," said Dudley. "He addresses the ball carefully, then whams away with all he's got on those tee shots. You can tell pretty well what sort of a job a fellow will do in his work from the way he goes about his golf. And I've never seen a man who works harder than General Eisenhower at golf."

It was big news in golf publications when Eisenhower played well, and his round of 87 in the company of Byron Nelson was duly reported. When Ike shot an 84 at Augusta National, it made headlines. Not long after Eisenhower took office, the USGA constructed a putting green for him at the White House.

Many U.S. presidents have been golfers—Harding, Wilson, Taft, Kennedy, Nixon, Ford, Bush, and Clinton—but it was Eisenhower's powerful, outgoing personality that drew new fans to the sport. In fact, Ike was so identified as "the golfer in the White House" that when Democrat John F. Kennedy campaigned for president, Kennedy downplayed his own ability, which was considerably better than Eisenhower's, in order to distance himself from his Republican predecessor.

In 1958, Ike's contributions to the game were acknowledged by the presentation of the Eisenhower Trophy as the prize for the World Amateur Team championship. And in testimony to Eisenhower's identity as a golfer, spike marks from Ike's golf shoes today remain embedded in the floor of the Oval Office.

1952

- January: PGA Tour players will compete in 32 events with a total season purse of $498,016.

- January: LPGA Tour players will compete in 21 events with a total purse of $150,000.

- January 1: A new code of golf's Rules eliminates the stymie, increases the out-of-bounds penalty to stroke and distance, and legalizes center-shafted putters.

- January 7: Ex-carpenter Tommy Bolt wins a three-way playoff in the Los Angeles Open.

- January 24: Ted Rhodes, Bill Spiller, and amateur Eural Clark play in the Phoenix Open under a new PGA Tour rule that lets blacks enter a tournament if the sponsor agrees.

- February 17: Jackie Burke shoots 67-65-64-64—260, one stroke off the Tour's 72-hole record, on the Brackenridge Park course in San Antonio to win the Texas Open.

1952

Dwight D. Eisenhower, the newly elected President of the United States, helped initiate the American golf boom in the 1950s. Ike loved the game and made no secret of it. He was frequently photographed on the golf course with pals, and he even practiced his putting on the back lawn of the White House.

• March: The classic instruction book *Swing the Clubhead* by famed teacher Ernest Jones is published by Dodd, Mead, and Company.

• March 3: Jackie Burke wins the Baton Rouge Open, his third straight victory, in a playoff with Bill Nary and Tommy Bolt.

• March 9: Jackie Burke wins the St. Petersburg Open by eight shots for his fourth straight victory.

• March 16: Babe Zaharias wins her third Titleholders Championship by seven strokes over Betsy Rawls.

• March 18: Former Jacksonville city champion Bertha Johnston and Mary Dempsey are killed when a U.S. Navy Corsair fighter plane crashes on the 7th fairway at Timuquana C.C. in Jacksonville, Florida.

• April 6: Despite hitting into the water on Augusta National's famed 12th hole, Sam Snead fires a 72 in the final round to win the Masters.

Jack Burke Jr.

Burke's Four Straight Wins Include a 260

In 1952, Jack Burke Jr. won four straight PGA Tour events, the longest winning streak since Byron Nelson's 11 consecutive wins in 1945. On February 17, Burke won the Texas Open, shooting 67-65-64-64—260, one off Nelson's Tour record. He followed with victories in the Houston Open, the Baton Rouge Open, and the St. Petersburg Open.

Berg Breaks Three LPGA Records in Richmond

Patty Berg congratulates her putter after setting three LPGA records while winning the Richmond Open in Georgia. In the opening round, Berg shot 30-34—64, setting LPGA nine-hole and 18-hole records. Berg also broke the 54-hole scoring record when she finished with a 210 total. For her efforts, Berg won just $750.

Patty Berg

Spiller Helps Break Down Golf's Color Barriers

Bill Spiller was one of the first black golfers to play in a big-name golf tournament. In January 1952, Spiller, Ted Rhodes, and amateur Eural Clark teed it up in the Phoenix Open at Phoenix C.C. Earlier in the month, the PGA Tour passed a rule that allowed black players to enter a tournament if the sponsor agreed.

Bill Spiller

• April 28: Patty Berg's 64-74-72—210 to win the Richmond Open sets a women's record for lowest 54 holes. Her opening-day score also set the Tour's 18-hole record, and her opening 30 set the nine-hole record.

• May 25: Ben Hogan fires a final-round 67 and comes from six strokes off the pace to win the Colonial National Invitation by four strokes.

• May 26: Babe Zaharias, recently described in a Seattle newspaper column as looking "dead tired," undergoes surgery for a reported hernia at a Beaumont, Texas, hospital.

• June 7: After 20 years of trying, Great Britain/Ireland wins the Curtis Cup, beating the U.S. by a score of 5-4. American Grace DeMoss blows the final singles match when she shanks two shots and whiffs another on the 32nd hole.

• June 14: Less than a year after his wife died following childbirth, Julius

Alice and Marlene Bauer

Younger Bauer, Marlene, Wins Her First Pro Tourney

Marlene Bauer *(right)* poses with older sister Alice in a rare early-'50s color photo. The teenage Marlene, who turned professional back in 1950, captured her first LPGA tournament in 1952. Marlene prevailed in the Sarasota Women's Open for the first of her 25 official career victories.

Snead Dances to Victory in the Masters

Sam Snead celebrates after sinking a par putt on the 6th hole of the third round in the 1952 Masters. Snead led after three rounds, then won the tournament by four shots over Jack Burke Jr. In high winds, Snead closed with a round of 72, despite hitting into the water on the famed par-3 12th.

Sam Snead

Boros wins the U.S. Open at the Northwood Club in Dallas. He wins by four with a 281 total.

• June 25: Jim Turnesa wins the PGA Championship at Big Spring G.C. in Louisville, Kentucky. He defeats Chick Harbert, 1 up, in the 36-hole final.

• June 29: Louise Suggs shoots 284 to win the U.S. Women's Open by seven strokes at Bala G.C. in Philadelphia.

• July 11: Bobby Locke wins his third British Open in the last four years, beating Australia's Peter Thomson by one stroke at Royal Lytham & St. Annes G.C.

• August 3: Sam Snead and Louise Suggs win the individual titles at George S. May's All-American championship near Chicago.

• August 10: Julius Boros and Betty Jameson win George S. May's World Championship. The men's first prize is $25,000.

Turnesa, Harbert Sweat It Out in PGA

Jim Turnesa *(right)* and Chick Harbert were all smiles after winning 36-hole semifinal matches in the 1952 PGA Championship. Harbert beat Bob Hamilton, 2 & 1, while Turnesa knocked off Ted Kroll, 4 & 2. The grind continued when Turnesa and Harbert went the distance in the 36-hole final before Turnesa prevailed, 1 up.

George and Babe Zaharias

Chick Harbert, Jim Turnesa

Babe Keeps on Winning Despite Surgery

Babe Zaharias shares some quality time with her husband George. Babe endured a roller-coaster year in 1952. She won the Titleholders Championship by seven strokes in March, then underwent surgery for a reported hernia in May. Five months later, she was back in the winner's circle at the Women's Texas Open.

Boros Beats Porky, Ben in U.S. Open

In 1952, Julius Boros burst into the spotlight by winning the U.S. Open at the Northwood Club in Dallas. Here, Boros blasts out of a bunker at the 14th hole to within 18 inches of the cup. He finished at 281, four strokes better than Porky Oliver. Ben Hogan led after 36 holes, but he wilted in the heat and finished third.

Julius Boros

- August 10: George S. May, promoter of the World and All-American championships, discloses that in 1951 he paid Ben Hogan $15,000 to play. May says Hogan refused to play this year without a similar guarantee.

- August 22: Mickey Wright of La Jolla, California, wins her first national title when she beats Barbara McIntire, 1 up, in the final of the U.S. Girls' Junior championship.

- August 23: At Seattle G.C., 47-year-old Jack Westland defeats Al Mengert, 3 & 2, to become the oldest man in history to win the U.S. Amateur.

- August 30: USGA officials advise Jackie Pung, the new U.S. Women's Amateur champion, to refrain from dancing. The Hawaiian woman celebrated her 2 & 1 victory over Shirley McFedters in the final with a hula.

- September 26: Joseph C. Dey Jr., executive secretary of the USGA

Jackie Pung, Shirley McFedters

Pung Wins Women's Amateur, Does the Hula

Jackie Pung of Honolulu presents an orchid lei to her opponent, Shirley McFedters, after winning the 1952 U.S. Women's Amateur championship at Waverley C.C. in Portland, Oregon. After her 2 & 1 victory, Pung celebrated with a hula until USGA officials asked her to refrain from dancing. At right is Totten P. Heffelfinger, USGA president.

Louise Suggs

Suggs Shatters U.S. Open Scoring Record

In 1952, Louise Suggs broke the U.S. Women's Open scoring record by seven strokes when she fired 70-69-70-75—284 at Bala G.C. in Philadelphia. Suggs once again won the Women's Open by a big margin as her 284 captured the title by seven shots. In her 1949 Women's Open victory, Suggs beat runner-up Babe Zaharias by 14.

Westland Wins Amateur at Age 47

Jack Westland holed this six-footer at the Seattle G.C. on his way to beating Al Mengert *(right)* in the final of the 1952 U.S. Amateur, 3 & 2. Westland, the championship's oldest winner at 47, climaxed an illustrious amateur career. In 1931, he had finished runner-up in the Amateur to Francis Ouimet.

U.S. Amateur Championship

since 1934, is named executive director of the association.

• October 12: Dutch Harrison wins the Reno Open in Nevada. The field includes Shirley Spork, the only woman to accept a blanket invitation to LPGA members, and she finishes last.

• October 19: Babe Zaharias makes her first appearance on the LPGA Tour since surgery five months ago and finishes tied for sixth in the Betty Jameson Open in San Antonio.

• October 26: Babe Zaharias wins her first tournament since surgery in May, capturing the Women's Texas Open.

• October 28: Betsy Rawls leads the LPGA with $14,505.

• December 6: Julius Boros tops the PGA Tour in earnings with $37,032.

• December 6: Jackie Burke wins the Vardon Trophy with an average of 70.54. He and Sam Snead lead with five Tour victories.

HOGAN ENTERS THREE MAJORS, WINS ALL THREE

In 1953, Ben Hogan took most of the year off, yet he still won six events. Moreover, he also became the only man to win three modern majors in one year—the Masters, U.S. Open, and British Open. Hogan chose not to play in the PGA Championship, since his bad legs couldn't handle the 36-hole match-play rounds. Also, the PGA that year conflicted with the British Open.

In April, Hogan arrived at the Masters striking the ball better than ever. His score of 70-69-66-69—274 shattered the tournament record by five strokes. Hogan called it "the best four rounds of golf in a tournament I've ever had." In May, Hogan won the Pan American Open in Mexico City, then won the 72-hole pro-am at the Greenbrier. Next, he picked up his fourth Colonial National Invitation Tournament title with a five-stroke victory.

The U.S. Open was played at treacherous Oakmont Country Club, but Hogan was poised from the start. He opened with a 67 and was in the driver's seat the whole tournament. On the 71st hole—a heavily bunkered, 292-yard par-4—Hogan drove the green and two-putted for a birdie.

On the final hole, Hogan rifled a 5-iron to just seven feet from the cup. He made the putt for another birdie, a back nine of 33, a score of 71, and a winning total of 283, the lowest 72-hole score ever at Oakmont. He won by six shots over Sam Snead.

Hogan played in the British Open for the first time, thanks to the urging of Walter Hagen, Tommy Armour, and Bobby Cruickshank. He arrived early at Carnoustie, a public course in Scotland, and spent two weeks in careful study of the layout. He had never played a true links course and was also forced to play with the smaller British golf ball.

Hogan's legend had grown since his comeback from the shattering auto accident. He was widely admired in Great Britain, which surprised him, and a devoted following wanted him to win this championship. "I began to feel a pressure that I've never before experienced about a tournament," Hogan said later. "A great many people have built up in their minds a mythical Hogan who wins whenever he wants to win. Well, it does not work out that way."

It did work out this weekend, however, as Hogan opened 73-71-70 and was tied with Roberto De Vicenzo after 54 holes. His final round was a masterpiece. Drilling tee shots to strategic positions, firing irons to the firm greens, and playing the occasional masterful pitch—one of which he holed—Hogan arrived at the last hole certain of victory.

Some 12,000 people lined the fairway, and other players paused to watch him pass. Those who were there remember a great stillness as he walked up to the green. When he holed the final putt for a 68 to win, a thunder of appreciation burst from the crowd. Hogan bowed gently. It was a satisfying moment for Hogan, who walked off with his third major in three attempts.

1953

• January: PGA Tour players will compete in 32 events with a total season purse of $562,704.

• January: LPGA Tour players will compete in 24 events with a total purse of $120,000.

• January 25: A third-round 63, which equals the course record, helps Lloyd Mangrum win the Phoenix Open at Phoenix C.C. It is his third win in the Tour's first five events.

• January 27: The USGA announces it will assume sponsorship of the U.S. Women's Open, to be staged in June for a purse of $7,500.

• February 15: Hometown prodigy Tony Holguin, age 26, captures the Texas Open at Brackenridge Park in San Antonio.

• February 27: Betty Jameson presents the Glenna Collett Vare Trophy to the LPGA to be awarded to the pro who has the year's lowest scoring average.

Playing the best golf of his illustrious career, Ben Hogan outdid himself in 1953.
Hogan blasted from this bunker at the 4th hole on his way to winning the '53 Masters
with a 274, a tournament record. He won the U.S. Open by breaking the scoring
record at Oakmont C.C., and he finished his season by winning the British Open.

• March 1: Babe Zaharias wins the Sarasota Women's Open by seven strokes. Louise Suggs refuses to sign the scorecard after Babe is given a controversial ruling on the 15th hole.

• March 2: Cary Middlecoff wins a five-way, 18-hole playoff in the Houston Open.

• March 8: Patty Berg wins the Titleholders by nine strokes over runner-up Betsy Rawls.

• April 5: Babe Zaharias wins the Babe Didrikson Zaharias Open in her hometown of Beaumont, Texas.

• April 11: Babe Zaharias will undergo cancer surgery in

Beaumont, Texas. Her doctor, W.E. Tatum, says she'll never play golf of championship caliber again. The news gets more press coverage than the Masters.

• April 12: Ben Hogan sets a new 72-hole scoring record at the Masters when he shoots 274 to win by five strokes over Porky Oliver.

Babe Zaharias, Dr. W.E. Tatum

Terrible Tommy Throws a Fit in Tucson

By 1953, Tommy Bolt had earned the reputation of "Terrible Tommy" for his temper tantrums on the course. Here we see the Terrible One toss his putter after missing a short putt in the '53 Tucson Open. Nevertheless, Bolt came back and shot a final-round 65 to win by one stroke over Chandler Harper.

Tommy Bolt

Zaharias Undergoes Exploratory Surgery

The day before undergoing exploratory surgery, Babe Zaharias talked with her physician, Dr. W.E. Tatum, at the Beaumont C.C. in Texas. Zaharias had just won her hometown's Babe Zaharias Open. It was the Babe's last victory before doctors discovered she had cancer. Tatum predicted she'd never again play championship golf.

Patty Berg

Berg Laps the Field in Titleholders

Veteran Patty Berg was still at the top of her game when she teed off on the 1st hole in the 1953 Titleholders. Amateur Bee McWane *(left)* was paired with Berg for the opening round at Augusta C.C. Patty waltzed through the tournament and won by nine strokes over runner-up Betsy Rawls.

• April 17: Babe Zaharias undergoes cancer surgery in Beaumont, Texas. Doctors predict she may be able to participate in sports in the future.

• April 20: President Dwight D. Eisenhower breaks 90 for the first time at Augusta National G.C. when he shoots an 88 and beats Senator Robert Taft in a dollar Nassau.

• April 30: Defending champion Lloyd Mangrum, Cary Middlecoff, and Jack Burke withdraw from the Pan American Open in Mexico City when they learn that Ben Hogan has received a $5,000 guarantee. Hogan will win the event.

• May 17: Betty Hicks blows a chance to win the LPGA's Nevada Women's Open when her ball lands in a bunker on a par-4 hole. Someone has etched the word "death" in the bunker. Rattled, Hicks makes a 7 and loses to Patty Berg in a three-way playoff.

• May 22: Tommy Bolt, who led the Colonial National Invitation with a 67 after the first round, breaks two

1953

Ben Hogan

Hogan Shoots 69 in the Sunshine at Masters

Ben Hogan putted out in the sunshine before a huge gallery on the 18th hole of the 1953 Masters. Hogan scored a 69 to take the 36-hole lead, and he was never headed. Ben fired a record three sub-70 rounds to win by five strokes. Hogan said it was the best golf he had ever played.

Betty Hicks

Baseball Players Golf Tournament

Yogi Goofs Around at Baseball Tournament

A quartet of New York Yankees monkey around at the Baseball Players Tournament in Miami in February 1953. Yogi Berra pool-cues one toward the cup, while Ed Lopat *(left)* and Joe Collins kneel by his side. The serious one standing is pitcher Allie Reynolds, who emerged as the tournament's winner.

Ugly Prank Costs Hicks a Victory in Nevada

Betty Hicks *(kneeling)* blew a chance to win the 1953 Nevada Women's Open when her ball landed in a bunker, where someone had etched the word "death." Rattled, Hicks made a 7 and lost the tournament in a playoff with Patty Berg. Hicks is shown here with Marilynn Smith *(left)* and Fay Crocker.

---

clubs and tosses another into the water during a second-round 81.

• May 24: Ben Hogan wins his fourth Colonial National Invitation, in his hometown of Fort Worth, Texas.

• June 13: Ben Hogan sets a 72-hole course record at Oakmont C.C. by shooting 283 and wins the U.S. Open by six strokes over runner-up Sam Snead.

• June 28: Betsy Rawls wins the first USGA-sponsored Women's Open in an 18-hole playoff with Jackie Pung, at C.C. of Rochester in New York. Patty Berg led by eight strokes after 36 holes.

• July 3: Babe Zaharias, nearly three months after her cancer surgery, plays nine holes in Tampa, Florida, and shoots 38.

• July 7: Walter Burkemo wins the PGA Championship at the Birmingham C.C. in Michigan, claiming a 2 & 1 victory over Felice Torza in the final.

Burkemo Squeaks by Torza for PGA Title

Walter Burkemo and Felice Torza, finalists in the 1953 PGA Championship, look at a periscope used by many spectators to see the action at Michigan's Birmingham C.C. In the 36-hole final, Burkemo edged Torza, 2 & 1, to win his only major championship. Walter was PGA runner-up in 1951 and 1954.

Ben Hogan Parade

Hogan Treated to Ticker-Tape Parade in New York

New Yorkers honor Ben Hogan with a ticker-tape parade after he won the 1953 British Open. It was his third major championship of the year, as he also took the Masters and U.S. Open. Previously, the only other golfer to receive ticker-tape treatment in New York was Bobby Jones, after he completed the Grand Slam.

Walter Burkemo, Felice Torza

• July 10: In his only British Open, Ben Hogan wins by four strokes. He now holds the British, Masters, and U.S. Open crowns. Hogan did not play in the PGA, as he was practicing for the British Open at Carnoustie, Scotland.

• July 21: After his British Open victory, Ben Hogan is welcomed back to the United States with a ticker-tape parade down Broadway in New York City.

• August 2: Babe Zaharias completes 72 holes in George S. May's All-American Open in Chicago, her first competitive rounds since April's cancer surgery. Babe, sitting on a collapsible seat between shots, finishes 15th.

• August 9: Lew Worsham holes a 135-yard wedge shot on the final hole to win the World Championship in Chicago. He wins by one stroke over Chandler Harper. It is a dramatic ending to the first nationally televised tournament.

Ben Hogan

Oakmont No Match for Determined Hogan

Ben Hogan was grim throughout his march to the 1953 U.S. Open title. Hogan, striding from Oakmont C.C.'s 10th tee, was on his way to a first-round 67 and the U.S. Open lead. With fierce concentration, Hogan humbled old Oakmont with a 5-under-par 283, winning by six strokes for his fourth Open in six years.

Gene Littler

Rawls Beats Pung in Open Playoff

In 1953, Betsy Rawls *(right)* got her hands on the U.S. Women's Open trophy for the second time, at the C.C. of Rochester in New York. Rawls and Jackie Pung *(left)* finished tied at 302, then entered a playoff. Rawls won easily, firing a 71 to Pung's 77. Pung would lose another heart-breaker in the Open in 1957.

Jackie Pung, Betsy Rawls

Littler Outclasses Morey in U.S. Amateur

The classic-swinging Gene Littler, age 23, emerged as a player of national stature when he won the 1953 U.S. Amateur at the Oklahoma City Golf and C.C. In the final against Dale Morey, Littler blasted from this bunker at the 26th green. Morey, in trouble, conceded the hole and Littler went 3 up. He won on the final green, 1 up.

- August 9: Louise Suggs leads the LPGA Tour in season earnings ($19,816) and victories (eight). Patty Berg wins the Vare Trophy with a 75.00 average.

- August 29: Mary Lena Faulk wins the U.S. Women's Amateur with a 3 & 2 victory over Polly Riley at Rhode Island C.C.

- September 5: The United States defeats Great Britain/Ireland, 9-3, in the Walker Cup Match at the Kittansett Club in Massachusetts.

- September 19: Gene Littler defeats Dale Morey, 1 up, in the 36-hole final to win the U.S. Amateur at the Oklahoma City Golf and C.C.

- October 3: The U.S. team defeats Great Britain, 6½-5½, in the Ryder Cup Match at Wentworth, England.

- December 12: Lew Worsham leads the PGA Tour in earnings with $34,002. Lloyd Mangrum wins the Vardon Trophy with an average of 70.22. Ben Hogan is Player of the Year.

ZAHARIAS BEATS CANCER, WINS U.S. OPEN

Babe Zaharias, the great athlete and larger-than-life personality, announced in January that she would play the LPGA's full schedule in 1954. This was no small news. Babe had undergone surgery for colon cancer the previous April and had missed the rest of the 1953 season. Without its biggest gate attraction, the women's tour was starved for publicity. Babe's return would guarantee revived interest in the LPGA.

Zaharias was a winner and a colorful character, but she was not universally loved. She could be cocky and brash, once playing a loud harmonica while Louise Suggs attempted to putt. But without doubt, Zaharias was the greatest woman athlete the world had seen. She played all sports with ease, and in 1932 won two Olympic gold medals in track and field. Zaharias became a serious golfer rather late in life, but with wonderful results. In 1950 and '51, she won a dozen LPGA events.

Babe's running conversation with galleries and cocky exuberance had made her the LPGA's top drawing card, and interest in her 1954 return was great. Her

first event, the Sea Island Invitational in January, disappointed many, as she suffered from dizziness and shot 81-82-83. But Zaharias grew stronger, and the following week she finished seventh in the Tampa Women's Open. In February, she tied for first in the St. Petersburg Women's Open before losing a playoff. Then, Babe won the Miami Women's Open and the Sarasota Women's Open back to back. "I feel wonderful," she said. "I think I'm here to stay."

Babe won at Washington, D.C., in the spring and set her sights on the U.S. Women's Open, which she had won in 1948 and 1950. This year's Open was played on the hilly Salem Country Club course in Peabody, Massachusetts,

and Zaharias jumped to a six-stroke lead after opening 72-71. However, Babe and the other players knew that Saturday's double round would severely test her endurance.

On a mild, cloudless day, Babe fired a 73 in the morning and had a 10-stroke lead. With the victory in her grasp, she took a nap in the clubhouse between rounds. Late in the afternoon round, Babe began to tire. She started pushing her tee shots and bogied four holes coming in. It didn't matter, though, as she won by a whopping 12 strokes. As she approached the final green, she was nearly mobbed by well-wishers.

At the presentation ceremony, Babe was subdued. "My prayers have been answered," she said. "I wanted to show thousands of cancer sufferers that the operation I had, colostomy, will enable a person to return to normal life.... This is my answer to them."

Two years later, she lost her battle with cancer. An irrepressible personality and great champion, Babe Zaharias drew attention to women's golf in a day when few people cared to watch. Today, she is remembered as America's first sports heroine.

1954

- January: PGA Tour players will compete in 26 events with a total season purse of $600,819.

- January: LPGA Tour players will compete in 21 events with a total purse of $105,000.

- January 11: Little-known Fred Wampler, 1950 NCAA champion,

wins the Los Angeles Open. The field includes black players Ted Rhodes and Charles Sifford, who finish in the money.

- January 15: In the first round of the Bing Crosby Pro-Am, Porky Oliver makes a 16 on Cypress Point's par-3 16th hole. He shoots 36-50—86.

- January 23: At its annual meeting, the USGA says women competitors may now wear shorts in USGA-sponsored championships.

- January 24: In his hometown, U.S. Amateur champion Gene Littler stuns the professionals by winning the San Diego Open by four strokes.

1954

After major cancer surgery, Babe Zaharias returned to the LPGA Tour with her doctors' blessings. Weakened by the disease, she started 1954 slowly, but victories in February and May meant that the Babe was back. When she endured Saturday's double round to win the 1954 U.S. Women's Open, Babe capped off one of golf's most dramatic comeback stories.

• **February 20:** In what she describes as her greatest thrill in sports, Babe Zaharias completes her comeback by winning the Serbin Open at Bayshore C.C. in Miami Beach, Florida.

• **February 20:** Ted Kroll ties the PGA Tour record with a 60 in the third round of the Texas Open.

• **February 21:** Chandler Harper finishes with three straight rounds of 63 to win the Texas Open on San Antonio's Brackenridge Park course. Harper ties the PGA Tour's 72-hole scoring record of 259.

• **March 7:** Despite leg cramps, Babe Zaharias wins the Sarasota Women's Open by nine strokes.

• **March 14:** Louise Suggs shoots a tournament-record 293 to win the Titleholders by seven strokes.

• **March 26:** Amateur Arnold Palmer takes the first-round lead with a 65 in the Azalea Open in Wilmington, North Carolina. He'll tie for seventh.

Alice Bauer

The USGA Gives In, Lets Women Wear Shorts

LPGA professional Alice Bauer was glad to be back in shorts. Bauer was one of many women forced to wear skirts after the USGA squelched shorts in USGA events. The association relented in 1954, and women competitors in USGA championships were allowed to return to more casual wear.

Gene Sarazen

Sarazen's Back at It in PGA Seniors

Gene Sarazen proved his durability by winning the 1954 PGA Seniors Championship in Dunedin, Florida, at the age of 52. Sarazen thus became the first man to win the U.S. and British Opens, the Masters, the PGA, and the PGA Seniors. Gary Player would equal the feat, as would Jack Nicklaus.

Lionel Hebert, Johnny Palmer, Chandler Harper

Harper Wins Texas Open with a Record 259

Chandler Harper *(right)* fired three straight rounds of 63 to win the 1954 Texas Open and tie the PGA Tour's 72-hole record of 259. Harper humbled San Antonio's Brackenridge Park, an A.W. Tillinghast design that took a beating over the years. Johnny Palmer *(center)* was second and Lionel Hebert *(left)* finished third.

• April 7: Doug Ford, Bill Nary, and Marty Furgol are fined by the PGA Tour for unbecoming conduct during the Greater Greensboro Open, in which Ford (the event's winner) and Nary nearly came to blows.

• April 11: Amateur Billy Joe Patton loses the Masters by two strokes after he tries to carry the water fronting the 13th green, fails, and makes a 7. Patton finishes at 290. Ben Hogan and Sam Snead tie for first at 289.

• April 12: In an 18-hole playoff for the Masters, Sam Snead defeats Ben Hogan, 70-71.

• May 14: The USGA is constructing a green on the south lawn of the White House so that President Dwight D. Eisenhower can practice.

• May 25: The U.S. Supreme Court opens public courses to black golfers when it rules that the city of Houston must operate municipal courses on an integrated basis.

Sam Snead

Snead Edges Out Hogan in Masters Playoff

Sam Snead hits from the trees along Augusta National's 2nd fairway. Snead won the 1954 Masters, but it wasn't easy. Sam and Ben Hogan benefitted from amateur Billy Joe Patton's final-round double bogey. Snead and Hogan tied for first with 289s—the highest winning score in Masters history—and Sam won the playoff, 70-71.

Billy Joe Patton

Suggs Prevails by Seven in Titleholders

Louise Suggs gets a kiss from three-year-old fan Bill Wylie after her opening round of 73 in the 1954 Titleholders Championship at Augusta C.C. Suggs went on to post another monster victory. She finished the tournament with a score of 293, winning by seven strokes and setting a new 72-hole Titleholders record.

Louise Suggs, Bill Wylie

Patton's Bad Iron Shot Costs Him Masters

Carefree amateur Billy Joe Patton, the sentimental favorite at the 1954 Masters, had a legitimate chance to become the event's first amateur champ. But in the final round, Patton tried to carry the creek at the 13th hole. He failed, made a 7, and finished two strokes out of a playoff.

• June 11: Wally Ulrich shoots a 60 in the second round of the Virginia Beach Open, tying the PGA Tour record.

• June 19: Ed Furgol, whose left arm is crippled from a childhood accident, wins the U.S. Open at Baltusrol G.C. in Springfield, New Jersey. He wins by a stroke over Gene Littler. The Open is televised nationally for the first time.

• June 28: Tommy Bolt wins the Insurance City Open. In the third round, Bolt became the third PGA Tour player this year to shoot a 60.

• July 3: Babe Zaharias caps her comeback from cancer surgery by winning the U.S. Women's Open by 12 strokes at Salem C.C. in Massachusetts. "My prayers have been answered," says Babe.

• July 9: Peter Thomson, a 24-year-old Australian, wins the British Open at Royal Birkdale in England. Jim Turnesa, who ties for fifth, is the highest American finisher.

Chick Harbert

Harbert Fights off Burkemo in PGA Final

Chick Harbert dons a gaucho hat against the noonday sun during the final of the 1954 PGA Championship, at Minnesota's Keller Golf Course. Harbert beat Walter Burkemo, the defending champion, 4 & 3, in the 36-hole match. It was a sweet victory for Harbert, who lost the 1952 PGA on the last hole of the final.

Little Riley Wins Fifth Southern Amateur

Short of stature and not a long hitter, Polly Riley was nevertheless one of America's best amateurs. In 1954, she won her fifth Southern Women's Amateur championship. While she never won the U.S. Women's Amateur, she captured most other major amateur titles and played on six Curtis Cup teams.

Polly Riley

Arnold Palmer

A Kid Named Palmer Wins U.S. Amateur

Arnold Palmer, age 24, began his reign as golf's most charismatic player by winning the 1954 U.S. Amateur. Palmer edged Robert Sweeny, 1 up, in a thrilling final at the C.C. of Detroit. For the first time in a national championship, the USGA roped the fairways from tee to green.

• July 27: Chick Harbert defeats Walter Burkemo, 4 & 3, in the final to win the PGA Championship at Keller Golf Course in St. Paul.

• August 15: Diminutive Bob Toski wins $50,000 when he finishes first at George S. May's World Championship in Chicago. Patty Berg wins the women's pro title.

• August 22: Australians Peter Thomson and Kel Nagle win the second Canada Cup Match at Laval-sur-le-Lac G.C. in Montreal. The U.S. team of Sam Snead and Jimmy Demaret finishes third.

• August 28: Arnold Palmer, age 24, wins the U.S. Amateur at the C.C. of Detroit. When Palmer defeats

Robert Sweeny, 43, on the last hole of the 36-hole final, a brass band plays "Hail to the Chief."

• September: Joe DiMaggio purchases a set of clubs for his wife, Marilyn Monroe, and says, "She takes a hell of a cut, and hits a long ball when she hits it."

Bob Toski, Mrs. George S. May

Toski Wins $50,000, Gives Mrs. May a Hug

Bob Toski had just won golf's biggest purse when he hugged Mrs. George S. May, the wife of the sponsor who put up the money. The diminutive Toski won a check for $50,000 for his victory in George S. May's World Championship at Tam O'Shanter C.C. near Chicago. Toski won by a single stroke over two others.

Barbara Romack

Romack Whips Wright in U.S. Women's Amateur

Barbara Romack grins and hugs the Robert Cox Cup, the prize for winning the 1954 U.S. Women's Amateur. At Allegheny C.C. near Pittsburgh, Romack defeated Mickey Wright, 4 & 2. Delayed by thunderstorms, the match lasted 29 hours and 15 minutes before Romack won.

Furgol Nips Littler by One in U.S. Open

Despite a withered left arm, Ed Furgol claimed an inspiring victory in the 1954 U.S. Open, at Baltusrol G.C. in New Jersey. Furgol finished at 284 to edge Gene Littler by a stroke. The title earned Furgol $6,000 and the 1954 PGA Player of the Year Award.

Ed Furgol

• September 3: The U.S. sweeps the foursomes matches to regain the Curtis Cup from Great Britain/Ireland, 6-3, at Merion G.C.

• September 19: Barbara Romack, age 21, defeats Mickey Wright to win the U.S. Women's Amateur at Allegheny C.C. in Sewickley, Pennsylvania.

• September 26: Patty Berg is the leading money winner on the LPGA Tour with $16,011, and Babe Zaharias wins the Vare Trophy with a 75.48 scoring average.

• November: Arnold Palmer, age 25, and Mickey Wright, age 19, turn professional.

• December 19: Bob Toski, the PGA Tour's leading money winner, sets a record with $65,819. He leads the Tour with four victories.

• December 19: Ed Furgol is the PGA Tour's Player of the Year, and E.J. "Dutch" Harrison wins the Vardon Trophy with an average of 70.41.

BERG ADDS TWO MORE MAJORS TO RECORD LIST

Patty Berg's reputation as one of golf's great entertainers overshadows her skill as a player. Berg's golf clinic remains a comedic masterpiece, but Patty was also one of history's greatest women players, and in 1955 she had one of her best years.

Berg was a red-headed, freckle-faced extrovert. Her stocky build kept her swing from looking as smooth as that of rival Louise Suggs, but, starting with her perfect grip, the swing was without flaws. A great bunker player, Berg hit a driving sort of shot, the ball starting low, then climbing. At times, she was quite long off the tee.

Berg was the daughter of a Minneapolis grain merchant. As a child, she was a champion speedskater and quarterbacked a neighborhood football team. Her amateur golf career was spectacular, and she won 29 championships, including the U.S. Women's Amateur, in seven years. Patty turned pro in 1940, with no organization for women pros and very few tournaments. In her early pro career, she mostly gave clinics and exhibitions for Wilson Sporting Goods. She joined a struggling new organization, the

Women's Professional Golf Association, in 1946, and in 1948 helped found the LPGA, serving as its president.

By the beginning of 1955, the 37-year-old Berg had won 40 events, including four Western Opens, five Titleholders, and the Women's Open. Berg's first win of '55 was the St. Petersburg Women's Open in February, and by spring she bid for her sixth Titleholders Championship. Georgia's Augusta Country Club, adjacent to Bob Jones's Augusta National, was a wooded, hilly course with elevated greens and many bunkers. Suggs took the first-round lead with a 71, and Patty was five strokes behind.

However, Suggs was stricken with a bad case of hay fever before the second round. While her long game remained sound, the allergies ruined her short game and her scores soared. As evidenced by her five titles here, Berg loved this golf course. In the second round, she fired a 68, breaking Babe Zaharias's course record by two strokes. She followed with 74-73—291, breaking the tournament record by two shots.

By mid-June, both Suggs and Berg were playing at a hot pace. Louise had won three events when Patty cruised to her fifth Western Open win. Suggs took the St. Louis Women's Open, but Patty won the All-American and her third straight World Championship, retiring the trophy. In the last tournament of the year, Berg shot 4-under-par for 72 holes and won the Clock Open.

Berg finished the year with $16,492 and became the first player to lead the LPGA in earnings and scoring average in the same season. The Associated Press named her Woman Athlete of the Year. Berg was a real rock of the LPGA Tour. By career's end, she would win 57 tournaments. More impressively, her 15 major victories remain an LPGA record.

1955

• January: PGA Tour players will compete in 36 events with a total season purse of $782,010.

• January: LPGA Tour players will compete in 27 events with a total purse of $135,000.

• January 9: In a unique format, the Los Angeles Open hosts tourna-

ments for PGA and LPGA Tour players. Gene Littler and Louise Suggs are the winners.

• January 23: Babe Zaharias wins the Tampa Open for the third time.

• February 17: Mike Souchak fires a PGA Tour record of 27 on the back nine at San Antonio's Brackenridge

Park. He shoots a record-tying 60 in the first round of the Texas Open.

• February 20: Mike Souchak's four rounds of 60-68-64-65—257 in the Texas Open set an all-time PGA Tour record. Souchak wins by seven.

• February 24: After a first round of 79, Babe Zaharias withdraws from

The colorful Patty Berg dominated the LPGA Tour in 1955. At the age of 37, Patty was at the peak of her considerable skills. She won two majors, capturing her fifth Women's Western Open and smashing the tournament record to win a sixth Titleholders. Berg led the money list with $16,492 and won the Vare Trophy with a 74.47 scoring average.

the Sarasota Open and her doctor orders her not to play again "for some time." George Zaharias, Babe's husband, says she is ill and exhausted.

• March 13: Patty Berg smashes the tournament record with a 72-hole total of 291 and wins her sixth Titleholders Championship. Babe

Zaharias, back in action, ties for seventh.

• April 10: Cary Middlecoff wins the Masters, thanks to a second-round 65. Ben Hogan finishes second, seven strokes behind.

• April 17: Sam Snead wins his fifth Greater Greensboro Open.

• May 1: Gene Littler beats a limited field of PGA Tour players by 13 strokes to win the Tournament of Champions and $10,000. Singer Frankie Laine, who had Littler in the Calcutta, wins $72,900.

• May 1: Babe Zaharias wins the Betsy Rawls-Peach Blossom Open in Spartanburg, South Carolina.

Golf Teacher Monti Gives Pros a Lesson

Eric Monti hit very few bunkers in his surprising two-stroke win in the 1955 Miami Beach Open. Monti, a bespectacled, 36-year-old Los Angeles teaching professional who gave lessons to film stars, fired a cool 68 in the final round for a 72-hole total of 270, 18-under-par.

Eric Monti

Mike Souchak

Middlecoff Runs Away with the Masters

After holing a 75-foot putt for eagle at the 13th hole in the second round of the 1955 Masters, Cary Middlecoff hits this iron shot to the green at Augusta National's 15th. He then made birdie on his way to a blazing 65. Middlecoff won by seven strokes over runner-up Ben Hogan. It was Doc's second major championship. He captured the U.S. Open title back in 1949.

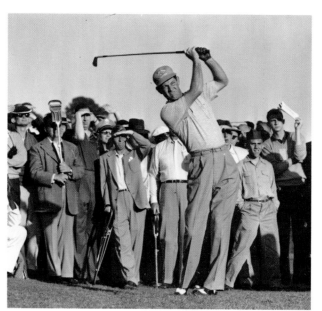

Cary Middlecoff

Souchak Shoots Record 257 to Win Texas Open

Mike Souchak shot 60-68-64-65—257, 27-under-par, in the 1955 Texas Open at Brackenridge Park in San Antonio. The 257, which broke the PGA Tour record, has never been equalled. The score of 60 tied a Tour record that has since been broken. Souchak's 27 on the back nine of the first round, which broke the Tour record, has been equalled only once.

• May 21: The American team routs Great Britain, 10-2, in the Walker Cup Match at St. Andrews, Scotland.

• June 17: The first machine to adjust the lie and loft of golf clubs, the Sam Snead Adjusto-Matic, is marketed by the Adjusto-Matic Company.

• June 18: Ben Hogan appears to have the U.S. Open wrapped up, but Jack Fleck, an Iowa professional who has never won on Tour, birdies two of the last four holes at San Francisco's Olympic C.C. to tie Hogan.

• June 19: To the amazement of the golf world, unknown Jack Fleck

defeats Ben Hogan, 69-72, in an 18-hole playoff for the U.S. Open championship.

• June 22: Babe Zaharias undergoes spinal surgery to remove a disc. She sustained the injury pushing her car out of sand. Her doctor says the surgery is not connected to her cancer surgery two years ago.

Littler, Laine Clean Up in Las Vegas

Curt Littler plays with a handful of silver dollars that his father Gene won in the 1955 Tournament of Champions. Dad prevailed by a whopping 13 strokes at the Desert Inn C.C. in Las Vegas. Littler won the $10,000 first prize, but singer Frankie Laine, who had Littler in the Calcutta, raked in $72,900.

Gene and Curt Littler

Holy Smokes! Fleck Upsets Hogan in U.S. Open

In one of golf's greatest upsets, Jack Fleck *(left)* beat Ben Hogan in a playoff for the 1955 U.S. Open crown. Hogan, here fanning Fleck's hot putter, was unable to match the Davenport, Iowa, professional on the greens. Fleck's putting was boldly accurate, and he fired a 69 to Hogan's 72. The world of golf was stunned.

Hogan Winds Up in U.S. Open Playoff

Ben Hogan found the rough on the first hole of this playoff with Jack Fleck for the 1955 U.S. Open, held at the Olympic Club near San Francisco. Hogan never expected to be in a playoff. He appeared to have won his fifth Open when he finished regulation play at 287. Then Fleck, a municipal course pro, made two birdies to tie. Fleck was playing with Ben Hogan golf clubs.

Jack Fleck, Ben Hogan

Ben Hogan

• June 26: Patty Berg wins the Women's Western Open for the fifth time, at Maple Bluff C.C. in Madison, Wisconsin.

• July 2: Fay Crocker of Montevideo, Uruguay, wins the U.S. Women's Open at Wichita C.C. The final day features 96-degree heat and 35-mph winds.

• July 7: Mobster Anthony Capezio, 53, dies of a heart attack while playing the 4th hole of White Pines C.C. near Chicago.

• July 8: For the second year in a row, Peter Thomson wins the British Open, played on the Old Course at St. Andrews. With most U.S. pros staying at home, Ed Furgol is the only American to finish among the top 20.

• July 17: The first LPGA Championship is completed at Orchard Ridge C.C. in Fort Wayne, Indiana. It's 54 holes at stroke play, followed by match play to determine money distribution. Beverly Hanson is the first LPGA Champion.

Doug Ford

Ford Beats Middlecoff in PGA Final

Playing against Cary Middlecoff in the 36-hole final of the 1955 PGA Championship, at Meadowbrook C.C. in Michigan, Doug Ford hit this bunker on the 23rd hole. Ford's bunker shot was close enough for one putt, and they halved the hole to remain even. Ford won four of the next 10 holes to win the match, 4 & 3, and became PGA Champion in his first try.

After Nine Tries, Ward Wins Amateur

In the 1955 U.S. Amateur, Harvie Ward of North Carolina nails this 175-yard iron shot and hits the green on his way to a semifinal victory. The following day, Ward—after nine tries—won the championship. He defeated Bill Hyndman, 9 & 8, in 36 holes at the C.C. of Virginia near Richmond.

Harvie Ward

• July 26: Doug Ford, playing in his first PGA Championship, prevails with a 4 & 3 victory over Cary Middlecoff in the final, at Meadowbrook C.C. in Northville, Michigan.

• August 4: Babe Zaharias is stricken with cancer again and needs to undergo radiation therapy. "It's a rub of the green," Babe says. "This is my greatest battle."

• August 14: Julius Boros wins the $50,000 first prize when he captures George S. May's World Championship near Chicago. Patty Berg wins the women's pro division and $5,000.

• August 20: Arnold Palmer gets his first professional victory when he wins the Canadian Open by four strokes at Weston G.C. in Toronto.

• August 27: Pat Lesser defeats Jane Nelson, 7 & 6, to win the U.S. Women's Amateur at Myers Park C.C. in Charlotte, North Carolina.

Fay Crocker

Uruguay's Crocker Wins U.S. Women's Open Title

In 1955, Fay Crocker became the first foreign-born winner of the U.S. Women's Open. Crocker, of Montevideo, Uruguay, won that nation's amateur title 20 times. Crocker led the Women's Open after every round and won by four strokes. Babe Zaharias, battling with cancer, was unable to defend her title.

Thomson Tames St. Andrews in British Open

Australian Peter Thomson *(right)*, on his way to his second straight British Open championship, looks over the Old Course at St. Andrews with veteran professional Henry Cotton. Thomson had just gained the lead with a 54-hole total of 209. For the first time, the BBC provided live coverage of the final round.

Boros Again Wins George May's World Championship

Julius Boros embraces his wife and four-year-old son, Jay, after winning George S. May's World Championship at Tam O'Shanter C.C. near Chicago. Boros captured the $50,000 first prize, which was the largest in golf. The smooth-swinging, easy-going Boros also won the World Championship in 1952.

Julius Boros

Henry Cotton, Peter Thomson

• September 17: Harvie Ward, after nine tries, wins the U.S. Amateur at the C.C. of Virginia, near Richmond. Ward defeats Bill Hyndman, 9 & 8, in the final.

• September 25: Patty Berg leads LPGA money winners with $16,492 and wins the Vare Trophy with a 74.47 average.

• October 1: John Wood "Woody" Platt wins the first U.S. Senior Amateur, at Belle Meade C.C. in Nashville.

• November 6: The United States defeats Great Britain, 8-4, in the Ryder Cup Match, at Thunderbird Ranch and C.C. in Palm Springs, California.

• November 26: Babe Zaharias re-enters John Sealy Hospital in Galveston, Texas, for treatment of cancer.

• December 18: Doug Ford is the PGA Tour's Player of the Year. Sam Snead wins the Vardon Trophy with a 69.86 average, and Julius Boros leads in money with $63,121.

AMATEUR VENTURI NEARLY CAPTURES THE MASTERS

The Masters has a history of being good to amateurs. Thanks to host Bob Jones, the supreme amateur of them all, amateurs were always welcomed as part of the field. And in 1956, an amateur almost won the prestigious event. Ken Venturi, a 24-year-old from San Francisco, was invited to the 1956 Masters by special invitation from the committee of past champions. Recently out of the Army, Venturi was a hot, young talent and a protégé of Byron Nelson.

In the opening round, Venturi and Billy Joe Patton—who almost won the Masters as an amateur in 1954—were paired together. Immediately, they began an assault on the rain-softened course. Venturi shot a 32 on the front nine, Patton a 34. At the par-5 13th, both men eagled, and the gallery ovation rivaled a Sunday finish. Patton finished with a 70, but Venturi shot 66 and led the tournament. On a blustery Friday when no one else broke 70, Venturi fired a 69 to tie the tournament's 36-hole record of 135. Cary Middlecoff was in second place, four behind.

On Saturday, Venturi shot a shaky 40 on the front nine and lost the lead to Middlecoff, who fired a 35. On the back nine, their scores were reversed. Each closed with a 75, and Venturi regained his four-stroke lead. Traditionally, the leader played with former champion Nelson in the final round. But tournament officials, who believed a pairing with his teacher would give Venturi an unfair advantage, chose to pair him with veteran Sam Snead.

Neither Venturi nor Middlecoff played well on the final round's front nine, as each shot 38. Jackie Burke, meanwhile, was making a charge. Burke had started the day eight shots off Venturi's lead, but with a solid final round and Venturi bogeying the 10th, 11th, and 12th, Burke was just three strokes behind. Middlecoff trailed by two.

Venturi's game was cracking. After a difficult par at the 13th, he bogied the 14th and 15th. Burke, playing ahead with Mike Souchak, pulled to within one of Venturi. Middlecoff double bogeyed the 16th to drop from contention. "Man, play some golf and you'll win this one," Souchak told Burke at the 17th tee. "They're shooting double bogeys out here."

Burke complied, holing a birdie putt on the 17th. On the 17th, Venturi's 9-iron approach shot went over the green. Rattled, he hit a weak chip and missed the 12-foot par putt. Venturi was now a stroke behind Burke, who had parred the final hole from a greenside bunker for a 71—289.

A shaken Venturi pulled himself together and hit his final-hole second shot within 15 feet of the flagstick. He missed the putt and, without embarrassment, burst into tears. "This one was a bitter disappointment," Venturi said. "I hope and pray some day I'll be able to wear one of those green jackets." Sadly, he never would.

1956

- January: PGA Tour players will compete in 36 events with a total season purse of $847,070.

- January: LPGA Tour players will compete in 26 events with a total purse of $140,000.

- January 13: The A.P. names Patty Berg Woman Athlete of the Year.

- January 15: By a five-stroke margin, Cary Middlecoff wins the Bing Crosby Pro-Am for the second straight year.

- January 22: From the site of the Tampa Women's Open, LPGA players and fans have an emotional conversation with ailing Babe Zaharias, via radio hook-up.

- January 26: President Dwight D. Eisenhower is awarded the Ben Hogan Trophy. The award is made to a person who overcomes a handicap to continue to play golf. Eisenhower suffered a heart attack on September 24, 1955.

- January 28: The USGA inserts an anti-gambling clause into the Rules

1956

Ken Venturi, an amateur, burst upon the national golf scene when he fired a 66 to take the first-round lead in the 1956 Masters. Venturi opened 66-69-75 to take a four-stroke lead after three rounds. On Sunday, however, he made six bogeys on the back nine and watched Jackie Burke zoom past him for the victory.

of Amateur Status. The clause is designed to put a stop to high wagering via Calcuttas.

• January 29: Jimmy Demaret, now age 45, wins the Thunderbird Invitational in California.

• February 5: Louise Suggs wins the first LPGA event to be staged in

Havana, Cuba—the Havana Biltmore Invitational.

• March 5: Mickey Wright wins the first LPGA tournament of her 16-month professional career, capturing the Jacksonville Open.

• March 11: Bob Jones attends the presentation ceremonies after Louise

Suggs wins her third Titleholders Championship in 10 years.

• March 29: Babe Zaharias re-enters John Sealy Hospital in Galveston, Texas, for tests.

• April 8: Amateur Ken Venturi, who led for three rounds, closes with an 80 and loses the Masters.

Jack Burke Jr.

Burke Leapfrogs Venturi to Win Masters

In the 1956 Masters, Jackie Burke Jr. escapes from the dogwood trees lining Augusta National's 15th fairway to surge to the final-round lead. When amateur Ken Venturi and Cary Middlecoff faltered, Burke came from eight strokes behind to win the tournament with a final-round 71.

President Eisenhower, Rep. Jack Westland

Suggs Tops Again in Titleholders

At Georgia's Augusta C.C., Louise Suggs topped the leader board after 36 holes and went on to win the 1956 Titleholders. The Georgia native obviously enjoyed home cooking—this was her third Titleholders victory in 10 years. Fellow Georgian Bobby Jones attended the presentation ceremonies.

Louise Suggs

Eisenhower Honored with Ben Hogan Trophy

President Dwight D. Eisenhower receives the Ben Hogan Trophy from Rep. Jack Westland, a former U.S. Amateur champion. The trophy is awarded annually to the golfer making the greatest comeback from a physical disability to continue to play golf. Ike had suffered a heart attack on September 24, 1955.

• April 8: Jackie Burke closes with a 71 to win the Masters by a stroke.

• April 15: Sam Snead wins his sixth Greater Greensboro Open in a sudden-death playoff with Fred Wampler.

• May 27: Don January eagles the final hole at Preston Hollow C.C. to win the Dallas Centennial Open by one stroke over Doug Ford. January holed out from a bunker.

• June 9: Great Britain/Ireland beats the U.S. in the Curtis Cup Match, 5-4, at Princes G.C. in England.

• June 16: By one stroke, Ben Hogan fails to win his fifth U.S. Open title. The victor is Cary Middlecoff, who picks up his second Open gold medal with a score of 281 at Oak Hill C.C. in Rochester, New York.

• June 24: Marlene Bauer Hagge wins the LPGA Championship, her fourth victory of the year, in a sudden-death playoff with Patty Berg, at Forest Lake C.C. in Detroit.

Don January

January Wins in Dallas with Dramatic Eagle

Don January, a native of Abilene, Texas, describes his opening-round 64 in the 1956 Dallas Centennial Open. January's score set the course record at Preston Hollow C.C. On the final hole of the tournament, January blasted his ball out of a bunker and into the cup for an eagle and a one-stroke victory over Doug Ford and Dow Finsterwald. It was his first career victory.

Cary Middlecoff, Ben Hogan

Middlecoff Nips Hogan for the U.S. Open Title

Two of the era's premier players, Cary Middlecoff *(left)* and Ben Hogan, pose with the 1956 U.S. Open championship trophy at Oak Hill C.C. in Rochester, New York. Middlecoff and Hogan were close to a playoff for the title until Hogan bogied the 71st hole. Middlecoff, 35, won his second U.S. Open crown. He also won in 1949.

Rawls Wins the Betsy Rawls Open

Betsy Rawls went to her hometown of Spartanburg, South Carolina, to become the Tour's first three-time winner of 1956. Rawls won the laurels with a victory in her namesake tournament— the Betsy Rawls-Peach Blossom Open. Earlier in the year, she won the Babe Zaharias Cancer Fund Open.

Betsy Rawls

• June 24: Ben Hogan and Sam Snead team to win the Canada Cup for the United States at Wentworth, England. They win by 14 strokes.

• July 6: Peter Thomson of Australia wins his third straight British Open crown, at Hoylake in England. Few Americans enter.

• July 15: Billy Casper, age 25, gets his first PGA Tour victory at the Labatt Open.

• July 24: Jackie Burke wins the PGA Championship at Blue Hill C.C. in Canton, Massachusetts.

• July 26: Ann Gregory, of Chicago Women's G.C., becomes the first

black woman to play in a USGA tournament when she tees off in the U.S. Women's Open in Duluth, Minnesota.

• July 28: Jack Nicklaus, age 16, equals the course record with a third-round 64 at the Marietta C.C. and wins the Ohio Open. Nicklaus started golf just six years ago.

Marlene Stewart

Stewart Wins Women's Amateur, College Title

Marlene Stewart, a diminutive Canadian, became one of the world's top women amateurs. Here she shows the form that helped her win both the 1956 Women's National Collegiate title and the '56 U.S. Women's Amateur. Stewart was a student at Rollins College in Florida.

Golf Inventions Border on the Ridiculous

Some poor chap probably shelled out good money for this silly contraption, which guaranteed he would keep his head down. Throughout the century, the U.S. Patent Office has been flooded with inventions guaranteed to make golfers play like Walter Hagen, Ben Hogan, or Jack Nicklaus. Few of the greats ever used such gadgetry.

Training Device

• July 28: Amateur Barbara McIntire makes a 30-foot eagle putt on the final hole to tie Kathy Cornelius in the U.S. Women's Open, at Northland C.C. in Duluth, Minnesota.

• July 29: In the playoff of the U.S. Women's Open, Kathy Cornelius beats Barbara McIntire, 75-82.

• August 12: Ted Kroll wins the $50,000 first prize in the World Championship of Golf.

• August 26: Mike Souchak birdies the last six holes to shoot 62 and win the St. Paul Open.

• September 14: In her hospital room, Babe Zaharias receives an award for "outstanding service in the field of cancer education and control." Hospitalized with cancer since March 29, Zaharias says, "I'll lick this thing yet."

• September 15: Harvie Ward wins the U.S. Amateur. He defeats Chuck Kocsis, 5 & 4, in the final at Knollwood Club in Illinois.

Ted Kroll, Jack Burke Jr.

Burke Claims His Second Major of the Year

Jackie Burke *(right)* is congratulated by Ted Kroll after winning the 1956 PGA Championship, at Blue Hill G.C. in Canton, Massachusetts. Burke came from behind to defeat Kroll, 3 & 2, in the 36-hole match. Burke became the second player to win the Masters and PGA in the same year. Sam Snead did it in 1949.

Peter Thomson

Zaharias Succumbs to Cancer

The funeral of the world's greatest woman athlete, Mildred "Babe" Didrickson Zaharias, was held in her hometown of Beaumont, Texas, after the Babe died of cancer on September 27, 1956. A winner of two Olympic gold medals in track and field, Zaharias was a sparkplug of the budding LPGA Tour and won the Women's Open three times.

Babe Zaharias's Funeral

British Champ Thomson Strong in U.S.

Australian Peter Thomson, who would win his third straight British Open in 1956, also proved he could play in the U.S. by winning the '56 Texas International in Dallas. Thomson fired a final-round 63, then won a three-way playoff with Cary Middlecoff and Gene Littler. He holds the flag from the 2nd hole, where he clinched the title.

• September 22: Canadian Marlene Stewart, age 22, defeats JoAnne Gunderson, 17, to win the U.S. Women's Amateur at Meridian Hills C.C. in Indianapolis.

• September 27: Babe Zaharias, history's greatest woman athlete, is dead of cancer at age 42. A winner of two Olympic gold medals in track and field, Zaharias also counted three U.S. Women's Open titles among her many golf victories.

• October 22: Marlene Hagge is the LPGA's leading money winner with $20,235, and Patty Berg's scoring average of 74.57 wins the Vare Trophy. Hagge leads with eight victories.

• December 16: Jackie Burke is the PGA Tour's Player of the Year.

• December 16: Ted Kroll is the PGA Tour's top money winner with $72,835. Cary Middlecoff wins the Vardon Trophy with a 70.35 average. Mike Souchak leads with four victories.

1957

USGA SUSPENDS WARD, DISQUALIFIES PUNG

The United States Golf Association, which rarely flexed its muscles, unleashed a nasty right-left combination in 1957, as it invoked punishing penalties on two American golf stars. Founded in 1894, the USGA was largely a volunteer organization. The association conducted the nation's open and amateur championships and served as arbiter of the Rules of Golf in the United States. Rarely did the USGA impose strict penalties, but in 1957 two such penalties forever altered the careers of amateur Harvie Ward and professional Jackie Pung.

In 1957, the 31-year-old Ward was the greatest amateur star since Bobby Jones. He had been a member of the U.S. Walker Cup team in 1953 and 1955 and had won the British Amateur in 1952. More significantly, he had won the U.S. Amateur in 1955 and 1956. As the 1957 season began, fans speculated whether Ward could win a record third straight Amateur in September. In June, however, Ward's amateur career fell apart.

Ward worked as a salesman for Edward E. Lowery's automobile dealership in San Francisco. In May 1957, Lowery was indicted on California tax-evasion charges. In testimony before a grand jury, he said he had paid Ward's expenses to two tournaments in 1954.

The national press picked up on the story and the USGA couldn't ignore this obvious violation of the Rules of Amateur Status. In June, the USGA's executive committee questioned Ward about his tournament expenses. Ward confirmed that he had been subsidized by Lowery, and on June 7 the USGA stripped Ward of his amateur status for one year. The USGA's action kept Ward out of the 1957 U.S. Amateur. In 1958, he was reinstated.

Later in 1957, a USGA ruling severely punished professional Jackie Pung. The rotund Mrs. Pung, a Hawaiian, was a former U.S. Women's Amateur champion and a gallery favorite on the LPGA Tour. On June 30, she finished as the apparent U.S. Women's Open champion with a 72-hole score of 298 at Winged Foot Golf Club in Mamaroneck, New York.

Pung was celebrating when she was told she had been disqualified. Her signed scorecard had a correct final-round total of 72 but showed a 5 on the 4th hole, rather than the correct score of 6. The championship and the $1,800 prize were awarded to Betsy Rawls, who shot 299, the second-lowest score. Ironically, Rawls had defeated Pung in a 1953 playoff to win her second Women's Open.

Immediately after Pung's disqualification, *New York Times* golf writer Linc Werden passed the hat for Mrs. Pung, collecting about $2,500. Pung remained a popular player but would never win a major title. In a year that could have belonged to Ward and Pung, the USGA stood out as the biggest story.

1957

- January: PGA Tour players will compete in 32 events with a total season purse of $820,360.

- January: LPGA Tour players will compete in 26 events with a total purse of $147,830.

- January 6: Nancy Lopez, who will win 44 LPGA events in her first 15 years on Tour, is born in Torrance, California.

- January 13: Jay Hebert wins the Bing Crosby National Pro-Am. Ken Venturi, in his pro debut, finishes fifth.

- January 17: Mickey Wright shoots 104 in the first round of the Tampa Women's Open. She is penalized 24 strokes for having an extra club for 12 holes.

- February 17: Mary Lena Faulk breaks the LPGA's 72-hole scoring record by five strokes. She shoots 71-67-73-68—279 to win the St. Petersburg Women's Open.

The USGA made some difficult Rules calls in 1957, and one ruling cost Jackie Pung the U.S. Women's Open title. Pung celebrated her apparent victory in the Open with daughter Barnett, but their happiness was short-lived as the USGA disqualified Pung for signing an incorrect scorecard. The title was awarded to Betsy Rawls.

• **March 17:** For the seventh time, Patty Berg wins the Titleholders Championship. She breaks the 72-hole tournament record with a 296.

• **April 7:** Doug Ford lets out a war whoop after holing a bunker shot on the final hole to win the Masters with a final-round 66. Ford was trailing Sam Snead by three strokes as the round began but beat Snead by three.

• **April 28:** Don January, George Bayer, Ernie Vossler, and Doug Higgins are suspended for 30 days for deliberately shooting high scores in the third round of the Kentucky Derby Open. The four complained that they were not allowed to withdraw after making the cut.

• **April 28:** Patty Berg holes a 35-foot eagle putt on the final hole to defeat Wiffi Smith by one stroke and win her sixth Women's Western Open.

1957

Doug Ford

Ford Holes Out from Bunker to Win Masters

Doug Ford hit one of those shots heard around the world in 1957, when he holed out a bunker shot on the 72nd hole to win the Masters. Ford trailed Sam Snead by one stroke after 54 holes, but he closed with a 66 for a three-stroke victory. Ford also won the 1957 Los Angeles and Western Opens.

Locke Notches Win No. 4 in British Open

Arthur D'Arcy "Bobby" Locke *(left)* receives the British Open trophy from H. Gardiner-Hill, captain of the Royal and Ancient Golf Club in St. Andrews. Locke negotiated the Old Course in 279 for 72 holes, equaling his own tournament record. It was the South African's fourth British Open title.

Faulk Sets Record by Shooting 279

Mary Lena Faulk of Thomasville, Georgia—a straight hitter who was deadly with fairway woods—broke the LPGA's 72-hole scoring record in 1957. Faulk shot 71-67-73-68—279 to win the St. Petersburg Women's Open by three strokes over veteran Louise Suggs. Faulk had turned pro just two years earlier.

Mary Lena Faulk

Bobby Locke, H. Gardiner-Hill

- May 12: Jimmy Demaret wins the Arlington Hotel Open. It's his third victory of the year, and the last of his 31 career victories.

- June 7: Defending U.S. Amateur champion Harvie Ward is stripped of his amateur status by the USGA for accepting expense money for tournaments.

- June 9: Louise Suggs wins the LPGA Championship at Churchill Valley C.C. in Pittsburgh. Wiffi Smith wins the driving contest with a 310-yard smash to a baked-out fairway.

- June 9: At the Rubber City Open in Akron, Ohio, Arnold Palmer chips in from 25 feet for a birdie to defeat Doug Ford on the sixth hole of sudden-death.

- June 16: In an 18-hole playoff, Dick Mayer defeats Cary Middlecoff, 72-79, to win the U.S. Open at the Inverness Club in Toledo, Ohio. Mayer sank a nine-foot putt on the 72nd hole to tie Middlecoff and go into the playoff.

1957

Don January, George Bayer, Ernie Vossler

Tour Pals Suspended for 30 Days

Roommates Don January, George Bayer, and Ernie Vossler *(left to right)* entered the 1957 Colonial National Invitation, their first tournament after a 30-day suspension from the PGA Tour. The three were suspended for deliberately shooting high scores in a Tour event after they were not allowed to withdraw from it.

Mayer Beats the Doc in U.S. Open

Dashing Dick Mayer blasts out of a bunker on the 7th hole in the fourth round of the 1957 U.S. Open, held at the Inverness Club in Toledo, Ohio. On the 72nd hole, Mayer made a nine-foot putt to tie Cary Middlecoff at 282. Mayer beat Middlecoff the following day in an 18-hole playoff, shooting a 72 to Doc's 79.

Suggs Wins Her Fourth of the Four Majors

Louise Suggs won the LPGA Championship in 1957, giving her at least one victory in each of the LPGA's four major championships. It was Suggs's 10th major. She had previously won the Women's Open twice, the Titleholders three times, and the Women's Western Open four times. Three of those wins came when Suggs was an amateur.

Louise Suggs

Dick Mayer

• June 19: Ben Hogan is awarded $5,000 in damages from the A.S. Barnes Publishing Company of New York for publishing a book using photographs of Hogan's technique.

• June 30: The USGA disqualifies apparent Women's Open winner Jackie Pung after she signs an incorrect scorecard. Runner-up Betsy

Rawls is crowned champion at Winged Foot G.C. Club members and reporters pass the hat, collecting $2,500 for Pung.

• July 5: South African Bobby Locke wins his fourth British Open, at St. Andrews, Scotland. Locke equals his own tournament record with 279 for 72 holes.

• July 21: Lionel Hebert defeats Dow Finsterwald, 2 & 1, in the 36-hole final of the PGA Championship at Miami Valley C.C. in Dayton, Ohio. It is Hebert's first PGA Tour victory.

• August: Dick Mayer adds the World Championship to his U.S. Open title. He wins $50,000.

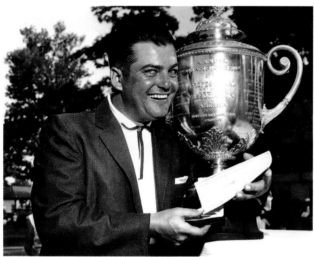

Lionel Hebert

Hebert Tops Finsterwald in PGA Final

Lionel Hebert was still revved up after winning the 1957 PGA Championship and the $8,000 first-prize check. Hebert, of Lafayette, Louisiana, beat Dow Finsterwald in the final, 2 & 1, at Miami Valley C.C. in Dayton, Ohio. It was Hebert's first PGA Tour victory, and it came in the last PGA Championship conducted at match play.

Argentine De Vicenzo Wins the All-American

Roberto De Vicenzo bogies this hole, the 7th at Tam O'Shanter C.C. near Chicago. Nevertheless, the Argentina native went on to win George S. May's 1957 All-American tournament, despite a closing round of 63 by Gene Littler, who finished second. De Vicenzo also won the 1957 Colonial NIT.

JoAnne Gunderson

Gunderson Wins First of Five Women's Amateurs

The powerful JoAnne Gunderson, age 18, rips one out of the rough and surges into a 5-up lead on her opponent, Ann Casey Johnstone, on the 26th hole of the 1957 U.S. Women's Amateur final. Gunderson won three of the next four holes to win, 8 & 6. It was the first of her five U.S. Women's Amateur championships.

Roberto De Vicenzo

• August: Patty Berg, who won last week's All-American, also wins the women's World title at Tam O'Shanter C.C. near Chicago.

• August 18: Ken Venturi wins the St. Paul Open at Keller Golf Course, shooting 66-67-65-68—266 for his first PGA Tour victory.

• August 24: Long-hitting JoAnne Gunderson of Seattle, age 18, wins the U.S. Women's Amateur at Del Paso C.C. in Sacramento, California.

• August 31: The U.S. team wins the Walker Cup Match, 8-3, over Great Britain/Ireland at the Minikahda Club in Minneapolis.

• September 14: Hillman Robbins Jr. of Memphis wins the U.S. Amateur at The Country Club in Brookline, Massachusetts. He defeats Dr. Frank M. Taylor Jr., 5 & 4.

• September 14: Sam Snead equals the PGA Tour record with a 60 at Glen Lakes C.C. in the second round of the Dallas Open.

Robbins Outclasses Taylor in U.S. Amateur

Hillman Robbins Jr. *(left)* of Memphis, Tennessee, and Dr. Frank Taylor of Pomona, California, wish each other good luck before teeing off in the final of the 1957 U.S. Amateur, held at The Country Club in Brookline, Massachusetts. Robbins went on to defeat Taylor, 5 & 4, to claim his only Amateur championship.

Hillman Robbins, Frank Taylor

Snead Fires a Record-Tying 60 in Dallas

Sam Snead holes this birdie putt on the 13th green of the 1957 Dallas Open, held at Glen Lakes C.C. On this day, Snead shot a blistering 60, tying the PGA Tour record for 18 holes. Snead's round of 11-under-par put him at 12-under after 36 holes. He won by 10 shots.

Sam Snead

Great Britain/Ireland Ryder Cup Team

Britain Wins Its First Ryder Cup in 24 Years

Great Britain won the 1957 Ryder Cup Matches, 7½-4½, at Lindrick G.C. in Yorkshire, England. Here, British players hoist captain Dai Rees on their shoulders after Britain won for the first time since 1933. For the first time ever, the U.S. lacked a big-name star.

• October 5: Great Britain upsets the United States, 7½-4½, in the Ryder Cup Matches at Lindrick G.C. in Yorkshire, England. The British sweep six of eight singles matches.

• October 6: Patty Berg leads the LPGA Tour in earnings with $16,272, while she and Betsy Rawls tie with five victories. Louise Suggs wins the Vare Trophy with a 74.64 average.

• October 12: *All-Star Golf,* the first TV series to show filmed matches between pros, debuts on ABC.

• November 10: Charlie Sifford becomes the first black player to win a Tour event, the Long Beach Open.

• December 15: Dick Mayer is named the PGA Tour's Player of the Year and, with $65,835, is the Tour's leading money winner.

• December 15: Dow Finsterwald wins the Vardon Trophy with a 70.30 average. Arnold Palmer leads the Tour with four wins.

YOUNG, FREEWHEELING PALMER PREVAILS IN MASTERS

In 1958, total prize money topped $1 million for the first time in PGA Tour history, and a sparkling collection of young talent poised for a run at golf's new riches. There was Ken Venturi, who had turned pro in 1956 after a sterling amateur career; smooth-swinging Dow Finsterwald; the Hebert brothers, Lionel and Jay; taciturn Doug Ford; mighty little South African Gary Player; and straight-hitting Art Wall.

Then there was Arnold Palmer, a dashing, young strongman from Western Pennsylvania. Palmer, age 28, had grown up on the Latrobe Country Club golf course where his father, Deacon, was head pro. With Deacon as his only teacher, Palmer had learned a slashing, hard-hitting style of play. On the greens, he used his old Tommy Armour putter with the delicate touch of a locksmith.

There was no pretense about him, and Palmer seemed to have an easy conviviality with his fans, known as Arnie's Army, who trailed after him. The charismatic Palmer freewheeled his way around the golf course. Muscles bulging and shirttail flapping, he slashed his ball over hill and

bunker, crashed his way out of trees, rifled his tee shots incredible distances, and made monumental birdie putts.

Palmer hadn't enjoyed the career of a typical gentleman amateur. He attended Wake Forest University but dropped out and joined the Coast Guard after his teammate and pal, Buddy Worsham, died in an automobile accident. Palmer made little dent in amateur golf until 1954, when he won the U.S. Amateur, beating socialite Bob Sweeny, 1 up. Three months later, Palmer turned pro. He won his first pro event, the Canadian Open in 1955, and followed that with two wins in 1956 and four in '57. Clearly,

Palmer was on the verge of playing great golf in 1958.

After a good winter, in which he won the St. Petersburg Open, Palmer joined the Tour's elite for the annual rite of spring—the Masters. After 54 holes, he and Sam Snead were tied at 5-under 211. In the final round, Palmer made the turn in 36 and pulled two strokes ahead of Snead.

On the back nine, Palmer bogied the 10th hole. On the par-5 13th, however, he smashed his 3-wood second shot to the green, 18 feet from the hole, and made the putt for an eagle 3. In high winds, Palmer fired a closing 73 to take a one-stroke lead over Fred Hawkins and defending champion Doug Ford, then sat in the clubhouse watching on television as they played the 18th hole.

Each needed a birdie to tie Arnold at 4-under-par 284. Hawkins had a 12-foot putt and Ford was about 10 feet away. Success by either would have forced the tournament into an 18-hole playoff. Both missed. Arnold Palmer had won the Masters, his first major championship. "This is the greatest thrill in my life, bar none," Palmer said. "This is my fondest dream come true."

1958

- January: PGA Tour players will compete in 39 events with a total season purse of $1,005,800. It's the first time the season purse has topped $1 million.

- January: LPGA Tour players will compete in 25 events with a total purse of $158,600.

- January: Ken Venturi wins the Thunderbird Invitational.

- January: The USGA abandons "current" and "basic" golf handicaps. Now there will be only one handicap.

- January 6: Frank Stranahan wins the Los Angeles Open, shooting 275.

- January 12: For the second year in a row, Mickey Wright wins the Sea Island Invitational.

- January 20: Betsy Rawls captures the Tampa Women's Open at Palma Ceia G.C.

- February: For the first time in seven years, there is no San Diego

1958

Defending champion Doug Ford helps a jubilant Arnold Palmer into the first green jacket of his career. Palmer won the 1958 Masters by one stroke over Ford and Fred Hawkins. Arnie's most significant score came Sunday on the par-5 13th, where he reached the green in two and holed an 18-foot putt for an eagle.

Open on the PGA Tour. It will resume next season.

• February 2: For the second week in a row, Ken Venturi is the PGA Tour's winner with a victory in the Phoenix Open.

• February 2: Gene Sarazen wins his second PGA Seniors Championship.

• February 16: Unknown Bill Johnston wins the Texas Open.

• March 2: For the third time in six weeks, Ken Venturi wins a PGA Tour event, the Baton Rouge Open.

• March 2: Fred Hawkins wins the Jackson Open in Mississippi—a 36-hole PGA Tour event.

• March 11: Billy Casper grabs his second Tour event of the year, the New Orleans Open, resumed for the first time in 10 years. Casper's victory comes at City Park Golf Course.

• March 16: Beverly Hanson wins the Titleholders Championship with a score of 299.

Edsel Curry, Frank Stranahan

Stranahan Collects First First-Place Check

Frank Stranahan *(right)* accepts the $7,000 check for winning the 1958 Los Angeles Open from Edsel Curry, president of L.A.'s Junior Chamber of Commerce. Stranahan previously played the PGA Tour as an amateur and won one Tour event. He captured the Durham Open way back in 1945.

Venturi Wins Three Tour Events in Six Weeks

Ken Venturi, poised at the finish of another fine swing, proved his talents as a professional in 1958. In a six-week period during the spring, Venturi won the Thunderbird Invitational, the Phoenix Open, and the Baton Rouge Open. He led the '57 Tour with four victories.

Sanders Hits the Big Time With Western Victory

Flashy Doug Sanders flashes a grin after winning his first tournament as a professional, the 1958 Western Open, held at Red Run G.C. in suburban Detroit. Sanders, a colorful dresser with an unorthodox swing, shot 275 for 72 holes. As an amateur, he won the Canadian Open in 1956.

Doug Sanders

Ken Venturi

- April 6: Arnold Palmer vaults into the national spotlight when he wins his first Masters with a 4-under-par 284. Doug Ford and Fred Hawkins tie for second.

- April 20: South African Gary Player prevails in the Kentucky Derby Open. It's the 22-year-old's first PGA Tour victory.

- May 4: Tommy Bolt wins the Colonial National Invitation Tournament.

- May 18: Sam Snead wins the Greenbrier Invitational.

- May 18: Billy Maxwell wins the inaugural Memphis Open, shooting 267 at Colonial C.C. in Tennessee.

- June: Phil Rodgers of the University of Houston proves the victor in the NCAA championship, and Houston takes its third straight team title.

- June 1: Doug Sanders takes the Western Open at Red Run G.C. in Royal Oak, Michigan.

1958

President Eisenhower

World Amateur Trophy Named After Eisenhower

President Dwight D. Eisenhower was honored in 1958 when the trophy for the World Amateur Team championship was christened the "Eisenhower Trophy." The trophy's inscription read: "To foster friendship and sportsmanship among Peoples of the World." In the inaugural event, the U.S. and Australia tied for first with 918 strokes, at St. Andrews in Scotland.

Peter Thomson

Thomson Ties Record of Young Tom Morris

Australian Peter Thomson chips onto the 3rd green at Hoylake in the 1958 British Open. Thomson went on to win the Open for the fourth time in five years. Peter was the ninth golfer to win the British four times, but only one other man—Young Tom Morris—claimed the event four times in five years.

Bolt Dances to Victory in U.S. Open

Tommy Bolt breaks into an impromptu jig after sinking this putt on the 9th hole at Tulsa's Southern Hills C.C., which gave him a one-stroke lead over Gary Player in the final round of the 1958 U.S. Open. Bolt led after every round and went on to beat Player by four strokes. It was his only win in a major.

Tommy Bolt

• June 8: Sam Snead wins the Dallas Open at Oak Cliff C.C.

• June 8: Mickey Wright claims her first major title, the LPGA Championship, at Churchill Valley C.C. in Penn Hills, Pennsylvania. Wright beats runner-up Fay Crocker by six strokes.

• June 14: Native Oklahoman Tommy Bolt wins his first major championship, the U.S. Open, at Southern Hills C.C. in Tulsa. Bolt leads after every round and defeats runner-up Gary Player by four strokes.

• June 22: Patty Berg wins her seventh Women's Western Open championship, at Kahkwa C.C. in Erie, Pennsylvania. Her first Western victory was in 1941. No other woman has won a major title as often.

• June 23: Billy Casper claims the first Buick Open Invitational at Warwick Hills C.C. in Grand Blanc, Michigan.

Beverly Hanson

Hanson Rubs It In at Titleholders Championship

Beverly Hanson of Fargo, North Dakota, repairs the damage after braving the weather to take the third-round lead at the 1958 Titleholders. The following day, Hanson won the championship with a 74—299. It was her second major victory; she also won the 1955 LPGA Championship.

Wright's First Major Victory Comes in the LPGA

Mickey Wright, a fourth-year professional, shows off her prize money for winning the first of her 13 major championships—the 1958 LPGA Championship. The classic-swinging Californian won by shooting 288 for 72 holes at Churchill Valley C.C. near Pittsburgh. Fay Crocker was second, six strokes back.

Mickey Wright

• June 28: Mickey Wright, age 23, wins the U.S. Women's Open. Wright leads after every round at Forest Lake C.C. in Detroit.

• July 4: At Royal Lytham & St. Annes G.C. in England, Peter Thomson wins a 36-hole playoff with Dave Thomas, 139-143, to win his fourth British Open title.

• July 12: Dan Sikes of Jacksonville, Florida, wins the U.S. Amateur Public Links championship at Silver Lake G.C. in Orland Park, Illinois.

• July 15: Patty Berg claims her second tournament of the year, the American Women's Open at Brookview C.C. in her hometown of Minneapolis.

• July 17: For the first time, PGA Tour players tee off in a PGA Championship conducted at stroke play, rather than match play. Stroke play is better suited for television.

• July 20: Dow Finsterwald wins the PGA Championship at Llanerch C.C. in Havertown, Pennsylvania. Billy Casper is runner-up.

Player Wins the Derby Open for First Tour Win

South African Gary Player burst onto the American golf scene with a victory in the 1958 Kentucky Derby Open. Player was inspired by the success of fellow countryman Bobby Locke to try the PGA Tour. Player won this event at the tender age of 22, and he would win his first major championship a year later.

Patty Berg

Berg Wins Last of Record 15 Major Championships

In 1958, 40-year-old Patty Berg captured the Women's Western Open for the last of her record 15 major victories. Berg won seven Westerns, seven Titleholders Championships, and one U.S. Women's Open. Berg would still play competitively for many years. In fact, 33 years later in the summer of 1991, she would score a hole-in-one.

Gary Player

• July 27: Art Wall gets his second victory in four weeks when he wins the Eastern Open.

• August: The All-American Open and World Championship of Golf are off the PGA Tour schedule. Sponsor George S. May, tired of feuding with the pros, also complained of a "circus" atmosphere.

• August 9: The team from Great Britain and Ireland retains the Curtis Cup by tying the United States, 4½-4½, at Brae Burn C.C. in West Newton, Massachusetts. The British team had won the cup in 1956.

• August 15: Judy Eller becomes the first two-time winner of the U.S. Girls' Junior championship, at the Manor C.C. in Rockville, Maryland. She won her first title last year.

• August 23: Anne Quast, low amateur in the 1958 U.S. Women's Open, stops Barbara Romack's bid for a second U.S. Women's Amateur championship. Quast defeats the 1954 champion, 3 & 2, at Wee Burn C.C. in Darien, Connecticut.

Dow Finsterwald

Finsterwald Wins First PGA at Stroke Play

Dow Finsterwald chips to the 5th green at Llanerch C.C. in Havertown, Pennsylvania. The crowd saw Finsterwald win the PGA Championship in its first year at stroke play. In the final round, Dow overtook third-round leader Sam Snead when he fired an outgoing 31. He finished with 276, two strokes better than Billy Casper.

George Bayer

Ailing Smith Elected to Hall of Fame

Horton Smith was inducted into the PGA Hall of Fame in 1958. Smith led professional golfers with eight victories in 1929 and twice won the Masters. He also served as PGA president from 1952–54 and remained active in golf administration. Stricken with Hodgkin's disease in 1957, he died in 1963.

Horton Smith

Powerful Bayer Wins Two Late in the Year

Big George Bayer hits back into the correct fairway after slicing his drive across an adjacent fairway at the 1958 Los Angeles Open. Bayer, the decade's longest hitter, went on to enjoy a fine year. Late in the fall, he won two official PGA Tour titles: the Havana Open and the Mayfair Inn Open.

- September 8: Mickey Wright wins the Dallas Women's Open.

- September 8: PGA Champion Dow Finsterwald wins his second event of the year, the Utah Open.

- September 13: Charles Coe, low amateur in the 1958 U.S. Open, wins his second U.S. Amateur championship. Coe defeats Tommy Aaron, 5 & 4, in the 36-hole final at the Olympic Club in San Francisco.

- September 14: Beverly Hanson, with a scoring average of 74.92, grabs the Vare Trophy and is the LPGA's leading money winner with $12,639.

- September 14: Mickey Wright's five official victories lead the LPGA Tour.

- September 21: Little-known John McMullin wins the PGA Tour's Hesperia Open in California.

- October 13: At the Old Course at St. Andrews, Scotland, the U.S. and

1958

Eller Edges Wheeler in U.S. Girls' Junior Championship

Judy Eller *(left)* of Old Hickory, Tennessee, receives the Vare Trophy from Glenna Collett Vare *(center)*, six-time U.S. Women's Amateur champion. Eller had just defeated Sherry Wheeler *(right)*, 1 up, in the final of the 1958 U.S. Girls' Junior. Eller, the defender, was the first to win the championship twice.

Charles Coe, John Ames

Judy Eller, Glenna Collett Vare, Sherry Wheeler

Coe Tops Aaron for Second Straight Amateur

Charles Coe *(left)* of Oklahoma City receives the U.S. Amateur championship trophy from USGA President John Ames after winning the event for the second time. On this day, Coe defeated Tommy Aaron in the final, 5 & 4. Aaron, in the background with his head down, would go on to win the 1973 Masters.

Australia tie for the first World Amateur Team championship.

• November 16: Big-hitting George Bayer is the winner in the PGA Tour's Havana Open in Cuba.

• December 7: George Bayer wins his second tournament in the last three events, the Mayfair Inn Open.

• December 7: Bob Rosburg, with a scoring average of 70.11, claims the PGA Tour's Vardon Trophy.

• December 7: Arnold Palmer leads the Tour with $42,607.50. Ken Venturi leads with four wins.

• December 7: Dow Finsterwald, winner of the PGA Championship,

claims the PGA Tour's Player of the Year Award.

• Helen Dettweiler, a founder of the LPGA Tour, wins the first LPGA Teacher of the Year Award.

• Veteran Tour player Horton Smith is elected to the PGA Hall of Fame.

RAWLS'S SUPER YEAR GIVES TOUR NEEDED BOOST

The skill of Betsy Rawls's golf game is often overshadowed by her contemporary role in the business of golf. A diplomatic woman of keen intelligence, Rawls has enjoyed great success as an administrator. When she retired from competition in 1975, she was hired by the LPGA as the Tour's first tournament director. In 1981, she began a long reign as executive director of the McDonald's Championship, and she is the first woman to serve on the Rules Committee of the U.S. Open.

It was as a player, however, that the soft-spoken woman from Spartanburg, South Carolina, made her greatest impact. And 1959, her greatest season, was the year in which Rawls set new standards in women's golf.

In 1959, the LPGA Tour featured a few dozen players who traveled a tournament circuit of small and medium-sized towns. The Tour desperately needed a new star, as the great Babe Zaharias had died of cancer and superstar Patty Berg was age 41 and past her prime. The LPGA's press coverage rested largely on the slender shoulders of the reserved Louise Suggs.

By 1959, Rawls had been on the Tour for eight years and had 28 wins. Her quiet, unassuming way had earned her many friends, but few headlines. At age 31, she had failed to ignite the excitement that Babe had brought to women's golf earlier in the decade. Rawls was more of a scholastic sort. At the University of Texas, she had earned degrees in both mathematics and physics and was Phi Beta Kappa.

On the course, Rawls was a premier shot-maker, a wizard around the greens, and an excellent putter. And in 1959, Rawls took women's golf to a higher level. She set new marks in victories, money winnings, and scoring, and her record-breaking season put her into the LPGA Hall of Fame. Beginning February 23 with a victory in the Lake Worth Open in Florida, and ending September 27 with a win in the Opie Turner Open, Rawls won 10 tournaments, or nearly 40 percent of the LPGA's 26-event schedule. Included were wins in the LPGA Championship and Women's Western Open.

It was the first time that any LPGA player had won tournaments in double figures. Her winnings, $26,774, broke Marlene Hagge's 1956 record by more than $6,000. Moreover, Rawls lowered the LPGA scoring average record by nearly a half-stroke, giving the LPGA a leap in credibility. In a day when the LPGA played courses set up at over 6,400 yards, she set a scoring-average record of 74.03.

Rawls would win another 17 tournaments before the end of her career. She is one of only two women to win the U.S. Women's Open four times, and she was inducted into the World Golf Hall of Fame in 1987. She spent 25 years on Tour, but 1959 was her shining moment. At a time when the LPGA needed appealing new champions, Betsy Rawls became the Tour's brightest star.

1959

- January: PGA Tour players will compete in 43 events with a total season purse of $1,225,205.

- January: LPGA Tour players will compete in 26 events with a total purse of $202,500.

- January 18: Art Wall gets off to a fast start in what will be his best year when he wins the Bing Crosby National Pro-Am.

- January 25: Arnold Palmer wins the Tour's fourth tournament of the year, the Thunderbird Invitational.

- February 8: Gene Littler ties Bobby Locke's tournament record of 268 when he wins the Phoenix Open.

- February 15: Gene Littler nabs his second straight tournament, the Tucson Open.

- March 14: In the third round of the Pensacola Open, Bob Rosburg needs only 19 putts in 18 holes.

- March 15: Louise Suggs claims her fourth Titleholders Championship.

Betsy Rawls had good reason to kiss caddie Warren Vander Voort. Rawls had just won the 1959 Mount Prospect Women's Open on her way to a record-breaking season on the LPGA Tour. Rawls won 10 tournaments, setting a new money record of $26,774. She also captured the Vare Trophy with a record scoring average of 74.03.

• March 30: Art Wall captures his second Tour event of the year, the Azalea Open.

• April: Jack Nicklaus wins the North and South Amateur championship.

• April 5: Art Wall birdies five of the last six holes to shoot 66 and win the Masters, by a stroke over Cary Middlecoff.

• April 12: The Babe Zaharias Open at Beaumont C.C. in Texas is Betsy Rawls's second win in a row and third of the year.

• April 19: Jackie Burke wins the Houston Classic in a playoff.

• April 26: Mike Souchak wins the Tournament of Champions in Las Vegas and the Tour's third-largest first prize, $10,000.

• May 1: At Colonial C.C. in Fort Worth, Texas—a course known as Hogan's Alley—46-year-old Ben Hogan wins his fifth Colonial National Invitation Tournament.

Arnold Palmer, Art Wall Jr.

Wall Masters Palmer in Exciting Sunday Showdown

Art Wall Jr. gets an assist from Arnold Palmer with the traditional green jacket after winning the 1959 Masters. Palmer, the defending champion, was tied for the lead with Stan Leonard going into the final round, six shots ahead of Wall. However, Wall closed with a record-tying 66 for a winning 284 total.

Littler Prevails in Phoenix, Tucson Opens

Gene Littler strokes this birdie putt into the cup on the 8th hole at Arizona C.C. in the 1958 Phoenix Open. Not only did Littler win this event, but his 268 tied the tournament record set by Bobby Locke. The following week, Littler drove down the road and won the Tucson Open.

Gene Littler

- **May 3:** Runner-up the previous week, Betsy Rawls captures the Land of the Sky Women's Open in Asheville, North Carolina.

- **May 16:** The United States wins the Walker Cup for the 16th time, defeating Great Britain, 9-3, at Muirfield in Scotland.

- **May 31:** Little-known Don Whitt claims his second straight PGA Tour event, as he captures the Kentucky Derby Open.

- **June 7:** Betsy Rawls wins her fifth tournament of the season, the Triangle Round Robin at New Jersey's Canoe Brook C.C.

- **June 13:** Saturday thunderstorms at the U.S. Open at Winged Foot G.C. in Mamaroneck, New York, force the USGA to stage the fourth round, for the first time in history, on Sunday.

- **June 14:** Billy Casper, age 27, wins his first U.S. Open championship with a one-stroke victory over Bob

Barbara McIntire, Louise Suggs

McIntire, Suggs Haul in the Hardware

Barbara McIntire *(left)* and Louise Suggs *(right)* celebrate amateur and professional wins in the 1959 Titleholders. McIntire, who won the amateur division, went on to win the U.S. Women's Amateur later in the year. Suggs, meanwhile, picked up her fourth Titleholders and 11th major title.

Aging Hogan Wins His Fifth Colonial NIT

At age 47, The Hawk still had what it took to win. Ben Hogan lines up this putt at Fort Worth's Colonial C.C. on his way to winning the 1959 Colonial National Invitation Tournament. Hogan and Fred Hawkins tied at 285, and Hogan won the playoff. It was his fifth win on the course known as Hogan's Alley.

Ben Hogan

Rosburg. Claude Harmon, the host professional, finishes in a tie for third with Mike Souchak.

• June 27: At Churchill Valley C.C. near Pittsburgh, the scene of her 1958 LPGA Championship, Mickey Wright wins the U.S. Women's Open for the second year in a row. Louise Suggs finishes second.

• July 3: South African Gary Player wins the British Open at Muirfield in Scotland, edging Fred Bullock and Flory Van Donck. It is Player's first major championship.

• July 5: Art Wall grabs his fourth Tour event of the year, the Buick Open, with a 282.

• July 6: Betsy Rawls prevails in the LPGA Championship, her sixth win of the year, at Sheraton C.C. in French Lick, Indiana. Patty Berg finishes runner-up.

• July 12: Brawny Mike Souchak wins the Western Open at Pittsburgh Field Club in Fox Chapel, Pennsylvania.

Mike Souchak

Souchak's the Victor in Breezy Tournament of Champions

In the third round of the 1959 Tournament of Champions, Mike Souchak barely missed a birdie when his ball struck the flagstick on the 2nd green and bounced out of the hole. Souchak was unfazed. Despite high winds, he went on to win the tournament and the $10,000 first prize.

It's Whitt by a Nose in Kentucky Derby Open

Little-known Don Whitt *(right)* compares his first-prize check with runner-up Jim Ferree after winning the 1959 Kentucky Derby Open in Louisville. Whitt edged Ferree by one stroke, firing 274 to collect the $2,800 first prize. It was Whitt's second straight PGA Tour victory.

Rosburg Strokes Just 19 Putts

Modern-day television commentator Bob Rosburg hit a lot of great shots in the 1950s and '60s, but he was known as the PGA Tour's finest putter. On March 14, 1959, Rossie needed only 19 putts in the third round of the Pensacola Open, tying the Tour putting record for 18 holes.

Bob Rosburg

Jim Ferree, Don Whitt

• July 18: Bill Wright of Seattle becomes the first black player to win a USGA championship when he defeats Frank H. Campbell, 3 & 2, to win the U.S. Amateur Public Links at Wellshire G.C. in Denver.

• July 19: Gene Littler captures the Insurance City Open for his fourth victory of the year.

• July 19: Mickey Wright wins her second tournament in two weeks, the Alliance Machine International Open.

• July 26: Betsy Rawls wins her second Women's Western Open and the fifth major title of her career. She first won the Western in 1952.

• August 2: Putting whiz Bob Rosburg claims his first major title, the PGA Championship, as he edges Jerry Barber and Doug Sanders at Minneapolis G.C.

• August 16: Mike Souchak wins his third Tour event of the year, the Motor City Open.

Barbara McIntire

McIntire's the Victor in U.S. Women's Amateur

Barbara McIntire relies on the moral support of her caddie as they survey the 15th green in the quarterfinals of the 1959 U.S. Women's Amateur, at Congressional C.C. outside Washington, D.C. McIntire defeated Anne Quast on the 20th hole with a par. She went on to win the championship by defeating Joanne Goodwin in the final, 4 & 3.

Mickey Wright

Player Prevails in British Open

Gary Player weathers a poor first round in the 1959 British Open, shooting 75 at Muirfield in Scotland. Nevertheless, Player went on to win the Open by two strokes over Fred Bullock and Belgium's Flory Van Donck. Player's opening round was the highest by a British Open champion in 30 years.

Gary Player

Wright is Victorious Again at Churchill Valley

Mickey Wright tips her visor on her way to victory in the 1959 U.S. Women's Open. The Open was held at Churchill Valley C.C. near Pittsburgh—one of her favorite hangouts. A year earlier, Wright won the LPGA Championship on the very same course. She shot 288 in the LPGA and 287 in the Open.

• August 16: Betsy Rawls wins her eighth LPGA tournament of the season, the Seattle Open.

• August 29: Barbara McIntire, age 24, who nearly won the 1956 U.S. Women's Open, wins the U.S. Women's Amateur championship. She defeats Joanne Goodwin, 4 & 3, in the 36-hole final.

• August 30: Gene Littler claims his fifth title of the season, the Miller Open.

• August 30: Betsy Rawls wins the Waterloo Women's Open in Iowa for her ninth victory of the year, breaking the LPGA record set by Louise Suggs and Marlene Hagge.

• September 7: For the second time in five weeks, Dow Finsterwald tops the PGA Tour field with a win in the Kansas City Open. He won the Carling Open earlier.

• September 14: Julius Boros captures the Dallas Open at Oak Cliff C.C.

Dow Finsterwald, Don Essig

Finsterwald Nips Fairfield in Kansas City Open

Dow Finsterwald *(left)* and Don Essig joke over Finsterwald's $2,800 first-prize check in the 1959 Kansas City Open. But Finsterwald was dead serious when he won the tournament in a playoff with Don Fairfield. It was Finsterwald's second win in a month. Essig was low amateur in the K.C. tourney.

Underrated Boros Prevails in Dallas Open

Until he won his second U.S. Open in 1963, Julius Boros was probably one of the most unappreciated golfers on the PGA Tour. Boros won his first U.S. Open in 1952, and he led the Tour in earnings in both 1952 and 1955. In 1959, he captured the Dallas Open, one of his 18 career victories.

Julius Boros

• **September 19:** Jack Nicklaus prevails in the U.S. Amateur championship at the Broadmoor G.C. in Colorado Springs, Colorado. He defeats Charles Coe, 1 up, in the final round.

• **September 27:** Betsy Rawls captures the Vare Trophy with a

scoring average of 74.03. On the strength of her 10 wins, she sets a new money record of $26,774.

• **October 4:** Billy Casper wins the Portland Open. It will be his first of three victories in the event.

• **November 7:** The United States wins back the Ryder Cup, which it

had lost in 1957, by defeating the British team, 8½-3½, at Eldorado C.C. in Palm Desert, California.

• **November 15:** Billy Casper captures his third tournament of the year, the Lafayette Open.

• **November 22:** For the second week in a row, Billy Casper is in the

Jack Nicklaus

Nicklaus Tops Andrews, Coe to Claim U.S. Amateur

Jack Nicklaus missed few birdie opportunities on his way to winning the 1959 U.S. Amateur, but this long putt on the 10th green stopped inches short. At the Broadmoor G.C. in Colorado Springs, Nicklaus won this semifinal match against Gene Andrews. He then defeated Charles Coe, the defending champion, for the title.

Goggin Prevails in Both Senior Tournaments

Willie Goggin plays from the rough in the 1959 U.S. National Senior championship. Goggin won this event, for the second year in a row, and also captured the '59 PGA Seniors Championship. Goggin won the PGA Seniors with a borrowed set of woods.

Willie Goggin

winner's circle as he claims the Mobile Open in Alabama.

• November 29: Arnold Palmer, winless since May, captures the West Palm Beach Open in Florida.

• December 6: Art Wall, with a scoring average of 70.35, wins the PGA Tour's Vardon Trophy.

• December 6: Art Wall is named Player of the Year. He leads in earnings with $53,167.60.

• December 6: Gene Littler leads the PGA Tour with five wins. Art Wall and Billy Casper have four each.

• *Golf* magazine begins publication.

• Deane Beman wins the British Amateur championship, defeating fellow American Bill Hyndman in the final at Sandwich, England.

• Harry Cooper, Jock Hutchison, and Paul Runyan are elected for induction into the PGA Hall of Fame.

PALMER CHARGES TO WIN MASTERS, U.S. OPEN

Arnold Palmer vaulted into the spotlight in 1960 as a player of near-mythic proportion. Like a knight charging after the Holy Grail, Palmer galloped to final-round surges to win his second Masters and his only U.S. Open. He very nearly won the British Open to cap the best performance by any golfer since 1953, when Ben Hogan won the same three tournaments.

In April, Palmer badly wanted to regain the Masters title he had first claimed in 1958. He opened with a brilliant 67 to take the lead. A 73 in the second round and a 72 in the third kept him atop the leader board. But Ken Venturi, one stroke behind as the final round began, was closing fast. Extraordinary play gave Venturi a one-stroke lead after the 16th hole. Squinting into the setting sun, Palmer mounted his now-famous "charge." He birdied the last two holes and beat Venturi by a stroke.

In June, Palmer arrived at Denver's Cherry Hills Country Club for the U.S. Open with five season wins in his pocket. Here, though, Palmer was in trouble from the start. He tried to drive the green of the 1st hole, a downhill par-4 of 346 yards, but drove into a hazard and made a double bogey. At the end of the third round on Saturday, Palmer trailed Mike Souchak by seven strokes. More than a dozen players were ahead of Arnie.

The final round would be played on Saturday afternoon. During lunch, Palmer asked companions, "I may shoot 65. What would that do?" "Nothing," said golf writer Bob Drum. "You're too far back." "The hell I am," Palmer snapped. "A 65 would give me 280, and 280 wins Opens."

Three times Palmer had tried to drive the 1st green, and three times he had failed. On Saturday afternoon, Palmer went for it again. He hit a smoking tee shot, his ball bounded through a belt of rough fronting the green, and it rolled onto the putting surface 20 feet from the hole. He nearly holed his eagle putt, and he made his birdie.

At the 2nd hole, Palmer chipped in for another birdie. A wedge shot to within one foot gave him a birdie at the 3rd, and he birdied from 18 feet at the 4th. He was now only three strokes behind Souchak, and galleries raced to Palmer's side. Arnie made a curling 20-footer for a birdie on the 6th, and he sank a six-foot birdie putt at the 7th. He made the turn in 30 strokes.

Souchak faltered. Amateur Jack Nicklaus and Ben Hogan were paired together, and Nicklaus led for a time before he three-putted twice on the back nine. Hogan, tied for the lead, tried daring shots on the final two holes, but he hit into the water both times. Palmer, meanwhile, was steady on the back nine and played the final two holes safely. He holed his last par putt for a 65 and the 280 he had wanted. When the winning putt fell, he flung his white visor into the air. It was a spectacular victory for the PGA Tour's most charismatic star.

1960

- January: PGA Tour players will compete in 41 events with a total season purse of $1,335,242.

- January: LPGA Tour players will compete in 25 events with a total purse of $186,700.

- January 9: Dow Finsterwald wins the Los Angeles Open.

- January 17: Mickey Wright wins the first LPGA tournament of the season, the Sea Island Invitational.

- February 7: Arnold Palmer prevails in the Palm Springs Desert Classic with a 90-hole score of 338.

- February 28: Mickey Wright wins her second tournament of the year, the Tampa Open. Patty Berg and Joyce Ziske tie for second.

- February 28: Arnold Palmer claims the Texas Open for his second victory of the year.

- March 6: At the Baton Rouge Open, Arnold Palmer wins his second tournament in a row.

Arnold Palmer *(left)* poses with Miss Golf, Glenda Gunter, and former winner Claude Harmon at the 1960 Masters. It's hard to tell what Arnie's doing with his fingers, but perhaps he's predicting how many tournaments he would win in 1960. He ended up with eight Tour victories; no one between 1950 and the present has won more tournaments in a year.

• March 13: Arnold Palmer makes it three in a row with a victory in the Pensacola Open.

• March 13: Fay Crocker captures the Titleholders Championship, shooting 303 for 72 holes.

• March 27: At the age of 47, Sam Snead wins the De Soto Open.

• April: Barbara McIntire wins her second Women's North and South Amateur championship.

• April 8: Arnold Palmer birdies the last two holes to beat Ken Venturi by one stroke at the Masters.

• April 10: Betsy Rawls wins the Babe Zaharias Open, staged in

memory of the late LPGA star, at the Beaumont C.C. in Texas. Country-western music is piped to the practice tee.

• April 17: Sam Snead claims the Greater Greensboro Open for the seventh time. His first victory in the tournament was in 1938.

Sam Snead, C.W. "Moon" Wyrick

Snead Notches Win No. 7 at Greater Greensboro

Sam Snead *(left)* was given a big basket by C.W. "Moon" Wyrick to haul away his money after winning the 1960 Greater Greensboro Open and another first-prize check. Sam, then 48, captured his seventh—but not his last—GGO by shooting 270 for 72 holes. Snead's first Greensboro victory came in 1938.

Arnold Palmer

Rawls Wins U.S. Open, Enters Hall

July 1960 was a heck of a month for Betsy Rawls. On July 23, she prevailed in the U.S. Women's Open, shooting 292 and winning by a stroke over Joyce Ziske. A week later, she was named to the Women's Golf Hall of Fame. Rawls was just the fifth woman named to the ultra-exclusive Hall.

Betsy Rawls

Palmer Kicks Off Masters with a Super 67

Arnold Palmer got off to a great start with a 5-under-par 67 in the opening round of the 1960 Masters. Palmer followed with rounds of 73-72-70 for a 72-hole total of 282. He birdied the final two holes to edge Ken Venturi by one stroke and win his second of four Masters titles.

• **May 8:** Jerry Barber wins the Tournament of Champions and the PGA Tour's second-largest first-prize check—$16,000 (the Masters is first at $17,500).

• **May 21:** Leading narrowly, 2-1, after foursomes play, the United States defeats Great Britain/Ireland, 6½-2½, to win the Curtis Cup. The Match is played at Lindrick G.C. in Worksop, England.

• **June:** Dick Crawford of the University of Houston wins the NCAA championship. Houston wins its fifth straight team title.

• **June:** The final round of the Canada Cup Match at Ireland's Portmarnock G.C. attracts more than 30,000 fans. The U.S. team of Sam Snead and Arnold Palmer wins the cup.

• **June 18:** After the third round of the U.S. Open at Cherry Hills C.C. in Denver, Arnold Palmer trails Mike Souchak by seven strokes. After the round is over, Palmer

McIntire Proves the Queen of Amateur Golf

Barbara McIntire hits from the rough on the 11th hole in her 1960 Curtis Cup match with British standout Elizabeth Price. They halved the match and the U.S. team won the Curtis Cup, 6½-2½. In 1960, McIntire won the British Ladies' Amateur and Women's North and South Amateur.

Joyce Ziske

Jerry Barber

Barber Digs into Dollars at Tournament of Champions

Jerry Barber and his wife enjoy a handful of the 10,000 silver dollars Barber won in the 1960 Tournament of Champions in Las Vegas. It was Barber's first big win since the 1954 All-American Open. Jerry won the T. of C. by setting a tournament record of 268, which would stand until 1986.

Barbara McIntire

Ziske Bests the Rest at Western Open

Joyce Ziske, a former Curtis Cup player from Milwaukee, was a strong player with a classic swing. In 1960, she proved her professional mettle by winning the Women's Western Open, finishing 4-under-par at Chicago's Beverly C.C. She would lose that year's U.S. Women's Open by one stroke.

---

predicts he'll win the tournament in the afternoon.

• June 18: In the final round of the U.S. Open, Arnold Palmer drives the green of the par-4 1st hole and shoots 65 to win by two strokes. Amateur Jack Nicklaus finishes second, and his 282 is the lowest amateur score in the event's history.

• June 29: Joyce Ziske wins the Women's Western Open, finishing 4-under-par at Chicago's Beverly C.C.

• July: Judy Bell of Colorado Springs, Colorado, wins her third Broadmoor Ladies Invitational in her hometown. She also won in 1957 and 1958.

• July 4: Mickey Wright captures her third tournament of the year, the LPGA Championship in French Lick, Indiana.

• July 9: Kel Nagle beats Arnold Palmer by one stroke in the British Open at St. Andrews, Scotland. Palmer's appearance keys American interest in the Open.

1960

Arnold Palmer, Jack Nicklaus

Nicklaus Better Than the Pros in U.S. Open

Arnold Palmer *(left)* and amateur Jack Nicklaus *(right)* finished one-two in the 1960 U.S. Open. The young Nicklaus, reigning U.S. Amateur champion, beat every pro except Palmer to win the silver medal. Palmer fired a winning total of 280 to Nicklaus's 282. It was the best showing by an amateur since 1933, when Johnny Goodman won.

Wright Claims Her Second LPGA Championship

Mickey Wright makes a rare miscue on this bunker shot in the final round of the 1960 LPGA Championship in French Lick, Indiana. While the flub cost her a bogey on the 6th hole, it was of little consequence. Wright went on to win her second LPGA Championship in three years.

Mickey Wright

• July 9: American Art Wall Jr. wins the Canadian Open at St. Georges Golf and C.C. in Toronto.

• July 17: Canadian Stan Leonard wins the American PGA Tour's Western Open at the Western Golf and C.C. in Michigan. Leonard defeats Art Wall on the first hole of sudden-death.

• July 23: Betsy Rawls wins a record fourth U.S. Women's Open, by one stroke over Joyce Ziske at Worcester C.C. in Massachusetts. Judy Torluemke, age 15, wins low-amateur honors.

• July 24: Jay Hebert nips Jim Ferrier by one stroke to win the PGA Championship at Firestone C.C. in

Akron, Ohio. Jay's brother Lionel won the PGA in 1957.

• August 27: JoAnne Gunderson defeats Jean Ashley, 6 & 5, to claim her second U.S. Women's Amateur championship, at the Tulsa C.C.

• September 1: Mickey Wright wins the Tour's Eastern Open at Range

Jay Hebert

Another Hebert Wins the PGA Championship

Jay Hebert poses with the trophy after winning the 1960 PGA Championship at Firestone C.C. in Akron, Ohio. Hebert won $11,000 when he beat runner-up Jim Ferrier by a single stroke. Hebert's brother Lionel won the PGA in 1957, the last year in which it was conducted at match play. They are the only brothers to win the PGA.

Stan Leonard

Crawford, Houston Win at NCAAs

Dick Crawford chips onto the 12th green on his way to a quarterfinal victory over Terry Dill in the 1960 NCAA championship. Crawford, from the University of Houston, went on to win the individual title, his second in a row. Crawford also helped Houston to the team championship, its fifth straight.

Dick Crawford

Canadian Leonard Wins Western Open Playoff

Stan Leonard, a Canadian, was part of the growing foreign influence on the U.S. PGA Tour. Playing here with Gary Player, Dennis Hutchinson, and Harold Henning—all from South Africa—Leonard won the 1960 Western Open by defeating Art Wall on the first hole of a sudden-death playoff.

End C.C. in Dillesburg, Pennsylvania. It's her fifth victory of the year.

• September 5: Johnny Pott captures his first official PGA Tour title, the Dallas Open.

• September 17: Deane Beman wins the U.S. Amateur, beating Robert W. Gardner in the final, 6 & 4, at St. Louis C.C.

• September 18: Mickey Wright claims her third straight LPGA tournament, the Memphis Open.

• September 25: Billy Casper wins the Portland Open for the second year in a row. Casper shoots 266.

• October 1: The U.S. dominates the World Amateur Team championship, winning by 42 strokes at Merion G.C. in Pennsylvania.

• October 2: Mickey Wright becomes the first LPGA Tour player to average fewer than 74 strokes per round when she averages 73.25 and wins her first Vare Trophy.

JoAnne Gunderson

The Great Gundy Nabs Women's Amateur

JoAnne Gunderson was known as The Great Gundy before she became Mrs. Carner. A dominant force in amateur golf, JoAnne showed the same exuberance with which she would charm galleries as a professional. Body english didn't help her make this putt in the semifinals of the 1960 U.S. Women's Amateur, but she won the championship anyway.

Nagle Prevails in Historic British Open

Australian Kel Nagle holds two trophies presented to him after winning the British Open on its 100th anniversary. The larger cup was the permanent trophy and the smaller cup was presented to Nagle to mark the Open's centenary. Nagle edged Arnold Palmer by one stroke to win.

Kel Nagle

U.S. Defeats Ireland in Canada Cup

Many of the 30,000 fans who attended the final round of the 1960 Canada Cup Match in Ireland swarmed around Arnold Palmer. Ireland had victory in sight until Christy O'Connor blew the individual title when he staggered to a 7. Palmer and Sam Snead won the cup for the United States.

Arnold Palmer

• October 2: Mickey Wright leads the Tour in victories with six.

• October 2: Louise Suggs ends the year as the Tour's leading money winner with $16,892.

• October 3: For the second week in a row, Billy Casper tops PGA Tour players, winning the Hesperia Open.

• October 16: Billy Casper matches Arnold Palmer's early-season feat by winning his third straight Tour event, the Orange County Open.

• December: Fred Corcoran, former LPGA tournament director and PGA Tour official, wins the William Richardson Award for his outstanding contributions to golf.

• December 11: Arnold Palmer's eight victories this season are the most since Sam Snead's 11 wins in 1950. Palmer ends the year as the PGA Tour's leading money winner with a record $75,262.85.

• December 11: With a scoring average of 69.95, Billy Casper claims the Vardon Trophy.

Billy Casper

Casper Rattles Off Three Consecutive Victories

Billy Casper had many opportunities to give the victory salute in the 1960s. Matching Arnold Palmer's feat of the previous spring, Casper won three straight PGA Tour tournaments in 1960. Billy's victories came in the early fall and included the Portland Open, Hesperia Open, and Orange County Open.

Jack Nicklaus, Makota Tanaka

Nicklaus & Co. Breeze to World Amateur Team Title

Jack Nicklaus led the U.S. to the 1960 World Amateur Team championship when he blazed around Merion G.C. in Ardmore, Pennsylvania, with an opening 66. Nicklaus, comparing scorecards with Makota Tanaka, the low Japanese player with a 76, joined Deane Beman, Bob Gardner, and Bill Hyndman to win by 42 strokes.

• December 11: The PGA Tour names Arnold Palmer Player of the Year.

• Barbara McIntire becomes only the third American to capture the U.S. Women's Amateur and the British Ladies' Amateur when she defeats Philomena Garvey in the final of the British.

• Mike Brady, Jimmy Demaret, and Fred McLeod are elected to the PGA Hall of Fame.

• Betsy Rawls, winner of four U.S. Women's Open championships, is inducted into the LPGA Hall of Fame. She is the fifth member of the exclusive club.

• Golf Architect Dick Wilson, believed by many to be the designer of the decade, completes Laurel Valley C.C. in Ligonier, Pennsylvania.

• Bellerive C.C., a future U.S. Open site designed by Robert Trent Jones, opens in St. Louis.

PICTURE-PERFECT WRIGHT CLAIMS THREE MAJORS

In a career of record rounds and great victories, Mickey Wright's 1961 season stands out. It was the year in which, at age 26, she became golf's golden girl.

Wright's success fulfilled a number of predictions. As a youngster, her dedication and rippling swing inspired awe. Before she was 20, she had won the U.S. Girls' Junior, finished second in the U.S. Women's Amateur, and placed fourth in the 1954 U.S. Women's Open. Paired in that Women's Open with Babe Zaharias, the youngster outdrove Babe on a number of holes, prompting Zaharias to exclaim, "What are you tryin' to do, copy my swing?"

Mickey didn't need to mimic Babe's fire-and-fall-back style— her own swing was much better. Wright's classic swing was later acclaimed by Ben Hogan and Byron Nelson as the best ever. She kept the clubface square throughout, generated tremendous power with her strong lower body, and struck the ball precisely at the bottom of her forward swing. A perfectionist, she sought out the best instructors.

From 1957–60—ages 22–25— Wright won 18 tournaments,

including two U.S. Women's Opens and two LPGA Championships. As 1961 began, Wright was poised for a record-breaking romp. On the Florida swing, she won at St. Petersburg and Miami. In April, she captured the Title-holders, a women's version of the Masters and a major championship. On June 25 at Baltusrol Golf Club in New Jersey, she arrived at the Women's Open. Players of that era will ever refer to the 1961 championship as "Mickey's Open." Hitting soaring tee shots and rifling towering long iron shots at the flagsticks, she played Saturday's final 36 holes in 69-72 and won by six strokes. It was her third U.S. Women's Open championship in four years.

Wright also took titles in Columbus, Georgia; Waterloo, Iowa; Spokane, Washington; Sacramento, California; and her hometown of San Diego. On October 15, she won her third major title of the year, the LPGA Championship in Las Vegas. In 1961, Wright played in only 17 tournaments, but she won 10 of them. She garnered $22,236, or nearly 10 percent of the LPGA's 1961 prize money.

In 1962, Mickey would again win the Titleholders, and in May of that year capture her first Women's Western Open. As defender of the Women's Open and LPGA Championship, she became the only woman in history to own all four of the LPGA Tour's major titles at once.

Wright would go on to win 82 official tournaments, including 13 major championships. She twice shot rounds of 62, an 18-hole LPGA scoring record that has stood for nearly 30 years. Wright thoroughly dominated golf from 1961–64, but in 1969 she retired from full-time competition. "All I ever wanted to be was the greatest woman golfer in the world," she said, "and I quit when I believed I had done that."

1961

- January: PGA Tour players will compete in 45 events with a total season purse of $1,461,830.

- January: LPGA Tour players will compete in 24 events with a total purse of $288,750.

- January: The USGA raises the value of prizes an amateur can accept in any one tournament from $100 to $200.

- January: The number of golfers in the U.S. reaches five million.

- January: The PGA Tour drops the caucasian clause in its constitution and, for the first time, blacks can become members.

- January 29: South African Gary Player wins his second official PGA Tour event, the Lucky International, and a first prize of $9,000.

- February 14: Louise Suggs defeats a field of men and women pros in the Royal Poinciana Invitational at Palm Beach Par-3 G.C. in Florida. The field includes Sam Snead,

Mickey Wright dons the jacket and hoists the trophy that signify the Titleholders Championship. Wright toted lots of hardware in 1961, as she also captured the U.S. Women's Open, the Western Open, and seven other events, including her own Mickey Wright Open in her hometown of San Diego.

Gardner Dickinson, and Dow Finsterwald. Men and women play from the same tees.

• February 26: Arnold Palmer wins his third tournament of the year, the Baton Rouge Open.

• March 19: Bob Goalby fires a record eight consecutive birdies in the final round, setting a new PGA Tour record and winning the St. Petersburg Open with a score of 261. It's his second victory of the year.

• April 10: Gary Player wins his first green jacket and $20,000 when he shoots 8-under-par 280 to capture the Masters. Arnold Palmer, who double bogeyed the 72nd hole, and amateur Charles Coe tie for second.

• April 30: Arnold Palmer shoots 270 to win his second straight Texas Open.

• April 30: Mickey Wright claims the LPGA's first major of the year, the Titleholders Championship.

Tournament of Champions

Snead Pockets 10 Grand with 80th Career Victory

Sam Snead may have had difficulty fitting 10,000 silver dollars into those tomato cans in which he reportedly buried his money, but Sam loved the windfall. The Slammer, nearly 49, won the jackpot for finishing first in the 1961 Tournament of Champions in Las Vegas. Snead won by seven strokes for his 80th career victory.

Gary Player

Goalby Cards Eight Birds in a Row

Bob Goalby was smokin' in the final round of the 1961 St. Petersburg Open. At the Pasadena G.C., he carded eight consecutive birdies, becoming the first Tour player to do so. Since then, only two players have equaled the feat—Fuzzy Zoeller at the 1976 Quad Cities Open, and Dewey Arnette at the 1987 Buick Open. Goalby won the St. Petersburg event with a 261.

Bob Goalby

Player Prevails in Masters by a Single Shot

Gary Player drives from the 2nd tee in the third round of the 1961 Masters. Player birdied this hole and went on to win with a 280, one shot better than Arnold Palmer and amateur Charles Coe. It's a good thing Player didn't fall back into a playoff, since he was atrocious in such affairs, winning three and losing 11 in his PGA Tour career.

• May 7: Sam Snead, 48, wins the Tournament of Champions.

• May 21: Doug Sanders wins his second straight Tour event, the Hot Springs Open.

• June: Jack Nicklaus of Ohio State wins the NCAA championship, and Purdue captures the team title.

• June 4: Sam Snead and Jimmy Demaret win the Canada Cup by 12 strokes over the Australian team at Dorado G.C. in Puerto Rico. Snead is medalist.

• June 4: Veteran Cary Middlecoff prevails in the Memphis Open at Colonial C.C. in his hometown. It is the last of his 39 career victories.

• June 4: Mary Lena Faulk wins her second tournament of the year, and first major, when she captures the Women's Western Open at Belle Meade C.C. in Nashville.

• June 17: Gene Littler wins the U.S. Open, his first major championship. Littler is the only player at Oakland Hills C.C. to break par twice, as he

Charlie Coe, Gary Player

Amateur Coe Falls Just Short in the Masters

Amateur Charles Coe *(left)* finished runner-up to Gary Player *(right)* in the 1961 Masters. Coe's performance wasn't a total surprise, as he had been among the game's best amateurs since the late 1940s. Coe won the 1949 and 1958 U.S. Amateurs, and he pushed Jack Nicklaus to the last hole in the final of the 1959 Amateur.

Littler Ekes Out the Win in U.S. Open

Gene Littler *(left)* gets a much deserved handshake from Gardner Dickinson after winning the 1961 U.S. Open. Not only did Littler fight off Doug Sanders and Bob Goalby by a stroke, but he closed with a 68 and shot 7-under on the difficult Oakland Hills course. Despite his 29 career Tour wins, this was Littler's only victory in a professional major.

Doug Sanders

Sanders Claims Five of His 20 Career Wins

Doug Sanders's 20 career Tour victories included five in 1961: the New Orleans Open, Colonial NIT, Hot Springs Open, Eastern Open, and Cajun Classic. Sanders was one of the few 20-plus winners who never nabbed a major. He did finish runner-up three times, including the 1961 U.S. Open, which he lost by a stroke.

Gene Littler, Gardner Dickinson

fires a 281 to defeat Doug Sanders and Bob Goalby by a stroke.

• June 18: Mary Lena Faulk captures her third straight victory on the LPGA Tour when she wins the Eastern Open.

• July 1: Mickey Wright wins her second major championship of the season and her third U.S. Women's Open, at Baltusrol G.C. in Springfield, New Jersey. Wright plays the par-5s in 7-under-par to win by six strokes.

• July 14: Arnold Palmer captures his first British Open, after finishing second the previous year. Palmer shoots 284 at Royal Birkdale G.C. in England to hold off runner-up Dai Rees.

• July 31: Jerry Barber sinks putts of 20, 40, and 60 feet on the last three holes to tie Don January in the PGA Championship at Olympia Fields C.C. in Illinois. They'll meet in the first stoke-play playoff in tournament history.

Mary Lena Faulk, Roy Smith

Faulk Tallies Three Straight Victories

Mary Lena Faulk accepts the winner's check from Roy Smith, owner of Range End C.C. in Pennsylvania, after the 1961 Women's Eastern Open. It was Faulk's third straight victory. In the preceding weeks, she won the Women's Western Open and the Triangle Round Robin.

Jackie Burke

Mickey Wright

Wright's 69 Leads to Easy Open Victory

Mickey Wright, who practiced the plumb-bob technique, used it to find the line of this birdie putt in the third round of the 1961 U.S. Women's Open. Wright made the birdie on her way to a spectacular 69 on the famed Lower Course at Baltusrol G.C. She went on to win the tourney by six strokes over runner-up Betsy Rawls. The victory was Wright's third Women's Open championship in four years.

Burke Claims the Trophy at Buick Open

Jackie Burke, age 38, grasps the trophy after winning the 1961 Buick Open Invitational in Grand Blanc, Michigan. Though its history stretches from 1958 through the present, the Buick Open always has been a lesser Tour event. It was discontinued in 1970 and 1971 and became a second-tour event from 1973–76.

• August 1: Jerry Barber defeats Don January, 67-68, for the PGA title.

• August 6: Mickey Wright wins her sixth LPGA event of the year, the Waterloo Women's Open.

• August 6: Doug Sanders wins his fourth Tour event of the year, the Eastern Open.

• August 26: Anne Quast Sander sets a record in winning the U.S. Women's Amateur at Tacoma C.C. in Washington when she defeats Phyllis Preuss, 14 & 13, in the final.

• August 27: Mickey Wright wins her seventh LPGA tournament of the year, the Spokane Women's Open at Esmeralda G.C. in Washington.

• September 2: The U.S. ties the largest winning margin in Walker Cup history by defeating Great Britain, 11-1. The Match is played on the American West Coast for the first time, at Seattle G.C.

• September 4: Earl Stewart Jr. wins the PGA Tour's Dallas Open at his home course, Oak Cliff C.C.

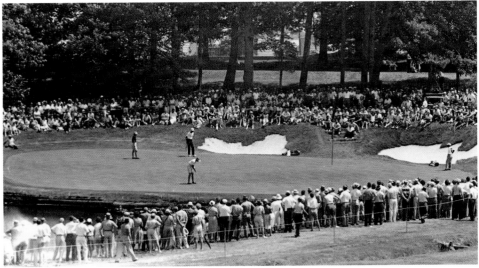

Baltusrol Golf Club

Baltusrol Plays Host to Women Pros

Huge trees frame the 4th green of the Lower Course at Baltusrol G.C. in Springfield, New Jersey, which hosted the 1961 U.S. Women's Open. Prior to '61, this esteemed club had hosted four U.S. Opens, three U.S. Amateurs, and two U.S. Women's Amateurs, but never a U.S. Women's Open. Baltusrol hosted the Women's Open for a second time in 1985.

Host Pro Stewart Wins in Dallas

Earl Stewart hits from the 10th fairway in the final round of the Dallas Open, which he won with a score of 278. Stewart knew this course, Oak Cliff C.C., better than any of the other participants since he was the host professional. Stewart actually became the first host pro ever to win a PGA Tour event. The victory earned him $4,300.

Earl Stewart

• September 16: Jack Nicklaus wins his second U.S. Amateur, at Pebble Beach G.L. Nicklaus outclasses Dudley Wysong, 8 & 6, in the final.

• September 24: Billy Casper wins his third straight Portland Open.

• October 1: Playing before her hometown fans in a tournament named for her, Mickey Wright wins the Mickey Wright Open at Mission Valley C.C. in San Diego. It is her third straight victory.

• October 1: The 1955 U.S. Open champion, Jack Fleck, claims the $3,500 first prize in the Bakersfield Open in California.

• October 8: Tony Lema wins his first official PGA Tour event, the 36-hole Hesperia Open in California.

• October 14: The United States team wins the Ryder Cup, defeating Great Britain/Ireland, 14½-9½, at Royal Lytham & St. Annes in England.

1961

Monti Proves His Worth in Ontario Open

The man behind the neat glasses is Eric Monti, a virtual unknown to fans of the PGA Tour. Monti, a Los Angeles teaching pro who instructed movie stars, made a name for himself when he won the 1955 Miami Beach Open. He captured his second Tour victory in 1959, and in '61 he claimed another—the Ontario Open in California.

Arnold Palmer

Palmer Cleans Up in Not-So-Jolly England

One of the few places where Arnold Palmer was *not* cheered in 1961 was England. First he edged Welshman Dai Rees in the British Open, and here he helps the U.S. to victory over Great Britain in the Ryder Cup Matches, held at Royal Lytham & St. Annes. Palmer won three matches and halved another.

Eric Monti

- October 15: Mickey Wright captures her third major championship of the year, the LPGA Championship at Stardust C.C. in Las Vegas. Louise Suggs finishes second.

- October 15: Little-known Eric Monti wins a PGA Tour event, the Ontario Open in California.

- October 22: Louise Suggs wins her sixth tournament of the season when she captures the San Antonio Civitan at Brackenridge Park.

- October 22: For the first time, Mickey Wright is the LPGA Tour's leading money winner with $22,236 for the season. She also leads in victories with 10.

- October 22: Mickey Wright wins the Vare Trophy with a scoring average of 73.55.

- December: PGA Tour players vote to name Jerry Barber the Tour's Player of the Year.

- December: The Golf Writers Association of America names

1961

Jerry Barber, Lou Strong, Don January

Barber Wins PGA Thanks to Monster Putts

Diminutive Jerry Barber *(left)* defeated Don January *(right)* in a playoff for the 1961 PGA Championship, at Olympia Fields C.C. in Illinois. Barber, age 45, reached the playoff by sinking putts of 20, 40, and 60 feet on the last three holes. He outgunned January, 67-68, in the 18-hole playoff.

Jack Nicklaus

Brewer Ends Drought With Three Tour Wins

Gay Brewer, who joined the PGA Tour in 1956, didn't get his first victory until 1961. He ended up winning three tournaments in '61, including two back-to-back. Brewer won the Carling Open in August, and in November he captured the Mobile Open in Alabama and the West Palm Beach Open in Florida.

Gay Brewer

Nicklaus Wraps Up U.S. Amateur on 12th Hole

At the 1961 U.S. Amateur final at Pebble Beach G.L., Jack Nicklaus chips to within eight feet of the cup on the 12th hole. Jack's opponent, Dudley Wysong, missed a 20-foot putt on this green to lose both the hole and the match, 8 & 6. This would be the last Amateur for Nicklaus; he'd have bigger fish to fry.

USGA executive director Joe Dey winner of the William Richardson Award for his contributions to the game.

• December: Orlando's Dave Ragan and Mickey Wright team in an alternate-shot competition to win the Haig & Haig Scotch Mixed Foursome championship at the Pinecrest Lake Club in Avon Park, Florida.

• December 3: Gay Brewer wins his second straight tournament, the West Palm Beach Open in Florida.

• December 10: Gary Player ends the year as the PGA Tour's leading money winner with $64,540.45.

• December 10: Arnold Palmer and Doug Sanders lead the PGA Tour in victories with five apiece. Palmer wins the Vardon Trophy for the lowest scoring average, 69.85.

• Johnny Farrell, Lawson Little, and Henry Picard are inducted into the PGA Hall of Fame.

NICKLAUS EDGES POPULAR PALMER IN U.S. OPEN

The 1962 U.S. Open was the setting for one of those classic encounters that marks the end of one era and the beginning of another. The decade had thus far belonged to the charismatic Arnold Palmer, the darling of the galleries. In this Open, however, Palmer was outdueled by Jack Nicklaus, a stocky rookie who played with Teutonic stoicism, and their playoff marked the end of Palmer's reign as golf's undisputed king.

According to veteran golf writer Robert Sommers, Palmer's reign actually began in 1957. "We saw it that year at the PGA tournament in Baltimore," said Sommers. "He had already won three tournaments that year, and galleries flocked to him. He was just so dashing and played with such flair." By June 1962, Palmer's stature had grown even greater. In the previous four years, he had won three Masters, the U.S. Open, and the British Open. In '62, he had won the Masters and three straight spring PGA Tour events.

Palmer was not only playing the best golf of his career, but he would be battling for the U.S. Open title at Oakmont Country Club, near his hometown of Latrobe, Pennsylvania. His gallery, made up of the usual members of Arnie's Army, was swelled by local admirers. "They were out in full force—and full throat—to root him on," said Nicklaus, who was paired with Palmer the first two rounds.

Nicklaus, after dominating the amateur ranks, was in his first season as a pro. Immensely talented, he hit the ball prodigious distances and enjoyed a delicate putting touch, all of which served him well at Oakmont. After three rounds, he was two shots behind leaders Bobby Nichols and Palmer, who had missed three two-footers in the third round.

In the final round, Palmer played right behind Nicklaus. With 10 holes to go, Arnie had a three-stroke lead, and it was his U.S. Open to win. The 480-yard, par-5 9th hole was pivotal. Nicklaus birdied. Behind him, Palmer fluffed a greenside chip, bogied, and saw his lead shrink to one. When Palmer hit a bunker and bogied the short 13th, they were tied. Both men parred in and finished at 283.

The playoff gallery belonged to Palmer. Noisy as wrestling fans, a few shouted insults at Nicklaus. Unfazed, the stoic, deliberate Nicklaus played his way into a two-stroke lead through 17 holes. Nicklaus then drove into a nasty lie in the left rough, but—when Palmer missed with his approach shot—Jack felt he could play conservatively and still win. Nicklaus hacked out, then hit a 9-iron to the green, where he two-putted for a bogey and a 71. Palmer double bogied for a 74.

These two historic battlers would have other encounters, and they would become fast friends. But in 1962, Jack Nicklaus, winning a playoff for the U.S. Open, cut short the Palmer era and began an era of his own.

1962

- January: PGA Tour players will compete in 49 events with a total season purse of $1,790,320.

- January: LPGA Tour players will compete in 32 events with a total purse of $338,450.

- January: Jack Nicklaus begins his first year on the PGA Tour.

- January: For the first time, the number of golf courses in the United States tops 7,000.

- February 7: Sam Snead claims the Royal Poinciana Invitational. Playing against LPGA and PGA Tour players from the same tees, Snead wins over runner-up Mickey Wright.

- February 11: Defending champion Arnold Palmer wins the Phoenix Open by 12 strokes.

- February 18: Phil Rodgers, who earlier won the Los Angeles Open, gets his second victory of the year when he wins the Tucson Open, held at El Rio Golf and C.C. for the last of 18 straight years.

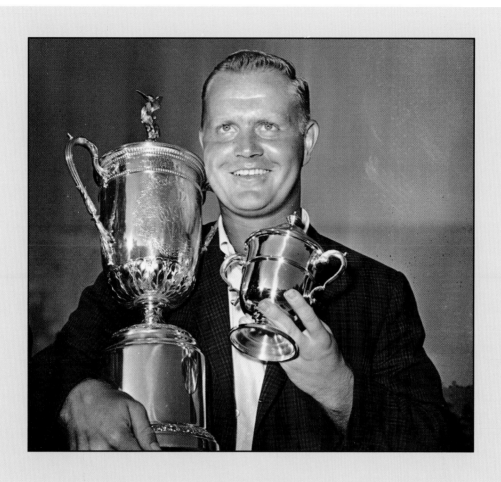

Jack Nicklaus poses with his trophies after winning the 1962 U.S. Open at Oakmont C.C. in Pennsylvania. Nicklaus tied Arnold Palmer at 283, then beat Arnie in a playoff, 71-74, even though the tournament was held near Palmer's hometown of Latrobe. For Palmer, this was one of his four runner-up finishes in the Open from 1962 through 1967.

• March 25: Billy Casper captures the inaugural Doral Open on the Blue Course at Doral C.C. in Miami.

• April 8: Arnold Palmer shoots 280 to tie Gary Player and Dow Finsterwald in the Masters.

• April 9: Arnold Palmer wins his third green jacket in five years when he shoots 37-31—68 in a playoff with Gary Player (71) and Dow Finsterwald (77) at the Masters.

• April 29: Mickey Wright wins the Titleholders Championship for the second straight year.

• April 29: Arnold Palmer wins his third straight Texas Open.

• May 6: For the second week in a row, Arnold Palmer is in the winner's circle, as he claims the Tournament of Champions in Las Vegas.

• May 13: Arnold Palmer makes it three in a row with a victory in the Colonial National Invitation Tournament.

Sam Snead

Nancy and Bobby Nichols

Snead Beats the Ladies in Par-3 Tourney

Sam Snead, easily recongized by his trademark hats, captured the 1962 Royal Poinciana Invitational at Palms Springs G.C. in Florida. This fascinating tournament was played on a par-3 course and included a mixed field of men and women pros, all playing from the same tees. Mickey finished second in 1962. Louise Suggs won in '61.

Palmer Prevails in Masters Playoff

Arnold Palmer and his fanatical army of supporters try to coax in a 35-foot putt, struck on the 18th green in a playoff at the 1962 Masters. Palmer missed the putt, but his tap-in gave him a 68 and a win over Gary Player (71) and Dow Finsterwald (77). It was Palmer's third Masters victory, after having won in 1960 and 1958.

Nichols Honored with Ben Hogan Award

Bobby Nichols smooches his wife Nancy after winning the 1962 Houston Classic at Memorial Park G.C. Bobby defeated Dan Sikes and Jack Nicklaus in sudden-death when he scored an eagle on the first hole. Nichols, whose body was ravaged by an auto wreck as a teenager, received the 1963 Ben Hogan Award for his courageous comeback.

Arnold Palmer

• May 13: Mickey Wright wins the Women's Western Open at the Montgomery C.C. in Alabama. It's her second major championship of the year and her third tournament victory.

• June: University of Houston's Kermit Zarley wins the NCAA championship, leading the Cougars to their sixth team championship in seven years.

• June 5: Two days after the Babe Zaharias Open is scheduled to end, the tournament is called and Betsy Rawls and Kathy Cornelius are declared co-winners. Heavy rains had flooded the Beaumont C.C. course in Texas.

• June 10: Sandra Haynie captures her first official LPGA Tour event. Haynie, six days after her 19th birthday, wins the Austin Civitan Open in her hometown of Austin, Texas.

• June 17: Young Sandra Haynie wins for the second straight week at the Cosmopolitan Open.

Mickey Wright

Wright Rings Up 10 More Tour Victories

A year after her 10-victory season of 1961, Mickey Wright triumphed 10 more times in 1962. Included were victories in two majors, the Titleholders and Women's Western Open, giving her four different major titles in the two-year period. Also in '62, Wright won four straight events and captured her third straight Vare Trophy.

Paul Bondeson, Billy Casper

Casper Captures the First-Ever Doral Open

Billy Casper *(right)* shakes the hand of runner-up Paul Bondeson after winning the 1962 Miami Invitational, a.k.a. the Doral Open. It was the premiere of the event, held at Doral C.C.'s Blue Course. In the last 30-plus years, the event has become a permanent fixture on the PGA Tour. Neither the course nor the yardage (6,939) has ever changed.

• June 17: Rookie Jack Nicklaus shatters Arnie's Army by defeating Palmer in a playoff, 71-74, for the U.S. Open title at Oakmont C.C. near Pittsburgh. Nicklaus and Palmer had tied at 283.

• June 30: In driving rain at the Dunes Golf and Beach Club in Myrtle Beach, South Carolina,

Murle Lindstrom comes from five strokes behind to win the U.S. Women's Open. It's her first victory.

• July 8: Kathy Whitworth, age 22, wins the first of what will become 88 official victories in her LPGA career. Her inaugural victory comes in the Kelly Girl Open in Maryland.

• July 13: Masters champion Arnold Palmer wins his second major of the year and his second straight British Open, as he shoots a British Open-record 276 at Troon G.C. in Scotland.

• July 14: Defending champion Richard H. Sikes wins his second U.S. Amateur Public Links title.

Richard Sikes

Haynie, 19, Wins Back-to-Back Tour Events

Less than a week after her 19th birthday, Sandra Haynie captured her first LPGA Tour victory—the 1962 Austin Civitan Open. Beginner's luck? Hardly. Haynie captured the Cosmopolitan Open the very next week. Haynie first made her mark as a 14-year-old, when she won the 1957 Texas State Publinx.

Sikes Claims Second Straight U.S. Publinx

Richard H. Sikes, a student at the University of Arkansas, captured the 1962 U.S. Amateur Public Links title at Sheridan Park G.C. in Tonawanda, New York. Despite a field of 2,241 competitors, Sikes won the event for the second year in a row. Only Carl Kauffmann (1927–29) had ever accomplished that feat.

Sandra Haynie

Murle Lindstrom

Lindstrom Reigns Supreme in Women's Open

Murle Lindstrom had never won an LPGA tournament before claiming the 1962 U.S. Women's Open. But despite pouring rain at Dunes Golf and Beach Club in Myrtle Beach, South Carolina, she came from behind to win by two, shooting 301. Lindstrom remains the last woman to win the Open with a 300-plus score.

• July 22: Gary Player claims his third major, the PGA Championship, at Aronimink G.C. in Newtown Square, Pennsylvania. He had previously won the British Open and the Masters.

• August 12: Arnold Palmer wins his seventh and final tournament of the season, the American Classic.

• August 18: The U.S. wins the Curtis Cup Match at Broadmoor G.C. in Colorado Springs.

• August 26: Doug Sanders wins his second straight PGA Tour event, the Oklahoma City Open.

• August 26: Mickey Wright wins her third straight LPGA event, tying a record, with a victory in the Salt Lake City Open.

• September 1: JoAnne Gunderson claims her third U.S. Women's Amateur, at the C.C. of Rochester in New York. Gunderson, who defeats Ann Baker in the final, 9 & 8, says it's the best performance of her career.

1962

Labron E. Harris Jr.

Harris Wins the U.S. Amateur on Final Hole

Labron E. Harris Jr. drops his putter and praises the heavens after holing out in the 1962 U.S. Amateur. This 36-hole final, on Pinehurst C.C.'s No. 2 Course, went down to the wire, with Harris defeating Downing Gray, 1 up. From 1959–63, the much more famous Jack Nicklaus and Deane Beman won the other four U.S. Amateurs.

George Sancken, Kathy Whitworth

Young Whitworth Puts the Heat on Wright

After coming up empty in her first three years on Tour, Kathy Whitworth captured her first LPGA victories in 1962—the Kelly Girl Open and the Phoenix Thunderbird Open. Nevertheless, the Texan still found a major roadblock in Mickey Wright. In '62, Whitworth finished runner-up to Wright six times, including three events in a row.

• September 3: Mickey Wright sets a new record with her fourth straight LPGA Tour win at the Spokane Open. It's her eighth win of the year. For the third week in a row, Kathy Whitworth is runner-up.

• September 16: Rookie Jack Nicklaus wins his second official PGA Tour event, the Seattle Open.

• September 17: Charles Evans Jr., age 72, plays in his 50th U.S. Amateur championship, at the No. 2 Course at Pinehurst, North Carolina.

• September 22: Labron Harris, five holes down to Downing Gray midway through the final of the U.S. Amateur, rallies to win, 1 up.

• September 23: Jack Nicklaus makes it two straight when he captures the Portland Open in Oregon.

• September 30: Mickey Wright claims her ninth tournament of the year, winning the San Diego Open in her hometown. Kathy Whitworth is again runner-up.

Arnold Palmer

Evans Plays in Yet Another U.S. Amateur

Chick Evans, the boy wonder of golf back in the 1910s, became the first golfer to play in 50 U.S. Amateur championships when he teed off in the 1962 version. Evans, 72 years old in '62, rose from the caddie ranks to win one U.S. Open, one Western Open, two U.S. Amateurs, and eight Western Amateurs.

Chick Evans

Palmer Wins British Open, Breaks Scoring Record

Almost single-handedly, Arnold Palmer revived American interest in the British Open. In 1962, he won the championship for the second year in a row, firing 276 over 72 holes at Troon in Scotland. It was the lowest score in the 102-year history of the British Open. Palmer shot a course-record 67 in the third round.

• October 13: The United States edges Canada by eight strokes to win the third World Amateur Team championship at the Fuji Golf Course in Kawana, Japan.

• October 19: Maureen Orcutt, a *New York Times* reporter and former Curtis Cup player, wins the inaugural U.S. Senior Women's Amateur championship at Manufacturers' Golf and C.C. in Oreland, Pennsylvania.

• October 21: Mickey Wright wins her 10th tournament of the season, the Carlsbad Cavern Open in New Mexico. Kathy Whitworth is second for the ninth time this year.

• November 4: Mickey Wright ends the LPGA season with a scoring average of 73.67 and wins the Vare Trophy.

• November 4: For the second straight year, Mickey Wright is the LPGA Tour's leading money winner with $21,641. As in 1961, she finishes with 10 wins.

JoAnne Gunderson

Gunderson Claims Amateur Title No. 3

JoAnne Gunderson claimed her third of five U.S. Women's Amateurs in 1962, trouncing Ann Baker in the final, 9 & 8, at the C.C. of Rochester in New York. The tournament featured interesting contestants. Tennis great Althea Gibson lost in the second round, while Mrs. George M. Trainor defeated her daughter, Anne Trainor, in a second-round match.

Gary Player

Player Picks Up Major No. 3 at PGA Championship

Gary Player tips his hat and waves his scorecard at Aronomink G.C. in Newtown Square, Pennsylvania, after firing a 69 to take the third-round lead in the PGA Championship. Player, who had previously won the British Open and the Masters, racked up his third major when he won the PGA the following day.

• November 4: Mary Mills is named Rookie of the Year on the LPGA Tour.

• November 11: Arnold Palmer and Sam Snead team to give the U.S. a two-stroke victory over host Argentina in the Canada Cup Matches.

• December 9: Arnold Palmer is the PGA Tour's Player of the Year. He captures his second straight Vardon Trophy with a scoring average of 70.27.

• December 9: Arnold Palmer, who won a Tour-high seven tournaments, is the year's leading money winner with $81,448.33.

• Pine Tree C.C., designed by Dick Wilson, opens for play in Boynton Beach, Florida. It will boast such members as Sam Snead, JoAnne Carner, and Jim McKay.

• The USGA's new book, *Golf Rules in Pictures,* is published. It will become a best-seller over many years.

'FAT JACK' HAS LAST LAUGH, WINS TWO MAJORS

When Jack Nicklaus defeated Arnold Palmer in a playoff for the 1962 U.S. Open at Oakmont Country Club, a lot of golf fans were disappointed. Most were members of Arnie's Army, and seeing their hero defeated by a rookie from Ohio didn't sit well. Some of them started to run down Nicklaus, calling him "Fat Jack." Jack may have been a little chubby, but the extra poundage had no effect on his brilliant game.

Nicklaus's performance in the major championships of 1963 virtually sealed his position as golf's top superstar. Nicklaus added his first Masters and PGA Championship titles to his career list, and he almost won the British Open. He wasn't a contender in the U.S. Open, another playoff loss for Palmer, but three out of four ain't bad.

At 23 years of age, Nicklaus became the youngest Masters champion in history by riding a second-round 66. The weather was rough in the third round, and a 74 really didn't put him out of contention. He virtually cruised on in Sunday afternoon, being even par stepping onto the 18th tee. Just ahead, Tony Lema rolled

in a 25-foot curling putt for birdie to pull within one shot of Nicklaus. All Fat Jack needed to do was to remain at par to get his first green jacket.

Nicklaus hooked his tee shot into a muddy area trampled by the gallery. It was ruled casual water, and Nicklaus dropped his ball onto a dry spot. He lofted an 8-iron onto the green. His approach putt rolled past, and he had to sink a three-footer to avoid a playoff. It was a nervous putt, but he smoothly drained it.

Bad final-hole hooks seemed to be Nicklaus's problem in the other 1963 major championships. On the final hole of the British Open at Royal Lytham & St. Annes, Nicklaus hooked his tee shot into

the lip of a bunker. He made bogey and missed getting into the playoff with Bob Charles and Phil Rodgers by one stroke. The next week, Nicklaus flew from London to Dallas to play in the PGA Championship at Dallas Athletic Club's Blue Course.

After three rounds at the PGA, Nicklaus was a full three shots behind Bruce Crampton. However, Jack eagled the 1st hole of the final round, triggering a serious charge. Nicklaus took the lead with a birdie on the 15th hole, but he again unleashed a final-hole hook by snapping a lay-up 3-iron into the rough. He chipped out of the rough short of the creek and lofted a 9-iron 20 feet above the cup. The ball rolled back to four feet from the hole, and he sunk the putt for a 68 and his first PGA Championship.

Nicklaus won three other events in 1963, including the Palm Springs Classic, the Tournament of Champions, and the Sahara Invitational, and he finished second to Palmer on the money list with $100,040. However, it was his extraordinary performances in the 1963 majors that forever turned Fat Jack into the Golden Bear.

1963

- January: PGA Tour players will compete in 43 events with a total season purse of $2,044,900.

- January: LPGA Tour players will compete in 34 events with a total purse of $345,300.

- January 7: Arnold Palmer captures the Los Angeles Open.

- January 20: Despite shooting a final-round 74 at Pebble Beach, Billy Casper wins the Bing Crosby National Pro-Am by one shot over five golfers.

- February 3: Jack Nicklaus shoots a 65 to win an 18-hole playoff at the Palm Springs Golf Classic by eight strokes over Gary Player.

- February 10: Mickey Wright wins her second straight event, the St. Petersburg Women's Open.

- February 12: Arnold Palmer nabs his third consecutive Phoenix Open, shooting a final-round 70 at Arizona C.C. to win by one over Gary Player.

Arnold Palmer *(right)* topped Jack Nicklaus *(left)* on the 1963 money list, $128,230-$100,040, but the year clearly belonged to the Golden Bear. Nicklaus, age 23, became the youngest player ever to win the Masters. He also claimed the PGA Championship, won three other events, and finished one stroke out of a British Open playoff.

• February 17: Don January breaks 70 all four rounds to win the Tucson Open by 11 shots.

• March 17: Rookie Raymond Floyd, 20 years and six months old, becomes the youngest player since 1928 to win a PGA Tour event, shooting a final-round 69 to win the St. Petersburg Open.

• March 24: Dan Sikes wins the Doral Open by one shot over 50-year-old Sam Snead.

• April 7: Jack Nicklaus gets a free drop out of casual water on the 18th hole and makes par to win his first Masters, by one stroke over Tony Lema. At 23, Nicklaus becomes the youngest Masters winner.

• April 28: Phil Rodgers shoots a final-round 65 at Oak Hills C.C. to win the Texas Open by two shots.

• April 28: Marilynn Smith claims the Titleholders Championship.

• May 5: Jack Nicklaus wins the Tournament of Champions in Las Vegas by five shots.

Raymond Floyd

Sikes Nips 50-Year-Old Snead in Doral Open

Dan Sikes rejoices after making a 30-foot putt on the 13th hole during the final round of the 1963 Doral Open. It turned out to be a pivotal putt for Sikes, as he won by a mere one stroke over 50-year-old Sam Snead. Sikes, a former attorney, won the U.S. Amateur Public Links championship in 1958.

Floyd's the Youngest Winner in 35 Years

Rookie Raymond Floyd, a mere 20 years and six months old, sits on his bag during the 1963 St. Petersburg Open. Floyd closed with a splendid 67-69 to defeat third-round leader Dave Marr. Floyd thus became the youngest player to win a PGA Tour event since Horton Smith in the 1928 Oklahoma City Open.

Dan Sikes

Bo Wininger

Unknown Wininger Wins Again in New Orleans

You won't find Bo Wininger's name in the record book too often, but he was a big name in New Orleans in the 1960s. Wininger closed with a 69 to win the 1963 Greater New Orleans Open—for the second year in a row. The 1963 event was held for the first time at Lakewood C.C., which would host the tourney continuously from 1963–88.

• May 12: Julius Boros wins the Colonial National Invitation Tournament by four strokes.

• May 19: Mickey Wright takes her second event in a row at the Muskogee Civitan.

• May 25: The United States wins the Walker Cup Match, defeating Great Britain/Ireland, 12-8, at the Ailsa Course at Turnberry, Scotland.

• May 26: Mickey Wright prevails in the Dallas Civitan Open.

• June 2: Mickey Wright ties her own LPGA Tour record of four consecutive wins with her victory at the Babe Zaharias Open.

• June 22: R.H. Sikes of the University of Arkansas claims the NCAA championship, with Oklahoma State winning the team title.

• June 23: Mickey Wright captures the Women's Western Open in Madison, Wisconsin.

1963

Julius Boros

Boros Digs Out of Trouble, Wins U.S. Open

The 13th hole of the 1963 U.S. Open playoff proved to be a thorny problem for Julius Boros, as he hit into the trees and ended up with a double bogey. Nevertheless, Boros finished with a 70 on the course that played so difficult throughout the week—the Country Club course in Brookline, Massachusetts. He won the playoff over Jacky Cupit and Arnold Palmer, who scored 73 and 76, respectively.

Beman Tops Again in U.S. Amateur

In the early 1960s, Deane Beman was considered a prototypical amateur. He had already won the 1959 British Amateur and 1960 U.S. Amateur and was making a good living in the insurance business. In 1963, he defeated Richard Sikes in the final, 2 & 1, to win his second U.S. Amateur championship.

Deane Beman

Masters Tournament

Nicklaus, Palmer Dominate the Masters

Jack Nicklaus *(yellow shirt)* and Arnold Palmer *(white shirt, no hat)* practice together prior to the 1963 Masters, an event the two dominated from 1958–66. Palmer won it four times and Nicklaus three during that period. Palmer led the Tour in earnings in 1963 thanks to seven Tour wins, including the Los Angeles and Western Opens.

• June 23: Julius Boros, Arnold Palmer, and Jacky Cupit tie for the U.S. Open title at The Country Club in Brookline, Massachusetts, with a score of 293, the highest winning score since 1935.

• June 24: Julius Boros shoots a 70 to win the 18-hole U.S. Open playoff by three strokes over Jacky Cupit

and six strokes over Arnold Palmer. Boros, 43, is the oldest player ever to win a U.S. Open.

• July 1: Arnold Palmer comes back by shooting 67 in an 18-hole playoff at the Cleveland Open to defeat Tommy Aaron and Tony Lema by three shots.

• July 6: Doug Ford wins the Canadian Open by one stroke over Al Geiberger.

• July 12: Jack Nicklaus hooks his tee shot into a bunker on the final hole at Royal Lytham & St. Annes to allow Bob Charles and Phil Rodgers to tie for first after 72 holes of the British Open.

Mickey Wright, Marilynn Smith

Red-Hot Wright Racks Up 13 Victories

Mickey Wright *(left)* jokes around with Marilynn Smith after Smith beat her by a stroke in the 1963 Titleholders Championship. The loss was no big deal for Wright, who finished the season with a whopping 13 Tour victories, breaking the LPGA record by three. She captured two majors: the LPGA Championship and the Women's Western Open.

Ford Holds Off Geiberger in Canadian Open

Doug Ford edged Al Geiberger by a stroke to win the 1963 Canadian Open, at Scarborough Golf and C.C. in Toronto. Geiberger nearly won it with a final-round 65, but Ford's total of 280 stood up. It was the last big win for Ford, who counted a Masters, a PGA Championship, and two Canadian Open titles among his 19 Tour victories.

Doug Ford

- July 14: Bob Charles shoots 140 to win a 36-hole British Open playoff by eight shots over Phil Rodgers. Charles becomes the first left-handed golfer to win a major championship.

- July 17: Jack Nicklaus wins the PGA Championship's long-drive contest at Dallas Athletic Club with a whack of 340 yards.

- July 20: Mary Mills captures the U.S. Women's Open at Kenwood C.C. in Cincinnati by three strokes over Sandra Haynie and Louise Suggs.

- July 21: Despite 110-degree heat, Jack Nicklaus shoots a final-round 68 to win his first PGA Championship, at Dallas Athletic Club.

- July 21: The U.S. Ryder Cup team is named, and Jack Nicklaus isn't on it. He isn't eligible because he hasn't completed his PGA apprenticeship.

- July 29: Arnold Palmer shoots a 70 in an 18-hole playoff to defeat Julius Boros by one and Jack Nicklaus by three in the Western Open, at Beverly C.C. in Chicago.

1963

Mary Mills

Mills Makes Women's Open Her First Win

In 1962, Mary Mills won the LPGA Tour's first Rookie of the Year Award, even though she didn't win a tournament. Her first win came in 1963 and it was one to remember. Mills, thanks to a second-round 70, prevailed in the U.S. Women's Open by three strokes over Sandra Haynie and Louise Suggs, at Kenwood C.C. in Cincinnati.

Charles, Rodgers Meet in British Playoff

Bob Charles *(left)* and Phil Rodgers *(right)* tied after four rounds of the 1963 British Open, at Royal Lytham & St. Annes in England. Each was lucky to be on top. Jack Nicklaus seemingly had the tournament wrapped up, but he hit a duck hook into a bunker on the last hole for his second consecutive bogey.

Bob Charles, Phil Rodgers

• August 11: Mickey Wright wins her eighth LPGA event of the year, the Waterloo Women's Open.

• August 11: Tom Weiskopf, age 20, defeats Labron Harris Jr. to win the Western Amateur.

• August 18: Mickey Wright wins the Albuquerque Swing Parade.

• August 24: Anne Quast Sander defeats Peggy Conley, 2 & 1, in the final of the U.S. Women's Amateur at Taconic G.C. in Williamstown, Massachusetts.

• September 14: Deane Beman defeats R.H. Sikes, 2 & 1, to win the U.S. Amateur at the Wakonda Club in Des Moines, Iowa.

• September 22: Mickey Wright captures the Visalia Ladies Open for her 11th win of the year, breaking the LPGA Tour record.

• September 29: Mickey Wright wins her namesake tournament, the Mickey Wright Invitational, in her hometown of La Jolla, California.

Bob Charles

Charles Becomes First Lefty to Win a Major

Bob Charles rips out a chunk of bad grass during the 36-hole playoff of the 1963 British Open. Charles beat Phil Rodgers by a full eight strokes, 140-148, to win the title. In doing so, Charles made history: The New Zealander became the first left-handed golfer to win a major professional championship.

Trio Meets in Open Playoff

After four rounds of the 1963 U.S. Open at The Country Club in Massachusetts, these three men were tied for first at 293—Julius Boros *(left)*, Arnold Palmer *(center)*, and Jacky Cupit. Cupit held a two-stroke lead at the par-4 71st hole but he double bogeyed, allowing Palmer and Boros—both former U.S. Open champions—to gain a tie.

Julius Boros, Arnold Palmer, Jacky Cupit

• October: Julius Boros is named PGA Player of the Year.

• October 13: Mickey Wright shoots 10-over-par at Stardust C.C. in Las Vegas, but she still wins the LPGA Championship by two shots over Mary Mills and Mary Lena Faulk. It's her third win in a row and her 13th of the season.

• October 13: The United States claims the Ryder Cup Match by defeating Great Britain/Ireland, 23-9, at East Lake C.C. in Atlanta.

• October 15: Horton Smith, winner of 30 Tour events, dies at age 55.

• October 27: The U.S. team of Jack Nicklaus and Arnold Palmer wins the Canada Cup at Golf de Saint-Nom-La-Breteche in Paris by three strokes over Spain. Nicklaus wins the individual title.

• November 17: Mickey Wright is the leading LPGA Tour money leader with a record $31,269. Her 13 victories break the Tour's record by three.

Labron Harris

U.S. Wins 18th Walker Cup in 19 Competitions

American Labron Harris chips out of bad rough during the 1963 Walker Cup Matches at the Ailsa Course in Turnberry, Scotland. Harris won two foursomes matches and a singles match to help the U.S. defeat Great Britain/Ireland, 12-8. The States' record in the Matches now stood at 18-1-0. The Americans hadn't lost since 1938.

Casper Nabs the Vardon, Excels in Ryder Cup

Billy Casper won two events in 1963—the Insurance City Open and the Bing Crosby National Pro-Am, which he won by a stroke over five others. He also secured his second of five career Vardon Trophies, averaging 70.58, thanks to his always-adept putting stroke. In October, Casper won four matches to lead the U.S. to a 23-9 Ryder Cup victory.

Billy Casper

Christy O'Connor

Despite O'Connor, Brits Fall in Ryder Cup

Christy O'Connor celebrates after winning a four-ball match during the 1963 Ryder Cup Matches, at East Lake C.C. in Atlanta. O'Connor, of Great Britain/Ireland, won this match by sinking a 40-foot birdie putt on the 18th hole. Overall, the Americans routed the Brits, 23-9. This was the first year that four-ball matches were held.

- November 17: Mickey Wright wins her fourth consecutive Vare Trophy with an average of 72.81, another LPGA record.

- November 17: Clifford Ann Creed is named LPGA Rookie of the Year.

- November 24: Arnold Palmer is the leading PGA Tour money winner with $128,230. It's the first time any golfer on the PGA Tour has reached $100,000 in a season. Palmer breaks the record of $81,448, which he set last year.

- November 24: Jack Nicklaus also reaches six digits in earnings ($100,040) to finish second on the Tour's money list.

- November 24: Arnold Palmer leads the PGA Tour with seven victories. Jack Nicklaus has five wins.

- November 24: Billy Casper wins his second career Vardon Trophy with a season scoring average of 70.58.

VENTURI BEATS THE HEAT, WINS U.S. OPEN

As he walked onto the 72nd green of the 1964 U.S. Open at Congressional Country Club in Bethesda, Maryland, Ken Venturi looked awful. He was tired and sweaty. Yet he lined up a 10-foot putt and knocked it into the hole. "My God!" he yelled. "I won the Open." Venturi's victory in the 1964 U.S. Open was one of the most thrilling major championship triumphs of the 1960s. But before he won the U.S. Open title, Venturi's career was one of the saddest stories in the history of golf.

In 1956, Venturi almost became the only amateur to win the Masters, but he closed with an 80 to lose by one shot to Jack Burke Jr. The next year, Venturi turned pro and proceeded to win 10 tournaments in his first four years. In early 1962, he suffered a pinched nerve that nearly paralyzed his right side, and his game collapsed. By the beginning of 1964, Venturi was starting to feel better physically but had not regained his confidence. He began to feel better about his game when he posted some good finishes in the spring. He barely got into the Open, shooting 77-70 in the regional qualifier.

On the weekend of the Open, the weather got extremely hot, and Venturi opened with a 72 to put himself four shots behind Arnold Palmer. A second-round 70 left him six shots behind Tommy Jacobs. In those days, the final two rounds were played on Saturday, and on this particular Saturday, the temperature would soar up to 100 degrees. Playing with Raymond Floyd, Venturi's third round got off to a surprising start. His 10-foot birdie putt on the 1st hole initially stopped on the lip, yet as he walked up to the ball, it dropped in.

Venturi had four more front-nine birdies for a 30 and was 6-under-par until the 17th hole, when he sat on the edge of his bag suffering from the heat. He bogied 17 and 18 but still shot 66. Venturi staggered into the clubhouse, and Dr. John Everett saw him lying down in the locker room. The doctor diagnosed him to be suffering from heat prostration, and he gave him some tea and salt tablets.

As the fourth round began, Dr. Everett started following Venturi around, handing him a wet towel. Joe Dey, executive director of the USGA, also walked along with him to at least sanction Venturi's slow play. Surprisingly, Venturi was still playing well. Jacobs started making bogeys, and Venturi's 18-foot birdie putt on 13 pumped him up. As he stepped onto the 18th tee, he was four strokes ahead of Jacobs.

"Hold your head up, Ken," said Dey. "You're the champion now." Venturi sunk that 10-footer for par and a 70, while golf fans looked on in amazement and admiration. The next year, the USGA decided to no longer play the final two rounds in one day. As for Venturi, he went on to win two more 1964 tournaments and become the Player of the Year. It was a remarkable comeback for a slightly disabled, physically exhausted golfer.

1964

• January: PGA Tour players are scheduled to compete in 41 events with a total season purse of $2,301,063.

• January: LPGA Tour players are scheduled to compete in 33 events with a total season purse of $351,000.

• January 18: Arnold Palmer makes a 9 on the par-3 17th hole at Pebble Beach G.L. and misses the cut at the Bing Crosby Pro-Am.

• January 20: Tony Lema shoots a 76 on a windy, rainy day at Pebble Beach to win the Bing Crosby Pro-Am. Al Balding, tied for the lead after 54 holes, fires an 88.

• February 2: Tommy Jacobs birdies the second extra hole to defeat 53-year-old Jimmy Demaret in a playoff for the Palm Springs Golf Classic. Demaret missed a two-foot putt on the first playoff hole.

• February 2: Players threaten to boycott next week's Phoenix Open in a dispute over television rights.

1964

Ken Venturi suffered from heat prostration during the final day of the 1964 U.S. Open at Congressional C.C. Searing heat and a 36-hole double round were the culprits. When Venturi proved the victor, it was more than just a triumph over heat and illness; it was a comeback from a four-year slump.

• February 3: The Phoenix Open reaches a compromise with the PGA Tournament Committee over television rights, ending the boycott threat.

• February 23: Sam Snead, age 51, wins the PGA Seniors Championship in his first appearance.

• March 15: Australian Bruce Devlin wins his first career PGA Tour event, shooting a final-round 70 to win the St. Petersburg Open.

• March 22: Billy Casper shoots a final-round 70 to win the Doral Open in Miami by one shot over Jack Nicklaus.

• March 22: Carol Mann wins the Women's Western Open at Scenic Hills C.C. in Pensacola, Florida. It is the 23-year-old's first Tour victory.

• April 5: Julius Boros shoots a final-round 66 to tie Doug Sanders for the Greater Greensboro Open title. Boros birdies the first extra hole to win.

Harney Ends Drought with Win in L.A.

Paul Harney chips to the 6th green during the final round of the 1964 Los Angeles Open, at Rancho Municipal Golf Course. Harney finished 66-71—280 to win by a shot over Bobby Nichols. Harney's victory ended a 4½-year slump. Ironically, he would win the Los Angeles Open again in 1965.

Paul Harney

Devlin Wins in St. Pete for First PGA Tour Win

In March 1964, 26-year-old Bruce Devlin captured his first PGA Tour victory, the St. Petersburg Open. Devlin, a native of Australia, had already established himself with victories in the Australian, French, and New Zealand Opens. Devlin earned this homely trophy in 1966 after winning the Carling World Open.

Arnold Palmer

Palmer's Even-Year Streak Continues

In 1964, Arnold Palmer continued his streak of winning the Masters every other year. He won in 1958, 1960, 1962, and again in '64, this time by a relatively easy six shots over Dave Marr and defending champion Jack Nicklaus. Palmer became the first to win four green jackets; Jimmy Demaret and Sam Snead won three apiece.

Bruce Devlin

- April 12: Arnold Palmer wins his fourth career Masters, prevailing by six strokes over Jack Nicklaus and Dave Marr.

- April 27: Marilynn Smith hits a 3-iron one foot from the 18th hole to make birdie and defend her Titleholders Championship, winning in a playoff over Mickey Wright.

- May 10: Billy Casper shoots a final-round 70 to win the Colonial NIT by four shots over Tommy Jacobs.

- May 17: Mickey Wright wins the Muskogee Civitan Open by nine strokes. It's her third consecutive victory.

- June 14: Tony Lema wins his second straight event, the Buick Open in Grand Blanc, Michigan.

- June 20: Suffering from heat prostration, Ken Venturi hangs on to win the U.S. Open at Congressional C.C. in Washington, D.C., by four strokes over Tommy Jacobs. It's his first win in four years.

Mann Kicks Off Career with Win in Western Open

The 6'3" Carol Mann, the tallest golfer ever on the LPGA Tour, captured her first Tour victory in 1964, the Women's Western Open at Scenic Hills C.C. in Pensacola, Florida. She would win 38 official events from 1964–75. Mann, a natural left-hander, learned to play golf right-handed at the age of nine.

Judy Kimball, Marilynn Smith

Winner Smith Nearly Gets Her Head Bashed In

Marilynn Smith *(right)* did defend her Titleholders Championship in 1964 but was lucky to do so. Playing partner Judy Kimball missed a putt on the 11th green and swung her putter in anger, almost hitting Marilynn in the head. Kimball finished in fourth place and Smith won by a stroke over Mickey Wright.

Carol Mann

• June 28: Tony Lema birdies the first extra hole to defeat Arnold Palmer in a playoff for the Cleveland Open. It is Lema's third win in four weeks.

• July 10: Tony Lema wins the British Open by five shots over Jack Nicklaus on the Old Course at St. Andrews, Scotland.

• July 11: Ruth Jessen ties Mickey Wright after 72 holes at the U.S. Women's Open at San Diego C.C.

• July 12: Mickey Wright claims her third straight event by defeating Ruth Jessen, 70-72, in an 18-hole playoff for the U.S. Women's Open. It is Wright's fourth Women's Open title.

• July 16: Bobby Nichols shoots a tournament-record 64 in the first round of the PGA Championship at Columbus C.C. in Ohio.

• July 19: Bobby Nichols wins the PGA Championship with a record 271, three shots better than Arnold Palmer and Jack Nicklaus. Nicklaus finished with a 64.

Marilynn Smith

Nichols Wins PGA in Jack's Backyard

Bobby Nichols sinks the putt that put him ahead to stay in the 1964 PGA Championship. The 15-foot birdie putt came on the 3rd hole of the final round at Columbus C.C. in Ohio, and it gave him a one-stroke lead over Arnold Palmer. Nichols went on to win by three over runners-up Palmer and Jack Nicklaus, who was playing in his hometown.

Bobby Nichols

Smith Fires a Record 66 at Titleholders

Marilynn Smith posted a score of, yes, 66 in the second round of the 1964 Titleholders. In doing so, she broke three tournament records: lowest score for 18 holes (breaking the previous best of 68), lowest score on the back nine (she fired 31), and lowest score for 36 holes (she shot 139).

Ruth Jessen

Jessen Wins Five Times But Loses U.S. Open

Ruth Jessen had the best year of her LPGA career in 1964, winning five tournaments. She also finished runner-up to Mickey Wright three times, including a playoff loss in the U.S. Women's Open. Jessen shot an admirable 72 in the playoff at San Diego C.C., but Wright—playing in her hometown—shot 70 for the victory.

- July 19: Ruth Jessen comes back to defeat Mickey Wright by three strokes for the Yankee Women's Open in Flint, Michigan.

- July 26: Ken Venturi's comeback continues with a one-stroke victory over four players at the Insurance City Open in Hartford, Connecticut.

- August 1: Johnny Miller defeats Enrique Sterling, 2 & 1, to win the U.S. Junior Amateur at Eugene C.C. in Oregon.

- August 2: Australian Kel Nagle, age 43, wins his first PGA Tour event, the Canadian Open, by two shots over Arnold Palmer.

- August 9: Chi Chi Rodriguez wins the Western Open at Tam O'Shanter C.C. by one shot over Arnold Palmer.

- August 22: Barbara McIntire defeats JoAnne Gunderson, 3 & 2, in the final of the U.S. Women's Amateur at Prairie Dunes C.C. in Hutchinson, Kansas.

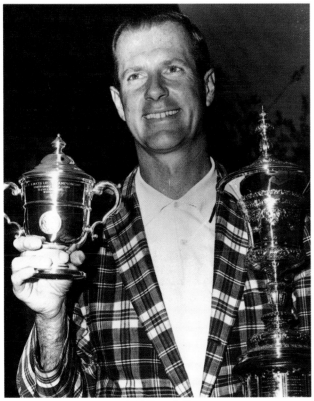

Bill Campbell

Amateur Campbell Finally Wins the Big One

Bill Campbell of West Virginia was one of the top amateurs in the 1950s and 1960s, winning numerous local and regional events. In 1964, he finally won the U.S. Amateur after playing the event 21 times. He later captured the U.S. Senior Amateur in 1979 and 1980 and was named president of the USGA in 1982.

Once Again, Wright Sweeps the Honors

At the 1964 Milwaukee Jaycee Open, Mickey Wright suffered from a stomach ulcer as well as oppressive heat and humidity. She won anyway. Wright led the Tour in victories for the fifth year in a row (with 11), led in earnings for the fourth straight year ($29,800), and won her fifth straight Vare Trophy, setting a scoring record with 72.46.

Kel Nagle

Nagle Beats Out Palmer for Canadian Open Title

Australian Kel Nagle closed 66-67 to overtake Arnold Palmer in the 1964 Canadian Open at Pine Grove C.C. in Quebec. It was the first Tour victory for the 43-year-old Nagle, who had made his mark in other important tournaments. Nagle won the 1960 British Open (where he also edged out Palmer) and teamed with Peter Thomson to win the 1954 Canada Cup.

Mickey Wright

- August 23: Ken Venturi wins the American Golf Classic at Firestone C.C. in Akron, Ohio.

- August 30: Bobby Nichols captures the PGA Tour's richest event, the $200,000 Carling Open, earning a first prize of $35,000. Arnold Palmer finishes one stroke behind.

- September 7: Texan Charles Coody wins his first career PGA Tour event, the Dallas Open, at Oak Cliff C.C.

- September 12: The United States defeats Great Britain/Ireland, 10½-7½, to win the Curtis Cup Match at Royal Porthcawl G.C. in Wales.

- September 13: Tony Lema wins the World Series of Golf, held for the winners of the four major championships.

- September 19: Bill Campbell defeats Ed Tutwiler, 1 up, in the final of the U.S. Amateur at Canterbury G.C. in Cleveland.

1964

Nicklaus and Palmer Team to Win Canada Cup

Jack Nicklaus *(left)* and Arnold Palmer hold miniatures of the Canada Cup after winning the 1964 championship for the United States in Kaanapali, Maui. Nicklaus fired a tournament-record 276 and Palmer shot 278. Hawaiian Ted Makalena *(second from right)* and South African Gary Player *(far right)* each shot 279.

Jack Nicklaus, Arnold Palmer, Ted Makalena, Gary Player

Charles Coody, Don Cherry, Rocky Thompson

Coody Beats Fellow Texans in Dallas Open

Charles Coody, Don Cherry, and Rocky Thompson *(left to right)* examine a scorecard after two rounds of the 1964 Dallas Open. These were the three leaders after two rounds and, ironically, they were all from Texas. Coody was a native of Fort Worth and the other two were from Wichita Falls, Texas. Coody went on to win the tournament.

Barbara McIntire

McIntire Tops Gunderson in U.S. Amateur

Two marquee names met in the final of the 1964 U.S. Women's Amateur, at Prairie Dunes C.C. in Kansas— Barbara McIntire *(pictured)* and JoAnne Gunderson. Barbara had won the championship in 1959 and lost a playoff in the 1956 U.S. Open; JoAnne was a three-time Amateur champ. In this head-to-head meeting, McIntire emerged with a 3 & 2 victory.

• October 4: Mary Mills upsets Mickey Wright by two strokes to win the LPGA Championship at Stardust C.C. in Las Vegas. It is the third-year pro's first victory.

• November 8: Mickey Wright wins her 10th event, the Tall City Open, and sets an LPGA 18-hole record with a 62. Wright entered the final round 10 strokes behind and birdied both extra holes to beat Sherry Wheeler in a playoff.

• November 22: Miller Barber shoots a final-round 67 to win the Cajun Classic, his first Tour victory.

• November 22: Mickey Wright finishes the season with her 11th win, the Mary Mills Mississippi Gulf Coast Invitational.

• November 22: Jack Nicklaus tops the Tour with $113,284.50, beating Arnold Palmer by $81.18.

• November 22: Arnold Palmer wins his third career Vardon Trophy with a scoring average of 70.01.

Chi Chi Wins Western as Well as the Lucky

In a familiar ritual, Chi Chi Rodriguez drops his hat over the cup after sinking a birdie putt in the 1964 Western Open. Rodriguez spent a quarter-century on the PGA Tour, but only in '64 did he win more than one Tour event. He captured both the Western Open, at Tam O'Shanter C.C. near Chicago, and the Lucky International.

Tony Lema

Lema Wins British Open, Pens the Book Golfer's Gold

Champagne Tony Lema had never been to the Old Course at St. Andrews prior to 1964. But once he got there for the '64 British Open, he won the championship with a score of 279. It was his first and only major title. The victory prompted him to write the book *Golfer's Gold* about life on the PGA Tour.

Chi Chi Rodriguez

• November 22: Jack Nicklaus, Billy Casper, and Tony Lema each finish the year with four victories, tops on Tour.

• November 22: Ken Venturi is named PGA Player of the Year.

• November 22: Mickey Wright is the leading LPGA money winner with $29,800. Wright wins her fifth consecutive Vare Trophy with a scoring average of 72.46.

• November 22: Susie Berning is named LPGA Rookie of the Year.

• November 22: Mickey Wright is inducted into the LPGA Hall of Fame.

• December: Mickey Wright is voted Associated Press Female Athlete of the Year for the second consecutive year.

• December 6: The United States wins the Canada Cup at Royal Kaanapali G.C. in Maui, Hawaii, by 11 strokes over Argentina. Jack Nicklaus wins the individual title.

Snead Wins No. 8 at Greensboro —at Age 52

Sam Snead's record of being the oldest winner on the PGA Tour can be broken, but with the success of the Senior PGA Tour, few will even give it a try. With all the money available on the Senior Tour, why would some of the better players give up all those chances for big money to return to the PGA Tour to break Snead's record? Most probably will not, unless a player wants to add one more record to his list of accomplishments. At any rate, Snead's win in the 1965 Greater Greensboro Open at age 52 years, 10 months, and 23 days will probably last well into the 21st Century.

Snead's victory in 1965 was actually two records. In addition to being the oldest PGA Tour winner, Snead also won his eighth career Greater Greensboro Open. The closest any other golfer has gotten to dominating a single tournament is six victories, held by Snead himself at the Miami Open and Jack Nicklaus at the Masters.

Back in 1965, there was really nothing much else for Snead to do but take on the likes of youngsters such as Billy Casper, Tommy Aaron, Tony Lema, Arnold Palmer, Nicklaus, and others. Other than the PGA Seniors Championship, which Snead won for the second year in a row back in March, there were no tournaments for senior golfers. Snead had to just keep battling the flatbellies and limberbacks.

Snead was probably just as limber and flatbellied as most regular Tour players when he arrived at Sedgefield Country Club in April. Ironically, with seven previous Greater Greensboro Open victories, he was being hailed by the tournament as its greatest champion. The week was designated "Sam Snead Week." "I guess they wanted to honor me," remembers Snead. "They had a big dinner for me and Ed Sullivan was there to emcee." Sullivan told the folks at the dinner, "Wouldn't it be nice if Sam won?" He didn't realize he was predicting a victory, but it turned out he was.

The Greensboro turned into a "really big shooo," as old Ed would say. Snead shot 68 and 69 to tie Casper for the second-round lead. A third-round 68 gave Snead a two-shot lead over rookie Labron Harris Jr., the 1962 U.S. Amateur champion. During the final round, Phil Rodgers posted a 31 on the front nine to catch Snead. But on the 13th hole, Slammin' Sammy rolled in a 60-foot birdie putt to reclaim the lead.

"That putt was from China to Japan, but it won the tournament," Snead said. Yes, it did. Sammy coasted in for another 68 to defeat Rodgers, Casper, and Jack McGowan by five shots. It was Snead's record-setting 81st Tour win, and his $11,000 first-place check was the largest of his career. "Heck, that was more than I made in Greensboro in my life," said Snead. "I think someone could break my record. It's like someone shooting 59. That was done again, so why can't someone else break my record?"

1965

- January: PGA Tour players are scheduled to compete in 36 events with a total purse of $2,848,515.

- January: LPGA Tour players are scheduled to compete in 33 events with a total purse of $356,316.

- January: Ken Venturi, 1964 U.S. Open champion, undergoes surgery for a circulatory problem afflicting his right hand.

- January 11: Paul Harney shoots 12-under-par to defend his Los Angeles Open title.

- January 17: Wes Ellis defeats Billy Casper in a playoff at the San Diego Open.

- January 30: The USGA announces that the final two rounds of the U.S. Open will be played over two days instead of one. Also, the U.S. Amateur moves from match play to stroke play.

- February 14: Rod Funseth shoots a final-round 67 at the Phoenix Open to claim his first PGA Tour victory.

1965

Sam Snead won the 1965 Greater Greensboro Open at the age of 52 years, 10 months, and 23 days, making him the oldest PGA Tour winner ever. Snead took the lead for good on the 13th hole of the final round, when he holed a putt that was "from China to Japan," as he put it. It was Snead's eighth win at Greensboro, setting another Tour record.

• March 1: Sam Snead wins the PGA Seniors Championship for the second consecutive year.

• March 7: Doug Sanders beats Jack Nicklaus in a playoff at the Pensacola Open.

• March 14: Doug Sanders stays hot and wins the Doral Open by a shot.

• March 21: Kathy Whitworth wins the LPGA season opener, the St. Petersburg Open.

• March 28: Dick Hart wins the Azalea Open at Cape Fear C.C. in Wilmington, North Carolina, in an eight-hole playoff with Phil Rodgers. It's the second-longest playoff in Tour history.

• April 4: Sam Snead wins his eighth career Greater Greensboro Open and establishes two PGA Tour records: oldest winner at 52 years, 10 months and most career victories at a single event.

• April 8: Jack Nicklaus shoots a Masters-record 271 to win by nine strokes.

Sanders Wins Back-to-Back in Florida

Doug Sanders agonizes over a missed putt in the 1965 Jacksonville Open. Sanders had won each of the previous two weeks, first at the Pensacola Open (in a playoff over Jack Nicklaus) and then at the Doral Open (by one over Bruce Devlin). Sanders's try for three in a row fell short, although he would win this tournament the following year.

Doug Sanders

Mayer Enjoys Brief Fling in New Orleans

Dick Mayer chipped in on the final green to win the 1965 Greater New Orleans Open at Lakewood C.C. The victory ended an eight-year drought; he hadn't won since claiming the 1957 U.S. Open. Nevertheless, Mayer wouldn't win again after New Orleans. He became a teaching pro in Arlington, Texas, until he died two decades later.

Dick Mayer

Tony Lema, Bing Crosby, Bruce Crampton

Crosby's Buddy Adds Name to Tourney

Bing Crosby *(center)* poses with the winner of the 1965 Bing Crosby National Pro-Am, Bruce Crampton *(right)*, as well the runner-up, Tony Lema. Crosby was the first celebrity to lend his name to a PGA tournament, but in 1965 he got some company. For the first time, old buddy Bob Hope lent his name to the Desert Classic.

• April 12: Mickey Wright, age 30, announces she will retire from full-time competition in 1966—a decision she will delay by three years.

• May 2: Arnold Palmer wins the Tournament of Champions in Las Vegas by two strokes over Chi Chi Rodriguez.

• May 11: Bruce Crampton shoots a final-round 66 to win the Colonial NIT, delayed two days by rain.

• May 16: Dick Mayer breaks out of an eight-year slump to win the Greater New Orleans Open.

• June: Ken Venturi undergoes a second surgery for a circulation problem in his hand, which has hampered his play.

• June 13: Susie Maxwell closes with the only sub-70 score of the week, a 69, to win the Women's Western Open in Chicago.

• June 21: Gary Player becomes the third golfer in history to win all four

Doug Sanders, Jackie Gleason

Floyd's Win at St. Paul One of Few

Raymond emerged as the winner in the 1965 St. Paul Open, his only victory from 1964–68. Actually, Floyd did little in his first 11 years on Tour, 1963–73, finishing in the top 20 on the money list only once (1969). His after-hours carousing was blamed for much of the problem. He took his game much more seriously after getting married.

Raymond Floyd

Gleason Passes the Bucks to Sanders

Actor Jackie Gleason always had to be where the action was, and here he poses with Doug Sanders, the winner of the 1965 Doral Open. Sanders earned $11,000, about enough to buy the ring on Jackie's finger. Gleason would eventually have his own event, Jackie Gleason's Inverrary Classic, which would begin in 1972.

Nicklaus Wins Masters with Record Score

Jack Nicklaus strolls down the fairway during the 1965 Masters. During the tournament, Masters founder Bobby Jones rolled onto the course in a wheelchair to watch Nicklaus play. He was amazed at what he saw, as Jack shot 271 to win by nine shots over Arnold Palmer and Gary Player. Nicklaus smashed the Masters record by three strokes.

Jack Nicklaus

professional majors, as he defeats Australian Kel Nagle, 71-74, in an 18-hole U.S. Open playoff at Bellerive C.C. in St. Louis.

• June 25: Marty Fleckman wins the individual title at the NCAA championships and leads Houston to the team championship.

• June 27: Randy Glover ties the PGA Tour record for the fewest putts in a round. He takes only 19 putts to shoot 68 in the final round of the St. Paul Open at Keller Golf Course.

• July 3: Carol Mann shoots 2-over-par to win the U.S. Women's Open by two shots at Atlantic City C.C.

Defending champion Mickey Wright withdrew before the tournament because of a thumb injury.

• July 4: Billy Casper, who recently shed 40 pounds after going on an exotic diet that included buffalo meat, shoots a final-round 64 to win the Western Open at Tam O'Shanter C.C. near Chicago.

Casper's Safe Play Leads to Low Scores

Billy Casper closed with a 64 to win the 1965 Western Open at Tam O'Shanter C.C. near Chicago. Casper's golfing strategy was to play conservatively: hit irons off the tee of tree-lined fairways, lay up short of water hazards, and avoid going for pins cut behind bunkers. His conservative approach led to a lot of low scores on tough courses. In 1965, he won his third Vardon Trophy.

Billy Casper

Mann Rolls to Victory in Women's Open

Carol Mann watches her 14-foot putt drop during the final round of the 1965 U.S. Women's Open, at Atlantic City C.C. in New Jersey. Mann shot 290 and won the tournament by two strokes over Kathy Cornelius. Mann would capture 35 more LPGA tournaments in her career, but never another major.

Carol Mann

Hart Survives Sudden-Death at Cape Fear

In 1965, Dick Hart ventured into Cape Fear C.C. in Wilmington, North Carolina, and endured eight grueling holes of sudden-death. Hart won the tournament, the Azalea Open, over Phil Rodgers in the second-longest sudden-death playoff in PGA Tour history. Sarah Kittle, Miss Wilmington, presented him with his check.

Sarah Kittle, Dick Hart

- July 9: Arnold Palmer and Tony Lema collapse in the final round of the British Open at Royal Birkdale to let Peter Thomson win his fifth career British crown.

- July 17: Gene Littler closes with a 66 to beat Jack Nicklaus by a shot at the Canadian Open at Mississauga G.C. in Toronto.

- July 25: Kathy Whitworth wins her third event in a row, the Buckeye Savings tournament in Cincinnati.

- August 1: Jack Nicklaus breaks 70 all four rounds to win the Thunderbird Classic in New York.

- August 8: Jack Nicklaus wins his second tournament in a row, eagling the 71st hole to win the Philadelphia Golf Classic by one shot.

- August 15: Dave Marr pops out of a three-year slump to win the PGA Championship at Laurel Valley G.C. in Ligonier, Pennsylvania. Runners-up Billy Casper and Jack Nicklaus finish two strokes back.

1965

Jean Ashley

Ashley Shocks Sander in U.S. Women's Amateur

Jean Ashley won the 1965 U.S. Women's Amateur at Lakewood C.C. in her home state of Colorado. Her 5 & 4 victory in the final against Anne Quast Sander stunned her home-state fans. Sander, who had routed Phyllis Preuss in the 1961 Women's Amateur, 14 & 13, was a three-time Amateur champion and expected to win a fourth.

Kel Nagle, Gary Player

Player Becomes Youngest to Win Each Major Title

Gary Player *(right)* defeated Kel Nagle *(left)* in a playoff, 71-74, for the 1965 U.S. Open championship, at Bellerive C.C. in St. Louis. Player thus became the third golfer to win all four major championships, joining Gene Sarazen and Ben Hogan. Player, at age 29, became the youngest to do it.

• August 23: Tony Lema wins the $35,000 first prize at the $200,000 Carling World Open—the richest event of the year. Arnold Palmer finishes second, two strokes behind.

• August 28: Jean Ashley defeats Anne Quast Sander, 5 & 4, to win the U.S. Women's Amateur at Lakewood C.C. in Denver.

• September 4: The United States and Great Britain/Ireland tie at 11 points each in the Walker Cup Match at Baltimore C.C.'s Five Farms Course.

• September 12: Gary Player wins the $50,000 first prize at the World Series of Golf, held for the winners of the four major championships.

• September 18: Bob Murphy shoots 3-over-par to win the U.S. Amateur by one stroke over Bob Dickson, at Southern Hills C.C. in Tulsa, Oklahoma.

• September 26: Sandra Haynie wins her first LPGA major, the LPGA Championship, at Stardust C.C. in Las Vegas.

1965

Jack Nicklaus, Dave Marr, Billy Casper

Marr's 8-Iron Earns Him PGA Title

The man in the middle, Dave Marr, captured the 1965 PGA Championship, edging runners-up Jack Nicklaus *(left)* and Billy Casper *(right)* at Laurel Valley G.C. in Ligonier, Pennsylvania. Marr won by two strokes thanks to a spectacular shot on the last hole. Marr fired an 8-iron to within three feet of the cup. He tapped in for par and a score of 280.

Peter Thomson

Sophomore Maxwell Cops Her First Major

Susie Maxwell, the 1964 LPGA Rookie of the Year, won her first event in May 1965, the Muskogee Civitan Open. A month later, she captured this cup for winning the Women's Western Open, a major championship. Maxwell would win 11 LPGA tournaments, and four would be majors (including three Women's Opens).

Susie Maxwell

Thomson Claims Cup No. 5 at British Open

Peter Thomson's victory in the 1965 British Open marked the fifth time he won the prestigious event. Only Harry Vardon, with six victories, claimed more. Winning five British Opens is the greatest record of any Australian in any major championship. The '65 British was held at Southport in England for the first and only time.

• October 3: South Africa wins the Canada Cup by eight shots over Spain at Club de Campo in Madrid. Gary Player wins the individual title.

• October 9: The U.S. defeats Great Britain/Ireland, 19½-12½, to win the Ryder Cup at Royal Birkdale G.C. in Southport, England.

• October 30: Gary Player, who shot 62s in the first and third rounds, wins the Australian Open.

• November 7: Gay Brewer birdies the first extra hole to defeat Bob Goalby in a playoff for the inaugural Hawaiian Open, at Waialae C.C. in Honolulu.

• November 28: Kathy Whitworth wins the Titleholders Championship by 10 strokes.

• November 28: Kathy Whitworth leads the LPGA in earnings with $28,658. She's also tops in victories with eight and claims the Vare Trophy with a scoring average of 72.61.

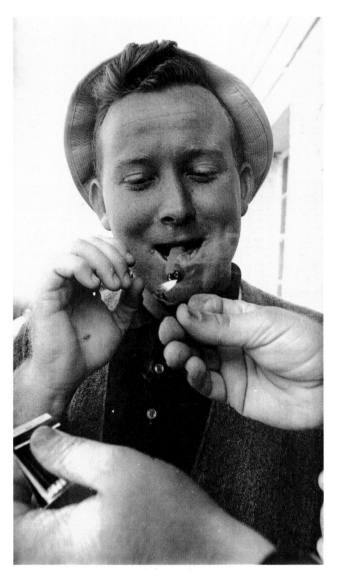

Bob Murphy

Murphy Wins the U.S. Amateur at Stroke Play

Bob Murphy, a 22-year-old senior at the University of Florida, lights a cigar before the third round of the 1965 U.S. Amateur, at Southern Hills C.C. in Tulsa, Oklahoma. Murphy would eventually win the championship by a stroke over Bob Dickson, 291-292. This was the first time the event was held at stroke play.

Kathy Whitworth

Whitworth Wins Coveted Titleholders Trophy

Kathy Whitworth still has a round to go, but she can't wait to get her hands on the Titleholders trophy. Back in 1958, a teenage Whitworth played in the Titleholders after riding in a bus from New Mexico with her mother. Whitworth captured the event in 1965, by a stroke over Peggy Wilson, for her first major championship.

• November 28: Margie Masters is named LPGA Rookie of the Year.

• November 28: Jack Nicklaus is the leading PGA Tour money winner with $140,752.14.

• November 28: Dave Marr is named PGA Player of the Year.

• November 28: Billy Casper wins his third career Vardon Trophy with a scoring average of 70.85.

• November 28: Jack Nicklaus leads the PGA Tour in victories with five, including the Masters.

• December 11: Gay Brewer and Butch Baird win the first PGA

National Fourball at PGA National G.C. in Palm Beach Gardens, Florida. Brothers Lionel and Jay Hebert finish second. Favorites Arnold Palmer and Jack Nicklaus are seventh.

• December 31: Kathy Whitworth is named Associated Press Female Athlete of the Year.

CASPER WINS U.S. OPEN AS ARNIE FALLS APART

The Billy Casper who won the 1966 U.S. Open at the Olympic Country Club in San Francisco was quite a bit different than the Casper who won the 1959 Open. The previous Casper was a rather chubby golfer who could putt well enough to cover up the rest of his game. The new Billy lopped off quite a bit of weight, down to about 185 pounds, thanks to an exotic diet that included avocado pears and buffalo meat. The new-look Casper would win the 1966 U.S. Open title in what would be the most electrifying Open of the post–World War II era.

Casper's victory would come at the expense of Arnold Palmer, who would suffer one of the worst collapses in golf history—at least one of the most memorable. However, in the early portion of the tournament, two other men stole the headlines. In the first round, obscure Al Mengert posted the top score, 67. In the next round, Rives McBee—an assistant pro from Midland, Texas—shot a tournament-record 64. But when Saturday ended, the cream had risen to the top, as Palmer led with a 207, three shots ahead of Casper.

The two were paired together in the final round. Palmer roared out with a 32 on the front nine to take a whopping seven-stroke lead over Casper and the rest of the field. When he stepped onto the 10th tee, it seemed the Open was securely Palmer's. The only problem was that Arnie was convinced he had the Open won and started thinking about breaking Ben Hogan's 1948 tournament record of 276. All it would take was a 36 to break the record. Palmer concentrated on immortality, while Casper just tried to ensure he would finish second.

However, when Palmer bogied the 10th and 13th holes, his lead was down to five shots. The big swing came on the par-3 15th.

Palmer made another bogey and Casper made a birdie to cut the lead to three shots with three holes to go. Then Palmer blew up. The 16th was a difficult, 604-yard par-5, and Arnie hooked his tee shot into the trees. That led to another bogey, and the down-the-middle Casper made another birdie. Palmer carded another bogey on 17, and Casper's par tied Arnie. Palmer made a difficult two-putt par on 18, and Casper's par tied him to set up an 18-hole playoff the next day.

To the distress of Arnie's Army, the playoff was a near-repeat of the fourth round. A 33 on the front nine gave Palmer a two-stroke lead, but the back nine bit him again. Casper tied him with a birdie to bogey on 11, then—on holes 13-16—Billy outgunned Palmer by four shots. Casper won the playoff by four.

Olympic must hate superstars. Eleven years earlier, Jack Fleck upset Ben Hogan to win the U.S. Open, and 21 years later, Scott Simpson surprised Tom Watson to win the Open. Olympic has invited the USGA to come back in the early 21st Century. The pattern is set for a future superstar to lose his major career. We'll see.

1966

- January: PGA Tour players are scheduled to compete in 36 events with a season purse of $3,704,445.

- January: LPGA Tour players are scheduled to compete in 37 events with a season purse of $509,500.

- January: In a Rules change, it is no longer a penalty if a ball hit from off the green, but within 20 yards of the hole, strikes an unattended flagstick.

- January 9: After a third-round 62, Arnold Palmer closes with a 73 to win the Los Angeles Open.

- January 23: Don Massengale bounces back from a third-round 76 with a final-round 70 at Pebble Beach to win the Bing Crosby National Pro-Am by one stroke over Arnold Palmer.

- January 31: Ken Venturi comes back from his hand ailment to win the Lucky International Open in his hometown of San Francisco. It is his last PGA Tour victory.

1966

Billy Casper had reasons to smile in 1966, as he won four Tour events and led in earnings with $121,944. The big day came when he defeated Arnold Palmer in a playoff, 69-73, for the U.S. Open title at the Olympic Club in San Francisco. Palmer led the playoff until the 13th hole, where Casper holed a 50-foot birdie putt.

• February 6: Doug Sanders beats Arnold Palmer in a playoff for the Bob Hope Desert Classic.

• March 13: Phil Rodgers wins the Doral Open in Miami by one shot over Jay Dolan.

• March 27: Doug Sanders wins his second 1966 PGA Tour event,

beating Gay Brewer by one shot in the Jacksonville Open.

• April 3: Doug Sanders birdies the second extra hole to defeat Tom Weiskopf in a playoff for the Greater Greensboro Open.

• April 10: Gay Brewer three-putts the 72nd green to fall back into a tie

for the Masters with Jack Nicklaus and Tommy Jacobs at even-par 288.

• April 11: Jack Nicklaus (70) tops Tommy Jacobs (72) and Gay Brewer (78) in the Masters playoff.

• April 18: Arnold Palmer outduels Gay Brewer in a playoff at the Tournament of Champions.

Venturi Wins the Lucky for Last Tour Victory

Ken Venturi's career was plagued by physical ailments, including a circulatory problem in his right hand. Venturi had surgery on the hand in both January and June of 1965. He managed to win the 1966 Lucky International Open in his hometown of San Francisco, but it was the last Tour victory of his career.

Dudley Wysong, Terry Dill

Wysong Triumphs in Phoenix, Threatens in PGA

Dudley Wysong *(left)* receives congratulations from Terry Dill after winning the 1966 Phoenix Open, which concluded on Valentine's Day. Wysong birdied the par-5 18th hole to win by a stroke over Gardner Dickinson. The unheralded Wysong also made noise in the 1966 PGA Championship, finishing in second place thanks to a third-round 66.

Ken Venturi

• April 18: Carol Mann wins the Raleigh Ladies Invitational by one shot when Kathy Whitworth calls a two-stroke penalty on herself on the last hole.

• May 1: Harold Henning captures the Texas Open in San Antonio by three shots. It is the South African's only victory on the PGA Tour.

• May 5: Major thunderstorms flood Champions G.C. in Houston, forcing the Houston Golf Association to postpone the Houston Champions International. It will be rescheduled for November 17–20.

• May 22: Even though he shot a 5-over 75 in the final round, Bruce Devlin wins the Colonial NIT in Fort Worth, Texas, by one shot over R.H. Sikes.

• May 25: Jim Barnes, who won 20 Tour events from 1916–37, dies at age 79.

• June 19: Arnold Palmer has a seven-stroke lead over Billy Casper with nine holes to go in the U.S.

Palmer Blows Seven-Stroke Lead at U.S. Open

Arnold Palmer misses a putt on the 14th hole during the final round of the 1966 U.S. Open, at the Olympic Club in San Francisco. On the back nine, Palmer lost seven strokes to Billy Casper, 39-32, to fall into a playoff with Casper. If Palmer had closed with a modest 37, he would have tied the U.S. Open scoring record of 276.

Jack Nicklaus

Nicklaus Nabs His Second Straight Masters

Jack Nicklaus won the 1966 Masters to become the first to win the title back-to-back. Nicklaus was tied after three rounds with Tommy Jacobs, then finished regulation tied with Jacobs and Gay Brewer. Jack won the playoff, shooting 70 to Jacobs's 72 and Brewer's 78. Nick Faldo (1989–90) would be the only other man to win successive Masters.

Arnold Palmer

Open at Olympic Club in San Francisco. He blows the lead with a 39 on the back nine.

• June 20: Billy Casper outguns Arnold Palmer, 69-73, to win the 18-hole U.S. Open playoff.

• June 25: Bob Murphy of the University of Florida wins the individual title at the NCAA championships. Houston wins its third straight team title.

• June 26: Billy Casper wins the Western Open at Medinah C.C. in Chicago by three shots.

• July 3: Sandra Spuzich shoots 9-over-par but wins the U.S. Women's Open by one stroke over Carol Mann, at Hazeltine National G.C. in Chaska, Minnesota.

• July 9: Jack Nicklaus wins the British Open at Muirfield by one shot over Doug Sanders and Dave Thomas. Nicklaus becomes the fourth player to win all four major professional championships.

Gay Brewer

Brewer Blows His Chance to Win the Masters

A boy perches on his father's shoulders to watch Gay Brewer putt during a three-way playoff for the 1966 Masters. Brewer fell into the playoff after he blew a three-foot par putt on the 72nd hole, tying him with Jack Nicklaus and Tommy Jacobs at 288. Brewer then posted an awful 78 to lose the playoff to Nicklaus.

Al Geiberger

Jack Wins British for Fourth Major

Jack Nicklaus won the 1966 British Open, giving him a victory in each of the four major professional championships. Nicklaus shot 282 to win by a stroke over Doug Sanders and Dave Thomas, at Muirfield in Scotland. Nicklaus was so impressed with the course that he would pattern his own course, Muirfield Village, after the design.

Jack Nicklaus

Geiberger Passes Snead to Win PGA Championship

Al Geiberger captured his only major title—on either the PGA Tour or the Senior Tour—when he won the 1966 PGA Championship at Firestone C.C. in Akron, Ohio. Geiberger shot 68-72-68-72—280 to finish at even-par and win by four strokes over Dudley Wysong. Sam Snead, 54 years old, led after two rounds.

• **July 17:** Seventy players sign a petition threatening to boycott the PGA Championship if they're not given more say in running the Tour. The boycott won't materialize.

• **July 24:** Al Geiberger wins the PGA Championship by four shots over Dudley Wysong at Firestone C.C. in Akron, Ohio.

• **July 24:** Tony Lema and wife Betty are killed when a private plane crashes onto the 7th hole at The Sportsman's Club in Lansing, Illinois. Lema was on his way from the PGA Championship to an exhibition in Chicago.

• **July 30:** The United States defeats Great Britain/Ireland, 13-5, to win the Curtis Cup Match at the Cascades Course at Virginia Hot Springs Golf and Tennis Club.

• **August 13:** JoAnne Gunderson Carner defeats Marlene Stewart Streit, 1 up, in a 41-hole final to win the U.S. Women's Amateur, at Sewickley Heights G.C. in Pennsylvania.

Carner Needs 41 Holes to Win Amateur

JoAnne Gunderson Carner won her fourth U.S. Women's Amateur in 1966, but she needed 41 holes to do it. In the longest final match in tourney history, Carner defeated Marlene Stewart Streit at Sewickley Heights G.C. in Pennsylvania. Streit could have won on the 36th hole, but her 13-foot putt hit the back of the cup and popped out.

Don Massengale

Massengale Fires Four 70s to Win in Canada

Don Massengale hoists the Seagram's Gold Cup after winning the 1966 Canadian Open at Shaughnessy Golf and C.C. in Toronto. Bringing new meaning to consistency, Massengale won the event by shooting 70-70-70-70—280. He also won the 1966 Bing Crosby National Pro-Am. These were the only two PGA Tour victories of his career. He would win twice on the Senior Tour in the early 1990s.

Sandra Spuzich

Spuzich Wins Open on Tough Hazeltine Track

Sandra Spuzich shot 75-74-76-72—297, 9-over-par, but still won the 1966 U.S. Women's Open at Hazeltine National G.C. in Chaska, Minnesota. Spuzich finished a stroke ahead of Carol Mann, who rimmed a putt for birdie on the 72nd hole. The success of the tournament at Hazeltine led the USGA to host the men's Open there in 1970.

JoAnne Gunderson Carner

- August 14: Kathy Whitworth wins for the third straight week, at the Lady Carling Open.

- September 2: Mickey Wright wins the Ladies World Series of Golf at Springfield C.C. in Ohio.

- September 3: Bruce Devlin wins the $35,000 first prize at the Carling World Open at Royal Birkdale G.C. in Southport, England. Billy Casper finishes a shot back.

- September 3: Deane Beman and Gary Cowan tie for the U.S. Amateur championship after the regulation 72 holes, at Merion G.C. in Ardmore, Pennsylvania. Beman double bogeyed the last hole.

- September 4: Gary Cowan shoots 75 to defeat Deane Beman by one shot in an 18-hole playoff for the U.S. Amateur.

- September 25: Gloria Ehret shoots 6-under-par to win the LPGA Championship at Stardust C.C. in Las Vegas. Mickey Wright is second.

Lema, Three Others Die in Plane Crash

PGA Tour golfer Tony Lema, wife Betty, and two other people were killed when this private plane crashed at The Sportsman's Club in Lansing, Illinois. The plane hit the ground and bounced into a water hazard on the 7th hole. Lema was on his way from the PGA Championship to an exhibition in Chicago.

Tony Lema Plane Crash

Gary Cowan

Hundreds Mourn Loss of Tony and Betty Lema

About 1,000 mourners turned out for the funeral of Tony and Betty Lema in Oakland, California. Lema, the 1964 British Open champion, was one of the most popular players on Tour. In 1964, he and Gwilym S. Brown wrote a book called *Golfer's Gold,* which gave golf fans a true inside feeling of the PGA Tour.

Tony and Betty Lema's Funeral

Cowan Edges Beman in U.S. Amateur Playoff

Gary Cowan *(pictured)* needed 90 holes to defeat Deane Beman in the 1966 U.S. Amateur, at Merion G.C. in Ardmore, Pennsylvania. After each finished at 285, Cowan took the playoff, 75-76. Beman double bogied the 72nd hole to fall into the playoff. Cowan, a Canadian, became the first foreigner to win the title since 1932.

• October 2: Don Massengale shoots four consecutive 70s to win the Canadian Open by three shots over Chi Chi Rodriguez.

• October 10: Tour players threaten to quit the PGA and form their own association if the PGA doesn't designate a special section for them.

• November 13: The U.S. team of Jack Nicklaus and Arnold Palmer wins the Canada Cup at Yomiuri G.C. in Tokyo by five shots over South Africa. George Knudson of Canada wins the individual title by one stroke over Nicklaus.

• November 20: Arnold Palmer wins the rescheduled Houston Champions International by one shot over Gardner Dickinson.

• November 27: Kathy Whitworth wins the Titleholders Championship.

• November 27: Billy Casper is the leading PGA Tour money winner with $121,944.92. He leads the Tour with four victories.

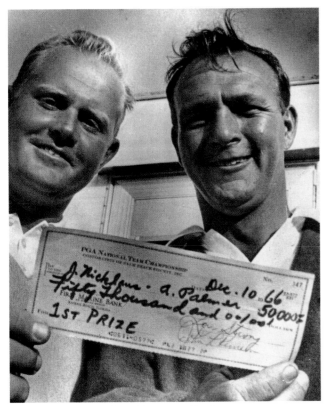

Jack Nicklaus, Arnold Palmer

Nicklaus, Palmer Split $50,000 Prize in Team Event

Jack Nicklaus *(left)* and Arnold Palmer display their $50,000 first-prize check for winning the 1966 PGA National Team Championship. The $275,000 purse made the event the richest of the year. From 1965 to 1966, the PGA Tour's total purse soared from $2.8 million to $3.7 million. Six players reached $100,000 in earnings in '66.

Whitworth Wins Nine, Leads in Tour Earnings

Kathy Whitworth blasts out of a bunker at Augusta C.C. en route to victory in the 1966 Titleholders Championship. In '66, Whitworth again led in victories (nine) and earnings (a record $33,517). Because of financial problems, this would be the last Titleholders for six years. Only one more would be held, in 1972.

Kathy Whitworth

• November 27: Billy Casper wins his fourth career Vardon Trophy with a scoring average of 70.27. He's named Player of the Year.

• December 4: Sandra Haynie wins the final LPGA event of the season, the Pensacola Ladies Invitational at Scenic Hills C.C. It's her fourth win of the year.

• December 4: Kathy Whitworth is the leading LPGA Tour money winner with $33,517. She leads the Tour with nine victories.

• December 4: Kathy Whitworth wins her second career Vare Trophy with a scoring average of 72.60. She is named Player of the Year.

• December 4: Jan Ferraris is named LPGA Rookie of the Year.

• December 10: Arnold Palmer and Jack Nicklaus win the PGA National Team Championship, splitting the first prize of $50,000. The purse of $275,000 is the biggest of the year, although it's unofficial money.

'67 OPEN SIGNALS THE DAWN OF MODERN GOLF

The 1967 U.S. Open on the Lower Course at Baltusrol in New Jersey was won by Jack Nicklaus, but it was much more than a Golden Bear victory. It was the debut of a funny-swinging Texan out of El Paso named Lee Trevino, and it was also the final U.S. Open appearance of Ben Hogan. Many claim that the '67 Open signaled the birth of golf's modern era.

The Open also sparked Nicklaus's career, as he had wallowed in a minor slump before the victory. He had missed the cut in the Masters and had yet to win a tournament in 1967. Putting was his problem. However, the week before the U.S. Open, Nicklaus acquired a white-painted, bull's-eye putter called White Fang. The new weapon inspired Jack to slightly alter his putting stroke, and that not only ensured his second U.S. Open victory, but it eventually allowed him to break Hogan's tournament record of 276.

Hogan, though, was still alive and kicking. He was exempted by the USGA to play in the Open, and even though he was 54 years old, he expected to win. "I figure to win any tournament I enter,"

said Hogan just before the Open. Nicklaus figured he would win too. After tallying nine one-putt greens during a practice-round 62 with Arnold Palmer, Nicklaus said, "If I win the Open, I'll break the record." Nevertheless, it took a while for Nicklaus to make his move. Palmer was the leader after two rounds, and Jack's third-round 72 kept him one shot out of the lead, held by amateur Marty Fleckman.

Things changed on Sunday, as Nicklaus started sinking putts. After holing a 22-foot birdie on the 7th hole, Jack took a two-stroke lead over Palmer. The fans still wanted Palmer to win. From the gallery, someone yelled,

"C'mon, Fatso, duck-hook it into the woods!" Nonetheless, White Fang kept draining putts, and by the time Nicklaus reached the 18th tee, he was two shots ahead of Palmer thanks to seven birdies.

The 18th hole was a testy par-5 with a creek, and Nicklaus pushed a 1-iron into the rough. He laid up short of the creek and rifled another 1-iron onto the green, 22 feet from the hole. White Fang rolled that putt in for a 65 and a 72-hole record of 275. It was a somewhat sad ending for Hogan, who finished 34th with a 292. "Hell can't be hotter than this," he said.

While Nicklaus's victory was exciting, a lot of golf fans were amazed at the unknown Mexican-American Texan. Nobody had ever heard of Trevino. He was an assistant pro at Horizon Hills Country Club in El Paso and was playing in just his second U.S. Open. But by finishing fifth, Trevino jumped into the public eye. Instead of going back to El Paso, he was invited to several PGA Tour events, and he won $26,472 before the year was out. The 1967 Open was the swan song for Hogan, but the young Lee Trevino was just warming up.

1967

- January: PGA Tour players are scheduled to compete in 37 events with a total purse of $3,979,162.

- January: LPGA Tour players are scheduled to compete in 32 events with a total purse of $435,250.

- January: The Canada Cup changes its name to the World Cup.

- January 22: Jack Nicklaus shoots a final-round 68 to win the Bing Crosby National Pro-Am.

- January 29: Arnold Palmer wins the Los Angeles Open by five shots.

- January 29: Sam Snead wins the PGA Seniors Championship by nine strokes.

- February 12: Julius Boros edges Ken Still by one shot to win the Phoenix Open, despite Still's final-round 63.

- March 12: Julius Boros wins his second tournament of the year, edging Arnold Palmer and George Knudson by one shot at the Florida Citrus Open.

Lee Trevino didn't win the 1967 U.S. Open, but his appearance was significant as he jumped into the public eye for the first time. The 27-year-old Texan finished in fifth place behind standouts Jack Nicklaus, Arnold Palmer, Don January, and Billy Casper. Trevino would soon challenge the quartet for Tour supremacy.

• March 19: Marilynn Smith opens the LPGA Tour season by winning the St. Petersburg Orange Classic.

• March 19: Jim Colbert ties the PGA Tour record for the fewest putts for nine holes with eight on the front nine of the Jacksonville Open. He shoots 69 and ties for third.

• March 26: Gay Brewer moves into third place in the PGA Tour record book by shooting 26-under-par in winning the Pensacola Open. The record is 27-under-par held by Ben Hogan and Mike Souchak.

• April 7: Jack Nicklaus, the winner the last two years, misses the 36-hole cut at the Masters.

• April 8: Ben Hogan, age 54, ties the nine-hole Masters record with a 30 on the back nine at Augusta National and shoots a third-round 66.

• April 9: Gay Brewer closes with a final-round 67 to win the Masters by one stroke over Bobby Nichols. Brewer shoots 280.

Julius Boros

Ageless Boros Still at the Top of His Game

At age 47, Julius Boros seemed to catch a second wind in 1967, as he won three PGA Tour events—the Phoenix Open, Florida Citrus Open, and Buick Open. A year later, he'd claim the PGA Championship. Boros was nicknamed "The Moose," but he actually displayed a soft touch around the green.

Bob Hope Desert Classic

Nieporte Edges Sanders in Bob Hope Desert Classic

Tom Nieporte holds the Eisenhower Trophy after winning the 1967 Bob Hope Desert Classic, by one stroke over defending champion Doug Sanders. NBC commentator Joe Garagiola holds the microphone for President Dwight Eisenhower. Bob Hope *(far right)* and Sanders *(far left)* participate in the ceremony.

• April 30: Chi Chi Rodriguez shoots a final-round 66 to win the Texas Open by one shot.

• May: The women's Titleholders Championship is canceled due to financial losses.

• May 20: The United States wins the Walker Cup Match, defeating Great Britain/Ireland, 13-7, at Royal St. George's G.C. in England.

• May 21: Dave Stockton wins the Colonial NIT for his first Tour victory.

• June 2: For the second straight year, Tour players threaten to boycott the PGA Championship unless they are given more control of the Tour.

• June 10: Mickey Wright shoots a 62 in the second round of the Bluegrass Invitational. It ties an LPGA record, but it won't go into the books because players were allowed to improve lies in the fairways.

Gay Brewer, Bobby Nichols

Brewer Bounces Back to Claim Masters Title

Gay Brewer *(left)* and Bobby Nichols stride off the 18th green after the final round of the 1967 Masters. Brewer won the tournament with a 280 total, while Nichols finished runner-up. Brewer had lost a heart-breaker at Augusta a year earlier; five years later, he would suffer a near-fatal ulcer attack just prior to the tournament.

Stockton Sparks Career with Win at Colonial

Dave Stockton captured his first PGA Tour event in 1967, the esteemed Colonial NIT, thanks to successive rounds of 65-66. Stockton won 11 Tour events in his career, including two PGA Championships. His biggest honor came in 1991, when he was named non-playing captain of the U.S. Ryder Cup team.

Dave Stockton

Dave Hill

Hill Scores First of Four Wins in Memphis

Dave Hill claimed 13 PGA Tour events in his career, and four of them came at Colonial C.C. in Memphis, Tennessee. Hill won the 1967 and 1969 Memphis Invitationals, and though the name was changed to the Danny Thomas Memphis Classic, he prevailed in 1970 and 1973. Hill won in '67 by a shot over Johnny Pott.

• June 11: Mickey Wright wins the Bluegrass Invitational by seven strokes.

• June 18: Jack Nicklaus's final-round 65 at Baltusrol G.C. in New Jersey enables him to set the 72-hole U.S. Open record of 275 and beat Arnold Palmer by four strokes.

• June 20: A compromise agreement is reached in the dispute between the players and the PGA.

• June 24: Hale Irwin wins the NCAA championship, with Houston taking its fourth straight team title.

• July 2: French amateur Catherine Lacoste shoots a final-round 79 at the Virginia Hot Springs Golf and Tennis Club, but she wins the U.S. Women's Open by two shots to become the event's first amateur winner.

• July 3: Billy Casper tops Art Wall in an 18-hole Canadian Open playoff, 65-69, at Montreal Municipal G.C.

Jack Nicklaus

Records Fall at Baltusrol in U.S. Open

Jack Nicklaus shot a tournament-record 275 (71-67-72-65) to win the 1967 U.S. Open at Baltusrol G.C. in New Jersey. Nicklaus, needing a birdie on the final hole to break Ben Hogan's score of 276, drained a 22-foot putt for the record. An estimated crowd of 88,000—a record for the Open—witnessed the action.

Roberto De Vicenzo

Beard Beats Palmer with Final-Hole Birdie

Frank Beard took home the $23,000 first-place check after winning the 1967 Houston Champions International in a thrilling finish. Both Beard and Arnold Palmer were tied at 9-under entering the final hole, but Beard won by a stroke after draining an 18-foot birdie putt. Beard surpassed $100,000 in 1967 for the first of five straight years.

Frank Beard

De Vicenzo, Age 44, Captures British Open

Roberto De Vicenzo of Argentina prevailed in the 1967 British Open, held at Hoylake in England for the final time. Roberto shot 278, two strokes off the tournament record, to defeat defending champion Jack Nicklaus by two strokes. De Vicenzo, age 44, thus became the first golfer from South America to win a major championship.

• July 12: Jack Klass files a $1.25 million suit against the LPGA over a rule requiring its players to be at least 18 years old. His 10-year-old daughter, Beverly, has played in three events this year.

• July 15: Roberto De Vicenzo wins the British Open at Hoylake by two strokes over Jack Nicklaus.

• July 16: Kathy Whitworth sinks a 50-foot birdie putt on the 72nd hole to win the LPGA Championship by one over Shirley Englehorn, at Pleasant Valley C.C. in Massachusetts.

• July 23: Don Massengale shoots a final-round 66 to tie Don January at 281 for the PGA Championship at Columbine C.C. in Denver.

• July 24: Don January fires a 69 to defeat Don Massengale in an 18-hole playoff for the PGA Championship.

• July 26: A judge dismisses Jack Klass's lawsuit against the LPGA.

• August 6: Jack Nicklaus captures the Western Open at Beverly C.C. in

1967

Catherine Lacoste

Massengale Bows to January in PGA

Don Massengale misses a birdie putt on the 2nd hole of the final round in the 1967 PGA Championship. Massengale closed with a blistering 66 to tie fellow Texan Don January at 281, then January won the play-off, 69-71. The tourney took place on Denver's Columbine C.C. course, a 7,436-yard track made easier by the mile-high air.

Jack Nicklaus

Amateur Lacoste Prevails in Women's Open

Catherine Lacoste became the first amateur to win the U.S. Women's Open with her victory in the 1967 championship, at the Virginia Hot Springs Golf and Tennis Club. She won by two strokes despite closing with a 79. Lacoste, of Paris, France, was the daughter of tennis great Rene Lacoste.

Don Massengale

Nicklaus Earns Two $50,000 Paychecks

Jack Nicklaus displays the $50,000 check he earned for winning the 1967 Westchester Classic. Checks of $50,000 were rare in the 1960s, but Nicklaus won two of them in '67, the other coming at the World Series of Golf. Even though the World Series money was unofficial, Nicklaus set the Tour's season record for earnings with $188,998.

Chicago by two shots over Doug Sanders.

• August 13: Arnold Palmer wins the American Golf Classic at Firestone C.C. in Akron, Ohio. It is Palmer's 50th Tour victory.

• August 19: Mary Lou Dill defeats Jean Ashley, 5 & 4, to win the U.S.

Women's Amateur at Annandale G.C. in Pasadena, California.

• August 20: Charlie Sifford, age 45, wins his first PGA Tour event, the Greater Hartford Open, shooting a 64 in the final round.

• August 20: Kathy Whitworth wins the Women's Western Open.

• August 30: Jack Nicklaus wins the largest first prize of the season, $50,000, at the Westchester Classic, which is delayed three days by rain.

• September: Croquet-style putting, used by Sam Snead in recent years, is made illegal in a change to the Rules of Golf, effective January 1, 1968.

Casper Earns His Dough in Canada, Scotland

In 1967, Billy Casper did most of his damage outside the U.S. He won two playoffs in Canada—a 65-69 victory over Art Wall in the Canadian Open, and a sudden-death triumph over Al Geiberger in the Carling World Open. Casper lost another playoff at St. Andrews, Scotland, falling to Gay Brewer, 68-72, in the Alcan Golfer of the Year tournament.

Bob Dickson

Dickson Gets Big Kisses, Wins Little Slam

Bob Dickson gets kisses from his sister Ann *(right)* and his sister-in-law after winning the 1967 U.S. Amateur at Broadmoor G.C. in Colorado Springs. He shot 285 to win by a stroke over Marvin Giles III. Dickson also won the '67 British Amateur, thus becoming the first golfer in 32 years to win the "Little Slam."

Billy Casper

- September 2: Bob Dickson wins the U.S. Amateur at Broadmoor G.C. in Colorado Springs.

- September 2: Francis Ouimet, who won the 1913 U.S. Open as a 20-year-old amateur, dies.

- September 4: Billy Casper birdies the first extra hole to defeat Al

Geiberger in a playoff in the last Carling World Open, at Board of Trade G.C. in Toronto.

- September 10: Jack Nicklaus wins the first prize of $50,000 (unofficial money) at the World Series of Golf.

- October 9: Gay Brewer defeats Billy Casper in a playoff, 68-72, to

win the $50,000 first prize at the Alcan Golfer of the Year tournament in St. Andrews, Scotland.

- October 22: The U.S. defeats Great Britain/Ireland, 23½-8½, to win the Ryder Cup at Champions G.C. in Houston. It is the widest victory margin in Ryder Cup history.

Marty Fleckman

Fleckman Wins the First Tour Event He Enters

Marty Fleckman was one of golf's great flash-in-the-pans. In 1967, as an amateur, he led the U.S. Open after three rounds before closing with an 80 to finish in 18th place. Later in the year, he won the first event he entered as a pro, the Cajun Classic in Louisiana. He never again won a PGA Tour event.

Arnold Palmer, Gardner Dickinson

Palmer, Dickinson Shine in Ryder Cup Match

Arnold Palmer *(left)* and Gardner Dickinson smile after their outstanding performances in the 1967 Ryder Cup Matches, at Champions G.C. in Houston. Palmer and Dickinson won all of their matches, five points each, to lead the U.S. to a 23½-8½ victory over Great Britain/Ireland. Ben Hogan served as the States' non-playing captain.

• November 12: The United States wins the World Cup at Club de Golf in Mexico. Arnold Palmer wins the individual title by five shots over Jack Nicklaus.

• November 19: Kathy Whitworth is the leading LPGA Tour money winner with $32,937. She also leads in victories with nine.

• November 19: Kathy Whitworth wins the Vare Trophy, averaging 72.74. She is named Player of the Year.

• December 3: Starting in his first tournament since qualifying for the PGA Tour, Marty Fleckman defeats Jack Montgomery in a playoff for the Cajun Classic in Louisiana.

• December 3: Jack Nicklaus is the leading PGA Tour money winner with $188,988.08. He leads the Tour with five victories and is named Player of the Year.

• December 3: Arnold Palmer wins the Vardon Trophy with a scoring average of 70.18.

AARON'S ERROR COSTS DE VICENZO THE MASTERS

The USGA Rules of Golf are considered the best way to ensure that the golfer who wins a tournament does so ethically. Hardly any golf professional ever violates rules, but a surprise accidental violation in the 1968 Masters is considered by golf fans to be the most unfair enforcement of the Rules of Golf.

Actually, it was the saddest loss of a tournament in the history of the game. Bob Goalby was declared the winner of the Masters after apparently tying reigning British Open champion Roberto De Vicenzo of Argentina. On Sunday, the two were red-hot and dueling it out on the back nine of Augusta National. Playing in front of Goalby, De Vicenzo sank a five-foot birdie putt on the par-4 17th hole and, despite a bogey on the 18th hole, posted what millions of television fans thought was an 11-under 277. Goalby was in a bit of trouble on the final hole, but he managed to drop in a five-foot par putt to shoot a 66 and post another 277.

Then the world of golf went into shock. De Vicenzo's playing partner, Tommy Aaron, who was keeping De Vicenzo's scorecard, had mistakenly marked down a par-4 on No. 17, even though Roberto had birdied the hole. Instead of giving De Vicenzo his rightful 65, Aaron had given him a 66. De Vicenzo didn't notice the mistake, signed the scorecard, and was rushed off to a television interview. Everyone was beginning to think about an 18-hole playoff the next day.

In the meantime, Aaron pointed out the mistake to the Rules Committee, and after consulting USGA Rule 38, Paragraph 3, they declared Goalby as the winner and De Vicenzo the runner-up. The rule simply stated that if a golfer incorrectly marked his scorecard lower than what he actually shot, he would be disqualified, and if it was marked higher, then the score was considered to be official. Once the scorecard is signed, it cannot be changed. Therefore, the 66 that De Vicenzo signed off on was considered official, giving him a total of 278, one shot behind Goalby.

An hour later, De Vicenzo refused to be angry at Aaron. He told the media, "It's my fault. Tommy feels like I feel, very bad. I think the rule is hard." The loss was even sadder for De Vicenzo, considering that day was his 45th birthday. Goalby wasn't all that happy either. He told the press, "I'd be a liar to say I was happy to win. I regret the way I won. I wish I was in a playoff tomorrow."

Goalby had a reason to be unhappy. The next year at the Masters, a lot of golf fans started running Goalby down, declaring he didn't deserve to own a green jacket. It was a sad rules violation, but there was one positive result. The PGA Tour started setting up scorecard-checking tents behind the 18th green to make certain no other golfer would ever blow a tournament the way De Vicenzo blew the Masters. It was a lousy birthday present.

1968

- January: PGA Tour players are scheduled to compete in 45 events with a season purse of $5,077,600.

- January: LPGA Tour players are scheduled to compete in 34 events with a total purse of $550,185.

- January 14: Johnny Pott birdies the first sudden-death hole to defeat Billy Casper and Bruce Devlin in a playoff for the Bing Crosby National Pro-Am.

- January 28: Billy Casper shoots 14-under-par to win the Los Angeles Open by three over Arnold Palmer.

- February 11: Tom Weiskopf beats Al Geiberger by one shot to win the Andy Williams San Diego Open. It's the first victory of his career.

- February 25: A week after winning the Phoenix Open, Canadian George Knudson nabs the Tucson Open by one stroke.

- March 10: Gardner Dickinson wins the Doral Open despite a bogey

1968

Roberto De Vicenzo *(far right)* sweats it out while Masters officials decide what to do about his erroneous scorecard. Tommy Aaron *(upper left)* discusses his blunder with tourney officials. Aaron, De Vicenzo's playing partner, recorded that Roberto scored a 66 in the final round. In reality, he shot a 65. The misunderstanding cost De Vicenzo a spot in a playoff with Bob Goalby.

and double bogey on the last two holes. Tom Weiskopf is one stroke back after finishing with two bogeys.

• April 14: Roberto De Vicenzo birdies the 17th hole of the Masters to tie Bob Goalby for the lead. Playing partner Tommy Aaron marks down a par on the scorecard instead of birdie. De Vicenzo doesn't notice the mistake and signs an incorrect scorecard.

• April 14: The Masters tournament committee declares Bob Goalby Masters champion. Roberto De Vicenzo finishes second, one shot behind, as he is credited with the 66 he signed for instead of a 65.

• April 21: Carol Mann sets an LPGA 54-hole record of 200 and wins the Lady Carling Open by 10 strokes.

• April 21: Steve Reid birdies the third extra hole to defeat Gary Player in a playoff for the Azalea Open in North Carolina. It's his first PGA Tour victory.

1968

Weiskopf Nabs Two Tour Wins

After going winless his first three years on Tour, Tom Weiskopf broke through with two victories in 1968—the Andy Williams San Diego Open and the Buick Open. He soared to No. 3 on the money list with $154,946. In October, however, Weiskopf began six months of active duty with the Army Reserves.

Tom Weiskopf

Dickinson Hangs on to Win at Doral

Gardner Dickinson closed the 1968 Doral Open with a bogey and a double bogey, but he still won the tournament by a stroke over Tom Weiskopf, who bogied the last two holes. Dickinson was credited with helping his wife, Judy Dickinson, with her golf game. Judy, still active, has earned over $1.5 million on the LPGA Tour.

Gardner Dickinson

Bob Goalby

Goalby's Masters Win Marred by Controversy

Bob Goalby's only career victory in a major championship came with a huge asterisk, as he won the 1968 Masters following the De Vicenzo scorecard controversy. Many fans gave Goalby a lot of flack, saying he didn't deserve to win. What should be noted, however, is that Goalby shot 277—one of the best scores in Masters history.

- **April 28:** Miller Barber wins the first Byron Nelson Golf Classic, formerly the Dallas Open, at Preston Trail G.C. in Dallas.

- **May 5:** Roberto De Vicenzo recovers from his Masters loss by winning the Houston Champions International by one shot over Lee Trevino.

- **May 5:** Carol Mann wins her third straight tournament, the Shreveport Kiwanis Open.

- **June 2:** A week after winning the Memphis Open, Bob Lunn wins the Atlanta Classic.

- **June 15:** The United States defeats Great Britain/Ireland, 10½-7½, to

win the Curtis Cup Match at Royal County Down G.C. in Newcastle, Northern Ireland.

- **June 16:** Lee Trevino becomes the first golfer ever to break 70 in all four rounds of the U.S. Open. He beats Jack Nicklaus by four shots at Oak Hill C.C. in Rochester, New York, to win his first official event.

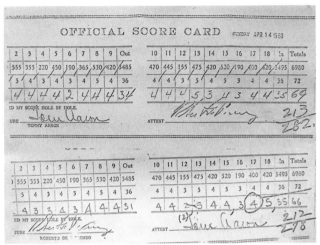

Roberto De Vicenzo's Masters Scorecard

Aaron Turns a Birdie into a Par

This is the scorecard that caused the controversy in the 1968 Masters. Roberto De Vicenzo's final round is on the bottom. He actually shot a 3 on the 17th hole, but Tommy Aaron jotted down a 4. After the 18th hole, on which he flubbed an easy par putt, an irritated De Vicenzo barely looked at the scorecard before signing it.

George Knudson

Casper Wins Six, Breaks $200,000 Barrier

Judge Charles Murray *(right)*, president of the Colonial C.C., presents the trophy to Billy Casper for winning the 1968 Colonial NIT. Casper dominated the circuit in 1968, winning six events while no one else claimed more than two. He also captured his fifth Vardon Trophy and became the first golfer in Tour history to earn $200,000.

Billy Casper, Judge Charles Murray

Knudson Wins Back-to-Back in Arizona

George Knudson of Toronto took home $20,000 after winning the Tucson Open in February 1968. He then donned the hat of the Conquistadores, sponsors of the tournament. Just a week earlier, he claimed the Phoenix Open. Knudson first made his mark in 1966, when he took individual honors in the Canada Cup Match.

• June 22: Florida ends Houston's four-year hold on the NCAA crown, while Oklahoma State's Grier Jones takes the individual title.

• June 23: Left-hander Bob Charles wins the Canadian Open by two shots over Jack Nicklaus, at St. Georges Golf & C.C. in Toronto.

• June 24: Rookie Sandra Post defeats Kathy Whitworth in an 18-hole playoff, 68-75, to win the LPGA Championship at Pleasant Valley C.C. in Sutton, Massachusetts.

• July 7: Susie Maxwell Berning wins the U.S. Women's Open by

three strokes over Mickey Wright, at Moselem Springs G.C. in Fleetwood, Pennsylvania.

• July 13: Gary Player shoots 1-over-par 289 but wins the British Open at Carnoustie, Scotland, by one shot over Jack Nicklaus and Bob Charles.

1968

Bert Yancey, Lee Trevino

Trevino Passes Yancey to Claim U.S. Open Title

Bert Yancey *(left)* congratulates Lee Trevino for winning the 1968 U.S. Open, at Oak Hill C.C. in Rochester, New York. Trevino tied the Open's 72-hole record by shooting 69-68-69-69—275. Yancey led after three rounds, breaking the 54-hole record with a 205. However, Bert closed with a 76 to finish in third place, six shots back.

Berning Captures Women's Open

Seven weeks after getting married, Susie Maxwell Berning won the 1968 U.S. Women's Open at Moselem Springs G.C. in Fleetwood, Pennsylvania. Berning opened with a 69 and led after every round, finishing at 5-over 289. Mickey Wright closed with a 68, a record final-round score for the Open, but finished three strokes back in second place. Berning would win the Open three times in all.

Susie Maxwell Berning

Julius and Armen Boros

Boros, Age 48, Nips Palmer for PGA Title

Julius Boros poses with wife Armen after winning the 1968 PGA Championship, at Pecan Valley C.C. in San Antonio. At age 48, Boros became the oldest golfer to win a major championship. Arnold Palmer had a chance to win his only PGA title, but he missed several make-able birdie putts in the final round and finished a shot back.

• July 21: Julius Boros, age 48, wins the PGA Championship by one stroke over Arnold Palmer and Bob Charles, at Pecan Valley C.C. in San Antonio. Boros thus becomes the oldest winner of a major championship.

• July 21: Arnold Palmer's $12,500 paycheck at the PGA Championship makes him the first golfer ever to reach $1 million in career earnings.

• July 27: Carol Mann's victory in the Supertest Canadian Open in Toronto is her third LPGA victory in a row and seventh of the year.

• August 4: Jack Nicklaus gets his first victory of the year at the Western Open, at Olympia Fields C.C. in Illinois.

• August 11: Jack Nicklaus wins again, defeating Frank Beard and rookie Lee Elder in a playoff for the American Golf Classic in Akron, Ohio. Elder loses on the fifth extra hole.

JoAnne Carner

Carner Wins Her Fifth Women's Amateur

JoAnne Carner triumphed in the 1968 U.S. Women's Amateur—her fifth such victory. Carner defeated Anne Quast Welts in the final, 5 & 4, at Birmingham C.C. in Michigan to move within one of Glenna Collett's six Amateur titles. Carner would lose in the first round of the 1969 championship and turn pro several months later.

Whitworth's Winnings Reach New Heights

Kathy Whitworth raises the putter that helped her win the 1968 Canyon Classic. Runners-up Mary Mills *(left)* and Donna Caponi cheer her on. For Whitworth, it was one of four victories she posted from October 27–November 24. She finished the year with 10 wins and took home $48,379—$15,000 more than any LPGA player had ever won.

Kathy Whitworth

Gary Player

Player Weathers Carnoustie to Prevail in British Open

Gary Player won the 1968 British Open at Carnoustie, Scotland, with a total of 289—the highest winning Open score in 20 years. Battering winds, as well as a devilish 7,200-yard course, contributed to the high scores. It was the second British Open victory for Player, who had been in a drought since winning the 1965 U.S. Open.

• August 14: Tour players announce that they will break from the PGA and run their own tour in 1969.

• August 17: JoAnne Gunderson Carner defeats Anne Quast Sander, 5 & 4, in the final of the U.S. Women's Amateur, at Birmingham C.C. in Michigan. It is Carner's fifth Women's Amateur title.

• August 18: Julius Boros wins the PGA Tour's top first prize, $50,000, at the Westchester Classic in New York.

• August 18: Kathy Whitworth shoots a final-round 62 to win the Holiday Inn Classic by six shots over Carol Mann.

• August 31: Bruce Fleisher shoots 4-over-par to win the U.S. Amateur at Scioto C.C. in Columbus, Ohio. Vinny Giles finishes a shot back.

• September 1: A week after winning the Philadelphia Classic for his first career victory, Bob Murphy wins the Thunderbird Classic.

Fleisher Nips Giles by One in U.S. Amateur

Bruce Fleisher of Miami won the 1968 U.S. Amateur at Scioto C.C. in Columbus, Ohio. Fleisher, a month short of his 20th birthday, thus became the fourth-youngest winner of the championship. Marvin Giles III finished second by a stroke for the second straight year. Giles would finish runner-up by five strokes in 1969.

Jack Nicklaus

Nicklaus Frustrated by Runner-Up Finishes

Jack Nicklaus signs an autograph at the 1968 British Open. The perturbed look on his face reflected his frustrating year. Nicklaus finished runner-up to Gary Player in the British Open, second to Lee Trevino in the U.S. Open, and runner-up to Bob Charles in the Canadian Open. He didn't get his first win until August, at the Western Open.

Bruce Fleisher

• September 13: Ted Makalena, winner of the 1966 Hawaiian Open, dies at age 34. Five days earlier, he broke his neck diving into shallow surf at Waikiki Beach.

• September 15: Arnold Palmer, who earlier in the week announced his support for the players breaking away from the PGA, wins the first Kemper Open, held at Pecan Valley C.C. in Sutton, Massachusetts.

• October 10: A court restraining order banning activities of the American Professional Golfers, the new players group, is lifted. Meanwhile, both the PGA and APG have held qualifying tourneys.

• October 26: Tom Weiskopf, third on this year's money list, starts six months of active duty with the Army Reserves.

• November 10: Lee Trevino wins his second career event, the Hawaiian Open. He dedicates the victory to his friend, Ted Makalena, who died two months earlier.

Judy Rankin

Rankin Grabs First Win at Corpus Christi

Judy Torluemke was a teenage star in the late 1950s and early '60s and she joined the LPGA Tour in 1962. But it wasn't until 1968, a year after she married Yippy Rankin, that she earned her first Tour victory. Rankin won the Corpus Christi Open for her first of 26 career LPGA wins. The other 25 all came in the 1970s.

Bob and Gail Murphy

Murphy, a Rookie, Cracks $100,000 Mark

Rookie Bob Murphy gets a kiss from wife Gail after winning the 1968 Thunderbird Classic at Upper Montclair C.C. in New Jersey. A week earlier, Murphy won the Philadelphia Classic. He finished the year with $105,595, becoming the first Tour rookie ever to earn six figures. Murphy would win just three more Tour events in his career.

• November 17: Canada wins the World Cup Match by two shots over the United States in Rome, Italy.

• November 24: Billy Casper is the leading PGA Tour money winner with $205,168, thus becoming the first player to break $200,000 in a single year. Casper finishes with six wins, four more than anyone else.

• November 24: Billy Casper wins the Vardon Trophy for the fifth time, with an average of 69.82.

• November 24: No PGA Tour Player of the Year Award is given.

• December 1: Kathy Whitworth tops the LPGA with $48,379. She is named Player of the Year.

• December 1: Carol Mann wins the Vare Trophy with an average of 72.04. She ties Kathy Whitworth for the lead in Tour victories with 10.

• December 7: The dispute between the players and the PGA is settled by the formation of the Tournament Players Division within the PGA.

POOR-PUTT MOODY DRIVES TO U.S. OPEN TITLE

In an era when Jack Nicklaus, Gary Player, and Lee Trevino were the dominant players, any other golfer who won the U.S. Open was a surprise. The biggest shocker in any post–World War II U.S. Open occurred in 1969, when Orville Moody, a retired Army master sergeant, won the event at Champions Golf Club in Houston.

At the time of the Open, Moody had been on the Tour only for a year and had finished 103rd on the 1968 money list. Earlier in the season, he lost a playoff at the Greater Greensboro Open to Gene Littler, and that was the only time he had been in contention in his career. His strong suit was hitting the ball long and straight, but he couldn't putt a lick. Using a cross-handed grip, Moody often missed easy birdie putts.

At the '69 Open, Moody was nothing more than a player in the field, but Champions Golf Club helped his game. The course was 6,967 yards with creeks, ponds, deep bunkers, and 50,000 trees. Moody's good long game worked well on such a difficult design. Also, the greens were Bermuda grass rather than bent grass, meaning they were slower and more friendly to poor putters like Moody. "Champions was really good for me because I was hitting the ball straight and long," said Moody. "That's what you had to do there to make pars. I made a lot of pars and a few birdies and that helped me hold up until the end."

The end was just about the only time any spectator at Champions even noticed Moody. He was just hanging out making pars, while Miller Barber led the pack. Things changed quickly in the third round when Moody shot a 68 to pull within three shots of Barber. Moody and Barber were paired together in the final round, and Moody's par pulled him into a tie after five holes. Moody took the lead on the 8th hole when Barber—on the way to a 78—made his fifth bogey. A bogey on the 10th hole dropped Moody back into a tie.

Both nearly blew the Open on the par-3 12th, as each pushed their tee shots right of the green. Moody got down in two for par, but Barber duffed his recovery into the bunker and made double bogey. Moody hung on with pars to take a one-shot lead to the 18th hole. There, he nailed a solid drive and shot an 8-iron to within 10 feet of the hole. He missed the birdie putt but won the Open anyway.

It took him a while to understand how important that victory was. He did win the World Series of Golf later in the year (beating out the winners of the other three majors), but that was an unofficial victory, and that U.S. Open win was his only official win until he joined the Senior PGA Tour in 1983. "A lot of times I could have won tournaments had I been a better putter," he said. "If I'd known about the long putter then, I might have won 25 tournaments."

1969

- January: PGA Tour players are scheduled to compete in 47 events with a total purse of $5,465,878.

- January: LPGA Tour players are scheduled to compete in 29 events with a total purse of $597,290.

- January: The Houston Open won't be held because the Houston Golf Association will be hosting the U.S. Open at Champions G.C.

- January 12: Charlie Sifford, age 46, birdies the first extra hole to beat Harold Henning in a playoff for the Los Angeles Open.

- January 19: U.S. Women's Amateur champion JoAnne Carner shoots even-par to beat the pros at the LPGA Burdine's Invitational in Miami.

- January 19: Rain cancels the third and fourth rounds of the Kaiser International Open at Silverado C.C. in Napa Valley. Miller Barber is declared the winner. A second event is scheduled for October.

Orville Moody gets a smooch from wife Doris after winning the 1969 U.S. Open at Champions G.C. in Houston. He parred the final four holes to win by a stroke over Deane Beman, Al Geiberger, and Bob Rosburg. Moody, age 35, joined the PGA Tour just two years earlier after serving a 14-year stint in the U.S. Army.

• January 22: Joseph C. Dey, executive director of the USGA, is appointed commissioner of the newly formed Tournament Players Division of the PGA of America.

• February 16: Gene Littler shoots 263 to win the Phoenix Open, breaking the tournament record by five shots.

• March 2: Tom Shaw wins the Doral Open by one stroke over Tommy Aaron despite a double bogey on the final hole.

• March 23: Raymond Floyd birdies the first extra hole to defeat Gardner Dickinson in a playoff for the Greater Jacksonville Open. It is Floyd's first win in four years.

• March 30: Former Georgia Tech football placekicker Bunky Henry wins a PGA Tour event, as he beats four players by one shot at the National Airlines Open in Miami.

• March 30: Red-hot Kathy Whitworth wins her third LPGA event in a row, the Port Malabar Invitational in Florida.

Tom Shaw

Shaw Barely Hangs On at Doral, AVCO

Tom Shaw sinks a 30-foot birdie putt on the 7th hole in the second round of the 1969 Doral Open. Shaw would double bogey the tournament's last hole but still win by a stroke over Tommy Aaron. Later in the year, Shaw almost blew the AVCO Classic in Massachusetts. He closed with a 77 but won by a shot over Bobby Stanton.

JoAnne Carner

Georgia Tech Kicker Henry Wins PGA Tournament

Bunky Henry holds son Brad, while wife Katy hangs on to a $40,000 check, after Bunky won the 1969 National Airlines Open in Miami. Many have said that the mechanics of kicking a football are much like those of swinging a golf club. Henry was living proof; he used to be a placekicker at Georgia Tech.

Brad, Bunky, and Katy Henry

Amateur Carner Beats the Pros at Burdine's

The 1969 LPGA season opened with the richest tournament on the schedule, the $35,000 Burdine's Invitational in Miami, but it was won by an amateur, JoAnne Carner, who couldn't collect the first prize. Carner, age 29, turned pro a year later. She remains the last amateur to win on the LPGA circuit.

• April 6: Gene Littler prevails in a four-man sudden-death playoff with Orville Moody, Julius Boros, and Tom Weiskopf at the Greater Greensboro Open. He wins with a birdie on the fifth playoff hole.

• April 13: George Archer hits his second shot into water on the par-5 15th at Augusta National, but he saves par and wins the Masters by one stroke over Billy Casper, Tom Weiskopf, and George Knudson.

• April 20: Gary Player wins the Tournament of Champions by two shots over Lee Trevino. The event has moved from Las Vegas to La Costa C.C. in Carlsbad, California.

• April 20: Kathy Whitworth ties Mickey Wright's LPGA record for most consecutive wins with four, as she beats Wright in a playoff at the Lady Carling Open.

• May 4: Larry Hinson beats Frank Beard on the third playoff hole to win the Greater New Orleans Open.

Charlie Sifford

Old Man Sifford Musters a Win in Los Angeles Open

Charlie Sifford, age 46, defeated Harold Henning in a playoff in the 1969 Los Angeles Open. It was his second of two career PGA Tour victories. Sifford turned professional in 1948 but didn't join the PGA Tour until 1960. He was still earning good money on the Senior PGA Tour in 1992—at age 70.

George Archer, Tom Weiskopf

Archer Nips Weiskopf, Two Others, to Claim Masters

George Archer *(left)* receives congratulations from Tom Weiskopf after winning the 1969 Masters with a 281. Archer tapped in for par on the 18th green to win by one stroke over Weiskopf, Billy Casper, and George Knudson. Archer overcame a scare on the par-5 15th, where he knocked his second shot into water yet was still able to save par.

• May 11: Deane Beman defeats Jack McGowan in a sudden-death playoff to win the Texas Open, the first PGA Tour victory of his career.

• June 8: Billy Casper's final-round 67 gives him a four-stroke victory in the Western Open at Midlothian C.C. in Chicago.

• June 15: Former Army sergeant Orville Moody comes out of nowhere to win the U.S. Open. He defeats Deane Beman, Al Geiberger, and Bob Rosburg by a shot at Champions G.C. in Houston.

• June 29: Donna Caponi shoots a final-round 69 to win the U.S. Women's Open at Scenic Hills C.C.

in Pensacola, Florida. She nips Peggy Wilson by one shot for her first career victory.

• July 12: Tony Jacklin becomes the first Englishman in 18 years to win the British Open, at Royal Lytham & St. Annes in England. Bob Charles is runner-up for the second straight year.

Deane Beman

Beman Wins in Texas for First Tour Victory

Deane Beman displays his check after winning his first career PGA Tour event, the 1969 Texas Open. Beman is known more for his outstanding amateur career (two U.S. Amateur titles, four Walker Cup teams) and his long stint as PGA Tour commissioner (1974 to the present). But in between, he won four official events in a six-year Tour career.

Beard in Midst of Five-Year Hot Streak

After winning the 1969 Westchester Classic, Frank Beard took home the season's largest paycheck, $50,000. Beard, age 30, led the 1969 circuit in earnings with $164,707—one of five straight years he reached $100,000 (1967–71). However, because of alcohol-related problems, Beard's game went downhill in the 1970s.

Frank Beard

Tony Jacklin

England's Jacklin Prevails in British Open

Tony Jacklin hoists the British Open trophy after claiming the 1969 title at Royal Lytham & St. Annes in England. Jacklin shot 280 to win by two strokes over Bob Charles and become the first Englishman in 18 years to win the British Open. Sandy Lyle, in 1985, would be the next Englishman to claim the coveted crown.

- July 27: Betsy Rawls, age 41, shoots 1-over-par to win the LPGA Championship at Concord G.C. in Kiameshia Lake, New York.

- July 27: Tommy Aaron beats Sam Snead in a playoff for the Canadian Open title. Aaron is still without a Tour victory because this is an unofficial event.

- August 3: Frank Beard wins the Westchester Classic by a stroke over Bert Greene. His $50,000 first prize is the highest of the year in an official event.

- August 9: Hollis Stacy, age 15, becomes the youngest winner of the U.S. Girls' Junior championship, at Brookhaven C.C. in Dallas.

- August 16: Frenchwoman Catherine Lacoste defeats Shelly Hamlin, 3 & 2, to win the U.S. Women's Amateur at Las Colinas C.C. in Irving, Texas.

- August 16: Civil rights protestors disrupt play during the third round of the PGA Championship, targeting Gary Player.

1969

Donna Caponi

Rawls Enjoys One Last Hurrah

Mike Strauss gives Betsy Rawls a check for winning the 1969 LPGA Championship, at Concord G.C. in Kiameshia Lake, New York. This was the last major title for the 41-year-old Rawls. She would win three more lesser events in the early 1970s and then begin a six-year stint as the LPGA's tournament director.

Mike Strauss, Betsy Rawls

Caponi Wins Women's Open with Closing 69

Donna Caponi won the 1969 U.S. Women's Open at Scenic Hills C.C. in Pensacola, Florida. Caponi closed with a 69, the lowest final round ever shot by a Women's Open winner, and won by a stroke over Peggy Wilson, 294-295. Play was suspended for 15 minutes when Caponi was on the last fairway, but she came back and finished with a birdie.

Catherine Lacoste

Lacoste Wins Women's Amateur

Two years after winning the U.S. Women's Open, Catherine Lacoste won the 1969 U.S. Women's Amateur, at Las Colinas C.C. in Irving, Texas. The unusual feat compared to that of another person of French descent, Francis Ouimet, who claimed the 1913 U.S. Open and 1914 U.S. Amateur. Also in 1969, Lacoste won the national amateur titles of Britain, France, and Spain.

• August 17: Raymond Floyd wins the PGA Championship at NCR C.C. in Dayton, Ohio, for the first major championship of his career. Despite closing with a 74, he wins by a shot over Gary Player.

• August 23: The U.S. defeats Great Britain/Ireland, 10-8, in the Walker Cup Match at Milwaukee C.C.

• August 30: Steve Melnyk shoots 286 to win the U.S. Amateur at Oakmont C.C. near Pittsburgh. Vinny Giles finishes second for the third straight year.

• September 6: Nancy Lopez, age 12, wins the New Mexico Women's Amateur, routing 23-year-old Mary Bryan in the final, 10 & 8.

• September 7: Larry Ziegler wins the Michigan Golf Classic, then discovers that the tournament doesn't have the funds to pay out its $100,000 purse. The PGA says it will pay half of the purse.

• September 7: Orville Moody wins the World Series of Golf, held for the four major champions.

Raymond Floyd

Floyd Holes 35-Footer to Win PGA Championship

A second-line player in his first six years on Tour, Raymond Floyd broke through with three victories in 1969, including one in the PGA Championship. Floyd shot 69-66-67-74—276 to hold off Gary Player by a shot, at NCR C.C. in Dayton, Ohio. Floyd's 35-foot birdie putt on the 70th hole was the difference.

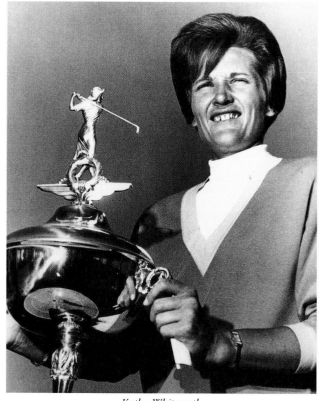

Kathy Whitworth

Whitworth Rips Off Four Wins in a Row

Kathy Whitworth holds the trophy after winning the 1969 Lady Carling Open in Palmetto, Georgia. This was Whitworth's fourth straight victory, the others coming in the Orange Blossom Open, Port Charlotte Invitational, and Port Malabar Invitational. Only Mickey Wright, in both 1962 and '63, had ever won four consecutive LPGA events.

• September 20: The U.S. ties Great Britain/Ireland, 16-16, in the Ryder Cup Match at Royal Birkdale G.C. in England. The U.S. keeps the trophy.

• September 28: Billy Casper wins the $55,000 first prize in the Alcan Golfer of the Year tournament. In a stunning finish, Casper birdies the last four holes and Lee Trevino triple bogeys the 17th to lose by one.

• October 5: The U.S. team of Lee Trevino and Orville Moody beats Japan by eight strokes to win the World Cup at Singapore Island C.C. in Singapore. Trevino wins the individual title.

• October 6: Walter Hagen—winner of five PGAs, four British Opens, and two U.S. Opens—dies of throat cancer at age 76.

• November 2: Carol Mann is the LPGA Tour's leading money winner with $49,152. She leads the Tour in victories with eight, one more than Kathy Whitworth.

1969

Hagen Dies of Throat Cancer at Age 76

Pallbearers carry the body of Walter Hagen, who—on October 6, 1969—died of throat cancer at age 76. Hagen, the first great professional golfer, died on his 20-acre estate near Traverse City, Michigan. Arnold Palmer *(right)* was one of the pallbearers at the funeral, which was held in Birmingham, Michigan.

Walter Hagen's Funeral

Dey Named to Head the Players Division

After 34 years as executive secretary of the USGA, Joseph C. Dey became commissioner of the new Tournament Players Division of the PGA of America in 1969. The pressure was on Dey to smooth relations between the players and the club professionals. He did a commendable job, as dissension decreased and purses increased in his five years at the post.

Steve Melnyk

Melnyk Wins by Five Shots in U.S. Amateur

Steve Melnyk points out his winning score in the 1969 U.S. Amateur, at Oakmont C.C. near Pittsburgh. His 70-73-73-70—286 won by five strokes over Marvin Giles, who finished runner-up for the third year in a row. Oakmont played so tough that only three men fired rounds under par during the entire tournament.

Joseph C. Dey

- November 2: Kathy Whitworth wins her fourth career Vare Trophy with a scoring average of 72.38. She is named LPGA Player of the Year.

- November 30: Arnold Palmer wins the new Heritage Golf Classic at Harbour Town G.L. in Hilton Head, South Carolina. Palmer is the only player to break par on the new course, designed by Pete Dye and Jack Nicklaus.

- December 7: After not winning for 14 months, Arnold Palmer wins for the second straight week, at the Danny Thomas Diplomat Classic.

- December 7: Frank Beard leads the Tour with $164,707.

- December 7: Dave Hill wins his first Vardon Trophy, averaging 70.34. Orville Moody is named PGA Tour Player of the Year.

- December 7: No PGA Tour player finishes with more than three victories. Dave Hill, Billy Casper, Jack Nicklaus, and Raymond Floyd win three times.

CASPER FINALLY MASTERS AUGUSTA NATIONAL

Prior to 1970, the Masters had always been a source of frustration for Billy Casper. He had won two U.S. Opens and a total of 44 career PGA Tour events, but never a Masters. Casper must have wondered if he would ever slide his arms into a green jacket.

Augusta National had been a real pain in the behind in 1969. Casper was the third-round leader but suffered a terrible collapse on the front nine of the final round. On the par-4 9th, he hit his second shot into a bunker on the left side of the green, then duffed his bunker shot. He completed the front nine with a 40. He charged back with a back-nine 34, but a final-round 74 wasn't good enough to tie eventual winner George Archer. Casper finished tied for second place with George Knudson and Tom Weiskopf.

Casper finally won the Masters in 1970, but by no means was it a stroll through the azaleas. In the final round, Casper was just one of seven players within one or two shots of the lead, as Gene Littler, Gary Player, Bert Yancey, Tommy Aaron, Dave Hill, and Dave Stockton were also in the hunt. Casper topped the leader board after seven holes of the final round, but he double bogied the par-5 8th hole. However, he rebounded with a birdie on 9 to pull into a tie with Littler and Yancey, a stroke ahead of Player.

Casper played a solid back nine, with a bogey at the 11th and birdies at Nos. 13 and 15. With the exception of Littler, the rest of the field started blowing putts. Casper and Littler each had makeable birdie putts on 17 and 18, but they missed them both to end up in a tie at 279. Player hooked his approach shot on 18 into the bunker and made bogey to finish at 280. Nobody else came close, and an 18-hole playoff was set up for the next day.

Casper had always been an excellent putter, and his stroke didn't let him down in the playoff. On the front nine, Casper totaled six one-putt greens on the first seven holes, and he made the turn at 3-under-par and five strokes ahead of Littler. Both Casper and Littler shot even par on the back nine, giving Casper a 69-74 victory. That afternoon, Archer slid a green jacket on Casper. After 15 years on Tour, and at the age of 38, he had won his first Masters.

Augusta National wasn't the only ghost Casper exorcised in 1970. The year prior, he had missed the cut at the Avco Classic after posting an embarrassing 81. But in '70, he stormed back and won the darned thing by three shots. He also captured the early-season Los Angeles Open as well as the IVB-Philadelphia Classic, marking the eighth consecutive year in which he won multiple tournaments. For his efforts, he was named Player of the Year. It would be the last great season for the aging Casper, but with a Masters jacket finally on his back, it was surely a satisfying one.

1970

- January: PGA Tour players are scheduled to compete in 55 events, including satellite events, with a total season purse of $6,751,523.

- January: LPGA Tour players are scheduled to compete in 21 events with a total purse of $435,040, both figures down from last year. It is the fewest number of events since 1954.

- January: The Buick Open in Grand Blanc, Michigan, is off the PGA Tour after 12 years. The Hawaiian Open takes a year off the Tour.

- January: Danny Thomas ties in the Danny Thomas Memphis Classic with the St. Jude's Children's Research Hospital to raise money for the charity.

- January 11: Billy Casper defeats Hale Irwin on the first playoff hole to win the Los Angeles Open.

- January 25: Bert Yancey nips Jack Nicklaus by a stroke to win the Bing Crosby National Pro-Am.

- February 1: Sam Snead wins his fourth PGA Seniors Championship.

1970

Billy Casper chips to the 7th green during the second round of the 1970 Masters.
Casper, who let a Masters victory slip away from him in 1969, shot 279 in the
1970 tournament to force a playoff with Gene Littler. Casper soundly
defeated Littler, 69-74. Billy went on to lead the Tour in victories (four) and was
named Player of the Year.

• February 7: U.S. Vice President Spiro Agnew, playing in the Bob Hope Desert Classic pro-am, hits pro partner Doug Sanders on the head with an errant shot on the 1st hole.

• February 12: The LPGA season gets underway without Mickey Wright, who has retired from full-time competition at age 34. Joining the Tour is amateur great JoAnne Carner, age 30.

• March 1: Mike Hill wins the Doral-Eastern Open by four shots.

• March 23: Don January beats Dale Douglass in a playoff at the Greater Jacksonville Open.

• April 10: Lee Trevino was invited but he's not in the field for the Masters. He declined the invitation, saying the Augusta National course doesn't suit his game.

• April 13: Billy Casper wins his first Masters title by beating Gene Littler, 69-74, in an 18-hole playoff.

Homero Blancas

Blancas Nips Trevino, Littler at Colonial

Homero Blancas hoists the trophy after winning the 1970 Colonial NIT, in which he held off Lee Trevino and Gene Littler by a stroke. Blancas, who won four Tour events in his career, is most famous for a round of golf he shot in the 1962 Oil Premier Invitational, an amateur tourney in Longview, Texas. Blancas fired a 55.

Jupiter Hills Club

Fazio's Jupiter Hills Course Opens for Play

Jupiter Hills Club, designed by George Fazio, opened in Jupiter, Florida, in 1970. The esteemed course features oak and mahogany trees—not palm—and is filled with hills and dales and nooks and crannies. The course bears a resemblance to the great Pine Valley layout—not surprising considering that Fazio used to be pro at Pine Valley.

Shirley Englehorn

Englehorn Rides a 30-Day Hot Streak

After averaging about a win every other year, Shirley Englehorn won four times in 1970, all within 30 days. From May 17–June 13, Englehorn won the Johnny Londoff Chevrolet tournament, the O'Sullivan Ladies Open, the Lady Carling Open, and the LPGA Championship. Shockingly, she never again won another Tour event.

• May 3: Jack Nicklaus defeats Arnold Palmer in a playoff for the Byron Nelson Classic. The two were paired all day in a 36-hole finale.

• May 10: Struggling pro Gibby Gilbert gets his first victory, beating Bruce Crampton in a playoff at the Houston Champions International. Ben Hogan, age 57 and competing in his first tournament in three years, finishes ninth.

• May 17: Homero Blancas sets the tournament record of 273 to win the Colonial NIT.

• May 24: Perennial bridesmaid Tommy Aaron wins his first PGA Tour event, the Atlanta Classic.

• June 13: Shirley Englehorn wins her fourth Tour event in 30 days, the LPGA Championship at Pleasant Valley C.C. in Sutton, Massachusetts. She shoots 285 to beat Kathy Whitworth.

• June 14: Hugh Royer wins the Western Open at Beverly C.C. in Chicago.

Jacklin Breezes to Victory in U.S. Open

Fans cheer on Tony Jacklin at the 1970 U.S. Open. Jacklin shot 71-70-70-70—281 to win by seven strokes. Jacklin's first round was the most impressive, as winds blew at 40 mph and no one else shot under 73. Jacklin became the first Englishman to win the U.S. Open since Ted Ray in 1920.

Tony Jacklin

Dave Hill

Yancey's Depression Hinders His Golf Game

Bing Crosby *(left)* congratulates Bert Yancey, winner of the 1970 Bing Crosby National Pro-Am. Yancey would win only one more Tour event, in 1972. Bert had a great golf swing but was often depressed. His mental illness caused physical problems, and his mental-health drugs caused his hands to shake.

Bing Crosby, Ed Crowley, Bert Yancey

Hill Points the Finger at Hazeltine

Dave Hill, the man who ripped into the design of Hazeltine National G.C. during the 1970 U.S. Open, finished a distant second in the tournament to Tony Jacklin. The PGA Tour fined him $150 for his comments. Hill won one event in 1970, the Danny Thomas Memphis Classic, and finished 10th on the money list.

• June 19: After shooting a second-round 69 in the U.S. Open at Hazeltine National G.C. in Chaska, Minnesota, Dave Hill criticizes the course's design. He says it's a good farm ruined.

• June 21: Englishman Tony Jacklin runs away with the U.S. Open, beating Dave Hill by seven strokes.

He becomes the first Englishman to win the U.S. Open in 50 years.

• June 27: The University of Houston wins its 12th NCAA championship in 15 years, at Scarlet G.C. at Ohio State University. John Mahaffey of Houston wins the individual title.

• July 5: Kermit Zarley wins the Canadian Open at London Hunt and C.C. in Ontario.

• July 5: Defending champion Donna Caponi wins her second U.S Women's Open, edging Sandra Haynie and Sandra Spuzich by a shot at Muskogee C.C. in Oklahoma.

Tommy Aaron

Aaron Finally Sheds the Bridesmaid Label

Though a fine player throughout the 1960s, Tommy Aaron was mostly known for two things: A) signing the incorrect scorecard that cost Roberto De Vicenzo the 1968 Masters, and B) never finishing better than second. After nine years on Tour, Aaron finally won in 1970, as he captured the Atlanta Classic in his native state of Georgia.

Nicklaus Downs Sanders— Literally—in British Playoff

Not only did Jack Nicklaus beat Doug Sanders in a playoff in the 1970 British Open, but Nicklaus almost conked him in the head with his putter. After sinking the winning shot at St. Andrews, Jack threw the club sky-high, not realizing Doug's whereabouts. Nicklaus won the playoff, 72-73, after they had tied at 283.

Doug Sanders, Jack Nicklaus

• July 11: Doug Sanders misses a three-foot par putt on the 18th green at St. Andrews to allow Jack Nicklaus to tie him for the British Open championship. Third-round leader Lee Trevino fades with a 77.

• July 12: Jack Nicklaus wins the British Open playoff, 72-73, after driving over the par-4 18th green.

• July 19: Judy Rankin wins the only LPGA event held during a 31-day stretch, the Springfield Jaycee Open.

• July 26: Arnold Palmer and Jack Nicklaus win the PGA Tour Four Ball at Palmer's home course, Laurel Valley G.C. in Pennsylvania. It will be Palmer's only win of the season.

• August 1: Gary Koch defeats Mike Nelms, 8 & 6, to win the U.S. Junior Amateur at Athens C.C. in Georgia.

• August 2: Bruce Crampton wins the $50,000 first prize at the Westchester Classic in New York.

• August 8: The United States defeats Great Britain/Ireland,

Records Fall as Caponi Wins U.S. Women's Open

Donna Caponi won the 1970 U.S. Women's Open—her second in a row—at Muskogee C.C. in Oklahoma. Caponi shot 69-70-71-77—287 to nip Sandra Haynie and Sandra Spuzich by a stroke. Along the way, Caponi set Open records for lowest 36- and 54-hole totals, and she equaled Mickey Wright's record for the lowest 72-hole score.

Sandra Haynie

Donna Caponi

Haynie Named LPGA Tour's Player of the Year

Sandra Haynie received a postseason award in 1970—and it wasn't for best slacks. Haynie was named the LPGA Tour's Player of the Year after finishing second on the money list with $26,626. The Tour's total purse in 1970 was only $435,040, down $160,000 from the year before. However, the purse would more than double by 1972.

11½-6½, to win the Curtis Cup Match at Brae Burn C.C. in West Newton, Massachusetts.

• August 9: Jane Blalock claims her first LPGA victory at the Atlanta Lady Carling Open.

• August 15: Hollis Stacy wins her second straight U.S. Girls' Junior title by defeating Janet Aulisi, 1 up, at Apawamis Club in Rye, New York.

• August 16: Dave Stockton wins the PGA Championship by outdueling Arnold Palmer and Bob Murphy at Southern Hills C.C. in Tulsa, Oklahoma.

• August 22: Martha Wilkinson beats Cynthia Hill, 3 & 2, to win the U.S. Women's Amateur at Wee Burn C.C. in Darien, Connecticut.

• August 30: Bobby Nichols wins the year's biggest first prize, $60,000, in the Dow Jones Open. It's the only year the tournament is held.

1970

Crampton Earns 50 Grand at Westchester

Bruce Crampton took home the largest paycheck of the 1970 season, $50,000, after winning the Westchester Classic in New York. Crampton, a physical fitness devotee, was known for his iron-man schedule. His heavy workload helped him become just the fifth Tour player to reach $1 million in career earnings, a mark he reached in 1973.

Craig Stadler, John W. Brown

Stadler Prevails in World Junior Championship

John W. Brown *(right)*, chairman of the 1970 World Junior championship, presents the first-place trophy to a husky Craig Stadler. The manly looking Stadler turned 17 in 1970. Craig went on to become a two-time All-American at Southern California, and in 1973 he captured the U.S. Amateur championship.

Bruce Crampton

• September 5: Lanny Wadkins edges Tom Kite by one stroke to win the U.S. Amateur at Waverley C.C. in Portland, Oregon.

• September 12: JoAnne Carner takes her first LPGA victory since turning pro, the Wendell-West Open.

• September 14: Jack Nicklaus wins the World Series of Golf, held for the four major championship winners.

• September 27: The first Southern Open, to be called the Green Island Open for one year, is played at Green Island C.C. in Columbus,

Georgia. It is won by Mason Rudolph.

• October 10: Jack Nicklaus beats Lee Trevino, 2 & 1, in the final of the Picadilly World Match Play Championship in England.

• October 25: Sandra Haynie is named LPGA Player of the Year.

Dave Stockton

Stockton Wins PGA After Hot Third Round

Dave Stockton mops his brow after the third round of the 1970 PGA Championship, held in 100-degree heat at Southern Hills C.C. in Tulsa, Oklahoma. Stockton shot a 66 on Saturday, then closed with a 73 to beat Arnold Palmer and Bob Murphy by two strokes. On Sunday, Stockton hit into the pond on the 13th hole but recovered for bogey.

Lanny Wadkins

Wadkins Outguns Kite in U.S. Amateur Championship

Lanny Wadkins nipped Tom Kite to win the 1970 U.S. Amateur, at Waverley C.C. in Portland, Oregon. Both players broke the championship's 72-hole scoring record, but Wadkins beat Kite by a stroke, 279-280. In a wild finish, each player scored birdie, double bogey, birdie on the last three holes. Wadkins holed out from 20 feet.

She won just two events but finished second on the money list with $26,626.

• October 25: Kathy Whitworth leads the LPGA Tour in earnings with $30,235.

• October 25: Shirley Englehorn leads the LPGA Tour in victories with four—all of which came within a 30-day span.

• October 25: Gary Player wins his sixth Australian Open title.

• November 15: Australia's team of Bruce Devlin and David Graham wins the World Cup Match at Jockey G.C. in Buenos Aires.

• December 13: Lee Trevino is the leading PGA Tour money winner with $157,037. He also wins the Vardon Trophy, averaging 70.64.

• December 13: Billy Casper is named PGA Tour Player of the Year after leading the Tour with four victories.

Even though Lee Trevino had won the 1968 U.S. Open, had captured four other PGA Tour events, and was 1970's leading money winner, many golf fans considered him to be nothing more than a flash in the pan. His oddball golf swing and clowning on the golf course didn't earn him much respect. Early in 1971, Jack Nicklaus told Trevino that he didn't realize how good a golfer he was. If you took the game seriously, Nicklaus told him, you could be one of the game's all-time great players.

In the U.S. Open, Nicklaus would regret his advice. Merion Golf Club's tight fairways and tricky greens were made to order for Trevino's game, and Super Mex roared home in the final round with a back-nine 33 to swirl past hotshot amateur Jim Simons and tie Nicklaus at even-par 280.

The playoff the next day sealed Trevino's reputation as a jokester. As both players were ready to begin the playoff on the first tee, Trevino greeted the Golden Bear by tossing a rubber snake at him. Trevino danced about with the snake on his driver, and he showed the world of golf that he

TREVINO WINS THREE BIG ONES IN 21 DAYS

was relaxed despite facing the game's greatest player in the country's biggest golf event. Relaxation worked for Trevino as he led the playoff the whole way. He posted a 68 to Nicklaus's 71 to win his second U.S. Open Championship.

The win gave Trevino instant credibility among golf fans, but the events of the next three weeks lifted him to a new level. At the Canadian Open at Montreal's Richelieu Valley Country Club, Trevino became quite popular among the French-speaking Canadians. The gallery hooted and hollered for Trevino, and he responded. Trailing Art Wall Jr. by two shots going into the final round, Super Mex rallied with

three birdies on the back nine to force another playoff. He left the rubber snake in the bag this time, but he holed an 18-footer for a birdie on the first playoff hole to become the first golfer to win the U.S. and Canadian Opens in the same year since Tommy Armour in 1927.

That would have made for a great year for Trevino, but his hot streak wasn't over. His low-flying shots worked well at the British Open at Royal Birkdale. After three rounds, he held a one-shot lead over Englishman Tony Jacklin and Taiwanese golfer Lu Liang Huan (Mr. Lu, to the British fans). After a front-nine 31 on Sunday, Trevino took a five-stroke lead over Mr. Lu. A horrid double bogey on the par-5 17th cut his lead to just one shot. But both birdied the final hole, and that was good enough for Trevino to win his third national championship in 21 days.

That afternoon, when defending champion Nicklaus gave Trevino the claret jug, he jokingly told the crowd, "I should have kept my mouth shut." Indeed, if Jack hadn't been so friendly to Trevino, the legend of Super Mex may never have come to pass.

1971

- January: PGA Tour players are scheduled to play in 63 events, including satellite events, with a total season purse of $7,116,000. The schedule includes the new U.S. Match Play Championship.

- January: LPGA Tour players are scheduled to play in 21 events with a season purse of $558,550.

- January 10: Bob Lunn wins the Glen Campbell Los Angeles Open on the fourth hole of a sudden-death playoff with Billy Casper.

- January 17: Tom Shaw wins the Bing Crosby National Pro-Am.

- January 22: It takes a 5-under-par 137 to make the cut at the Phoenix

Open, the lowest cut score ever on the PGA Tour.

- January 24: Miller Barber wins the Phoenix Open with a 23-under 261.

- February 6: Alan Shepard becomes the first human to hit a golf shot on the moon. He hits a 6-iron during an Apollo 14 moon walk.

1971

In 1971, Lee Trevino *(right)* faced the great Jack Nicklaus in a playoff for the U.S. Open title, but the pressure hardly fazed him. On the playoff's first tee, the Merry Mex tossed a rubber snake at Nicklaus, then danced around with the snake on his clubhead. Trevino, looking worry-free throughout the playoff, beat Nicklaus, 68-71. Here, Trevino jokes around with Gary Player.

• February 14: Arnold Palmer comes back to life at the Bob Hope Desert Classic. He beats Raymond Floyd in a playoff for his first individual title in 14 months.

• February 21: Ruth Jessen wins the Sears Women's World Classic, by beating Sandra Palmer. The $60,000 purse is the LPGA's biggest ever.

• February 21: J.C. Snead, Sam Snead's nephew, claims his first PGA Tour title, the Tucson Open.

• February 28: Jack Nicklaus wins the PGA Championship at PGA National G.C. in Palm Beach Gardens, Florida. Nicklaus becomes the first to win all four majors twice.

• March 7: J.C. Snead wins for the second time in three weeks at the Doral-Eastern Open.

• March 14: Arnold Palmer wins the Florida Citrus Invitational.

• March 28: Gary Player wins his second tournament in a row, the National Airlines Open.

1971

Walt Disney World Course

Courses Open for Play at Disney World

Florida's Walt Disney World boasts five highly regarded resort courses, and the first two—Palm and Magnolia—opened in 1971. In this photo, the park's tram zooms by in the background. Beginning in December 1971, these two courses hosted the Walt Disney World Open Invitational, a PGA Tour event. Jack Nicklaus won the first three Disney tournaments.

Shaw Prevails in Crosby, Hawaiian

Tom Shaw, who suffered a broken back in an automobile accident in 1966, won four career PGA Tour events including two in 1971—the Bing Crosby National Pro-Am and the Hawaiian Open. Unfortunately, Shaw's game soon went downhill. His second comeback came in 1989, when he became a six-figure earner on the Senior Tour.

Tom Shaw

Palmer Blows Crosby, Wins Four Others

Arnold Palmer misses a birdie attempt in the final round of the 1971 Bing Crosby National Pro-Am. Palmer collapsed on the back nine and lost to Tom Shaw. However, Palmer won four tournaments on the year and earned a career-best $209,603, third on the Tour's money list. He would never again finish in the top 20 in earnings.

Arnold Palmer

• April 11: Charles Coody holds off 23-year-old Johnny Miller and PGA Champion Jack Nicklaus in the final round of the Masters. Coody finishes the tournament birdie-birdie-par-par to win by two shots.

• April 25: Jack Nicklaus shoots 9-under-par to win the Tournament of Champions by eight strokes.

• April 25: Lee Trevino, without a victory in the last 12 months, wins the Tallahassee Open.

• May 9: Sandra Haynie wins her third LPGA Tour event in a row, shooting 13-under-par to win the San Antonio Alamo Open by six strokes.

• May 9: Jack Nicklaus successfully defends his Byron Nelson Classic title by beating Jerry McGee and Frank Beard by two strokes.

• May 16: Rookie Hubert Green shoots even-par 280 to win the Houston Champions International. It's his first PGA Tour victory.

1971

Jack Wins the PGA— in February

Jack Nicklaus *(shown putting)* led wire-to-wire to claim the 1971 PGA Championship at PGA National G.C. in Palm Beach Gardens, Florida. He thus became the first golfer to twice win all four major professional championships in a career. The PGA of America staged the tournament in February to avoid the summer heat of Southern Florida.

Gary Player

Player Musters a Playoff Win

Gary Player reacts after sinking a birdie on the 71st hole of the 1971 Jacksonville Open. Player won the event in a playoff with Hal Underwood, then grabbed the National Airlines Open the next week. Despite the Jacksonville victory, Player's lifetime mark in playoffs was 3-11. Only Ben Crenshaw, 0-8 through 1992, boasted an uglier mark.

Jack Nicklaus

- May 27: Great Britain/Ireland tops the U.S., 13-11, in the Walker Cup Match at St. Andrews.

- June 6: Gardner Dickinson, age 43, beats Jack Nicklaus in a playoff to win the Atlanta Golf Classic.

- June 13: Kathy Whitworth wins the LPGA Championship by four strokes at Pleasant Valley C.C. in Sutton, Massachusetts.

- June 19: Amateur Jim Simons takes the lead with a third-round 65 in the U.S. Open at Merion G.C.

- June 20: Jack Nicklaus and Lee Trevino tie for first at even-par 280 at the U.S. Open.

- June 21: Lee Trevino wins the U.S. Open, defeating Jack Nicklaus in a playoff, 68-71. On the first tee, Trevino tosses a rubber snake at Nicklaus.

- June 26: Ben Crenshaw becomes the first freshman to win the NCAA individual title, and he leads Texas to the team championship.

JoAnne Carner

Carner Blows Away Foes for Women's Open Title

JoAnne Carner proved her worth as a professional by claiming the 1971 U.S. Women's Open—her first major pro title—at the Kahkwa Club in Erie, Pennsylvania. Carner shot 288, a full seven strokes better than runner-up Kathy Whitworth and 11 better than anyone else. No other woman besides Carner has won the U.S. Girls' Junior, U.S. Women's Amateur, and U.S. Women's Open titles.

J.C. Snead

J.C. Breaks Out of His Uncle Sam's Shadow

Jesse Carlyle Snead, nephew of the legendary Sam Snead, joined the PGA Tour in 1968. He broke through in 1971 to claim his first two victories—the Tucson Open and Doral-Eastern Open—and he earned a spot on the '71 Ryder Cup team. Prior to joining the Tour, J.C. played baseball in the Washington Senators' farm system.

Lee Trevino

No One Can Match Trevino's Three Titles

Lee Trevino, ever the prankster, displays a mink-covered golf tee during a practice round for the 1971 U.S. Open. Legends Bobby Jones, Gene Sarazen, and Ben Hogan had won the British and U.S. Opens in the same year, but only Trevino claimed the national titles of Britain, the U.S., and Canada in one year.

• June 27: JoAnne Carner wins her first U.S. Women's Open title, beating Kathy Whitworth by seven shots at the Kahkwa Club in Erie, Pennsylvania.

• July 4: Lee Trevino wins the Canadian Open at Richelieu Valley G.C. in Montreal. Art Wall misses a 15-foot putt to win after a 15-minute delay because of a commotion in the gallery. Wall then loses a playoff.

• July 10: Lee Trevino beats Taiwan's Lu Liang Huan by one stroke to win the British Open, at Royal Birkdale G.C. in England. It's his third national title in 21 days.

• July 18: Bruce Crampton shoots 5-under-par to win the Western Open.

• July 25: Arnold Palmer wins the Tour's richest event, the $250,000 Westchester Classic in New York.

• August 1: Arnold Palmer teams with Jack Nicklaus to successfully defend the National Team title.

The Machine Continues to Crank Out the Wins

Gene Littler, nicknamed "The Machine" because of his consistent swing, was among the top 60 money winners on Tour 25 times in 26 years. Though 40 years old in 1971, he was still going strong, winning both the Monsanto Open and Colonial NIT. Also in '71, Littler made the Ryder Cup team for the sixth consecutive time.

Gene Littler

Charles Coody

Jessen's Back from Surgery, Wins Tourney

Ruth Jessen won the largest check on the 1971 LPGA Tour, $10,000, for winning the season-opening Sears Women's World Classic in Florida. It was perhaps Jessen's most gratifying victory, as she was coming back from thyroid surgery. The GWAA awarded her the Ben Hogan Award in honor of her comeback.

Ruth Jessen

No Choke This Time; Coody Wins Masters

Sparked by an opening-round 66, Texan Charles Coody won the 1971 Masters by two strokes over Jack Nicklaus and Johnny Miller. Later in the year, he won the World Series of Golf and the $50,000 first prize. A year earlier, Coody led the Masters with three holes to go but bogied the last three holes to finish fifth.

• August 14: Hollis Stacy becomes the only player to win consecutive U.S. Girls' Junior titles by defeating Amy Alcott, 1 up, on the first extra hole of the final at Augusta C.C.

• August 21: Laura Baugh wins the U.S. Women's Amateur, defeating Beth Barry, 1 up, in the final at Atlanta C.C.

• August 29: DeWitt Weaver wins the first U.S. Professional Match Play Championship over Phil Rodgers.

• September 4: Gary Cowan holes out a 9-iron on 18 to win the U.S. Amateur by three shots over Eddie Pearce at Wilmington C.C. in Delaware.

• September 12: Charles Coody wins the World Series of Golf.

• September 12: Johnny Miller wins the first PGA Tour title of his career, the Southern Open Invitational.

• September 18: The United States wins the Ryder Cup at Old Warson C.C. in St. Louis, 18½-13½.

Laura Baugh

Baugh Reaches Peak at 16, Wins U.S. Women's Amateur

Laura Baugh, an L.A. teenager in hot pants, won the 1971 U.S. Women's Amateur, becoming the youngest on record to do so. The 16-year-old Baugh defeated Beth Barry, 1 up, at Atlanta C.C. Baugh, named *Golf Digest's* Most Beautiful Golfer in 1972, joined the LPGA Tour at age 18. In 20 years on Tour, she never won a tournament.

Miller Claims His First Victory—the Southern Open

Johnny Miller weathers a rain delay during the 1971 Southern Open at Green Island C.C. in Columbus, Georgia. Miller, who turned pro in 1969, won this tournament for his first of 23 career Tour victories. Miller was also the first of nine Tour pros who made the Southern Open their first career triumph.

Johnny Miller

• October 9: Gary Player beats Jack Nicklaus, 5 & 4, to win the Picadilly World Match Play Championship in England.

• October 17: Kathy Whitworth leads the LPGA Tour in victories with five and earnings with $41,181. She's named Player of the Year.

• October 31: Jack Nicklaus wins the Australian Open by eight strokes.

• November 14: The U.S. team of Jack Nicklaus and Lee Trevino beats Japan by 12 shots to win the World Cup at PGA National G.C. in Florida. Nicklaus wins the individual title.

• November 24: Black golfer Lee Elder plays in the South African PGA Championship at the invitation of Gary Player. Elder goes on to finish 34th.

• November 28: Hale Irwin wins the Heritage Classic for his first PGA Tour victory.

1971

After Years of Suffering, Bobby Jones Passes On

Robert Tyre "Bobby" Jones Jr., America's greatest and most beloved golfer prior to World War II, died in 1971 at age 69. For the last 20 years of his life, Jones suffered from a crippling spinal ailment that gradually paralyzed his arms and legs. On December 18, Jones died at his home in Atlanta.

Kathy Whitworth

Once Again, Whitworth Sweeps Postseason Honors

In 1971, Kathy Whitworth led the LPGA Tour in earnings ($41,181), won the Vare Trophy, and was named Player of the Year. In other words, it was another run-of-the-mill season for Whitworth, who would claim the above honors at least seven times each. Whitworth did win her first major in four years in '71—the LPGA Championship.

Bobby Jones

- December: Lee Trevino is named Athlete of the Year by the Associated Press.

- December 12: Ten PGA Tour players won the first tournament of their careers in 1971 to tie the record for the most first-time winners.

- December 12: Arnold Palmer's four wins result in his 17th consecutive year with at least one Tour victory.

- December 12: Jack Nicklaus and Lee Trevino tie for the most PGA Tour wins with five. Nicklaus leads in earnings with $244,490.

- December 12: Lee Trevino wins his second straight Vardon Trophy with a season scoring average of 70.27. He is also named PGA Tour Player of the Year.

- December 18: Bobby Jones, winner of 13 major championships, dies at the age of 69.

NICKLAUS TAKES A SWING AT THE GRAND SLAM

Golf's professional Grand Slam, winning all four majors in one year, is the most difficult accomplishment in the game. No golfer has ever accomplished the feat, although Ben Hogan got close with three major victories in 1953 and Bobby Jones won the four majors of his day in 1930 (U.S. and British Opens and Amateurs). Whoever wins the Masters each year is the only Grand Slam candidate, and if that Masters champion goes on to win the U.S. Open, the pressure from both the media and golf fans becomes heavy.

In 1972, Jack Nicklaus became the first player since Arnold Palmer in 1960 to win the first two legs of the Grand Slam. Nicklaus didn't pull off the ultimate feat, but he put together a sensational year—the best of his career. Jack won seven PGA Tour events (the first man to do so since Arnold Palmer in 1963) and became the first golfer to win more than $300,000 in a single year.

His Masters victory was a classic Nicklaus championship. He shot a 1-over-par 37 on the front nine of the first round, but rallied with a 31 on the back nine to post

a 68. He was never in trouble throughout the tournament. Even though he shot a bad-weather 74 in the final round, he won the Masters by three shots over Bruce Crampton, Tom Weiskopf, and Bobby Mitchell. None of the three got close enough to threaten Nicklaus, even though he double bogied the par-5 15th, a mandatory birdie hole, in the final round.

Two months later, at the U.S. Open at Pebble Beach, Nicklaus shot a 290, a seemingly high score but one that was good enough to win by three over Crampton. The Grand Slam pressure was on. "I feel proud to be in the company of Jones," Nicklaus told the media after his victory. The grand feat

was still a long shot, but Nicklaus felt he was going to pull it off because the British Open was being played at Muirfield Golf Club, the place where he won his first British Open in 1966.

The only problem would be defending champion Lee Trevino. Trevino never seemed to be scared of Nicklaus, especially after beating him in a playoff for the U.S. Open the year before. In fact, after three rounds, Trevino was more concerned about beating Tony Jacklin because Nicklaus was six shots back. Yet, while Trevino was dueling it out with Jacklin, the Golden Bear fired a final-round 66 to post a 279 total. Trevino was in trouble on the par-5 17th but chipped in for par. That secured his second British Open and eliminated Nicklaus's ultimate dream. Jack finished in second place, one stroke behind the Merry Mex.

The pressure was off Nicklaus a month later at the PGA Championship. He finished six shots behind Gary Player and it was no big deal. Nicklaus didn't win the Grand Slam in 1972, but with two majors, seven wins, and $320,542, he certainly couldn't complain.

1972

- January: PGA Tour players are scheduled to play in 71 events, including satellite events, with a total season purse of $7,596,749.

- January: LPGA Tour players are scheduled to play in 30 events with a season purse of $988,400. Included is the $110,000 Dinah Shore-Colgate Winners Circle.

- January: Spalding introduces the Top-Flite ball, the first two-piece ball with a durable cover.

- January 9: Marlene Hagge wins the Burdine's Invitational. It is the last of her 25 career victories.

- January 10: George Archer wins the Glen Campbell Los Angeles

Open in an 18-hole playoff over Tommy Aaron and Dave Hill.

- January 16: Jack Nicklaus prevails in the Bing Crosby National Pro-Am, beating Johnny Miller in a playoff.

- February 13: Bob Rosburg, age 45, wins his first PGA Tour event in 11

Jack Nicklaus won the first two legs of the 1972 Grand Slam, grabbing the Masters and U.S. Open by three strokes each. He made a great run in the third major, closing with a 66 at the British Open, but his 279 total fell a stroke short of winner Lee Trevino's mark. In the PGA Championship, Nicklaus finished six shots back.

years at the Bob Hope Desert Classic in California.

• February 27: Tom Weiskopf beats Jack Nicklaus by one stroke to win the new Jackie Gleason's Inverrary Classic in Fort Lauderdale, Florida. He earns the biggest prize of the year—$52,500.

• March 6: Jack Nicklaus wins the rain-delayed Doral-Eastern Open. Sam Snead, age 59, finishes fourth.

• March 15: Gene Littler undergoes surgery for cancer. Doctors remove a tumor from under his left arm.

• April 2: Arnold Palmer triple bogeys the 16th hole and loses the

Greater Greensboro Open by one stroke. George Archer beats Tommy Aaron in a playoff.

• April 9: Despite shooting a final-round 74, Jack Nicklaus hangs on to win the Masters by three shots over Bruce Crampton, Bobby Mitchell, and Tom Weiskopf.

George Archer

Archer Again Wins Multiple Tournaments

In 1972, George Archer won both the Los Angeles Open and Greater Greensboro Open, marking the fourth time in five years that he won two tournaments. Archer finished third on the money list in 1972, but his game declined afterward because of physical ailments. In his day, Archer was one of the premier putters on the PGA Tour. He later emerged on the Senior Tour.

Bruce Devlin

Mitchell's the Winner in T. of C.

Bobby Mitchell *(holding check)* made little noise on Tour until he won the Cleveland Open in 1971. The victory earned him an invitation to the 1972 Tournament of Champions, where he defeated the champion of all champions, Jack Nicklaus *(far right)*. Mitchell prevailed on the first hole of sudden-death. He never again won on Tour.

Tournament of Champions

Devlin Wins a Tourney, Unveils a Course

Australian Bruce Devlin displays his $25,000 check for winning the 1972 Houston Open in the city that became his home. Since 1966, Devlin has helped design more than 140 golf courses. In 1972, he and Robert von Hagge unveiled their most famous creation: The Links at Key Biscayne, a public layout in Florida.

• April 16: Jane Blalock beats Carol Mann and Judy Rankin by three shots to win $20,000 at the first Dinah Shore-Colgate Winners Circle.

• April 23: Bobby Mitchell birdies the first extra hole to defeat Jack Nicklaus in a playoff and win the Tournament of Champions.

• May 7: Betty Burfeindt wins the Sealy Golf Classic, her second victory in three weeks.

• May 14: Jerry Heard wins the Colonial NIT by two shots.

• May 20: Jane Blalock is disqualified from the Bluegrass Invitational after her fellow competitors accuse

her of cheating by moving the ball when replacing it on the green.

• May: The LPGA suspends Jane Blalock through 1979. She responds with a lawsuit and wins an injunction against the suspension.

• May 21: Lee Trevino claims his first victory of the year, beating

Heard Dances to Victory in Colonial NIT

Jerry Heard *(right)* and his caddie do a little jig during the third round of the 1972 Colonial National Invitation Tournament. Heard, one of the most laid-back golfers on Tour, captured both this tournament and the Florida Citrus Open in the spring of '72. He would win two more Tour events in his career and be struck by lightning at the 1975 Western Open.

Sandra Palmer

Jerry Heard

Palmer Prevails in Last-Ever Titleholders

Sandra Palmer captured the 1972 Titleholders Championship, edging Judy Rankin and Mickey Wright by a stroke at Pine Needles Golf and C.C. in Southern Pines, North Carolina. This was the first Titleholders since 1967, and it offered a paltry first prize of $3,000. Because of financial difficulties, the tourney would never be held again.

Chi Chi Rodriguez

Rodriguez Spends Time with the Kids

Chi Chi Rodriguez signs autographs after the first round of the 1972 Byron Nelson Classic, which he would win with a birdie putt in sudden-death over Billy Casper. Chi Chi's love for children has never been a secret. The Chi Chi Rodriguez Youth Foundation has helped teach the game of golf to thousands of disadvantaged youngsters.

---

rookie John Mahaffey by four strokes at the Danny Thomas Memphis Classic.

• May 29: The Titleholders comes back on the LPGA schedule for one year, at Pine Needles Resort in Southern Pines, North Carolina. Sandra Palmer wins by 10 strokes.

• June 4: Doug Sanders nabs the Kemper Open for the last of his 20 Tour wins. He beats Lee Trevino by one stroke.

• June 10: The United States defeats Great Britain/Ireland, 10-8, in the Curtis Cup Match at Western Gailes, Ayrshire, Scotland.

• June 11: Kathy Ahern wins the LPGA Championship by six strokes over Jane Blalock.

• June 18: Jack Nicklaus's 290 total beats Bruce Crampton by three shots in the U.S. Open at Pebble Beach G.L. His final-round 74 comes in heavy winds. Nicklaus has now won the year's first two majors.

Sanders Wins Kemper Open for Last Tour Win

Doug Sanders emerged as the winner of the 1972 Kemper Open, which was held throughout the 1970s at Quail Hollow C.C. in Charlotte, North Carolina. Sanders holed out a putt from the fringe of the 18th green for the victory. It turned out to be the last of 19 Tour wins for Sanders, who turned 40 years old in 1973.

Jack Nicklaus

Pros Can't Handle Juiced-Up Pebble Beach

Jack Nicklaus putts on the 18th green at Pebble Beach G.L. in the 1972 U.S. Open. Tour golfers had played Pebble Beach yearly during the Bing Crosby National Pro-Am; but for the Open, the USGA raised the rough and slicked the greens. Golfers were overwhelmed by the tough track, and only Nicklaus (292) shot better than 295.

Doug Sanders

• June 24: Ben Crenshaw and Tom Kite tie for the NCAA individual crown and their Texas club wins the team title, at Cape Coral C.C. in Florida.

• June 25: Jim Jamieson wins the Western Open by six strokes at Sunset Ridge C.C. in Winnetka, Illinois.

• July 2: Susie Maxwell Berning wins the U.S. Women's Open on the rugged West Course at Winged Foot G.C. in Mamaroneck, New York. Her 11-over-par total bests Kathy Ahern, Pam Barnett, and Judy Rankin by a stroke.

• July 3: Australian David Graham defeats fellow Australian Bruce

Devlin in a playoff to win the Cleveland Open. It's his first Tour victory.

• July 9: Gay Brewer wins the Canadian Open by one shot over Dave Hill and Sam Adams.

• July 15: Lee Trevino successfully defends his British Open title, edging

Lee Trevino

Chip Shot Saves Trevino in Tense British Open

In 1972, Lee Trevino defended his British Open title at Muirfield in Scotland, although he was lucky to do so. Trevino got into trouble on the par-5 17th hole and it looked like Tony Jacklin would catch him. However, the Merry Mex chipped in for a par to save his lead, then parred the final hole for the win.

Jim Jamieson

Jamieson Basks in Glory at Western Open

The chubby Jim Jamieson rarely was much of a factor on Tour. In fact, with the exception of 1972, he never finished among the top 40 on the money list. But in June of '72, he enjoyed his four rounds of fame by blowing away the field at the Western Open, winning by six strokes. In August, he tied for second in the PGA Championship.

Tom Kite

Texas Mates Kite and Crenshaw Tie in NCAAs

The careers of Tom Kite (*pictured*) and Ben Crenshaw are remarkably intertwined. Both learned how to play golf from Harvey Penick at Austin C.C. in Texas, and both went to the University of Texas. In 1972, they tied for the NCAA championship and were declared co-champions. Through 1992, Kite had 17 Tour wins; Crenshaw had 16.

Jack Nicklaus by one stroke at Muirfield G.C. in Scotland. It ends Nicklaus's bid for the Grand Slam.

• August 6: Gary Player nearly holes out a 9-iron on the 16th hole at Oakland Hills C.C. in Birmingham, Michigan, to win the PGA Championship. He beats Tommy Aaron and Jim Jamieson by two strokes.

• August 12: Nancy Lopez defeats Catherine Morse, 1 up, in the final of the U.S. Girls' Junior championship at Jefferson City C.C. in Missouri.

• August 13: Jack Nicklaus wins his fifth Tour event of the year, the Westchester Classic.

• August 19: Mary Budke tops Cynthia Hill, 5 & 4, in the final of the U.S. Women's Amateur at St. Louis C.C.

• August 27: Jack Nicklaus wins his sixth tournament of the year, edging Frank Beard, 2 & 1, in the final of the U.S. Match Play Championship.

Gary Player

After Ulcer Attack, Brewer Wins in Canada

In 1972, 40-year-old Gay Brewer suffered a near-fatal ulcer attack on the eve of the Masters. Nevertheless, he bounced back and won the '72 Canadian Open. His comeback earned him the Ben Hogan Award for his "courage in the face of trying circumstances." In 1973, Brewer earned $93,502, a career high.

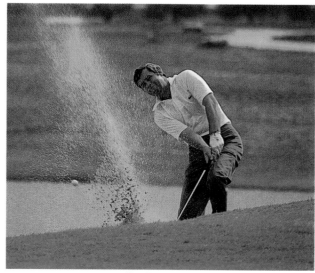

Gay Brewer

Player Wins PGA Thanks to Super 9-Iron Shot

Gary Player won the 1972 PGA Championship at Oakland Hills C.C. in Birmingham, Michigan. On Sunday, Player nearly blew this tournament, as he bogied 14 and 15 and knocked his tee shot far to the right on 16. However, he hit a 9-iron over a tree and water to within four feet of the hole. He tapped in for birdie and won by two shots.

Lanny Wadkins, Del Webb

Wadkins Strikes It Rich in Vegas

Del Webb presents a first-place check to rookie Lanny Wadkins, winner of the 1972 Sahara Invitational in Las Vegas. Wadkins, the 1970 U.S. Amateur champion, enjoyed an outstanding rookie year in '72, finishing 10th in earnings. Wadkins, known for his aggressive swing, would win more than $5 million on Tour.

• September 2: Vinny Giles wins the U.S. Amateur at Charlotte C.C. in North Carolina.

• September 10: Gary Player wins the World Series of Golf.

• September 24: Sandra Haynie wins for the second straight week at the Lincoln-Mercury Open.

• October 1: Deane Beman wins the first Quad Cities Open by one shot over rookie Tom Watson.

• October 8: Gay Brewer wins the $65,000 first prize—bigger than any U.S. event's—at the Pacific Masters in Japan. Gene Littler, in his first tournament since cancer surgery, finishes fifth.

• October 22: Betsy Rawls earns the last of her 55 LPGA Tour victories at the GAC Classic.

• October 29: Rookie Lanny Wadkins takes his first PGA Tour victory at the Sahara Classic.

• November 5: Kathy Whitworth leads the LPGA Tour in earnings

David Graham

Graham Sparks Career with Win in Cleveland

David Graham moved from Australia to the United States after going bankrupt as a club pro in Tasmania. He barely made any money in his first year on the PGA Tour, 1971, but he took home $57,827 in 1972, thanks to a victory in the Cleveland Open. The victory earned him an exemption, and he went on to win nearly $2 million on Tour.

Giles Wins Last Amateur at Stroke Play

The U.S. Amateur was held at stroke play for the last time in 1972, and Marvin "Vinny" Giles took the title. Giles, a three-time runner-up, won by three strokes over Mark Hayes and Ben Crenshaw at Charlotte C.C. in North Carolina. Giles never turned pro. Instead, he became an agent for Tom Kite and Lanny Wadkins.

Marilynn Smith

Smith Wins Last of 22 LPGA Tournaments

In 1972, at age 43, Marilynn Smith won her last of 22 LPGA events—the Pabst Ladies Classic. A year earlier, Smith became the first player in LPGA history to record a double eagle, as she tamed a par-5 at Pine Ridge G.C. in Baltimore during the Lady Carling Open. In 1973, she became the first female TV commentator of a men's golf tournament.

Vinny Giles

---

with $65,063 and ties Jane Blalock with five wins.

• November 5: Kathy Whitworth wins her fourth consecutive Vare Trophy, averaging 72.38. She is named LPGA Player of the Year.

• November 12: Taiwan wins the World Cup team title, beating Japan

by two shots at Royal Melbourne G.C. in Australia.

• December 3: Jack Nicklaus shoots 21-under-par to win his seventh tournament of the year, the Walt Disney World Open Invitational.

• December 3: Jack Nicklaus leads the PGA Tour in wins with seven

and earnings with $320,542. He is named Player of the Year.

• December 3: Arnold Palmer did not win a tournament in 1972, ending a 17-year streak.

• December 3: Lee Trevino wins his third straight Vardon Trophy, averaging 70.89.

WEISKOPF HEATS UP AS SPRING TURNS TO SUMMER

Golf has always been a funny game. One day a golfer can't do anything right, and the next day he or she looks like Arnold or Sandra Palmer. Even the pros struggle with consistency. On average, 85 percent of their annual earnings come from about four out of 30 tournaments. They get hot and play well, then cool down. One of the hottest players in the history of the PGA Tour was Tom Weiskopf in the summer of 1973.

Before 1973, Weiskopf had won five PGA Tour events in eight years, which positioned him as one of the game's better players—although not quite at the level of a Jack Nicklaus, Lee Trevino, or Arnold Palmer because he hadn't won a major. Actually, Nicklaus's shadow loomed over him a lot. Both were natives of Ohio—Weiskopf from Massillon, Nicklaus from Columbus—and Weiskopf, three years younger, had followed Nicklaus on the Ohio State golf team. When Weiskopf joined the PGA Tour in 1965, analysts fell in love with his swing, but everyday golf fans still paid homage to the Golden Bear.

However, fans started to pay attention to Weiskopf at the 1973

Colonial NIT in Fort Worth, Texas, the start of his hot summer. When he holed out on 18, Weiskopf was a stroke behind Bruce Crampton, but the Australian double bogied 18 to let him win by one shot. Pumped up, Weiskopf went on to win the Kemper Open in Charlotte by three shots. The next week, he won the IVB-Philadelphia Classic by four shots. With three wins under his belt by the time he got to Troon, Scotland, for the British Open, Weiskopf felt he might just win his first major.

He did. In the first two rounds, Weiskopf shot 68 and 67. In the final round, Nicklaus loomed over his head, shooting a 65 despite

rainy weather. But that didn't scare Weiskopf, as he shot a 70 to tie the British Open record of 276 set by Arnold Palmer in 1962. He won by three shots over Johnny Miller and four over Nicklaus. "I will never consider myself a great player until I win a major championship," Weiskopf had said. A week later, he flew back to North America and played in the Canadian Open in Quebec. He was still hot, winning his second national championship by two shots for his fifth win in the last eight tournaments. Later in the year, he won the World Series of Golf, an exhibition at the time, and the South African PGA.

Weiskopf's hot summer was clearly the hallmark of his career. The $245,463 he won in 1973 was the most he had ever accumulated in a season and the most he would ever win. Moreover, he would capture only six more PGA Tour wins in his next dozen or so years on the circuit and would never again win a major. Disappointing? Perhaps. But as Weiskopf looks back on his career, he can take solace in that he was once the greatest player in golf—better than Nicklaus—even if it was for just a summer.

1973

• January: PGA Tour players are scheduled to play in 75 events with a season purse of $8,657,225.

• January: LPGA Tour players are scheduled to play in 36 events with a season purse of $1,471,000.

• January: The World Open, a 144-hole tournament to be played over

two weeks, will be the first PGA event with a $100,000 first prize.

• January: The Titleholders, the third LPGA major, is permanently canceled due to financial difficulty.

• January 7: Rod Funseth wins the Glen Campbell Los Angeles Open by three shots over four golfers.

• January 21: Bruce Crampton takes his second desert tournament in a row, winning the Dean Martin Tucson Open by five shots.

• January 28: Jack Nicklaus defeats Raymond Floyd and Orville Moody in a playoff at the Bing Crosby National Pro-Am at Pebble Beach.

1973

In the summer of 1973, Tom Weiskopf captured five PGA Tour events in a two-month stretch. He won the Colonial NIT in May, the Kemper Open and IVB-Philadelphia Classic in June, and the British Open and Canadian Open in July. Outside of this hot streak, Weiskopf won 11 tournaments in a quarter-century on Tour.

• **February 11:** Arnold Palmer shoots 343 to win the 90-hole Bob Hope Desert Classic. It is the last victory of his 60-win career.

• **February 25:** Lee Trevino wins the Jackie Gleason Inverrary-National Airlines Classic by one shot over Forrest Fezler.

• **March 11:** Kathy Whitworth wins the $100,000 S&H Green Stamp Classic, earning $20,000.

• **March 25:** Jack Nicklaus beats Miller Barber in a playoff for the Greater New Orleans Open.

• **April 9:** Tommy Aaron shoots a final-round 68 to beat J.C. Snead by

a stroke to win the Masters. The tournament finishes on Monday because of a Saturday rainout.

• **April 15:** Mickey Wright wins the Colgate-Dinah Shore Winners Circle for the last of her 82 wins.

• **April 22:** Jack Nicklaus wins the Tournament of Champions.

Bruce Crampton

Crampton Wins Four PGA Events

Bruce Crampton enjoyed his best year in 1973 at age 37, as he won the Phoenix Open, Tucson Open, Houston Open, and American Golf Classic. He also became the first foreign player to win the Vardon Trophy since 1937. Crampton finished runner-up to Jack Nicklaus in the 1972 Masters and U.S. Open as well as the 1973 PGA Championship

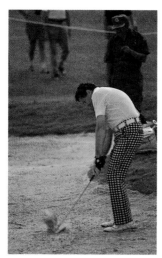

Rod Funseth

Hope, Boone, Reagan Meet at Golf Tourney

Three patriotic Americans—Bob Hope, Pat Boone, and Ronald Reagan *(left to right)*—pose together at a golf tournament. In 1973, Hope presided over his ninth Bob Hope Desert Classic in California. Reagan, governor of California at the time, was one of the few recent U.S. Presidents who wasn't obsessed with golf.

Bob Hope, Pat Boone, Ronald Reagan

Funseth Wins by Three in Los Angeles Open

Rod Funseth captured the 1973 Glen Campbell Los Angeles Open, winning by three strokes. Funseth won three more Tour events, his last being the 1978 SDJ-Greater Hartford Open, and later joined the Senior Tour. In 1983, Funseth teamed with Roberto De Vicenzo to win the Liberty Mutual Legends of Golf. He died of cancer two years later.

- April 29: Lanny Wadkins wins the Byron Nelson Classic on the first extra playoff hole.

- May 13: Tom Weiskopf wins the Colonial NIT by one shot.

- May 20: Dave Hill wins the Danny Thomas Memphis Classic—his fourth victory in Memphis.

- June: A federal judge overturns the LPGA's suspension of Jane Blalock, ruling it is an anti-trust violation for her fellow players to make such a judgment.

- June 3: Tom Weiskopf wins the Kemper Open by three shots over Lanny Wadkins.

- June 10: Tom Weiskopf stays hot and wins the IVB-Philadelphia Golf Classic by four shots.

- June 10: Mary Mills wins the LPGA Championship, shooting 4-under-par at Pleasant Valley C.C. in Sutton, Massachusetts. Betty Burfeindt finishes a shot back.

1973

Mary Mills

Rankin Begins Five Years of Standout Golf

In 1973, Judy Rankin won four LPGA events, finished second on the money list with $72,989, and won the Vare Trophy, averaging 73.08. The stellar season kicked off a five-year stretch in which she was hailed as the new-age LPGA superstar. Rankin would vault to the top of the money list in both 1976 and '77.

Judy Rankin

Mills Wins LPGA for Third Major Championship

Mary Mills acknowledges the crowd after sinking a long putt in the 1973 LPGA Championship, at Pleasant Valley C.C. in Sutton, Massachusetts. Mills won the tournament by a stroke over Betty Burfeindt, giving her three major championships in her career. Three weeks later, Mills won the Lady Tara Classic for her last-ever victory.

Jack Nicklaus, Tommy Aaron

Aaron Wins Masters in Native Georgia

Jack Nicklaus slides the green jacket on Tommy Aaron, winner of the 1973 Masters. Aaron shot a 68 in a cool, breezy final round to rally from four shots back and defeat J.C. Snead by one stroke. Both of Aaron's career victories came in his native state of Georgia, as he also won the Atlantic Classic in 1970.

• June 17: Johnny Miller shoots a tournament-record 63 in the final round to win the U.S. Open at Oakmont C.C. near Pittsburgh. He wins by one shot over John Schlee, as Tom Weiskopf finishes third.

• June 17: Canada's Jocelyne Bourassa wins the LPGA's La Canadienne Golf Championship.

• June 23: Ben Crenshaw of Texas wins his third consecutive NCAA individual title.

• June 24: Bruce Crampton takes his fourth victory of the year at the American Golf Classic.

• July 1: After leading through three rounds of her first pro event, the Lady Tara Classic, 18-year-old Laura Baugh shoots a 75 and ties for second, a shot behind Mary Mills.

• July 1: Billy Casper shoots 12-under-par to win the Western Open.

• July 11: Gene Sarazen, age 71, aces the 8th hole in the first round of the British Open.

Weiskopf Nearly Adds U.S. Open to Win List

Not only did Tom Weiskopf win five times in the summer of 1973, but he nearly won the U.S. Open. With leader Johnny Miller in the clubhouse, Weiskopf needed to birdie the last three holes to tie. He birdied one and finished two strokes back. A frequent challenger in the Open, Weiskopf finished second, third, fourth, and fourth from 1976–79.

Johnny Miller

Miller Roars to Open Title with a Final-Round 63

After three rounds of the 1973 U.S. Open, four men shared the lead and Johnny Miller *(pictured)* was six strokes behind. But with a closing 63—the lowest round in U.S. Open history—Miller won the title by a stroke over John Schlee, 279-280, at Oakmont C.C. near Pittsburgh. Miller had nine birdies and one bogey in the final round.

Tom Weiskopf

• July 14: Red-hot Tom Weiskopf wins the British Open at Royal Troon in Scotland. Johnny Miller and Neil Coles tie for second.

• July 22: Susie Maxwell Berning successfully defends her U.S. Women's Open title by shooting 2-over-par at the C.C. of Rochester in New York.

• July 22: Gene Littler wins the St. Louis Children's Hospital Classic 16 months after cancer surgery.

• July 29: Tom Weiskopf wins the Canadian Open at Reichelieu Valley Golf & C.C. near Montreal. It is his fifth win in the last eight tournaments.

• August 12: Jack Nicklaus wins his third PGA Championship, at Canterbury G.C. in Cleveland. It is his 14th major championship, breaking Bobby Jones's total of 13.

• August 18: Carol Semple wins the U.S. Women's Amateur, defeating Anne Quast Sander in the final, 1 up, at Montclair G.C. in New Jersey.

1973

Nicklaus Claims a Record 14th Major Championship

Jack Nicklaus's victory in the 1973 PGA Championship marked his 14th major title, breaking Bobby Jones's 43-year-old record. Nicklaus captured the PGA by four strokes over Bruce Crampton at Canterbury G.C. in Cleveland. He also won six other '73 events, led in earnings with $308,362, and was named Player of the Year.

Craig Stadler

Stadler Topples Giles, Strawn in U.S. Amateur

The U.S. Amateur reverted back to match play in 1973 and 20-year-old Craig Stadler emerged as the winner. Stadler defeated David Strawn in the final, 6 & 5, at the Inverness Club in Toledo, Ohio. In the semis, Stadler beat defending champion Vinny Giles, who was exhausted after playing in the Walker Cup Matches the week before.

Jack Nicklaus

- **August 25:** The United States tops Great Britain/Ireland, 14-10, to win the Walker Cup Match at The Country Club in Massachusetts.

- **September 2:** The U.S. Amateur is back to match play. Craig Stadler defeats David Strawn, 6 & 5, to win at the Inverness Club in Toledo, Ohio.

- **September 9:** Tom Weiskopf's 36-hole total of 137 beats Jack Nicklaus, Tommy Aaron, and Johnny Miller in the World Series of Golf.

- **September 9:** Gary Player, sidelined earlier in the year by abdominal surgery, wins the Southern Open by one shot over Forrest Fezler.

- **September 22:** The United States breaks away from an 8-8 tie after two days to capture the Ryder Cup, 16-10, at Muirfield G.C. in Scotland.

- **September 23:** Kathy Whitworth wins her third LPGA Tour event in a row, the Portland Ladies Open in Oregon.

Susie Maxwell Berning

Berning Captures Her Third U.S. Women's Open

In 1973, Susie Maxwell Berning won her second straight U.S. Women's Open and third overall, prevailing by five strokes at the C.C. of Rochester in New York. Berning pared down her schedule in the 1970s after she became a mother. In 1989, she and daughter Robin became the first mother and daughter to compete in the same LPGA event.

Teenage Alcott Piles Up the Amateur Trophies

Seventeen-year-old Amy Alcott shows off the dozens of golf trophies she had already accumulated. The one near her hand is the biggest of all, one that signifies her victory in the 1973 U.S. Girls' Junior championship. Alcott won the title after becoming a finalist in 1971 and medalist in 1972.

Amy Alcott

- October 8: Jack Nicklaus wins the first Ohio-Kings Island Open at the Jack Nicklaus Golf Center near Cincinnati.

- November 4: Kathy Whitworth wins her seventh tournament of the year, and the fifth in the last two months, at the Lady Errol Classic.

- November 4: Kathy Whitworth leads the LPGA Tour in earnings with $82,864 and victories with seven. She is named LPGA Player of the Year.

- November 4: Judy Rankin wins the Vare Trophy with an average of 73.08.

- November 4: Playing in his first PGA Tour event as a pro, Ben Crenshaw shoots a final-round 66 to win the San Antonio Texas Open.

- November 9: Gibby Gilbert's 62 breaks the course record on Pinehurst C.C.'s No. 2 Course. It comes in the first round of the 144-hole World Open.

1973

Barber Rakes In $100,000 at 144-Hole World Open

Miller Barber strung together a cute streak of winning exactly one PGA Tour event a year from 1967–74. But one of those victories, in the 1973 World Open in North Carolina, carried the weight of two or more. The event was played over 144 holes and offered a first prize of $100,000—the largest in PGA Tour history.

Kathy Whitworth

Miller Barber

Whitworth's Long Reign of Dominance Nears Its End

Kathy Whitworth piled up seven more victories in 1973, though none of the marquee variety (e.g., the S&H Green Stamp Classic). Whitworth led in earnings for the eighth and last time (with a record $82,864) and was named Player of the Year for the seventh and final time. Never again would a golfer dominate the Tour like Whitworth had done.

- November 17: Miller Barber wins the World Open to capture the $100,000 first prize. Rookie Ben Crenshaw finishes second.

- November 25: The United States wins the World Cup Match in Marbella, Spain, by six strokes over South Africa. Johnny Miller wins the individual title.

- December 1: Jack Nicklaus wins the Walt Disney World Open Invitational for the third consecutive year. He becomes the first player to reach $2 million in career earnings.

- December 1: Jack Nicklaus leads the Tour in earnings with $308,362 and victories with seven. He is named PGA Tour Player of the Year.

- December 1: Five PGA Tour players win more than $200,000 and 14 win more than $100,000.

- December 1: Bruce Crampton wins the Vardon Trophy, averaging 70.57. He finishes with four victories, tying Tom Weiskopf for the second most on Tour.

MILLER CASHES IN WITH EIGHT TOUR WINS

Winning at least one major championship in a year is generally considered to be the foundation for winning the Player of the Year Award. But Johnny Miller proved in 1974 that a golfer doesn't have to win a major title to be crowned the PGA Tour's top player. His performance in 1974 was the best by any golfer since Arnold Palmer's great year in 1960, and no golfer has done as well since. Miller won eight PGA Tour events, all non-majors, and set a record for the most money won in a season. The closest any golfer has gotten to Miller's 1974 domination was Tom Watson with six victories during 1980.

Miller's 1974 season started in a rather odd manner. The first tournament of the year was the Bing Crosby National Pro-Am, and he was lucky to win it. Rain and hail bombed Pebble Beach, and after three rounds Miller had a four-stroke lead. More rain caused the final round to be canceled, and he was declared the winner. But it wasn't raining the next two weeks in the Arizona desert. He beat Lanny Wadkins by a stroke at the Phoenix Open and made it three in a row by beating

Ben Crenshaw by three strokes at the Dean Martin Tucson Open. Through all three tournaments, Miller was 37-under-par. He then finished fourth at the Bob Hope Desert Classic and fifth at the Los Angeles Open, as he rolled up an amazing 24 consecutive rounds of par or less.

Miller's fourth victory was at the Sea Pines Heritage Classic at Hilton Head, South Carolina, and he seemed primed to win the Masters. However, he didn't come close. He tied for 15th in what would be his best major finish of the year. But two weeks later, Miller won the Tournament of Champions, despite shooting a first-round 75. He seemed to be taking the rest of the summer off,

as he finished tied for 35th in the U.S. Open with a bloated score of 302, but he got back to the winner's circle in late August by shooting 19-under-par at the Westchester Classic in New York.

Soon, dollar signs started to fill Miller's eyes. A $60,000 first-place check at the World Open at Pinehurst got him thinking about breaking Jack Nicklaus's money-winning record. Miller went home to Napa Valley to play in the Kaiser International at Silverado Country Club, a course he had never done well on even though he lived next to the 8th hole. Yet he broke 70 in all four rounds to win $30,000 and break Nicklaus's record.

His season-ending total of $353,021.59 remained the Tour's highest until 1978, when the total PGA Tour purse increased by $2 million. Miller was delighted but a bit surprised at playing so well. "I'm going to have to sit down and do a lot of thinking about next year," he said. "This has been sort of ridiculous, and I've got to keep everything in perspective." Yet he added, "I would never trade this year for one major title, no matter what anyone says."

1974

• January: PGA Tour players are scheduled to play in 57 events with a total season purse of $8,165,941.

• January: LPGA Tour players are scheduled to play in 35 events with a season purse of $1,752,500.

• January: The Tournament Players Championship is a new showcase

event on the PGA Tour schedule. This year, it will be played in Atlanta. The U.S. Pro Match Play Championship is off the Tour schedule.

• January: Deane Beman, age 35, retires from competition after six years on the PGA Tour. He is named the commissioner of the Tournament

Players Division and will take over for the retiring Joe Dey on March 1.

• January: Under a new policy, top players will be required to play in designated events each year. There are three designated events this year—the Colonial, Kemper, and World Open.

1974

Johnny Miller's eight PGA victories in 1974 remain the most by a Tour player since 1960. Three of Miller's wins came in January, at the Bing Crosby National Pro-Am, the Phoenix Open, and the Dean Martin Tucson Open. Miller opened with 24 straight rounds of par or better. He would bust out of the gate in similar fashion in 1975.

• January 6: Johnny Miller shoots a final-round 70 at Pebble Beach G.L. to win the rain-shortened Bing Crosby National Pro-Am by four shots.

• January 13: Johnny Miller wins again, breaking 70 all four rounds at the Phoenix Open to win by one shot over Lanny Wadkins.

• January 20: Johnny Miller wins the Dean Martin Tucson Open by three shots over Ben Crenshaw. He becomes the first player ever to win the Tour's first three events of the year.

• February 3: Jack Nicklaus wins the Hawaiian Open by three shots over 21-year-old rookie Eddie Pearce. Johnny Miller finished 11th in his first tournament since his last victory.

• February 17: Sam Snead, age 61, almost catches Dave Stockton in the final round of the Glen Campbell Los Angeles Open, but Stockton birdies the last hole to prevail by two strokes.

1974

Snead, Age 61, Finishes One Back in L.A. Open

Dave Stockton was a hole away from winning the 1974 Glen Campbell Los Angeles Open, as he led by a stroke over 61-year-old Sam Snead *(pictured)*. On the 18th tee, Snead told Stockton how he once won this tournament with a birdie—back in 1945! Stockton felt Snead was trying to intimidate him, but Dave birdied 18 to clinch the win.

Muirfield Village Golf Club

Jack's Muirfield Village Course Opens for Play

Pictured is the par-3, 156-yard 12th hole at Muirfield Village G.C. in Dublin, Ohio. The course, which opened in 1974 and was named after Muirfield in Scotland, was designed by Jack Nicklaus and Desmond Muirhead, a self-described "earth-form artiste." Muirfield Village would host the Memorial Tournament beginning in 1976.

Sam Snead

• March 24: Johnny Miller wins his fourth event of the year, the Sea Pines Heritage Classic, by three shots over Gibby Gilbert. Miller's first 24 rounds of 1974 are even-par or better.

• April 14: Gary Player wins the Masters by two shots over Tom Weiskopf and Dave Stockton.

• April 21: Jo Ann Prentice beats Jane Blalock and Sandra Haynie in a playoff to win the LPGA's biggest prize, $32,000, at the Colgate-Dinah Shore Winners Circle.

• April 28: Johnny Miller wins his fifth event of the year, shooting a final-round 69 to win the Tournament of Champions by one

stroke over Brian Allin and John Mahaffey.

• May: Muirfield Village G.C., designed by Jack Nicklaus and Desmond Muirhead, opens for play outside Columbus, Ohio.

• May 19: Native American Rod Curl wins the Colonial NIT—the

Joe Dey, Deane Beman

Beman Succeeds Dey as PGA Tour Commissioner

In 1974, at the age of 35, Deane Beman *(right)* quit playing the PGA circuit and took over as the Tour's commissioner. Beman's plans were to boost the Tour purses and make the PGA Tour a major contributor to charities. Beman took over the commissionership from Joseph Dey *(left)*, who retired from the post at the age of 67.

Gary Player

Player Recovers from Surgery, Wins Masters

A determined Gary Player examines his ball during the 1974 Masters. Player, who underwent kidney surgery in 1973, bounced back to win at Augusta National. With two holes to go, Gary led Tom Weiskopf and Dave Stockton by just one stroke. But his 9-iron approach on 17 landed six inches from the hole, and he tapped in for a title-clinching birdie.

Hubert Green

Green, Mac Beat the Sneads at Disney

Hubert Green played the villain in 1974 when he and Mac McClendon won the Walt Disney World National Team Championship, defeating 62-year-old Sam Snead and nephew J.C. Snead by one stroke. Green, 34 years younger than Sam, won four events in 1974 and finished third on the money list with $211,709.

Tour's first designated event—by one shot over Jack Nicklaus.

• May 19: JoAnne Carner breaks a three-year winless drought at the Bluegrass Invitational. She'll win again next week.

• June 16: Hale Irwin shoots 7-over-par but still wins the U.S. Open, on the West Course at Winged Foot G.C. in Mamaroneck, New York. Forrest Fezler finishes second, two shots back.

• June 22: Freshman Curtis Strange of Wake Forest eagles the last hole of the NCAA championship, giving him a one-stroke individual victory and his team the title by two strokes.

• June 23: Sandra Haynie wins the LPGA Championship, shooting 4-under-par at Pleasant Valley C.C. in Sutton, Massachusetts.

• June 30: Tom Watson wins the first PGA Tour event of his career, the Western Open. It's the first of 17 Western Opens at Butler National G.C. outside Chicago.

Though 7-Over-Par, Irwin Claims U.S. Open

Hale Irwin's first of three U.S. Open titles came in 1974, when he shot 7-over-par 287 on Winged Foot G.C.'s West Course in Mamaroneck, New York. Irwin made 13 birdies, 18 bogeys, and a double bogey but still won by two over Forrest Fezler. Tom Watson, the third-round leader, collapsed with a final-round 79.

Hale Irwin

Rod Curl

Curl, a Native American, Prevails in Colonial NIT

At 5'5", Rod Curl was the shortest golfer on the PGA Tour in 1974. Curl, a Wintu Indian, won the '74 Colonial NIT to become the first and only Native American to capture a PGA Tour event. Unfortunately, Curl's one-stroke victory over Jack Nicklaus turned out to be his only career triumph.

• July 13: Gary Player shoots a final-round 70 at Royal Lytham & St. Annes to win the British Open by four shots over Peter Oosterhuis. It's Player's second major title of the year.

• July 21: Sandra Haynie wins the U.S. Women's Open at La Grange C.C. in Illinois, giving her victories in both LPGA majors. Haynie birdies the last two holes to beat Carol Mann and Beth Stone by one shot.

• July 28: Bobby Nichols breaks 70 all four rounds to win the Canadian Open by four shots over Larry Ziegler.

• August 3: The United States beats Great Britain, 10-4, in the Curtis Cup Match at San Francisco G.C.

• August 4: Victor Regalado, a native of Mexico, wins the PGA Tour's Pleasant Valley Classic.

• August 10: Nancy Lopez wins her second U.S. Girls' Junior title.

1974

Watson Arrives with Victory in Western Open

Tom Watson of Kansas City won his first PGA Tour event in 1974—the Western Open. Previously, Watson had frittered away chances in the 1973 Hawaiian and World Opens as well as the 1974 U.S. Open. In high school, Watson earned the nickname "Huckleberry Dillinger" for his freckled face and his fierce intensity.

Gary Player

Player Rolls to Third Career Win in British Open

Gary Player kisses the British Open trophy after winning the 1974 championship at Royal Lytham & St. Annes in England. Player shot 282, four shots better than Peter Oosterhuis, for his third British Open victory. Later in the year, Player was among 13 golfing greats inducted into the new PGA World Golf Hall of Fame.

Tom Watson

Sandra Haynie

Haynie Wins Both the LPGA and Women's Open

Only two LPGA major championships were held in 1974, and Sandra Haynie won them both. Haynie defeated JoAnne Carner by two shots in the LPGA Championship, and she edged Carol Mann and Beth Stone by one in the U.S. Women's Open, at La Grange C.C. in Illinois. In the Open, Haynie sank birdie putts of 70 and 15 feet on the last two holes.

• August 11: Lee Trevino and Jack Nicklaus duel it out in the final round of the PGA Championship at Tanglewood Golf Course in Clemmons, North Carolina. Both shoot 69s, but Trevino wins by one shot.

• August 17: Cynthia Hill wins the U.S. Women's Amateur, defeating Carol Semple, 5 & 4, in the final at Broadmoor G.C. in Seattle.

• August 25: Johnny Miller wins the Westchester Classic.

• August 31: Jerry Pate defeats John Grace, 2 & 1, in the final of the U.S. Amateur at Ridgewood C.C. in New Jersey.

• September 2: Jack Nicklaus wins the first Tournament Players Championship by two shots over J.C. Snead at Atlanta C.C.

• September 8: Lee Trevino wins a seven-hole, sudden-death playoff with Gary Player to capture the World Series of Golf.

PGA World Golf Hall of Fame Opens Its Doors

President Gerald Ford conducts the grand opening of the PGA World Golf Hall of Fame, which opened in Pinehurst, North Carolina, in September 1974. Thirteen famous male and female golfers were inducted, including Arnold Palmer, Jack Nicklaus, and Gary Player *(seated left to right)*. President Ford played nine holes with the Hall of Famers and shot a 48.

Hall of Fame Grand Opening

Lee Trevino

Regalado's the First Mexican to Win on the PGA Tour

Victor Regalado of Tijuana, Mexico, plays his ball from the trees during the final round of the 1974 Pleasant Valley Classic. Regalado won the tournament by a stroke over Tom Weiskopf to become the first native of Mexico to capture a PGA Tour event. Lee Trevino is of Mexican descent, of course, but he was born in Dallas.

Trevino Outguns Nicklaus for PGA Title

Lee Trevino used a putter he found in a house he was renting to win the 1974 PGA Championship, at Tanglewood G.C. in North Carolina. Trevino, leading by a stroke after 54 holes, dueled it out with Jack Nicklaus in the final round. Each shot 69 on Sunday, and Trevino won by a stroke.

Victor Regalado

• September 11: The PGA World Golf Hall of Fame opens in Pinehurst, North Carolina.

• September 11: The new Hall of Fame's first members are Patty Berg, Walter Hagen, Ben Hogan, Bobby Jones, Byron Nelson, Jack Nicklaus, Francis Ouimet, Arnold Palmer, Gary Player, Gene Sarazen, Sam Snead, Harry Vardon, and Babe Zaharias.

• September 15: Johnny Miller wins his seventh event of the year, the $300,000 World Open, which has been pared down to 72 holes. Miller wins in a playoff over Frank Beard, Jack Nicklaus, and Bob Murphy.

• September 15: Sandra Haynie wins the Charity Golf Classic. It's her sixth win of the year.

• September 29: Johnny Miller's eighth season victory, the Kaiser International Open, comes in his hometown of Napa Valley, California. He wins by eight strokes over Billy Casper and Lee Trevino.

1974

Carner Wins Six, Begins a Decade of Excellence

After winless seasons in 1972 and '73, JoAnne Carner ignited a 12-year winning streak in 1974. Carner won a half-dozen events in '74 and took home her first of five Vare trophies. She also set an LPGA record for earnings with $87,094. Carner would finish in the top 10 on the money list for each of the next 11 years.

Jan Stephenson

JoAnne Carner

Australia's Stephenson Joins the LPGA Tour

Jan Stephenson was a top junior golfer in Australia, winning the New Wales Schoolgirl title five times. After winning four events on the Australian LPGA circuit, she moved to the United States in 1974 and joined the LPGA Tour at age 22. Stephenson was named the LPGA's Rookie of the Year in '74. She won her first tournament two years later.

• November 3: Hubert Green teams with Mac McLendon to win the Walt Disney World National Team Championship by one stroke over 62-year-old Sam Snead and nephew J.C. Snead.

• November 3: Johnny Miller wins eight PGA Tour events, the most since 1960, and a Tour-record

$353,021, nearly $115,000 ahead of second-place Jack Nicklaus. Miller is named PGA Player of the Year.

• November 3: Lee Trevino wins his fourth Vardon Trophy with an average of 70.53.

• November 24: South Africa wins the World Cup at Lagunita C.C. in

Venezuela thanks to Bobby Cole's score of 271.

• December 8: JoAnne Carner leads the LPGA Tour with $87,094 and is named Player of the Year. Carner wins the Vare Trophy with an average of 72.87. She ties Sandra Haynie for the lead in Tour victories with six.

NICKLAUS WINS THE GREATEST MASTERS OF ALL

Augusta National has witnessed its share of great drama. But if you were to ask avid Masters fans, many of them would tell you the best Masters ever was the 1975 battle between Jack Nicklaus, Tom Weiskopf, and Johnny Miller. With three of the greatest players of the 1970s locked in the duel, this became a golf fan's dream-come-true.

Nicklaus eventually won the Masters by one shot over Miller and Weiskopf. Jack played admirable golf, breaking 70 three times, but his competitors turned in spectacular rounds. Weiskopf shot a 66 on Saturday, while Miller came in with a record-setting finish of 65-66. Hale Irwin shot a 64 on Sunday, although it wasn't enough to crack the top three.

The Masters made the turn to greatness during the third round. After starting with a 68 and a 67, Nicklaus seemed to have the Masters wrapped up. Nobody in the gallery paid any attention to Miller, who opened with a 75, until they looked at the leader board and noticed Johnny ringing up birdie after birdie. He birdied six holes in a row, starting with the 2nd hole, and cruised on in

with a 65. Weiskopf, as mentioned, shot a 66, and after Nicklaus chugged in with a 73, Weiskopf took the lead.

The next day was even more exciting. By the time they got to the back nine, Nicklaus and Weiskopf were tied for the lead and Miller was right on their tails. Then the real fun began. Weiskopf took a one-stroke lead over Jack with birdies on 14 and 15. Nicklaus tied him with his own birdie on 16, which Weiskopf watched from the tee. Weiskopf bogied 16, three-putting from 100 feet. Miller birdied 17 to tie Weiskopf and—heading to the final hole—the two were one behind Nicklaus.

Both Miller and Weiskopf hit perfect tee shots on 18, and Miller hit his second shot 15 feet from the cup. Weiskopf followed with a second shot eight feet from the cup on the same line as Miller's putt. So the stage was set: If either man could make his birdie putt, he would meet Nicklaus in a playoff. Miller lined up the putt and seemed to hit it perfectly...yet the ball curled to the left just before it reached the hole. Now Weiskopf had the chance to tie Nicklaus, but his putt rolled to the right of the hole.

Nicklaus had thus claimed his fifth career Masters, and he would go on to win the PGA Championship at Firestone (beating Bruce Crampton by two strokes). Weiskopf was really disappointed. "How do you describe pain?" he asked the press. Miller wasn't that unhappy considering his fabulous comeback from an opening-round 75. "I'm not upset," he told the media. "I'm funny this way. I don't get down on myself when I don't win. I gave it my best, and 66 and 65 are not too shabby." No kidding! None of the players were all that shabby. They were the greatest players at the greatest Masters.

1975

- January: PGA Tour players are scheduled to play in 51 events, including satellite events, with a total season purse of $7,895,450. The purse is down from the previous year.

- January: LPGA Tour players will play in 33 events with a season purse of $1,742,000.

- January: The Atlanta Classic and Tournament Players Championship are the only designated events.

- January: The LPGA will shorten its courses this year, with the goal being lower scores.

- January: Retired PGA Tour player Don January decides to return to the

Tour after two years away, because his golf architecture business is in decline due to the recession.

- January 12: Johnny Miller shoots 24-under 260 and wins the season-opening Phoenix Open by 14 shots.

- January 19: Johnny Miller shoots 25-under-par to win the Dean

1975

Jack Nicklaus shot 68-67-73-68—276 to win the 1975 Masters, edging Johnny Miller and Tom Weiskopf by a stroke. Both Miller and Weiskopf could have tied Nicklaus with birdies on the last hole, but Miller's 15-foot birdie putt curled to the left and Weiskopf's eight-foot attempt rolled to the right.

Martin Tucson Open by nine shots. He carded his second 61 in two tournaments.

• January 26: Gene Littler wins the Bing Crosby National Pro-Am.

• February 9: Johnny Miller wins the Bob Hope Desert Classic by three shots.

• March 2: Bob Murphy wins Jackie Gleason's Inverrary Classic and the Tour's biggest first prize—$52,000.

• March 2: Amy Alcott, age 19 and playing in her third LPGA event, wins the Orange Blossom Classic.

• March 13: The Houston Gulf Coast Classic, an LPGA Tour event

scheduled to begin tomorrow, is canceled because the sponsor doesn't have the money for the purse.

• March 29: Jane Blalock wins the Karsten-Ping Classic a week after winning $13,500 in damages (plus legal fees) in her anti-trust suit against the LPGA.

Johnny Miller

Miller Laps the Field in Phoenix, Tucson Opens

Johnny Miller threw it into high gear in early 1975. On January 12, he won the Phoenix Open by a whopping 14 strokes. The next week, he shot 25-under to claim the Dean Martin Tucson Open by nine shots. And on February 9, he nabbed the Bob Hope Desert Classic by three strokes, capping off a phenomenal 13-month stretch of golf.

Lee Elder

Elder Breaks the Color Barrier at the Masters

In 1975, Lee Elder became the first black golfer invited to the Masters, earning the invitation because of his victory in the 1974 Monsanto Open. Elder would eventually be inducted into the NCAA Hall of Fame—even though he never went to college. He was so honored because of his gracious contributions to colleges and the underprivileged.

• March 30: Jack Nicklaus, thanks to a second-round 63, wins the Sea Pines Heritage Classic.

• April 10: Lee Elder becomes the first black golfer to play in the Masters. Elder earned the invitation by winning the 1974 Monsanto Open.

• April 13: Jack Nicklaus wins a thrilling Masters by one shot over Tom Weiskopf and Johnny Miller. Both Weiskopf and Miller missed makeable birdie putts on the final green.

• April 19: Arnold Palmer travels to Europe and wins the Spanish Open.

• April 20: Sandra Palmer leads from start to finish to win the Colgate-Dinah Shore Winners Circle.

• May 12: Tom Watson booms home with a 65 to win the Byron Nelson Classic in Dallas by two shots over Bob E. Smith.

Gene Littler

Littler Rebounds from Cancer, Wins Three

At age 45, Gene Littler enjoyed one of his best years in 1975, winning the Bing Crosby National Pro-Am, the Danny Thomas Memphis Classic, and the Westchester Classic. Littler had undergone surgery for cancer of the lymph system in 1972. He earned the Bob Jones and Ben Hogan Awards for his courageous comeback.

Kathy Whitworth

After 75 Victories, Whitworth Enters Hall

Kathy Whitworth was inducted into the LPGA Hall of Fame in 1975. It's hard to figure why she wasn't admitted earlier, since her victory in the '75 LPGA Championship was her 75th on Tour. Whitworth defeated Sandra Haynie by a stroke in the LPGA Championship, at Pine Ridge G.C. in Baltimore.

Tom Weiskopf

Weiskopf Recovers from Tough Masters Loss

In one of golf's more historic moments, Tom Weiskopf bangs his putter after missing an eight-foot putt on the 72nd hole of the 1975 Masters. The birdie attempt would have tied him for the title with Jack Nicklaus. Weiskopf rebounded to win the '75 Greater Greensboro Open and Canadian Open. He finished third on the money list.

• May 18: Billy Casper takes his 51st and last PGA Tour victory at the First NBC New Orleans Open.

• May 29: The U.S. defeats Great Britain/Ireland, 15½-8½, in the Walker Cup Match at St. Andrews.

• June 1: Kathy Whitworth wins the LPGA Championship by one shot over Sandra Haynie, at Pine Ridge Golf Course near Baltimore.

• June 22: John Mahaffey shoots a final-round 71 at Medinah C.C. in Chicago to tie Lou Graham at the U.S. Open. Ben Crenshaw double bogeys the 71st hole to finish one behind.

• June 23: Lou Graham shoots an even-par 71 to defeat John Mahaffey by two shots in the U.S. Open playoff.

• June 27: Lee Trevino, Bobby Nichols, and Jerry Heard are hospitalized after being struck by lightning during the second round of the Western Open.

Lou Graham

Mahaffey Falls Short in U.S. Open Playoff

John Mahaffey came up a stroke shy of winning the 1975 U.S. Open, at Medinah C.C. near Chicago. Mahaffey shot a 71 in the final round of regulation, then fired a 73 in an 18-hole playoff with Lou Graham. Graham mirrored the scores, shooting 73 on Sunday and 71 on Monday. Mahaffey would become known for his outstanding iron play.

Jane Blalock

Blalock Goes 12 Years Without Missing Cut

Jane Blalock pocketed $10,000 for winning the 1975 Karsten-Ping Open, one of the richest LPGA events of the year. Blalock never won a major title, but she did capture 29 LPGA Tour events. She also achieved one of the most astounding records in golf: 299 consecutive Tour events without missing the cut, from 1969-80.

Graham Wins U.S. Open, as Well as the World Cup

Lou Graham defeated John Mahaffey, 71-73, in a playoff to claim the 1975 U.S. Open, one of six career victories. Graham could have won the Open with a par on the 72nd hole, but he hit his approach shot into a bunker and settled for a bogey. Later in the year, Graham teamed with Johnny Miller to win the World Cup in Bangkok, Thailand.

John Mahaffey

• June 28: Jay Haas of Wake Forest wins the individual title at the NCAAs, and Wake Forest successfully defends its team title.

• June 30: Hale Irwin wins the Western Open by one stroke.

• July: The LPGA hires Ray Volpe as its first commissioner.

• July 5: Art Wall, age 51, wins the Greater Milwaukee Open by one shot over Gary McCord.

• July 13: Tom Watson shoots 71 to defeat Jack Newton by a stroke in an 18-hole British Open playoff at Carnoustie, Scotland. It's Watson's first major championship.

• July 13: Rookie Roger Maltbie shoots a final-round 64 to win the Ed McMahon Quad Cities Open. It's his first Tour victory. He'll win again next week.

• July 20: Sandra Palmer wins the U.S. Women's Open at Atlantic City C.C. in New Jersey. JoAnne Carner, Sandra Post, and 18-year-old

Tom Watson

Jack Nicklaus

Maltbie Wins Two in a Row, Loses Check

Roger Maltbie captured back-to-back tournaments as a Tour rookie in 1975—the Quad Cities Open in Illinois and the Pleasant Valley Classic in Massachusetts. He also made a rookie mistake at the latter event, as he accidentally left his $40,000 winner's check in a restaurant near the course. The sponsor issued him a new check.

Watson Beats Newton in British Playoff

Three weeks after blowing the 1975 U.S. Open (he shot 67-68-78-77), an angry Tom Watson went to Carnoustie, Scotland, and captured the British Open. Watson holed a long birdie putt on the 72nd hole, putting him in an 18-hole playoff with Australian Jack Newton. Watson outgunned Newton, 71-72, for the title.

Roger Maltbie

Nicklaus Tallies Five Wins, Including PGA Championship

Besides his memorable Masters victory, Jack Nicklaus won four other Tour events in 1975, including the PGA Championship at Firestone C.C. in Akron, Ohio. Nicklaus claimed his fourth PGA title by shooting 276, two strokes better than Bruce Crampton. At Firestone, Nicklaus won the World Series of Golf five times.

---

amateur Nancy Lopez finish four strokes back.

• July 27: Tom Weiskopf birdies the first extra hole to defeat Jack Nicklaus in the Canadian Open at Royal Montreal G.C.

• August 3: Gene Littler, age 45, birdies the first extra hole to defeat 55-year-old Julius Boros in a playoff at the Westchester Classic. Littler aced the 14th hole of the final round.

• August 10: Jack Nicklaus finishes two strokes ahead of Bruce Crampton to win his fourth PGA Championship, at Firestone C.C. in Akron, Ohio. Crampton shot a PGA Championship-record 63 in the second round but he followed with a third round of 75.

• August 16: Beth Daniel, age 18, defeats Donna Horton, 3 & 2, in the final of the U.S. Women's Amateur at Brae Burn C.C. in West Newton, Massachusetts.

Amy Alcott

Alcott Wastes No Time Getting Her First Victory

Amy Alcott joined the LPGA Tour in January 1975, and in February—on the weekend of her 19th birthday—she won the Orange Blossom Classic. Alcott would go on to win a tournament in each of her first 12 years on Tour. Of those in the LPGA Hall of Fame, only Louise Suggs and Betsy Rawls could make that claim.

Irwin Kicks Off Four-Year Hot Streak

At the peak of his career in 1975, Hale Irwin captured two tournaments—the Western Open and Atlanta Classic. He also began a phenomenal streak in which he made the cut in 86 consecutive tournaments (through 1978). Byron Nelson (113) and Jack Nicklaus (105) are the only men to surpass Irwin's mark.

Hale Irwin

Daniel Wins Women's Amateur

Fresh-faced Beth Daniel captured the 1975 U.S. Women's Amateur, defeating Donna Horton in the final, 3 & 2, at Brae Burn C.C. in West Newton, Massachusetts. Daniel, age 18, clinched the title with a 15-foot birdie putt on the 16th hole. She would win the Amateur again in 1977 and join the Tour in 1979.

Beth Daniel

• August 24: Al Geiberger wins the Tournament Players Championship by three strokes at Colonial C.C. in Fort Worth, Texas.

• August 29: Andy North ties the PGA Tour record for the lowest nine holes, shooting 27 on the par-34 back nine at En-Joie G.C. at the B.C. Open. He shoots 63.

• August 31: Fred Ridley defeats Keith Fergus, 2 up, in the final of the U.S. Amateur at the C.C. of Virginia.

• September 7: Tom Watson wins the World Series of Golf.

• September 10: Willie Anderson, Fred Corcoran, Joseph C. Dey, Chick Evans, Tom Morris Jr., John H. Taylor, Glenna Collett Vare, and Joyce Wethered are inducted into the PGA World Golf Hall of Fame.

• September 14: Jack Nicklaus beats Billy Casper on the first hole of a playoff at the World Open in Pinehurst, North Carolina.

January Rejoins Tour, Wins the Texas Open

In the early 1970s, Don January *(seated)* retired from the PGA Tour to concentrate on his golf course architecture business. But with business down due to the country's recession, he rejoined the Tour in 1975 at age 45. It was a heck of a comeback, as he won the '75 San Antonio Texas Open and claimed the 1976 Vardon Trophy.

Sandra Palmer

Palmer Claims Dinah Shore, U.S. Women's Open

Sandra Palmer made her two 1975 victories count, as she won the Tour's most lucrative tournament (Colgate-Dinah Shore Winners Circle) and its most prestigious (U.S. Women's Open). In the latter, she won by four strokes at Atlantic City C.C. in New Jersey. Palmer led the '75 Tour in earnings and was named Player of the Year.

Don January

• September 21: The United States defeats Great Britain/Ireland in the Ryder Cup, 21-11, at Laurel Valley G.C. in Ligonier, Pennsylvania.

• October 19: Don January makes his return to the Tour successful by winning the San Antonio Texas Open. He birdies the second playoff hole to defeat Larry Hinson.

• October 26: Jack Nicklaus leads the PGA Tour in victories with five and earnings with $298,149. He is named PGA Tour Player of the Year. Bruce Crampton wins the Vardon Trophy, averaging 70.51.

• November 23: Sandra Palmer leads the LPGA Tour in earnings with $76,374 and is named LPGA Player of the Year. Sandra Haynie and Carol Mann lead the Tour with four victories apiece.

• December 7: The United States team of Johnny Miller and Lou Graham wins the World Cup in Bangkok, Thailand.

MARRIAGE, 5-WOOD HELP FLOYD WIN MASTERS

When the 1970s began, Raymond Floyd was considered to be a viable superstar candidate. In 1969, he had won three tournaments, including the PGA Championship, and seemed destined for a decade of success. Eventually he achieved that goal, but in the early 1970s Floyd was a virtual nothing on the PGA Tour. From 1970–74, he lagged way back on the money list and didn't win a single tournament.

Some golf experts felt Floyd was just too wild and crazy off the golf course, partying and chasing women. Then he met Maria, and the couple got married. Marriage was the difference in Floyd's return to PGA Tour stardom, as Maria calmed him down and got him more interested in his golf game.

Floyd got back into the winner's circle by capturing the 1975 Kemper Open in Charlotte, North Carolina, but not everybody in the world of golf was sure Floyd was really back. The next year at the Masters, Floyd was not considered a contender. In fact, when he stepped to the first tee, his name wasn't on the initial leader board. The scoring committee felt he was just part of the field. A front-nine 32 changed their minds rather quickly. A back-nine 33 gave Floyd a score of 65, one of the best starts in the history of the Masters. His name was placed on the leader board— right at the top.

One reason Floyd did so well was his idea of bringing a 5-wood to Augusta National. He knew that birdies on the four par-5s were essential to posting good scores, and he thought a 5-wood would be an excellent club to loft soft second shots onto the par-5s' greens. He birdied all four par-5s in the first round, and he had three birdies and an eagle on the par-5s during his second-round 66. During his third-round 70, Floyd again birdied all four par-5s, and when the day ended he had an eight-stroke lead over second-place Jack Nicklaus. For all intents and purposes, this tournament was sewn up.

The wind started blowing during Sunday's final round, but all that did was cause Floyd to start parring par-5s. He parred Nos. 2, 8, and 13, but a birdie on the difficult par-3 12th made up the difference. He decided not to go over the water in two shots on the par-5 15th, but he ended up birdieing the hole anyway. Floyd's fourth-round 70 was more than enough to win the Masters, as he finished eight strokes ahead of Ben Crenshaw, who shot a final-round 67. Sunday's wind prevented Floyd from setting a new 72-hole Masters scoring record, as his 271 tied Nicklaus's 1965 mark.

After Floyd's victory, 5-woods became popular. In fact, in the coming years, 5-woods replaced 4-woods as the standard third wood in a set of clubs. As for Floyd, he got better with age, winning 15 more PGA tournaments, including the 1982 PGA Championship and 1986 U.S. Open. In 1992, he became the first player to win on both the PGA Tour and the Senior Tour.

1976

- January: PGA Tour players are scheduled to play in 49 events with a total season purse of $9,157,522.

- January: LPGA Tour players are scheduled to play in 32 events with a season purse of $2,527,000.

- January: The LPGA announces a new tournament, the Ladies' Masters, to be played at Moss Creek Plantation on Hilton Head Island, South Carolina.

- January: The USGA sets an overall distance standard for golf balls. They must not exceed an average of a 280-yard drive under standard test conditions by a mechanical golfer.

- January: The Masters announces it will go to a sudden-death playoff, instead of 18 holes, in case of a tie.

- January 11: Johnny Miller wins his third consecutive Tucson Open to start the season.

- January 18: Rookie Bob Gilder wins the second PGA Tour event he

1976

Raymond Floyd tips his visor to the gallery on his way to victory in the 1976 Masters. Floyd, with the help of his 5-wood, fired 21 birdies and an eagle and led from start to finish. Entering Sunday's round, he had an eight-stroke lead, which he maintained. Floyd shot 271, tying Jack Nicklaus's 72-hole Masters record.

enters, the Phoenix Open, by two shots over Roger Maltbie.

• January 25: Ben Crenshaw breaks out of a two-year slump by winning the Bing Crosby National Pro-Am by two shots over Mike Morley. Jack Nicklaus shoots 37-45—82 in the last round.

• February: The scheduled Ladies' Masters changes its name to the Women's International after objections from Augusta National.

• February 1: Ben Crenshaw wins the Hawaiian Open by four shots.

• February 8: Johnny Miller continues to excel in the desert with

a three-shot win in the Bob Hope Desert Classic.

• February 8: Jan Stephenson claims her first LPGA Tour victory at the Sarah Coventry-Naples Classic.

• February 22: Hale Irwin beats Tom Watson by two to win the Glen Campbell Los Angeles Open.

1976

Green Wins Three Events in a Row in March

Pre-tournament favorite Hubert Green signs autographs during the 1976 Masters. Green won three straight Tour events in March—the Doral-Eastern Open, Greater Jacksonville Open, and Sea Pines Heritage Classic—then took a week off to rest and prepare for the Masters. His strategy didn't work, as he finished in 19th place.

Craig Stadler, Ben Crenshaw

Crenshaw Emerges from Slump, Wins Three Tourneys

In 1976, Ben Crenshaw *(right)* burst out of a long slump to win three tournaments: the Crosby, Hawaiian Open, and Ohio Kings Island Open. He also finished second on the money list—his best showing ever. Gentle Ben, pictured here with Craig Stadler, hadn't won since he captured his first start as a professional, 2½ years earlier.

Hubert Green

• March 1: Jack Nicklaus wins his second Tournament Players Championship.

• March 8: Hale Irwin pars the sixth playoff hole to defeat Kermit Zarley in the Florida Citrus Open.

• March 28: Hubert Green wins the Sea Pines Heritage Classic. The

previous two weeks, he won the Doral-Eastern Open and Greater Jacksonville Open.

• April 4: Al Geiberger wins the Greater Greensboro Open, as Hubert Green takes the week off.

• April 4: Judy Rankin wins her second LPGA event of the year, the

Colgate-Dinah Shore Winners Circle, and a first prize of $32,000.

• April 11: Raymond Floyd ties the tournament record of 271 to win the Masters by eight shots over Ben Crenshaw. Hubert Green is 19th.

• April 12: Clifford Roberts, age 82, steps down as chairman of the

Roger Maltbie

Maltbie Beats Irwin in First-Ever Memorial

In 1976, Roger Maltbie needed four sudden-death holes to defeat Hale Irwin in the inaugural Memorial Tournament, held at Jack Nicklaus's new Muirfield Village course in Dublin, Ohio. The Memorial, played in May, would become one of the premier tournaments held between the Masters (April) and U.S. Open (June).

Judy Rankin

Rankin Becomes First on Tour to Reach $100,000

Judy Rankin reached an important milestone in 1976 when she became the first LPGA player to earn $100,000 in a season. Actually, Rankin soared to $150,734, thanks to six wins including the lucrative Colgate-Dinah Shore Winners Circle. Rankin also benefitted from a Tour purse that jumped from $1.74 million in 1975 to $2.53 million in '76.

Hale Irwin

Irwin Beats Zarley on Sixth Hole of Sudden-Death

Hale Irwin hits out of the woods during the fourth sudden-death hole of the 1976 Florida Citrus Open. Irwin and Kermit Zarley remained gridlocked through two overtime holes on Sunday. After darkness suspended play, they played four more holes on Monday, with Irwin prevailing. Two weeks earlier, Hale won the Los Angeles Open.

Masters after 42 years. Bill Lane takes over.

• April 18: Don January, age 46, wins the MONY Tournament of Champions by five shots over Hubert Green.

• May 9: Sally Little holes out from a greenside bunker for a birdie on

the last hole to beat Jan Stephenson by one shot at the Women's International.

• May 16: Lee Trevino wins his first PGA Tour event in 14 months, the Colonial NIT.

• May 30: Roger Maltbie beats Hale Irwin on the fourth playoff hole to

win the first Memorial Tournament, at Muirfield Village G.C. in Ohio.

• May 30: Betty Burfeindt beats Judy Rankin by one shot in the LPGA Championship.

• June 6: Pat Bradley wins a four-woman playoff at the Girl Talk Classic. It's her first Tour victory.

Jerry Pate

U.S. Open Goes Down to Wire; Pate Prevails

In 1976, Jerry Pate starred in a thrilling U.S. Open at Atlanta Athletic Club. Four men—John Mahaffey, Tom Weiskopf, Al Geiberger, and Pate—had a chance to win on the 72nd hole. Mahaffey hit into water, while Weiskopf and Geiberger drove poorly and were forced to play short of the hazard. Pate hit a 5-iron two feet from the hole and birdied to win.

Burfeindt Nips Rankin at LPGA

Long-hitting Betty Burfeindt edged Judy Rankin by one stroke to win the 1976 LPGA Championship, at Pine Ridge G.C. near Baltimore. It was Burfeindt's fourth career victory, and she finished the season 11th on the money list. Two years earlier, Burfeindt underwent thyroid surgery.

Betty Burfeindt

Bradley Nabs the Girl Talk for First Win

In her third season on Tour, Pat Bradley ignited her career with her first-ever LPGA victory, the 1976 Girl Talk Classic. Bradley grew up in New England and became known as much for her skiing exploits as her golfing ability. On Tour, Bradley impressed golfers with her intense concentration.

Pat Bradley

• June 6: Tom Kite scores his first PGA Tour victory, beating Terry Diehl on the fifth hole of a playoff at the IVB-Bicentennial Golf Classic.

• June 12: The United States beats Great Britain/Ireland, 11½-8½, to win the Curtis Cup Match at Royal Lytham & St. Annes in England.

• June 20: Rookie Jerry Pate wins the U.S. Open by two strokes over Tom Weiskopf and Al Geiberger at Atlanta Athletic Club. It is his first PGA Tour win.

• June 27: Al Geiberger wins the Western Open by a stroke over Joe Porter. Bob Dickson blows a five-stroke 54-hole lead with an 80.

• July 10: Johnny Miller shoots a final-round 66 to win the British Open by six shots over Jack Nicklaus and Seve Ballesteros at Royal Birkdale G.C. in England. Ballesteros, age 19, led after three rounds.

• July 11: Judy Rankin becomes the first LPGA player to reach $100,000

1976

JoAnne Carner

Carner Tops Palmer in Women's Open

JoAnne Carner defeated Sandra Palmer in a playoff at the 1976 U.S. Women's Open, on the pesky Rolling Green G.C. course in Springfield, Pennsylvania. The track measured just 6,066 yards, but the co-leaders finished at 8-over-par 292. On Monday, Carner topped Palmer, 76-78, for her second Women's Open title.

Geiberger Wins by a Stroke in Western Open

The week after he blew an opportunity to win the 1976 U.S. Open, Al Geiberger took his hot game to Chicago for the Western Open. This time he prevailed, winning by a stroke over Joe Porter. Like many of his 11 career victories, Geiberger's win came on a very difficult course, Butler National G.C.

Al Geiberger

Tom Kite

Kite Soars to Victory in IVB-Bicentennial

Tom Kite, who would become more famous for the amount of money he earned rather than the tournaments he won, claimed his first Tour victory in the 1976 IVB-Bicentennial Classic. He defeated Terry Diehl on the fifth extra playoff hole. Beginning in '76, Kite earned over $100,000 for the first of 17 straight years.

---

in earnings in a year with her 17th-place finish in the U.S. Women's Open.

• July 12: JoAnne Carner beats Sandra Palmer, 76-78, in a U.S. Women's Open playoff, at Rolling Green G.C. in Springfield, Pennsylvania. They had tied at 8-over 292.

• July 18: David Graham wins the $60,000 first prize at the American Express Westchester Classic.

• July 25: U.S. Open champion Jerry Pate wins the Canadian Open by four shots over Jack Nicklaus.

• August 16: Dave Stockton rolls in a 13-foot par putt on the final hole

to edge Raymond Floyd and Don January by a shot in the rain-delayed PGA Championship at Congressional C.C. in Bethesda, Maryland.

• September 5: Bill Sander defeats Parker Moore, 8 & 6, in the final of the U.S. Amateur at Bel-Air C.C. in Los Angeles.

Fuzzy Zoeller

Miller Overcomes Seve in British Open

Johnny Miller closed with a rousing 66 to win the 1976 British Open at Royal Birkdale in England. After 54 holes, a 19-year-old hot-shot named Seve Ballesteros led the tournament by two strokes, but Seve closed with a 74. Miller ended up winning by six shots over Ballesteros and Jack Nicklaus. It was his second major victory.

Johnny Miller

Zoeller Cards Eight Birdies in Quad Cities Open

Fuzzy Zoeller made a name for himself in the first round of the 1976 Ed McMahon Quad Cities Open. Zoeller tied the Tour record with eight birdies in a row at Oakwood C.C. in Coal Valley, Illinois. He shot 63 in the round but lost the tournament by a stroke. Zoeller got the nickname "Fuzzy" from his initials, Frank Urban Zoeller (F.U.Z.).

- September 5: Jack Nicklaus earns $100,000 for winning the World Series of Golf. Previously a four-man exhibition, the World Series is now an official event with an elite field of about 20 players.

- September 8: Tommy Armour, James Braid, Tom Morris Sr., Jerry Travers, and Mickey Wright are inducted into the PGA World Golf Hall Of Fame.

- September 12: Raymond Floyd wins the World Open in a playoff over Jerry McGee.

- September 26: Donna Caponi Young wins her second straight tournament, The Carlton, and a season-high first prize of $35,000. It is the only year the event is played.

- October 9: David Graham beats Hale Irwin on the third extra hole in the Picadilly World Match Play Championship in England.

- October 24: Seve Ballesteros, 19, tops the European Order of Merit.

Stockton Holes 10-Foot Putt to Win PGA Title

Dave Stockton urges a birdie putt into the hole during the final round of the 1976 PGA Championship, at Congressional C.C. in Bethesda, Maryland. Though thunderstorms forced the final round to Monday, Stockton prevailed. On the final green, he holed a 10-foot par putt to avoid a playoff with Don January and Raymond Floyd.

Jack Nicklaus

Dave Stockton

Nicklaus Earns $100,000 at World Series of Golf

Jack Nicklaus won both the 1976 Tournament Players Championship and the World Series of Golf, as the World Series became an official event for the first time and offered a season-high $100,000 to the winner. Nicklaus led the '76 Tour in earnings ($266,438) for the eighth and final time. He also won his fifth Australian Open.

• November: A federal judge rules that the LPGA's Moss Creek event can be called the Ladies' Masters, as sponsors had planned for 1977.

• November 3: Donna Caponi Young wins her third straight tournament on the LPGA circuit, the Japan Classic.

• November 7: Jack Nicklaus leads the PGA Tour in earnings with $266,438. He is named PGA Tour Player of the Year.

• November 7: Ben Crenshaw and Hubert Green lead the PGA Tour in victories with three each. Don January wins his first Vardon Trophy, averaging 70.56.

• December 7: Spain, with Manuel Pinero and Seve Ballesteros, wins the World Cup at Mission Hills C.C. in Palm Springs, California.

• December 7: Judy Rankin leads the LPGA Tour in wins with six and in earnings with $150,734. Rankin also wins the Vare Trophy and is named Player of the Year.

WATSON TOPS NICKLAUS; A NEW KING IS CROWNED

In the 1960s, Jack Nicklaus—10 years younger than Arnold Palmer—succeeded Arnie as golf's top player. In the 1970s, a whole crop of golfers—all seven to 13 years younger than Nicklaus—were looking to climb the king's hill and grab his crown. The group included Lanny Wadkins, Tom Watson, Ben Crenshaw, Jerry Pate, John Mahaffey, and Tom Kite, but the one that proved to be the next generation's superstar was Watson, nearly 10 years younger than Nicklaus.

By 1975, Watson had established himself as a quality player, winning two PGA Tour events and the 1975 British Open. Though he went winless in 1976, he soared to the top of the charts in 1977. To start the season, Watson won both the Bing Crosby National Pro-Am and the Andy Williams San Diego Open. When he went to Augusta National for the Masters, he began to challenge Nicklaus face-to-face. Watson was the third-round leader at Augusta, and even though Nicklaus buried six birdies on the first 13 holes on Sunday, Watson hung right there with him. Nicklaus finished the fourth round with a 66, but Watson's 67 was good enough to defeat Nicklaus by a stroke to give him his first career Masters.

Neither Watson nor Nicklaus were in contention at the U.S. Open, but when they flew across the Atlantic to play in the British Open at Turnberry, the face-to-face duel began anew. In the pleasant weather of the first three rounds, Nicklaus shot 68-70-65. Amazingly, Watson matched each round—68-70-65—and the two of them entered the final round three strokes ahead of the field.

Nicklaus and Watson were paired together in the final round, and it was more of a match-play than stroke-play finale. With six holes remaining, Nicklaus was three strokes ahead of Watson, but then Watson rolled in a 60-foot birdie putt on the 15th hole to tie. As they walked off the green, Watson said to Nicklaus, "Isn't this what golf is supposed to be like?" Nicklaus mumbled "yes," and when he two-putted from four feet for a par on the par-5 17th—compared to Watson's birdie—Watson claimed the lead.

Now it was down to the last hole. Nicklaus hit a poor tee shot into the rough and Watson was up the middle. Watson lofted a soft 8-iron two feet from the cup. It looked like everything was over. It wasn't. Nicklaus blasted out of the rough onto the green and rolled in a 32-foot birdie. Watson was a bit nervous knowing he had to make that birdie to win, but he made it to shoot 268, a British Open record, and defeat Nicklaus for a second time that year.

By winning two majors face-to-face with the Golden Bear, Watson had proven he could beat anybody. When he returned to the United States, Watson won the Western Open and became the leading money winner for the year. He would lead the Tour in earnings from 1977–80 and become golf's new undisputed king.

1977

- January: PGA Tour players are scheduled to play in 48 events with a total season purse of $9,688,977.

- January: LPGA Tour players are scheduled to play in 35 events with a season purse of $3,058,000.

- January: The Tournament Players Championship has a permanent home, Sawgrass C.C. near Jacksonville, Florida. The Greater Jacksonville Open drops off the schedule.

- January 16: Bruce Lietzke wins the Joe Garagiola Tucson Open for his first PGA Tour victory. He birdies the fourth playoff hole to defeat Gene Littler.

- January 23: Tom Watson wins the Bing Crosby National Pro-Am by a shot over Tony Jacklin.

- January 30: Tom Watson wins the Andy Williams San Diego Open by five shots.

- February 6: Bruce Lietzke wins the Hawaiian Open.

This photo, taken at the 1977 Masters, reflects the changing of the guard on the PGA Tour. Tom Watson *(right)* won the Masters by two strokes over Jack Nicklaus *(background)*, then outlasted Jack in a classic final-round face-off at Turnberry for the British Open title. Watson, not Nicklaus, now reigned as golf's best player.

• February 27: Judy Rankin wins the Bent Tree Classic for her second straight victory.

• March: The PGA of America announces a sudden-death format for the PGA Championship.

• March 20: Mark Hayes wins the Tournament Players Championship by two shots over Mike McCullough with a 289. In a windy second round, players averaged a 79.

• March 27: Australia's Graham Marsh beats Tom Watson by a stroke to win the Heritage Classic and become another first-time winner.

• April: Bruce Crampton, age 41 and winner of 14 PGA Tour events, announces he is quitting the Tour to go into the oil business.

• April 3: Kathy Whitworth wins the Colgate-Dinah Shore Winners Circle by one shot over Sally Little and JoAnne Carner.

Palmer Teams with President in Crosby

Arnold Palmer putts during the 1977 Bing Crosby National Pro-Am. Standing behind him are *(left to right)* Hale Irwin, former President Gerald Ford, and Darius Keaton. Keaton was Irwin's amateur partner, while Ford partnered Palmer. The President had his own fans, called "Ford's Forces," to supplement Arnie's Army.

Andy Bean

Big-Hitting Bean Claims First Victory

Andy Bean joined a long list of first-time winners in 1977 when he clinched the Doral-Eastern Open by a single stroke. Bean possessed a deft putting touch as well as the ability to hit the ball a country mile. (He would lead the Tour in driving distance in 1985.) A record 11 players won their first tournament in 1977.

Bruce Lietzke

Lietzke Triumphs in Tucson, Hawaii

Bruce Lietzke exploded onto the scene in 1977 with wins in both the Joe Garagiola Tucson Open and the Hawaiian Open. His winnings soared into six digits for the first of 16 straight seasons, a feat surpassed only by Tom Kite and Tom Watson. Lietzke would eventually cut down his schedule so he could do what he really loved: fish, race cars, and spend time with his family.

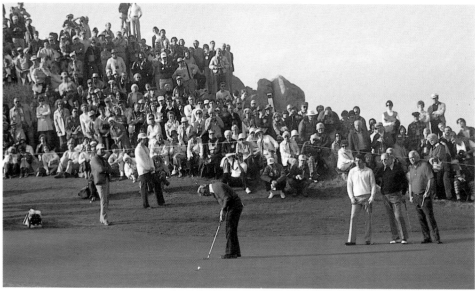

Bing Crosby National Pro-Am

- April 10: Tom Watson's final-round 67 is good enough to win the Masters by two strokes over Jack Nicklaus, despite Nicklaus's final-round 66.

- April 17: Jack Nicklaus wins his fifth Tournament of Champions, defeating Bruce Lietzke in a three-hole playoff.

- April 17: Sandra Palmer wins the Women's International.

- May 1: Veteran Gene Littler wins the Houston Open, the 25th and last official victory of his career.

- May 8: Raymond Floyd wins the Byron Nelson Classic by two shots over Ben Crenshaw.

- May 15: Ben Crenshaw wins the Colonial NIT by one shot.

- May 23: One year after he started the Memorial, Jack Nicklaus wins his own tournament at Muirfield Village G.C.

- May 23: Jack Nicklaus's $45,000 first prize at the Memorial makes

Mark Hayes

Hayes Claims the TPC in Ponte Vedra

Mark Hayes captured the 1977 Tournament Players Championship, which boasted a total purse of $300,000. After three years of moving around, the TPC finally settled in Ponte Vedra, Florida, home of the PGA Tour. The 27-year-old Hayes, who was given a 10-year Tour exemption for claiming the event, never won again.

Ben Crenshaw

Crenshaw Wins One, Almost Two, in Texas

Ben Crenshaw, a Texan through and through, won the 1977 Colonial NIT in Fort Worth, Texas, by one stroke over John Schroeder. A week earlier, Ben finished runner-up in the Byron Nelson Classic in Dallas. Over the years, Crenshaw has been lauded for his extraordinary putting ability—as well as his knowledge of golf history.

Chako Higuchi

Japan's Higuchi Claims LPGA Championship

Chako Higuchi, Japan's premier woman professional, became the third foreign player to win a major title on the LPGA Tour. Higuchi won the 1977 LPGA Championship in North Myrtle Beach, South Carolina. Two foreign players had previously won the U.S. Women's Open—Fay Crocker of Uruguay and Catherine Lacoste of France.

---

him the first golfer in Tour history to win $3 million in official money.

• June 10: Al Geiberger shoots a second-round 59 in the Danny Thomas Memphis Classic at Colonial C.C. to become the first PGA Tour golfer to break 60 in an official event. In a seven-hole stretch, he makes six birdies and an eagle.

• June 11: Southern California's Scott Simpson wins his second consecutive NCAA championship. Houston wins the team title.

• June 12: Chako Higuchi of Japan wins the LPGA Championship at Bay Tree Golf Plantation in North Myrtle Beach, South Carolina.

• June 19: Despite a death threat, Hubert Green shoots a final-round 70 to win the U.S. Open by a shot over Lou Graham at Southern Hills C.C. in Tulsa, Oklahoma. It is the first tournament to receive 18-hole television coverage.

• June 26: Tom Watson wins the Western Open by one stroke.

Al Geiberger

Mr. 59! Geiberger's the First to Break 60

On June 10, 1977, Al Geiberger became the first player to break 60 in an official PGA Tour event. His 13-under 59 in the second round of the Danny Thomas Memphis Classic electrified the sports world. He played a stretch of seven holes in 8-under, and on the 18th hole he canned an eight-footer for birdie. He won the tournament and earned the nickname "Mr. 59."

Stacy Holds Off Lopez in Women's Open

Hollis Stacy won her first of three U.S. Women's Opens in 1977 at Hazeltine National G.C. in Chaska, Minnesota. After three rounds, Stacy stood two strokes ahead of 20-year-old phenom Nancy Lopez, but both closed with 74s and Lopez finished second. These two, along with third-place finisher JoAnne Carner, were former U.S. Girls' Junior champions.

Hollis Stacy

Hubert Green

Despite Death Threat, Green Wins U.S. Open

Hubert Green had a police escort on his way to winning the 1977 U.S. Open at Southern Hills C.C. in Tulsa, Oklahoma. Green led the Open by a stroke after the third round, but that night he received a death threat. Seemingly unrattled, Green fired a final-round 70 and beat Lou Graham by one stroke.

• July 3: Judy Rankin wins her fourth tournament of the year, the Peter Jackson Classic.

• July 9: Tom Watson outduels Jack Nicklaus, 65-66, in the final round to beat him in the British Open at Turnberry, Scotland. Watson birdies the final hole for the victory.

• July 24: After a 14-month slump, Lee Trevino wins the Canadian Open by four shots over Peter Oosterhuis. It's held at Glen Abbey G.C. in Oakville, Ontario, for the first time.

• July 24: Hollis Stacy, age 22, wins the U.S. Women's Open at Hazeltine National G.C. She wins by two strokes over Nancy Lopez, who's playing in her first tournament as a professional.

• August 6: Judy Rankin's victory in the Colgate European Women's Open is her fifth of the year.

• August 9: Evan Williams wins the National Long Drive Championship

Pat Bradley

Bradley's No Fan of Mission Hills' 18th

Pat Bradley points out Rancho Mirage, California— specifically, the nightmarish 18th hole at Mission Hills C.C., where the Colgate-Dinah Shore Winners Circle annually concluded. "That hole has cost me a lot of money," Bradley said. Bradley didn't win the 1977 Dinah Shore—Kathy Whitworth did—but Pat won the Bankers Trust Classic and finished eighth in earnings.

Evan "Big Cat" Williams

Williams Booms 'Em in Long Drive Contest

Evan "Big Cat" Williams unleashed a tee shot of 353 yards to win the 1977 Long Drive Championship in Pebble Beach, California. "I just relax, delay the release of my hands, use strong leg action, and let 'er rip," said Williams. In the 1990s, John Daly became famous for a similar philopsophy. "Grip it and rip it," Daly said.

Wadkins Wins PGA in First Sudden-Death

Lanny Wadkins, winless for nearly four years, captured the 1977 PGA Championship at Pebble Beach G.L. Wadkins won in a sudden-death playoff—the first ever in a major championship— when he beat Gene Littler with a par on the third extra hole. On the back nine of the final round, Littler bogied five of six holes.

Lanny Wadkins

at Pebble Beach with a drive of 353 yards, 24 inches.

• August 13: Beth Daniel wins her second consecutive U.S. Women's Amateur, defeating Cathy Sherk, 3 & 1, in the final at Cincinnati C.C.

• August 14: Lanny Wadkins makes up five strokes on the final nine at Pebble Beach G.L. to tie Gene Littler in the PGA Championship. Wadkins pars the third playoff hole to win in sudden-death.

• August 23: Bobby Locke, John Ball, Herb Graffis, and Donald Ross are inducted into the PGA World Golf Hall of Fame.

• August 26: The United States wins the Walker Cup Match, 16-8, over Great Britain/Ireland at Shinnecock Hills G.C. in Southampton, New York.

• August 28: Hale Irwin shoots 20-under-par 264 on Pinehurst C.C.'s No. 2 Course to win the Hall of Fame Classic by five shots.

Debbie Massey

Rookie Massey Scores a Victory in Japan Classic

Debbie Massey, an outstanding amateur who was a two-time member of the U.S. Curtis Cup team, achieved immediate success on the LPGA Tour. In her first year, she won the Mizuno Japan Classic and finished 15th on the money list to capture Rookie of the Year honors. Massey would serve as the Tour's player president in 1982.

Tom Watson

Watson Smashes British Open Scoring Record

Tom Watson clutches the British Open trophy after an historic duel with Jack Nicklaus at Turnberry, Scotland. Watson and Nicklaus were tied after three rounds, but Watson closed with a 65 to Jack's 66. Tom's final-hole birdie earned him the victory, and his 268 total broke the championship's 72-hole scoring record by eight strokes.

• September 4: Hollis Stacy sets a 72-hole LPGA scoring record of 271 in winning the Rail Muscular Dystrophy Classic by eight shots.

• September 5: Inspired by his PGA victory, Lanny Wadkins wins the World Series of Golf by five shots over Hale Irwin and Tom Weiskopf.

• September 5: John Fought defeats Doug Fischesser, 9 & 8, in the final of the U.S. Amateur at Aronimink G.C. in Newtown Square, Pennsylvania.

• September 17: The United States wins the Ryder Cup, beating Great Britain/Ireland, 12½-7½, at Royal Lytham & St. Annes in England.

• September 29: Former Masters chairman Clifford Roberts dies at age 84 of an apparently self-inflicted gunshot wound on the grounds of Augusta National G.C.

• October 9: Bill Rogers, a non-winner on the PGA Tour, takes the $65,000 first prize at the Pacific Club Masters in Japan.

1977

Judy Rankin

Rankin Again Ranks No. 1 on LPGA Circuit

In 1977, Judy Rankin enjoyed her last great season, leading the LPGA Tour in earnings ($122,890) for the second straight year and tying in victories (five). She also won her second straight Vare Trophy and Player of the Year Award. In 28 events in '77, Rankin finished in the top 10 an amazing 25 times—an LPGA record that still stands.

Shoal Creek Country Club

Gorgeous Shoal Creek Course Opens for Play

Pictured is the 18th green of Shoal Creek C.C., a lauded course that opened in 1977. Designed by Augusta National fan Jack Nicklaus, it has some of that great course's characteristics. Large pines and an abundance of azaleas give life, and a creek meanders throughout. The course cuts through the Oak and Double Oak Mountains.

• November 6: Tom Watson leads the PGA Tour in wins with four and earnings with $310,653. He also wins the Vardon Trophy with a 70.32 average and is named PGA Player of the Year.

• November 6: Eleven players won their first PGA Tour event in 1977, setting a record.

• November 6: Johnny Miller fails to win a PGA Tour event for his first winless year since 1970. He finishes 48th on the money list.

• November 13: Judy Rankin leads the LPGA Tour in earnings with $122,890 and ties Debbie Austin in victories with five. Rankin also wins the Vare Trophy, averaging 72.16,

and is named the LPGA Tour's Player of the Year.

• December 11: Spain, with Seve Ballesteros and Antonio Garrido, wins the World Cup at Wack Wack C.C. in the Philippines. Gary Player wins the individual title with a score of 289.

ROOKIE LOPEZ RACKS UP FIVE WINS IN A ROW

A rookie year is always tougher for golf professionals compared to rookies in other sports. Golf pros have to get used to traveling around the country by themselves and dealing with tournament golf courses for the first time. Few rookies even win a tournament, and when one does, he or she is likely to be named Rookie of the Year. That's been the case for most years except for 1978, when Nancy Lopez, a 21-year-old rookie from New Mexico, turned pro and played her first year on the LPGA Tour.

Lopez was the 1978 Rookie of the Year, but that was the least of her achievements. She won an unbelievable nine LPGA Tour events including the LPGA Championship, which was part of five consecutive wins. She was also named Player of the Year and was the LPGA's leading money winner. No rookie, not even Jack Nicklaus, burst onto the scene like Lopez did.

Though no one ever dreamed of nine first-year wins, Lopez entered 1978 as a heralded rookie because of her sensational amateur career. She had won the USGA Girls' Junior twice, the Western Junior three times, the AIAW National

Collegiate title, and the Mexican Amateur. Her greatest amateur feats, though, occurred in 1969 and 1975. In '69, she won the New Mexico State Amateur—at age 12. And in '75, she finished second in the U.S. Women's Open—as an 18-year-old.

For all intents and purposes, Lopez wrapped up the 1978 Rookie of the Year Award by March. On February 26, she won the Bent Tree Classic, then won the next event, the Sunstar Classic. Two months later, Lopez began the hottest winning streak in LPGA Tour history. Starting on May 14, she won the Baltimore Classic, Coca-Cola Classic, and Golden Lights Championship in successive weeks. She took the next week off to get ready for the LPGA Championship at the Jack

Nicklaus Golf Center in Ohio.

Lopez captured the LPGA Championship for her first major, and she won it like she had been doing all year. A second-round 66 led to a 13-under-par 275 and a six-shot win over Amy Alcott, supposedly the next LPGA superstar until Lopez turned pro. By winning the Bankers Trust Classic the next week, Lopez had thus won five tournaments in six weeks. The only one she didn't win was the Peter Jackson Classic, which she didn't attend.

Lopez finished the year with two more victories to win $189,813, another LPGA record. Her phenomenal success made her a household name and gave a needed boost to the LPGA Tour. Lopez would shrug off the sophomore slump in 1979 by winning eight more events, giving her 17 by age 22. From 1980–92, she would give birth to three daughters, yet still find time to win 29 more LPGA Tour events. Is Lopez the best woman golfer of all time? Some may argue that Mickey Wright was the greatest. Whatever the case, no one— woman or man—ever had a greater rookie year than Nancy Lopez in 1978.

1978

- January: PGA Tour players are scheduled to play in 48 events with a total season purse of $10,337,332.

- January: LPGA Tour players are scheduled to play in 37 events with a season purse of $3,925,000.

- January 8: Tom Watson wins the Joe Garagiola Tucson Open.

- January 16: Miller Barber, age 46, shoots a final-round 65 to win the Phoenix Open. It's the last of Barber's 11 Tour victories.

- January 23: Tom Watson pars the second extra hole to defeat Ben Crenshaw in a playoff for the Bing Crosby National Pro-Am.

- February 26: Jack Nicklaus birdies the last five holes to win Jackie Gleason's Inverrary Classic by one shot over Grier Jones.

- February 26: Rookie Nancy Lopez takes her first LPGA victory, shooting 1-over-par at the Bent Tree Classic in Sarasota, Florida.

Nancy Lopez *(center)* poses with members of her family. Lopez wowed the sports world in 1978 by compiling nine victories—including five in a row. Lured by her compelling smile and extraordinary golfing skills, thousands flocked to LPGA events to get a glimpse of Lopez, the biggest hit on Tour since Babe Zaharias.

• March: The USGA says it will introduce a rule banning balls that correct a slice or a hook in flight.

• March 12: Nancy Lopez wins her second consecutive event, the Sunstar Classic in Los Angeles.

• March 19: Despite shooting a final-round 75, Jack Nicklaus wins the Tournament Players Championship by a shot over Lou Graham.

• April 2: Seve Ballesteros, not yet 21, prevails in the Greater Greensboro Open. It is his first PGA Tour victory.

• April 2: Sandra Post wins the Colgate-Dinah Shore Winners Circle, beating Penny Pulz in a sudden-death playoff.

• April 9: Gary Player, age 42, closes 34-30—64 to win the Masters. Hubert Green misses a three-foot putt on the last hole to finish a shot behind, along with Tom Watson and Rod Funseth.

1978

Seve Ballesteros

Young Ballesteros Makes His Mark in U.S.

In 1978, 21-year-old Spaniard Seve Ballesteros won the Greater Greensboro Open. Ballesteros, who won the World Cup at age 19, would become known for his fierce determination, long drives, and incredible ability to recover from trouble. "He can get up and down from a parking lot," wrote one scribe.

Tom Watson

Once Again, Watson Proves He's the Best

A year after dethroning Jack Nicklaus as golf's top player, Tom Watson secured his top spot in 1978. Watson paced the Tour in wins (five), led in earnings (a record $362,429), copped the Vardon (70.16), and was named Player of the Year—all for the second year in a row. A playoff victory in the Crosby highlighted his season.

Bill and Beth Rogers

Rogers Wins the Hope, Plus a New Automobile

Bill Rogers can't believe he just won the 1978 Bob Hope Desert Classic, his first PGA Tour victory. His wife Beth holds the keys to a new car just presented to them by Bob Hope. Later in the year, Rogers lost a Western Open playoff to Andy Bean. In 1981, Rogers would make headlines with a globe-trotting winning spree.

• April 16: Gary Player comes from seven shots back with a closing 67 to win the MONY Tournament of Champions.

• April 23: Gary Player wins the Houston Open by one shot over Andy Bean to claim his third consecutive PGA Tour victory.

• April 30: Sam Snead, age 65, and Gardner Dickinson team to win the first Legends of Golf for players 50 and over.

• May: It is announced that Europeans will be added to the Great Britain/Ireland team in the Ryder Cup Matches, beginning in 1979.

• May 7: Jan Stephenson wins the Women's International by four strokes. Amateur Beth Daniel is second.

• May 14: Lee Trevino becomes the first to break 270 at Colonial C.C. in Fort Worth, Texas, and wins the Colonial NIT with a 268.

Tom Watson, Gary Player

Player, 42, Edges Three Others by a Stroke in Masters

Tom Watson, 1977 Masters champion, slips the green jacket on 1978 victor Gary Player. Player, the Masters' oldest winner at age 42, was down seven strokes after three rounds, but he closed 34-30—64 to win by a stroke over Hubert Green, Rod Funseth, and Watson. Watson could have tied with a par on 18, but he bogied.

Lopez's Streak Ends at Lady Keystone Open

Nancy Lopez mulls over a putt with caddie Roscoe Jones during the 1978 Lady Keystone Open, at Hershey C.C. in Pennsylvania. Lopez was hoping to win the sixth consecutive tournament in which she entered, but she ended up 15 strokes behind winner Pat Bradley. Lopez had won seven of the previous 14 LPGA Tour events.

Nancy Lopez, Roscoe Jones

- May 21: Jim Simons shoots a final-round 74 at Muirfield Village but still wins the Memorial Tournament by one shot over Bill Kratzert.

- May 21: A week after winning the Greater Baltimore Classic Nancy Lopez wins again, beating JoAnne Carner in a playoff at the Coca-Cola Classic in New Jersey.

- May 29: Nancy Lopez makes it three in a row, shooting a final-round 65 to win the Golden Lights Championship by three over JoAnne Carner.

- June 4: Nancy Lopez takes the week off, and JoAnne Carner wins the Peter Jackson Classic by eight shots with a closing 64.

- June 11: Andy Bean wins his second straight event, the Danny Thomas Memphis Open, in a playoff over Lee Trevino.

- June 11: Nancy Lopez shoots 13-under-par to win the LPGA Championship at its new home, the Jack Nicklaus Golf Center in Kings Island, Ohio.

1978

Andy North

North Hangs On to Win U.S. Open

Andy North won the 1978 U.S. Open at Cherry Hills C.C. near Denver. North needed just a bogey-5 on 18 to win by a stroke over Dave Stockton and J.C. Snead, and that's what he got. Andy hit his tee shot into rough, his approach into more rough, and his third shot into a bunker. However, he chipped his bunker shot to within four feet of the hole and sank the putt.

Bruce Lietzke

Lietzke Captures Canadian Open

Bruce Lietzke beat Pat McGowan by a stroke in the 1978 Canadian Open, held at Glen Abbey G.C. in Oakville, Ontario, which would become the tournament's permanent home course. Lietzke possessed considerable golfing skills, which came to light after statistics were first kept in 1980. At various times, Lietzke led the Tour in greens in regulation, par-breakers, eagles, and total driving.

Simons Edges Out Kratzert in Memorial

Jim Simons emerged as the winner in the 1978 Memorial Tournament, as he prevailed by a stroke over Bill Kratzert. Simons, who won the NBC New Orleans Open a year earlier, challenged occasionally in the late 1970s and early '80s. He first entered the spotlight in 1971, when he led the U.S. Open after the third round— as an amateur.

Jim Simons

• June 18: Andy North makes a four-foot putt for a bogey on the 72nd hole to beat J.C. Snead and Dave Stockton by one stroke in the U.S. Open, at Cherry Hills C.C. near Denver.

• June 18: Nancy Lopez wins the Banker's Trust Classic in Rochester, New York. Her victory sets an

LPGA record of five consecutive wins in tournaments played (though not five events in a row).

• June 25: Bruce Lietzke captures the Canadian Open by one shot over Pat McGowan.

• June 25: Pat Bradley wins the Lady Keystone Open. Nancy Lopez's

winning streak ends as she finishes 15 strokes behind.

• July 2: Andy Bean ties Bill Rogers with a closing 66 at the Western Open, then beats Rogers in a playoff for his third win of the year.

• July 9: The eight-hole playoff between Lee Elder and Lee Trevino

1978

Bean Wins Three Tournaments in a Month

Andy Bean soared to No. 3 on the money list in 1978 thanks to three Tour wins within a month. Bean claimed a five-stroke victory in the Kemper Open and then, the next week, won the Danny Thomas Memphis Classic in a playoff over Lee Trevino. Three weeks later, Bean beat Bill Rogers in a Western Open playoff.

John and Susie Mahaffey

Mahaffey Nips Watson, Pate in PGA Playoff

John Mahaffey and wife Susie celebrate his playoff victory in the 1978 PGA Championship, at Oakmont C.C. near Pittsburgh. After three rounds, Mahaffey trailed leader Tom Watson by seven strokes. But John closed with a 66 to tie Watson and Jerry Pate at 276. Mahaffey made a 12-foot birdie putt on the second extra hole for the victory.

Andy Bean

at the Greater Milwaukee Open matches the second longest in PGA Tour history. Elder eventually wins.

• July 15: Jack Nicklaus wins his third British Open with a final-round 69 at St. Andrews, Scotland. Ben Crenshaw, Raymond Floyd, Tom Kite, and Simon Owens finish two behind.

• July 23: Jack Nicklaus wins his second tournament in a row, the IVB-Philadelphia Classic.

• July 23: Hollis Stacy wins her second straight U.S. Women's Open, beating JoAnne Carner and Sally Little by one shot at the C.C. of Indianapolis.

• August 6: John Mahaffey wins a playoff at the PGA Championship at Oakmont C.C. near Pittsburgh. Mahaffey closes with a 66, then defeats Tom Watson and Jerry Pate on the second extra hole.

• August 6: Nancy Lopez wins her eighth event of the year, the Colgate European Open in England.

Jack Nicklaus

Nicklaus Wins British Open, Plus the TPC

One of Jack Nicklaus's great streaks was that he finished among the top four on the Tour money list for 17 consecutive seasons (1962–78). A victory in the British Open highlighted his '78 season, as he won by two strokes at St. Andrews, Scotland. Nicklaus won three 1978 Tour events, including the Tournament Players Championship.

Hollis Stacy

Stacy Wins Her Second Straight Women's Open

Hollis Stacy won the 1978 U.S. Women's Open, her second in a row, at the C.C. of Indianapolis. Stacy, just 24 years old, shot 70-75-72-72—289 to defeat JoAnne Carner and Sally Little by a stroke. Little closed with a 65, a Women's Open record. Carner missed her chance at victory by finishing bogey-par-par.

Greg Rita, Dr. Gil Morgan

Morgan Rakes in the Dough at World Series

Dr. Gil Morgan, an optometrist, and caddie Greg Rita align a putt during the 1978 World Series of Golf. Morgan won the event by beating Hubert Green on the first hole of a playoff. Thanks to the $100,000 first prize, as well as his check for winning the Glen Campbell Los Angeles Open, Morgan finished No. 2 on the Tour's money list.

• August 13: John Mahaffey follows up his PGA victory with a win in the American Optical Classic.

• August 19: Cathy Sherk wins the U.S. Women's Amateur at Sunnybrook G.C. near Philadelphia.

• August 22: Billy Casper, Harold Hilton, Dorothy Campbell Hurd

Howe, Bing Crosby, and Clifford Roberts are inducted into the PGA World Golf Hall of Fame.

• September 3: John Cook wins the U.S. Amateur at Plainfield C.C. in New Jersey.

• September 17: Ron Streck closes 63-62 in the San Antonio Texas

Open to set the PGA Tour record for the best consecutive two rounds. He wins by one stroke.

• October 1: Dr. Gil Morgan pars the first extra hole to win a playoff with Hubert Green at the World Series of Golf, taking the $100,000 first prize.

Cook Knocks Off Hoch in U.S. Amateur

John Cook topped Scott Hoch, 5 & 4, in the final of the 1978 U.S. Amateur, at Plainfield C.C. in New Jersey. Cook, a three-time All-American at Ohio State, was in the midst of a sensational amateur career. He won the 1974 World Juniors, finished runner-up in the 1979 U.S. Amateur, and helped the Buckeyes to the 1979 NCAA title.

John Cook

Bradley Finishes a Distant Second to Lopez

While Nancy Lopez stole the LPGA Tour headlines in 1978, Pat Bradley quietly finished second on the money list with $118,057—$71,756 behind Lopez. Bradley won three official events including the Lady Keystone Open, ending Nancy's five-tournament winning streak.

Pat Bradley

• November 5: Tom Watson again leads the PGA Tour in wins (five) and earnings ($362,429). He wins his second straight Vardon Trophy (70.16) and Player of the Year Award.

• November 5: Jack Nicklaus's three 1978 PGA Tour victories give him 17 consecutive years with at least

one victory, tying Arnold Palmer's record.

• November 12: Nancy Lopez wins her ninth LPGA event, the Colgate Far East Open in Malaysia.

• November 12: Nancy Lopez leads the LPGA Tour in wins (nine) and earnings (a record $189,814). She

wins the Vare Trophy with a record average of 71.76 and is named LPGA Player of the Year and Rookie of the Year.

• December 3: The United States wins the World Cup Match at Princeville Maka G.C. in Hawaii by 10 strokes over Australia. John Mahaffey wins the individual title.

LEGENDS OF GOLF SOWS SEEDS FOR SENIOR TOUR

Starting in the early 1970s, Fred Raphael, who produced the *Shell's Wonderful World of Golf* television series in the previous decade, began trying to sell a new project. Called the Legends of Golf, it would bring together the game's greats of the past, all of them 50 years and older, for a competition.

It took a few years of talking, but Raphael finally found a buyer, NBC, and in 1978 the Legends was born. Originally, Raphael was planning a taped series of seven shows, but NBC wanted the drama of a live tournament, so that's what it got. Little did anyone know that the success of the Legends of Golf would lead to an entire tour for senior pros.

The first Legends, won by Sam Snead and Gardner Dickinson, was a success, but it was the second event, in 1979, and its memorable playoff, that really sparked the explosion of senior golf. The protagonists were the teams of Roberto De Vicenzo, age 56, and Julius Boros, 59, against Tommy Bolt, 61, and Art Wall, 55. They had tied with best-ball totals of 15-under-par at Onion Creek Country Club in Austin, Texas. The playoff started with

pars for both teams on the 15th hole, but then things got wild.

De Vicenzo and Wall matched birdies on the 16th. Then De Vicenzo and Bolt both birdied the 17th. At the 18th, it was another pair of birdies for De Vicenzo and Bolt. They returned to the 15th, a demanding par-4 of 440 yards. Remarkably, De Vicenzo and Bolt birdied yet again, the fourth straight hole the teams had halved with birdies. Would it ever end? Finally, on the 17th, Wall and Bolt missed birdie tries, while De Vicenzo rolled in a five-footer for his fifth straight birdie (teammate Boros had done his part in regulation—he birdied the final hole to get them into the sudden-death affair).

The survival of the tournament was assured. Raphael had been able to come up with the $400,000 purse for the first two Legends events thanks only to generous contributions by NBC in the first year and the host club, Onion Creek, in the second. The playoff drama convinced Liberty Mutual to come aboard as sponsor for future years.

Even more, the quality of play in the playoff convinced people that these old golfers still had considerable skills—and that there was an audience for them. Soon, the Legends had company. The PGA Tour sponsored two senior events of its own in 1980, and the USGA started the U.S. Senior Open in the same year.

The timing was perfect, because the game's most popular player, Arnold Palmer, turned 50 in September 1979 and joined the new tour in its inaugural season. By 1985, the Senior PGA Tour was a powerful force in the game, with 27 events for a total purse of $6 million; by 1990, it had grown to 42 events and $18 million. The seniors who pocketed that cash owe thanks to Fred Raphael, and to the quartet of players who produced a playoff for the ages.

1979

• January: PGA Tour players are scheduled to play in 46 events with a total season purse of $12,801,200.

• January: LPGA Tour players are scheduled to play in 38 events with a total season purse of $4,400,000.

• January: Nancy Lopez marries sportscaster Tim Melton.

• January: The PGA Tour adopts a "one-ball rule," meaning players must play the same brand and type of ball for the entire round. The rule stops the practice of switching from a wound ball to a two-piece ball to gain an advantage on certain shots.

• February: 20th Century-Fox Film Corp. buys Pebble Beach G.L. and

other Monterey Peninsula properties for $71 million.

• February 5: Lon Hinkle wins the Bing Crosby National Pro-Am despite squandering a five-stroke lead with a 77 in the final round. He beats Mark Hayes and Andy Bean in a playoff.

1979

Roberto De Vicenzo played the key role in the 1979 Legends of Golf—the thrilling, nationally televised event that sparked the interest in seniors golf. The best-ball tournament, pitting De Vicenzo and Julius Boros vs. Tommy Bolt and Art Wall, went into sudden-death. De Vicenzo birdied five straight extra holes for the victory.

• March: PGA Tour headquarters moves from Chevy Chase, Maryland, to Ponte Vedra, Florida.

• March: TaylorMade introduces its first metal wood, triggering a new trend.

• March 25: Lanny Wadkins wins the Tournament Players Champi-onship in high winds at Sawgrass. The field averages 78.46 on Sunday, but Wadkins shoots a 72—283 to win by five.

• April 8: Raymond Floyd comes from six strokes behind in the final round to win the Greater Greensboro Open.

• April 8: Sandra Post wins her second consecutive Colgate-Dinah Shore Winners Circle, beating Nancy Lopez by one stroke.

• April 15: Fuzzy Zoeller wins the Masters in a playoff over Ed Sneed and Tom Watson on the second extra hole. Sneed bogeyed the last three holes to fall into a tie.

Pebble Beach Golf Links

Pebble Beach Area Sold for $71 Million

Pictured is the par-5 18th hole of Pebble Beach G.L., which plays along the rocky cliffs of the Pacific Ocean. In 1979, 20th Century-Fox Film Corp. bought Pebble Beach and other properties in Monterey Peninsula for $71 million. It was a pretty good deal. Ten years later, the Pebble Beach properties were sold to a Japanese company for $841 million.

Post Beats Lopez in Dinah Shore

Canada's Sandra Post, who won the 1978 Colgate-Dinah Shore Winners Circle, was surprised when she arrived at 1979's event. It had been customary for the champion to grace the cover of the tournament program and team with Dinah in the pro-am. But in '79, Nancy Lopez received both honors. Post got revenge, though, by beating Lopez by a stroke.

Sandra Post

Nelson Rises to No. 2 on Money List

Larry Nelson won the 1979 Jackie Gleason's Inverrary Classic for his first Tour victory. Nelson also won the '79 Western Open and lost a playoff in the Danny Thomas Memphis Classic. Nelson, a grinder his first five years on Tour, made the 1979 Ryder Cup team and finished No. 2 on the money list—the only top-five showing of his career.

Larry Nelson

• April 22: Tom Watson wins the MONY Tournament of Champions by six strokes.

• April 29: Roberto De Vicenzo and Julius Boros make five birdies in a six-hole, sudden-death playoff to win the Legends of Golf over Tommy Bolt and Art Wall.

• May 20: Nancy Lopez wins the Coca-Cola Classic in a five-way playoff over Bonnie Bryant, Hollis Stacy, Mickey Wright, and Jo Ann Washam.

• May 26: Gary Hallberg of Wake Forest wins the NCAA championship.

• May 27: Tom Watson wins the Memorial Tournament, his fourth win in eight starts. He shot 69 in a frigid, rainy, second round, a day when 42 players didn't break 80.

• May 31: The United States wins the Walker Cup over Great Britain/Ireland, 15½-8½, at Muirfield in Scotland.

1979

Sneed Bogies the Last Three Holes to Blow Masters

Ed Sneed smacks this chip far right of the flag on the 72nd hole of the 1979 Masters. Sneed bogied this hole, plus the two preceding it, to fall into a playoff with Tom Watson and eventual champion Fuzzy Zoeller. Sneed, who would win four small Tour events in his career, missed his one shot at real glory.

Ed Sneed, Fuzzy Zoeller, Tom Watson

Zoeller Wins Masters in Sudden-Death Playoff

Tom Watson has a few kind words to say about Fuzzy Zoeller, who just defeated him and Ed Sneed *(standing)* in the 1979 Masters. The three finished at 280, and then Zoeller won with a birdie on the second hole of sudden-death. Earlier in the year, the Fuzz claimed his first Tour victory at the Wickes-Andy Williams San Diego Open.

Ed Sneed

• June 3: Jerry McGee opens with a 61 and wins the Kemper Open.

• June 3: Nancy Lopez wins the Golden Lights Championship, her fifth win in nine events.

• June 10: Donna Caponi wins the LPGA Championship by three strokes over Jerilyn Britz.

• June 10: Andy Bean shoots a third-round 61 and wins the Atlanta Classic by eight strokes at 23-under-par 265.

• June 14: In the first round of the U.S. Open at the Inverness Club in Toledo, Ohio, Lon Hinkle plays the 8th hole by going up the 17th fairway.

• June 15: On the 8th hole at the Inverness Club, the USGA plants a tree overnight to prevent anymore shortcuts.

• June 17: Hale Irwin wins the U.S. Open with an even-par 284. After rounds of 68-67, Irwin closes with a 75 to win by two over Gary Player and Jerry Pate.

Hale Irwin

Irwin Sputters to Victory in U.S. Open

Hale Irwin hung on to win the 1979 U.S. Open, shooting 74-68-67-75—284 at the Inverness Club in Toledo, Ohio. After three rounds, Irwin led the field by three strokes. On the back nine on Sunday, he posted a 40 despite an eagle on 13. Nevertheless, Irwin won by two strokes over runners-up Gary Player and Jerry Pate for his second of three U.S. Open titles.

Bruce Edwards, Tom Watson

USGA's New Tree Blocks Hinkle's Shortcut

Pictured is the most famous tree in sports history. The 1979 U.S. Open was held at the Inverness Club in Toledo, Ohio, and during the first round Lon Hinkle took a shortcut. He cut the dogleg on the par-5 8th hole by hitting onto the 17th fairway. Overnight, USGA officials planted this tree to block the shortcut.

Tree at Inverness Club

Despite Cold Weather, Watson Stays Hot

Tom Watson walks off with his caddie after winning the 1979 Memorial Tournament. Watson had shot a 69 in the frigid second round, when the wind-chill factor dipped to 13 degrees and most players struggled just to break 80. For the third year in a row, Watson led the Tour in wins (five) and earnings (a record $462,636). He also won his third straight Vardon Trophy and Player of the Year Award.

• June 24: Lee Trevino wins his third Canadian Open.

• July 1: Gil Morgan wins the Danny Thomas Memphis Classic by sinking a 60-footer in sudden-death.

• July 8: Larry Nelson wins the Western Open in a playoff over Ben Crenshaw.

• July 15: Jerilyn Britz wins the U.S. Women's Open with an even-par 284 at the Brooklawn C.C. in Fairfield, Connecticut.

• July 22: Seve Ballesteros, age 22, becomes the youngest winner of the British Open since the turn of the century. He wins by three strokes at Royal Lytham.

• July 22: Sam Snead, 67, becomes the first player to shoot his age in a PGA Tour event, the Quad Cities Open. He shoots a 67 in the second round and a 66 in the fourth round.

• July 29: Amy Alcott wins the Peter Jackson Classic in the first year the Canadian event is designated a major by the LPGA.

Seve Ballesteros

Ballesteros Wins British for First Major Title

Seve Ballesteros, age 22, captured his first major championship by winning the 1979 British Open, at Royal Lytham & St. Annes in England. Seve's 283 beat Jack Nicklaus and Ben Crenshaw by three strokes. On the 70th hole, Ballesteros hit a wild tee shot into a nearby car park, yet he reached the green in regulation and wound up birdieing the hole.

Arnold Palmer

Palmer Turns 50, Ready for Senior Golf

The most important event Arnold Palmer attended in 1979 was his birthday party. Palmer, who won just $9,276 on the '79 PGA Tour, turned 50 years old on September 10 and thus became eligible for the senior tournaments that would soon arise. The Senior Tour would get a big boost from Arnie's enormous drawing power.

Sam Snead

Snead Shoots His Age, 67, Then Betters It

Sam Snead, in his 43rd and final year on the PGA Tour, added one more feather to his straw hat in the 1979 Quad Cities Open. In the second round, Snead became the first golfer to equal his age in a PGA Tour event, as he shot 67. Two days later, he fired a 66. Snead credited his longevity to clean living and an unending love for the game.

• July 29: Sam Trahan sets a PGA Tour record for fewest putts in a round with 18 in the final round of the IVB-Philadelphia Classic. He finishes 72nd in the tournament.

• August: Louise Suggs and Walter J. Travis are inducted into the World Golf Hall of Fame.

• August 5: David Graham wins the PGA Championship in sudden-death over Ben Crenshaw at Oakland Hills C.C. in Birmingham, Michigan. Graham shoots a final-round 65.

• September 2: Mark O'Meara beats defending champion John Cook in the final of the U.S. Amateur at Canterbury G.C. in Cleveland.

• September 10: Arnold Palmer turns 50 years old.

• September 16: The United States wins the Ryder Cup, 17-11, at the Greenbrier in White Sulphur Springs, West Virginia. It is the first year Europeans are added to the Great Britain/Ireland side.

Jerilyn Britz

Graham Outshines Crenshaw in PGA Playoff

For the third straight year, the PGA Championship went to sudden-death, and David Graham won the 1979 version at Oakland Hills C.C. in Birmingham, Michigan. In the final round, Graham shot a sensational 65, marred only by a double bogey on the 18th hole. David then defeated Ben Crenshaw with a birdie on the third extra hole.

Former Teacher Britz Claims Women's Open

Jerilyn Britz closed 69—284 to win the 1979 U.S. Women's Open, at Brooklawn C.C. in Fairfield, Connecticut. Britz, a former teacher who joined the LPGA Tour at age 30, defeated Debbie Massey and Sandra Palmer by two strokes. On Sunday, Massey strung together birdies on holes 15–17, but then double bogied the 18th hole.

David Graham

- September 23: Rookie John Fought wins the Anheuser-Busch Classic after taking the Buick Open a week earlier. He never wins again on the PGA Tour.

- September 28: Nancy Lopez sets an LPGA record with 10 birdies in the second round of the Mary Kay Classic.

- September 30: Lon Hinkle wins the World Series of Golf with a score of 272.

- October 7: Lou Graham wins the San Antonio-Texas Open, his third victory in 11 weeks. He had won three in 14 previous years on Tour, and he'll never win again.

- October 21: Tom Watson leads the PGA Tour money list with $462,636, about $180,000 ahead of second-place Larry Nelson. His five victories also top the Tour.

- October 21: Tom Watson is named PGA Player of the Year and wins the Vardon Trophy with a 70.27 scoring average.

O'Meara Thumps Cook in U.S. Amateur

Mark O'Meara blew away defending champion John Cook, 8 & 7, in the final of the 1979 U.S. Amateur, at Canterbury G.C. in Cleveland. O'Meara, a Long Beach State student, played sensational golf in the final match, reaching 24 of the 29 greens in regulation. O'Meara would become PGA Tour Rookie of the Year in 1981.

Nancy Lopez

Lopez Records Another Record-Breaking Season

By 1979, a few LPGA Tour players had grown tired of all of the praise heaped on Nancy Lopez, although Nancy's sister shows her support here with a kiss on the cheek. Lopez deserved all of the accolades in '79, as she won eight events, set a Tour record for earnings ($197,488), and broke her own record for scoring average (71.20).

Mark O'Meara

• October 21: Jack Nicklaus's streak of 17 consecutive years with a victory ends, leaving him tied for the record with Arnold Palmer.

• November 3: Nancy Lopez finishes the season with eight LPGA victories, giving her 17 in her first two full years on Tour.

• November 3: Amy Alcott and Jane Blalock tie for second in LPGA victories with four each.

• November 3: Nancy Lopez leads in earnings with $197,488, wins the Vare Trophy with a scoring average of 71.20, and is the LPGA Player of the Year.

• November 6: Chick Evans, the winner of the 1916 and 1920 U.S. Amateur and 1916 U.S. Open, dies at age 89.

• December 18: Don January, just 26 days past his 50th birthday, wins the PGA Seniors Championship by eight strokes.

'OVER THE HILL' NICKLAUS CAPTURES U.S. OPEN

On January 21, 1980, Jack Nicklaus turned 40 years old. He was coming off his worst season, by far, since joining the PGA Tour in 1962: After finishing no worse than fourth on the money list in his first 17 seasons, he dropped to 71st in 1979, going winless for the first time. Were his skills declining to the point where he was no longer a serious threat to add to his 15 major professional titles? Had he reached a point where he was no longer driven to be the best?

During the 1980 season, Nicklaus answered a resounding "no" to those questions. The 1979 slump, combined with turning 40, had given him a determination to prove he wasn't over the hill. And at the U.S. Open at Baltusrol Golf Club in Springfield, New Jersey, he showed he was still a major performer.

Nicklaus had won the 1967 U.S. Open at Baltusrol with a record total of 275. Thirteen years later, he broke that mark with a 272, holding at least a share of the lead after each round. In 1980's first round, he also tied the 18-hole U.S. Open record of 63. But the victory didn't come easily.

Japan's Isao Aoki, paired with Nicklaus for all 72 holes, put up such a pitched battle that Nicklaus needed a birdie-birdie finish to win by two strokes.

At the outset of this event, Nicklaus was pressed by Tom Weiskopf, who also opened with an Open-record 63. Nicklaus putted better than he had in years, though he did fail on a four-foot birdie attempt on the 18th hole which would have given him a 62. Weiskopf quickly fell back, leaving Aoki to pick up the chase. After three rounds, Aoki's 68-68-68 had matched Nicklaus's 63-71-70. Lon Hinkle was one stroke back, while Tom Watson and others were two behind.

But the final round evolved into a Nicklaus-Aoki duel. Nicklaus grabbed a two-stroke lead after nine holes despite a 1-over-par 35. On the back nine, Nicklaus hit every fairway and every green to finish with a 2-under 68. But Aoki stayed on his heels. The final two holes at Baltusrol were par-5s, the 17th a monstrous 630-yarder. Aoki, trailing by two strokes, hit his third shot to within five feet of the stick. Nicklaus kept him at bay by holing a 20-footer for a birdie that preserved the two-stroke margin. On the 543-yard 18th, Aoki nearly pitched in for an eagle, but Nicklaus again matched Aoki's birdie. The scoreboard by the 18th green carried an appropriate message: "JACK IS BACK."

Nicklaus proved it again two months later at the PGA Championship at Oak Hill Country Club in Rochester, New York. With a 6-under-par 274, he coasted to a seven-stroke win over Andy Bean, becoming the first player since Ben Hogan in 1948 to sweep the U.S. Open and PGA. In a year where Tom Watson won six PGA Tour events plus the British Open, Jack Nicklaus stole the show.

1980

- January: PGA Tour players are scheduled to play in 45 events for a total season purse of $13,371,786.

- January: LPGA Tour players are scheduled to play in 40 events for a total season purse of $5,150,000.

- January: The PGA Tour schedules two events for senior players, the beginning of what will become the Senior PGA Tour. The USGA schedules the first U.S. Senior Open.

- January: The PGA Tour begins compiling statistics in categories such as driving distance, driving accuracy, greens in regulation, putting, etc.

- January 13: Craig Stadler wins the PGA Tour-opening Bob Hope Desert Classic, his first Tour victory.

- March 2: With temperatures in the 30s and winds gusting to 40 mph, Dave Eichelberger shoots a 74 in the final round to win the Bay Hill Classic.

1980

Jack Nicklaus, age 40, won the 1980 U.S. Open at Baltusrol G.C. in New Jersey, setting the U.S. Open scoring record. Jack shot 63-71-70-68—272 to break the record of 275, which he himself set in 1967 on the same course. Isao Aoki, paired with Nicklaus for all four rounds of the '80 Open, finished in second place, two shots back.

• March 9: Johnny Miller wins Jackie Gleason's Inverrary Classic.

• March 16: Raymond Floyd chips in to beat Jack Nicklaus in sudden-death at the Doral-Eastern Open.

• March 16: JoAnne Carner wins the Honda Civic Classic, her fourth win in six starts and second in a row.

• March 23: Lee Trevino wins the Tournament Players Championship by one stroke over Ben Crenshaw.

• April 6: Craig Stadler wins by six at the Greater Greensboro Open.

• April 6: Donna Caponi Young wins the Colgate-Dinah Shore Winners Circle.

• April 10: Tom Weiskopf makes a 13 at the par-3 12th during the first round of the Masters.

• April 13: Spain's Seve Ballesteros runs away with the Masters, leading by 10 strokes with nine holes to play and winning by four. Gibby Gilbert and Jack Newton finish second.

Craig Stadler

Stadler Wins the Hope for First Pro Title

Craig Stadler holds his ball up high after winning his first pro tournament, the 1980 Bob Hope Desert Classic. He earned $50,000 and a new car. It was a sweet victory for Stadler, an accomplished amateur golfer who struggled during his first four years on Tour, 1976–79. Stadler later won the 1980 Greater Greensboro Open.

Bill Murray in Caddyshack

Eichelberger Wins Chilly Bay Hill

Dave Eichelberger won the 1980 Bay Hill Classic in frigid conditions at the Bay Hill Club in Orlando. During the final round, temperatures dipped into the 30s and winds reached 40 mph. Eichelberger closed 74—279 for the title.

Dave Eichelberger

Murray, Rodney Yuck It Up in Caddyshack

Bill Murray plea-bargains with a gopher during the 1980 film *Caddyshack*. This was perhaps the most popular golf movie of all time. It was certainly the funniest, with Murray, Chevy Chase, Ted Knight, and Rodney Dangerfield at their wackiest. The film's plot, though, was flimsy; it mostly poked fun at the WASPy country club set.

• April 20: Tom Watson prevails in the MONY Tournament of Champions.

• April 27: Tommy Bolt and Art Wall, playoff losers a year ago, win the Legends of Golf.

• May 4: At the Michelob-Houston Open, Curtis Strange blows a six- stroke lead in the final round, then wins a sudden-death playoff over Lee Trevino.

• May 11: Tom Watson wins the Byron Nelson Classic, his third win in three starts and fifth of the year.

• May 25: David Graham makes a 30-foot putt for birdie on the 72nd hole to beat Tom Watson by one stroke at the Memorial Tournament.

• May 31: Jay Don Blake of Utah State wins the NCAA championship in a playoff over Hal Sutton of Centenary.

• June 1: John Mahaffey wins the first Kemper Open at its new home,

Donna Caponi

Red-Hot Caponi Begins Two-Year Winning Spree

Donna Caponi captured the 1980 Colgate Dinah Shore Winner's Circle, one of five LPGA tournaments she won in 1980 and one of 10 she claimed from March 1980 through October 1981. These would also be the last victories for Caponi, as she never was the same after undergoing knee surgery in 1982.

JoAnne Carner

Carner Wins Five in "Off" Year

Most every recount of JoAnne Carner's prolific career glosses over her exploits of 1980. It was one of the few years that she didn't capture a major championship, set a significant record, or receive a national award. Nevertheless, she did win five LPGA tournaments, plus she set a personal record with $185,916.

Graham Wins a Thriller at Memorial

David Graham won the 1980 Memorial Tournament in spectacular fashion, holing a 30-footer for birdie in the final to defeat Tom Watson by a stroke. Throughout his career, the Australian Graham won numerous tournaments around the world. In 1980 alone, he won the Mexican Open, Rolex Japan, and Brazilian Classic.

David Graham

Congressional C.C. in Bethesda, Maryland.

• June 7: The United States defeats Great Britain/Ireland in the Curtis Cup, 13-5.

• June 8: Sally Little wins the LPGA Championship by three strokes over Jane Blalock.

• June 14: Patty Sheehan of San Jose State wins the AIAW championship.

• June 15: Jack Nicklaus holds off Isao Aoki to win the U.S. Open at Baltusrol G.C. in New Jersey.

• June 22: Don January wins the Atlantic City Senior, the first senior event run by the PGA Tour.

• June 29: Roberto De Vicenzo wins the U.S. Senior Open at Winged Foot G.C. in Mamaroneck, New York.

• July 6: Scott Simpson takes his first PGA Tour victory, the Western Open, on greens made brown and bumpy by a disease at Butler National G.C.

Nancy Lopez

Lopez Reaches 20th Victory in Third Season

Nancy Lopez won three LPGA tournaments in 1980, giving her 20 for her first three seasons, and earned a personal high of $209,078. She also captured the 1980 JCPenney Classic with Curtis Strange. As in every other year of her career, Lopez came up empty in the U.S. Women's Open, closing with a 77 to finish 14 shots out.

Seve Ballesteros

Seve Becomes the Youngest to Win Masters

Spain's Seve Ballesteros won the 1980 Masters with an impressive score of 275, four shots better than runners-up Gibby Gilbert and Jack Newton. Ballesteros, winner of the 1979 British Open, became the youngest Masters champion ever, winning just four days after his 23rd birthday. Seve would try on the green jacket again in 1983.

• July 13: Amy Alcott wins the U.S. Women's Open by nine strokes at Richland C.C. in Nashville.

• July 19: Jodie Mudd wins the U.S. Amateur Public Links championship.

• July 19: Isao Aoki ties the British Open's 18-hole record with a 63 at Muirfield in the third round.

• July 20: Tom Watson wins the British Open by four strokes over Lee Trevino.

• July 27: Howard Twitty goes six extra holes to defeat Jim Simons at the Greater Hartford Open.

• August 10: Jack Nicklaus wins the PGA Championship by seven strokes at Oak Hill C.C. in Rochester, New York.

• August 10: Pat Bradley wins the Peter Jackson Classic at St. George's Golf & C.C. in Toronto.

• August 16: Juli Simpson Inkster wins the U.S. Women's Amateur four weeks after her wedding.

1980

Roberto De Vicenzo

De Vicenzo Wins the First U.S. Senior Open

Roberto De Vicenzo *(right)* captured the inaugural U.S. Senior Open in 1980, shooting 285 to win by four shots at Winged Foot G.C. in Mamaroneck, New York. The USGA decided to sponsor the championship after the recent swell of interest in senior golf. The Open, for golfers 55 and older, was televised nationally the last two days.

Hal Sutton

Mahaffey Wins Kemper Open at Congressional

John Mahaffey watches his putt roll toward the cup on the 72nd hole of the 1980 Kemper Open. The ball dropped in for birdie, and he won the tournament with a score of 275, 13-under-par. The Kemper was played for the first time at Congressional C.C. in Bethesda, Maryland, the course that U.S. Presidents and Senators have called home.

John Mahaffey

Sutton Romps to Victory in U.S. Amateur

Hal Sutton shoots out of a bunker during the 1980 U.S. Amateur, at the C.C. of North Carolina at Pinehurst. Sutton, a 22-year-old from Shreveport, Louisiana, trounced Bob Lewis Jr. in the final, 9 & 8. Sutton would qualify for the PGA Tour in 1981, win a Tour event in 1982, and win the PGA Championship in 1983.

• August 17: Arnold Palmer wins the Canadian PGA Championship, which is not a PGA Tour event, over Isao Aoki and Gary Player. It will be his last victory in a non-senior event.

• August 24: Tom Watson finishes 65-65 to win the World Series of Golf by two strokes over Raymond Floyd.

• August 31: Hal Sutton wallops Bob Lewis, 9 & 8, in the final of the U.S. Amateur at the C.C. of North Carolina in Pinehurst.

• September: Henry Cotton and Lawson Little are inducted into the World Golf Hall of Fame in Pinehurst, North Carolina.

• September 7: Beth Daniel beats a 12-player field in the inaugural World Championship of Women's Golf.

• September 14: With a fifth-place finish at the United Virginia Bank Classic, Beth Daniel becomes the first LPGA player ever to surpass $200,000 in earnings in a season.

Beth Daniel

Daniel Named LPGA Tour's Player of the Year

Beth Daniel earned the LPGA Tour's Player of the Year Award in 1980. The 23-year-old won four tournaments, including the Chevrolet World Championship of Women's Golf. She also became the first Tour player to reach $200,000 in season earnings, and she led the circuit with $231,000.

Aoki Puts Three of the Game's Superstars to the Test

Isao Aoki made three Hall of Famers sweat a little in 1980. In the U.S. Open, Aoki battled Jack Nicklaus for four rounds before succumbing to Jack by two strokes. Isao shot a 63 in the third round of the British Open, although Tom Watson won the crown. Also, Aoki finished runner-up to Arnold Palmer in the Canadian PGA Championship.

Isao Aoki

• September 28: Ben Crenshaw wins the Anheuser-Busch Classic. He had finished second six times since his last victory in January 1979.

• October: The Tournament Players Club at Sawgrass opens in Ponte Vedra, Florida. The first "stadium course" will host the Tournament Players Championship.

• October 12: Tom Watson leads the PGA Tour money list with $530,808. He is named PGA Player of the Year.

• October 12: Tom Watson finishes the year with six PGA Tour victories, plus the British Open. Lee Trevino has three wins.

• October 12: Lee Trevino wins the Vardon Trophy, averaging 69.73.

• October 19: Brothers Danny and David Edwards win the Walt Disney World National Team title.

• October 19: Sandy Lyle leads the European Tour money list for the second year in a row.

1980

Amy Alcott

Alcott's Red-Hot in the U.S. Women's Open

Amy Alcott put on a heroic performance to win the 1980 U.S. Women's Open, at Richland C.C. in Nashville. Despite 100-degree temperatures each day, Alcott shot 280 to win by nine strokes and break the Open record by four shots. Alcott, a youthful 24 and from Southern California, was able to handle the heat better than others.

Tom Watson

Sally Little

Little Wins by Three at LPGA

Sally Little barely missed this shot on the 17th hole of Jack Nicklaus G.C. in Ohio, but she could smile anyway. On the next hole, Little wrapped up her first major, the LPGA Championship, by a three-stroke margin. In her career, Little won one LPGA, one Dinah Shore, and one du Maurier.

Watson's British Victory One of Seven Total Wins

Tom Watson raises his arms in victory after winning the 1980 British Open, his third, with a score of 271 at windswept Muirfield in Scotland. This was the greatest of all seasons for Watson, as he also won six PGA Tour events, including the World Series of Golf, and led in earnings for the fourth straight year.

• October 19: Pat Bradley wins $50,000 in the first J&B Gold Putter Award Putt-Off in Las Vegas.

• November 9: Beth Daniel leads the LPGA money list with $231,000. She is the LPGA Player of the Year.

• November 9: Amy Alcott wins the Vare Trophy, averaging 71.51.

• November 9: Donna Caponi and JoAnne Carner finish with five LPGA victories, Beth Daniel and Amy Alcott with four, and Nancy Lopez with three.

• November 16: Charlie Sifford wins the Suntree Classic in Melbourn, Florida. It's the second of the year's two official Senior PGA Tour events.

• December 7: Arnold Palmer wins the PGA Seniors Championship at Turnberry Isle C.C. in North Miami, Florida. It's Palmer's first win as a senior.

• December 14: Nancy Lopez and Curtis Strange win the JCPenney Mixed Team Classic.

ROGERS GOES ON WORLDWIDE WINNING SPREE

In six years on the PGA Tour, Bill Rogers had developed a reputation as a steady player, but not as a winner. He had captured only one event, the 1978 Bob Hope Desert Classic, and in 1979 he finished sixth on the money list without a Tour victory. His sole win that year was at the Suntory World Match Play in England. Apparently, he was saving it up for one glorious year.

Rogers won three PGA Tour events in 1981 and was fifth on the money list with $315,411, but that was only part of the story. He also won the British Open, one tournament in Japan, and two in Australia for a total of seven victories worldwide. Six of those wins came in a whirlwind four-month span from July through November, where Rogers jetted around the world and seemingly won wherever he traveled.

The year got off to a slow start, with Rogers missing the cut in five of six events during one stretch. His game returned at the Sea Pines Heritage Classic, where he built a six-stroke lead during the final round and hung on to win by one. In June, he tied for second, three strokes behind David Graham, at the U.S. Open.

Rogers's biggest triumph—and the only major title of his career—came at the British Open, which was held at Royal St. George's Golf Club in Sandwich, England. He shot rounds of 66 and 67 on Friday and Saturday to take a five-stroke lead after 54 holes. In the final round, a double bogey on the par-5 7th cut his margin to a single stroke over Bernhard Langer. But birdies on the 9th and 10th sent Rogers on his way to a 71 and a four-stroke triumph. At 4-under 276, he was the only player to break par on the rugged links.

A month later, Rogers started an amazing end-of-the-year run. He won five of his last eight events, finishing second, third, and fourth in the other three. It started at the World Series of Golf, where Rogers shot a final-round 67 to hold off Tom Kite, the year's other hot player (Kite had 21 top-10 finishes but only one victory), by one stroke. Rogers then won the Suntory Open in Japan, the Texas Open on the PGA Tour, the New South Wales Open, and the Australian Open. During that time, Rogers traveled from the U.S. to Japan, back to the U.S., to England, to Japan, to Australia, back to the U.S., and to Australia again, with a final stop-off in New Zealand before returning to the U.S. for the off-season.

Alas, that hectic schedule may be one reason Rogers was never the same again. Worn down, he had a mediocre year in 1982. Then his swing left him, he lost confidence, and, he says, the game ceased to be fun. Rogers would win only once more, at the 1983 USF&G Classic. From 1984 on, he didn't even rank among the top 100 money winners, and he quit the Tour after 1988 to become a club pro. He had packed nearly all of his success into one calendar year.

1981

- January: PGA Tour players are scheduled to play in 45 events with a total purse of $14,175,393.

- January: LPGA Tour players are scheduled to play in 40 events with a total purse of $5,800,000.

- January: The Senior PGA Tour now totals five events.

- January 11: Johnny Miller wins the season-opening Joe Garagiola-Tucson Open, his fourth career victory in Tucson.

- February 2: John Cook wins a five-way playoff at the Bing Crosby National Pro-Am, which is cut to 54 holes and finishes on Monday due to bad weather.

- February 22: Johnny Miller takes his second victory of the year at the Glen Campbell Los Angeles Open.

- March 8: Tom Kite wins the American Motors Inverrary Classic by one stroke over Jack Nicklaus. Nicklaus misses a four-foot par putt on the final hole.

In 1981, from August 30 on, Bill Rogers won five tournaments in eight events entered. He won in the United States (World Series of Golf, Texas Open), Japan (Suntory Open), and Australia (New South Wales Open, Australian Open). He didn't do too badly in the other three events either, finishing second, third, and fourth.

• March 22: Raymond Floyd wins the Tournament Players Championship and a $250,000 bonus for winning the Doral-Eastern Open and TPC back-to-back.

• April 5: Larry Nelson chips in on the 72nd hole to tie Mark Hayes, then wins in sudden-death at the Greater Greensboro Open.

• April 5: Nancy Lopez closes fast to win the Colgate-Dinah Shore with a final-round 64.

• April 12: Tom Watson wins the Masters, beating Jack Nicklaus and Johnny Miller by two strokes.

• April 19: Lee Trevino wins the MONY Tournament of Champions.

• April 19: Beth Daniel wins a five-way playoff at the Florida Lady Citrus. Amateur Patti Rizzo is one of the losers.

• April 26: Gene Littler and Bob Rosburg win the Liberty Mutual Legends of Golf at Onion Creek C.C. in Austin, Texas.

1981

Nancy Lopez

Lopez Closes Strong to Claim Dinah Shore

Nancy Lopez won the 1981 Colgate Dinah Shore, closing 64—277 to beat out Carolyn Hill by two strokes. Lopez had shot 277 in the tournament in 1979 but fell one stroke short. This was not a major championship victory for Lopez, as the Dinah Shore wasn't declared a major until 1983.

Johnny Miller, Dean Wendt

Miller Wins a Pair of Events Early in the Year

Johnny Miller yawns before teeing off in the rain-delayed Bing Crosby National Pro-Am. Amateur Dean Wendt *(right)* had a hot partner in Miller. Three weeks earlier, Johnny won the Joe Garagiola-Tucson Open. Three weeks later, he would capture the Los Angeles Open. He would also finish runner-up in the Masters.

• May 10: Bruce Lietzke beats Tom Watson in a playoff to win the Byron Nelson Classic, ending Watson's string of three straight wins in the event.

• May 17: Kathy Whitworth gets her first victory in three years, the Coca-Cola Classic, moving within one of Mickey Wright's 82 victories.

• June 14: Donna Caponi wins the LPGA Championship for the second time in three years.

• June 21: David Graham shoots a nearly flawless 67 in the final round to pass George Burns and win the U.S. Open at Merion G.C. in Ardmore, Pennsylvania.

• June 28: Jerry Pate ends a winless drought of nearly three years at the Danny Thomas Memphis Classic. He jumps into a lake to celebrate.

• July 5: Jan Stephenson wins the Peter Jackson Classic.

• July 13: Arnold Palmer wins the U.S. Senior Open in an 18-hole

1981

Ray Floyd

Floyd Cashes In with Back-to-Back Victories

Raymond Floyd studies a putt in the rain at the 1981 Doral-Eastern Open. Floyd struck it rich in a two-week stretch, winning at Doral and then capturing the lucrative Tournament Players Championship. On top of that, he received a $250,000 bonus for winning the two Florida events back-to-back.

Watson Still Going Strong, Wins Masters

After winning four consecutive Player of the Year Awards, Tom Watson cooled off—slightly—in 1981. He did capture a major championship, his second Masters, by two strokes over Jack Nicklaus and Johnny Miller, and he won two other events. Watson finished third on the money list and also led in a statistical category—sand saves.

Donna Caponi

Caponi Nabs LPGA with a Birdie on Final Hole

Donna Caponi smiles after holing a birdie putt on the 72nd hole to win the 1981 LPGA Championship. Caponi, Jerilyn Britz, and Pat Meyers were all tied going into the final hole, but Britz and Meyers both parred to finish a stroke back. Caponi won five events in 1981 and became the third LPGA player to reach $1 million in career earnings.

Tom Watson

playoff over Billy Casper and Bob Stone at Oakland Hills C.C. in Birmingham, Michigan.

• July 17: Jack Nicklaus follows an opening 83 at the British Open with a 66 in the second round.

• July 19: In the British Open at Royal St. George's G.C. in

Sandwich, England, Bill Rogers is the only player to break par for four rounds. His 4-under 276 wins by four strokes.

• July 19: At the Quad Cities Open, Dave Barr outlasts four playoff foes to win on the eighth hole of sudden-death.

• July 25: Kathy Whitworth, who has never won a U.S. Women's Open, leads this year's Open after three rounds at LaGrange C.C. in LaGrange, Illinois.

• July 26: Pat Bradley wins the U.S. Women's Open by outdueling Beth Daniel, 66-68, in the final round.

1981

Jerry Pate

Pate Takes a Swim After Winning in Memphis

Jerry Pate does a perfect swan dive into a lake near the 18th green at Colonial C.C., the site of his victory in the 1981 Danny Thomas Memphis Classic. Pate had said if he won the tournament, he would "bathe in victory," and he made good on his promise. Two of Pate's favorite hobbies, by the way, are fishing and water skiing.

David Graham

Graham Heats Up on Sunday to Win U.S. Open

Australian David Graham rejoices after winning the 1981 U.S. Open, at Merion G.C. in Ardmore, Pennsylvania. Graham, down by three strokes to George Burns after 54 holes, closed with a 67 to win by three. His 273 total was one off the U.S. Open record, and he became the first foreign player to win the title since Tony Jacklin in 1970.

Arnold Palmer

Palmer Wins Senior Open

Arnold Palmer won the second U.S. Senior Open, at Oakland Hills C.C. Palmer, Bob Stone, and Billy Casper all closed at 289, but Palmer won the playoff with a 70 to Stone's 74 and Casper's 77. Palmer, age 51, was able to play in the Open because the minimum age was dropped from 55 to 50.

• July 26: Kathy Whitworth's U.S. Women's Open check of $9,500 makes her the first LPGA player to hit $1 million in career earnings.

• July 26: John Mahaffey wins the first Anheuser-Busch Classic at its new home, Kingsmill G.C. in Williamsburg, Virginia.

• August 2: Peter Oosterhuis earns his only career Tour win, the Canadian Open.

• August 2: Donna Caponi wins the Boston Five Classic, her fifth victory of the year.

• August 9: Hometown boy Larry Nelson captures the PGA Champi-

onship by four strokes at Atlanta Athletic Club.

• August 15: Juli Inkster wins her second consecutive U.S. Women's Amateur championship.

• August 16: Jan Stephenson shoots an LPGA-record 198 for 54 holes to win the Mary Kay Classic.

1981

Pat Bradley

Bradley Nips Daniel by One in Women's Open

Pat Bradley broke the U.S. Women's Open scoring record in winning the 1981 edition at La Grange C.C. in Illinois. Bradley closed with a blistering 68-66—279 to edge Beth Daniel, who finished 69-68—280. Both players birdied the final hole. Actually, Daniel almost eagled the hole, but her approach shot just missed falling in.

Stephenson Wins a Major, Breaks a Record

Jan Stephenson captured three LPGA tournaments in 1981, including her first major, the Peter Jackson Classic. She won the event by a stroke over future Hall of Famers Nancy Lopez and Pat Bradley at Summerlea C.C. in Dorion, Quebec. Also, Stephenson shot 65-69-64—198 at the 1981 Mary Kay Classic to break the Tour's 54-hole record.

Jan Stephenson

Nathaniel & Kathryn Crosby

Bing's Son Nate Wins Dramatic U.S. Amateur

Nathaniel Crosby hugs his mom, Kathryn Crosby, widow of actor Bing Crosby. Nate, age 19, won the 1981 U.S. Amateur at the Olympic C.C. in San Francisco, 15 miles from the Crosby home. In a thrilling finale, he beat Brian Lindley, 1 up in 37 holes. Crosby won it by holing a 20-foot birdie putt on the first extra hole.

• August 23: Beth Daniel wins the World Championship of Women's Golf for the second consecutive year.

• August 29: The U.S. wins the Walker Cup, 15-9, at Cypress Point Club in Pebble Beach, California.

• August 30: Bill Rogers wins the World Series of Golf.

• September: Lee Trevino and Ralph Guldahl are inducted into the World Golf Hall of Fame.

• September 6: Nathaniel Crosby, the son of singer Bing, wins the U.S. Amateur championship in a 37-hole final against Brian Lindley at the Olympic Club in San Francisco.

• September 20: The United States defeats Europe, 18½-9½, in the Ryder Cup Matches at Walton Heath G.C. in Surrey, England.

• September 20: Tom Weiskopf wins the new LaJet Classic in Texas.

• October 4: Bill Rogers wins a playoff in the Texas Open.

Larry Nelson

Inkster Edges Goggin in U.S. Women's Amateur

Juli Inkster won the 1981 U.S. Women's Amateur with a dramatic 1-up victory in the final over Australian Lindy Goggin, at Waverley C.C. in Portland, Oregon. Down a hole with two to go, Inkster birdied the 17th and 18th to leap-frog Goggin for the win. Inkster thus became the first golfer in 41 years to claim back-to-back Women's Amateurs.

Nelson Claims PGA Title Thanks to Two 66s

Larry Nelson cruised to a four-stroke victory in the 1981 PGA Championship, at Atlanta Athletic Club. Nelson, a Vietnam veteran, won this tournament in the middle two rounds, in which he shot 66-66. Earlier in the year, Nelson won the Greater Greensboro Open in sudden-death after holing out from a bunker on the 72nd hole.

Juli Inkster

- October 15: Jim Holtgrieve wins the first U.S. Mid-Amateur championship, which is for amateurs age 25 and over.

- October 18: Tom Kite is the PGA Tour's leading money winner with $375,699. He has only one victory but posts 21 top-10 finishes in 26 events.

- October 18: Tom Kite wins the Vardon Trophy, averaging 69.80.

- October 18: Raymond Floyd, Bruce Lietzke, Tom Watson, and Bill Rogers lead the PGA Tour with three wins each.

- October 18: Bill Rogers is the PGA Player of the Year.

- November 8: Patty Sheehan gets her first LPGA victory at the Mazda Japan Classic—and does a somersault on the final green.

- November 8: Beth Daniel birdies the final hole to finish solo second at the Mazda Japan Classic, enabling her to pass JoAnne Carner and lead the final money list with $206,978.

1981

Kathy Whitworth

After 82 Career Wins, Whitworth Hits $1 Million

In July 1981, Kathy Whitworth became the first LPGA Tour player to earn $1 million in official career earnings. JoAnne Carner and Donna Caponi would reach that figure a month later. Whitworth compiled 81 victories before reaching a million. By contrast, Alice Ritzman topped $1 million in 1992 without ever winning *any* tournaments.

Jim Holtgrieve

Holtgrieve Prevails in First U.S. Mid-Amateur

At Bellerive C.C. in St. Louis, Jim Holtgrieve captured the 1981 U.S. Mid-Amateur, an inaugural USGA event for men age 25 and older. The Mid-Amateur was created to give middle-aged amateurs a chance at a national title. For years, the U.S. Amateur had been dominated by hot-shot college-age golfers on the fast track to the PGA Tour.

• November 8: JoAnne Carner wins the Vare Trophy (71.75) and is Player of the Year.

• November 8: Donna Caponi leads the LPGA Tour with five victories.

• November 22: Bill Rogers wins the Australian Open, his seventh victory of the year worldwide.

• December 2: Steve Scott, the American record-holder in the 1,500 meters, sets the record for a round of golf on a regulation course at 29:33.05. He shoots a 92.

• December 6: Miller Barber wins the PGA Seniors Championship at Turnberry Isle C.C. in North Miami, Florida.

• December 6: Miller Barber leads the Senior Tour money list with $83,136. He captures two of the year's five official events.

• December 6: Tom Kite and Beth Daniel team to win the JCPenney Classic at Broadmoor C.C. in Largo, Florida.

WATSON HOLES CHIP SHOT TO WIN U.S. OPEN

In most other years, Craig Stadler or Raymond Floyd would have been solid choices for Player of the Year with the credentials they racked up in 1982. Stadler won four tournaments, including the Masters, and led the PGA Tour's money list; Floyd counted the PGA Championship among his three victories. Nonetheless, the year belonged to Tom Watson. Not only did he sweep the U.S. and British Opens, but Watson also produced one of the most memorable shots of the century.

The scene was the U.S. Open, final round, on the par-3 17th hole at Pebble Beach Golf Links. Watson, tied with Jack Nicklaus, had missed the green long and left with a 2-iron. He was 18 feet from the hole, with a good lie in the deep rough. But with the green sloping away from him, it was going to be difficult to stop the ball close to the hole.

Nicklaus, who had already finished with a 69, admitted afterward that he was anticipating a fifth Open championship which would have pushed him past Ben Hogan, Bobby Jones, and Willie Anderson for the all-time record. Watson had other ideas. He told

his caddie, Bruce Edwards, that he was going to chip the ball in—and he did. The birdie gave Watson a one-stroke lead, while another birdie at the par-5 18th gave him a two-stroke victory and his first U.S. Open title.

Watson had his chances in the Open before. He had led after three rounds in 1974, after two rounds in 1975, and entered the final round two strokes out of the lead in 1980. But his country's championship had always slipped out of his grasp.

This time, he entered the final round tied for the lead with Bill Rogers at 4-under-par thanks to a third-round 68. But the biggest threat on the final day would come from the 42-year-old

Nicklaus, who had won the Open at Pebble Beach 10 years before. On Sunday, Nicklaus grabbed a share of the lead when he birdied holes 3, 4, 5, 6, and 7. Jack would go on to bogey the 8th and 11th, then birdie the 15th, leaving Watson to match his 4-under total.

Watson was 4-under for the tournament through the first 10 holes on Sunday. He shot an even-par 36 on the front nine and made a key save on the par-4 10th. His second shot on No. 10 drifted toward the beach on the right but settled into a playable lie on the bank short of the green. He popped it out to 25 feet and made the putt for par. On the par-5 14th, Watson holed a 40-footer from the back of the green for birdie to take a one-stroke lead. But he gave it back on the 16th where he drove into a fairway bunker and bogied.

Would Watson become a modern-day Sam Snead, unable to win a U.S. Open title despite his many victories in other events? It seemed possible, especially when he missed the green with his tee shot on the 17th. Instead, he authored one of the Open's greatest shots ever.

1982

- January: PGA Tour players are scheduled to play in 46 events with a total season purse of $15,089,576.

- January: LPGA Tour players are scheduled to play in 38 events with a total season purse of $6,400,000.

- January: Senior PGA Tour players are scheduled to play in 11 official

events (six more than last year) for a total season purse of $1,372,000.

- January: The Tournament Players Championship is scheduled to move from Sawgrass C.C. in Ponte Vedra, Florida, to the new TPC at Sawgrass, which is at PGA Tour headquarters a few miles away.

- January: The LPGA moves into its new headquarters in Sugar Land, Texas, near Houston.

- January 3: Johnny Miller wins $500,000 in the first Sun City World Challenge in South Africa.

- February 7: Jim Simons makes up a five-stroke deficit on Craig Stadler

Tom Watson *(right)* won the 1982 U.S. Open at Pebble Beach G.L. in a classic duel with Jack Nicklaus. Watson won by two strokes thanks to his memorable chip-in on the 17th hole. Former U.S. President Gerald Ford *(left)* has long been a devoted golfer. Unfortunately, he became famous for his wayward, crowd-scattering drives.

in the last 12 holes to win by two at the Bing Crosby National Pro-Am.

• February 14: By capturing the Hawaiian Open, Wayne Levi becomes the first player to win on the PGA Tour using an orange ball.

• February 21: Tom Watson beats Johnny Miller in a playoff at the Glen Campbell Los Angeles Open after Miller bogeys the last two regulation holes.

• February 28: Tom Kite chips in on the first playoff hole to capture the Bay Hill Classic.

• March 21: Jerry Pate wins the first Tournament Players Championship held at the TPC at Sawgrass, and he celebrates by tossing Commissioner Deane Beman and course architect Pete Dye into the pond next to the 18th green, then jumping into the water himself.

• April: John Laupheimer takes over as LPGA commissioner, replacing Ray Volpe.

Kathy Whitworth

Whitworth Passes Wright with 83rd Victory

In 1982, Kathy Whitworth won her 83rd Tour event, the Lady Michelob, to break Mickey Wright's record for career victories. Whitworth would go on to win 88 events. With Nancy Lopez cutting back her schedule in recent years and greater competition on Tour, it's hard to fathom any golfer breaking Whitworth's record.

Stadler Wins Masters, Leads Tour in Earnings

Craig Stadler's greatest year was clearly 1982, when he won the Masters, claimed three other tournaments, and led the PGA Tour in earnings. Stadler won the Masters in a playoff after Dan Pohl bogied the first hole of sudden-death. Stadler also took the prestigious World Series of Golf, beating Raymond Floyd in a playoff.

Craig Stadler

• April 4: Danny Edwards wins the Greater Greensboro Open.

• April 4: Sally Little closes with a 64 and wins the Nabisco Dinah Shore Invitational.

• April 11: Craig Stadler wins the Masters when Dan Pohl bogeys the first hole of sudden-death. Stadler had blown a five-stroke lead with a 40 on the final nine.

• April 18: Lanny Wadkins wins the MONY Tournament of Champions.

• April 18: Kathy Whitworth wins the CPC International by nine strokes to tie Mickey Wright's career record of 82 victories.

• April 25: Sam Snead and Don January win the Liberty Mutual Legends of Golf by 12 strokes.

• May 16: Kathy Whitworth wins the Lady Michelob, setting an LPGA record with her 83rd career victory.

• May 16: Jack Nicklaus wins the Colonial National Invitation.

1982

Jan Stephenson

Stephenson Wins LPGA, Sparks Controversy

Jan Stephenson captured the 1982 LPGA Championship, beating out JoAnne Carner by two strokes. In 1981 and '82, Stephenson caused a storm of controversy with her sensuous poses in *Fairway*, the LPGA Tour's official magazine. Stephenson once was offered $150,000 to pose for *Playboy*, but she declined.

Miller Barber

Barber Fires a 65 to Claim Senior Open

With an eye-popping 65 in the final round, Miller Barber won the 1982 U.S. Senior Open at Portland G.C. in Oregon. Barber won by four strokes over Gene Littler and Dan Sikes, and his 65 was three strokes better than anyone else shot all week. Here he accepts the championship cup, called the Francis Ouimet Trophy.

• May 29: Freshman Billy Ray Brown wins the NCAA championship and leads Houston to the team title.

• May 30: Raymond Floyd wins the Memorial Tournament when Roger Maltbie blows a six-stroke lead after 36 holes.

• June 6: Craig Stadler wins his second straight Kemper Open.

• June 13: Raymond Floyd wins the Danny Thomas Memphis Classic.

• June 13: Jan Stephenson beats JoAnne Carner by two strokes at the LPGA Championship.

• June 20: Tom Watson wins the U.S. Open at Pebble Beach G.L. Watson breaks a tie with Jack Nicklaus by chipping in on the 71st hole.

• June 26: Bob Gilder ends the third round of the Manufacturers Hanover Westchester Classic with a double eagle.

Raymond Floyd

Records Fall as Floyd Wins PGA Championship

Raymond Floyd won the 1982 PGA Championship at Southern Hills C.C. in Tulsa, Oklahoma, beating out Lanny Wadkins by three strokes. Floyd opened with a 63, tying the PGA Championship 18-hole record. His opening 63-69—132 broke the event's 36-hole mark, and his 63-69-68—200 set a 54-hole record. He closed with a 72.

Laupheimer Named the New LPGA Commissioner

In April 1982, John Laupheimer was named commissioner of the LPGA Tour, taking over for Ray Volpe. From 1982–88, the growth of the Tour would double in terms of total purse and number of televised events. Nevertheless, Laupheimer would be forced to resign in July 1988 because players thought their Tour was growing too slowly.

John Laupheimer

Tom Watson

Watson Wins Open with Classic Chip Shot

Pictured is Tom Watson's historic chip shot on the par-3 17th of Pebble Beach G.L., which helped him beat Jack Nicklaus in the U.S. Open. Watson, playing out of rough 18 feet from the hole, chipped onto the fringe of the green and watched the ball beeline to the cup. Four weeks later, Watson won his fourth British Open.

• June 27: Bob Gilder wins the Manufacturer's Hanover Westchester Classic.

• July 4: Sandra Haynie, a winner the previous week, takes the Peter Jackson Classic by one stroke.

• July 4: Tom Weiskopf birdies the last hole to beat Larry Nelson by

one at the Western Open. It is Weiskopf's last PGA Tour victory.

• July 11: Miller Barber finishes with a 65 and captures the U.S. Senior Open at Portland G.C. in Portland, Oregon.

• July 18: Tom Watson takes advantage of the collapses of Bobby

Clampett and Nick Price to win the British Open at Royal Troon in Troon, Scotland.

• July 25: Janet Alex passes JoAnne Carner and Beth Daniel with a final-round 68 to win the U.S. Women's Open at Del Paso C.C. in Sacramento, California.

Lopez Marries Baseball's Ray Knight

Six months after divorcing Cincinnati sportscaster Tim Melton, Nancy Lopez *(left)* married Ray Knight *(right)* on October 29, 1982. Knight, a solid-hitting third baseman, played for Cincinnati from 1974–81 before moving to Houston in 1982. Lopez gave birth to their first of three children in November 1983.

Juli Inkster

Nancy Lopez, Ray Knight

Inkster Makes It Three Amateurs in a Row

Juli Inkster won the 1982 U.S. Women's Amateur, her third in a row, at Broadmoor G.C. in Colorado Springs. Inkster defeated Cathy Hanlon in the final, 4 & 3, for her 18th straight match-play victory in the Amateur. No one since Virginia Van Wie (1932–34) had won three consecutive titles.

JoAnne Carner

Carner Enters Hall After 35th Career Victory

JoAnne Carner packed a lot of excitement into 1982, the top highlight being her victory in the World Championship of Women's Golf, which gave her 35 career wins and clinched her spot in the LPGA Hall of Fame. Carner led the '82 Tour in wins (five), earnings, and scoring, and finished runner-up in the Women's Open and the LPGA Championship.

- August 5: Raymond Floyd ties the PGA Championship single-round record with a 63 at Southern Hills C.C. in Tulsa, Oklahoma.

- August 6: The United States romps to a Curtis Cup victory over Great Britain/Ireland, 14½-3½, at Denver C.C.

- August 8: Raymond Floyd wins the PGA Championship by three strokes over Lanny Wadkins. A double bogey on the final hole leaves Floyd with a 272 total, one above the 72-hole tournament record.

- August 15: Tim Norris shoots 25-under-par 259, two strokes off the PGA Tour record for 72 holes, to win the Sammy Davis Jr.-Greater Hartford Open.

- August 21: Juli Inkster wins her third straight Women's Amateur.

- August 22: JoAnne Carner wins the World Championship of Women's Golf and qualifies for the LPGA Hall of Fame.

Calvin Peete

Peete Breaks Through with Four Tour Victories

After just one victory in six previous years on Tour, Calvin Peete won four tournaments in 1982—including the Greater Milwaukee Open, which he won in 1979. Peete, the straightest driver on Tour from 1981–90, grew up on a farm in Florida. He had 18 brothers and sisters through two marriages by his father.

Janet Alex

Alex Romps to Victory in U.S. Women's Open

Janet Alex came out of nowhere to win the 1982 U.S. Women's Open, at Del Paso C.C. in Sacramento, California. Alex, who had never won an LPGA tournament and had never finished better than 26th in the Women's Open, won by six strokes with a 283 total. Alex closed with a rousing 68, the best round of the tournament.

• August 29: JoAnne Carner wins the Henredon Classic on the fifth hole of sudden-death. Playoff opponent Sandra Haynie falls into a creek while following through on her second shot and makes a bogey.

• August 29: Craig Stadler defeats Raymond Floyd in a playoff for the World Series of Golf.

• September: Julius Boros and Kathy Whitworth are inducted into the World Golf Hall of Fame.

• September 5: Calvin Peete shoots 63-63 in the middle rounds and wins the B.C. Open by seven strokes.

• September 5: Jay Sigel wins the U.S. Amateur.

• September 6: JoAnne Carner wins for the third straight week at the Rail Charity Classic.

• October 29: Nancy Lopez, divorced in April, marries baseball star Ray Knight.

• October 31: Craig Stadler leads the Tour money list with $446,462.

Don January

January Claims PGA Seniors at PGA National

Don January cashed in quickly on the budding Senior PGA Tour. He finished second on the money list in 1981 and '82, and first in 1983 and '84. His two 1982 victories included the PGA Seniors Championship, which he won with an even-par 288 at its new permanent home, PGA National G.C. in Palm Beach Gardens, Florida.

Sigel Cruises by Tolley to Claim U.S. Amateur

Jay Sigel captured the 1982 U.S. Amateur at The Country Club in Brookline, Massachusetts, beating David Tolley in the final, 8 & 7. Sigel, age 38, had finished runner-up in the 1961 U.S. Junior Amateur. He may have turned pro had he not accidentally punched his left hand through a glass door, causing nerve damage.

Jay Sigel

- October 31: Tom Kite wins the Vardon Trophy with an average of 70.21.

- October 31: Craig Stadler and Calvin Peete each finish with four PGA Tour victories, while Raymond Floyd, Tom Watson, Bob Gilder, and Lanny Wadkins finish with three each.

- October 31: Tom Watson is the PGA Player of the Year.

- November 7: JoAnne Carner leads the LPGA Tour money list with $310,399 and is the LPGA Player of the Year.

- November 7: JoAnne Carner wins the Vare Trophy, averaging 71.49.

- November 7: JoAnne Carner and Beth Daniel each finish with five LPGA Tour victories.

- December 5: Don January wins the PGA Seniors Championship.

- December 5: Miller Barber leads the Senior Tour money list with $106,890.

First Skins Game Is A Made-for-TV Success

It began as an idea by television producer Don Ohlmeyer. Golf, he noticed, was completely absent from network television from September until January. Why not breach the gap by taking four of golf's biggest names and have them play a skins game—a format familiar to average golfers—on Thanksgiving weekend? Surely, he figured, people would want to watch golf's stars playing in the sunshine when the weather was dreary throughout much of the country.

Skeptics abounded. Television people doubted golf could earn high ratings during football season. Golf purists felt the event smacked too much of an exhibition instead of a legitimate competition. Nonetheless, Ohlmeyer sold his idea to NBC, and he got Jack Nicklaus, Arnold Palmer, Gary Player, and Tom Watson to agree to play at Desert Highlands, a new Nicklaus-designed course near Phoenix. The Skins Game was born.

It says something about golf in the 1980s that three of the game's competitors were over 40 years old—stars of another era. The lack of a superstar was a recurring theme of the decade. Though

Watson qualified as a major Tour star in 1983, his career would soon enter a decline, with no single player able to take over.

Unlike skins in your weekend foursome, these stars weren't playing for their own money. The stakes were $10,000 for each of the first six holes, $20,000 for the next six, and $30,000 for the last six—a total of $360,000. If no player won a hole, the money would carry over, creating the potential for big payoffs. In the 1983 Skins Game, there were two such jackpots. Palmer drained a 35-foot birdie putt for $100,000 on the 12th hole. And Player claimed $150,000 by sinking a four-footer for a birdie on the 17th. Player won overall honors

with a total of $170,000, while Palmer claimed $140,000, Nicklaus $40,000, and Watson $10,000.

But what happened afterward proved to be the big story. Watson thought Player had gotten away with a Rules violation on the 16th hole, and he engaged Player in a heated discussion after the round. *New York Times* columnist Dave Anderson happened to be nearby, and he reported what he heard. "I'm accusing you, Gary. You can't do that. I'm tired of this," Watson said. What Player had done, according to Watson, was remove or flatten a leaf near his ball on a chip to the 16th green. Since the leaf was growing, not loose, it could not be disturbed. Player said it was all a misunderstanding, that he did not move the leaf. In a sense, it was a moot point, since Watson didn't say anything on the spot.

Nonetheless, the Skins Game was a TV hit. It drew the highest ratings of any golf event of the year, except for the major championships, assuring its return in years to come. Now, golf's "off-season" is littered with televised events—though none bigger than the Skins Game.

1983

- January: PGA Tour players are scheduled to play in 45 events with a total season purse of $17,588,242.

- January: LPGA Tour players are scheduled to play in 36 events with a total purse of $7 million.

- January: Senior PGA Tour players are scheduled to play in 18 events.

- January: Monday qualifying is eliminated on the PGA Tour's new "all-exempt" Tour. The top 125 money winners from the previous year are exempt for all non-invitational events.

- January: The new Panasonic Las Vegas Pro-Celebrity Classic has the largest PGA purse ($750,000).

- January: The Nabisco Dinah Shore has been designated as a major championship on the LPGA Tour.

- January 9: Gil Morgan beats Curtis Strange and Lanny Wadkins in a playoff to win the season-opening Joe Garagiola-Tucson Open.

1983

Gary Player was at the center of controversy in the inaugural Skins Game.
Tom Watson accused Player of illegally moving a leaf on the 16th hole, and
the two hooked up in a heated discussion. It's not surprising that tensions ran high;
the hole was worth $120,000. Nobody won the hole but Player claimed
the next, worth $150,000.

• January 16: Gil Morgan wins the Glen Campbell Los Angeles Open.

• January 30: Bob Gilder defeats Rex Caldwell on the eighth hole of a playoff at the Phoenix Open.

• February 6: Rex Caldwell finishes second to Tom Kite at the Bing Crosby National Pro-Am.

• February 13: Isao Aoki holes out from 128 yards for an eagle on the 72nd hole to beat Jack Renner by one stroke at the Hawaiian Open.

• March 6: Johnny Miller wins the Honda Inverrary Classic.

• March 28: Hal Sutton wins the Tournament Players Championship when John Cook, who was tied for the lead, double bogeys the final hole.

• April 3: Amy Alcott wins the Nabisco Dinah Shore by two strokes.

• April 11: Seve Ballesteros wins the Masters after going 4-under-par on the first four holes on Sunday.

Hal Sutton

Despite a 77, Couples Wins His First Pro Event

Fred Couples, one of the Tour's most talented young golfers, captured his first victory at the 1983 Kemper Open. He almost blew it, though, as he shot a 5-over 77 on Sunday to fall into a five-way playoff. He then beat T.C. Chen, Barry Jaeckel, Gil Morgan, and Scott Simpson in sudden-death.

U.S. Open Rain Delay

Sophomore Sutton Wins TPC, Leads Tour in Money

In his second season on Tour, 25-year-old Hal Sutton led the 1983 circuit in earnings with $426,668. In March, he won the Tournament Players Championship, held for the second year at TPC at Sawgrass in Ponte Vedra, Florida. Sutton won by one stroke over Bob Eastwood and two over John Cook, who double bogeyed the tough 18th hole.

Fred Couples

Lightning, Thunder Interrupt U.S. Open

The second round of the 1983 U.S. Open at Oakmont C.C. was suspended for 2½ hours because of a severe electrical storm. Two spectators were struck by lightning; they went to the hospital but were soon released. The final round was also interrupted by thunderstorms. The last few holes had to be played on Monday.

• April 24: Lanny Wadkins beats Raymond Floyd by one stroke to win the MONY Tournament of Champions.

• May: Bob Hope and Jimmy Demaret are inducted into the World Golf Hall of Fame. Hope joins Bing Crosby as the only two entertainers in the Hall.

• May 1: Roberto De Vicenzo and Rod Funseth win the Liberty Mutual Legends of Golf.

• May 26: The U.S. defeats Great Britain/Ireland, 13½-10½, in the Walker Cup in Hoylake, England.

• May 29: Hale Irwin wins the Memorial Tournament.

• May 29: Patty Sheehan finishes with a 63 and wins the Corning Classic by eight strokes.

• June 5: Fred Couples wins a five-way playoff for his first PGA Tour victory at the Kemper Open.

• June 12: Miller Barber wins the Senior Tournament Players

1983

Alcott Wins Dinah Shore, Hits $1 Million

Amy Alcott won the 1983 Nabisco Dinah Shore, which was declared a major championship for the first time. It also offered the largest purse in LPGA Tour history, $400,000. A month later, Alcott became the sixth woman golfer to reach $1 million. She celebrated by buying champagne for the press.

Amy Alcott

Tillie Stacy, Hollis Stacy

Irwin Claims First of Two Memorials

With a score of 281, Hale Irwin captured the 1983 Memorial Tournament at Muirfield Village G.C. in Dublin, Ohio. Irwin was often in the thick of this tournament. He won the 1985 Memorial with the same score, and he lost two Memorial playoffs—one in 1976 to Roger Maltbie and another in 1991 to Kenny Perry.

Hale Irwin

Stacy Wins Three Events, Including a Major

Hollis Stacy gets a peck on the cheek from her mom, Tillie Stacy. Hollis, who comes from a family of 10 children, won three tournaments in 1983, including a major championship—the Peter Jackson Classic. Stacy, who won the 1969 U.S. Girls' Junior at age 15, would later get into golf course architecture.

Championship at Canterbury G.C. in Cleveland.

• June 12: Patty Sheehan comes from seven strokes behind, outscoring Sandra Haynie, 66-75, to win the LPGA Championship.

• June 19: On Sunday, Tom Watson takes a three-stroke lead in the U.S.

Open at Oakmont C.C. in Pennsylvania. Watson is tied with Larry Nelson when a thunderstorm suspends play with the last group on the 14th green.

• June 20: Playing his last three holes on Monday morning, Larry Nelson finishes 65-67 in the last two rounds, the best in U.S. Open

history, to beat Tom Watson by one stroke and Gil Morgan by three.

• July 3: Hollis Stacy wins the Peter Jackson Classic at Beaconsfield G.C. in Montreal.

• July 4: Mark McCumber beats Tom Watson by one at the Western Open.

Hal Sutton

Sutton Holds Off Nicklaus for PGA Title

Hal Sutton rode a first-round 65 to victory in the 1983 PGA Championship, at Riviera C.C. in Pacific Palisades, California. Sutton shot 65-66-72-71—274 and led after every round of the tournament. Jack Nicklaus added drama with a final-round 66, but the Golden Bear finished one stroke back.

Tom Watson

Watson Captures His Fifth British Open Title

Tom Watson hoists the trophy after winning the 1983 British Open title, his fifth. Watson shot 275 to edge Andy Bean at Royal Birkdale G.C. in Southport, England. All five of his victories came on different courses. Only the legendary Harry Vardon, with six victories, ever won the British more often.

• July 17: Tom Watson wins his fifth British Open, at Royal Birkdale G.C. in England.

• July 24: Hal Sutton blows a six-stroke lead at the Anheuser-Busch Classic. Calvin Peete wins.

• July 25: Billy Casper beats Rod Funseth in an 18-hole playoff for the U.S. Senior Open at Hazeltine National G.C. in Chaska, Minnesota.

• July 30: Andy Bean is penalized two strokes for tapping in a putt with the handle of his putter during the third round of the Canadian Open. He shoots a 77.

• July 31: Andy Bean shoots a final-round 62 at the Canadian Open and finishes two strokes out of a playoff. John Cook beats Johnny Miller on the sixth playoff hole.

• July 31: Jan Stephenson wins the U.S. Women's Open with a 6-over-par 290 total at Cedar Ridge C.C. in Broken Arrow, Oklahoma. JoAnne

1983

Pat Bradley

Bradley Reaches Her First Money Milestone

In April 1983, Pat Bradley became the fourth LPGA player to reach the $1 million mark. In later years, she would become the first to reach $2 million, $3 million, and $4 million. From 1978–92, Bradley took home six figures each year but one. Only in 1988, when she was diagnosed with hyperthyroidism, did she fall short.

Seve Ballesteros, Craig Stadler

Ballesteros Slips on Another Green Jacket

Seve Ballesteros, the 1983 Masters champion, sits beside 1982 champion Craig Stadler *(right)*. Ballesteros, who shot 4-under on the first four holes Sunday, finished at 280 to win by four strokes over Tom Kite and Ben Crenshaw. This was the second green jacket for Seve, who turned just 26 two days earlier.

Carner, who shot an 81 in the first round, finishes just one stroke back.

• August 7: Hal Sutton beats Jack Nicklaus by one stroke in the PGA Championship at Riviera C.C. in Pacific Palisades, California.

• August 21: JoAnne Carner captures the Chevrolet World

Championship of Women's Golf, her first win of the year after seven runner-up finishes.

• August 28: Nick Price wins the World Series of Golf.

• September 4: Jay Sigel wins his second consecutive U.S. Amateur, defeating Chris Perry in the final.

• September 11: Mark Lye comes from eight strokes behind on the final day to win the Bank of Boston Classic.

• September 25: Four times a runner-up this year, Rex Caldwell wins his only career event, the LaJet Coors Classic.

Jay Sigel

Sigel Breezes to Second Straight Amateur Victory

In 1983, Jay Sigel claimed his second straight U.S. Amateur championship, at North Shore C.C. in Glenview, Illinois. Sigel trounced Chris Perry in the final, 8 & 7. Jay also won the 1983 Mid-Amateur, becoming the first man to win two USGA events in the same year since Bobby Jones in 1930.

Carner Again Leads in Earnings, Scoring

JoAnne Carner's two victories didn't tell the whole story of her 1983 season. Carner finished runner-up seven times (including the U.S. Women's Open after an opening 81), led in earnings for the second straight season, and won the Vare Trophy for the third consecutive year. It would be her last great season.

JoAnne Carner

Larry Nelson

Nelson Closes 65-67 to Capture U.S. Open

Larry Nelson won the 1983 U.S. Open at Oakmont C.C. in Pennsylvania, but he needed an extraordinary performance to do it. Nelson closed 65-67—280 to beat Tom Watson by a stroke. No golfer had ever shot 132 for 36 holes in the Open before. In fact, no one had ever done better than 136.

• October 15: Gene Littler fires an 8-under-par 28 on the front nine during the third round of the Suntree Classic. He shoots a 63.

• October 16: The United States edges Europe, 14½-13½, in the Ryder Cup Matches at PGA National G.C. in Palm Beach Gardens, Florida.

• October 30: Hal Sutton leads the PGA Tour with $426,668. He is the PGA Player of the Year.

• October 30: Raymond Floyd wins the Vardon Trophy, averaging 70.61.

• October 30: No player finishes with more than two victories on the PGA Tour. Hal Sutton, Fuzzy Zoeller, Lanny Wadkins, Calvin Peete, Gil Morgan, Mark McCumber, Jim Colbert, and Seve Ballesteros win two each.

• November 13: Pat Bradley closes with a 64 to win the Mazda Japan Classic by seven strokes.

Billy Casper

Casper Outlasts Funseth in Senior Open Playoff

Billy Casper defeated Rod Funseth in a playoff at the 1983 U.S. Senior Open, at Hazeltine National G.C. in Minnesota. Both finished at 288 and each shot 75 in the 18-hole playoff. Casper then sank a 10-foot birdie putt on the first sudden-death hole for the victory. Richard King, incidentally, shot 103 in the fourth round.

Jan Stephenson

Stephenson Wins Sweltering Women's Open

In 1983, Jan Stephenson claimed her third different major championship when she won the U.S. Women's Open, at Cedar Ridge C.C. near Tulsa, Oklahoma. Stephenson shot 6-over 290 to win by a stroke over Patty Sheehan and JoAnne Carner. Temperatures reached 100 degrees each day, affecting scores. Most failed to break 300.

• November 13: JoAnne Carner leads the LPGA money list with $291,404.

• November 13: JoAnne Carner wins her third straight Vare Trophy with a scoring average of 71.41.

• November 13: Patty Sheehan and Pat Bradley lead the LPGA Tour with four victories each. Sheehan is the LPGA Player of the Year.

• November 27: Jack Nicklaus, Arnold Palmer, Gary Player, and Tom Watson meet in the first Skins Game at Desert Highlands in Scottsdale, Arizona. Player wins the most money, $170,000.

• December 4: Don January leads the Senior Tour with $237,571. He also leads the tour with six victories in the 13 events he enters.

• December 4: Seve Ballesteros wins the $300,000 first prize at the Sun City Challenge in South Africa, his sixth victory of the year worldwide.

BALLESTEROS WINS A CLASSIC AT ST. ANDREWS

With two holes remaining, the 1984 British Open had reduced itself to a thrilling confrontation: the two best players in the world, Tom Watson and Seve Ballesteros, battling on golf's most historic venue, the Old Course in St. Andrews, Scotland. It wasn't quite a head-to-head match-up, as Ballesteros was playing in the next-to-last pairing, Watson in the last. But that only added an element of uncertainty to a tense situation.

Certainly, both players wanted the tournament badly. Watson had won five British Opens (1975, 1977, 1980, 1982–83), and a sixth would tie him with the legendary Harry Vardon for the most British Open titles. Spain's Ballesteros, who had won in 1979, always viewed Britain as practically his home turf, and he valued its championship above all others. And both considered a British Open at ageless St. Andrews to be the most special championship of all.

This was clearly a marquee match-up. Watson had eight major titles under his belt, including the 1977 and '81 Masters and the 1982 U.S. Open along with his British triumphs.

Ballesteros, seven years younger at 27, already had three—the 1980 and '83 Masters plus his British title. Watson had led the PGA Tour money list four times, while Ballesteros had topped the European Tour three times.

When the final round began, Watson was tied for the lead with Australia's Ian Baker-Finch, two strokes ahead of Ballesteros and Bernhard Langer. Baker-Finch faded quickly, finishing with a 79. Langer tied for second but wasn't really a factor in the closing drama. Watson, though, couldn't pull away, and he fell into a tie for the lead with Ballesteros with a bogey on the 12th hole. They remained gridlocked through the 16th hole.

The 17th at the Old Course, the Road Hole, was one of the most famous, and toughest, holes in golf, with a deep bunker to the left and a road to the right, which guarded the green on a long second shot. Ballesteros made his par, hitting the green with a 6-iron out of the left rough. Then it was Watson's turn. He drove into the fairway but couldn't decide between a 2- or 3-iron for his approach. He chose the 2-iron but hit it long and to the right, the ball bounding onto the road. From there, a wall blocked a full backswing for his pitch, although he was able to punch the ball onto the green.

Moments before Watson addressed his 30-foot par putt, Ballesteros delivered a crucial blow up ahead at the 18th green. On that short par-4, Ballesteros hit his second to within 15 feet, holed the putt, and punched the air in exultation. Watson heard the roar, then missed his putt. Suddenly it was over, barring a Watson miracle that was not to come. Ballesteros had his second British Open. For Watson, it was a career turning point in the wrong direction. He would never again win a major title.

1984

- January: PGA Tour players are scheduled to play in 46 events with a total season purse of $21,251,382.

- January: LPGA Tour players are scheduled to play in 38 events with a total season purse of $8 million.

- January: Senior PGA Tour players are scheduled to play in 24 events with a total season purse of $5,156,000.

- January: The Seiko-Tucson Match Play Championship is introduced with a combined purse of $1 million for regular and senior divisions.

- January 8: Tom Watson wins the Seiko-Tucson Match Play, defeating Gil Morgan in the final match, 2 & 1. Gene Littler wins the senior portion.

- January 20: In the PGA Seniors Championship, Arnold Palmer shoots a tournament-record 63 to take an eight-stroke lead after two rounds.

Seve Ballesteros pumps his fist after birdieing the 72nd hole of the 1984 British Open at St. Andrews. Tom Watson, putting for par on the 71st hole, heard the roar and moments later missed his putt. That two-stroke swing gave Ballesteros a two-stroke lead and clinched his second British Open victory.

• January 22: Arnold Palmer takes his second PGA Seniors title, finishing 79-71.

• February 5: Hale Irwin is saved at the Bing Crosby National Pro-Am when his tee shot on the 18th hole caroms off a rocky beach back onto the fairway. He birdies the hole and beats Jim Nelford in a playoff.

• February 12: Jack Renner, foiled by Isao Aoki a year ago, wins the Hawaiian Open.

• March 4: Nancy Lopez wins the Uniden Invitational four months after giving birth to her first child.

• March 11: Tom Kite shoots a final-round 65 to win the Doral-Eastern Open by two strokes over Jack Nicklaus.

• March 18: Chris Johnson scores her second LPGA victory, one week after her first win, at the Tucson Conquistadores Open.

• March 18: Gary Koch wins a playoff at the Bay Hill Classic.

Eastwood Finally a Winner After 12 Years

Bob Eastwood had struggled through 12 seasons on the PGA Tour before breaking through in a big way. In 1984, Eastwood won his first tournament, the USF&G Classic in New Orleans. Later in the year, he won the Danny Thomas-Memphis Classic and finished third in the World Series of Golf. He was 24th on the money list, his best finish.

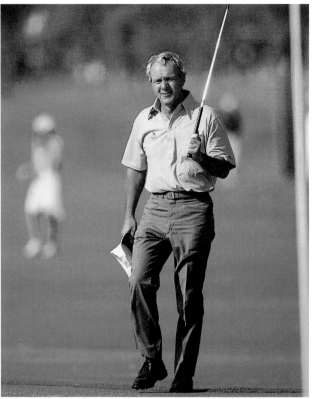

Arnold Palmer

Palmer Grabs Another PGA Seniors Championship

Arnie proved he still had it with a whirlwind performance in the 1984 PGA Seniors Championship. Palmer fired a tournament-record 63 in the second round to vault to an eight-stroke lead. Though he slumped with a 79 in the third round, he fired a closing 71 to win his second PGA Seniors title.

Bob Eastwood

- March 25: In her eighth year on the LPGA Tour, Betsy King gets her first victory at the Women's Kemper Open.

- April 1: Fred Couples outduels Lee Trevino and Seve Ballesteros to win the Tournament Players Championship.

- April 8: Rookie Juli Inkster beats veteran Pat Bradley in a playoff at the Nabisco Dinah Shore.

- April 15: Ben Crenshaw shoots a 68 in the final round and takes the Masters for his first major title.

- April 22: Nick Faldo wins his first PGA event, the Heritage Classic.

- May 6: Tom Watson wins the MONY Tournament of Champions.

- May 20: Peter Jacobsen beats Payne Stewart in a playoff at the Colonial National Invitation.

- May 27: Jack Nicklaus wins the Memorial Tournament in a playoff over Andy Bean.

1984

Betsy King

Irwin's Bank Shot Saves Win at Pebble Beach

Hale Irwin can thank a certain rock on Pebble's beach for his victory in the 1984 Crosby. Irwin pulled his drive on the 72nd hole and his ball headed for the beach. Fate, and the rock, intervened and Irwin's ball bounded back to the fairway. He birdied the hole, then won in a playoff.

Hale Irwin

After Seven Years, King Breaks Through

In 1984, Betsy King finally won an LPGA tournament, the Women's Kemper Open. Since joining the Tour in 1977, King had neither won an event nor reached six figures in season earnings. But from 1984–92, she would win at least two tournaments each season and finish above $200,000 every year.

• June 3: Greg Norman wins his first PGA Tour event, the Kemper Open.

• June 3: Patty Sheehan wins her second consecutive LPGA Championship, by 10 shots.

• June 9: The U.S. nips Great Britain/Ireland, 9½-8½, to win the Curtis Cup at Muirfield in Scotland.

• June 10: Patty Sheehan wins the McDonald's Kids Classic, as well as a $500,000 bonus for adding that win to her LPGA Championship.

• June 17: In the U.S. Open at Winged Foot G.C. in Mamaroneck, New York, Greg Norman holes a 45-foot putt for a par on the 72nd hole and ties Fuzzy Zoeller.

• June 18: Fuzzy Zoeller romps in an 18-hole playoff over Greg Norman, 67-75, to win the U.S. Open.

• June 24: Tom Kite wins the Georgia-Pacific Atlanta Classic, marking the first time in his career he's won more than one tournament in a year.

1984

Gary Koch

Koch Sensational in His Native Florida

Native Floridian Gary Koch loved playing on his home turf. Koch won his fourth Florida PGA Tour event when he captured the 1984 Bay Hill Classic in Orlando. Gary won the tournament in 1977 when it was called the Florida Citrus Open. He also captured the 1976 Tallahassee Open and 1983 Doral-Eastern Open in the sunshine state.

Debbie and Fred Couples

Couples the Winner at Players Championship

Fred Couples gets a victory hug from wife Debbie after capturing the 1984 Tournament Players Championship, by a stroke over Lee Trevino. Couples took the lead in the second round with an 8-under-par 64 on the tricky Stadium Course at TPC—Sawgrass. Surprisingly, the talented Couples wouldn't win again until 1987.

• June 24: Arnold Palmer wins the Senior Tournament Players Championship.

• July 1: Greg Norman wins the Canadian Open by two strokes.

• July 1: Miller Barber beats Arnold Palmer by two strokes at the U.S. Senior Open.

• July 8: Tom Watson beats Greg Norman in a playoff for the Western Open title.

• July 15: Ronnie Black closes with a 63 to win the Anheuser-Busch Classic.

• July 15: Hollis Stacy wins her third U.S. Women's Open at Salem C.C.

in Peabody, Massachusetts. Amy Alcott double bogeys the 72nd hole to finish two back.

• July 22: Seve Ballesteros takes his second British Open at the Old Course in St. Andrews, Scotland. Ballesteros wins by two after he birdies the 72nd hole and Tom Watson bogeys the 71st.

Juli Inkster

Inkster Nabs Dinah Shore, Then Grabs the du Maurier

No one was surprised when Juli Inkster broke through for a major victory in her first full year as a professional. Inkster, who edged Pat Bradley in a playoff at the 1984 Nabisco Dinah Shore, had won three straight U.S. Women's Amateurs before turning pro. Inkster also captured the '84 du Maurier Classic.

Sheehan Blows Away the Field at LPGA

For the second consecutive year, Patty Sheehan won the LPGA Championship—and she did it with flair. In the third round, Sheehan shot a career-best 63 en route to a 10-stroke victory. It was her 10th victory and second major championship after only 3½ seasons as a professional. Sheehan also won the 1984 Vare Trophy.

Patty Sheehan

Fuzzy Zoeller

Zoeller Routs Norman in U.S. Open Playoff

Fuzzy Zoeller's spirits sank on the 72nd hole of the 1984 U.S. Open at Winged Foot G.C., as Greg Norman saved par with a 45-foot putt. The putt put Zoeller in a tie with Norman and the two went at it the next day in an 18-hole playoff. The happy-go-lucky Fuzz kept his cool and sprinted to a 67-75 victory.

- July 29: Juli Inkster wins the du Maurier Classic (formerly the Peter Jackson Classic) at St. George's Golf & C.C. in Toronto. It's her second major championship of the year.

- August 12: Don January wins the du Maurier Champions with a Senior Tour-record 194 for 54 holes.

- August 19: Lee Trevino, age 44, shoots four rounds in the 60s to win the PGA Championship at Shoal Creek C.C. in Birmingham, Alabama.

- August 19: Nancy Lopez wins the Chevrolet World Championship of Women's Golf.

- August 26: Denis Watson wins the NEC World Series of Golf thanks largely to a 62 in the second round.

- September 2: Scott Verplank wins the U.S. Amateur.

- September 2: Mary Beth Zimmerman cards eight consecutive birdies in the Rail Charity Classic.

Ben Crenshaw

Crenshaw Wins Masters for His First Major Title

Few victories have proven as popular as Ben Crenshaw's win in the 1984 Masters. Crenshaw, one of the game's top players, had never won a major championship. "I don't think there will ever be anything sweeter for me," Crenshaw said. Ben won it with a final-round 68.

Stacy Claims Her Third Career U.S. Women's Open

Hollis Stacy was an old hand at winning USGA events when she captured the 1984 U.S. Women's Open at Salem C.C. in Massachusetts. It was Stacy's sixth USGA title. She won the U.S. Girls' Junior three straight times, and this was her third victory in the Women's Open.

Greg Norman

Norman Claims Two Tour Wins

Greg Norman may have lost a playoff in the 1984 U.S. Open, but he won the Kemper Open two weeks prior to the U.S. Open and captured the Canadian Open two weeks after. They were his first two wins on Tour. The Shark's aggressive style of play would eventually draw legions of fans.

Hollis Stacy

• September 9: George Archer, age 44, wins his first tournament in eight years, the Bank of Boston Classic.

• September 22: Vicki Fergon ties the LPGA 18-hole record with a 62 at the San Jose Classic. The next day, she'll shoot a 79 and finish tied for 11th.

• September 23: Denis Watson wins $162,000 at the Panasonic Las Vegas Invitational.

• October 6: Ayako Okamoto rolls to an 11-stroke victory at the Hitachi Ladies British Open.

• October 28: Tom Watson leads the PGA Tour money list with $476,260. He is the PGA Player of the Year.

• October 28: Calvin Peete wins the Vardon Trophy, averaging 70.56.

• October 28: Tom Watson and Denis Watson finish with three victories each on the PGA Tour.

Jack Nicklaus

Jack's Birdie Worth $240,000 in Skins Game

Jack Nicklaus didn't have a great season in 1984, winning only the Memorial, but Jack cashed in at the Skins Game. His birdie on the last hole was worth $240,000. The birdie earned Nicklaus almost as much as he won that entire season on the PGA Tour, when he banked $272,595.

Miller Barber

Barber Shaves Arnie at U.S. Senior Open

Miller Barber edged Arnold Palmer to win the 1984 U.S. Senior Open at Oak Hill C.C. in Rochester, New York. Barber was a true pioneer of the Senior Tour, leading the circuit in earnings its first two years (1981–82) and finishing second the next two seasons. Barber was nicknamed "Mr. X" because of his fondness for solitude.

Trevino's Hot Putter Helps Him in PGA

Lee Trevino may have found the woods during the 1984 PGA Championship, but his hot putter helped him to victory. Trevino, using a putter he recently purchased in Holland, shot 69-68-67-69—273 at Shoal Creek C.C. in Birmingham, Alabama. Gary Player, age 48, shot a second-round 63. He finished in second place, four strokes back.

Lee Trevino

- November 4: Betsy King leads the LPGA Tour money list with $266,771. She is the LPGA Player of the Year.

- November 4: Patty Sheehan wins the Vare Trophy, averaging 71.40.

- November 4: Patty Sheehan and Amy Alcott finish with four victories each on the LPGA Tour. Betsy King, Ayako Okamoto, and Kathy Whitworth have three each.

- November 25: Jack Nicklaus birdies the 18th hole to take a $240,000 skin (two-thirds of the total purse) and win the Skins Game at Desert Highlands in Arizona.

- December 9: Peter Thomson wins the PGA Seniors Championship.

- December 9: Don January leads the Senior Tour with $328,597.

- December 9: Miller Barber leads the Senior Tour with four wins. Don January and Arnold Palmer have three.

TIDE FINALLY TURNS, AS EUROPE CLAIMS CUP

During the early 1980s, the balance of power in golf started to shift away from the United States toward Europe. The process began with Spain's Seve Ballesteros, who by 1984 had captured two British Opens and two Masters. In 1983, the Europeans nearly upended the U.S. in the Ryder Cup at PGA National Golf Club in Palm Beach Gardens, Florida, the Americans escaping with a 14½-13½ victory.

And while Europe was churning out more and more players of high caliber to join Ballesteros—Bernhard Langer won the 1985 Masters, Sandy Lyle the 1985 British Open, and Nick Faldo and Ian Woosnam were making a mark—American golf was plagued in the mid-'80s by an onset of parity. Tom Watson, once dominant, began to decline, Jack Nicklaus was in his mid-40s, and no one emerged to replace them.

The time was ripe for Europe to win the Ryder Cup, something it had not done since 1957 (when it was just Great Britain against the U.S.), managing only a tie in 1969 in the last 13 biennial meetings. With Watson and Nicklaus not making the 1985 U.S. squad, the Americans lacked the intimidation

factor. And with the event being held at The Belfry in Sutton Coldfield, England, the Europeans had a raucous home crowd on their side.

The United States led only after the first day, 4½-3½. The turning point came at the end of the second morning's foursomes. Craig Stadler of the U.S. had a two-foot putt on the 18th hole for a win. When he missed, the overall standings were even at 6-6. Europe won three matches in the afternoon to take a 9-7 lead into the final day of singles, which consisted of 12 matches.

The Europeans had been led the first two days by Spaniards Ballesteros and Manuel Pinero, who teamed to win 3½ of a

possible four points. Pinero, off first in singles, dealt the Americans a major blow by beating Lanny Wadkins, 3 & 1. Ballesteros managed only a half-point against Tom Kite but it was a come-from-behind effort, as he stormed from three down with five to play.

In the final day's early matches, only Stadler won for the Americans. With Paul Way beating Raymond Floyd, Sandy Lyle topping Peter Jacobsen, and Bernhard Langer handling Hal Sutton, the Europeans stood only a point away from victory. They got that point when Andy North of the U.S. hit his tee shot into the water on the 18th hole and his opponent, Sam Torrance, scored a winning birdie. With Howard Clark and Jose Maria Canizares adding wins in later matches, Europe took the singles, 7½-4½, for a convincing overall victory, 16½-11½.

Two years later, the Europeans proved this win wasn't a freak occurrence, as they won the Ryder Cup on American soil for the first time. They kept the Cup in 1989 with a tie before the United States finally regained it—by one point—in 1991.

1985

• January: PGA Tour players are scheduled to play in 47 events with a total season purse of $25,290,526.

• January: LPGA Tour players are scheduled to play in 38 events with a total season purse of $9 million.

• January: Senior PGA Tour players are scheduled to play in 27 events

with a total season purse of $6,076,000.

• January 13: At the Bob Hope Classic, Lanny Wadkins plays the last five holes of regulation 5-under and beats Craig Stadler on the fifth playoff hole after both finish 27-under-par.

• January 27: Lanny Wadkins shoots a tournament-record 264 to win the Los Angeles Open by seven strokes.

• February 10: Mark O'Meara, winner of last week's Bing Crosby National Pro-Am, wins the Hawaiian Open.

1985

Seve Ballesteros *(left)* sprays Ryder Cup captain Tony Jacklin with champagne after the European squad won the 1985 Ryder Cup, 16½-11½, at The Belfry in Sutton Coldfield, England. It was the first time the United States lost since 1957. Manuel Pinero led Europe with four points, and Ballesteros had 3½.

• March 10: Fuzzy Zoeller, six months after back surgery, wins the Hertz Bay Hill Classic.

• March 31: Calvin Peete finishes with a 66 to win the Tournament Players Championship.

• April: Kathryn Crosby, widow of Bing, withdraws the Crosby name from the PGA Tour event at Pebble Beach when AT&T comes in as title sponsor.

• April 7: Alice Miller wins the Nabisco Dinah Shore.

• April 12: After opening with an 80, Curtis Strange shoots 65 in the second round of the Masters.

• April 14: Leader Curtis Strange falters in the Masters by hitting shots into the water on the 13th and 15th. Bernhard Langer wins with a closing 68.

• April 28: After setting an LPGA 36-hole record with a 129 total (64-65), Judy Clark finishes 75-75 in the S&H Classic. Alice Miller wins.

1985

Wadkins Wins Bob Hope Classic with Fierce Charge

Lanny Wadkins put on a show to win the 1985 Bob Hope Classic. Wadkins went 5-under over the last five holes of regulation to tie Craig Stadler. The two battled it out in sudden-death before Wadkins won it on the fifth playoff hole. It was one of three victories for Wadkins in '85, and he was named PGA Player of the Year.

Calvin Peete

Accurate Peete Prevails in Players Championship

Calvin Peete, the son of a Florida migrant worker, blazed his way to glory by winning the biggest event of his career, the 1985 Tournament Players Championship. The straight-hitting Peete eased down the narrow fairways of the Stadium Course at TPC—Sawgrass, shooting a final-round 66.

Lanny Wadkins

• May 12: Payne Stewart double bogeys the 72nd hole and the first playoff hole to lose the Byron Nelson Classic to Bob Eastwood.

• May 12: Kathy Whitworth, age 45, wins the United Virginia Bank Classic, her 88th and last LPGA Tour victory.

• May 19: Corey Pavin shoots a tournament-record 266 to win the Colonial National Invitation.

• May 19: Jack Nicklaus Jr. wins the North and South Amateur.

• June 2: Nancy Lopez shoots a final-round 65 and wins the LPGA Championship by eight strokes.

• June 9: Alice Miller shoots her fourth straight 68 to win the McDonald's Championship, by eight strokes over Nancy Lopez.

• June 16: T.C. Chen, the leader of the U.S. Open, double hits a chip on the 5th hole of the final round and makes a quadruple bogey to blow a four-stroke lead. He finishes one

Alice Miller

Miller Wins Four Tourneys in Career Year

Alice Miller came out of nowhere to enjoy the finest year of her career in 1985. In April, Miller won the Nabisco Dinah Shore, a major, then added three more tournaments, including the prestigious McDonald's Championship. She finished the year as third-leading money winner with $334,525. Miller wouldn't win again for six years.

Fuzzy Recovers from Back Surgery to Win at Bay Hill

Fuzzy Zoeller captured the 1985 Hertz Bay Hill Classic with final rounds of 66-67. It was quite a comeback story for the Fuzz, who had ruptured a couple of discs in his back in the summer of 1984. He underwent surgery in September, and by February of '85 he was back on Tour. The Bay Hill victory came on March 10.

Fuzzy Zoeller

behind winner Andy North, at Oakland Hills C.C. in Michigan.

• June 23: Arnold Palmer rolls to an 11-stroke victory in the Senior Tournament Players Championship.

• June 23: Alice Miller wins the Mayflower Classic, setting a season record with $318,250.

• June 30: Miller Barber takes his third U.S. Senior Open, at Edgewood Tahoe C.C. in Nevada.

• July 7: Curtis Strange wins the Canadian Open. Jack Nicklaus finishes second for the seventh time.

• July 14: Kathy Baker wins the U.S. Women's Open at Baltusrol G.C. in

New Jersey. Nancy Lopez falls from contention with a closing 77.

• July 21: Scotland's Sandy Lyle becomes the first British player to win the British Open since Tony Jacklin in 1969. He beats Payne Stewart by one stroke at Royal St. George's G.C. in Sandwich, England.

Nancy Lopez

Lopez Laps the Field in LPGA Championship

Nancy Lopez ran the gamut of emotions in the 1985 LPGA Championship. In the opening round, Lopez was distressed after being penalized two strokes for slow play. Nevertheless, she finished the round with a rousing 65. Lopez posted another 65 on Sunday to win by eight strokes.

Chen Follows Double Eagle with Quadruple Bogie

T.C. Chen of Taiwan caused a stir in the 1985 U.S. Open. First, he scored a double eagle on the 2nd hole on his way to the first-round lead. Then, on the 5th hole of the final round, he double hit a chip shot and took a quadruple bogey. That erased his four-shot lead; he lost by one stroke.

T.C. Chen

• July 27: Lee Elder sets a Senior Tour 18-hole record with a 61 in the Merrill Lynch/Golf Digest Commemorative Pro-Am.

• July 28: Pat Bradley nips Jane Geddes to take the du Maurier Classic at Beaconsfield C.C. in Montreal.

• August 4: Scott Verplank's victory in the Western Open is the first by an amateur on the PGA Tour since Gene Littler won in San Diego in 1954.

• August 4: Don January becomes the first player to pass $1 million in Senior PGA Tour earnings.

• August 11: Hubert Green holds off Lee Trevino to win the PGA Championship at Cherry Hills C.C. in Englewood, Colorado.

• August 11: Nancy Lopez sets an LPGA record with a 72-hole total of 268 and wins the Henredon Classic by 10 shots.

Bernhard Langer

Langer Captures Masters After Strange Squanders Lead

Germany's Bernhard Langer won the 1985 Masters at the expense of Curtis Strange, as Strange blew a four-stroke lead on the final nine holes. While Langer fired a closing 68, Strange hit into the water guarding the 13th and 15th greens. After 36 holes, Bernhard had trailed the leaders by six strokes.

North Wins U.S. Open Title by a Single Stroke

Andy North was the beneficiary of T.C. Chen's double hit of a chip shot in the 1985 U.S. Open, at Oakland Hills C.C. in Birmingham, Michigan. North, a smooth putter, thus won his third official PGA Tour event. Two of the three wins were U.S. Opens, as he also won the championship in 1978.

Kathy Baker

Baker Enjoys Day of Fame at Women's Open

Kathy Baker, the 1982 National Collegiate champion, proved the victor in the 1985 U.S. Women's Open at Baltusrol G.C. in Springfield, New Jersey. Baker won by three strokes over runner-up Judy Clark. It was the only time Baker won or finished runner-up in a major championship, as she left the LPGA Tour at an early age.

Andy North

- August 14: Former football star John Brodie turns 50 and decides to take a crack at the Senior Tour.

- August 18: Muffin Spencer-Devlin shoots a 28 on the final nine to win the MasterCard International.

- August 22: The United States defeats Great Britain, 13-11, in the Walker Cup at Pine Valley G.C. in New Jersey.

- August 25: Roger Maltbie shoots four rounds in the 60s to win the NEC World Series of Golf.

- September 1: Sam Randolph, runner-up last year, wins the U.S. Amateur.

- September 9: Senior Tour player Rod Funseth dies of cancer at the age of 52.

- September 15: Europe defeats the U.S., 16½-11½, in the Ryder Cup at The Belfry in Sutton Coldfield, England. It's the first time the U.S. has lost the Cup since 1957.

Scott Verplank

Verplank, an Amateur, Wins Western Open Title

Scott Verplank became the first amateur to win a Tour event since 1954 when he captured the 1985 Western Open. Verplank, a college star at Oklahoma State, won the NCAA championship in 1986, then turned professional later in the year. In succeeding years, he struggled with his game because of serious elbow problems.

Hattori, 16, Wins U.S. Women's Amateur

Michiko Hattori, 16 years and 11 months old, won the 1985 U.S. Women's Amateur, defeating Cheryl Stacy in the final at Fox Chapel C.C. in Pittsburgh. Hattori became the third-youngest winner of the Amateur; Laura Baugh was the youngest at 16 years and two months, while Beatrix Hoyt was 16 years and three months. Hattori, of Japan, was also the first woman of an Asian country to win.

Michiko Hattori

Sandy Lyle

Scotland's Lyle Captures British Open for First Major

Sandy Lyle of Scotland became an international threat in 1985 when he won his first major championship, the British Open, at Royal St. George's in Sandwich, England. A 5 on the final hole could have cost Lyle the win, but David Graham and Bernhard Langer—still on the course—couldn't rally. Payne Stewart sneaked into second place.

• September 15: JoAnne Carner, age 46, wins the Safeco Classic, becoming the oldest winner ever on the LPGA Tour.

• October 13: Mike Fetchick wins the Hilton Head Seniors International on his 63rd birthday, making him the oldest senior player to win.

• October 27: Curtis Strange leads the PGA Tour money list with $542,321. He and Lanny Wadkins lead with three victories.

• October 27: Don Pooley wins the Vardon Trophy with a scoring average of 70.36 despite finishing 46th on the money list.

• October 27: Curtis Strange and Lanny Wadkins lead the PGA Tour with three victories each.

• October 27: Lanny Wadkins is the PGA Player of the Year.

• November: JoAnne Carner is inducted into the World Golf Hall of Fame.

Curtis Strange

Strange Wins Three, Leads Tour in Earnings

Curtis Strange, undaunted by a painful loss in the Masters, salvaged his 1985 season by winning three tournaments: the Honda Classic, Panasonic-Las Vegas Invitational, and Canadian Open. Strange led the PGA Tour with $542,321, thanks largely to the $171,000 he won in Las Vegas.

Hubert Green

Carner Wins Tourney at Age 46

JoAnne Carner captured the 1985 Safeco Classic at the age of 46, thus becomming the oldest winner in LPGA Tour history. Still not through, Carner would finish runner-up in an LPGA tournament each year from 1986 through 1990, and then again in 1992 at the age of 53.

JoAnne Carner

Green Claims PGA Championship at Cherry Hills

Hubert Green *(left)* emerged from three seasons of mediocrity by winning the 1985 PGA Championship at Cherry Hills C.C. in Denver. Lee Trevino *(right)* led Green by two strokes after two rounds, but then the Merry Mex closed 75-71. Hubie finished with a steady 70-72 for the victory.

• November 10: Jane Blalock wins the Mazda Japan Classic, her 29th and final LPGA victory.

• November 10: Nancy Lopez leads the LPGA with $416,472. Her 70.73 scoring average is a record.

• November 10: Nancy Lopez leads the LPGA Tour with five victories.

Alice Miller has four wins, Pat Bradley and Amy Alcott three each.

• November 23: Gary Player wins the first Senior Tour event he enters, the Quadel Seniors Classic.

• November 24: Peter Thomson leads the Senior Tour money list with $386,724.

• November 24: Peter Thomson wins a record nine events on the Senior PGA Tour, giving him 11 for his career. He'll never win another senior event.

• December 7: The brother/sister team of Larry and Laurie Rinker wins the JCPenney Mixed Team Classic.

THE GRAND MASTER ENJOYS ONE LAST HURRAH

Jack Nicklaus played his first Masters in 1959. Entering the 1986 Masters, he had won the tournament a record five times and established the 72-hole record of 271 in 1965. But never had he played a finer or more dramatic round at Augusta National than he did in 1986, at the age of 46, when he claimed his sixth green jacket.

It had been six years since Nicklaus won a major, two since he had won a tournament, and some wrote him off as a Masters contender. The Golden Bear shot a 69 in the third round to go into Sunday four strokes off the lead held by Greg Norman (the leader after 54 holes of all four major championships during the year). Through eight holes of the final round, Nicklaus was even par for the day and did not seem to be a major threat. But then lightning struck.

Nicklaus birdied the 9th hole, then played the back nine in 30 strokes, tying the tournament record. He birdied the 10th and 11th with long putts, bogied the 12th, and came back with a birdie at the 13th. He still trailed Seve Ballesteros by four strokes, but no matter. Nicklaus eagled the par-5 15th with a 12-foot putt and nearly scored a hole-in-one on the par-3 16th before making a three-footer for birdie.

Two-time Masters champion Ballesteros had grabbed the lead with eagles at the 8th and 13th holes, but, perhaps shaken by the roars greeting Nicklaus's heroics up ahead, faltered badly at the 15th. His 4-iron second shot on the 15th dived into the water short and left of the green, leading to a bogey. Suddenly, it was tied. Nicklaus had one more birdie in him, accomplishing it with a 10-foot putt on the 17th. Ballesteros posted yet another bogey to knock himself out of it, but the game was by no means over. Nicklaus parred the 18th to finish the tournament at 9-under, with a finishing 65, and there were several players still on the course with a chance.

Nick Price, who had set the Masters' 18-hole record with a 63 the day before, fell three shots short with a 71 on Sunday. That left Norman and Tom Kite. Kite, playing with Ballesteros, had matched the Spaniard's eagle at the 8th hole in the day's first dramatic moment. He came to the 18th hole at 8-under, needing a birdie to tie, and hit his approach to within 10 feet. His putt looked good, but it just missed on the low side.

Now it was down to Norman. The Australian had seemingly shot himself out of it with a double bogey on the 10th, his second of the week on that hole. Then, suddenly, he birdied four straight holes starting at the 14th to go 9-under. A par on the 18th would force a playoff. But Norman blocked his 4-iron approach well to the right, pitched on, and missed a 15-foot putt. Nicklaus had his 18th major championship as a professional, and it was perhaps the most memorable of them all.

1986

- January: PGA Tour players are scheduled to play in 46 events for a total season purse of $25,442,242.

- January: LPGA Tour players are scheduled to play in 36 events with a total season purse of $10 million.

- January: Senior PGA Tour players are scheduled to play in 28 events.

- January: The Panasonic Las Vegas Invitational will offer $1,150,000 in official money, making it the first Tour event with a seven-figure purse.

- January: Two new events with $1 million purses are scheduled on the PGA Tour—The International and the Vantage Championship.

- January: The PGA Tour will award $2 million to players in the season-long Vantage Cup bonus pool, determined by a points system.

- January: The Stadium Course at PGA West, designed by Pete Dye and billed as the toughest course in the world, opens for play.

In the 1986 Masters, 46-year-old Jack Nicklaus remained back in the pack after 62 holes. However, he then authored one of the greatest charges in major championship history. In the final 10 holes, Nicklaus posted these scores: birdie, birdie, birdie, bogey, birdie, par, eagle, birdie, birdie, par. A back-nine 30 gave him his sixth Masters title.

• January 11: Calvin Peete shoots a tournament-record 267 to win the MONY Tournament of Champions, which has become a season-opening event.

• February 9: Charles Owens becomes the first player to win using a long putter at the Senior Tour's Treasure Coast Classic.

• February 13: Mac O'Grady calls PGA Tour Commissioner Deane Beman a "little Hitler" for deducting a $500 fine (stemming from a 1984 incident) from his winnings. He will be suspended for his comments.

• February 16: Gary Player leads all the way in winning the General Foods PGA Seniors Championship.

• February 23: Doug Tewell finishes 66-63 and wins the Los Angeles Open by seven strokes.

• March 2: Kenny Knox wins the Honda Classic despite a third-round 80 in chilly, 45-mph winds. He remains the last Tour player to win a tournament with a round of 80 or higher.

1986

PGA West—Stadium

The Stadium Course Opens at PGA West

Pete Dye, asked by the Landmark Land Co. to design the toughest course in the world, obliged with the Stadium Course at PGA West in La Quinta, California. Dye incorporated small greens and pot bunkers into this brutally tough desert track. The course played host to the Skins Game from 1986–91.

Knox Wins Honda Despite a Round of 80

The pros faced nasty weather in the 1986 Honda Classic in Coral Springs, Florida. In the third round, they endured cold winds that blew up to 45 mph. Kenny Knox shot 80 that day yet still won the tournament, closing 70—287. Through 1992, Knox remained the last player to win an official PGA Tour event with a round of 80 or above.

Kenny Knox

Sutton Prevails in Phoenix, at Memorial

In 1986, Hal Sutton captured both the Phoenix Open and the Memorial Tournament. Sutton finished sixth on the money list, his best performance since he led all money winners in 1983. In subsequent years, Sutton lost confidence and his play suffered greatly. In 1992, he employed the Houston Astros' team psychiatrist as a caddie.

Hal Sutton

• March 30: John Mahaffey prevails in the Tournament Players Championship.

• April 6: Pat Bradley leads all the way to win the Nabisco Dinah Shore.

• April 12: Nick Price breaks the 18-hole Masters record with a 63.

• April 13: Jack Nicklaus, 46, becomes the oldest winner of the Masters, beating out Greg Norman, Tom Kite, and Seve Ballesteros down the stretch.

• May 4: Greg Norman shoots 27-under-par for five rounds and wins the $207,000 first prize at the Panasonic Las Vegas Invitational.

• June 1: Greg Norman beats Larry Mize on the sixth playoff hole to win the Kemper Open.

• June 1: Pat Bradley beats Patty Sheehan by one stroke at the LPGA Championship.

• June 15: Raymond Floyd, 43, becomes the oldest winner of the

1986

Mac O'Grady

Teed-Off O'Grady Calls Beman Nasty Names

1n 1986, Mac O'Grady blew his stack after being fined $500 by PGA Tour Commissioner Deane Beman (stemming from a 1984 incident). O'Grady responded to the fine by calling Beman a "thief with a capital T" and a "little Hitler." For those comments, O'Grady was suspended six weeks. O'Grady appealed to a federal court, but to no avail.

Nabisco Dinah Shore

Bradley Strolls to Victory in Dinah Shore

Pat Bradley *(at center in yellow sweater)* won the 1986 Nabisco Dinah Shore, leading all the way. It was the first of three majors she won in 1986, the best season of her Hall of Fame career. A big swinger and long hitter when she turned pro, Bradley had since refined her game in favor of accuracy.

Juli Inkster

Inkster Wins Four Events

Juli Inkster built up an eight-stroke lead after 54 holes in the 1986 McDonald's Championship. She won the event despite a final-round 77. This was Inkster's most productive season, as she also captured the Women's Kemper Open, Lady Keystone Open, and Atlantic City Classic.

U.S. Open, at Shinnecock Hills G.C. in Southampton, New York.

• June 22: Chi Chi Rodriguez takes his first Senior Tour title, the Senior Tournament Players Championship.

• June 29: Bob Murphy captures the Canadian Open for his first win in 11 years.

• June 29: Dale Douglass beats Gary Player by one stroke to win the U.S. Senior Open at Scioto C.C. in Ohio.

• July 6: Mac O'Grady wins his first Tour event, the Sammy Davis Jr.-Greater Hartford Open.

• July 8: Players and spectators are evacuated from the course during a

practice round for the U.S. Women's Open due to a toxic cloud of smoke from a train derailment near NCR G.C. in Dayton, Ohio.

• July 14: Jane Geddes gets her first career victory, beating Sally Little in an 18-hole playoff for the U.S. Women's Open.

Raymond, Christina, and Maria Floyd

Floyd, Age 43, Becomes Oldest Open Winner

Raymond Floyd poses with wife Maria and six-year-old daughter Christina after winning the 1986 U.S. Open at Shinnecock Hills in Southampton, New York. Floyd, at age 43, closed with a 66 to become the oldest winner of the championship. It was also his first U.S. Open victory in 23 years on the Tour.

Bob Tway

Douglass Turns 50, Goes on a Binge

Dale Douglass turned 50 on March 5, 1986, and 18 days later he captured the Senior Tour's Vintage Invitational. Before the year was over, he had won three more events. He even reeled in the big one, the U.S. Senior Open. Douglass defeated Gary Player by one stroke at Scioto C.C. in Columbus, Ohio.

Dale Douglass

Tway Holes Out from Bunker to Claim PGA

Bob Tway holes this bunker shot on the 72nd hole to defeat Greg Norman in the 1986 PGA Championship. Tway was the first of four men to stun Greg Norman with miraculous shots. Other Norman killers included Larry Mize (1987 Masters), Robert Gamez (1990 Nestlé Invitational), and David Frost (1990 USF&G Classic).

• July 18: Greg Norman ties the 18-hole British Open record with a 63 at Turnberry, Scotland.

• July 20: Greg Norman wins the British Open by five strokes for his first major championship.

• July 27: Pat Bradley wins the du Maurier Classic at the Board of Trade C.C. in Toronto for her third major title of the year. She defeats Ayako Okamoto in a playoff.

• August 2: Great Britain/Ireland defeats the U.S., 13-5, in the Curtis Cup at Prairie Dunes C.C. in Hutchinson, Kansas. It's the first time they have won the cup on American soil.

• August 3: Tom Kite comes from seven strokes behind in the final round to win the Western Open.

• August 9: Greg Norman takes a four-stroke lead after three rounds of the PGA Championship at the Inverness Club in Toledo, Ohio. He has now led after 54 holes of all four major championships this year.

Geddes's First Win Comes at Women's Open

Jane Geddes won the 1986 U.S. Women's Open at NCR G.C. in Dayton, Ohio, but she needed an 18-hole playoff to do it. After each tied at 287, Geddes defeated Sally Little, 73-71, for the title. It was Geddes's first LPGA Tour victory. The very next week, she won the Boston Five Classic.

Bob Tway

Tway Can't Hold Back Tears After PGA Win

PGA Champion Bob Tway wipes away tears after accepting the Wanamaker Trophy. At the halfway point, Tway was nine strokes off the lead. Despite a third-round 64, Tway trailed Greg Norman by four strokes. But in the final round, Tway outscored Norman 70-76, thanks to his incredible bunker shot on the 72nd hole.

Jane Geddes

• August 11: Bob Tway holes out a bunker shot for a birdie on the 72nd hole of the PGA Championship to break a tie and beat Greg Norman, who finishes with a 76. The final round is played Monday because of rain.

• August 17: Ken Green wins The International, a new event with a Stableford format (points are awarded for scores on each hole).

• August 17: Pat Bradley charges from eight strokes behind to win the Nestlé World Championship of Women's Golf with a closing 63.

• August 17: Cindy Mackey wins the MasterCard International Pro-Am by 14 strokes, tying the LPGA record for victory margin.

• August 24: Dan Pohl wins his second event of the year at the NEC World Series of Golf.

• September 1: Betsy King comes from behind to win the Rail Charity Classic with a closing 63.

Great Britain/Ireland Curtis Cup Team

Great Britain/Ireland Wins Curtis Cup Match

Amateurs representing Great Britain and Ireland pose together after winning the 1986 Curtis Cup, held at Prairie Dunes C.C. in Hutchinson, Kansas. Great Britain/Ireland broke America's 13-match winning streak. It was just its third win in 24 total meetings, and its first on American soil.

Bradley Nabs a Couple More Major Championships

After winning the Dinah Shore, Pat Bradley won two more majors in 1986, the LPGA Championship and du Maurier Classic. However, neither one was easy. Bradley edged Patty Sheehan by one in the LPGA, and she outdueled Ayako Okamoto in sudden-death in the du Maurier. At season's end, Bradley was named LPGA Player of the Year.

Pat Bradley

Dan Pohl

Pohl Captures Colonial NIT, World Series of Golf

Dan Pohl, the Tour's longest driver back in 1980 and '81, showed finesse from the sand when he won the 1986 NEC World Series of Golf. It was his second win of the season, and his career, even though he had been on Tour since 1978. Pohl finished fifth on the 1986 money list.

• September 3: Arnold Palmer makes a hole-in-one on the 3rd hole at the TPC at Avenel in the Chrysler Cup pro-am. It's the second straight day he has aced the same hole.

• October: Cary Middlecoff is inducted into the PGA World Golf Hall of Fame.

• October 26: Ben Crenshaw wins the Vantage Championship when the fourth round is canceled by rain.

• October 26: Bob Tway wins $500,000 for finishing first in the Vantage Cup bonus pool.

• October 26: Scott Hoch wins the Vardon Trophy, averaging 70.08.

• November 2: Greg Norman leads the PGA Tour money list with $653,296, just $516 ahead of Bob Tway.

• November 2: Bob Tway leads the PGA Tour with four victories. Fuzzy Zoeller has three. Tway is also the PGA Player of the Year.

Greg Norman

Norman's a Winner in U.S., Australia, Europe

Greg Norman, who led after 54 holes of every major championship in 1986, was clearly the world's best player. He won four tournaments in Australia, three in Europe, and two in the U.S. Despite his heavy activity outside the United States, Norman still managed to lead the U.S. PGA Tour in earnings, with $653,296.

Norman Holds Best Scorecard at British Open

In the second round of the 1986 British Open, Greg Norman navigated old Turnberry G.L. in 63 strokes on his way to winning his first major. The 63 equaled the lowest mark in British Open history. Norman had eight birdies and an eagle in the round. He could have finished with a 62, but he three-putted the 18th green. Norman ended up winning by five strokes over Gordon Brand.

Greg Norman

Arnold Palmer

Palmer Aces Same Hole Twice at Avenel

Arnold Palmer proved he still had the magic at the 1986 Chrysler Cup at TPC—Avenel. Palmer scored a hole-in-one on the 3rd hole—then aced the same hole the next day. Unfortunately, Palmer faded a little in '86. It was the first year he did not win a Senior Tour event, although he'd win one more in 1988.

• November 2: Greg Norman wins the Adelaide Open, winning for the third straight week in Australia and the fifth straight event he has entered, including two in Europe.

• November 9: Pat Bradley leads the LPGA Tour money list with $492,021, which is $200,000 more than second-place Betsy King.

• November 9: Pat Bradley is the LPGA Player of the Year. She also wins the Vare Trophy (71.10) and leads in victories (five).

• November 23: Bruce Crampton leads the Senior PGA Tour in earnings ($454,299) and victories (seven).

• November 30: Fuzzy Zoeller wins $370,000 of the $450,000 purse at the Skins Game.

• November 30: Greg Norman wins the Western Australian Open for his ninth victory of the year (three in Europe, four in Australia, two in the United States).

MIZE HOLES CHIP SHOT, BREAKS SHARK'S HEART

The 1987 Masters might have been Greg Norman's third consecutive major championship victory. Instead, it was the second straight time he was victimized in a miracle finish. Norman had made the 1986 British Open his first major title after coming close several times. At that point, he was age 31 and seemed well on his way to winning multiple majors. The next major was the 1986 PGA Championship, where Norman lost only when Bob Tway holed out for a birdie from a greenside bunker on the 72nd hole. It was the first time anybody had won a major by holing a shot from off the final green to break a tie—but not the last time.

In golf's very next major, the 1987 Masters, Norman again found himself in the thick of a thriller. The final round was a see-saw battle among multiple contenders, the leader board changing so fast it was hard to keep up. One of the key figures was Larry Mize, who grabbed the lead with birdies at 12 and 13, gave it back with bogeys at 14 and 15, then regained a share of it by sinking a five-foot birdie putt on the final hole. Mize was an Augusta native and went to high school there, though he had lived much of his childhood in Columbus, Georgia. He had won one tournament in his first five years on Tour, though he was better known for blowing several others.

Mize, however, reached a playoff with a 285, as did Seve Ballesteros. The Spaniard, shaking off bad memories from his shaky Masters finish the year before, got into sudden-death with birdies on 15 and 17 and by saving par from a bunker on the 18th. Norman had an up-and-down day—six birdies and six bogeys, with a 25-foot birdie putt on 17 the key blow down the stretch. His birdie putt from a similar distance on 18 looked good, but it narrowly missed on the low side. He too entered the playoff.

Three players finished one shot back in the tightest Masters finish ever. Third-round co-leaders Ben Crenshaw and Roger Maltbie shot 74s, while Jodie Mudd couldn't quite sustain an early charge of birdie-eagle-birdie on the first three holes. On the first hole of sudden-death, No. 10, Mize had the best birdie chance but missed from 10 feet. Ballesteros knocked his 25-foot birdie putt five feet past, and when he missed the comebacker, his Masters was over.

Norman and Mize moved to the par-4 11th, where Mize put himself in trouble with a second shot well to the right of the green. Norman hit the fringe for a likely par. Mize, about 45 yards from the hole, pitching to a slick green, faced a much tougher shot than Tway in the PGA the year before. But the result was the same. The ball found the hole, sending Norman to defeat and, perhaps, to despair. Through 1992, Norman had still not added another major championship.

1987

- January: PGA Tour players are scheduled to play in 46 events with a total purse of $32,106,093.

- January: LPGA Tour players are scheduled to play in 36 events with a total purse of $11,400,000.

- January: Senior PGA Tour players are scheduled to play in 35 events.

- January: The Vantage Championship is replaced by the season-ending, $2 million Nabisco Championships.

- January: The PGA Tour's Vantage Cup will be replaced by the Nabisco Grand Prix, which awards $1 million to the top 30 season-long points earners.

- January 18: Corey Pavin holes a 25-foot birdie putt on the final hole to beat Bernhard Langer at the Bob Hope Chrysler Classic.

- February 1: Johnny Miller finishes with a 66 to win the AT&T Pebble Beach National Pro-Am, the last of his 23 PGA Tour victories.

1987

Larry Mize leaps toward the heavens after winning the 1987 Masters. Mize won on
the second hole of sudden-death, the 11th at Augusta National. He was 45 yards from
the pin and hoping just to get up and down for a par. But miraculously, he pulled out
his sand wedge and chipped it in, sending Greg Norman to another agonizing defeat.

• February 8: Nancy Lopez gets her 35th LPGA career victory, qualifying for the LPGA Hall of Fame.

• February 15: Chi Chi Rodriguez wins the General Foods PGA Seniors Championship.

• March 8: Mark Calcavecchia wins the Honda Classic. A year earlier, having lost his Tour exemption, he caddied for Ken Green in the same event.

• March 15: Payne Stewart shoots a tournament-record 264 and wins the Bay Hill Classic. He donates his first prize of $108,000 to the Florida Hospital Cancer Center.

• March 15: Don Pooley scores a $1 million ace on the 17th hole at the Bay Hill Classic ($500,000 for himself, the rest for charity).

• March 29: Sandy Lyle beats Jeff Sluman in a sudden-death playoff for the Tournament Players Championship.

1987

Johnny Miller

Miller's Final Win Comes at Pebble Beach

Johnny Miller, the hero of the early 1970s, returned to his old form in the 1987 AT&T Pebble Beach National Pro-Am. Miller shot a final-round 66 on America's favorite public course for the victory. This would be the last of Miller's 23 PGA Tour wins. He would go on to become a popular commentator on NBC.

Stewart Donates Check to Charity

Payne Stewart won the 1987 Hertz Bay Hill Classic with a 20-under 264, then donated his $108,000 first-place check to the Florida Hospital Golden Circle of Friends. The donation was "in memory of my father, William Louis Stewart, who died of cancer two years previous to this day." Payne hadn't won a tournament since 1983, and he wouldn't win again until 1989.

Payne Stewart

Betsy King

King Claims Dinah Shore in Sudden-Death

After 10 years on Tour, Betsy King claimed her first major in 1987, the Nabisco Dinah Shore. King holed a bunker shot on the 70th hole at Mission Hills C.C., then defeated Patty Sheehan in sudden-death. King, one of the most active Christian players on Tour, also won the 1987 Samaritan Award for her humanitarian and charitable efforts.

• **March 29:** Pat Bradley wins the Standard Register Turquoise Classic and becomes the first LPGA player to pass $2 million in career earnings.

• **April 5:** Betsy King wins her first major championship, beating Patty Sheehan in a playoff at the Nabisco Dinah Shore.

• **April 12:** Larry Mize wins a playoff for the Masters title over Greg Norman and Seve Ballesteros by chipping in on the second sudden-death hole.

• **May 2:** Jan Stephenson, tied for the 54-hole lead at the S&H Classic, is injured in an auto accident and won't play the next day.

• **May 24:** Chi Chi Rodriguez wins for the third straight week at the Silver Pages Classic. He made eight straight birdies in the second round.

• **May 24:** Jane Geddes nips Betsy King by one stroke to win the Mazda LPGA Championship, as both close with 67s.

Jay Randolf, Richard J. Ferris, Don Pooley

Pooley's Hole-in-One Worth $1 Million

Don Pooley *(right)* earned a $500,000 check after acing the 17th hole at the 1987 Hertz Bay Hill Classic. Another $500,000 went to the Arnold Palmer Children's Hospital. Here, Richard J. Ferris, chairman of Allegis Corporation, presents the check to Pooley, and NBC reporter Jay Randolph gets the quotes. In May, Pooley won the Memorial.

Grooves Too Close in Ping Eye 2s

The great groove controversy, which would drag on for more than five years, began in 1987. The USGA and PGA Tour declared that the new Ping Eye 2 irons didn't conform to the Rules of Golf, saying the grooves were too close together. Karsten Manufacturing, makers of the Eye 2 irons, disagreed and took the matter to court.

Lyle Mines for Gold on the PGA Tour

Sandy Lyle, a premier European player since the late 1970s, struck it rich on the PGA Tour in the late 1980s. His first U.S. victory came in the Greater Greensboro Open in 1986, and in 1987 he captured the lucrative Tournament Players Championship. The following year, he would win three events in the United States and rake in 726,934 American dollars.

Sandy Lyle

Ping Eye 2 Irons

• May 28: The United States defeats Great Britain/Ireland, 16½-7½, to win the Walker Cup at Sunningdale G.C. in Berkshire, England.

• May 31: Scott Hoch, who opened 67-64-67 for a four-stroke lead, closes with a 78 to lose the Memorial Tournament to Don Pooley.

• June 7: Chi Chi Rodriguez wins the Senior Players Reunion Pro-Am, his fourth consecutive victory in tournaments entered (he took last week off).

• June 14: J.C. Snead, age 46, beats Seve Ballesteros in a playoff at the Manufacturers Hanover Westchester Classic.

• June 14: Gary Player wins the Mazda Senior Tournament Players Championship at Sawgrass C.C. in Ponte Vedra, Florida.

• June 21: Scott Simpson shoots a 32 on the back nine to win the U.S. Open by one stroke over Tom Watson at the Olympic Club in San Francisco.

Jane Geddes

Geddes Edges King in LPGA Championship

Jane Geddes won nine events in her first 10 years on Tour, 1983–92, and five of them came in 1987. The biggest of the five was the Mazda LPGA Championship. Both she and Betsy King shot 67s in the final round, and Geddes prevailed by a shot. Geddes, one of the longest hitters on Tour, finished third on the 1987 money list.

Scott Simpson

Simpson Squeaks by Watson to Win U.S. Open

Few observers picked Scott Simpson to win the 1987 U.S. Open when play started at San Francisco's Olympic Club. The favorite was Tom Watson, who went to nearby Stanford. But Simpson came into his own, firing a 32 on the back nine in the final round to nip Watson by a stroke. Simpson also won the 1987 Greater Greensboro Open.

• June 23: The USGA rules that Ping Eye 2 irons don't conform to the Rules because the grooves are too close together, but they will be allowed in USGA competition until 1990 and won't be illegal under the Rules of Golf until 1996.

• July 12: Ayako Okamoto blows a six-stroke lead in the final round and loses to Jody Rosenthal at the du Maurier Classic at Islesmere G.C. in Laval, Quebec.

• July 12: Gary Player shoots four rounds in the 60s to roll to victory in the U.S. Senior Open at Brooklawn C.C. in Fairfield, Connecticut.

• July 19: Nick Faldo pars all 18 holes in the final round and wins the British Open by one stroke at Muirfield, Scotland.

• July 28: England's Laura Davies, age 23, defeats Ayako Okamoto and JoAnne Carner in an 18-hole playoff in the U.S. Women's Open at Plainfield C.C. in New Jersey.

Nick Faldo and Family

Faldo Wins British by Parring Last 18 Holes

Nick Faldo poses with his family after winning the 1987 British Open, at Muirfield in Scotland. Faldo ended this tournament with neither a whimper nor a bang; he brought new meaning to consistency by parring every hole of the final round. Paul Azinger bogied the 17th and 18th holes to lose by one stroke.

Strange Nabs Three Tour Victories in Hot Summer

Curtis Strange burned it up in the summer of 1987, capturing the Canadian Open, Federal Express St. Jude Classic, and NEC World Series of Golf in a two-month stretch. Strange was proving you no longer needed to be a mega-winner to earn mega-bucks. With three total wins, Strange won a record $925,941.

Curtis Strange

Laura Davies's U.S. Open Celebration

Davies Wins the Open, Throws a Party

Laura Davies *(top center)* celebrates with British and American friends after her surprising win in the 1987 U.S. Women's Open. Davies, who had not yet qualified for the LPGA Tour, overpowered JoAnne Carner and Ayako Okamoto to win the championship in a playoff. The LPGA quickly extended her an exemption from qualifying for the Tour.

• July 30: Mike McGee ties a PGA Tour record by taking 18 putts in the first round of the Federal Express St. Jude Classic.

• August 9: At PGA National G.C. in Palm Beach Gardens, Florida, Larry Nelson beats Lanny Wadkins in a playoff for the PGA Championship.

• August 22: The Beatrice Western Open, delayed for two days by heavy rains, finally gets underway. Due to flooding at Butler National G.C., nine holes are played at the nearby Oak Brook Village G.C.

• August 23: Kay Cockerill wins her second straight U.S. Women's Amateur.

• August 30: Curtis Strange wins the NEC World Series of Golf.

• August 30: Billy Mayfair wins the U.S. Amateur championship.

• September 20: Jan Stephenson, who missed a month and a half of action after her automobile accident in April, wins the Safeco Classic.

Nelson Outduels Wadkins in Heated PGA

Larry Nelson beat Lanny Wadkins on the first hole of sudden-death to win the 1987 PGA Championship, at PGA National G.C. in Palm Beach Gardens, Florida. As one might expect, Florida in August was hot and muggy. The weather, combined with the difficult course, produced the highest winning score in the tournament's 62-year history—287.

Larry Nelson

Okamoto Tops Tour in Earnings

Ayako Okamoto, treated like a queen in her home country of Japan, waves to the cameras after the 1987 Mazda Japan Classic, the LPGA Tour's last event of the season. Okamoto didn't win—she finished second— but her runner-up finish pushed her into first place on the money list. She also won Player of the Year honors.

Ayako Okamoto

- September 27: Europe defeats the U.S. in the Ryder Cup, 15-13, at Muirfield Village G.C. in Dublin, Ohio. It's the first Ryder win for Europe on American soil.

- October 4: Al Geiberger, playing in his fourth senior event, wins the Vantage Championship, the Senior Tour's first $1 million event.

- November: Robert Trent Jones and Betsy Rawls are inducted into the PGA World Golf Hall of Fame.

- November 1: Tom Watson takes the $360,000 first prize at the Nabisco Championships of Golf.

- November 1: Curtis Strange leads the PGA Tour money list with

$925,941. His $175,000 Nabisco Grand Prix bonus is included in the total.

- November 1: Curtis Strange and Paul Azinger finish with three victories each to lead the PGA Tour Azinger wins the PGA Player of the Year Award.

Trevino Scores Hole-in-One at Skins Game, Wins $310,000

Lee Trevino is congratulated by caddie Herman Mitchell after scoring a hole-in-one at the 1987 Skins Game. Trevino aced the 17th hole at PGA West and thus won the skin, worth $175,000. He earned a total of $310,000 in the event, beating out Jack Nicklaus, Arnold Palmer, and Fuzzy Zoeller.

European Ryder Cup Team

Europe Claims First Cup on American Soil

The European Ryder Cup team, led by captain Tony Jacklin *(third from left)*, repeated its 1985 victory by barely edging a frustrated United States squad, 15-13. It was only the second time in 30 years that the U.S. had lost, and it was its first loss ever on American soil. Seve Ballesteros led Europe with four points.

Lee Trevino

- November 1: Dan Pohl wins the Vardon Trophy, averaging 70.25.

- November 8: Ayako Okamoto nips Betsy King for both the money title ($466,034 to $460,385) and LPGA Player of the Year honors.

- November 8: Jane Geddes leads the LPGA Tour with five victories.

- November 8: Betsy King wins the Vare Trophy, averaging 71.14.

- November 29: Lee Trevino aces the 17th hole at the Skins Game for $175,000 and wins with $310,000.

- December 6: Ian Woosnam wins the winner-take-all Million Dollar Classic in South Africa.

- December 13: Chi Chi Rodriguez leads the Senior Tour with $509,145. He also leads with seven victories, two more than Bruce Crampton.

- December 20: Nancy Lopez and Miller Barber team to win the Mazda Champions in Jamaica.

When Curtis Strange won the Memorial Tournament three weeks before the 1988 U.S. Open, runner-up Hale Irwin proclaimed Strange the best player in the world. It was a defensible case. Strange had led the PGA Tour money list in 1985 and 1987, winning three times each year, and he had already won twice in 1988.

Still, Strange was 33 years old and had never won a major championship. His main contenders for unofficial "No. 1" status—Seve Ballesteros, Greg Norman, and 1988 Masters champion Sandy Lyle—all had. But with perfect timing, Strange took care of that deficiency in the '88 U.S. Open at The Country Club in Brookline, Massachusetts.

Strange entered Open Sunday as the 54-hole leader, although Englishman Nick Faldo—the 1987 British Open champion—was right on his tail. Neither played especially well, but no one behind them made much of a move. Faldo, who had won the '87 British with a final round of 18 pars, seemed determined to use the same method here. He parred the first 14 holes but still trailed by a stroke. Finally, he birdied the

STRANGE WINS U.S. OPEN ON WAY TO $1 MILLION

15th from five feet to grab a share of the lead. He immediately gave it back by hitting into a bunker on the par-3 16th and making a bogey.

Strange was not as sharp as he'd been in the first three rounds, but he regained the lead by holing a 25-foot putt for a par on the 16th. On the 17th, however, he watched his treacherous, downhill birdie putt from 15 feet roll six feet past. He missed that one and the game was tied again. On the 18th, Strange avoided another bogey by getting up and down from the front bunker, blasting to within a foot of the hole. Faldo

missed a birdie try from 18 feet, setting up the second U.S./Great Britain clash in a U.S. Open at The Country Club. The first was 75 years earlier, when 20-year-old Francis Ouimet beat Englishmen Harry Vardon and Ted Ray.

This too would be an American victory, as Faldo stumbled in the playoff with a 40 on the back nine to shoot a 75. Strange, one-putting for par six times, managed an even-par 71. The key hole was the 13th. Strange turned a one-stroke lead into a three-stroke margin by holing an 18-foot birdie putt while Faldo three-putted for a bogey.

Strange didn't stop with the U.S. Open. He assured that 1988 would be his best year ever by claiming his fourth victory at the Nabisco Championships, the finale to the PGA Tour season, in a sudden-death playoff over Tom Kite at Pebble Beach Golf Links. The $360,000 first-place check—plus a $175,000 season-long bonus—made Strange the first player ever to crack $1 million in PGA Tour earnings, as he reached $1,147,644. Faldo, meanwhile, would go on to claim the mantle of world's best player in 1989, 1990, and—arguably—1992.

1988

• January: PGA Tour players are scheduled to play in 47 events with a total season purse of $36,959,307.

• January: LPGA Tour players are scheduled to play in 36 events with a total season purse of $12,510,000.

• January: Senior PGA Tour players are scheduled to play in 37 events.

• January: The $1 million Nabisco bonus pool will be awarded to the top 30 players on the PGA Tour money list. There will be no season-long points system.

• January: The Vardon Trophy will now be based on a scoring average adjusted to the average score of the field each week.

• January 30: The USGA says square-grooved irons will remain legal, but Ping Eye 2 irons don't conform because grooves are too close together.

• January 31: Sandy Lyle comes from seven strokes behind to tie Fred Couples at the Phoenix Open. Lyle wins the playoff.

1988

In 1988, when Curtis Strange became the first PGA Tour player to reach $1 million in season earnings, he owed a nod of gratitude to Nabisco. Strange's win in the season-ending Nabisco Championships earned him $360,000; and since he finished as the leading money winner, he received a $175,000 bonus from Nabisco's bonus pool.

• January 31: Chi Chi Rodriguez wins $300,000 of the $360,000 total in the first Senior Skins Game, beating Gary Player, Arnold Palmer, and Sam Snead.

• February 14: Gary Player wins the General Foods PGA Seniors Championship by three strokes.

• March 6: Orville Moody finishes with a 63 to win the Vintage Chrysler Invitational by 11 strokes.

• March 16: Mary Bea Porter, playing in a qualifying tournament for the Standard Register Turquoise Classic, saves the life of a small boy who had nearly drowned in a swimming pool.

• March 27: Mark McCumber wins the Tournament Players Championship by four strokes over Mike Reid.

• April 3: Amy Alcott's record 274 wins the Nabisco Dinah Shore.

• April 10: Sandy Lyle birdies the 72nd hole from a fairway bunker to win the Masters by one stroke.

1988

Orville Moody

Moody Wins by 11 at Vintage Invitational

With the help of the long putter, Orville Moody's career rebounded on the PGA Senior Tour. In 1988, the former U.S. Open champion tied the Senior Tour record for victory margin when he won the Vintage Chrysler Invitational by 11 strokes. Moody shot a final-round 63 at the Vintage Club in Indian Wells, California.

Sandy Lyle

Chip Beck

Lyle's Bunker Shot Helps Him Claim Masters

Sandy Lyle tees off at Augusta National G.C. during the 1988 Masters. Lyle won the tournament on the 72nd hole with a spectacular bunker shot. Sandy hit a 7-iron from an uphill lie to the green, then holed a 10-foot birdie putt that gave him a one-stroke victory over Mark Calcavecchia. Lyle finished at 281.

Beck Shoots 26-Under at USF&G

Soft-spoken Southerner Chip Beck nearly broke the PGA Tour's 72-hole record for most strokes under par in 1988. Beck won the USF&G Classic in New Orleans by shooting 26-under, just a stroke off the record set by Mike Souchak and Ben Hogan. Beck finished the season second on the PGA Tour money list, winning $916,818.

• May 1: Bruce Crampton and Orville Moody win on the sixth extra hole of a playoff over Lou Graham and Tommy Aaron at the Liberty Mutual Legends of Golf.

• May 22: Sherri Turner outscores Amy Alcott, 67-74, to make up a six-stroke deficit and win the Mazda LPGA Championship.

• May 29: Sherri Turner wins the LPGA Corning Classic—her second victory in two weeks.

• June 12: Billy Casper wins the Mazda Senior TPC at the TPC at Sawgrass Valley Course.

• June 20: Curtis Strange defeats Nick Faldo, 71-75, in an 18-hole

playoff to win the U.S. Open, at The Country Club in Massachusetts.

• July 3: Jim Benepe, in the tournament on a sponsor's exemption and playing his first PGA Tour event, wins the Beatrice Western Open.

• July 3: Sally Little takes her first victory since 1982 at the du Maurier

Amy Alcott, Dinah Shore

Alcott Wins Dinah Shore with Record Total Score

Winless the previous year, Amy Alcott scorched Mission Hills C.C. with a record score of 274 to win the 1988 Nabisco Dinah Shore. Alcott was on her way to her best money season on the LPGA Tour, earning nearly $300,000. Ironically, this was her only win of the year; she did have 15 top-10 finishes.

Jim Benepe

Sluman Tames Oak Tree to Win PGA

Jeff Sluman won his first PGA Tour event in 1988, the PGA Championship at Oak Tree G.C. in Edmond, Oklahoma. Sluman, just 5'7", turned in one of the great finishing rounds in the championship's history. He shot a 65, which included an eagle on the par-5 5th hole, where he holed a 100-yard wedge. His 272 total won by three shots.

Jeff Sluman

Benepe Wins the Western, His First Tour Event

Jim Benepe turned more than a few heads when he won the 1988 Beatrice Western Open. Amazingly, Benepe had never played in a PGA Tour event before, and he snuck into this one only because he was given a sponsor's exemption. Benepe led the Canadian Tour's Order of Merit in 1987.

Classic at Vancouver G.C. in Coquitlam, British Columbia.

• July 16: Blaine McCallister shoots a 63 in the third round of the Hardee's Classic, giving him a total of 125 in consecutive rounds.

• July 17: Seve Ballesteros catches Nick Price with a final-round 65 and wins the rain-delayed British Open at Royal Lytham & St. Anne's in Lytham, England.

• July 19: John Laupheimer resigns as LPGA commissioner in response to calls for his ouster.

• July 24: Swedish rookie Liselotte Neumann outduels Patty Sheehan to win the U.S. Women's Open at Baltimore C.C.

• July 31: Chi Chi Rodriguez wins the Digital Seniors Classic for the third consecutive year.

• August 8: Gary Player beats Bob Charles in an 18-hole playoff, 68-70, to win the U.S. Senior Open.

Sherri Turner

Turner Comes from Behind to Claim LPGA

Little-known Sherri Turner used her long tee shots to great advantage in the 1988 LPGA Championship. Six strokes off the lead going into the final round, Turner roared in with a 67 and won. In the four previous years, she never fared better than 20th on the money list. In 1988, she finished first on Tour with $350,851.

Little Ends Drought with Win at du Maurier

After a six-year drought, South African Sally Little won a tournament in 1988. She picked a good one to win, the du Maurier Classic, a major championship for LPGA players. This was Little's first and last victory since undergoing both abdominal surgery and arthroscopic knee surgery in 1983.

Sally Little

Seve Ballesteros

Seve Captures British with a Closing 65

One of the most talented trouble-shot players in history, Seve Ballesteros hacked out of this jungle on his way to winning the 1988 British Open, at Royal Lytham & St. Annes in England. In the final round, Ballesteros fired a 65 to surpass Nick Price and win the British for the third time.

• August 14: Jeff Sluman catches Paul Azinger with a final-round 65 and wins the PGA Championship at Oak Tree G.C. in Oklahoma.

• August 20: Jack Nicklaus passes $5 million in Tour earnings.

• August 28: Mike Reid wins the NEC World Series of Golf in a playoff when Tom Watson misses a three-foot putt on the first extra hole.

• August 28: Eric Meeks wins the U.S. Amateur championship.

• September 4: Ken Green wins the Canadian Open, taming Glen Abbey G.C. with a 275.

• September 10: Ken Green wins the Milwaukee Open.

• September 18: Arnold Palmer takes his first victory in three years at the Crestar Classic.

• October 9: Walter Zembriski, a former construction worker and mini-tour player before he joined the

1988

Liselotte Neumann

Swedish Rookie Neumann Wins U.S. Women's Open

Sweden's Liselotte Neumann proved herself in America with her first LPGA Tour victory, the 1988 U.S. Women's Open. On the Five Farms Course at Baltimore C.C., Neumann outlasted Patty Sheehan to win by three strokes. Though a rookie on the LPGA Tour, Neumann excelled in Europe the three previous years.

Gary Player

Player Outduels Charles in Senior Open Playoff

Gary Player shoots from a bunker during the 1988 U.S. Senior Open at Medinah C.C. in Illinois. Player defeated Bob Charles in an 18-hole playoff, 68-70, for his second Senior Open in a row. Charles could have won the tournament the previous day, but he bogied holes 15, 16, and 17.

Senior Tour, wins the $135,000 first prize in the Vantage Championship.

• October 16: Corey Pavin shoots a 72-hole total of 259, two off the PGA Tour record, to win the Texas Open by eight strokes.

• October 29: At the Walt Disney World/Oldsmobile Classic, Bob Lohr

and Chip Beck tie at 25-under, then Lohr wins on the fifth extra hole.

• November: Peter Thomson, Tom Watson, and Bob Harlow are inducted into the PGA World Golf Hall of Fame.

• November 6: Sherri Turner leads the LPGA Tour with $350,851.

• November 6: Nancy Lopez is the LPGA Player of the Year. Colleen Walker wins the Vare Trophy, averaging 71.26.

• November 6: Five players finish the LPGA Tour with three victories each—Juli Inkster, Rosie Jones, Betsy King, Nancy Lopez, and Ayako Okamoto.

Ken Green

Radar Reid Nips Watson in World Series

Mike Reid captured the 1988 NEC World Series of Golf, winning on the first hole of a playoff after Tom Watson missed an easy par putt. It was just the second career victory for Reid in 12 years on Tour. Mike earned the nickname "Radar" for his uncanny accuracy off the tee, although he was never a long driver.

Mike Reid

Colorful Green Wins in Canada, Milwaukee

In 1988, Ken Green captured two tournaments back-to-back—the Canadian Open and Milwaukee Open. Green, one of the most colorful characters on Tour, would draw several fines in 1992. One was for throwing his putter into the Pacific Ocean at the U.S. Open; another came at the PGA Championship, when he said the Bellerive course "sucked."

• November 13: Davis Love Jr., noted golf instructor and father of PGA Tour player Davis Love III, dies in a plane crash.

• November 13: Seve Ballesteros wins the Visa Taiheyo Club Masters to finish the year with seven victories, each in a different country.

• November 14: Curtis Strange birdies the second playoff hole—No. 17 at Pebble Beach G.L.—to win the Nabisco Championships of Golf over Tom Kite.

• November 14: Curtis Strange leads the Tour money list with $1,147,644. He's the first man to surpass $1 million in earnings.

• November 14: Curtis Strange leads the PGA Tour with four victories. He is the PGA Player of the Year.

• November 14: Chip Beck wins the Vardon Trophy with an adjusted scoring average of 69.46.

• November 20: Lee Elder wins the Gus Machado Senior Classic a year

1988

Walker Finishes Fifth in Earnings, Tops in Scoring

Colleen Walker vaulted to fifth on the money list in 1988 with $318,116. She captured only one event, the Boston Five Classic, but she finished in the top 10 18 times. She also led the LPGA Tour in scoring average (71.26), birdies (325), rounds under par (55), and rounds in the 60s (29).

Nancy Lopez

Lopez Cops Fourth Player of the Year Award

In 1988, Nancy Lopez was named the LPGA's Player of the Year for the fourth time in her career. The Hall of Famer won three tournaments, lost two others in playoffs, and crossed the $2 million mark in career earnings. In '88, *Golf* magazine named her "Golfer of the Decade" for the period 1978–87.

Colleen Walker

after suffering a heart attack at the same event.

• November 22: The LPGA hires William Blue, a consumer marketing executive, as its new commissioner.

• November 27: Raymond Floyd wins $290,000 to capture the Skins Game.

• December 4: Rodger Davis beats Fred Couples in a playoff to win the $435,000 first prize in the Australia Bicentennial Classic.

• December 4: Amy Benz and John Huston team to shoot 21-under-par and win the JCPenney Classic in Largo, Florida.

• December 4: Bob Charles leads the Senior Tour money list with $533,929. Charles and Gary Player tie for the tour lead with five victories.

• December 11: Ben Crenshaw and Mark McCumber win the World Cup for the United States, finishing one stroke ahead of Japan.

HOCH, KITE, NORMAN, AND REID BLOW MAJORS

Major championships are often lost rather than won, but rarely have they been lost more dramatically—or agonizingly—than the four majors of 1989.

The horror show started with Scott Hoch at the Masters. He needed only to hole an 18-inch putt for a par in the gathering darkness at Augusta National to beat Nick Faldo on the first hole of sudden-death. Hoch, winner of only three PGA Tour events and no major championships in his career, took his time. Too much time. He studied the tiny putt from all angles, but when he finally pulled the trigger, he hit the downhill putt too hard to take the break, missing to the left. Faldo won with a birdie on the second extra hole.

At the U.S. Open, it was Tom Kite's turn to take a fall. Kite, age 39, had never won a major, but he held a three-stroke lead after four holes of the final round at Oak Hill Country Club. He lost it in one hole. On No. 5, Kite let his tee shot slide to the right, into a creek. A tree blocked his path to the green, so he laid up and pitched to 12 feet, giving himself a chance to save a bogey. Instead,

he knocked his first putt two feet past, then, shockingly, missed that one and ended up with a triple bogey.

Kite was never the same. He made two double bogeys on the back nine, finished with a 78, and tied for ninth, five strokes behind Curtis Strange.

Greg Norman blew the British Open in a different fashion—by hitting a drive too well. First, he shot a 64 at Royal Troon to reach a playoff with Wayne Grady and Mark Calcavecchia. Norman and Calcavecchia were tied going to the final hole, No. 18, of a four-hole aggregate playoff. There, Norman uncorked a drive of some 325 yards, the ball rolling into a fairway bunker he thought

unreachable. Norman's next shot found a bunker short of the green, from which he blasted over the green and out of bounds. He never even finished the hole, as Calcavecchia made a winning birdie.

The most painful finish was yet to come. Soft-spoken Mike Reid, another player looking for his first major title, led the PGA Championship by three strokes with three holes to play. One of the straightest drivers on the PGA Tour, the man they called "Radar" pushed his drive into a lake on the 16th hole at Kemper Lakes, eventually getting up and down for a bogey.

The par-3 17th was a nightmare. Reid's tee shot was too long, then he stubbed a chip 15 feet short and ran the putt two feet past. Whereas Hoch waited too long on his short putt at the Masters, Reid rushed his "tap-in." The result was the same—a stunning miss. The double bogey dropped him one stroke behind Payne Stewart, who had birdied the 18th up ahead. Reid parred the last hole to finish second. Like Hoch, Kite, and Norman before him, Reid could only ponder what might have been.

1989

- January: PGA Tour players are scheduled to play in 44 events with a total season purse of $41,288,787.

- January: LPGA Tour players are scheduled to play in 36 events with a total season purse of $14,190,000.

- January: Senior PGA Tour players are scheduled to play in 41 events.

- January: The Southwest Classic and Pensacola Open are off the fall PGA Tour schedule. The Southwest Classic becomes a senior event.

- January 15: Steve Jones wins the Bob Hope Chrysler Classic a week after winning the MONY Tournament of Champions.

- January 30: Dottie Mochrie wins her first LPGA Tour event, the Oldsmobile LPGA Classic, by beating Beth Daniel on the fifth hole of a playoff.

- February 5: Mark Calcavecchia takes the Nissan Los Angeles Open two weeks after winning the Phoenix Open.

Tom Kite was one of four men to blow a major in 1989. Kite had a three-stroke lead in the final round of the U.S. Open, but he lost it all when he took a triple bogey on the 5th hole. It was a tough pill for Kite to swallow. Though he would become the Tour's all-time leading money earner later in the year, he still hadn't won a major.

• February 12: Larry Mowry wins the General Foods Senior PGA Championship.

• February 28: The PGA Tour announces it will ban square-grooved irons as of January 1, 1990.

• March 12: Tom Kite and Davis Love III both double bogey the 72nd hole at the Nestlé Invitational, then Kite beats Love in a playoff.

• March 19: Tom Kite beats Chip Beck by one stroke to win the Players Championship.

• April 2: Juli Inkster leads all the way to win her second Nabisco Dinah Shore.

• April 9: Nick Faldo completes a 77 in the rain-delayed third round of the Masters, then closes with a 65. Faldo wins on the second hole of a playoff after Scott Hoch blows a two-foot putt on the first.

• April 9: Tom Watson passes Jack Nicklaus as the all-time leading money winner.

1989

Steve Jones

Jones Takes the T. of C., Hope, Canadian

Steve Jones, a journeyman pro from Artesia, New Mexico, stepped into the spotlight with a win in the 1989 MONY Tournament of Champions. The victory sparked him to two more wins—the Bob Hope Chrysler Classic and Canadian Open. Jones finished with $745,578.

Faldo Wins Masters as Hoch Blows a Gimme

Nick Faldo *(left)* won the 1989 Masters—barely. Scott Hoch had a chance to win on the first sudden-death playoff hole, but he studied a two-foot putt too long and blew it. Faldo won on the next hole. Here, Faldo poses with boyhood rival Sandy Lyle, a Scot who won the Masters in 1988.

Bies Wins with Extra-Long Putter

One of Don Bies's three 1989 wins came at the Murata Seniors Reunion, where—on the day before the tournament started—he picked up an elongated putter for the first time in his life. He used it all three days and ran away from the field by six shots. He used it the next week at The Tradition at Desert Mountain and won that event too.

Don Bies

Nick Faldo, Sandy Lyle

• April 16: Kenny Knox sets a PGA Tour record for fewest putts in a 72-hole tournament, 93, at the MCI Heritage Classic.

• April 16: Don Bies captures the first Tradition at Desert Mountain.

• April 23: Ken Green wins the Kmart Greater Greensboro Open a year after blowing the same event by missing a putt on the 72nd hole.

• April 30: Scott Hoch wins the Las Vegas Invitational on the fifth hole of a playoff against Robert Wrenn.

• May 21: Nancy Lopez closes with a 66 to win her third Mazda LPGA Championship.

• May 21: Bob Charles's 193 wins the NYNEX/Golf Digest Commemorative.

• June 11: Arizona State freshman Phil Mickelson wins the NCAA championship.

• June 11: Orville Moody wins the Mazda Senior TPC by two strokes at

1989

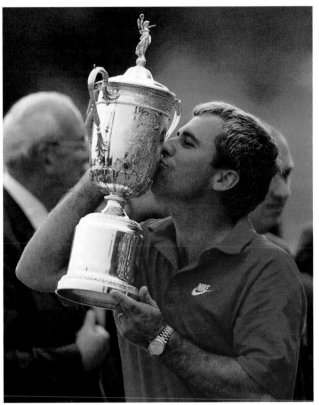

Curtis Strange

Strange Wins Open— His Second in a Row

Curtis Strange gladly walked through the open door when Tom Kite stumbled as leader of the 1989 U.S. Open, at Oak Hill C.C. in Rochester, New York. While Kite closed with a 78, Strange shot a final-round 70 to win his second straight Open, becoming the first player to accomplish the feat since Ben Hogan in 1950–51.

Lopez Nabs Her Third LPGA Championship

Despite motherhood, the career of Nancy Lopez just kept rolling along. Lopez, now 32 and the mother of two, blazed home with a closing 66 to pass leader Ayako Okamoto and win the 1989 LPGA Championship. This was Lopez's third win in the LPGA. Amazingly, she still hadn't won any other major championship.

Juli Inkster

Inkster Prevails Again in Nabisco Dinah Shore

Juli Inkster won the 1989 Nabisco Dinah Shore, cruising to a five-stroke victory. Inkster also captured the 1989 Crestar Classic. She had now won 13 Tour events in her career and, ironically, had won five different tournaments twice: the Dinah Shore, Crestar, Safeco Classic, Lady Keystone Open, and Atlantic City Classic.

Nancy Lopez

the TPC at Sawgrass Valley Course in Ponte Vedra, Florida.

• June 16: Two holes are closed because of wet conditions at the Northville Long Island Classic. The first round consists of 16 holes.

• June 16: Four players (Mark Wiebe, Nick Price, Jerry Pate, and Doug Weaver) ace the 6th hole at Oak Hill C.C. in Rochester, New York, during the first round of the U.S. Open.

• June 18: Curtis Strange becomes the first player since Ben Hogan (1950–51) to win consecutive U.S. Opens. Third-round leader Tom Kite stumbles to a 78.

• July 2: Orville Moody prevails in the U.S. Senior Open by two strokes over Frank Beard, at Laurel Valley C.C. in Ligonier, Pennsylvania.

• July 2: Tammie Green wins her first LPGA event, the du Maurier Classic, at Beaconsfield G.C. in Montreal.

King's Open Victory Highlights Banner Year

Betsy King won the 1989 U.S. Women's Open by four strokes over crowd-favorite Nancy Lopez, at Indianwood C.C. near Detroit. King enjoyed a monster year in '89, capturing six tournaments, winning the Player of the Year Award, and setting the LPGA record for earnings with $654,132. In 25 events, she finished in the top 10 20 times.

Doug Weaver, Jerry Pate, Nick Price, Mark Wiebe

Four Golfers Ace the 6th Hole at U.S. Open

At the 1989 U.S. Open, four golfers scored a hole-in-one in one day—and on the same hole! Doug Weaver, Jerry Pate, Nick Price, and Mark Wiebe *(left to right)* aced the 159-yard 6th hole in the second round at Oak Hill C.C. The odds of four pros acing the same hole on the same day were 8.7 million-to-1, according to the National Hole-in-One Association.

Betsy King

- July 16: Betsy King wins the U.S. Women's Open by four strokes over Nancy Lopez at Indianwood Golf & C.C. in Lake Orion, Michigan.

- July 23: Mark Calcavecchia wins a four-hole playoff against Greg Norman and Wayne Grady to take the British Open title at Royal Troon G.C. in Troon, Scotland.

- August 5: Vicki Goetze, age 16, wins the U.S. Women's Amateur.

- August 10: Karsten Manufacturing, maker of Ping clubs, sues the USGA over its ruling that makes Ping Eye 2 irons illegal as of 1996 and disallowed in USGA events as of 1990. The dispute is over the width of space between grooves.

- August 13: Payne Stewart wins the PGA Championship, shooting a 31 on the back nine at Kemper Lakes in Illinois. Mike Reid double bogeys the 17th to lose by one.

- August 17: Great Britain/Ireland nips the U.S., 12½-11½, to win the Walker Cup at Peachtree G.C. in Atlanta—its first win on U.S. soil.

1989

U.S. Women's Open

Indianwood Dresses Up for U.S. Women's Open

Bagpipers pipe in the new U.S. Women's Open champion, Betsy King, after she defeated the field on a Scottish-style course in Lake Orion, Michigan. The Women's Open drew record crowds, perhaps because of an attractive leader board that included King, Nancy Lopez, and Pat Bradley.

Great Britain/Ireland Walker Cup Team

Stewart Shoots 31 on Back Nine, Wins PGA

Payne Stewart

Payne Stewart rallied on the closing holes to win the 1989 PGA Championship, at Kemper Lakes Golf Course in Illinois. Stewart unleashed four birdies on the final five holes, shot 31 on the back nine, and won by a stroke over Mike Reid, Andy Bean, and Curtis Strange. Reid three-putted from four feet at the 17th hole.

Great Britain/Ireland Wins Walker Cup Match

Great Britain/Ireland nipped the United States, 12½-11½, to win the 1989 Walker Cup, held at Peachtree G.C. in Atlanta. Team members pose together after winning their countries' first Cup on American soil. The U.S. had gone 28-2-1 since the series began in 1922, and had been a near-perfect 14-0-1 on its home turf.

• August 27: David Frost wins the NEC World Series of Golf in a playoff over Ben Crenshaw.

• August 27: Bob Charles wins the Sunwest Bank/Charley Pride Classic for the third consecutive year.

• August 27: Chris Patton wins the U.S. Amateur championship.

• September 22: Hurricane Hugo strikes Charlotte, North Carolina, site of the Senior Tour's PaineWebber Invitational, which is canceled.

• September 24: Europe and the U.S. tie, 14-14, in the Ryder Cup Matches at The Belfry in Sutton Coldfield, England.

• October 1: Beth Daniel wins the Konica San Jose Classic, her fourth victory in her last six starts.

• October 8: Donnie Hammond shoots 258, one off the Tour record, to win the Texas Open. Hammond fires 65-64-65-64, 22-under-par, at Oak Hills C.C. in San Antonio.

Tom Kite

Kite Sets All-Time Records in Season and Career Earnings

Tom Kite clenches his fists after Payne Stewart misses a putt in a playoff for the 1989 Nabisco Championships. Stewart's miss gave Kite the victory. With a win in the Players Championship, Kite had thus won the year's two biggest paychecks. In 1989, Tom set the Tour's record for season earnings ($1,395,278) and career earnings ($5,600,692).

Daniel Prevails in Washington, Goes on a Tear

After a winless drought of more than four years, Beth Daniel began a 15-month winning binge in August 1989. That month, Daniel captured the Greater Washington Open for her first of 11 official Tour victories through October 1990. In 1989, she won four events and set the LPGA Tour scoring record with 70.38.

Beth Daniel

• October 8: Gary Player wins the lucrative RJR Championship.

• October 15: The first golf course in the Soviet Union opens, the nine-hole Tumba G.C. in Moscow.

• October 29: Tom Kite beats Payne Stewart in a playoff to win the $2.5 million Nabisco Championships at Harbour Town G.L. in Hilton Head Island, South Carolina.

• October 29: Tom Kite tops the Tour money list with $1,395,278. Also, Kite is now No. 1 in career earnings.

• October 29: Tom Kite and Steve Jones finish with three victories each to lead the PGA Tour. Kite is the PGA Player of the Year.

• October 29: Greg Norman wins the Vardon Trophy (69.49).

• November: Raymond Floyd, Roberto De Vicenzo, Nancy Lopez, and Jim Barnes are inducted into the PGA World Golf Hall of Fame.

1989

Europe and U.S. Tie, 14-14, in Ryder Cup Match

Seve Ballesteros looks on as Ryder Cup teammate Jose Maria Olazabal misses a putt at The Belfry in Sutton Coldfield, England. After European victories in 1985 and '87, the U.S. rallied in '89 to tie, 14-14, thanks to singles victories by Tom Watson, Mark McCumber, Lanny Wadkins, and Curtis Strange.

Seve Ballesteros, Jose Maria Olazabal

Mark Calcavecchia

Calcavecchia Prevails in British Open Playoff

Mark Calcavecchia captured the 1989 British Open at Royal Troon G.C. in Scotland. Calcavecchia beat Greg Norman and Wayne Grady in a new formula for a playoff—four holes to determine a winner. Mark finished with a flourish, stroking a 5-iron to within seven feet of the pin on the final hole, then holing out with a birdie.

Vicki Goetze

Goetze, Just 16, Wins U.S. Women's Amateur

Sixteen-year-old Vicki Goetze won the battle of the youngsters in 1989 to capture her first U.S. Women's Amateur. The straight-hitting Goetze defeated powerful Brandi Burton, 17, in the final at Pinehurst C.C. in North Carolina. The same summer, Burton won the U.S. Girls' Junior championship.

- November 5: Betsy King leads the LPGA Tour money list with $654,132. She is the LPGA Player of the Year.

- November 5: Beth Daniel wins the Vare Trophy, averaging 70.38.

- November 5: Betsy King leads the LPGA Tour with six wins. Beth

Daniel has four wins and Nancy Lopez three.

- November 26: Curtis Strange wins the Skins Game with earnings of $265,000.

- December 9: Bob Charles leads the Senior Tour with $725,887. He also leads with five wins.

- December 9: Lee Trevino, in his Senior Tour debut, finishes seventh at the GTE Kaanapali Classic.

- December 20: A Federal judge grants an injunction to Karsten Manufacturing, which stops the PGA Tour's ban of square-grooved irons pending the outcome of the company's lawsuit against the Tour.

SHOAL CREEK ADMITS TO BANNING BLACKS

The 1990 PGA Championship at Shoal Creek Country Club in Birmingham, Alabama, isn't remembered for Wayne Grady's victory in a rather unexciting tournament. Much more significant was the controversy surrounding the all-white Shoal Creek club in the month and a half leading up to the tournament—a time when the sport of golf had its consciousness raised.

The firestorm resulted from remarks made by Shoal Creek founder Hall Thompson in a story in the *Birmingham Post-Herald* on June 21. "The country club is our home and we pick and choose who we want," he said of club membership. "I think we've said that we don't discriminate in every other area except the blacks."

Thompson, no doubt, had no idea of the reaction his comments would inspire. After all, there was nothing unusual about a golf tournament being played at an all-white country club. Most of the clubs that had hosted PGA Championships and U.S. Opens had no black members, and neither did Augusta National, which hosts the Masters, nor nearly half of the clubs hosting events on the PGA Tour. The

difference is that none had publicly stated they wouldn't admit black members, and their tacit discrimination was ignored. Thompson's statements brought the issue into the spotlight.

The most immediate reaction came from two black groups, the Southern Christian Leadership Conference and the National Association for the Advancement of Colored People, which called for picketing and protests of the tournament. But the most important move came the next month when nearly all of the companies scheduled to sponsor the ABC telecast of the tournament dropped their support.

The PGA of America, the PGA Tour, and the USGA also reacted quickly. All said they would not

hold future tournaments at clubs that discriminate, either in policy or in practice. This meant clubs not only had to say they were willing to admit black (or women) members, but they would have to actually have them.

The PGA never considered moving the championship from Shoal Creek. But protests of the tournament were averted when the club, less than two weeks before the start of the event, admitted a black man, local businessman Louis Willie, as an honorary member.

The effects of Shoal Creek were felt after the tournament ended. Over the next few months, nine clubs withdrew as tournament sites, including Butler National and Cypress Point from the PGA Tour, Chicago Golf Club and Merion from USGA events, and Aronimink from the 1993 PGA Championship. But many more, including Augusta National, admitted minority and/or women members in order to comply with the new guidelines. It was just a first step—many pointed out the larger problems of low minority participation in the game—but it's a step that wouldn't have been taken without Shoal Creek.

1990

- January: PGA Tour players are scheduled to play in 44 events with a total season purse of $46,251,831.

- January: LPGA Tour players are scheduled to play in 37 events with a total season purse of $17,100,000.

- January: Senior PGA Tour players are scheduled to play in 42 events

with a total season purse of $18,323,968.

- January: The Ben Hogan Tour, a 30-event circuit of events with $100,000 purses, begins for players who do not have PGA Tour cards.

- January 12: Nabisco announces it will drop its sponsorship of a year-

end tournament and bonus pool after 1990.

- January 14: Robert Gamez wins the Northern Telecom Tucson Open in his first event as a rookie. David Frost shot 60 on Friday.

- January 21: Jack Nicklaus turns 50 years old.

Shoal Creek C.C. founder Hall Thompson may have had some support from his members, but—to the rest of the country—he was not a popular fellow. In 1990, Thompson admitted to banning blacks from his club. The NAACP was about to picket the club, until Shoal Creek accepted local black businessman Louis Willie as an honorary member.

• January 27: The USGA and Karsten Manufacturing settle their grooves dispute out of court. The USGA rules existing Eye 2 irons legal, but future clubs must conform to groove-width measurement standards.

• January 28: Arnold Palmer wins the Senior Skins Game.

• March 4: At the Doral Ryder Open, Greg Norman shoots a 62 to come from seven strokes behind and chips in for an eagle on the first extra hole to win a four-way playoff.

• March 18: Jodie Mudd holds off Mark Calcavecchia by one stroke to win the Players Championship.

• March 25: Robert Gamez holes a 7-iron from 176 yards for an eagle on the 72nd hole to beat Greg Norman by one stroke at the Nestlé Invitational.

• April 1: Betsy King wins the Nabisco Dinah Shore despite a closing 75.

King Takes the Title at Dinah Shore

Dinah Shore *(left)* helps Betsy King hoist the trophy after King won the 1990 Nabisco Dinah Shore. It was yet another sensational season for King, as she also won her second consecutive U.S. Women's Open and became the third LPGA player to reach $3 million. Her season included two of her four career holes-in-one.

Dinah Shore, Betsy King

Gamez the Latest to Stun the Shark

Robert Gamez won the first PGA Tour event he played in—the 1990 Northern Telecom Tucson Open. Two months later, he won the Nestlé Invitational in dramatic fashion, holing out with a 7-iron from 176 yards. The incredible shot was one more dagger in the heart of Greg Norman, who finished a stroke behind.

Robert Gamez

Nicklaus a Winner in His Senior Tour Debut

The biggest media event in Senior Tour history occurred in the spring of 1990, when Jack Nicklaus—50 years and two months old—appeared in his first senior event, The Tradition at Desert Mountain. Nicklaus played steadily throughout and wound up beating Gary Player by four shots. The event was reduced to three rounds by rain.

Jack Nicklaus

- April 1: Jack Nicklaus wins his Senior Tour debut, The Tradition at Desert Mountain.

- April 8: Nick Faldo becomes the first man since Jack Nicklaus (1965–66) to win back-to-back Masters. He beats Raymond Floyd in a playoff when Floyd hits into water on the second extra hole.

- April 15: Gary Player wins his third PGA Seniors Championship.

- April 29: David Frost holes out from a bunker for a birdie on the 72nd hole to beat Greg Norman by one at the USF&G Classic.

- May 27: Jan Stephenson wins the first JCPenney LPGA Skins Game.

- June 9: Phil Mickelson wins his second straight NCAA championship.

- June 10: Jack Nicklaus shoots a Senior Tour-record, 27-under-par 261 to win the Mazda Senior TPC.

- June 18: Hale Irwin, age 45, becomes the oldest winner of the

1990

Nick Faldo

Faldo Knocks Off Floyd in Masters Playoff

Nick Faldo proved his first Masters win was no fluke, as he won it for the second year in a row in 1990. Both victories came in a playoff, this one over 47-year-old Raymond Floyd. After each had tied at 278, Floyd blew his chance at victory when he hit into the pond on the second extra hole. Faldo needed only to two-putt, and he did.

Irwin Wins U.S. Open at Age 45

At age 45, Hale Irwin became the oldest U.S. Open winner ever when he won at Medinah C.C. in Illinois. Irwin was an early finisher when he holed a 45-foot birdie putt for a 67. He clearly believed his 280 total would win. It tied. Hale and Mike Donald each shot 74 in the playoff, and then Irwin won in sudden-death.

Hale Irwin

Shoal Creek Opens the Door to Willie

Louis Willie, president of Alabama's largest black-owned insurance company, poses in his Birmingham office. Protests of the 1990 PGA Championship at Shoal Creek C.C. were called off after the club admitted Willie as a member. However, other clubs refused to admit blacks and thus were dumped as PGA Tour sites.

Louis Willie

U.S. Open, at Medinah C.C. in Illinois. A 45-foot putt on the 72nd hole tied him with Mike Donald; they each shoot 74s in an 18-hole playoff, and Irwin wins on the first hole of sudden-death.

• June 21: Hall Thompson, founder of Shoal Creek C.C. in Birmingham, Alabama, site of this year's PGA

Championship, is quoted in the *Birmingham Post-Herald* as saying his club would not accept black members.

• June 24: Hale Irwin wins the Buick Classic.

• July: The PGA of America, PGA Tour, and USGA announce plans for

new policies of not holding tournaments at clubs with exclusionary membership policies or practices.

• July: Several corporations scheduled to advertise during the PGA Championship telecast withdraw sponsorship, citing discriminatory practices at Shoal Creek.

Sheehan, Up Nine, Blows Women's Open

Patty Sheehan's collapse in the final round of the 1990 U.S. Women's Open prompted her to burst into tears. Sheehan blew a nine-stroke lead at the halfway point of the tournament, held at Salem C.C. in Peabody, Massachusetts. She played the last 27 holes at 8-over-par and lost to Betsy King by a single stroke.

David Frost

Frost Chills Norman with Spectacular Shot

David Frost goes nuts after holing out from a bunker at the 1990 USF&G Classic. In order to force a playoff with Greg Norman, Frost needed to par the extremely difficult par-4 18th hole at English Turn Golf & C.C in New Orleans. Incredibly, Frost hit from tee to bunker to bunker to cup for a birdie and the win.

Patty Sheehan

• July 1: Cathy Johnston wins the du Maurier Classic at Westmount Golf & C.C. for her first LPGA Tour victory.

• July 1: Lee Trevino shoots a final-round 67 to pass Jack Nicklaus and win the U.S. Senior Open at Ridgewood C.C. in Paramus, New Jersey.

• July 15: Patty Sheehan has a nine-stroke lead in the U.S. Women's Open on a 36-hole final day. She plays her last 27 holes 8-over-par and loses by one to Betsy King.

• July 22: Nick Faldo coasts to a five-stroke victory over Payne Stewart and Mark McNulty in the British Open with a 270 total.

• July 29: Beth Daniel shoots a final-round 66 to come from five strokes behind and win the Mazda LPGA Championship at its new home course, Bethesda C.C. in Maryland. It is the Tour's first $1 million purse.

• July 31: Shoal Creek C.C. announces it will admit black businessman Louis Willie as an honorary,

Nick Faldo

Faldo Cruises to Victory in British Open

In 1990, Nick Faldo solidified his spot as golf's dominant player when he won his second major of the year and his second British Open. Faldo's victory on the Old Course at St. Andrews brought him close to tears. It was an easy victory for Faldo, as he won by five strokes over Payne Stewart and Mark McNulty.

Mickelson Wins U.S. Amateur, NCAA Title

In 1990, Phil Mickelson's smooth swing gave hope to all left-handed golfers. Mickelson won both the NCAA championship and the U.S. Amateur, prompting comparisons with Jack Nicklaus, the only other man to win both in the same year. Fittingly, Phil won the 1990 Jack Nicklaus Award as collegiate player of the year.

Phil Mickelson

Jack Nicklaus, Lee Trevino

Trevino Wins U.S. Senior Open, Tops $1 Million

Lee Trevino *(right)* is congratulated by Jack Nicklaus after winning the 1990 U.S. Senior Open at Ridgewood C.C. in Paramus, New Jersey. Nicklaus challenged Trevino until he bogied the 17th hole and fell two strokes behind. Trevino won seven times in 1990 and became the first senior to win $1 million in a year ($1,190,518).

non-paying member. Plans for a protest of the PGA Championship at Shoal Creek by black organizations are canceled.

• August 12: Wayne Grady wins the PGA Championship at Shoal Creek when Fred Couples misses three short putts on the final nine.

• August 26: Jose Maria Olazabal wins the NEC World Series of Golf with a tournament-record 262. He opened with a 61.

• August 26: Phil Mickelson wins the U.S. Amateur, becoming the first to win that title and the NCAA in the same year since Jack Nicklaus in 1961.

• September: Augusta National G.C. admits its first black member. Butler National G.C. and Cypress Point G.C., which do not have black members, withdraw as sites of PGA Tour events.

• September 4: William Blue steps down as LPGA commissioner.

Greg Norman

Norman Tops in Money, Despite Heartbreaks

Greg Norman lost both the 1990 Nestlé Invitational and USF&G Classic due to miraculous shots by his opponents, but he also won an event in dramatic fashion. Norman chipped in for eagle to win a playoff in the Doral Ryder Open. He also won the Memorial Tournament to finish first on the Tour in earnings with $1,165,477.

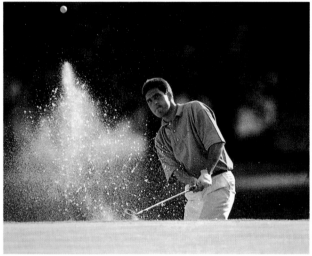

Jose Maria Olazabal

Olazabal's 262 Sets Record at World Series

In the 1990 NEC World Series of Golf, Jose Maria Olazabal conquered one of America's toughest courses, Firestone C.C. in Akron, Ohio. Olazabal fired a course-record 61 in the opening round, then finished with a winning score of 262, breaking the tournament record by a full five strokes.

• September 5: Pebble Beach G.L. and related properties are sold to a company owned by Japanese developer Minoru Isutani for $841 million.

• September 16: Patty Sheehan wins the Safeco Classic by nine shots over Deb Richard.

• October 7: Beth Daniel wins the Centel Classic, giving her a sweep of the LPGA's first two $1 million events.

• October 14: Bob Tway wins the Las Vegas Invitational in a playoff when John Cook's approach shot on the first playoff hole lands in the hole and bounces 15 feet away.

• October 28: Jodie Mudd wins the Nabisco Championships at Champions G.C. in Houston. He birdies the last two holes plus the first playoff hole against Billy Mayfair.

• October 28: Greg Norman leads the PGA Tour money list with $1,165,477. He also captures the

Wayne Grady

Grady Victorious in the PGA Championship

Australian Wayne Grady, who had only one previous win on Tour, posted a three-stroke victory in the 1990 PGA Championship at Shoal Creek C.C., shooting 6-under-par 282. Fred Couples finished three back, as he carded bogies on holes 13–16 during the final round. Gil Morgan closed with 18 consecutive pars to finish four back.

Levi's Four Wins Earn Him a Million

In 1990, little-heralded Wayne Levi won four tournaments, more than any other Tour player. Levi won the BellSouth Atlanta Classic, Centel Western Open, Canon Greater Hartford Open, and Canadian Open. He took home $1,024,647, second to Greg Norman's total, and was named PGA Tour Player of the Year.

Wayne Levi

Daniel Burns It Up, Wins Seven Times

After four victories late in 1989, Beth Daniel went hog-wild in 1990, winning seven official events including the LPGA Championship. The 5'11" Daniel became the first LPGA Tour player to reach $700,000 in a season—she won $863,578—and easily captured the Player of the Year Award. She also nabbed the Vare Trophy.

Beth Daniel

Vardon Trophy with an adjusted average of 69.10. Wayne Levi leads with four victories. Nick Faldo is the PGA Player of the Year.

• November: Gene Littler, Bill Campbell, Paul Runyan, and Horton Smith are inducted into the PGA World Golf Hall of Fame.

• November 4: Beth Daniel leads the LPGA money list with $863,578. She is also the LPGA Player of the Year and wins the Vare Trophy, averaging 70.54. Daniel leads the Tour with seven victories.

• November 18: The U.S. defeats Europe, 11½-4½, in the first

Solheim Cup for women professionals at Lake Nona G.C. in Orlando, Florida.

• December 16: Lee Trevino leads the Senior Tour in money with $1,190,518. He also wins the Byron Nelson Trophy with a scoring average of 68.89, and is high in victories with seven.

WOW! UNKNOWN DALY BOOMS HIS WAY TO PGA TITLE

Never has a golf hero been born so quickly as John Daly at the 1991 PGA Championship. Before the tournament, only a few avid golf observers knew that the 25-year-old was the longest hitter on the PGA Tour and that he had posted a couple of top-10 finishes in his rookie season. But by the time it ended, he was a hero for the masses.

The making of a legend, appropriately, began with a story straight out of a Hollywood script. Daly, the ninth alternate based on his money earnings for the year, was unlikely to even make the field at Crooked Stick Golf Club in Carmel, Indiana. By Tuesday, however, five players had withdrawn. Three alternates declined to make the trip to Indiana on the chance another player would drop out. Daly was willing. He hopped in his car at 5 p.m. Wednesday for the 7½-hour drive from his Memphis home, and when he arrived, he received a message that he was in. Nick Price had withdrawn that evening when he got word that his wife was about to deliver their first child.

In another fortuitous circumstance, Crooked Stick was tailor-made for a long hitter. It was the second-longest course ever to host a PGA Championship (7,289 yards) and the fairways were relatively wide. Daly was able to blast away with less fear of penalty for an errant drive than is usually found at a PGA Championship or U.S. Open. He could reach even the long par-4s—six of them were 440 yards or more—with 7-, 8-, or 9-irons.

The fans loved it. While his first-round 69 passed largely unnoticed, Daly began to gain attention with a 67 in the second round to take the lead. By the weekend, fans were flocking to see this swashbuckling blond kid crush the ball. And Daly, an engaging, man-of-the-people sort, fed on the crowd's energy, proving immune to the pressure that eats up so many first-time contenders in major championships.

His third-round 69 to take a three-stroke lead was an impressive display, marred only by a double bogey on the 8th hole, where he hit a sand wedge an impossible 150 yards, ending up in the water over the green. Daly never let anybody get closer than two strokes in the final round, and that was only on the 1st hole. He grabbed a five-stroke lead midway through the back nine, and a final-round 71 enabled him to win by three over Bruce Lietzke.

Already, Daly was a larger-than-life figure. He was invited to the Skins Game in November, an event reserved for the game's elite names. Some hailed him as the game's next dominant player—a premature assessment, it turned out, because of the erratic nature of both his game and his personal life (he would spend time in an alcohol rehab clinic 16 months later). But while long-term greatness was yet to be proved, there's no doubt that Crooked Stick made John Daly a star.

1991

• January: PGA Tour players are scheduled to play in 44 events with a total season purse of $49,628,203.

• January: LPGA Tour players are scheduled to play in 37 events with a total season purse of $18,435,000.

• January: Senior PGA Tour players are scheduled to play in 42 events with a total season purse of $19,788,218.

• January: Callaway Golf Co. introduces Big Bertha, the first metal wood with an oversized head.

• January 1: Charles Mechem takes over as the new LPGA Tour commissioner.

• January 13: Amateur Phil Mickelson, a 20-year-old at Arizona State, wins the PGA Tour's Northern Telecom Open.

• February 10: Corey Pavin and Mark O'Meara shoot 29-under-par for 90 holes at the Bob Hope Chrysler Classic. Pavin wins the playoff.

Rookie John Daly splashed onto the golf scene when he won the 1991 PGA Championship at Crooked Stick G.C. in Carmel, Indiana. Hours before the tournament started, Daly learned he had made the field as ninth alternate. Daly, unleashing his jaw-dropping 300-yard drives, won by three strokes. The victory was worth $230,000, plus much more in endorsements.

• March 2: Paul Azinger is disqualified from the Doral Ryder Open when a TV viewer calls the tournament after noticing Azinger move loose impediments in a hazard.

• March 31: Steve Elkington birdies the 72nd hole to win the Players Championship by one over Fuzzy Zoeller.

• March 31: Amy Alcott breaks her own record with a 15-under 273 to win the Nabisco Dinah Shore.

• March 31: The entire country is officially under the slope system for USGA handicaps.

• April 7: Jack Nicklaus, who had trailed by 12 strokes with two rounds to play, finishes 66-67 to prevail in The Tradition at Desert Mountain.

• April 14: Ian Woosnam of Wales wins the Masters, making it four straight years a player from Great Britain has taken the title. His 277 defeats runner-up Jose Maria Olazabal by a stroke.

Ian Woosnam and Family

Pint-Sized Woosnam Dons the Green Jacket

Ian Woosnam poses with his wife, Glendryth, and kids, Rebecca and Daniel, after donning the green jacket at the 1991 Masters. Woosnam, a native of Wales, shot 66-67 in the middle two rounds to win by a shot over Jose Maria Olazabal. Woosnam, only 5'4", actually led the European Tour in driving distance in 1985 and 1987.

Elkington Prevails in Players Championship

Steve Elkington displays the trophy symbolic of victory in the 1991 Players Championship, which he won by a stroke over Fuzzy Zoeller. The victory earned him $288,000, more than half of his season total. The Australian Elkington had captured only one previous Tour event, the 1990 Kmart Greater Greensboro Open.

Steve Elkington

Nabisco Dinah Shore

Alcott Wins Dinah Shore, Jumps in the Lake

Amy Alcott (*left*) took a swim next to the 18th green after winning the 1991 Nabisco Dinah Shore, at Mission Hills C.C. in Rancho Mirage, California. Also taking a dip were Shore and Bill Kurra, Alcott's caddie. Alcott won by eight strokes and shot 273, breaking her own tournament record.

• April 21: Jack Nicklaus wins the PGA Seniors Championship.

• May 19: Kenny Perry beats Hale Irwin in a playoff to win the Memorial Tournament.

• May 19: Pat Bradley edges Ayako Okamoto to win the $1.1 million Centel Classic.

• May 29: Hord Hardin steps down as chairman of the Masters. He's replaced by Jack Stephens.

• June 9: Billy Andrade wins the Buick Classic a week after winning the Kemper Open.

• June 9: Club pro Jim Albus scores an upset victory in the Senior Players

Championship at its new home, the TPC of Michigan in Dearborn.

• June 13: Spectator William Fadell is killed by lightning at the first round of the U.S. Open at Hazeltine National G.C. in Minnesota.

• June 17: Payne Stewart beats Scott Simpson in an 18-hole playoff for

Meg Mallon

Mallon Breaks Through, Grabs Two Major Titles

After finishing no better than third during her first four years on Tour, Meg Mallon won four times in 1991—including the LPGA Championship and U.S. Women's Open. When she won her first event, the Oldsmobile LPGA Classic, her caddie was writer Sonja Steptoe, who was carrying the bags to research a story. Mallon had to get her own yardages.

Baker-Finch Closes Strong to Win British

The 6'4" Ian Baker-Finch played like a giant in the 1991 British Open at Royal Birkdale G.C. in Southport, England. He closed 64-66—272 to win by two strokes over Mike Harwood. Baker-Finch shot 29 on the front nine of the final round, making five birdies on the first seven holes.

Phil Mickelson

Amateur Mickelson, 20, Wins on PGA Tour

Experts predicted that Phil Mickelson would be the game's next superstar, but few dreamed that he would win a Tour event before his 21st birthday. Mickelson, a 20-year-old left-hander, captured the 1991 Northern Telecom Open to become the first amateur to win a Tour event in six years. He would win his third NCAA championship in 1992.

Ian Baker-Finch

the U.S. Open, 75-77, when Simpson bogeys the last three holes to lose a two-stroke lead.

• June 30: Meg Mallon outduels Pat Bradley and Ayako Okamoto to win the Mazda LPGA Championship.

• July 7: Russ Cochran wins the Centel Western Open when Greg Norman bogeys five of the last six holes to lose a four-stroke lead.

• July 14: Meg Mallon shoots a final-round 67 to win the U.S. Women's Open at Colonial C.C. in Fort Worth, Texas.

• July 14: Bruce Fleisher, a 42-year-old non-winner who quit the Tour in 1984, captures the New England Classic.

• July 21: Jodie Mudd ties the British Open's 18-hole record with a 63 at Royal Birkdale G.C.

• July 21: Ian Baker-Finch plays the front nine in 5-under 29 and wins the British Open with a closing 66.

Payne Stewart

Stewart Beats Simpson in U.S. Open Playoff

Payne Stewart wore the appropriate red, white, and blue during the playoff of the 1991 U.S. Open, at Hazeltine National G.C. in Minnesota. Stewart won the 18-hole affair by defeating Scott Simpson, 75-77. Simpson, who bogied the 70th and 72nd holes, also bogied the last three holes of the playoff.

Nicklaus Tops Chi Chi in Senior Open

Two of America's favorite seniors, Jack Nicklaus *(pictured)* and Chi Chi Rodriguez, battled down the stretch in the 1991 U.S. Senior Open at Oakland Hills C.C. Rodriguez birdied the long, par-4 finishing hole to force an 18-hole playoff, but—on Monday—Nicklaus had one of his best rounds in years. His 65 beat Rodriguez by four shots.

Jack Nicklaus

Bradley Enters Hall of Fame

In 1991, Pat Bradley needed four Tour wins to reach the magical 30 mark, which would allow her automatic entry into the LPGA Hall of Fame. Bradley responded with wins in the Centel Classic, Rail Charity Golf Classic, and Safeco Classic. Then, with only one official domestic event remaining, Bradley captured the MBS LPGA Classic.

Pat Bradley

• July 29: Jack Nicklaus outduels Chi Chi Rodriguez, 65-69, to win a U.S. Senior Open playoff at Oakland Hills C.C. in Michigan.

• August 11: Rookie John Daly holds onto his 54-hole lead to win the PGA Championship, overpowering Crooked Stick G.C. in Carmel, Indiana, with his long drives.

• August 11: Dale Douglass wins the Showdown Classic when leader Charles Coody plays the last two holes in 5-over-par.

• August 25: Tom Purtzer beats Jim Gallagher and Davis Love III in a playoff to win the NEC World Series of Golf.

• August 25: Martha Nause eagles the final hole to win the Chicago Sun-Times Shoot-Out by one stroke.

• September 2: Pat Bradley shoots a Tour-record 197 for 54 holes to win the Rail Charity Classic by six shots.

• September 6: The U.S. wins the Walker Cup, 14-10, in Ireland.

1991

Martha Nause

Nause Wins Shoot-Out with a Dramatic Eagle

Martha Nause won the 1991 Chicago Sun-Times Shoot-Out in spectacular fashion, holing her 107-yard approach shot for an eagle on the final hole, a par-5. The shot gave her a round of 65, a career best, and allowed her to defeat Kris Monaghan by a stroke. It was Nause's second win of her 14-year career.

U.S. Ryder Cup Celebration

U.S. Wins Ryder Cup, Pops the Champagne

Fans wave the American flag and Payne Stewart douses Hale Irwin with champagne after the U.S. defeated Europe for the 1991 Ryder Cup, 14½-13½. Europe had a chance to tie, but Germany's Bernhard Langer missed a makeable putt on the final hole, giving the U.S. its first victory since 1983.

• September 15: Nancy Scranton plays the last seven holes 6-under to win the du Maurier Classic at Vancouver G.C. in Coquitlam, British Columbia.

• September 29: At the new Ocean Course at Kiawah Island Resort in South Carolina, the U.S. wins the Ryder Cup for the first time since 1983. The U.S. nips Europe, 14½-13½, when Bernhard Langer misses a six-footer on the final hole.

• September 29: With her third Tour win of the month, Pat Bradley qualifies for the LPGA Hall of Fame by winning the MBS Classic, her 30th career victory.

• October 6: Jim Colbert wins the $202,500 first prize at the Vantage Championship.

• October 11: Chip Beck ties Al Geiberger's 18-hole PGA Tour scoring record with a 59 in the third round of the Las Vegas Invitational on the Sunrise G.C. course.

Beck Equals Geiberger, Shoots a 59

Chip Beck tied Al Geiberger's PGA Tour record by shooting a 59 in the 1991 Las Vegas Invitational at Sunrise G.C. In the third round, Beck shot 29-30, scoring six birdies on the front nine and seven on the back. Hilton Hotels gave Beck $500,000 for achieving the feat. The 6,194-yard course was not used in 1992's Invitational.

Fred Couples

Chip Beck

Couples Prevails in First Johnnie Walker Championship

Fred Couples displays the trophy for winning the first Johnnie Walker World Championship, held in December 1991 at Tryall G.C. in Jamaica. The tournament brought together an international field of 28 elite players and offered a monstrous first prize of $525,000. Some speculated that the Johnnie Walker would someday become a major championship.

Pavin Leads in Earnings Despite Just Two Wins

Corey Pavin won two lesser Tour events in 1991, the Bob Hope Chrysler Classic and the BellSouth Atlanta Classic, yet he still was honored as the PGA of America's Player of the Year. No one else won more than two events, and Pavin led the Tour in earnings with $979,430. Ten top-10 finishes bolstered his income.

Corey Pavin

- October 13: Andrew Magee and D.A. Weibring shoot 31-under-par for 90 holes at the Las Vegas Invitational. Magee wins the playoff.

- October 27: John Brodie wins the Security Pacific Senior Classic.

- October 27: Bob Charles becomes the first senior to pass $3 million.

- November 3: Craig Stadler beats Russ Cochran in a playoff to win the Tour Championship at Pinehurst C.C. in North Carolina.

- November 3: Corey Pavin leads the PGA Tour money list with $979,430. He is also the PGA Player of the Year.

- November 3: Fred Couples wins the Vardon Trophy with an adjusted scoring average of 69.59.

- November 3: Nobody wins more than two tournaments on the PGA Tour.

- November 10: Pat Bradley leads the LPGA Tour with $763,118.

1991

John Brodie

QB Brodie Wins His First Senior Tour Event

After six years on the Senior Tour, John Brodie won his first tournament, the 1991 Security Pacific Senior Classic. Brodie, the former NFL quarterback and NBC commentator, claimed the win on the first hole of sudden-death. He hit a 9-iron shot within a foot of the cup and then tapped in with his elongated putter.

Andrew Magee

Magee, Weibring Shoot 31-Under in Las Vegas

In 1991, Andrew Magee *(pictured)* and D.A. Weibring set the PGA Tour record for most under par when they shot 31-under at the 90-hole Las Vegas Invitational. Magee fired 69-65-67-62-66—329, while Weibring shot 70-64-65-64-66—329. Magee defeated Weibring in sudden-death. During the tourney, three other players tied the previous record of 29-under.

- November 10: Pat Bradley is the LPGA Player of the Year. She also wins the Vare Trophy (70.66) and ties with Meg Mallon for the lead in wins (four).

- November 10: Jim Thorpe wins the Amoco Centel Championship, the first tournament for players between ages 40 and 50.

- November 13: Ian Woosnam wins the revived PGA Grand Slam of Golf, which includes the winners of the four majors.

- December 7: Jim Colbert equals the Senior Tour's 18-hole record with a 61 in the second round of the First Development Kaanapali Classic. He'll win the next day.

- December 15: Mike Hill leads the Senior Tour in money ($1,065,657) and wins (five).

- December 22: Fred Couples wins the $525,000 first prize at the Johnnie Walker World Championship, a new event with an elite field of 28 players.

COUPLES WINS MASTERS, $1 MILLION BY SPRING

Going into the 1992 Masters, Fred Couples was hotter than any PGA Tour player had been in years. It started at the Nissan Los Angeles Open, where he defeated Davis Love III in a playoff. Couples then tied for second at the Doral Ryder Open and lost a playoff to Corey Pavin at the Honda Classic. Next, Couples demolished the field at the Nestlé Invitational, winning by nine strokes.

Two wins and two seconds, all in four weeks. Not since Tom Watson in 1979 had a player finished first or second in four consecutive tournaments. The streak ended at the Players Championship, where Couples tied for 13th, but even there he broke the course record with a 63 in the third round. Worn down by being in contention for five straight weeks, it was time for a much needed week off before the Masters. But could he maintain his torrid pace when he returned?

That was only one question about Couples. Long considered one of the most talented players in the game, his desire and ability to rise to the big occasion were doubted by many. He answered the skeptics to no small degree

with his clutch performances in leading the U.S. to victory in the Ryder Cup in 1991. Still, at 32 years old, he had yet to win a major championship.

Couples showed in the second round of the Masters that his game was still sharp. He birdied five straight holes, starting at the 6th, and shot a 67. In the third round, he added a 69 for a 205 total, one shot behind Craig Parry, with 49-year-old Raymond Floyd two off the lead. The final round developed into a two-man duel between Couples and Floyd, as Parry three-putted his way out of contention on the front nine. Couples got off to a bit of a slow start himself, but then he showed he did have the nerve—and the

putting touch—to win a major title.

Couples took the lead by sinking birdie putts of 18 and 20 feet on the 8th and 9th holes, then made a six-foot par-saver on the 10th. He stayed ahead with a back nine of eight pars and a birdie, emerging unscathed from one big scare. That came on the par-3 12th, as his 8-iron tee shot barely cleared Rae's Creek, the ball staying on the bank instead of rolling back into the water as most do. It was a huge break, but maybe Couples was due for some good fortune. Twice earlier in the week, he had hit approach shots that landed in the hole and popped out.

Floyd, seeking to become the oldest player to win the Masters, stumbled in the middle of the round. He applied some pressure with birdies on the 14th and 15th, but he finished two strokes behind and settled for his second runner-up finish in three years. The victory pushed Couples's season earnings to over $1 million in less than four months. It also marked the end of his hot streak. But even without a victory the rest of the year, Couples had shown his mettle.

1992

- January: PGA Tour players are scheduled to play in 44 events with a total season purse of $53,648,581.

- January: LPGA Tour players are scheduled to play in 40 events with a total season purse of $20,935,000.

- January: Senior PGA Tour players are scheduled to play in 42 events

with a total season purse of $21,025,000.

- January 19: John Cook chips in on the third and fourth playoff holes to beat Gene Sauers at the Bob Hope Chrysler Classic.

- January 26: Arnold Palmer makes six birdies on the back nine and

wins the Senior Skins Game with $205,000.

- February 2: Mark O'Meara wins the AT&T Pebble Beach National Pro-Am for the third time in four years and fourth overall.

- February 9: Shelley Hamlin wins the Phar-Mor at Inverrary six

1992

Fred Couples was smokin' in the early weeks of 1992, finishing first or second in four straight tournaments including wins in the Los Angeles Open and the Nestlé Invitational (by nine strokes). Before April was over, he had captured the Masters for his first major title and had reached $1 million in season earnings.

months after a mastectomy. It's her first victory since 1978.

• February 19: Minoru Isutani, having trouble coming up with the money to pay off the loan, sells Pebble Beach to a Japanese partnership for $500 million, a year and a half after paying $841 million.

• March 1: Fred Couples beats Davis Love III in a playoff to win the Nissan Los Angeles Open.

• March 8: Raymond Floyd, age 49, wins the Doral Ryder Open, tying Sam Snead's PGA Tour record for most years from first to last victory (29 years). A fire destroyed Floyd's home two weeks ago.

• March 15: At the Honda Classic, Corey Pavin holes an 8-iron from 135 yards for an eagle on the 72nd hole, then beats Fred Couples in a playoff.

• March 15: Brandie Burton, age 20, earns her first LPGA Tour victory at the Ping/Welch's Championship.

John Cook, Bob Hope

Cook Heats Up in Hope Playoff

Eighty-eight-year-old Bob Hope *(center)* helps congratulate John Cook *(left)* for winning the 1992 Bob Hope Chrysler Classic. He did so in spectacular fashion, recording three birdies and an eagle to beat Gene Sauers on the fourth hole of sudden-death. Cook chipped in on the final two holes for the win, his first of three victories on the year.

Shelley Hamlin

O'Meara Continues His Run at Pebble Beach

Through 1992, Mark O'Meara had captured eight PGA Tour events—and four came in the AT&T Pebble Beach National Pro-Am. O'Meara won the 1992 event on the first playoff hole over Jeff Sluman. He also won the Pro-Am in 1985, 1989, and 1990. O'Meara led in putting in '92 with a 1.731 average.

Mark O'Meara

Hamlin, Fighting Cancer, Wins at Inverrary

Shelley Hamlin gave fans the most inspirational moment of the 1992 season, capturing the Phar-Mor at Inverrary just six months after a mastectomy. Hamlin, diagnosed with breast cancer in July 1991, won the Phar-Mor in February, shooting 72-68-66—206 to win by a stroke. It was Hamlin's first victory since 1978.

- March 29: Davis Love III rolls to a four-stroke victory in the Players Championship.

- March 29: Dottie Mochrie beats Juli Inkster in a playoff to win the Nabisco Dinah Shore.

- April: Hale Irwin, Chi Chi Rodriguez, Harry Cooper, and Richard Tufts are inducted into the PGA World Golf Hall of Fame.

- April 5: Lee Trevino nips Jack Nicklaus by one stroke to win The Tradition at Desert Mountain.

- April 5: Chi Chi Rodriguez passes Bob Charles for first place on the Senior PGA Tour career money list.

- April 12: Fred Couples gets his first major title, beating Raymond Floyd by two strokes in the Masters. Mark Calcavecchia shoots a Masters-record 29 on the final nine.

- April 19: Lee Trevino beats Mike Hill by one stroke to win the PGA Seniors Championship.

1992

Brandie Burton

Floyd Makes History, Wins on Both Tours

In 1992, Raymond Floyd became the first player to win on the PGA Tour and the Senior Tour in the same year. In March, at age 49, he won the Doral Ryder Open; in September, 16 days after his 50th birthday, he claimed the GTE North Classic. Floyd won two more senior events and planned to play on both tours in 1993.

Raymond Floyd

Sophomore Burton Hits Top of the Charts

Brandie Burton, a mere 20 years old, proved she was on the verge of greatness with a terrific 1992 season. She won only one tournament, the Ping/Welch's Championship, but she finished fourth on the money list and was among the leaders in virtually every statistical category. Burton won the Rookie of the Year Award in 1991.

Corey Pavin

Pavin Holes One from Downtown to Win Honda

Corey Pavin *(pictured)* needed a miraculous shot to cool off Fred Couples in March 1992. On the 72nd hole of the Honda Classic, Pavin holed an 8-iron from 135 yards for an eagle, tying Couples. He then beat Couples in a playoff with a birdie on the second extra hole. Pavin, winner of $979,430 in 1991, earned $980,934 in '92.

• April 25: Cathy Gerring is seriously burned in a hospitality-tent accident at the Sara Lee Classic.

• April 26: Davis Love III closes with a 62 to win the Kmart Greater Greensboro Open by six strokes.

• May 3: Danielle Ammaccapane wins the $1.2 million Centel Classic.

• May 3: Lee Trevino's victory in the Las Vegas Senior Classic is his third in a row in an individual event—and fourth in a row counting his Legends win with Mike Hill.

• May 10: Tom Kite wins the BellSouth Classic and becomes the first player to reach $7 million in earnings.

• May 17: Betsy King wins the Mazda LPGA Championship by 11 strokes, setting a 72-hole Tour record of 267.

• May 24: Pat Bradley, not invited to the first JCPenney LPGA Skins Game two years ago, wins the second playing of the event.

1992

Three Times a Charm for Ammaccapane

"Three" was the lucky number for Danielle Ammaccapane in 1992, as she won three tournaments and finished third in earnings, driving accuracy, putting, and sand saves. Ammaccapane was clearly part of the Tour's new generation of stars. She listed her favorite pastime as watching MTV and jogging to the music in front of the television.

Davis Love III

Love in the Springtime: Davis Wins Three in a Month

Davis Love III grabbed three Tour victories within a month in the spring of 1992. He earned $324,000 by winning the Players Championship *(pictured)*, claimed the MCI Heritage Classic by shooting 67-67-67-68—269, and closed with a 62 to win the Kmart Greater Greensboro Open. His season earnings reached $1,191,630, and he won three postseason events.

Danielle Ammaccapane

• May 30: Georgia freshman Vicki Goetze wins the NCAA title.

• June 6: Phil Mickelson of Arizona State wins his third NCAA title.

• June 14: Dave Stockton wins the Mazda Senior Players Championship when he birdies the 72nd hole and leader J.C. Snead double bogeys.

• June 20: Gil Morgan becomes the first player to go 10-under-par during a U.S. Open, getting as far as 12-under-par through seven holes of the third round. By the end of the day, he drops back to 4-under.

• June 21: Tom Kite wins the U.S. Open for his first major championship. Kite shoots an even-par 72

on a brutally windy day at Pebble Beach; many fail to break 80.

• July 12: Larry Laoretti gets his first Senior Tour victory at the U.S. Senior Open at Saucon Valley C.C. in Bethlehem, Pennsylvania.

• July 17: Nick Faldo sets a British Open record of 130 for 36 holes

1992

Betsy King

Kite Bumps Off the Monkey, Wins U.S. Open

Tom Kite plays along the ocean on the 9th hole of Pebble Beach G.L. during the 1992 U.S. Open. Kite bumped a 20-year-old monkey off his back by winning the championship, his first-ever major victory. Conditions were brutal in the final round, but Kite—long known for his amazing consistency—shot a cool 72 to win by two.

King's 267 in LPGA Is a Major Record

Betsy King won three LPGA Tour events and finished No. 2 on the money list in 1992, but her top highlight came at the Mazda LPGA Championship. She shot 68-66-67-66—267 on the Bethesda C.C. course to win by a full 11 strokes. King's 267 was the lowest 72-hole score ever in a major professional championship—by a woman *or* a man.

Tom Kite

Lee Trevino

Trevino Racks Up Five Victories by May

Lee Trevino won his second Senior Tour Player of the Year Award in 1992 thanks to a torrid spring. Between March 15 and May 24, he won five times, including a one-stroke victory over old rival Jack Nicklaus at The Tradition. It was likely Trevino's last hurrah as the No. 1 man, owing to a thumb injury and the arrival of Raymond Floyd.

---

with rounds of 66 and 64 at Muirfield in Gullane, Scotland.

• July 19: Nick Faldo birdies the 15th and 17th holes to beat John Cook by one stroke and win the British Open.

• July 27: Patty Sheehan beats Juli Inkster, 72-74, in an 18-hole playoff for the U.S. Women's Open title, at Oakmont C.C. in Pennsylvania.

• August 1: Teenage phenom Tiger Woods wins his second consecutive U.S. Junior championship.

• August 15: Vicki Goetze, age 19, wins her second U.S. Women's Amateur.

• August 16: Nick Price wins his first major title, the PGA Championship at Bellerive C.C. in St. Louis, as Gene Sauers and Jeff Maggert falter in the final round.

• August 16: Sherri Steinhauer wins the du Maurier Classic at St. Charles C.C. in Winnipeg, Manitoba.

Nick Faldo

Faldo, Best in the World, Wins British

Nick Faldo hits from the 13th tee at Muirfield G.C. during the 1992 British Open. Faldo won by a stroke over John Cook after Cook bogied the final hole. Faldo was arguably the best player in the world in 1992, leading the European Tour in earnings and winning the Johnnie Walker World Championship. He also finished second in the PGA Championship.

Dottie Mochrie

Colbert Wins Another Vantage Championship

Jim Colbert, often seen with this determined grin, finished third on the Senior Tour money list for the second year in a row in 1992. Colbert achieved such lofty status by winning the lucrative Vantage Championship each year. Each win was worth $202,500. It was an easy paycheck in '92, as rain cut the event to two days.

Jim Colbert

Mochrie Best All-Around on the LPGA Tour

Dottie Mochrie swept the LPGA honors in 1992. Mochrie led the Tour in victories (four), scoring (70.80), and earnings ($693,335). The determined Mochrie won two sudden-death playoffs, defeating Juli Inkster in the Nabisco Dinah Shore and winning a six-hole playoff over two others at the Sun-Times Challenge.

• August 30: Craig Stadler wins the NEC World Series of Golf.

• September 13: Nancy Lopez wins her second consecutive event, the Ping-Cellular One Championship.

• September 20: Raymond Floyd gets his first Senior Tour victory in his second event, the GTE North Classic. He's the first to win on both tours in the same year.

• October 4: Europe surprises the U.S., 11½-6½, to win the Solheim Cup in Edinburgh, Scotland.

• October 18: John Huston wins the Walt Disney World/Oldsmobile Classic with a final-round 62.

• November 1: Paul Azinger wins the Tour Championship at Pinehurst C.C. in North Carolina, keeping alive his streak of one victory in each of the last seven years.

• November 1: Fred Couples leads the PGA Tour money list with $1,344,188. He is the PGA Player of the Year and also wins the Vardon

Laoretti Puffs to Victory in Senior Open

Larry Laoretti, known for his trademark cigar, upset the heavyweights when he captured the 1992 U.S. Senior Open at Saucon Valley C.C. in Bethlehem, Pennsylvania. It was the first senior victory for Laoretti, who never played the regular tour. Laoretti also became known for driving around the senior circuit with his wife in a mobile home.

Larry Laoretti

Sheehan Ends Open Jinx, Wins in a Playoff

Patty Sheehan won the 1992 U.S. Women's Open at Oakmont C.C. in impressive fashion. She birdied the final two holes of regulation and then beat Juli Inkster in an 18-hole playoff. Sheehan had finished runner-up in the Open three times. In 1990, she blew a nine-stroke lead and lost to Betsy King.

Teenage Tiger Tops Again in U.S. Junior Championship

Eldrick "Tiger" Woods, a golf whiz since a toddler, made history in 1992 by becoming the first kid to win the U.S. Junior Amateur championship twice. Woods, who won in 1991 at age 15, beat Mark Wilson, 1 up, in the final in 1992. Woods, along with the older Phil Mickelson, was being touted as the game's next superstar.

Tiger Woods

Patty Sheehan

Trophy with an adjusted scoring average of 69.38.

• November 1: Fred Couples, Davis Love III, John Cook, and Nick Price lead the PGA Tour with three wins each.

• November 8: Fred Couples and Davis Love III both birdie the final hole to give the U.S. a one-stroke victory in the World Cup.

• November 8: Dottie Mochrie leads the LPGA money list with $693,335 and four victories. She is the LPGA Player of the Year and also wins the Vare Trophy with a scoring average of 70.80.

• November 11: Nick Price wins the PGA Grand Slam of Golf despite a second-round 62 by Tom Kite.

• December 13: Raymond Floyd wins the Senior Tour Championship.

• December 13: Lee Trevino leads the Senior Tour in earnings ($1,027,002) and wins (five).

INDEX